LIFE AND SOCIETY IN THE WEST

The Modern Centuries

LIFE AND SOCIETY IN THE WEST

The Modern Centuries

PETER N. STEARNS

Carnegie-Mellon University

HARCOURT BRACE JOVANOVICH, PUBLISHERS

San Diego   New York   Chicago   Austin   Washington, D.C.
London   Sydney   Tokyo   Toronto

For Sarah and Susan,
Kate and Martha,
Jo and Karin:
extended families still count.

Cover Photo: Steinberg Residence, La Jolla, California; Howard Oxley, Architect, inspired by Karyn Steinberg. Photo © 1986 Joan Hicks-Vandershuit.

ISBN: 0-15-550727-3

Library of Congress Catalog Card Number: 87-81883

Printed in the United States of America

Illustration Credits and Copyrights and Acknowledgments appear on pages 447–48, which constitute a continuation of the copyright page.

PREFACE

This book examines Western civilization during the past five centuries through the lens of social history. The focus on Western society allows us to understand the development of institutions and values that have shaped much of our own social environment and that describe the civilization whose activities, for better or worse, have influenced and shaken the entire modern world. The same focus allows us to grasp certain kinds of fundamental changes, including, but not confined to, the Industrial Revolution.

The social history approach picks up a development that has quietly revolutionized historical study in recent decades. Rather than concentrating on formal politics and great ideas alone, social historians turn their attention to the evolution of ordinary people and to such activities as family life and the rituals of health and illness. The result has been an explosion of new knowledge about the past and a massive expansion of the kind of historical perspective that can inform our understanding of the present—of why people today behave and think as they do. The social history approach also shifts attention from single events as the cornerstones of history—an election, a battle—to more basic concerns, such as changes in birthrates or new ways of defining work. At the same time, the rise of social history, precisely because of its novelty, has often been an ill-disciplined affair, more concerned with staking out new topics than with putting the pieces together or relating them to more familiar historical landmarks. This book seeks to capture the excitement of social history while building a more coherent integration, linking process and event, showing relationships between political change and social change.

Finally, our focus is modern, dealing with centuries in which Western society has been transformed in many ways. This panorama poses its own challenge to show how different developments interrelate without sketching too simple or tidy a picture.

Getting from Then to Now:
A Complex Fabric of Change

Between the sixteenth century and the twentieth century—that is, during the 450-year span before today—Western society generated a radically new set of institutions and a substantially novel culture. In 1500 almost all western Europeans adhered to basic Christian beliefs and belonged to the Catholic church. By 1950 their descendants professed various versions of Christianity and many had lost primary allegiance to any formal religion at all. In 1500 the dominant form of government was a monarchy; by 1950 this political institution had virtually disappeared, replaced most widely by democratic parliamentary regimes but in some places by new kinds of authoritarian systems. In 1500 the purpose of the family was rooted in its service as the chief unit for producing goods. By 1950 the family's production function had almost vanished, and the family itself had become the subject of confused debate—and even sharp attack from those, such as some feminists, who found it oppressive. In 1500 the average twenty-year-old in the West was a peasant waiting for a chance to marry and take over a plot of land; by 1950 the average twenty-year-old was launched on a career of factory or office work, after twelve to fourteen years of schooling, and hoping for advancement, a house in the suburbs, and individual fulfillment. In sum, the remaking of Western society involved a vast series of changes, many of them touching fundamental ways society and individuals operate. And although 450 years is no small period of time, it is clear that change of this basic sort has been unusually rapid as well.

The Economic and Technological Underpinnings of Western Society

The key to the direction of change in modern Western history lies in a progressive recasting of the economic framework of Western society. Steady, often undramatic technological improvements propelled Western society to world technological leadership by 1600, for the first time in history. Commercial activity, already swelling during the Middle Ages, expanded to new levels, as the West, again for the first time, took over the direction of worldwide trade. Changes of this sort prepared the still more fundamental shifts in the eighteenth and nineteenth centuries, as Western society underwent the world's first industrial revolution.

In other words, most Western history is defined in considerable measure by the underlying currents that led an agricultural society to become an urbanized, industrial society within a relatively short time. To be sure, there had been one comparable transformation in the human experience, when hunters and gatherers, initially in the Middle East (and later, independently, in Central America) learned how to farm. Like the process of industrialization that modern Western society pioneered, this transformation fundamentally altered systems of government, the places where people lived, the way they thought about the world around them. Like industrialization, the first agricultural revolution involved a long period of preparation, often unwitting, as ordinary people and leaders alike reacted to changes in their physical and social environment. But the agricultural revolution took many centuries to unfold, whereas the economic revolution that produced industrial society reached some completion within three to four hundred years. Again, in dealing with this economic and industrial core of the recent Western experience, one is dealing with a very unusual historical episode.

Two obvious issues therefore inform modern Western history: How did Western society achieve the possibility of major change? And what impact has this change had? The first question calls attention to distinctive features of the Western experience from 1500 to about 1850, including important changes within this early modern period both at society's summit, in political institutions and formal culture, and at its base, in family forms and the economic behavior of ordinary people. The second question organizes much of the history of the West since industrialization broke through, and indeed takes us easily to the contemporary era. Westerners are still debating questions about the functions of the family as a result of industrialization, including the roles of women, and about the place of leisure in a radically new kind of society. They also debate the function of the arts in an industrial environment and certainly continue to discuss how best to organize an effective industrial state.

These two leading issues—how the West got here, and what resulted—are also interconnected. One clear source of the West's ability to innovate was its growing influence in the wider world—the spread of early colonies and trading patterns that gave the West control over a growing portion of the world's wealth. Industrialization heightened the West's international position, but it also provided models for imitation that have produced new rivals for world influence in the twentieth century. Changes in the position of women played a role in the array of shifts that prepared the West's ability to industrialize, but the same changes generated questions that still agitate Western society. Portions of the West that converted to Protestantism saw particularly marked changes in the culture surrounding women; these same areas produced, and still produce, the most vigorous feminist challenges in Western industrial society. Again, the forces that produced the Western transformation help define that transformation and its results, so that preindustrial history is linked with more recent developments at many points.

The Unevenness of Historical Change

Seeing Western history, not just since the rise of factories but to an extent before, as organized around a central, sweeping transformation, involves several problems. First, by no means was *all* Western history since 1500 bent on generating and reacting to economic transformation; many developments were rather random, fitting no basic pattern or coherent direction. Second, other movements, such as the Renaissance and the Reformation (cultural and religious respectively), had consequences different in part from those intended by their proponents—leading to more change, particularly in the economic and social sphere, than they had wished. Certainly few people were aware of their own participation in a fundamental economic transformation at least until the eighteenth century. Third, no one sat down in 1600 to say, "Let's plan industrialization for a century or so hence." The record of early modern history must not be forced to make it seem more coherent or self-conscious than it was. Even after industrialization began, many developments remained separate from economic change, sometimes continuing earlier themes. For example, in the nineteenth-century and essentially to our own day, the military purposes of the modern state changed less than its technology did. Thus not every trend in modern Western history fits neatly together.

One key reason for this lack of neat fit—even in the nineteenth century, which served as the crucible of industrialization—involves the gap between the elite and ordinary people. A tempting way to visualize modern European history is to posit a shift in high culture and politics that forced the tradition-minded masses into new patterns of behavior and ultimately built the new economic framework. Indeed, changes in formal ideas and in government functions did contribute to the wider transformation of the modern West. But many elite interests were themselves traditional, or were irrelevant to the central changes. Nor were the ordinary people of Western society simply passive victims. They, too, produced new institutions and behaviors that would feed into industrialization, even though they had no explicit intention of doing so. The formula *elite equals dynamic, masses equals inert* does not work in Western history. This is one reason that the modern industrial and economic transformation cannot be viewed in any simple way. It involved causation from above, but also resistance from leading thinkers and statesmen, and a similar mixture of activity and resistance from the world of ordinary peasants and workers. Correspondingly, the *impact* of change was by no means uniform throughout society: it caused great disruption for established elites and their values, as well as for ordinary people, while bringing new opportunities at various levels as well. The complex combination of innovation and resistance, in different areas of society and at different levels, is itself a warning against seeing all of modern history moving neatly toward some single climax.

Nor is the theme of change uniform across the Western world. The same basic process of industrialization and reactions to industrialization that confirmed the parliamentary system in Britain brought Nazism for a time in Germany. The extension of Western civilization to most of North America created important divergences, as what ultimately became the United States and Canada participated in the broader pattern of Western change but with a number of cultural and social variants derived from their distinctive geography and early historical experiences.

The idea that modern Western history had a basic direction, then, must be balanced against the realization that change was uneven, that it did not describe all important historical developments, and that it involved a complex relationship between elite and mass participation. Furthermore, change in Western history is not the story either of triumphant progress or of tragic deterioration—at least it is not automatically such a story. Many elements in the transformation of Western society look "good": Western people have become richer, healthier, more democratic, less obviously superstitious. Many elements look "bad": A rich popular culture has been disrupted to allow room for industrialization, more adults work for other bosses rather than on their own account, the technology of war has become steadily more menacing. Therefore, identification of a central transformation beginning to take shape from roughly 1500 onward, and extending to our own time, allows questions to be asked about losses and gains. It is not, by definition, either an optimistic or a pessimistic vision. It focuses attention on how contemporary Westerners differ from their ancestors, and how these differences gradually developed. The differences include, among other things, important changes in the way society is assessed; moderns, for example, place more weight on long life as a measure of quality of existence than their predecessors did. But this evaluation should not lead to simple ideas about contemporary superiority over a boorish past, or of contemporary tragedy played against a nostalgic past. Attention to central themes of change should not preclude sympathetic understanding of the past in its own right, or a critical examination of the present.

The Western pattern of economic transformation has not been the only one in modern history, although it was indisputably the first. The ability of Japan and eastern Europe to copy Western technologies, and generate their own, provides additional basis for highlighting what was distinctive about the Western process, including some features that may seem undesirable in this comparative context.

The transformation of Western society, grounded in crucial economic changes, provides in sum a guidepost to the history of the last four and a half centuries, not a detailed map. It helps raise questions about the relationships among seemingly diverse developments. What did the witchcraft persecution of the sixteenth and seventeenth centuries have to do with changes in popular outlook and structures that in turn fed wider economic shifts? How did economic change relate to political revolutions or new artistic styles in the nineteenth century? The answers are not easy, for the process of change was not neatly lock-step. But the questions do allow a vision of the modern Western past that is not entirely random, not simply one period after another with no coherent relationship. For, despite their complexities, it is the ramifications of a central process of change that describe much of the evolving experience of Western people in the modern era.

Exploring the Western transformation links the past to contemporary experience in crucial ways. Issues such as what children are for and how they should be raised arose in new ways as part of Western society's premodern shifts and changed again as a result of industrialization. Such issues are still with us. The way we view children and youth is conditioned by the whole series of changes in modern Western society, including industrialization, and can be understood and assessed only in terms of this historical perspective. The same holds true for the role of the state in dealing with problems of poverty, which began to be redefined in the sixteenth and seventeenth centuries and flows from this initial modern shift to the present. It holds true, relatedly, for the treatment of criminals: the first modern prisons were built in the sixteenth and seventeenth centuries and, although much changed—among other things by the results of industrialization—remain a central Western response to the problem of crime. The list extends—to the eating habits of families, to the relationship between art and business—wherever basic shifts began to emerge in the 1500s and 1600s that would feed the wider process of change and link to twentieth-century patterns. We live today, obviously, in a rapidly changing world. But it is a world that has been changing for some time in ways to which we are still reacting. A grasp of what the Western transformation entailed, including what caused it, is central to our definition of the issues and directions of our own society. The contemporary West is an evolving response to basic, and still quite recent, upheavals in the Western past. This is as true for the concerns of ordinary life—such as romance, sports, and protest—as it is for the more familiar stuff of history, such as the structure of the state or the philosophies of the elite.

The Central Areas of Greatest Change

The best way to grasp the complexity of change as the modern West emerged and continued to evolve into our own time, without losing all sense of direction, is to focus on five interlocking areas of society's functioning. In each of these areas dramatic shifts developed between 1500 and 1700, with further changes building on the previous dynamic. Each area also involved both elite actors—great leaders, thinkers, or entrepreneurs of rare genius—and ordinary folk, who reacted to innovation and produced new departures of their own.

1. The first area is international relations. Western Europe began a historic rise in world power position after the explorations of the fifteenth century. It even managed to export Western values and institutions to new areas, notably in North America but also in Australia and New Zealand. It also was able to channel important proportions of the world's wealth into its own coffers.

2. The second area is internal political organization. With some preparation in the later Middle Ages and during the sixteenth century, the West pioneered a new political form, the nation-state, that began to come into its own in the 1600s. This nation-state involved levels of government organization new to the West, and links and loyalties between ordinary people and the state that were novel in any previous society.

3. The third area of great change featured the development of a commercialized economy and a social structure to match, in which control of money served as the basis for power and status. This involved, in turn, a new definition of gaps between haves and the have-nots within society.

The West would produce several versions of growing commercialization, first within the confines of an agricultural economy, then through industrialization and mass consumer power.

4. Technology is the fourth area of great change. Technological change helped boost the West's power in the world, with the development of mobile gunnery in the fifteenth century. Industrialization, three centuries later, consisted of a technological revolution and the introduction of recurrent technological shifts into the social fabric.

5. Finally, the development of modern Western society entailed basic changes in the ways people thought, or in *mentality*. These changes arose among intellectuals, and also in the outlook of ordinary people. In new, often deeply held ways of viewing nature, family, and the self lay causes of other changes—for example, in the roles of women or children—and also mirrors of shifts in technology, commerce, and politics. Because of its richness as cause and reflection of change, the subject of mentality or culture describes the reality of historical experience particularly well.

The great changes in the five facets of Western society did not occur neatly or in full harmony. Commercialization introduced new social divisions, where changes in outlook at times brought people closer together, across social divides. Some periods of time emphasized certain sectors over others; the sixteenth century, for example, emphasized developments in commerce and outlook more than politics or technology. Directions set at one point might be considerably altered at others, and we must especially consider how the West late in the 20th century fits, or diverges from, some of the patterns of its modern development. For all its complexity, however, the idea of five areas of great change does enable the student of modern Western history to envision the past as more than a series of scattered events. Understanding how people reacted to the great changes and contributed to them—and how their reactions and contributions differed according to social position, age, and gender—is the best way to see modern Western history for the human experience it was and still continues to be.

Acknowledgments

A number of people contributed to the preparation of this book. My thanks to Drake Bush and Craig Avery, for arranging the project and steering the manuscript into production, and to the rest of the staff at Harcourt Brace Jovanovich for making a big job more manageable. Three readers provided extremely useful comments, which substantially improved my initial work: Elinor Accampo, University of Southern California, Myron P. Gutmann, University of Texas at Austin, and Robert Moeller, University of California, Santa Cruz. Susan Tomsic typed the manuscript with efficiency and good humor.

I am also—I hope obviously—indebted to the many social historians who continue to expand and inspire the field, including, of course, the social history faculty at Carnegie-Mellon University and the contributors to the *Journal of Social History*. My colleagues teach me in many ways, as do my students, whose reactions and questions make social history so rewarding. Finally, my thanks to my family, most of whom also like to talk history.

Peter N. Stearns

CONTENTS

MAPS

ONE

EUROPE AROUND 1500: STAGES IN THE LATE MIDDLE AGES AND RENAISSANCE

1300ff Italian Renaissance
Giotto (1276–1337); Petrarch
(1304–1374); Leonardo da Vinci
(1452–1519); Machiavelli (1469–
1519); Michelangelo (1475–
1514)

1347–1348 Black Death begins a long, recurrent series of plagues in Europe

1418ff Portuguese expeditions, sponsored by Henry the Navigator, along African coast

1450ff Northern Renaissance
Erasmus (1469?–1536)

1453–1471 Wars of the Roses in England

1453 Fall of Constantinople to the Ottoman Turks

1455 First European printing press, Mainz, Germany

1461 Hundred Years' War between France and England ends

1462 Ivan III (the Great) frees much of Russia from Tartars

1479–1516 Ferdinand and Isabella unite Spain 1492   last Muslims expelled

1480 Moscow region free from Tartars

1485 Tudor dynasty established in England
1509–1547 Henry VIII

1492–1493 Columbus's first expedition to West Indies
1493 Second Columbus expedition; Spanish colonial administration in West Indies begins

1494ff French and Spanish invasions of Italy; beginning of decline of Italian Renaissance

1497–1499 Vasco da Gama (Portugal) rounds Africa, reaches India

1515–1547 Francis I king of France

1516–1556 Charles I founds Habsburg dynasty, rules Spain (as Charles V), Flanders, Holy Roman Empire

1519–1522 Magellan (Spain) circumnavigates the globe

1521–1559 Recurrent wars between Francis I and Charles V
1559 Treaty of Cateau-Cambrésis ends these wars, Spain emerges as leading continental power

CHAPTER
ONE

EUROPE IN 1500

MORE THAN MOST SOCIETIES around the world at this time, western Europe in 1500 was in busy transition. The most obvious changes were occurring at the elite level, in the cultural and political movement known as the Renaissance. Earlier artistic and literary styles, such as Gothic architecture and epic poetry, were increasingly challenged in the name of revived classical forms. Political theories that stressed the power of the ruler vied with the medieval legacy of feudal limitations and parliaments. Beneath the glittering surface of these new styles and ideas, western European people were also recovering from some of the problems that had beset late-medieval society. Population declines in the 1300s and 1400s, caused by ravaging plagues and inadequate agricultural resources, now began to be reversed (although plagues remained prevalent until about 1700). Technological improvements and commercial expansion, launched in earlier centuries, were rising to new levels. On various fronts, western Europe was shedding its medieval skin and taking on a new guise. High culture and ordinary family structures alike reflected striking new trends.

Change was also beginning to fuel a new Western influence in the wider world. In 1500, as at later points, the West was a cultural rather than a clear geographical expression—a society with certain shared values and institutions. But despite its somewhat imprecise definition, it was at this juncture rather small and still clearly inferior to the great Asian civilizations in many respects. It centered on France, the Low Countries, the British Isles, Italy, and Germany; embraced Spain and Portugal; and extended to Scandinavia and, less specifically, to central European regions such as Bohemia. A common religion, Christianity, and rather loose systems of government were the West's most obvious hallmarks as it approached the great changes that were to mark its evolution toward more modern forms.

Long overshadowed by the splendor the the Byzantine Empire and the Muslim Middle East, western Europe around 1500 was gaining greater wealth and diversity. In the centuries before 1500, western Europe had profited greatly by borrowing from more advanced societies: Western scholars learned new mathematics and philosophy from the Arabs, and the European upper classes acquired new tastes for spices from merchants' contact with East Asia and learned new technologies such as printing, paper manufacture, and gunpowder from various Asian centers as well. These lessons began to bear increasing fruit, as western Europe was also spared the distraction of dealing with a new wave of barbarian invasions—the Mongol hordes—that had affected most other parts of the Eurasian world during the 1300s. Recovering from its own adjustments to the declining vitality of specifically medieval culture, including major setbacks in the economy and in population levels, western Europe was entering a newly creative period, regaining a vitality it had displayed during the peak period of the Middle Ages three centuries before. Just when Muslim society in the Middle East was narrowing its cultural emphasis to concentrate on Islamic faith, European civilization was branching into a new array of literary and philosophical interests, along with exploring new regions. As China withdrew into greater isolation after about 1450, following an astounding but brief series of expeditions through the Indian ocean, Western voyagers, though less massively organized, were pushing into this same ocean and across the Atlantic as well.

Nevertheless, change was counterbalanced by the weight of continuity. Western Europe remained medieval in many ways. Monarchs talked of new ideas and built showy new palaces, but they continued to be limited by the military and political powers of the aristocracy. Popular culture, in its religious habits and its rhythm of work and festivals, remained highly traditional as well. In other words, neither the elite nor the masses was wedded to some new idea of change. Indeed, many innovations, such as Renaissance interests in secular art and literature, provoked reactions in the name of customary beliefs. This attempt to return to older ideals (here, of religion) was one source of the Protestant Reformation that surged after 1517, and the Catholic Reformation that followed.

This balance of important change with continuity was affected by the geographical variations within the West. Italy stood somewhat apart (as it had for centuries), divided politically into vibrant city-states and open to unusually pure classical influences that caused its Renaissance to appear earlier than, and to differ from, the Renaissance experienced elsewhere. Spain, one of Europe's powerhouses, was marked by a missionary fervor that had just driven the expulsion in 1492 of the Muslims from the Iberian peninsula. (Political unity was also a recent achievement in Spain.) The heart of medieval Europe—France, the Low Countries, and western Germany—remained pivotal in the formation of the new Europe.

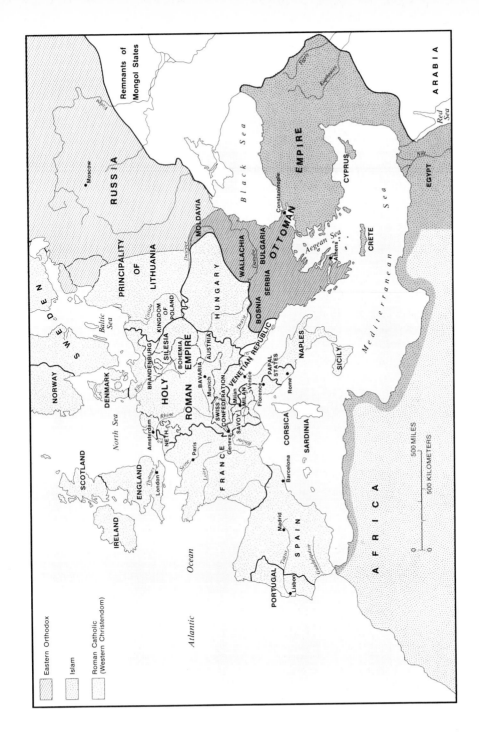

Western Europe was small, poor, and weak in comparison to the Ottoman Empire and the Muslim Middle East, but by 1500 it was growing in strength, wealth, and diversity of outlook. With Christianity as its common religion, trade and exploration becoming its impetus for growth, and agriculture its predominant way of life outside the thriving cities, western Europe reached south to Spain and Portugal, north Scandinavia, and east to portions of central Europe.

They were joined by an increasingly prosperous and venturesome England. But whereas France and England had well-established monarchies, Germany was divided into regional states only loosely aligned under a Holy Roman Emperor, chosen by this point from the Habsburg family, which directly ruled Austria. Thus not only political structures but also popular customs, including landholding patterns, divided western Europe into a multitude of regions. Finally, to the east, in what was clearly a separate society, Russia was beginning to awaken from two centuries of Mongol, or Tartar, control. Like the West, it was about to play a new role in the wider world. But it would find somewhat different sources of strength and would develop a fascinating love–hate relationship with the West.

This chapter focuses on how people in the West lived and organized their society around 1500. It captures some medieval traditions, changes such as the Renaissance that had been in the works for over a century, and other innovations that were just coming to the fore. It reflects a society rudely shocked by waves of disease and by agricultural setbacks occasioned by limited techniques and a climate that had been growing colder since about 1250. And it makes clear that western Europe, rather than declining under the challenge, sought relief in territorial expansion and change. The West in 1500 was hardly standing still, but the overview that follows shows the backdrop against which a new series of great changes would later challenge tradition, and reveals the forms of ongoing transition that explain why further change could take place.

The Peasant World in 1500

Western Europe—and indeed, the East as well—was still a peasant society in 1500. Between 80 percent and 90 percent of all western Europeans lived in the countryside, and most of these worked full-time or part-time in agriculture. Some peasants in southern Europe, such as those in Sicily, lived in larger agglomerations of a few thousand persons. In a few areas, as in parts of central Austria, peasants lived in isolated farmsteads. But most European peasants lived in relatively small villages of four hundred to eight hundred persons. Although many of the great events and virtually all the great styles and ideas of Western history would be products of the urban minority, the bustle of city life played against a predominantly peasant backdrop. Thus the deepest changes in Western society would be those that reached the countryside as well.

The Material Constraints of an Agricultural Society

Europe's rural character, which it shared with all other civilizations in the world in 1500, generated many aspects of life that seem strange today, when only about 10 percent of the population is now truly nonurban. Although conditions varied according to region and type of soil, peasants were characteristically poor. A typical village contained a few reasonably substantial property owners, who could employ labor; a larger number of owners of modest means, who could normally feed their fam-

Peasants at work in the sixteenth century. Community labor was a relaxed enterprise. Pieter Bruegel, *Wheat Harvest,* 1565.

ilies but little more; and another minority of landless or nearly landless
poor. This "diamond-shaped" social structure saw 15 percent to 20 percent of all peasants in the lowest category and another 10 percent to 20
percent in the top segment, with the rest in the middle.

Material life was generally hard for all groups. Most peasant households produced largely for themselves. Some sold a bit of their harvest
on the market; and this meager surplus, along with the output of large
estates owned by the church or the aristocratic landlords, kept the cities
alive. Most peasants bought and sold little, concentrating not on a specialty crop but on rounded, somewhat inefficient general production that,
they hoped, would assure subsistence. Housing, although diverse in
character and type by region and family status, was crude and crowded.
Animals were kept in or around the house, adding to the crowding and
to the problems of sanitation. Clothing was homespun from wool or flax
and was rarely washed. Festival costumes, in brighter colors, alone provided some contrast to the normal workday drab. Diets were meager and
consisted mainly of bread, usually made from rye, oats, or barley, augmented only occasionally with meat. Honey provided the only sweet-
ener. Because most water supplies were polluted with human and animal
wastes, drink consisted mainly of weak, homemade beer, the brewing of
which reduced its bacterial level somewhat.

Agricultural Production   The material constraints of rural life followed
from the prevailing methods of production. Western European farming
had never developed the high per-acre yields of East and South Asian

agriculture. This was partly inevitable: Most of western Europe lacked the climate or soil for growing rice, and the available grains were simply not as high in yield. Additionally, the West had not developed the extensive political organization necessary to construct elaborate irrigation projects; nor did many Westerners use human wastes for fertilizer, though animal wastes were widely used. A peasant family thus required a relatively large spread of five to nine acres or more simply to assure subsistence—a size that was possible because western Europe had never built the huge population levels characteristic of China or India. Another constraint on the food supply was that peasants had to leave a third of their land fallow each year to allow recovery of fertility. Spoilage of food during winter storage further reduced the food supply, particularly in late winter and early spring. It was true that during the Middle Ages, and particularly between about 900 and 1200, agricultural productivity had risen due to better knowledge of seeds, use of improved plows and animal yokes, and the clearing of new land. As a result, European population had grown, and farmers were required to reserve only about 20 percent of their annual harvest for seed. But these gains in farming production had stopped by about 1300.

When the long period of colder weather had set in during the thirteenth century, the West's agriculture had been severely strained; and Europe would see no major new improvements until the 1600s. In 1500, most peasants used tools and crops that their forefathers had used—with no sense that other methods were possible.

Limited food production was thus a fundamental feature of Western life. It set clear constraints on city growth; at least eight families had to farm to allow two to perform other tasks. It restricted the revenues available for governments and armies; although peasants were taxed and they supported kings and nobles through their taxes and rents, they could hardly be pressed too far. Given available farming methods, plus limited means of transportation in the form of animal-powered carts and barges, the food supply was periodically uncertain. Local famines occurred every few years because of crop disease or poor weather, and general shortages occurred more often. Life was a struggle and an uncertain one at that.

Health Conditions   The constraints of rural life showed clearly in its health conditions. Poor home sanitation practices and limited food resources caused frequent outbreaks of disease and high death rates, particularly among young children and the elderly. In this respect, cities were in an even worse condition, as death rates regularly surpassed birth rates and no city could sustain itself without some inflow of peasants from the countryside. Periodically major plagues swept through the countryside, as had the bubonic Black Death of the fourteenth century that had killed over one-quarter of the total population. Even in more normal times, up to 40 percent of all children died before reaching two years of age. The picture was less grim for those who survived childhood, and many villagers lived into their fifties and sixties. But even for middle-aged adults, death was no rarity. Women were vulnerable to death in childbirth, less from the event itself than from subsequent infection and fever. Ironically,

German peasant houses of the sixteenth century had thatched roofs, as this woodcut from Sebastian Müster's *Cosmography* (1543) shows.

rural society depended in a way on its high death rates, for without such rates the population would have soared well beyond the capabilities of the available local food supply. Peasant families burdened with too many children who did not die were condemned to growing poverty, as their diets would deteriorate below even the crude normal levels. The practice of infanticide remained, though at lower levels than in earlier centuries, as a recourse when ordinary death rates did not suffice to keep family size down.

Culture   The poverty of material life inevitably carried over into peasant culture in many ways. First, peasant life was frequently isolated. Many peasants never traveled out of their small region, which was why city-dwellers often viewed this population with such suspicion, and why peasants in their turn saw many strangers and outsiders as fearsome threats. Second, most peasants were illiterate. A village might contain a few literate people—the priest, perhaps a miller who needed to keep accounts, and in a few cases some scribe who would write marriage contracts or other documents for his rural clientele. Otherwise, peasant culture was oral—that is, passed down by word of mouth. Oral transmission almost assured that rural society was tradition-bound, for although local lore and popular ballads could introduce a few new elements from time to time, they had to stay within strict limits of style and length in order to be memorized. Deliberate change or dramatic extensions of available knowledge could not be welcomed.

Family Life   The material restrictions of Western life even dominated family organization. The family was above all an economic unit; most divisions of labor occurred within it, both in manufacturing and in farming. Women, who were required to devote considerable time to bearing and raising young children, were also vital to the family as a production unit. But women held an inferior place; as in most agricultural societies, patriarchal rule held firm, based on the fact that men monopolized most grain-growing activities and many key crafts. Women had their own vital sphere in caring for livestock, processing food, and assisting men in peak harvest periods; but theirs was a separate domain, generally considered to be inferior.

In rural society human relationships were thus cast in the mold of role-bound practicality and patriarchal will. Family affection was often limited. Marriages were typically contracted with an eye to economic survival, not happiness. A man wanted a wife who could contribute a modest dowry to the farm, often through some additional land or domestic animals; and he wanted a good worker. To the extent that women were allowed to formulate preferences, they were encouraged to seek a man with some property. Indeed, most marriages were arranged by a couple's parents, with only a brief courtship to determine whether the prospective partners could tolerate each other. Affection might develop as the marriage wore on, but it was not guaranteed and was not a primary feature of family life.

Children were also seen in terms of their economic role. Young children, who were simply drains on the family economy, frequently received scant attention. Swaddling was pervasive. Children were tightly wrapped during their first months to prevent freedom of movement that might damage them, and also to limit the amount of time busy parents would have to spend attending to their needs. Discipline was often severe, with a strong emphasis on whippings and spankings. When Europeans encountered people from other cultures, such as American Indians, they often provoked dismay by their readiness to punish children physically. Strong beliefs held that children were naturally willful, even sinful, and required equivalent discipline in order to learn proper respect and order. Discipline was certainly devoted to making children relatively willing

Children, who worked even while very young and were sometimes heavily disciplined, nevertheless had some time to play. Pieter Bruegel, *Children's Games*, 1560.

workers, for the peasant family required contributions of labor by children from about age five. Indeed, because most families normally employed no outside workers, children formed the bulk of the menial labor force. Although affection might develop between parents and children, and a playful approach to young children was common, emotional rewards were hardly the main point of parent–child relations.

Many family members had little daily contact with each other aside from work roles; they took their meals hastily and without much conversation. Not surprisingly, rates of violence within families and within the wider village community were high. Some crime and violence resulted from bands of landless men, whose desperation drove them to pillage; some resulted from attacks by members of the upper classes on a largely defenseless peasantry. The material tensions of rural life, compounded by close residence and frequent personal friction, and sometimes exacerbated by an excess of alcohol, created violence among villagers as well.

Work and Its Rewards   With all the constraints on rural culture came a richness that undoubtedly compensated for some of the problems. Work, which was typically rather leisurely except at harvest time, provided some satisfactions. Most adults were their own bosses, in terms of determining their day-to-day activities. Few men had to report to anyone on a daily basis; they owned their own land or at least controlled it. Although peasants worked long days and had no specific periods of leisure other than the night's sleep, they had neither the energy nor the desire for frenzied labor. Moreover, limited opportunities for selling or buying goods curbed any general sense that work should be pushed to a maximum. Except for a few (often resented) villagers bent on rising in the local social scale, there was little point to this kind of driving mentality for individual attainment. Labor had a strongly social quality; peasants knew all their workmates, who were usually family members or other villagers. Thus the workday was interspersed with naps, singing, and chatter.

Peasants were guided in some decisions by village elders or a village council when more than individual property was concerned. Villages collectively regulated their common lands, which were used by most villagers to provide firewood and grazing area for animals, and which were essential to the very existence of some landless folk. Common lands were not individually owned, and they served as an emblem of the community's desire to promote general security. Villagers also decided collectively when animals would be let loose for grazing on private lands after the harvest.

Although adult women were legally in their husband's charge and often were not allowed to own property in their own names, they also had a fairly independent sphere of activity that consisted of running the household, maintaining the nearby vegetable garden, and tending the livestock. Children worked for others, for their own parents, or for a local family to whom they were put out as servants. Although adult regulation of their behavior was often rigorous, most male children could hope to rise to ownership on their parents' death, which could cushion their lack of freedom to some extent. Heavily disciplined at times, both male and female children were also given free periods of play in which they encountered less intense adult supervision than their counterparts experience today. Because rural folk had little to teach their children other than discipline, religious values, and work skills, there was little sense that children's free time had to be "usefully" employed.

The Decline of Serfdom

To be sure, many peasants encountered larger restrictions on their freedom of action in the form of obligations owed to landlords. During the early Middle Ages most western European peasants had been serfs, at best semifree, forced to provide labor services and payments in produce to their landlords. Serfdom persisted in many parts of western Europe in 1500, and in some places it had even revived after the plagues of the fourteenth century. Many large estates were still held by monastic orders or other church bodies and by aristocratic landlords. Some peasants still owed money rents to the landlord, and perhaps limited work service on the estates. However, most peasants were no longer actually serfs; some were essentially free farmers, particularly in England.

This incomplete freedom of many rural people, especially on the Continent, would provoke bitter complaints from peasants for several centuries to come. It had already inspired many sweeping rural uprisings from the late Middle Ages onward. Furthermore, trends toward greater freedom for peasants in western Europe ran markedly counter to the growing enserfment of peasants in the Muslim world and in eastern Europe in the centuries before and after 1500. Peasant rebellions in the West more commonly expressed resentment at freedoms not yet completely accorded than at outright servitude.

Festivals   Work was also punctuated by a rich popular tradition of festivals, the chief form of rural leisure. Concentrated around the holy days such as Christmas, the carnival before Lent, and Easter, festivals dotted the yearly calendar, providing up to eighty days a year of merry diversion. They celebrated saints' days, the completion of planting and of harvest, and local triumphs such as the expulsion of the Muslim invaders from southern Italy centuries before. Many festivals embraced pre-Christian elements. In the Scandinavian midsummer festival, also found in parts of France, a tall tree was burned to assure that the sun would stay high in the sky.

Festivals served a number of social purposes. They helped cement ties within the village community, as the celebrations involved everyone. They helped alleviate potential discontent; young men could let off steam in fierce wrestling matches or tugs of war, which often pitted the unmarried against the younger married men. Indeed, festivals tolerated a certain amount of youthful violence, as when young people would pull down an outhouse or a wooden chimney. They also allowed an even larger number of villagers to enforce community standards. For example, a procession might gather to revile an older woman who was trying to marry a younger man. Masked figures were allowed to shout insults at passersby: the local landlord, the tax collector, a man accused of being betrayed or beaten by his wife. In this regard festivals provided a brief sense of the world turned upside down, in which actions or words normally prevented by rules of social order could provide relief. They featured abundant feasting, with unusual amounts of meat and drink for a people whose daily diets were far more limited; lots of games and competitions with a strong aggressive element, for a people who were normally supposed to be more circumspect in their behavior; and more than the usual opportunities for courtship and sexual activity as well.

The wearing of fancy costumes and masks typified the sense of release that festivals offered. To be sure, entertainments were often crude; in village festivals, people provided their own singing, sports, and dancing, with few if any "professionals" involved such as wandering jugglers or animal trainers.

Participation—a keen sense of involvement—was precisely the point of the festivals. Their intensity allowed many a peasant to get through ordinary days thinking of the last occasion or dreaming of the next one, in a society that did not allow time or energy for more regular doses of entertainment.

Peasant Beliefs   In addition to the values embodied in ordinary work and festival leisure alike, peasant culture offered something of a world-view, carefully preserved in the oral tradition, that made some sense of situations that might strike us as extremely harsh. A strong current of animism boiled beneath the surface of formal Christianity. Many peasants believed that natural objects were inspired by divine spirits for good or evil, and they had a host of rituals to conciliate the good spirits and fend off the evil ones. Rituals were available to prevent illness. A frog might be held up to the throat of a coughing child, in the belief that the sickness could be transferred to the animal—hence the phrase, "a frog in my throat." Rituals might be used to make a barren woman conceive, or to prevent the birth of unwanted children. "White magic," using rituals or charms to attract good fortune, was more common than defensive magic against evil spirits.

An intense, if not always entirely orthodox, Christianity overlay other popular beliefs. The year's calendar was organized around religious events. Symbolic gestures, such as making the sign of a cross in a new loaf of bread, brought Christianity into ordinary daily acts. Baptism of a newborn child included dropping salt, an ancient symbol of purity, on the infant's tongue to drive away demons and strengthen the child in the Christian faith. Church services were conducted in Latin; but there were also stories in the vernacular languages to demonstrate God's power and Christ's mercy, to show that improper behavior would be punished but that there was a better life after death awaiting the good Christian. Special religious charms helped ward off disaster.

In short, the peasant possessed a popular set of beliefs and ceremonies that could explain a difficult and often dangerous world and to some extent, even manage it. Illness and bad harvests were punishments for sin. Prayers and ceremonies were ways to prevent them, or to deal with them when they arrived. Priests offered sacraments and indulgences, or reductions of penalties for sin, to those who promised to live better or who accomplished special acts such as visiting a religious shrine. In a world that was uncertain, even terrifying—storms could ruin a crop; darkness made night fearsome—peasants had some power to act, and more power to hope.

A Traditional Outlook

The peasant world was also cushioned psychologically by its embracing community and tradition. Peasant youth often faced severe discipline but had few problems of choice. The future they could expect was the life of their own parents, quite familiar to them through daily work. The village community could be intrusive as it sought to discipline its members by labeling deviant acts as shameful, but it also provided a wide circle of acquaintances and tangible aid in times of trouble. Even the typical pattern of landholding expressed the spirit of community support. Most peasant owners held a set of divided strips rather than a single plot of land. This pattern resulted in part from accidents of inheritance, but it also followed from a desire to scatter each person's land among various fields that differed in fertility and exposure to bad weather. The result was that a peasant's holdings were hard to farm efficiently because of the travel time necessary to get from one plot to the next. Yet the pattern of holdings promoted the greater goal of security in a community environment. Children could be left to community supervision rather than allowed to interact intensely with parents alone. Through their common lands, communities could also help families provide for members who

A peasant community at play. Pieter Bruegel, *Peasant Dance*, c. 1566–1567.

lacked land, or who were retarded or mentally ill and so incapable of running a normal family farming operation.

Even death lost some of its sting in the environment of community and traditional religion. To be sure, plagues were "scourges of the devil" and seemed to bring hell to earth. But a normal death—from respiratory disease, for example—might allow a peasant to assemble his family around him, to put his affairs in order, and to die convinced, as were those gathered near, that all the proper ceremonies had been observed.

An outlook that included magical and religious beliefs and community support was widely shared throughout society among men and women alike, even among city folk and in the upper classes. Some women may have shared notions that they, who were considered inferior to men, were especially punished for sin or made dangerously lustful by their physical nature. But special beliefs about women, and separate roles within the family, did not create widely separate gender cultures. For example, common attitudes about the economy prompted women as well as men to participate widely in popular protests. At another level, there was little rush to distinguish between young boys and girls in dress. It was enough that later training through work linked boys to their fathers or to other men, and girls to adult women and *their* sphere.

It is possible today to look back on the traditional world of the western European peasant with nostalgia. These people knew how to die a good death, in contrast to more modern people who would seek to fight death to the last. They knew how to take care of the defective among them, save for the terrifyingly insane, rather than trying to cast them out in some special asylum. They knew how to join work and a rich social life, and they participated in a rewarding leisure—rather than passively allowing other people to entertain them.

Of course, this nostalgia must be balanced with a realistic outlook. Reliance on tradition and a fatalistic acceptance of many problems helped keep material conditions poor and death rates high. Family and community relations were hardly serene, as we have seen, and festivals expressed the undercurrent of fear and violence that ensnared this society. But it is true that rural traditions offered satisfactions as well as problems, true also that they limited any real sense of alternatives. Peasants were not entirely passive. Popular belief by 1500 included a strain of egalitarianism—a belief that inequality was improper, condemned by God. Thus English peasants, a hundred years before, had shouted the couplet: "When Adam delved and Eve Span, who was then a gentleman," in attacks on landlords and government tax agents. But along with the sporadic undercurrent of protest against injustice came a substantial belief that the present order had been ordained by God, that people should accept the station in life into which they had been born. Strong family discipline, with emphasis on the authority of parents (and particularly fathers), helped build this belief early in life. Not surprisingly, popular stories and ballads often stressed the goodness and bravery of rulers, particularly heroic figures such as King Arthur or "good king" Wenceslas of Bohemia. Above all, even when aroused, the western European peasantry could articulate no sense that any new system could serve them well. They frequently riorted in belief that their kings were good and only misled by bad advisers. When they attacked some injustice, they claimed that it was wrong because it contravened traditional arrangements: Landlords had taken land that once belonged to peasants, or had imposed dues that in the better society of the past had not been present.

Although the peasant world was by no means serene and certainly harbored tensions, it remained bounded by the need to appeal to tradition. This characteristic, as well as the comforts a traditional way of life provided, influenced how peasants would react to new sources of change.

The World of Cities

Urban and Rural Life: Differences and Similarities in Outlook

The minority of people who lived in cities often saw striking contrasts between their bustling lives and the suspicious isolation of the peasantry. Many townspeople viewed peasants as though they were animals, as in the Italian song called "The Peasant's Dirty Tricks":

> They are cunning in ill-doing
> The old ones as much as the young
> They all seem rogues to me
> There is no doing business with them
> Don't trust the peasant.

There was a considerable gap between urban and rural life, which contributed to the city-dwellers' suspicions. Most cities were small, in the range of ten thousand to twenty thousand inhabitants, and most recruited new residents from displaced or ambitious former peasants. But urban life focused on the manufacture of craft goods, from baking bread to producing the stained glass of the great cathedrals to fabricating the swords of the nobility. It involved extensive trade, contact with money—few townspeople could subsist on their own production—and more marked social gradations than the countryside, from wealthy merchants to impoverished beggars and unskilled haulers. The towns produced a greater diversity of entertainment, including popular plays or the jugglers and sword-swallowers who competed for attention in the busy squares. They supported more spectacles, including the public executions of criminals to which people thronged. And they were ravaged more by disease, because of crowding and poor sanitation.

Yet in many respects townspeople and rural peasants shared a number of common values. Even though cities included many different groups and outright strangers, they possessed a strong sense of community. Most policing activity, for example, was undertaken by community groups, rather than by professional law officers. Ordinary townspeople alternated in service on night watches, for although governments organized law courts and punishments, they did not yet extend to general police service.

Townspeople of all stations also participated in the festival traditions, adding only somewhat more elaborate trappings than villagers could afford but retaining the basic forms and purposes common to towns and countryside alike. Races, animal-baiting, feasts, and bonfires punctuated the urban year. On the most important occasions floats and parades celebrated key urban groups, such as the craft associations, students, or women who cared for children. Here as in rural festivals, the theme of ridiculing the powerful and those who did not live up to community standards prevailed. Husbands who had been beaten by their wives were paraded, riding backwards on donkeys, in many French town carnivals. Church rituals were parodied, and even parental authority might be teased in this topsy-turvy atmosphere; for example, in some processions sons mimicked spanking their fathers. City populations and main squares permitted more formal stage shows than were possible in the rural world, and a tradition of urban drama, both religious and profane, had developed in the Middle Ages that would later nourish Italian comedy and the plays of Elizabethan dramatists such as William Shakespeare.

Crafts, Guilds, and Merchants

Townspeople also shared work values with their rural brethren, as well as a fair variety of tasks, for although some craft work was more specialized than rural labor, it characteristically involved a variety of processes from raw material to finished product. The social context of work was also prominent in the cities. Most artisan masters, who owned their own shops, lived there as well, and they depended for their livelihood on assistance from other family members. Outsiders might be taken in as apprentices (teenagers who were learning the craft skill) or journeymen. These people were typically housed and fed by the master, so that a family environment—not necessarily a loving one—described the work. Some artisans developed a particular, virtually artistic, pride in their skill that peasants might lack, but both experienced the same rhythms of work, including long hours at relatively slow pace.

Manufacturing at the craft level was the major occupational sector in the cities. The community context of craft manufacturing was more fragile than that of peasant villages, though even peasants faced internal tensions because of the differences in the amounts of land they worked. Craft work featured artisan masters, skilled workers who owned the shop where the work took place; journeymen, who owned their tools and had completed their training, and who worked alongside the masters but did not run the shop; and apprentices, who were technically in a years-long period of training but who also did many menial tasks. The artisan tradition, and the guild organizations that were common in most specific trades, sought to limit rifts among the three groups of workers by regulating behavior and limiting the number of inferior workers—apprentices and journeymen—any master could employ. In theory an apprentice could serve a time as journeyman and then buy, inherit, or acquire through marriage the master's shop—thus achieving equality over a working lifetime. But tensions among the work groups, and also the exclusion of women from many (though not all) urban crafts, rubbed against group cohesion. No clear alternatives to group work values emerged, however, and symbolic support for such values, in the form of craft parades and costumes, remained high.

Market day in the city of Augsburg in the sixteenth century featured a procession of merchants.

Even the economic spirit of the cities did not differ completely from that of the peasantry. Cities were based on trade. Merchant activity was fundamental, and western Europe was already noteworthy for its vigorous merchant spirit, and particularly for the extensive powers that merchants wielded in urban governments. Some merchants made considerable fortunes. Western European cities already had substantial banking operations and far-flung overseas trading establishments. A spirit of capitalism, in the sense of investing amid risks but with goals of high profit, was already planted. Although it flourished most abundantly in the cities of Italy, where Mediterranean trade provided an unusual spur, extensive trading networks also operated out of many northern cities. In the Low Countries as in Italy, some urban merchants had even gained control of a rural-based manufacturing system. In this domestic, or putting-out, system, merchants bought raw materials (usually wool or flax) for distribution to workers in cottages, and then collected and sold the thread or cloth that resulted. Investment was modest, insofar as workers provided the tools and space, but the operation subjected labor to the control of profit-seeking merchants.

Although capitalist motives and organizations existed, they were not really typical of the urban economy. The characteristic urban economic institution, the guild, deliberately sought to *limit* individual profit-seeking in the name of collective security and harmony. Guilds of merchants in a given town thus regulated access to bargain materials, so that each guild member would have a share. And they tried to enforce some standards of dealing fairly with customers. Craft guilds not only limited the number of journeymen and apprentices a master might take, so that no one operation would grow too large, but they also restricted the total number of craftsmen in a given trade in one town as protection against the entry of unauthorized outsiders, lest overproduction reduce earnings. At the same time, craft guilds assured standards of training and judged the skill levels of apprentices as a protection to their art and for consumers. They tried to defend traditional procedures against new equipment that might devalue the worth of artisans and the quality of their products. Guilds also provided a community context for their members within the city, as members were marked by distinctive uniforms and social activities. The "double-edged" quality of community life, in providing identity but also constraint, showed in guilds' requirements that members participate in group activities; here too, community life was a protection but also an intrusive obligation.

Multiple Values and the Rise of Urban Influence

City dwellers around 1500 probably prided themselves on their wit compared to that of their slower country cousins. But despite differences in style and specific environment, they shared many fundamental viewpoints with their rural fellows. Religious values ran deep in the cities. Urban traditions allowed some mocking of pompous priests and other authorities, but piety was widespread. Indeed, many cities supported lay groups for expressions of piety in the two centuries prior to 1500. Nor were city people exempt from many of the superstitions that greeted problems of disease or natural calamity. Charms, incantations, and folk remedies were urban as well as rural responses to the threat of sickness, along with prayer and religious observance. Nevertheless, the network of urban centers that had grown up particularly during the Middle Ages provided distinct departures from rural ways, in terms of economic activity and even economic motives. Because of the cities' greater resources and diversity, cultural forms varied also. Urban and rural people alike were aware of the distinction between town and countryside; a rural value system that placed greatest emphasis on owning land jostled against the bases of urban status, which had more to do with skill and money. Not long before 1500, Christian writers had often criticized merchants' quest for profits, implying with the Bible that it would be difficult for anyone who dealt mainly with money to enter heaven. However, by 1500 Christianity had made its peace with the merchant class, and by this time the merchants, despite their distinct commercial outlook, had come to fit into society's shared values.

As well as engendering somewhat distinctive values, cities harbored their own problems. They were more dangerous than the countryside, and decidedly more prone to disease. Western Europe around 1500 was locked into a cycle of recurrent plague, particularly bubonic plague; this cycle had begun with devastating effect in the fourteenth century, and it would continue until the seventeenth century when various factors, including more effective policing of borders by stronger central governments, brought the problem under partial control. Plagues affected rural people too, but they spread much more widely in the cities, where they struck every decade or two, causing loss of life and economic disruption. Partly due to plagues, city populations could not sustain themselves; because their death rates were higher than their birth rates, they had to depend on immigration from the countryside for a stable population of workers. Plagues also brought social tensions. They spread most widely among the urban poor, whose squalid conditions almost invited epidemic disease. Fears of plague began to breed suspicions of the poor among wealthier groups. These new fears encouraged social divisions that would become steadily wider in the sixteenth and seventeenth centuries. Here too, cities took the lead.

The World of Power

Above the urban and rural worlds of the common people were those who wielded special kinds of power. Western society was sufficiently complex to generate a number of forms of power by 1500. Wealthy merchants possessed power through the goods and labor they could command. Some lent money to kings, and through this means—or simply because their abilities were recognized—they gained political as well as monetary power. Leading churchmen were also important centers of power. The Catholic church had long since developed a hierarchical organization from the ordinary faithful, through priests, to bishops, and finally to the pope in Rome. Priests had spiritual powers because they were held to be ordained by God through a special sacrament. They could offer other sacraments, including baptism and communion, to ordinary believers as a favored channel to salvation. Their power as special representatives of God was quite real in the world of 1500; but upper churchmen had additional resources. They commanded considerable wealth, because the church tithed (or taxed) ordinary believers and had substantial holdings in land. They could pressure political authorities to support their religious interests. Governments had often followed the church's lead in attacking heretics through military force and judicial executions. Churchmen also had power through their literacy and wide-ranging intellectual inquiry, in a world that was still mainly nonliterate. Ordinary priests might have little more formal knowledge than their parishioners, but leading churchmen received formal schooling. In 1500 the church sponsored most of what intellectual activity there was, or at least had done so until recently. Most schools and universities were church-run operations; theology, the study of God and His workings, was still officially the queen science.

Land as Power

Although the powers of knowledge, special access to God, and money were very real, the two primary sources of power in 1500 remained ownership of substantial landed estates and the control of military force. This is to say that the key power group in 1500 in most of western Europe remained the landed, military nobility. The importance of land for a power base is obvious. Despite the rise of cities, agriculture produced the greatest wealth in Western society. In most parts of western Europe, nobles controlled only a minority of all land outright. Yet they had more than enough to support their families on the basis of produce and rents from the peasants who actually worked their estates. Indeed, great nobles could afford a substantial court life and paid retainers to serve in their personal military forces. Their wealth far surpassed that of most merchants.

The military powers of the nobility were somewhat less preeminent than before, but were nonetheless substantial. During most of the Middle Ages, nobles had done the bulk of the fighting, for they alone could afford horses, swords, and armor. Peasants might be dragooned (or drafted) to help set up camps, but the common people did little in the way of combat. This pattern had begun to change, particularly in the century before 1400. In Italy, city governments supported paid military men who were not necessarily from the nobility. During the Hundred Years' War between England and France, the English began to use bowmen, drawn from peasant or yeoman ranks, whose weapons were quite effective against the noble cavalry of France. These developments began to eat away at the nobility's monopoly of military power. Nevertheless, in most areas nobles alone retained the right to carry swords. They continued to dominate the ranks of military leaders, even when their forces now included some footsoldiers and bowmen.

The continued military power of the nobility was demonstrated, between 1453 and 1471, in the Wars of the Roses in England. During these wars great nobles chose sides between two competing families, each vying for the king's throne. Each side recruited various lesser nobles and managed to generate substantial chaos in the kingdom as a whole. Although a new royal family, the Tudors, began to restore order after 1485, the independent military strength of the nobility remained a factor to reckon with in England and throughout most of western Europe for some time.

Members of the nobility often aligned with the reigning monarch, serving as his generals and chief administrators. Nobles were also closely linked to the church. Many of the leading churchmen, including monks, came from noble ranks. This was an excellent way to place younger sons who could not inherit the family estates, and it also served to promote the political interests of the class.

Hereditary Power

Noble status was passed on by inheritance. It was not impossible for a commoner to rise to noble rank, particularly by bureaucratic service to a king. But the hereditary principle of the nobility was jealously defended. Many nobles still operated as clan leaders, linking their families through marriage ties while seeking to oppose rival clans.

The hereditary and clan features of noble power placed a premium on patriarchal authority. Marriages were carefully arranged to further male advantage, whereas women were rarely consulted about choice of mate and often treated as little more than breeding stock. Patriarchalism ran stronger in the upper class than among ordinary people, where women's work was too vital to ignore. Noblewomen could develop only informal power by running a complex household and participating in arrangements for their children. They could participate in some of the activities of the culture of the nobility, which featured extensive ceremonies and entertainments as well as male-dominated hunts.

The position of the nobility was often resented by those outside its ranks, for the class, though small in size—often consisting of less than three percent of the total population—monopolized most privileges. Townspeople had a long history of resentment and often served as allies of kings against rebellious nobles, for quite apart from questions of power the nobles' fighting and courtly code downplayed the hardworking, money-making virtues of the merchant groups. Peasants had complaints as well. Periodic risings against the remaining obligations of serfdom and against the large estates were directed above all against the noble class. Peasants resented the nobles' attempts to monopolize hunting. Poaching and other "crimes" revealed the popular belief that the nobles were claiming more than their due.

Despite the fact that the obligations of peasants had tended to lessen from the later Middle Ages onward, rents and labor service could still be crushing burdens. Nobles' "war games" also brought hardship. Few people were actually killed in battle, but fighting forces lived off the land, depending on spoils rather than formal pay. They also brought disease and a multitude of vagabond-criminals in their wake. Peasants had scant power to resist an invading force. Lacking effective weapons and training, they could only appeal to their king for protection—or to the local noble.

The Powerful and the Powerless: A Common Culture

The division between the powerful and the powerless could be agonizing, but the gulf was not total. Medieval theorists had pictured society as a living organism: nobles as the fighting arms, the clergy as the soul, peasants as the sturdy feet. Although the functions and powers of each part clearly differed, each was essential for the survival of the social body. The picture was too neat, ignoring the conflicts of interest that obviously arose between the nobles and the peasants. But it was true that the nobility shared many concerns and values with the majority of commoners.

Grain was a measure of one's wealth in the sixteenth century, and manual labor the norm for most people—including women and children.

Their religious outlook was scarcely different: Christianity by way of the Catholic faith was the path to salvation. And although they might use doctors in cases of illness, and had enough wealth to flee population centers during plagues, the nobility shared with the common folk the variety of beliefs, from medicine through astrology and symbolic cures, of how to protect their health.

Powerful and powerless participated in other elements of the popular culture as well. Although the former had their own pastimes, including those like jousting that related to military training, they also participated in festivals. Noble sons took a prominent role in town processions, wearing masks and leading games with the best of them. Noble landlords helped patronize key village festivals, and even tolerated the festivals' symbolic attacks on the powerful. Many nobles were no more refined in their personal habits than most peasants. Although new codes of politeness had won some popularity in the noble class during the late Middle Ages, many nobles ate just as greedily, burped and spat just as publicly, and enjoyed ribald jokes about sex or urination just as much as many peasants did. Although many nobles lived in spacious palaces, they had no more sense of personal privacy than did ordinary people, conducting many activities among guests and retainers. The tension between the nobles' clearly separate status and their participation in the common culture was a legacy of medieval history that would persist well beyond 1500.

Tides of Change: The Renaissance

New currents were beginning to alter Western life on several fronts by 1500, often coexisting uneasily with the basic features of society inherited from the past. The most obvious set of changes was summed up in the movement known as the Renaissance. The Renaissance, which had taken shape in Italy over a century earlier and was now penetrating western Europe more generally, was above all an alteration of Western high culture—that is, the world of formal ideas, the most prestigious literature, and the arts. The Renaissance also had important, though more limited, changes in store for the organization and function of the state, here too working against previously dominant medieval patterns.

Italy, the initial center of the Renaissance, had long been organized in a welter of city-states and small kingdoms, in contrast to the feudal monarchies to the north. It boasted strong and indigenous contacts with classical antiquity, and unusually extensive trade, particularly around the Mediterranean. In short, Italy was something of an anomaly during the Middle Ages, and it now extended its distinctive qualities into an alternative cultural style.

Renaissance culture was first defined by great thirteenth- and fourteenth-century writers such as Dante, Petrarch, and Boccaccio, who knew and valued classical literature and scorned the rougher styles of many medieval writers. In addition to their concerns for stylistic elegance, these writers began to deal with more strictly secular subjects than had been popular in the Middle Ages. Petrarch wrote love poems to his Laura, and other poems praising his own valor in climbing mountains—a new sign of individualism and pride in purely human achievements. Boccaccio wrote earthy stories of love and lust, though he later apologized and returned to a stricter religious faith. The Italian Renaissance was quickly defined as well by new artists who developed a new system of perspective that allowed three-dimensional portrayals of nature. Using increasing realism, artists began to copy classical styles and subjects, painting gods and goddesses or strictly human themes in addition to Christian motifs. Technical advances in oil painting, as well as the development of perspective, added to the new artistic surge.

Seldom has an age produced as many cultural "greats" as did Renaissance Italy, led by the bustling commercial city of Florence. A new "service class" of architects built churches and public buildings in classical

Two aspects of the Renaissance style in painting were an emphasis on anatomic detail and a variety of expressions. Detail from Michelangelo's *Last Judgement*, Sistine Chapel, 1534–1541.

styles, using the square shapes and elaborate columns first devised in ancient Greece; the Gothic, the characteristic style of the Middle Ages, was progressively abandoned, even denounced. Painters became increasingly precise in their realism. Leonardo da Vinci advanced the realistic portrayal of the human body in art, even painting pictures of medical dissections. The statues of Michelangelo offered graphic displays of human musculature. Portraits of individual people also flourished, again with realism taking precedence over spirituality. Italian literature, after the first great Renaissance writers, was somewhat less lively. During the early 1400s many writers slavishly copied Latin and Greek forms, then shifted back to Latin in the process. Increasingly they emphasized secular, even practical, subjects and purely human beauty; great scorn was heaped on the rationalistic philosophical interests and styles of medieval writers.

During the later fifteenth century and into the early sixteenth, Italian writers, returning to use their own language, developed important statements of historical method and political theory. New interest arose in testing the authenticity of documentary evidence about the past, and a number of long-accepted church documents were shown to be forgeries. For these writers history, like art, should focus on the realities of the human condition. In his essay *The Prince*, Niccolò Machiavelli described the actual methods a ruler should use to gain and maintain power: how to employ cruelty, when to deceive and when to tell the truth, how to sway public opinion. Machiavelli combined detailed knowledge of current Italian politics with the use of Greek and Roman examples—a characteristic Renaissance mixture.

The Themes of the Italian Renaissance

Italian Renaissance culture involved a number of themes. It represented a dramatic shifting of interest, not only away from religion but also from much formal philosophy and science. Few Renaissance writers in any direct way attacked religion—but few were intensely pious. Scientific work continued, as in the study of optics, but for a time it took a back seat to the new, excited embrace of the artistic vision. Artists, in turn, became increasingly important, patronized by governments, aristocrats, and business leaders. No longer did the church monopolize the organization of culture, although the Renaissance papacy ardently collected secular art and literature at considerable expense. Artists, proud of their contributions as individuals, were known by name. Even music, previously composed for the most part anonymously and often maintained through memory, was now composed by identified individuals and carefully written down. Artistic individualism led to many jealous rivalries, and to some assertions that culture was improving because of the newly enlightened efforts of the leading figures. Renaissance reverence for the achievements of the ancients prevented any sweeping belief that human society could progress, but there was little question in Renaissance eyes that its culture was far superior to its medieval levels. The cultivation of artistic excellence and the confidence in the powers of individual creativity set the stage for a new disdain for unexamined traditionalism.

The overall spirit of the Italian Renaissance was summed up in the theme of humanism. *Humanism* initially meant a focus on classical literature, but it came to have the wider implication of placing humankind at the center of intellectual and artistic interest. Human activities, not acts of God, were the stuff of history and the proper subject for art and inquiry. Humans could achieve excellence in various fields, ranging from politics and war through courtly manners to art. Humankind was also capable of ethical behavior, if properly tutored; philosophers tended to discuss ethics somewhat separately from religion, in the style of ancient writers such as Cicero.

The Spread of the Renaissance Northward

As the Renaissance spread northward, from about 1450 onward, it retained many of the Italian emphases but typically in less radical form.

Northern humanists looked to classical art and literature, but they were more vigorous in their continued concern for religious values. "Christian humanism," indeed, is a term used to describe the Northern Renaissance tone. The most famous northern humanist, the Duthman Desiderius Erasmus (1469?–1536), rejected what he saw as the "pure paganism" of Italian literature. He urged that rulers be taught a careful combination of classical ethics and religion. He also worked to improve the text of the New Testament by making it correspond to the new standards of textual criticism. His goal was to enhance religion and make it more accessible:

> Christ wished his mysteries to be published as openly as possible. I wish that even the weakest woman should read the Gospel . . . and I wish [the Bible] were translated into all languages.

The religion of the northern humanists was not the religion of the medieval church. Erasmus wanted a pure, direct faith, rather than the elaborate speculations of the scholastic theologians. He wanted simple piety based on the immediate word of God, not the elaborate ceremonies of the church. Furthermore, many northern humanists were biting in their attacks on many traditional habits and institutions, and some added a frank appreciation of man's physical instincts. The French writer François Rabelais used a gross and earthy humor to ridicule aspects of contemporary religion and abstract philosophy while emphasizing the importance of simple prayer and sound education.

Northern artists were less quickly affected by the Italian Renaissance than leading writers were, and religious themes and Gothic styles predominated until after 1500. Soon, however, partly because of the importation of Italian craftsmen, classical styles began to take over in the building of palaces and leading public buildings in the north, and the new interest in realism and individualism began to affect painting and sculpture.

The Power Elite in the Renaissance

The culture of the Renaissance remained largely the province of an elite of rulers, wealthy aristocrats, and some rich urban businessmen. It did not fully embrace even upper-class women, and it was certainly not a mass movement. Ordinary people in the cities, particularly in Italy, shared in the Renaissance only by seeing the new public buildings; most of the new art was held in private hands. The peasant majority was entirely bypassed. In fact, Italian city-states ruthlessly exploited the countryside under their control, in the interest of financing urban improvements. Although a few cultural leaders such as Erasmus dreamed of spreading new knowledge to the common man, including more direct access to the Bible, the tone of Renaissance education was fiercely elitist. Renaissance interests in developing new classical knowledge and well-rounded human abilities certainly dictated a deep concern for education, and for its separation from strict church control and from the hand of the medieval universities. The profession of tutor, along with a variety of schools, developed to pass the new approach to knowledge on to new generations. But these schools were for wealthy and nobly born men (upper-class women were excluded from Renaissance education or at best given a very different version). Indeed, the Renaissance ideal of the classical education—with strong emphasis on Greek and Latin, ancient history, literature and ethics, but also moral training and practice in games and etiquette—became a standard for education for the male upper class of Western society well into the nineteenth century.

This is not to say that Renaissance culture had no impact on the common person. Northern playwrights in the earthy Renaissance tradition, such as Shakespeare later in the sixteenth century, won a wider popular audience in the larger cities. But overall, the cultural impact of the Renaissance on ordinary people was gradual at best, and by increasing the formality and secularism of high culture the Renaissance for a time created an even greater rift between elite and mass tastes than had existed during most of the Middle Ages.

The Renaissance also had ambiguous implications for women, even in the upper classes. Wealthy women could enjoy some features of Renaissance culture along with men, and their level of education rose a bit. Rabelais embraced both genders in his praise of sensual pleasures. But Renaissance styles of life tended to divide women and men in the upper classes: women became objects of beauty and sexual gratification, trained largely as ornaments, whereas men were schooled for worldly interests in business, politics, and war. The Renaissance did help launch an important discussion of women's roles, based on a tension between new interests and culture but no new functions, that we must return to in dealing with issues in Western society later. However, this new cultural ambiguity was largely an upper-class province.

The Renaissance was not, however, simply a cultural movement, and some of its other features had a wider outreach. Aside from Machiavelli's frank political theories, the Renaissance outlook had important implications for politics. Italian city-states, particularly during the fifteenth century, developed new forms and new functions. Venice, a leading trading center, was governed by a council drawn from the city's upper class. Other cities were ruled by individuals who based their government on raw military power or on merit, rather than on any claim to hereditary status. There were even some brief hints at democracy, as urban artisans sometimes sought a direct political voice; these recalled earlier centuries when popular participation in city government had been greater. City-state governments were not content with traditional roles in defense and the administration of justice. They patronized culture, tried to promote the urban economy, and even sketched rudimentary welfare measures for the city poor by bringing in grain during famine periods. The new interest in more rational and extensive administration brought a concern for censuses and other inquiries into popular conditions. It also promoted new diplomatic styles, as the city-states exchanged ambassadors and thus launched one of the standard features of subsequent Western foreign relations.

When Renaissance political impulses traveled to the north, they had more impact on the style than on the substance of monarchy. French, English, and Spanish kings increased their patronage of the arts and built more luxurious palaces. Francis I claimed new authority over the operations of the Catholic church in France. Leading monarchs from the new Tudor dynasty in England, particularly Henry VIII and Queen Elizabeth, ruled with strong hands. They took new interest in encouraging trading companies and colonial enterprises, and they even passed laws on the treatment of the poor. They were also somewhat franker in their aggressive ambitions than medieval kings had been, as they pursued wars of self-interest unadorned by apparent religious or legal justifications. Thus England pursued a lengthy effort to conquer Ireland, while France not only invaded Italy but also tried to construct alliance systems to counter the power of Habsburg-ruled Spain and the Holy Roman Empire. Despite these efforts, the actual structure and functions of northern European governments changed little as a result of the Renaissance. At most,

---

RENAISSANCE ITALIAN DIPLOMACY

Between 1450 and 1494 the Italian states played an absorbing diplomatic and military game, largely apart from the larger nations of Europe. They formed elaborate alliances, signed many mutual treaties, and essentially invented modern Western techniques of diplomatic relations. The guiding principle in this Italian system was the preservation of the balance of power. Francesco Guicciardini, a Florentine historian, put it this way:

> It was the aim of each [of the major Italian powers] to preserve its own territory and defend its own interest by carefully making sure that no one of them grew strong enough to enslave the others; and to this end each gave the most careful attention to even minor political events or changes.[1]

Venice was the most powerful single state, so Florence, Milan, and Naples typically united against it. But the system depended on careful reactions to any new move by any state, which kept Italian diplomacy in a perpetual state of hyperexcitement.

The political intensity of the Italian city-states overlapped with Renaissance culture. New rulers could feel that the state, too, was a work of art, their power an expression of their individual excellence. But the city-state style of government had distinct limitations. City states spent a great deal of time warring against each other. They were no match for the larger monarchies that had formed elsewhere in Europe. By the 1490s, when French and then Spanish kings had developed a firmer hold over their own countries, they understandably turned their attention to this rich but weak peninsula. Successive invasions reduced the independence of the city-states and sent Italian politics into a prolonged decline.

[1] *Opere in edite di Francesco Guicciardini*, ed. P. and L. Guicciardini, vol. 3, *Storia Fiorentine* ch. 11 (Florence: n. p., 1869), 105.

THE STRUGGLE BETWEEN THE HABSBURGS AND THE KINGS OF FRANCE: THE LEADING DIPLOMATIC ISSUE OF THE EARLY 1500s

A key diplomatic rivalry in 1500 and for some decades thereafter pitted the kings of France—from the Valois family—against the Habsburgs. This was a quarrel between dynasties, not nations. The French king was beginning to assert new powers over his people, forming a rudimentary professional army and playing down the role of the nobility and the medieval parliament. In a revealing statement in 1527, the head of France's highest court told Francis I that "we do not wish to ·dispute or minimize your power, that would be sacrilege, and we know very well that you are above the laws." But, in fact, there were a host of restrictions on the power of the king, including chronic shortage of money; the French monarchy had not set up a new kind of state. The Habsburgs had an even shakier power base. They had a territorial core in Austria, parts of Bohemia, and the Netherlands, and Habsburgs were regularly elected Holy Roman Emperor. This post gave them vague authority over Germany, but effective rule came from smaller states. The Habsburgs advanced their power not through new forms of government, but through marriage alliances. The marriage of a Habsburg son to the daughter of Ferdinand and Isabella of Spain put a single ruler on the thrones of Spain and the Holy Roman Empire during several decades of the sixteenth century. In the early 1500s, the Emperor Charles V accomplished a major feat by having family members marry into the royal family of Hungary and Bohemia, the royal family of Portugal, and the royal family of England.

These acts enhanced the personal rivalry between the Habsburgs and the Valois family. Charles feared new French controls over its outlying provinces and also the French invasions of Italy; France feared that the Habsburgs through their marriages might surround France on the east, north, and south by controlling German territories in the Netherlands and Spain. This rivalry produced clashes between France and Spain for control in Italy, as well as attempts to form wider alliances. France temporarily settled quarrels with its traditional rival, England. The French also made contacts with the Muslim Ottoman Empire, which formed a real threat to the Habsburg lands. France also encouraged opposition to the Habsburgs within the German states. A series of conflicts finally dragged to a close through a treaty of 1559, in which France abandoned its claims to Italian territories, where Habsburg Spain now had a strong foothold; but the Habsburgs renounced their claims to several key French provinces. This ended the last purely dynastic rivalry in European history.

the Renaissance slightly accelerated the gradual centralization and the development of nonfeudal armies that had begun in the later Middle Ages.

Trade and Exploration

A Background

Although a Renaissance high culture certainly existed, and a Renaissance politics had some meaning, there was no "Renaissance economy." The Italian city-states still benefited from their extensive trade, particularly their dominance of the Mediterranean. Venice for a time even extended colonies along the Adriatic Sea. In Florence, bankers and merchants were prominent as politicians and patrons of culture. Certainly the Renaissance worldliness was consistent with eager interest in trade. But trade had been gaining earlier in the Middle Ages, and the Renaissance does not mark a sharp rise in the amount or organization of commerce in the West.

Concurrent with the Renaissance, however, was a new surge of Western exploration and discovery, which ultimately brought Western-dominated trade routes to all the major oceans of the world. By 1500 the West's new global role was being launched, and it would evolve as one of the greatest changes of recent centuries. There had been hints of European interest in expansion before. In the tenth century, Viking ships from Scandinavia had crossed the Atlantic, reaching Greenland and then North America. But these adventurers quickly lost interest in their "Vinland," as they called the new continent, in part because they encountered Indian warriors whose weaponry was intimidating. During the eleventh century, Westerners from various countries participated in the crusades to the Holy Land. And in the fourteenth century a number of Italian travelers reached China and Southeast Asia, increasing European interest in this part of the world and augmenting a desire to import spices and other goods. This trade proved onerous to the Europeans, who could only offer crude items in return due to the more sophisticated manufacturing technology of Asia. To make up the balance, the Europeans had to send gold, which was hardly abundant in Europe.

Stimulated by the new contacts with Asia, eager to find better and more direct routes to the East, and spurred by their gold shortage, Europeans began to push out timidly. As early as 1291 an expedition from the Italian port of Genoa sailed into the Atlantic seeking a westward route to the Indies, but it was never heard from again. More modest expeditions from Spain and Italy reached the northwest Atlantic coast of Africa and Atlantic island groups, including the Canaries, in the fourteenth century. Europeans improved their nautical designs in the fifteenth century, developing round-hulled ships for the Atlantic that did not depend on oar propulsion. They also adopted the navigational compass from the Arabs, who had learned of it from the Chinese. Better equipped than ever before, western Europe was ready for its big push in trade and exploration.

The Drive for Exploration around 1500

The small kingdom of Portugal led the way. Portuguese kings had just driven out the Muslims, who still threatened from North Africa. This threat, and the surge of energy that sometimes accompanies expulsion of an occupation force, prompted the Portuguese to look for conquest in Africa. They hoped for exciting discoveries, damage to the Muslim invaders, and gold—for legends of African wealth were tantalizing. Beginning in 1434, guided by Prince Henry the Navigator, the government began sponsoring a series of expeditions down Africa's Atlantic coast, each going a bit farther than its predecessor. Finally the Portuguese pressed around the Cape of Good Hope, eager to reach India and also what they believed were treasure troves on Africa's East Coast. Vasco de Gama, aided by a Hindu pilot picked up in East Africa, did indeed reach India in 1497, returning with a small load of spices, and an annual trading voyage to India quickly developed. Soon the Portuguese ventured farther in the Indian ocean, reaching Indonesia by 1514, then China; by 1542 Portugal had sent an expedition to Japan. One ship, blown off course in the Atlantic, reached Brazil, where the Portuguese proclaimed their sovereignty. As a Portuguese poet later wrote, "And if there had been more world they would have found it."

Meanwhile, Spain, Portugal's larger neighbor, reached for a westward route to India. The Genoese sailor Christopher Columbus received royal backing and set off with three ships in 1492, reaching the West Indies. Follow-up expeditions under Spanish control—one was led by another Italian, Amerigo Vespucci—gave Spain official control over most of the new land, which was soon named America. And by 1519–1521 the Spanish had sailed around the world, passing beneath the southern tip of South America and claiming the Philippines on the way back to Europe.

Europe's new surge of exploration and trade had just begun in 1500, and some leading actors, including England and Holland, had yet to begin the effort. The main impact of the discoveries—trade, wealth, colonies—would also come later. Nevertheless, the unprecedented voyages of Spain and Portugal were a clear sign of Europe's ascendancy on the world scene. New skills in shipbuilding and navigation were combined with striking advances in gunnery. Using knowledge of the Chinese invention of gunpowder, fifteenth-century Europeans had gone well beyond the land mines that the Chinese had developed, fashioning cannons that could send shells a considerable distance and with some claim to accuracy. Here was the secret to Europe's new domination of the seas and coastal regions. Against some groups, such as the Indians of the Americas, Europe's muskets, superior iron weapons, and tools, gave it an edge in weapons on the land—but against most civilizations in Asia the European could as yet claim no such advantage. A new technological edge, focused particularly on a new advance in killing and intimidating, nevertheless serves as a basic explanation for Europe's new world role.

But Europe also had to develop the motives for using technology for expansionist purposes. Greed and God were constant companions in the European ventures. Rising trade interest and the specific problem of gold supply explains part of the motivation. Christian beliefs in the importance of conversion and its possession of apparently exclusive religious truth provided another spur. The culture of the Renaissance may have contributed, as well, by promoting new confidence in human powers and a new desire for achievement—although ironically the new trade patterns, by shifting attention away from the Mediterranean, would soon harm the Italian cities that had produced so much of the new merchant spirit. Once the expansionist thrust began, rivalries among European countries added fuel to the fire, as each major monarchy wanted its new colonies and trade. These rivalries gained greater importance in the sixteenth century.

Changes in Ordinary Life

The beginning of a profound shift in western Europe's world position in 1500 joined the cultural and political changes produced by the Renaissance to suggest a new spirit enlivening the summit of Western society. As ideas and styles changed because of the works of confident Renaissance intellectuals and artists, political leaders developed new tastes and new cunning. Meanwhile, the combined efforts of key rulers and eager merchant-adventurers pushed European flags around the oceans. Political tastes changed more than political forms did, however. And European expansion owed at least as much to earlier merchant ventures and to Christian beliefs as they did to any specifically Renaissance culture.

The concatenation of changes around 1500 would nevertheless have profound consequences for the ordinary people of European society. Renaissance tastes remained rather refined, certainly not quickly producing a popular response. But Renaissance political leaders had wider impact in seeking new taxes to support their new self-image and in bringing new warfare to several parts of Europe. New weapons challenged established habits in Europe as in other parts of the world. The castles of the nobility began to lose their central defensive functions in an age of cannon, and the destructive power of gunpowder created legitimate new fears among ordinary people, who were now more decisively surpassed in weaponry by professional soldiers than ever before. Explorations and new trade routes would ultimately bring new knowledge of the wider world to ordinary people, plus new products and new wealth—a major theme for the sixteenth and seventeenth centuries.

Ordinary people were also generating some changes of their own in the period that led to 1500. Although less dramatic in many cases than the flash of Renaissance art or the great discoveries, the two strands of grassroots change—technology and family structure—may have been just as significant in reshaping European life.

Changes in Technology

Agricultural methods changed little after the great medieval surge, and because agriculture remained Europe's fundamental economic sector, lack of change in this area was a major limitation on any overall technological transformation. But spurred partly by advances learned from contacts with Asia, technological innovation around 1500 focused particularly on manufacturing and mining, in addition to vital advances in shipbuilding and gunnery. Improvements in textile technology also lagged a bit at this point, although there were some changes. Despite the traditionalism of the guild structure, individual European craftsmen were clearly alert to the possibility of technological change.

Many key developments came from the hands of seemingly ordinary craftsmen. In mining, new uses of pulleys and pumps allowed the sinking of deeper shafts, and the production of coal and of metal ores increased fairly steadily. Still more striking were advances in metalwork, as artisans learned how to forge stronger iron and to shape a greater diversity of products. The development of guns and cannon was a key result of this general advance in the metalworkers' craft, which placed western Europe, for the first time in history, on at least a par with the metalworking techniques of the great civilizations of Asia.

One new invention was particularly significant, because it was so obviously linked with the culture of the Renaissance: the printing press. The West had imported knowledge of paper manufacture earlier from China by way of the Middle East; the first paper factory, in Italy, dates from the thirteenth century. Direct contacts with China taught Europeans of the existence of printing in the form of paper money and playing cards. But Chinese printing required that each word or phrase be separately carved on a wooden block, which was extremely time-consuming, and Chinese ideographs were far less adaptable to further printing advance than were the Roman letters of the European languages. Around 1455, several German artisans, including Johannes Gutenberg, experimented with movable type by placing individual letters on a wooden block that would then be rearranged to form new words. By aligning the letters on a large block in separate lines, whole pages could be printed at one time. One of the advantages was that the individual letters could be reused. Gutenberg's Bible, the first printed book in the West, was issued in 1456, and knowledge of the new process spread quickly over Europe. Books could now be printed in less time, at much lower cost, and in far greater quantities than ever before. Here too, Europe seized a new technological lead. By 1500 or shortly thereafter, substantial publishing houses had sprung up in several centers. Most specialized in religious books, but the writings of Renaissance figures such as Erasmus were widely disseminated as well.

The main impact of printing came after 1500. As in other fields, Western Europe in 1500 sat on the edge of far-reaching change. But there is no doubt about the long-range impact of printing, in making ideas of various sorts, both traditional and new, more accessible to a wider array of people than ever before. New technology here would stimulate rising literacy, another feature of the sixteenth century and beyond. Rising literacy would change the way many people thought about themselves and their world and would partially close some of the widening gaps between elite and popular cultures. This dynamic lay in the future; in

1500 printing served primarily to encourage new reading among the already literate sections of the elite.

Changes in Family Structure

Alterations in family structure were in many ways even more fundamental than changes in technology. By the fifteenth century, family structure through most of western Europe was beginning to shift to what has been called the "European-style" family. The label is prosaic enough, but it accurately suggests three features of the family style developing among peasants and artisans that were unusual for an agricultural society. First, ordinary people began marrying relatively late, usually around twenty-five or twenty-six for both men and women. A late age of marriage for men was not uncommon in agricultural societies, but the late age for women was distinctive and, among other things, tended to reduce the number of children born per family. This was simply because marriage occurred some time after puberty and so eliminated several child-bearing years. Second, a large minority of people did not marry at all—sometimes, depending on economic conditions, as many as a third of all adults. Because rates of illegitimate birth were rather low due to the supervision of tightly knit communities and strict religious standards, the effect of the unmarried segment on the whole population was a lower birth rate. Finally, society placed strong emphasis on the nuclear family rather than on the extended family, which was the medieval model; the key family unit was now the husband, the wife, and the children. Nuclear families kept in touch with other family members, including grandparents, but in decision-making and in control of the place of residence the nuclear family became increasingly supreme.

These various shifts in family structure tightened the linkage of the family with property—the peasant's land, the artisan master's shop. The goal of family policy was to limit the birth rate through delayed marriage, so that a given family was unlikely to have more children than it could provide for, always assuming the usual number of infant deaths. Marriage became very difficult for people who had no access to property through inheritance or, for women, no dowries; hence, there were many nonmarrieds, who often worked as dependent laborers for peasant families. The nuclear family, based as it was on the control of property, typically formed only when it was on a solid economic footing. By then older parents had either died or had yielded some or all of their property, often in return for some assurance of support in their later years.

Thus the European-style family contrasted with families in most other parts of the world, including Eastern Europe, in several basic respects. For one thing, it involved later marriage age. For another, it accepted a large minority that did not marry at all. Moreover, it generated a birth rate that was high by our modern standards but lower than average for an agricultural civilization. Finally, it emphasized the nuclear family over the extended family.

The characteristics of the emerging European-type family had a number of social implications. The family of the ordinary person now differed sharply from the patterns of the wealthier land-owning nobility. Nobles married young—at least the woman was young—and had more children than peasants and artisans did, because they had the wealth to support a family of substantial size and because they were eager to assure themselves of adequate heirs for the family line. This was the opposite of what would emerge as the modern family pattern in which poorer people began to have more children than did more substantial property owners. Indeed, the European-style family helped limit European population growth for several centuries. Despite economic advances, Europe did not generate the concentrated populations characteristic of India or China because of the strategies used to maximize access to some modest property.

The nuclear emphasis of the typical Western family may also have altered practical relations between husbands and wives. In terms of law and official ideology, the European family remained strictly patriarchal— that is, dominated by husband and father. But among ordinary people, who lived mainly in family units in which there were only two adults, women's work, support, and even informal participation in family decisions may have increased in importance.

The predominance of the nuclear family was qualified by some periods in the family cycle in which older relatives might be present. It was also qualified by the common presence of nonfamily members, such as apprentices or servants, within the household, which might limit private or intense relationships between husbands and wives. Nevertheless, the bonds of the nuclear family were strong enough to limit the development of separate gender cultures in western Europe, which in other agricultural societies was based on large numbers of same-sex kin in an extended family arrangement. The nuclear family may even have raised some questions about patriarchalism in practice, by making women's contribution to the household vital and highly visible. Certainly there was some gap between women's role in running the nuclear family, despite their somewhat separate tasks from those of men, and their official inferiority.

The development of the European-style family gave rise to other tensions, most obviously sexual ones. The western European family reserved a significant interval between puberty and marriage. Festivals played some role in alleviating tension by giving young unmarried men the chance to display aggression. But there is no question that community control over young people included a strong element of sexual control, or that youth in Western culture was unusually prolonged.

Tension also surfaced with older adults. Because many young adults had chafed under their parents' continued control of property, their sense of obligation to parents (if they became incapacitated, for example) was not always strong. There were few intense emotional links to cushion this generation gap, even though the formal culture, preached certainly by Christian leaders, urged respect for one's elders. This was one reason that older people so often had to have careful contracts drawn up when they surrendered property, to assure that they would not be abandoned. And a minority of the old, particularly from poor families, ended up in hospitals, which at this point in Europe were mainly places to go to die when there was no family available to provide care. Finally, the careful rationality of the European-style family did not guarantee the desired results. Even with late marriage, some families had more children than they could provide for. Villages attempted to alleviate this problem by having excess children placed in the homes of wealthier, particularly childless peasants (10 percent to 20 percent of all couples were biologically infertile). But having many children could still doom a family to poverty, and it helped account for the minority of people later unable to afford marriage.

For all its problems, the European-style family was a fascinating social product. It suggested an unusual attachment to property and avoidance of crowding. It also demonstrated that popular culture, although traditional in many ways, was capable of fundamental change.

The changes in popular life did not mesh neatly with developments in elite culture. (As we will see in later chapters, popular efforts at population control often ran counter to the interest of more active, belligerent governments that encouraged a growth which would spur the economy and provide more potential military recruits.) Although changes in technology and the expansion of commerce affected ordinary people as well as the elite, the high-cultural implications of the Renaissance remained far removed from new family patterns. The ordinary people of Europe remained intensely religious. They saw their identities in terms of family and community, not the self-conscious individualism of Renaissance heroes.

The Problem of Eastern Europe

In 1500 the patterns of Western society discussed in this chapter extended with wide variations from England through Germany. Italy's Renaissance was unique, as were the drive of Spain and Portugal for overseas expansion and the particular fervor of Spanish Catholicism after centuries of battle against Muslim occupation. Patterns of land tenure varied from the largely free farmers of England to pockets of intense serfdom in parts of France and Germany. National monarchies were taking shape in England, France, and Spain, but not in Italy, Germany, or the Low Countries, where regional governments—dukedoms, city-states, archbishoprics—largely prevailed.

Yet there was unity in the West, if only in the sense of a shared general culture. The institutions and some of the beliefs of Catholic Christianity were widespread. Other cultural influences spread fairly readily—hence the broad impact of some basic aspects of the Renaissance. Popular culture, though intensely local in some respects, with particular rituals, saints, and habits, also had some commonalities. The spread of the characteristic forms of the European-style family throughout most of the West was an evidence that, at the level of ordinary people, Western society had some rough coherence.

But the West was not the whole of Europe in 1500. An important zone of southeastern Europe formed part of the Turkish Ottoman Empire. The Turks, who had conquered the ancient Christian city of Con-

stantinople in 1453, were nearing the height of their power. They were
in firm control of Greece and the rest of the Balkans and ready to press
into Hungary. Ottoman control did not convert this part of Europe to
the Muslim religion, except for a minority, but it kept the southeast
rigorously separate from most developments in the West.

More important still was the separate status of Russia, just awakening
after two centuries of domination by the Mongol Tartars. Russia, like
most of the Balkans, had long since converted to the Orthodox version
of Christianity, which did not recognize papal authority. Russia's religion
had little contact with the intellectual and artistic currents of western
European Catholicism during the Middle Ages. Tartar control reduced
Russia's cultural vitality, if only by isolating priests and other intellectual
leaders. The literacy of the priests declined. Tartar domination also disrupted what had been a lively commerce, making Russia more thoroughly an agricultural society than the West. But as princes near Moscow,
who claimed descendance from earlier Russian kings, began to struggle
against the Tartar overlords beginning in the fourteenth century, the vast
country began to produce its own kind of dynamism. A large part of
Russia was freed by 1462, under the leadership of Ivan III (known as Ivan
the Great). Ivan organized a strong army, giving the new government a
military emphasis, and he used loyalties to Russia and to Orthodox
Christianity to win support for his campaigns. By 1480 the Mongols had
been decisively pushed back, and the revived Russian state contained a
vast territory running from the borders of Poland in the west, to the Ural
mountains in the east.

The rulers of the new Russia had a sense of mission. Ivan the Great
married the niece of the last Byzantine emperor; and because the Turks
had taken over this once-great empire, which had succeeded the Roman
Empire in the eastern Mediterranean, Ivan and his advisors now talked
of Russia as the "third Rome" and heir to the great imperial tradition.
Ivan accordingly called himself *tsar*, or "Caesar," and claimed leadership
over the Orthodox religion. These various missions combined with a
simpler desire for new territories—in part to push the Mongols still farther from Russia's heartland—to make Russia an expansionist power from
the 1500s onward. This was a key sign of the nation's new vigor, and it
parallelled the new colonial expansionism of the West at the same time.

But Russia was no extension of Western society. Under the tsars the
Russians developed a firmer tradition of central state dominance than was
true in the West, in part because the Russian nobility was supported by
no prior system of feudalism. Russia's cities remained small, in comparison with Western patterns. There was no strong merchant group, and
even most artisan production occurred in the countryside. Furthermore,
whereas in almost all areas of western Europe the peasantry had shaken
off the most rigid forms of serfdom, Russian peasants, once in freer control of their lands, were now subjected to extensive domination by landlords. From about 1500, noble landlords progressively reduced most Russian
peasants to serfdom, holding over them important legal rights and exacting labor service as well as taxes in produce. It was from the standpoint

of the ordinary people that the societies of Russia and the West were starkly different.

Yet Russia's new vigor would soon make it newly important in European affairs. And Russian awareness of the West increased at the elite levels. By the sixteenth century Russian tsars began importing Italian architects to help design churches and palaces, including the Kremlin, their capital enclave within Moscow. Russia thus partially entered a "zone" of general European culture, just as it began to engage in European diplomatic contacts. From 1500 onward, Russia and the West would become part of each other's history, without at all merging into a single civilization.

Between Russia and the West there were a number of important but loosely organized kingdoms, including Poland, Bohemia, and (except when under Ottoman control) Hungary. These areas were Catholic rather than Orthodox; they used a Latin alphabet for the Slavic (or in Hungary, Magyar) languages rather than the Cyrillic alphabet that Russia and many parts of the Balkans had imported from the Byzantine Empire. They too were less urbanized than the West, and the powers of their landed nobility and their system of serfdom resembled patterns in Russia more than those in the West. These buffer areas of eastern Europe thus stood culturally and geographically between East and West, and they would often form a battleground between the two societies.

Although they emerged from different traditions and had different emphases, western and eastern Europe did have this in common: Both were beginning to flex new muscles around 1500, and both were involved in significant change. This parallelism intertwines the two European neighbors to our own day.

But developments around 1500 were merely a starting point. Western politics and social forms remained far more medieval than novel; and even high culture, jolted by the Renaissance challenge, had yet to take on settled new forms. Far more sweeping innovations were to come in the decades after 1500—innovations that built on and sometimes even attacked the initiatives of the Renaissance thinkers, the seafaring discoverers, and the often anonymous groups who had introduced new technologies and new family forms. Ironically, the next definite step on the path of change came from people who thought they were fighting to restore past values: the reformers of the Christian religion.

FROM COMMERCIAL EXPANSION
AND THE REFORMATION
TO 1648

1501ff Beginnings of European-run African slave trade to the Americas

1503ff Beginning of importation of New World silver; price increase

1509ff Spanish conquest of much of Central and South America

1517 Martin Luther's Ninety-five Theses; beginning of Protestant Reformation

1534 Beginning of Church of England

1534 Foundation of Jesuit Order

1541–1564 Calvin in Geneva

1543 Vesalius's work on anatomy; Copernicus on astronomy

1545–1563 Council of Trent; Counter-Reformation

1550ff Religious Wars in Germany, France, Low Countries, England

1555 Peace of Augsburg recognizes religious division in Germany

1562–1598 Religious wars in France

1572 St. Bartholemew's Day Massacre

1589–1610 Henry IV king

1598 Edict of Nantes

1552–1556 Russian expansion in Central Asia

1553–1584 Ivan the Terrible first tsar in Russia

1556–1598 Philip II King of Spain

1558–1603 Queen Elizabeth I in England

1559ff Dutch wars against Spanish rule

1581 Dutch proclaim independence

1571 Spanish-Italian fleet defeats Turks at Lepanto

1580s–1590s Severe popular protest

1588 England defeats Spanish Armada

1590sff Chartering of the great international trading companies by England, Holland, France

1600ff Peak of witchcraft hysteria

1601 Elizabethan Poor Law (England)

1607ff English colonies in North America

1618–1648 Thirty Years' War

1648 Treaty of Westphalia

1642–1649 English civil wars

1649 Execution of Charles I

1647–1648 Widespread popular protest

CHAPTER

TWO

THE WINDS OF CHANGE: RELIGION AND ECONOMICS IN THE SIXTEENTH AND EARLY SEVENTEENTH CENTURIES

MANY OF THE DEVELOPMENTS already set in motion around 1500 continued during the following century. Although Italy faded, beset by foreign (mainly Spanish) occupation of several key centers plus the decline of Mediterranean trade, the Renaissance spirit still burned brightly in many facets of culture. Renaissance themes and styles in literature spread to writing in French, English, and German, with major writers such as Rabelais and Shakespeare leading the way. The Renaissance also affected scientific work through a new desire to investigate physical phenomena directly rather than simply echoing traditional opinion. European outreach and discovery also continued; the sixteenth century was the great age of Spanish conquest in Central and South America, and English, Dutch, and French explorers began their voyages to North America and elsewhere.

But the key themes of the sixteenth century stemmed from two more novel developments, one in the area of values and beliefs and the other in the area of economic growth: new trends in popular mentalities and in commercialization began to take shape. A new breed of religious reformer shattered the longstanding unity of Western Christendom. Lutherans, Calvinists, and other Protestant sects battled for allegiance; the Catholic Church responded with a reform and missionary movement of its own. The Reformation set a new political agenda, as European governments tried to come to terms with new religious diversity and to take advantage of the disarray of the Catholic Church to increase their own powers. The Reformation did more to strengthen the hand of many monarchs than the Renaissance had done, but it also encouraged new political ideas in opposition to traditional political concepts.

As the Reformation seized center stage, a major change in European economic life was also occurring, fueled by new wealth brought back from the Americas. New money encouraged greater commercial activity and important changes in social structure. It also affected family life.

The Reformation and the commercial revolution coexisted uneasily. The former called for a new devotion to God; the latter spurred a new interest in mammon. Although they were very different in inspiration, both the new religious and the new economic spirits combined in their impact on social stratification and on family habits. Furthermore, both currents affected ordinary people as well as the elite of western Europe. The Reformation inspired new philosophies, including new skepticism about formal religion of any sort, but it also touched the basic outlook of ordinary peasants and city-dwellers. Similarly, the commercial revolution gave new resources and functions to governments, but it also brought changes to many villages and groups of artisans.

Finally, both the Reformation and the economic trends caused considerable tension at various levels of European society, precisely because they challenged established habits. Wars erupted, sometimes bringing great hardship; popular cultural traditions were attacked; an unprecedented wave of popular protest burst forth in many parts of Europe, and this in turn brought experiments with new forms of social control. In several parts of Europe a frenzied attack on witchcraft resulted from the anxieties generated by change.

The Religious Transformation

Lutheranism

In 1517 a German monk, Martin Luther, posted a list called the Ninety-five Theses, or propositions, on the door of the castle church in Wittenberg, protesting the sale of indulgences by agents of the Catholic church in his region. Indulgences expressed the Catholic belief that priests could reconcile sinners to God if the sinners confessed and did penance. They were sold with the promise that they would serve as penance for sin and ease entry into heaven to anyone who paid the required fee. The basic beliefs behind this system, that God was merciful and channeled grace through the church, were old, but the "sales campaign" reflected the urgent need of the Renaissance church for tax funds to pay for its ambitious building program. To Luther, the practice was appalling, for Luther's reading of the Bible, particularly St. Paul, argued against any ability to gain salvation through earthly acts, not to mention outright payment.

The pope portrayed as the devil in this Lutheran woodcut. With the advent of the printing press, woodcuts became a prime means of disseminating religious ideas during the Reformation. To a largely illiterate society, such pictures were powerful propaganda.

He was willing to pit his reading of the Bible against the authority of the pope himself.

Luther's theses received wide attention in Germany, spurred by use of the new printing press (which would play a vital role in spreading ideas and bitter debates throughout the Reformation). Papal resistance to Luther's claims led Luther to more sweeping condemnations of Rome's power and to more elaborate statements of his own beliefs. Luther came to argue that salvation flowed not through good works, but through faith in God's word alone. Therefore, according to him, most traditional Catholic sacraments, and the special powers claimed for priests, were invalid. For Luther, authority rested in the Bible as the word of God, not in the church as a perpetual channel of divine wisdom. Each Christian should read and understand the Bible he believed, for the true church consisted not of any hierarchy of priests, but of all believers. Priests and monks possessed no special powers; *all* faithful Christians had equal merit regardless of what jobs they held. Luther's attack on the idea of special religious virtues for the clergy led him to denounce all forms of monasticism and to insist that ministers of God, who now had the role simply of calling God's word to the attention of the faithful, could marry. Luther himself later married a former nun.

42

TWO
*The Winds of
Change: Religion
and Economics in
the Sixteenth and
Early Seventeenth
Centuries*

Luther's theological arguments were extremely complex, and the Reformation that he inspired consisted in part of vigorous but abstract theological debate. But Luther himself came from the common people. The son of an ambitious, hard-driving copper miner, Luther had been trained for a career in law but disobeyed his father to enter a monastery. His training and intelligence were highly unusual, but Luther articulated many religious concerns shared by ordinary folk—particularly a distrust of church luxury and of the authority claimed by some priests. Luther may also have shared some psychological tensions not uncommon in ordinary families, though his specific turmoil was again unusual: Luther had defied his severe father. His desire to describe an all-powerful God may have translated the concerns many people felt in a time of changing family life to find a clear principle of divine authority.

To many peasants in Germany, Luther seemed to offer a more directly relevant message in his defiance of established authority and his praise for the freedom of the true Christian. Many German peasants were facing deteriorating conditions, mainly due to rising prices. Begging increased in cities and countryside alike. In 1524 the huge Peasant Revolt broke out in various parts of Germany. Peasants sought a complete end to serfdom, confiscation of church property, abolition of taxes and church

A scene depicting the pillage of a German monastery during the Peasants' Revolt of 1524–1526. From the contemporary chronicle of Abbot Jakob Murer of Eisenbach.

tithes, and other reforms that would free them from landlord and church control. The Peasant Revolt echoed many of Luther's arguments, as the rebels were firmly convinced that they were following the Word of God. Luther, however, was no social rebel; his idea of freedom was internal— a freedom won through faith in order to avoid sin. Hence Luther vigorously condemned the peasant rising, and the German nobility repressed it fiercely, killing perhaps as many as 100,000 people. Even in the longer run, Lutheranism encouraged an obedience to established secular authority, including the state, that may help explain why social and political protest were often more muted in Germany than elsewhere.

Luther also had rather conservative views on the position of women, believing that marriage and obedience to the husband were the woman's proper lot in life. By abolishing convents, Luther (and other Protestant leaders) actually eliminated an important alternative for women in several parts of Europe, enhancing their purely familial role. Protestants saw convents, like monasteries, as false centers of piety because they implied that special efforts, such as celibacy, could win God's grace; but although a wife was as holy as any other woman, it became harder, in Protestant lands by the 1530s, for a woman to be anything other than a wife. Catholics continued to allow religious vocations for women, but Protestants stressed family life as the only really appropriate destiny for women. Furthermore, although Luther's idea of male dominance in the family was not new, he may have emphasized it more fully, recalling the influence of his own powerful father, than many Catholics did in practice. Protestantism thus reduced flexibility for women, although, as we will see in this chapter, it had more promising implications as well.

Even though Luther's religious protest did not legitimate direct reforms in the social and economic conditions of ordinary people, it did have a genuine popular appeal, stemming in part from Luther's own roots among the common folk. Many peasants and townspeople liked the idea that they were on an equal spiritual footing with the ministers of the church. They liked the notion that they had direct access to God's truth, and that the Bible could be open to them. Luther's own use of the German language, and a vigorous translation of the Bible into German, helped make reality of his desire to right the relationship between religion and the people. Large numbers of ordinary Germans, and soon many Scandinavians as well, were aware of Luther's struggle with the Catholic church and directly converted to Lutheran principles.

But Luther's doctrines won attention from higher quarters as well. Many German humanists admired the Lutheran simplification of religion and Luther's reliance on the original biblical sources. They also liked his use of language, for the miner's son was a masterful stylist. Luther appealed to a sense of Germanness among many intellectuals, who had resented religious controls from Rome; Lutheranism thus reflected and encouraged an early form of national loyalty. Many German princes, rulers of the small states technically controlled by the Habsburg Emperor, found virtues in Lutheranism. Some were sincerely attracted to the new doctrines. But many saw in Luther's rebellion a chance to enhance their own power against the emperor, who remained loyally Catholic. Conversion to Lutheranism also gave princes a chance to seize church lands and property, and to control the new church. For Luther, having renounced the papacy, gave important powers of church control, including appointment of church leaders, to the hands of secular rulers. Acceptance of Lutheranism by many regional German princes encouraged conversions to the reformed religion by still larger numbers of subjects.

The various sources of support for Luther's stand made it impossible for Catholic authorities to repress the new movement. Both pope and emperor initially tried to drive out what they saw as a new heresy. Luther was excommunicated from the Catholic church, declared an outlaw of the empire. But the backing of key German princes, plus the popular conversions, protected the new movement, particularly in the northern and central reaches of the German-speaking lands. Furthermore, Emperor Charles V was distracted by his recurrent conflicts with France, which prevented full attention to the new challenges within his own loosely organized realm. As a result, in 1555 the emperor agreed to the Peace of Augsburg, which recognized that Germany would be religiously divided, each prince determining the religion of his own region. Most of northern and central Germany became Lutheran; most of the south and west remained Catholic. This settlement was no recognition of religious tolerance, for within each region religious conformity prevailed; and the settlement did not end religious strife in Germany. The Peace of Augsburg did attest, however, to the fact that for the first time in the history of Western Christianity, religious unity had officially been broken.

The rise of Lutheranism spurred religious protest movements—or Protestantism—in other parts of Europe as well, for the printing press quickly brought religious debate to almost all corners of Western society. By the middle of the sixteenth century, Lutheranism won not only Scandinavia but important conversions in eastern France and Switzerland.

Lutheran Reform in England   A number of English religious leaders also had contacts with Luther. Interest in religious reform and greater popular access to the Bible had developed in England even earlier, though specific reform movements had been driven underground. The wealth and frequent corruption of English Catholic leaders drew much hostility. But the formation of a separate English church owed still more to the marriage woes of its powerful king, Henry VIII. Henry desperately wanted a male heir, and his Spanish wife did not provide one. So Henry sought papal permission to dissolve his marriage, in favor of a new union with a woman named Anne Boleyn. The pope refused, and Henry appointed a new archbishop to head the English church, who in turn readily granted the annulment. Henry went on to remove the church fully from papal control. He also went on to marry five other wives in succession, putting two of them to death and leaving two daughters and a sickly son to fight over the English crown.

But Henry's new English church was not simply a ploy in an extraordinary royal dating game. Henry himself had serious interest in certain Lutheran ideas, and other Englishmen were also enthusiastic about religious reform. Henry and his ministers also were eager to get their hands on church properties; as a result, Catholic monasteries were closed and sold to the profit of the Crown. New money encouraged the formation of a larger and better-defined royal bureaucracy in England, which assured government control of the major appointments in the new church. Protestant influence in the English church increased during the brief reign of Henry's son, and then it retreated during the equally brief rule of his eldest daughter, a fervent Catholic. Much persecution and bloodshed accompanied these religious shifts in the mid-sixteenth century. Finally, under Queen Elizabeth (who ruled from 1558 to 1603), a distinctive and durable tone was imparted to the new church. Elizabeth was a Protestant, and she was firmly resolved to keep control of the church in English hands. But she also wanted religious peace, so she created the Anglican Church that would accept a broad range of doctrines and ceremonies, from the essentially Catholic to the fervently Protestant. Services were conducted in English, not Latin, and the clergy were allowed to marry. But the Church of England retained a hierarchy of bishops and many traditional forms of service.

Calvinism

Still another version of Protestantism developed under John Calvin, a Frenchman who settled in Geneva, one of the city-states of Switzerland. Calvin, initially destined for a career in the Catholic church, converted to Protestantism in 1533, believing that God had chosen him to reform the church. Asked to organize religion in Geneva, he proceeded to set up a church-dominated government while also writing an elaborate statement of his own doctrines. Even more than Luther, Calvin insisted that human efforts to obtain salvation were misguided. God had predestined the fate of every individual: "Our souls are but faint flickerings over against the infinite brilliance which is God." God alone was sovereign, and man had no free will. Most people, indeed, were destined for damnation. But against this pessimistic backdrop Calvin urged that individuals try to be good, worship God and enforce His principles in order to demonstrate that God had chosen them for salvation. Hence Calvin dictated a strict moral code opposed to dancing, card-playing, and luxurious living. And he insisted on full adherence to his own beliefs; dissenters were punished as rigorously in Calvin's Geneva—even executed—as they were in the strictest Catholic countries.

Calvinism described a much more complete rejection of Catholic traditions than did Lutheranism or Anglicanism. Calvin wanted no sacraments in his church, whereas Luther had retained two (baptism and the eucharist); sacraments implied that recipients could earn God's grace by performing certain ceremonies. Artistic decoration was also banned from Calvinist churches, lest it encourage image-worship. Calvin also wanted to curtail hierarchy in his church government. Calvinist churches selected their own ministers and were governed by elders of the congregation—the basis of government in Presbyterianism—or by somewhat wider councils of leading church members. Calvinism's strict moral code and the paradoxical belief in hard striving to demonstrate God's grace,

TWO
*The Winds of
Change: Religion
and Economics in
the Sixteenth and
Early Seventeenth
Centuries*

TEMPLE DE LYON, NOMME PARADIS.

A Calvinist church in Lyon, France, in 1564. Note the stark decor, designed to focus attention on receiving God's word.

even amid strict predestination in theory, led to active missionary efforts and an extraordinary religious energy. Calvin also believed, again more fully than Luther, in the validity of work in this world. Success on the job, including business, was part of the good religious life and was pleasing to God.

The Spread of Calvinism   Under Calvin, Geneva became a magnet for religious refugees from many countries. A number of these went home after Calvinist training to spread the good word in their own areas. In this manner, the main Protestant movement in France, the Huguenot church, was Calvinist in inspiration. A majority of Dutchmen became Calvinist, forming the Dutch Reformed Church. John Knox converted Scotland to Presbyterianism. Calvinism also won converts in Hungary and parts of Germany, and an important minority of English people accepted Calvinism, as well, in the second half of the 16th century. From this base Calvinism would spread to North America after 1600.

Often, as in England, Calvinism won only a minority, for rarely did it have the backing of established governments. But that minority were usually vigorous, convinced like Calvin himself of the absolute truth of their own beliefs. Because of their activism, and Calvinism's wide geographical reach, this religious system became the most important single Protestant force by 1600.

The religious uproar engendered still other dissenting groups. Anabaptist movements in various cities, particularly in Germany, sought a return to primitive Christianity, in which all believers would associate without any formal guidance, producing social equality as well as true spirituality. Anabaptists refused to serve established governments and particularly rejected military activity. These pure beliefs attracted only a small number of people, particularly among the urban poor. Most governments feared the revolutionary potential of this version of Protestantism and attacked Anabaptist strongholds. Nevertheless, the spirit of Anabaptism, which was a desire to seek an inner spiritual light and personal union with God, would survive in a number of small German sects and, later, in Quaker and Baptist movements born in England.

The Catholic Response: The Council of Trent

With all its varieties, Protestantism was no unchallenged wave in the religious turbulence of sixteenth century Europe. The Catholic church responded not only with repression, but by revitalizing its own faithful and reaffirming its doctrine. Like Protestantism, Catholicism was able to build on intense popular piety, so that the Catholic or Counter Reformation was not merely a response to Protestant threat. To be sure, the popes who initially reacted to the Reformation were still steeped in Renaissance goals, inclined to dismiss the seriousness of religious disputes, and eager to get on with building their own art collections. Their hesitations help explain why Protestantism continued to spread. Finally, however, pressed by church representatives from Germany, a new pope did agree to call a meeting of churchmen to consider the issue of internal reforms, and the resultant Council of Trent (1545–1563) really initiated the Catholic response.

The Council of Trent reaffirmed key Catholic doctrines, including the traditional sacraments, the authority of priests, and the Church's authority to proclaim valid religious truth. Thus the Council firmly rejected Protestant ideas, refusing to compromise for the sake of unity. But the Council also imposed higher educational standards on the clergy; it stopped the sale of indulgences; it took measures to reduce the corruption of clergy—for example, forbidding the holding of multiple offices; and it urged new attention to educating laymen in religion. Here was a solid basis for the spiritual renewal of the Catholic church. At the same time, a number of new religious orders arose to spread Catholic doctrine and oppose Reformation conversions with new missionary activity. An Italian woman founded the Ursuline order of nuns to provide better education for women and spread Catholic belief through the authority of wives and mothers. The Society of Jesus, known as the Jesuits, was launched in Spain, also to work to develop better education. The Jesuits were a tightly organized order under papal control; their concentration on education of the nobility gave them great political influence in Europe. The Jesuits also sponsored a vital missionary effort in the Americas and Asia; within

Europe, Jesuit zeal helped bring southern Germany, Hungary, and parts of eastern Europe, initially swayed by Protestantism, back to the Catholic fold.

Spurred by the new religious spirit, the papacy returned to more exclusively Catholic concerns. Renaissance interests in art were downplayed, and leading popes even ordered selective overpainting of nude figures in earlier masterpieces in the church's possession. The papacy also established a new Inquisition, modeled on church courts that had attacked religious rebels in the Middle Ages, to bring heretics to trial and to censor publications. The Index was established to prohibit books not in accord with Catholic doctrine by listing and forbidding to the faithful all disapproved titles, beginning with the works of the Reformers themselves.

The Results of the Religious Upheaval

The Reformation and the Catholic reaction it provoked reaffirmed the importance of religious observance and piety at all levels of Western society. The movement arose from deep concerns about salvation on the part of religious leaders such as Luther and a wide array of ordinary people who had to make decisions about what religious path to follow. These religious currents seemed to demonstrate the shallowness of some of the cultural developments of the Renaissance, whose secular spirit was now temporarily eclipsed. In government also, religion returned as a key policy issue. Princes and kings tried to use religious turmoil to the advantage of their own positions. French kings backed German Lutherans

---

SIR THOMAS MORE AND THE CRISIS OF CONSCIENCE

The Reformation caused great pain to many Northern humanists, whose religious loyalties lay mainly with a life of gentle piety rather than strife or doctrinal dispute. Erasmus, though sympathizing with many of Luther's objections to Church corruption, deplored the religious split. Another Renaissance humanist, Sir Thomas More in England, faced an even more agonizing situation, for he had taken service under Henry VIII as a chief minister of state. Erasmus and More had already debated this choice, Erasmus arguing for the purity of noninvolvement, More arguing that values had to be translated into action. Then came Henry's battle with the papacy. The king bribed and threatened many political and religious leaders to win approval of his new church, and most caved in. But More, though no fanatic, was a sincere Catholic, and to him this meant unswerving loyalty. He resigned his office in protest of the law that required the clergy to submit to the king, and he refused to take an oath recognizing the legitimacy of Anne Boleyn's child (the later Queen Elizabeth). For his act of principle, More, along with several other dissenters, was beheaded.

because they weakened the Habsburg empire. Also, many French nobles turned Protestant because this gave them a new weapon against the central authority of their own Catholic monarch. But religion was not just a policy tool; it *guided* policy as well. Until the middle of the seventeenth century, Protestant rulers often banded together against Catholic kings, who responded in kind. Europe's overseas ventures were also colored by religion, as Protestant English and Dutch explorers tried to counter the power of Catholic Spain.

Most Reformation churches shared with Catholic leaders one key traditional belief: that there was only one religious truth. Luther had no desire to set up a separate church, but rather to win all of Christendom to his way of thinking—which, he maintained, was only the original doctrine of Christ restated. Calvin and the newly vigilant papacy vied with each other in attacking heretics and burning "erroneous" books. This belief in a single truth was maintained by ordinary believers as well. Where Protestants and Catholics coexisted in the same town or region, they frequently attacked each other, disrupting religious processions and ravaging opponents' churches. Indeed, few regions could long embrace Protestants and Catholics alike: one side had to win out. This was a tragic but inevitable result of the deep-seated devotion to religion still envisaged in traditional ways by Protestants and Catholics alike.

Yet the Reformation, and to some extent the Catholic response, constituted new movements as well. Most obviously, despite the intent of leaders on both sides, religious unity was shattered. The fact of competing beliefs gave some Europeans a sense of choice in outlook that was new, and ultimately would help lead to a lessening of the importance of religion as an ingredient in the overall Western outlook. Even in the sixteenth century, the sight of religious dispute and intolerance led some observers to wonder about such fanatical devotion. Writers in the humanistic tradition of the Renaissance, such as Michel de Montaigne in France, publicly questioned narrow intolerance, arguing that other values, including respect for human life, were more important. The long-range implications of new religious disputes for weakening the primacy of religion were precisely that—long-range. But they do suggest the vital results of the remaking of the European religious map as a major break in Western history and illustrate how some of the key consequences of the Reformation ran counter to the intentions of those enmeshed in the initial turmoil.

War and Civil War

Outside of the religious sphere itself, the most immediate result of the Reformation and Catholic reaction was a series of devastating religious wars that pockmarked Europe's history from the mid-sixteenth century until the mid-seventeenth. Religious wars in France combined with battles between monarchy and nobility, and between Paris-based central government and independent-minded regions that had embraced Protestantism. Several bitter massacres, including an attack on Protestants on St. Bartholomew's Day in 1572, marked this strife, which seriously set

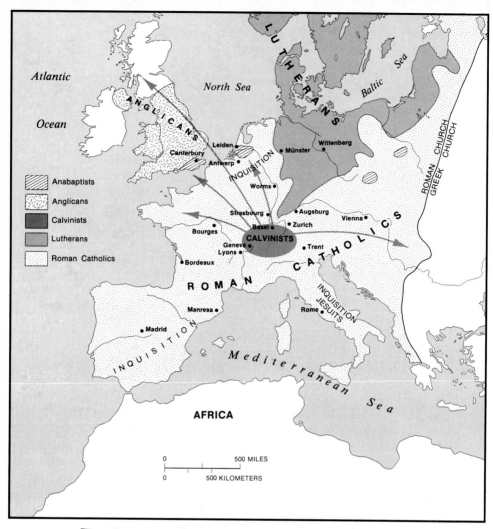

The religious complexity of western Europe after the Reformation shows dramatically in the geography of key Protestant faiths and in the important Catholic strongholds.

back the development of a stronger French monarchy. Religious wars here ended only with the granting of tolerance to Protestants in the Edict of Nantes, in 1598. Even after this, tensions simmered, and the rights of Protestants were limited again in the seventeenth century.

The Netherlands was another center of religious controversy. The Habsburgs had inherited the provinces of present-day Belgium and Holland, and these territories passed to Spain in 1536. The Dutch were already restive under foreign rule, for they had a strong tradition of local liberty. Then the majority of the Dutch converted to Calvinism, and they were pitted against one of the most fervent Catholic rulers in Europe, Philip II. Mutual slaughter resulted from 1559 onward, as the Spanish tried to wipe out Protestantism and fervent Calvinists responded in kind.

Spain was unable to put down the unrest, and in 1581 the northern provinces declared their independence (the south, which would ultimately become Belgium, remained Catholic and in Spanish hands). Queen Elizabeth of England provided some aid to the Dutch rebels, lest expanding Spanish power envelop her kingdom as well; and the English defeat of the Spanish fleet, the Armada, aimed against England aided the Dutch as well. Finally, in 1608 the Spanish essentially recognized Dutch independence.

Germany was yet another theater of religious war. Despite the Augsburg settlement, Lutherans and Catholics still competed for conversions, and Calvinists wanted recognition of their own. Tied to this quarrel was the endemic dispute between German princes and the Holy Roman Emperor. Outright war broke out in 1618, when Protestants tossed Catholic imperial officials out a window in Prague. Catholic forces were headed by the Habsburgs of Austria, with strong aid from Spanish armies. Scandinavian armies fought on the Protestant side, with Swedish troops roaming up and down the countryside for years. Late in the Thirty Years' War, French diplomats also aided the Protestant cause in order to weaken Spain. Finally, after battles that had devastated the German countryside and caused massive loss of life, in 1648 a peace settlement, the Treaty of Westphalia, was reached that enhanced the power of the local princes, gave new territory to France, and limited the power of the papacy in German religion. Through this treaty Calvinism joined Lutheranism and Catholicism as a legally permissible religion in Germany. Because of population loss and economic dislocation, plus the reduction of any central authority in Germany, the Thirty Years' War severely weakened this part of Europe for over a century. Many peasants had to sell their lands because they lacked enough money to rebuild their farms, which led to a network of large estates and a revival of serfdom. This was particularly true in eastern Germany, where Prussian landlords controlled most property and exacted substantial taxes and work services from the peasantry.

A final scene of religious war was England, where disputes among Catholics, Anglicans, and Calvinists contributed to civil war in the 1640s. Puritans reacted against an apparent revival of Catholic influence, after the tolerant reign of Elizabeth I. For a time after the execution of the king, Puritans ruled the country. The monarchy was soon restored, but religious disputes eased only with a new reform effort in 1688–1689, when the dominance of the Church of England was affirmed but with tolerance for other Protestant (though not Catholic) religious activities.

The Aftermath of the Religious Wars

The results of the various religious wars confirmed Europe's religious disruption. Germany, already divided politically, was now divided religiously, with the north–south division between Protestantism and Catholicism. While Lutheranism commanded most Protestant loyalty, Calvinist churches now had significant adherence, and the small Anabaptist current was by no means dead. Scandinavia and Scotland were solidly Protestant, but Holland, though dominated by Calvinism, had a

TWO
The Winds of
Change: Religion
and Economics in
the Sixteenth and
Early Seventeenth
Centuries

The Reformation and resulting religious wars described much of the action in the Europe of the late sixteenth and early seventeenth centuries, but they were not the only determinants of events. Indeed, intertwined with the Catholic–Protestant struggle was a battle for power among the monarchs of Europe. Spain was the leading state of Europe during most of the sixteenth century. Its monarchy was effectively centralized, its devotion to the Catholic faith intense, its coffers filled with the silver imported from the mines of its American colonies. Spanish armies, large and well-drilled, were known for their battle-toughness. Thus Spain had the means and the zeal to make its mark on Europe. It easily outdistanced its French rival, which was beset by internal strife. It held territory in Italy and the Low Countries, and it remained closely linked to the Austrian Habsburgs even after the two thrones separated following the reign of Charles V, with the severe Phillip II taking over for his father in Spain. The Spanish fleet, though relying on somewhat cumbersome ships, not only plied the Atlantic but also patrolled the Mediterranean. Spain commanded a Christian navy that inflicted a major defeat on the fleet of the Turkish empire, at Lepanto in 1571, that helped limit Turkish commerce and open parts of the Middle East to European trade.

But Spain's predominance was short-lived. It could not hold its European empire together, and it roused increasingly coherent opposition from other rulers. Spain also suffered from a relatively undeveloped merchant and banking establishment, which limited its ability to profit from its New World wealth. Spain did maintain its trading monopoly with its American holdings, despite facing piracy from British and other ships; but it saw much of its wealth pass to the hands of more sophisticated Dutch or other northern bankers. Specific political troubles included the costly Netherlands revolt, which ended in Dutch independence; and the disastrous failure in 1588 of its great fleet sent against Protestant England. Blown off course by a storm, the Spanish Armada was savaged by the smaller, more mobile English ships. Spain was still strong enough to play a significant role in the early phases of the Thirty Years' War in Germany, on the side of the Holy Roman Empire and Catholicism. But it could not put down the Protestant states, aided by Scandinavian armies and finally by French forces sent to weaken the Spanish-Austrian alliance above all. The Treaty of Westphalia recognizing Dutch independence and the religious division of Germany, was a decisive defeat for Spain, which now began to fade into the second rank of European powers, just as France began a new push for ascendancy.

significant Catholic minority in the south. England maintained a dominant Anglican church, but there were many other Protestant groups and a persistent, though now repressed, Catholic minority. Conquests in the sixteenth and seventeenth centuries gave England control of Ireland, and an Anglican-style church was established there as well, as the only official religion; but the majority of Irish people, bitter at foreign domination, remained firmly Catholic. In fact, Catholicism gained ground among the Irish peasantry, who had previously been inclined to combine Christianity on the surface with older, pagan beliefs. Most of southern Europe, of course, remained Catholic as well. The Reformation won few converts in Italy or Spain; Protestantism was a minority force in France, and by the seventeenth century a beleaguered one. Protestant success in the border countries of east-central Europe, such as Hungary, was largely rolled back by the Jesuit counterattack, leaving these areas, too, fairly solidly Catholic.

In the many parts of Europe where religious contest had been fierce, such as Germany, France, Holland and England, a certain *de facto* tolerance had been established by some point in the seventeenth century. But for the most part this tolerance was grudging—a recognition of the impossibility of restoring full religious unity, and not a matter of principle. The idea of a single religious truth and the importance of a universal church, and the resultant hatred of other faiths, remained too strong for any other result. Hence toleration was typically minimal and incomplete. Germany chose religion by region. France allowed Protestant ceremonies, through the Edict of Nantes, but then progressively narrowed this compromise during the seventeenth century, finally repealing the Edict outright. England, after bitter civil war, granted tolerance in 1689 to non-Anglican Protestants but did not allow them to hold political office or attend universities; Catholics were not part of this compromise. By the later seventeenth century, it was clear that religious unity was over for Western society as a whole and that in key parts of Europe this fact had been recognized. But the wounds were still fresh, for bitter religious conflict had dominated the political and military history of Europe between the mid-sixteenth and the mid-seventeenth centuries.

The Religious Upheaval and Changes in Basic Mentalities

Western Europe's working through of the Reformation and Catholic Reformation did more than provide the overriding theme for the events of a hundred tumultuous years. Religious change also set in motion basic shifts in the way Europeans thought and behaved, which would last well beyond the age of religious wars.

The alteration of the popular outlook or mentality constitutes one of the basic changes in Western society that began in the sixteenth and seventeenth centuries, ranking with shifts in the economic structure and the relations between state and people. The gradualness of this shift reduces its drama, to be sure—but other basic changes were gradual as well.

Alterations in mentalities are hard to measure; they leave behind less

5 4

TWO
*The Winds of
Change: Religion
and Economics in
the Sixteenth and
Early Seventeenth
Centuries*

RELIGION AND THE ENGLISH CIVIL WAR

The death of Queen Elizabeth in 1603 without an heir brought a new dynasty, the Stuarts, to the English throne. James I, already king of Scotland, lacked Elizabeth's tact and vision. He believed in the supremacy of king over parliament, which the Tudor rulers had managed successfully. Appointing many corrupt ministers, James also passed a number of measures that harmed British merchants. James and his son, Charles I, angered English and Scottish Protestants by trying to move the Church of England closer to Catholic practices and to impose a system of bishops on Scottish Presbyterians. A number of English Puritans fled the country, first to Holland and then to New England, seeking a purer religious atmosphere. Finally, various factions combined to oppose Stuart policies: merchants, nobles, and gentry eager to curtail royal power, parliamentarians, and Protestants. The Stuarts had supporters as well, and the civil war that broke out in 1642 was bitterly fought. Rebel forces seized and executed Charles I in 1649, and for a brief time Oliver Cromwell, a Puritan general, ruled as dictator amid huge disagreements over what religion should predominate and whether any diversity could be accepted. A number of popular movements sprang up seeking democracy or even some kind of socialism, combining extreme Protestant views with newer political ideas about equal voting rights or equal property rights. Cromwell himself concentrated on using his well-organized army to end civil strife and to conquer Ireland more fully. But on Cromwell's death, after a brief delay, Parliament recalled the dead king's son, who ruled as Charles II. Renewed Stuart rule, however, raised all the old issues about royal authority and religion, as Charles and particularly his successor James II seemed to work for toleration of Catholics. Parliament rebelled again, this time peacefully, and arranged that James be replaced by his daughter and her husband, a Dutch Prince. These new rulers, William and Mary, were firmly Protestant, and also promised to obey parliament. A real political change in England resulted, in what was called the Glorious Revolution, and limited toleration ended the worst of the religious disputes. Stuart attempts to regain power were decisively defeated, despite some support in Ireland and elsewhere.

direct evidence than do structural or political shifts. But their elusiveness should not mislead about the importance of what was underway. The process of redefining the mental contours of ordinary life, launched in this period of religious turmoil, would underlie many other features of Western social thought.

The Organization of Space and Time for Worship

Disagreements between Protestants and Catholics involved far more than quarrels over church affiliation and structure or even beliefs. When ordinary business people, artisans, or peasants were faced with a choice between rival religious systems, as happened in many parts of western Europe, they were implicitly debating basic issues of outlook and behavior. Fundamental changes in popular mentality began to take shape in the Western world during the sixteenth century, and although these changes reflected the new religious currents, they also helped cause them.

Protestants, for example, viewed urban space differently from tradi-

Apotheosis of the Virgin, an early seventeenth-century fresco by Il Domenichino. In this expression of the fervor and aims of the Counter-Reformation, the Virgin comes to the aid of the city of Naples, and Luther and Calvin are cast down.

5 6

TWO
*The Winds of
Change: Religion
and Economics in
the Sixteenth and
Early Seventeenth
Centuries*

tional Catholics. Catholic custom mixed together a host of elements of urban life: Religious processions wound through market squares, and shops were built up against churches. Protestants insisted on a stricter separation between places of worship and places for business and other secular activities. Because they attacked the worship of saints as idolatry, they naturally tried to forbid many popular religious processions that had long brought religion among ordinary people and served time-honored purposes of using ritual to placate nature. The Protestant approach urged prayer, rather than ritual. The result, in Protestant cities or sections of cities, was a separation between business and residential sections, on the one hand, and the rather austere churches and meetinghouses on the other.

Protestants and Catholics also differed in their sense of time. Protestants were urged to pray often, according to individual need and impulse. But Sundays were set aside as the time for organized, collective prayer and worship. The traditional Catholic calendar was more complex, as saints' days and other religious festivals punctuated the year. This complexity was compounded by the variety of local, even neighborhood, ceremonies. Protestantism produced a more universal church calendar by disallowing most local variants in favor of a standard religious schedule. It also reduced the intertwining of religious and ordinary days, by attacking most religious festivals as idolatrous and distracting.

Basic changes in the organization of space and time thus accompanied the conflict between Protestant and Catholic. Various terms have been applied to the new Protestant outlook developed among ordinary converts. In a way, the world of nature and daily life became less mystified, not in the sense that God was viewed as less powerful or less involved in judging individual conduct, but in the sense that ceremony and religious imagery were removed from so many times and places. Daily religion among Protestants depended on individual spirituality; it was not surrounded by processions, statues, or specially dressed priests and nuns. There was less need, in an ordinary month, to stop normal working activities to celebrate a religious patron or to participate in a ceremony designed to prevent annual flooding. Similar goals—success at work, avoidance of natural disaster—might be objects of prayer, but prayer was either individual and largely private, or was confined to the intensely religious weekly worship day.

Popular Religious Practices and Public Behavior

Although Protestantism generated or enhanced many of the most sweeping changes in popular culture, as Protestant styles differed measurably from Catholic among ordinary people, the Reformation was not the only force for change. Catholic leaders, too, attacked aspects of popular culture. This attack was underway a few decades before the Reformation began, and it was enhanced by the attempts to purify the Church in response to Protestant attack. Catholic leaders now identified many popular religious practices as superstitious or frivolous. They blasted many of the practices associated with the carnival before Lent, seeing them as pagan remnants or as so devoted to worldly pleasures that they distracted from the appropriate respect for God. Thus a Portuguese bishop in 1534 attacked popular religious plays: "Even if they represented the Passion of Our Lord Jesus Christ, or his Resurrection, or Nativity, . . . because from these plays arise much that is unfitting, and they frequently give scandal to those who are not very firm in our holy Catholic faith, when they see the disorders and excesses of these plays." In other words, many Catholic leaders shared with even more fervent Protestant purifiers a belief that there should be more separation between things sacred and things profane in popular life. They disliked the spontaneity and disorder that had long been part of popular religion and the mixture of religious and work or leisure activities in ordinary life. In effect, they were asking for greater personal discipline and restraint, as part of more solemn—in some ways narrower—ideas of what was proper behavior before God.

There were, to be sure, important differences between Protestant and Catholic views of popular traditions. Far more Protestant reformers wanted to ban traditional games and plays altogether. During Cromwell's brief rule in England, Puritan zealots tried to outlaw card playing, tavern drinking, dancing, animal performances such as bear-baiting and cock-fighting, and theater performances. A Dutch Calvinist attacked spring maypole dancing and the custom of filling children's shoes with little presents on the feast of St. Nicholas, near Christmas, a practice he termed "nonsense." Catholic purists were more eager to *modify* popular behavior. They urged less raucous carnivals, more attention to the serious ceremonies and fasting of Lent—rather than no carnivals at all. They did not try to abolish saints' days, but rather to make their celebration more strictly religious.

Nevertheless, after about 1500, popular Western culture was increasingly pressed for reform and restraint, a campaign for which Protestantism was a particularly sweeping expression. The attempt to reshape popular behavior involved members of the elite, such as Catholic bishops or Cromwellian leaders, trying to produce new orderliness among the masses. But it also involved ordinary people themselves attempting to fashion a new seriousness and decorum in their own world. It was an ordinary French printer, converted to Calvinism, who attacked preachers who became too emotional, or used coarse language in their sermons, "which they might have used in a brothel." And just as a Catholic bishop might attack wild popular dances, such as one called the "twirl" in which boys tossed girls into the air, so might an ordinary Puritan do the same in Elizabethan England. To the bishop, the twirl was "infamous" in exposing "what shames obliges us to hide . . . naked to the eyes of those taking part and those passing by." To the Elizabethan Puritan, dances provided opportunities for "filthy groping and unclean handling," and so acted as "an introduction to whoredom, a preparative to wantonness, a provocative to uncleanness, and an introit to all kinds of lewdness." Typically, the Puritan went further than the Catholic in the moralistic attack, but the division was not simply a matter of newly zealous leaders trying to bring the masses into line; representatives of the masses participated as well.

58

TWO
*The Winds of
Change: Religion
and Economics in
the Sixteenth and
Early Seventeenth
Centuries*

The Protestant and Catholic campaign against key aspects of traditional popular culture was not simply negative. Leaders of both faiths also worked to provide active alternatives to older religious habits. Protestants such as Luther wrote stirring hymns, and a vigorous new musical culture began to develop in many parts of Protestant Europe. Bible reading and other religious literature provided a new focus as well. Similarly, Jesuit and other Catholic leaders inspired new festivals and new saints, and they introduced more fervent preaching into popular religious ceremonies. In Italy and parts of France, organizations of Catholic laymen, called "confraternities," gained in size and vigor as part of the campaign to infuse popular piety with greater seriousness.

Positively and negatively alike, the effort to transform popular religion recast the way people thought about God and nature; moreover, it added up to a significant reshaping of popular ceremony—what we might call, using a more modern vocabulary, popular leisure, or the ways people spent their nonwork time. This effort did not produce a sudden revolution in habits. In later chapters we will see ongoing elements of the campaign well after 1650. Some goals failed outright; for example, the attack on popular drinking in seventeenth-century England made little headway, for taverns were too important as social centers. Some goals failed in part; despite Calvinist objections, some celebration of Christmas as a time for gift-giving and feasting survived in Holland and elsewhere. Yet although this effort to reshape popular culture was slow and its results spotty, it was a new force in ordinary life from the sixteenth century onward.

Between 1500 and 1650, alterations in popular culture already went beyond an attack on traditional ceremonies and what reformers were prone to call superstitions, plus the effort to provide a new set of religious outlets. Changes were greater in Protestant areas than in Catholic ones, but some similar forces were at work across religious lines, particularly in the ways information was acquired and in the evaluation of family life. The period from 1500 to 1650 was only the starting point for most key developments, not surprisingly given the tremendous barriers to rapid change in basic habits; in many cases effects would be even greater in later decades.

Changes in Literacy

The rise of literacy was a vital ingredient in the transformation of popular outlook, including religious belief. Protestantism explicitly encouraged higher literacy, because of the importance of giving ordinary people direct access to the word of God. To be sure, by the late sixteenth century Protestant leaders worried about untrammeled literacy and urged the faithful to come to church to hear long sermons that would elucidate the one "true" meaning of God's work; nevertheless, Protestantism and rising literacy continued to go hand in hand.

Catholic reformers had some interest in literacy as well, though it ranked lower in their priorities—behind more vigorous preaching, for example. But the rise of printing encouraged literacy generally, particularly in the cities. And there is no question that the ability to read began to become much more widespread in the century and a half after 1500.

In Venice, roughly 61 percent of a sample of witnesses in court trials could sign their names around 1450, but 98 percent could do so by 1650. In Durham, England, around 1570, roughly 20 percent of all court witnesses who were not churchmen were literate, but by 1630 the figure had climbed to 47 percent. Changes of this sort were merely a beginning; the rise of literacy would proceed even more rapidly after 1650. Certainly, in 1650 only a minority could as yet read at all. Urban people were far more likely to read than rural people, craftsmen more likely than peasants, men more likely than women, and, of course, Protestants more likely than Catholics. Reading ability, even when improved, often remained limited. Many sixteenth-century French Calvinists, for example, laboriously learned enough to pore over their Bible but never read more, and never learned to write.

Yet western Europe was turning from a society in which only a tiny elite was actively literate, and most of this within church ranks, to one in which a substantial minority could read. This was a major change. It greatly increased the openness of ordinary people to new ideas, first in religion and then in other matters. Growing literacy often had a spillover effect, as readers could pass ideas and information on to a wider circle of acquaintances who might not themselves be literate. The growth of large-minority literacy also reduced some of the traditional gap between elite and at least a middle rank of ordinary people, and this played against other developments that tended to heighten an elite–commoner gap.

Literacy not only opened a growing number of Westerners to new ideas; it may, itself, have constituted a change in outlook. People who come to rely on reading for their information certainly change in some respects from those who rely on the spoken word. Their memories worsen; their respect for elders, as sources of remembered knowledge, may decline; their rationality may increase, as knowledge is increasingly seen as something to be laid out, planned, dissected for appearance on a printed page, rather than embodied in more ornate, rambling, and often symbolic story form. Literacy, for the expanding minority involved, could thus join the larger effects of religious reform to producing a new mental arsenal that emphasized the possibility of controlling and organizing knowledge and, again, reducing spontaneous emotion.

Changes in the Concept of Love and the Family

Another important area of new thinking involved the family. Traditional Catholic preaching had of course praised the family, and marriage was viewed as a sacrament. But Catholic sermonizers had also been at pains to warn of dangers in family life, particularly from unbridled sexuality; and the chastity of the priesthood was viewed as part of a special holy state. Although Catholic writers had recognized the importance of the family for procreation, they often wrote as though the family had been necessitated mainly by human evil—to restrain human sensuality from even worse abuses.

60

TWO
*The Winds of
Change: Religion
and Economics in
the Sixteenth and
Early Seventeenth
Centuries*

This somewhat narrow view began to yield in the sixteenth century. A Counter-Reformation pamphlet of 1566, though still mentioning marriage as a means of helping people curb their lust, stressed the beauties of family companionship more strongly. Thus the first goal of marriage is the "very partnership of diverse sexes—sought by natural instinct, and compacted in the hope of mutual help so that one aided by the other may more easily bear the discomforts of life and sustain the weakness of old age."

Protestant writers, particularly by the early seventeenth century, took up this theme even more vigorously. In Protestantism, after all, the notion of a special holiness linked to chastity had officially disappeared; ministers could marry, and in most Protestant sects monasticism had been abolished. So it was natural that a more favorable view of the family would follow. Nevertheless, the vigor of Protestant sentiment was noteworthy. In Calvinist writing, particularly, the family began to be spoken of in terms of desirable love and passion. As one English writer put it in 1642, there must be "mutual love betwixt man and wife . . . else the end and right use of marriage will be perverted." Or again: "The first duty of Husbands is to Love their Wives (and Wives their Husbands) with a true intire Conjugal Love." In Puritan writing, a bad marriage now became one of life's true tragedies, because of the family's new and central importance in proper human life: "When love is absent between husband and wife, it is like a Bone out of joint; there is no ease, no order." And love now meant a complex set of interrelationships: true friendship between husband and wife, but also sensual passion and pleasure. Protestants wanted the family to serve as a center of training in the proper love of God, but this solemn duty was not judged incompatible with the new emotional bonds of family.

Under this kind of prompting, families began (at least by the seventeenth century) a long process of reorientation, again perhaps more quickly in Protestant than in Catholic areas but ultimately throughout the West. Many spouses had loved each other before. But there had been little overall social sanction for *deep* love, and indeed many warnings that love might distract from religious obligations. And certainly marriage had normally been formed more clearly on the basis of economic than emotional or sexual arrangements. Now, with love beginning to be encouraged, some shift could be noted, though it remained limited until after the seventeenth century. Courtship for some people began to involve new possibilities of rejecting a suitor on grounds that she (more commonly he) was not lovable. Whereas wealthy families still worried about property arrangements, poorer people began to increase their references to love in their marriage ceremonies. Another new phenomenon suggested emotional change in the family. A number of Protestants, including many women, began to keep diaries—itself a sign of new literacy and a new desire to record oneself, and one's emotions, as an individual. And diary records, along with personal letters, often referred to love between husband and wife, and sorrow when the spouse was absent.

The halting changes in family life, along with the larger religious changes of the period, had ambivalent implications for women. We have seen that Protestantism in some ways narrowed women's options. The abolition of convents meant that women were thrown back on family more fully than before. Luther and other Protestant leaders had vigorous views about women's domestic, child-bearing roles. At the same time, Protestantism did encourage more women to read, even if female literacy still lagged. It prompted women along with men to think of their own relationship to God, rather than rely on the institutional church as intermediary. The emphasis on family companionship certainly featured a new esteem for women as potential emotional equals. Traditional views, still vigorous in the seventeenth century, had emphasized women's special sinfulness—it was Eve, after all, who committed the first sin. Many writers held that women were more animal-like than men, less capable of restraint of passion. This approach was incompatible with the new trend that emphasized the wife as a man's first friend, and the new stress on family and friendship within family certainly suggested a new place for women within the domestic confines. Male authority in the family remained officially dominant, and there was much confusion still about women's roles and moral standing. But the confusion itself reflected some new currents, which in fact supplemented the earlier increase in husband—wife interaction as part of the European-style, predominantly nuclear family.

An Impetus for Change

The changes in popular outlook that were being suggested during the sixteenth and early seventeenth centuries were extensive. They involved rethinking popular leisure forms; redefining time and space in their religious implications; seeking greater orderliness and control, even in aspects of emotional life; reassessing the family. Changes of this magnitude would not come overnight. We are sketching the beginnings of a revolution in the mentality of ordinary people, not a completed process. Even these beginnings were uneven, due to differences between Protestant and Catholic, among social classes, between urban and rural, and between men and women. Nevertheless, a general impetus toward change was present, attested by the fact that Catholic as well as Protestant sermonizers picked up so many of its directions. And the change brought pain and confusion to those who found more literal traditionalism expressive of their needs and pleasures. This confusion was reflected in various forms of popular protest and scapegoating, discussed on pages 72–81.

New Currents in Science

The Rise of Experimentation

Although religious changes dominated the intellectual map of Western society through the early seventeenth century, and much of popular culture as well, they were not the only cultural changes. New work in science provided a vital undercurrent even as religious struggles poured over much of western Europe. Downplayed during the Renaissance and hardly

62

TWO
*The Winds of
Change: Religion
and Economics in
the Sixteenth and
Early Seventeenth
Centuries*

encouraged by the religious goals of Reformation and Counter-Reformation, the trickle of scientific research launched in the later Middle Ages was swelling nevertheless. For the Renaissance approach, though distracted from scientific work by the fascination with artistic expression, did have implications for science. The best Renaissance thinkers urged a critical assessment of received learning and suggested the possibility of new knowledge, despite their reverence for classical work. Along with this spirit came the new liveliness of commercial cities and the huge leaps in geographical knowledge made possible by the voyages of exploration: the physical world could and should be better known. Somewhat quietly amid the din of religious dispute, scientists in the sixteenth-century began to expand medieval experimental work in areas such as optics and to develop a belief that science was not simply a matter of memorizing what Greek and Hellenistic scholars had portrayed. Thus the Belgian physician Andreas Vesalius published, in 1543, a revolutionary new treatise of the human anatomy, complete with woodcuts, which provided unprecedented knowledge about the construction of the human body. In the same year, the Polish monk Nicolaus Copernicus published his attack on the received belief that the earth forms the center of the universe. This belief, current in the West (though not in other civilizations) since Hellenistic times, had supported Christian ideas about the centrality of God's creation of man—for if the earth served as the hub of God's physical

The cosmology of Copernicus is depicted in an engraving from Andreas Cellarius's *Atlas Coelestis* of 1660.

creation, it was natural to focus attention on human beings as the highest earthlings. But Copernicus, relying on new astronomical observations and particularly new geometrical calculations, dared to disagree. He disputed the Hellenistic model by arguing that the sun was the center of the universe, with earth and the other planets revolving around it. Here, as later scientists would recognize, was revolution indeed: not only new knowledge, but a new recognition that even the most venerable belief could be overturned by new observation and mathematical theory. And this brash scientific approach received sixteenth-century formulation as well, in the writings of the French royal doctor Ambroise Pare, who stated the new credo succinctly: "I should prefer to do everything by myself than to fall into error with the sages and even with all mankind. . . . Knowledge is a great thing, but only if it is based on experience."

The new approach to science, including Copernicus's own discovery, had its main impact later, in the seventeenth century, and we will take up the full scientific revolution in Chapter 3. It was perhaps crucial that the implications of the scientific discoveries were not at first discerned, due to the more pressing issues of Reformation and Counter-Reformation; for had they been realized, they might have been suppressed. Copernicus's work was dedicated to the pope with a preface by a Lutheran, but neither Catholic nor Protestant authorities really noticed. When they did notice, early in the seventeenth century, they attempted to banish the scientific challenge, but by then it was too late.

Changes in Medical Theory

Even in the sixteenth century, however, the new idea of revising established truth had wider cultural impact in the area of medicine. In the medieval period, medical theory—that is, the ideas about what caused disease and how the body functioned—had been based largely on the work of the Hellenistic physician, Galen. Previously, new discoveries had been fit into Galen's framework. Now, with a growing proliferation of medical texts resulting from the invention of printing, with some knowledge of Arab and Asian medical ideas, and with Vesalius's discoveries that many of Galen's anatomical notions were embarrassingly incorrect, the accepted framework began to crumble. Indeed, for a time there seemed to be no framework at all, as knowledge increased about individual diseases and what they did to the body, without any overarching theory. Trained doctors now argued bitterly about how to diagnose and treat disease. One group, for example, urged use of mercury-based compounds, which Galenists regarded as sheer poison; here, both sides were right, or wrong: Small amounts of mercury do aid in treating some diseases such as syphillis, but larger quantities are fatal. But the point was that a new uncertainty had been introduced in medical diagnosis and treatment. One effect, though ironic, was to encourage trained doctors to attack popular medical culture. Perhaps because Galenism was receding, there was a new need to insist on the importance of training and orthodoxy. In France and elsewhere, university-trained doctors blasted popular healers, charlatans, people who sold folk medicines, and many women, including midwives. One French doctor described the sources of unofficial medicine in sweeping and bitter terms: "vagabonds, atheists, exiles, priests, monks, shoemakers, carders, drapers, weavers, masons, madames and prostitutes"—all of whom were "reprobates . . . and abusers."

64

TWO
The Winds of
Change: Religion
and Economics in
the Sixteenth and
Early Seventeenth
Centuries

Medical views in Western Europe were still open-ended in the early seventeenth century. The use of traditional popular remedies, and reliance on religion as a health recourse, would long continue. But there was new uncertainty, new competition for authority in the health field, and an attack by scientists on elements of popular culture.

The Commercial Revolution

Far more important than science in changing the shape of Western society in the sixteenth century was the development of new commercial patterns, new sources of wealth, and new channels for distributing that wealth. Along with religious change, the commercial revolution of the sixteenth century provided the fundamental challenge to established patterns. Commercial pressures and opportunities help explain why some results of religious reforms took the shape they did—often quite apart from the original intentions of the reformers. Fundamentally, new economic pressures combined with the attacks on religious unity and the new doubts about a single religious truth relaxed religious intensity in favor of more explicit pursuit of material gain. Economic ties also helped keep Western society together even after religious institutions had sundered; Catholics and Protestants continued to trade actively except at the height of religious wars. Here too, the new economic culture of the West was just as fundamental as the new religious culture in the process of social change.

The commercial revolution of the sixteenth century had two basic features. First, the level of European trade rose sharply. This included an increase in the variety of goods available to many Europeans; enhanced size and importance for the merchant class; and a new tendency for some regions to specialize in the products they were best suited for, relying on market purchases for the rest. Second, western Europe began to establish a new position in international trade, which it was to retain until this day.

The Rise in Trade Abroad

The clearest single sign of economic change in the later sixteenth and early seventeenth centuries was a substantial increase in prices, which in turn resulted from the massive import of gold and silver from Spanish colonies in Latin America. Mines in Mexico and Peru poured out their precious ores. Between 1503 and 1650, 16 million kilograms of silver and 185,000 kilograms of gold entered Spain's principal port, Seville. The result was a huge stimulus to the Spanish economy, which however could not sustain the new demands placed upon it, and more generally to western Europe. Spain and then other parts of Europe began to produce goods to sell in the American colonies, and to a lesser extent in other parts of the world: olive oil, wines, textiles, steel cutlery and tools, and many luxury products. Price increases—first in Spain, then in Europe—showed that production could not yet keep pace with the new money supply. Many regions and social groups were damaged by the price increases. Traditional aristocratic landowners who received fixed rents, for example, saw their real earnings drop rapidly as their money bought less. But other groups, including many merchants, found in inflation an encouragement to new risk-taking and investment, because borrowing was cheaper when money was losing value. The very poor were also hit, as inflation drove up food prices.

Inflation and the new opportunities in colonial trade led to the formation of many large trading companies. Government backing allowed capitalists in England, Holland, and France to pool resources for trade with Asia or eastern Europe. Each government granted regional monopolies of trade to these giant companies. The Dutch East Indies Company thus long dominated trade with the islands of Indonesia, and by the early seventeenth century, the British East India Company began to establish a firm toehold on the subcontinent of India. Merchant operations of this sort, which increasingly pushed out traditional Arab and Indian international traders in much of Asia, also brought new resources into Europe. European merchants developed new managerial skills and banking facilities. They encouraged European production of manufactured products for sale in what was beginning to be a Western-dominated world commercial structure.

Increased Specialization

Rising prices, new opportunities for sale abroad plus growing prosperity in the most vigorous centers such as Holland and England encouraged a new level of specialization in production. Although most peasants continued to produce mainly for the subsistence of their own families and had little contact with wider markets, a growing minority pinned their hopes on market opportunities. Hence many wine-growing villages in France began to concentrate on this crop, relying on the market for other products they would need, including some basic foods. Some villages also began to concentrate on the production of processed foods such as cheeses, or even manufactured products such as shoes, for sale in wider markets. The Staffordshire region in England, for example, began to specialize in pottery production. Several Dutch cities produced painted tiles for sale across Holland and even in England and Germany. Craftsmen, in other words, were beginning to convert to larger-scale production for wider markets, at least in some key product lines, rather than concentrating on sales within a single city. This transformation bore some relationship to gradual improvements in manufacturing techniques, and it encouraged further production changes.

Western Europe's growing wealth and manufacturing also created a demand for grain from the Baltic regions of eastern Europe, including eastern Germany and Poland, where serfdom provided cheap labor. These new commercial relationships profited some landlords, but by reinforcing the use of oppressed peasant labor and helping maintain the importance of agriculture to these countries, western Europe helped keep eastern Europe economically backward in comparison to the surging West.

66

TWO
The Winds of
Change: Religion
and Economics in
the Sixteenth and
Early Seventeenth
Centuries

The Effects of Economic Change

Population Growth   The economic changes of the sixteenth and early seventeenth centuries furthered the alteration of Europe's economic position in the world, and the balance within Europe. Beyond that, these changes had three vital internal effects. First, Europe's population began to grow again. The growth was not massive, for among other things, despite a new interest in seeking improved methods in agriculture, there was no fundamental change in food production, which in turn limited the West's population potential. But growth in a few regions was truly rapid; in the Castile region of Spain, for example, population rose from 3 million to 6 million during the sixteenth century. On the other hand, population loss occurred in some regions, most notably Germany, as a result of the devastations of the Thirty Years' War, and many parts of western Europe remained rather sparsely settled. Overall, Europe's population probably increased by about 20 percent between 1500 and 1650, to a total of 100 million people. This growth was not sufficient to relieve frequent complaints about labor shortage, or to trigger revolutionary new economic forms; but it certainly put pressure on existing resources, including available land and food, and helps explain the growing suffering among the poor. Furthermore, along with population growth came some increase in urbanization. In 1500 there were only three cities in Western Europe with populations over 100,000: Paris, Naples, and Venice. This number now began to increase with the rapid growth of centers such as London and Amsterdam. New market opportunities plus crowding in the countryside accounted for new growth in the cities, although here too the change should not be exaggerated as Western society remained decidedly rural overall.

Increases in Prosperity   The second effect of economic change lay in the area of material culture. For many Westerners, and not just those at the summit of society, wealth increased as a result of new patterns of trade and manufacture. Most people still lived close to subsistence. Material life still involved widely fluctuating conditions and uncertainties; indeed, population growth made problems of periodic famines and hardship somewhat greater than before. But for many ordinary people, as well as many wealthy landlords and merchants, there was some improvement. For land-owning peasants and well-placed artisans, the definition of subsistence began to change somewhat. Although regional variations remained important between depressed areas such as Spain or Germany and more prosperous centers such as France, England, and the Low Countries, by 1650 the average European was almost certainly better off than an average person in any of the world's other civilizations—better housed, better fed, and with more material objects in his possession.

A prosperous if sober group of Dutch merchants express the new attributes of success in *Syndics of the Cloth Guild* by Rembrandt van Rijn (1662).

Counting up the number of tools, utensils, pieces of furniture, and items of clothing, one historian has estimated that a Westerner owned five times as many "things" as his or her counterpart in southeastern Europe— where prosperity had been at least as great as in the West a few centuries before.

People discerned this change at the time. An Englishman noted that whereas in the past a peasant and his family slept on the floor, owning only a pan or two as kitchenware, by the late sixteenth century a farmer might have "a fair garnish of pewter in his cupboard, three or four feather beds, so many coverlets and carpets of tapestry, a silver salt, a bowl wine . . . and a dozen spoons." Another Englishman, writing of his village life in the late 1580s, "noted three things to be marvelously altered . . . within his sound remembrance." The first was the increasing number of chimneys, as farming families kept themselves warmer and used more brick for construction; the second was a use of glass for windows, which provided more warmth and light and also more privacy than purely open exposures could do; and the third was the replacement of straw mats by beds and pillows. The writer could have rated the division into specialized rooms as well; sleeping quarters were now differentiated from kitchen and living space. Rural England indeed was being rebuilt.

Similar changes occurred elsewhere in the West. In Alsace, in what is now eastern France, rural craftsmen built and furnished half-timbered houses. Painted cabinets and bedsteads spread from Scandinavia and Holland through Germany and Austria, featuring warm colors and floral designs. Early in the seventeenth century, for the first time French peasants could afford some regular use of wine, rather than home-brewed beer. Here and elsewhere the use of glass for windows increased, and home furnishings became more substantial. Rural taverns spread as well, providing local farmers as well as travelers with more regular opportunities for socializing and entertainment.

68

TWO
*The Winds of
Change: Religion
and Economics in
the Sixteenth and
Early Seventeenth
Centuries*

Proletarianization   The third effect of economic change was the beginning of a new kind of social division among the common people—between those who owned house, land, tools, or some substantial property, and those who owned little but their bodies and could offer little but physical labor for their own support. What was beginning here was a process of "proletarianization," initially affecting only a minority of the common people, but later producing a permanently propertyless class compelled to work at others' hire and direction. For this group, increasing poverty and certainly increasing loss of personal independence were the result of economic change, as the poor tended, ironically and tragically, to grow poorer even amid increasing overall wealth.

Proletarianization, which shaped a new kind of labor force open to exploitation, resulted from several developments: one, population growth created a shortage of available land. Two, rising food prices hit hard at the poor. Three, landowners in many areas tried to take advantage of new market opportunities in the cities by tightening their control over a rural labor force. In many places, merchants bought out the established landlords on the estates and then installed more efficient labor controls, doing away with purely traditional obligations. Landlords of this sort, and also some noble landlords, pressed the nearby peasants to sell their small plots, expanding the estates and adding to the rural proletariat in the process. This expansion of large estates occurred to some extent all over western Europe, but it was most powerful in the eastern part of Germany and later in eastern Europe generally, and also in Britain and Ireland. In eastern Germany, aristocratic landlords called Junkers assailed once-free peasants in order to establish large estates to produce rye grains for export to urban markets and to England and the Low Countries. In England landlords in the sixteenth century mounted an enclosure movement. They beseeched Parliament to require that land be enclosed by hedge fences in their regions; peasant owners of small plots of land could not afford these hedges and so often had to sell out. Enclosure laws also allowed landlords to seize lands held in common by villagers. In Ireland, English conquest produced a similar result, creating new large estates worked by peasant laborers who had no land or only a plot too small to support their families.

Proletarianization also affected the cities. In the first place, many rural poor pressed into the cities, seeking occasional jobs or charity. In the second place, many craftsmen, seeking to take advantage of new sales opportunities, began to treat their journeymen-workers less as fellow artisans and more as paid employees with little or no chance to become masters in their own right. The idea of master and journeyman as co-producers, equal because of common skills even though the master owned the shop, began to give way to greater hierarchy. Guild traditions broke down, in many cases, as masters used the guilds to defend their own rights, and journeymen were forced to form separate associations to de-

The new proletariat. In this painting by Hans Wertinger (c. 1530), "free" German farm workers labor for a low wage. A wealthy commercial farmer, their employer (second from right), has just sold a sack of grain to the man at the extreme right.

fend their position as workers. Journeymen normally owned a few tools and had some skills, so they were not as desperate as were other elements of the proletariat. But they were increasingly separated from the middle ranks of the ordinary people, like masters who owned small shops for whom they worked for a money wage. Little wonder that a handful of labor strikes began to occur for the first time in this period, in trades such as printing, where the commercialization of employer–worker relations was particularly advanced. As workers, journeymen could seek to use collective action to assume power that they lacked as individuals, in defense of wages or other goals.

Like so many of the changes that altered ordinary life in the sixteenth and seventeenth centuries, the process of proletarianization was a gradual one. Many artisan settings would remain highly traditional for over a century yet. Many peasant owners still survived even in heavily enclosed regions of Britain. But there was a new force at work, which divided the ranks of ordinary people, created a new kind of labor force, and brought a new set of social problems for those at the top of society.

The clearest result of proletarianization in the sixteenth century was a new perception of the problem of poverty. The poor seemed more numerous and desperate than ever before. Begging and vagabond bands of criminals drew growing attention. And policymakers at various levels tried

TWO
*The Winds of
Change: Religion
and Economics in
the Sixteenth and
Early Seventeenth
Centuries*

to develop new strategies to counter this threat. New poor laws were one response. In England a law of 1531 authorized local magistrates to issue begging licenses only to those poor who were infirm—that is, incapable of work. All other beggars were criminals. In 1601 the Elizabethan Poor Law was passed. Pursuant to this law, local authorities were required to collect taxes to support the infirm poor, who were to be placed in almshouses and hospitals. The idea was to make each locality responsible for its own poor, to prevent them from wandering about and bothering respectable people. At the same time, the old distinction between worthy poor, who could not work because of illness, and others, was maintained, and vagabonds and beggars judged capable of work were to be jailed. This approach, in principle to be enforced by local magistrates, would remain England's main response to new poverty for over two centuries.

Another institution generated by the new division between propertied and propertyless was the prison. Criminals had previously been punished by whipping, mutilation, or execution, the latter often a great public event designed to intimidate other potential wrongdoers. But around 1600 the merchants who ran the city of Amsterdam came up with another solution for separating the criminal from the respectable rest of society: the large, institutional prison. The construction of prisons and the use of prison terms as punishment would gradually spread in western Europe.

Poor laws and prisons were limited responses in practice; older forms of punishment continued, and only a minority of captured criminals were imprisoned. In fact, poor laws did not prevent begging and vagabondage; nor did they fully replace more traditional charity from rich to poor or among the poor themselves. But in these early initiatives there was a new outlook that would become increasingly widespread: Poverty was a social problem. There was a new gap between many poor people and respectable people. Poverty should be approached through rational, general measures, and where possible the poor should be isolated. And there was a new fear abroad, shared by the elite and by smaller property owners alike: the fear that without property a person might not be trusted and was not capable of proper personal and social discipline. And this was a view that would have a long life indeed in modern Western society.

Economic Change and Changes in the European Mentality

The changes in outlook resulting from the religious and the economic shifts in European life were interrelated. A new society was beginning to take shape, one in which social and economic structures, as well as ways of thinking, would differ from those of the past. Both kinds of change were still tentative and incomplete, and in structure and outlook much of western Europe in 1650 was still traditional.

There were more precise interrelationships between the directions of these changes in outlook and in economic structure, however. New religious ideas, particularly those of Protestantism, emphasized personal achievement. The individual was encouraged to seek a more direct relationship with God. Many Protestants came to believe, particularly by the seventeenth century, that hard work and economic success were signs of God's favor. In many people's minds individual religious and material achievement became linked with personal discipline and the striving central to both. Because of this relationship, some theories have sought in Protestantism the origins of modern Western capitalism. Early in the twentieth century, the great German sociologist Max Weber posited this relationship directly. But this explanation is too simple. Capitalism—profit-seeking business activity based on investments of money—existed in the West before Protestantism did, and it continued to flourish in Catholic cities in Italy and France. Many Protestant areas, in contrast, remained economically backward. It was true, however, that the religious reformers placed a new emphasis on ordinary work life. Poverty was no longer a religious virtue; contemplation of God's mysteries was replaced by a life of striving; work in the world was seen as more glorious than attempts to isolate oneself in a cloistered existence. This new approach, partly echoed in Catholic attacks on beggars and random charity in the name of respectability and good order, helped fuel economic change and was fueled by it. And economic change helped enhance interests in secular life and gain, even as religious divisions called excessive spiritual devotion into question.

Economic change also abetted the tendency to demystify human surroundings. A tool lost its spiritual significance when it became commonplace. The increase of material possessions enhanced the idea that nature could be controlled, and did not have to be propitiated by special ceremonies as though it harbored a divine spirit.

Family Values

Economic changes certainly enhanced the new interest in family life. As housing became more spacious, family life became more pleasant and so a more attractive part of a person's goals. But the fact that new prosperity was directed to the home and its furnishings was not inevitable, but itself a sign that family values themselves were gaining ground. Moreover, the growth of market relationships supported the closeness of family. Increasingly, men saw their fellow workers as potential economic competitors; they were less likely, as in medieval times, to devote their emotional energies primarily to intense friendships. Family relationships, in contrast, were noncompetitive, and so the family took on new emotional significance as people withdrew from boundless loyalty and devotion to their fellows. What was occurring was a division between public life, where economic values and individual striving predominated, and a contrasting familial warmth. The division was just beginning, but it too would affect Western social life until the present day.

The enhancement of the values and material comforts of family life had important implications for gender relations, and here too a persistent pattern was beginning to take shape in the sixteenth century. Commercialization drew the workforce of men into several economic areas once open to women. A number of manufacturing guilds that had included women were now converted to men-only status. This shift, along with new attacks on women healers and the closing of many convents, showed how clearly new gender demarcations were tied to other facets of change in the Western world. Women's link to the family context—including productive labor within the household setting—became stronger than ever, although the emotional and material enhancement of family life compensated in part for the restrictions on women's roles. This was yet another theme that would expand in later centuries.

72

TWO
*The Winds of
Change: Religion
and Economics in
the Sixteenth and
Early Seventeenth
Centuries*

A Growing Preoccupation with Poverty

Apart from the fact that basic changes in the social outlook were still tentative and incomplete, the relationship between new popular beliefs and new social structures was coming into focus with all its complexities. In particular, it was hard for people to reconcile the economic basis of proletarianism with the new emphasis on family values or personal self-control. This was a key reason for the growing preoccupation with poverty and with separating the poor from respectable society. That is, if one believed that poor people were poor because they had failed to improve themselves and their families, lacked values, and hence required discipline, one could explain their intrusion on orderly social life. Changes both in social and economic structure and in popular mentality, launched in this age of Reformation and commercial revolution, were beginning to reshape Western society in durable ways. The complexity of the relationship between Western society's structure and its outlook would be lasting as well: the new industrial world emerging would be no simple or consistent environment, even when the changes took deeper root.

Changes in both outlook and structure had one result above all in this period: in challenging traditional patterns, they created confusion and dismay. A series of popular protests greeted new economic issues, including proletarianization, yet reflected new ways of thinking as well. And attacks on witches, discussed on page 77, focused concern about the new social structure and about new personal values alike.

Riots and Revolts

With agitation clustered in the last two decades of the sixteenth century and again in the 1640s, the period of religious and economic upheaval formed one of the truly great, and truly tragic, episodes of popular protest in Western history. Riots and rebellions covered Europe, from Sicily to Sweden, and from England to the east.

Causes of Resentment

The trigger for most popular risings was particularly severe famine, such as occurred in the 1580s and again from 1647 to 1649. Western society still lived too close to the bone to survive a year or two of unfavorable weather without major hardship. When the all-important grain crop failed, not just in scattered regions, as occurred quite commonly, but over large stretches of territory, there was trouble. Food shortages in the country-side caused some outright starvation but even more malnutrition, which was an invitation to death through respiratory or other disease. Food shortages in the cities meant rapidly rising prices as well as problems of availability. With food prices up, people had less money to spend on manufactured products; and this meant unemployment and falling wages for artisans who made clothes and furniture or built housing. Here was the worst kind of economic crisis; resources declined just as food prices reached a peak.

But although food crises prompted most popular risings, they did not explain the severity of the outbursts or the goals that protesters sought. Food shortages hurt worst when they occurred in the context of general price inflation. Between 1550 and 1600, the prices of necessities had risen between 70 percent and 100 percent. Many groups were hit by this pattern, but the ordinary laborers were most severely affected. Their wages rose, but because of population increases and displacements caused by land consolidation, they lagged well behind prices. Rising poverty for a large minority, then, underlay the popular anger.

Fueling the anger as well was resentment against what was seen as the injustice of new relationships between owners and workers. Particularly vivid was the zeal of many landlords to extend their estates and replace traditional obligations with low-paid wage labor. Here was a cause that could rouse not only the rural proletariat, but other observers as well, who felt that important traditional standards of justice were being violated. Thus spoke an English writer, Robert Crowley in 1550:

> The great farmers, the graziers, and rich butchers, the men of law, the gentlemen, the knights, the lords, and I cannot tell who; men that have no name because they are doers in all things that any gain hangeth upon. Men without conscience. Men utterly void of God's fear. Yes, men that live as though there were no God at all. Men that would have all in their own hands; men that would leave nothing for others; men that would be alone on the earth; men that be never satisfied, Cormo-rants, greedy gulls; yes, men that would eat up men, women and chil-dren, are the causes of sedition. They take our houses over our heads, they buy our grounds out of our hands, they raise our rents, they levy great (yes, unreasonable) fines, they enclose our commons. No custom, no law or statute can keep them from oppressing us in such sort, that we know not which way to turn us to live.

Many people, including those without property or threatened with its loss, believed that there was a natural justice, a moral code, that bound members of society in mutual obligations. This standard of justice did not call for absolute equality, but it did call for restraint and mutual assistance. Extensions of individual wealth, particularly the attempt to turn communal goods such as the common lands into private property, were condemned as unjust as well as harmful to many people. Around this standard of justice, seen as enshrined in tradition but now newly violated, intense, righteous protest could easily rally. A deeply felt moral code—as well as many empty stomachs—motivated the new currents of popular unrest.

There were other underlying reasons for the risings as well. Although most major Protestant groups urged obedience to the social order, the prospect of defying religious tradition and appealing to the spiritual rights of ordinary people, against the customary powers of priests, could encourage protest efforts. The religious wars caused great confusion and devastation in many regions. Governments and churches, both Protestant and Catholic, also pressed for new revenues during this period. They too were hit by inflation, which severely reduced the value of their taxes and tithes. Military ventures, such as the Thirty Years' War, cost money as well, for although most armies lived off the regions in which they fought, there was still some extra government expense for efforts such as those of Sweden or Spain. A number of popular risings were directed against tax collections. Printing and the increased rate of literacy also played their role in the new protest surge. Pamphlets often articulated grievances against governments or merchants of grain or bread, and there were now enough people who were able to read that they could pass the word along to the larger number of potential insurgents.

Widespread Agitation

Rioters in the 1580s seized on a number of specific targets. A southern French town, Romans, was seized in 1580 by a coalition of peasants and artisans led by a man named Jean Serve. Popular government was intended to replace a grasping upper class, which the rebels claimed would sell even human flesh if it made them a profit. But the upper class rallied and, allied with other propertied people, fell on the rebels and killed many of them. In Naples, in 1585, representatives of the government drew the people's wrath. Despite rising bread prices, the government had decided to ship flour to Spain, where there was also a shortage. A crowd seized one of the officials responsible for this decision and carved up his body, offering pieces of it for sale. All his belongings were destroyed, rather than stolen, in what was really a ritual sacrifice to express popular indignation at callous state action. Again, a brutal repression followed, with over 800 rebels brought to trial, 31 executed, 71 sent to the galley ships as rowers, and 300 exiled on pain of death.

Bad harvests brought renewed agitation in the 1590s, with risings from England through Hungary. Finnish peasants rebelled; so did rural laborers in parts of Britain. Again popular leaders emerged, along with a good bit of bloodthirstiness. One English agitator, blasting high grain prices, said that "we should cut off all the gentlemen's heads," and that "we shall have a merrier world shortly." In a French peasant rebellion, Catholics and Protestants worked side by side, subsuming religious differences in a common hatred of the upper classes and particularly taxes levied by landlords and governments. "They seek only the ruin of the poor people, for our ruin is their wealth." As in many of the risings there was a strong democratic flavor, with the rebels pledging mutual respect—"by faith and oath to love each other and cherish each other, as God commands"—

and making decisions in large assemblies. In this case, the movement was so strong that the royal government hesitated to repress it outright; rather, government agents encouraged Catholic–Protestant antagonisms until the rebels' military forces, now divided, could be successfully attacked.

Peasant agitation continued also in Germany and Austria, despite the defeat of the earlier Peasant Revolt (discussed on page 42). Religious enthusiasm remained as a spur, but the targets were the landlords, particularly those trying to increase work service obligations on the large estates. Some landlords were killed, and rioters often burned castles and records to destroy, they thought, the false legality of the landlords and restore popular control of the land. Several revolts spread over many regions, displaying remarkable organization and enough discipline to avoid random attacks on their enemies. Most rebels tried to make it clear that they accepted the authority of the state and were willing to pay legitimate taxes. But they wanted lighter burdens, more control of government troops, and legal restraint over landlord exactions which, they often claimed, were reducing them to slavery.

Risings continued in various parts of Europe in the early 17th century. The Thirty Years' War prompted many revolts in Germany and Austria, against the taxes and military exactions the war imposed. In some cases, Catholics and Protestants joined together, and unions of townsmen and peasants were common. Deep hostility to the upper classes emerged again; peasant songs expressed sentiments such as this: "The whole country must be overturned, for we peasants are now to be the lords, it is we who will sit in the shade."

More efficient royal government in France prompted widespread urban and rural risings in the 1630s against higher taxes, supplemented as usual by crop failures that drove prices up. Rebels in Normandy called themselves *Nu-pieds*, or "barefoot ones," to show how taxation was reducing everyone to beggary. Women played a prominent part in these French revolts, claiming the need to protect their children against starvation spurred by the food crisis; in a number of instances women mutilated the bodies of army officers who had been captured.

The wave of popular unrest crested in 1648. In England the demands of urban and rural laborers became part of the Civil War, leading to the formation of the radical groups that demanded democratic politics and economic socialism. A group called the Levellers produced remarkable organization in many parts of the country; in one case it was able to generate 100,000 signatures on a petition for political rights. But the group did not attempt outright armed insurrection, and it was ultimately put down. Risings of a more literal sort occurred in southern Italy, with people professing political loyalty while asking for reforms: "Long live the king and down with taxes and bad government"; "down with the food taxes and long live the King of Spain." Risings of this sort are called "church and king" riots, because of their interesting mixture of deeply felt grievance with equally strong obedience to established leaders. Loyalty to kings sometimes helped people target the upper classes—noble landlords and sometimes merchants—whom they saw as their real enemies. As in many other cases also, hostility to taxation focused particularly on food levies such as the sales tax on salt, which was seen as particularly unfair when people were starving.

76

TWO
The Winds of
Change: Religion
and Economics in
the Sixteenth and
Early Seventeenth
Centuries

Because of the widespread food shortage, caused by bad weather in 1647–48, but also springing from what was now a lively tradition of revolt, popular risings had unprecedented geographical sweep in 1648. It would be another two hundred years before unrest developed with such wide scope across the Continent. Risings in France were stimulated further by a simultaneous war by the nobles against the growing authority of the French king. A final round of peasant risings occurred in Austria and southern Germany. Swiss peasants, invoking the legends of William Tell, marched on their governments.

The Risings in Perspective

The wave of popular revolt largely ended after 1648. Better harvests and the termination of the Thirty Years' War helped calm passions. Outright repression, as usual, played a major role. Governments showed no mercy on popular rebels, only occasionally sympathizing with their misery and sometimes stalling for time because of tactical weakness. Soldiers attacked rebels fiercely. Leaders or accused leaders were executed in widely publicized ceremonies; sometimes their corpses or heads were kept on scaffolds as reminders of what real power was all about.

The rebellions, furthermore, had accomplished almost nothing. No political changes resulted from virtually a century of recurrent popular unrest. Individual landlords or businessmen might have hesitated in their profit-seeking course for fear of retaliation, but the basic trends of commercialization and an increasingly differentiated social structure continued.

Although the risings were ineffective, they mirrored the vast changes occurring in European society. Ordinary people had quite good ideas about what was causing their problems, and although they usually seized on personal targets rather than abstract formulations, their ideas were accurate. New class hostility between poor and rich was understandable in light of the growing profit-seeking of many landlords, merchants, grain millers, and artisan masters. Small wonder that popular rebels showed such fierceness in seizing and destroying the property of the wealthy, which they thought had been gained from their misery and labor—as they burned they often shouted, "It is the blood of the people!"

The popular rebellions were not only a cry of pain and outrage; they also suggested some changes in the thinking of the common people, which would crop up in later times as well. Aided by higher literacy, the popular capacity to organize and identify leaders was improving, even if it was not yet enough to beat down the forces of repression except in brief, local settings. The idea of equality—of harmony among the rebels, male and female, and of distaste for the wealthy—was increasingly formulated as well as a goal for social action. Also interesting were the hints of new political thinking, particularly of course in larger civil wars such as that in England in the 1640s. Some ordinary folk now turned against the monarchy; wanting the people to run the government directly. Far more rebels remained loyal to the king or simply had no large political ideas. But even these rebels were newly articulate in their belief that the government should be fair and should protect common people against material distress and against the depredations of the upper classes. Beliefs of this sort formed political expectations, even when they did not call the structure of government into question.

The common people have a long memory. Even as the wave of agitation died down after 1648, with such scant results, a recollection of the great defiances and of the new ideas about government and equality would remain in the popular mind, to be revived a century or more later. And the current of unrest itself did not entirely disappear. Important risings would resume later in the seventeenth century. In addition, bands of brigands, particularly in mountainous areas of France, Italy, or Spain, formed periodically to attack the landlords and express wider popular hostility against the new structure of Western society. New kinds of crime persisted as well, on a less formal basis. Smugglers brought in untaxed goods at many border points, secure in their belief that the government had no right to tax in the first place. Poachers tried to hunt on the landlords' great estates, seeking to supplement their diets but also protesting the closing off of so much land in the new regime of strict private property. They too believed that they were not disobeying any just law. The idea that the economy ought to be structured for the good of all, and that this "moral economy" was being violated for the benefit of a few, became deeply embedded in the minds of many ordinary people.

Witchcraft Hysteria

During the same decades that popular protest surged, a new fear of witchcraft spread across many parts of Western Europe and also, after 1630, in the English colony of Massachusetts. The unsettled conditions that had generated riots had helped fuel the fires of the witchcraft hysteria. Religious uncertainties were definitely involved; most of the witchcraft trials occurred in regions that had recently become Protestant or in areas, such as parts of southwestern Germany, where Protestant–Catholic division kept the controversy going. Although beliefs about witches were widely shared by both Catholics and Protestants, the anxiety did not pervade western Europe but settled in England and Scotland, Switzerland and southwestern Germany, a few parts of France and the Low Countries, and New England in America.

Witchcraft hysteria, though reflecting concerns about the new structure of Western society, was generated still more clearly by the confusions associated with changing outlook. Just as popular protest showed the depth of structural change, so the witchcraft trials revealed reactions to new ways of thinking and to local or personal institutions such as village or family.

Widespread Trials and Executions

During the sixteenth and seventeenth centuries, tens of thousands of people were tried and executed as witches. Scholars disagree widely on exactly how many were killed—some estimates run up to a million for Germany alone—but certainly the slaughter was considerable. Even more people were brought to trial; and more people still feared witches and being named a witch because of the trials. It has been estimated that in the English county of Essex one village in four had at least one witchcraft trial in this period. The fears of being accused of witchcraft, and the fears that caused people to claim that a neighbor was a witch, ran rampant in many parts of Western society. In general, witchcraft hysteria hit the largest cities rather early and then tended to fan out to smaller centers and the countryside, where the trials lasted well into the seventeenth century.

Who Were Accused

All sorts of people accused others of being witches. Teenagers were sometimes involved, as in some of the most famous cases in Salem, Massachusetts, and it may be assumed that some accusations reflected tensions of puberty or other adolescent insecurities. But older people participated, including sober magistrates and ministers of religion who conducted the trials on the assumption that standards existed that could determine who was and who was not a witch. The range of people accused of being witches was less great. There was a pronounced tendency to target some sectors of the population. By far the majority of accused witches were women, mostly single or widowed, and a disproportionate number were over fifty. Many accused witches, furthermore, had little or no property. There were exceptions: adult men, some of them prominent city officeholders, were tried for witchcraft.

Generally two kinds of problems could bring accusations of witchcraft. First was bizarre behavior, real or imagined. Suspected witches were accused of swearing allegiance to the Devil and attending satanic ceremonies where they ate, drank, danced, and copulated with their Master in various obscene rites. Many accused witches confessed to these practices. Some were coerced by the torture applied in the witchcraft trials. Many authorities justified torture on grounds that this would determine if the Devil was protecting his clients—if you suffered, you might not be a witch. But the effect was to produce far more confessions than would otherwise have been offered. Other "witches" did confess voluntarily. Magdelena Horn, in southwestern Germany in 1565, admitted that the Devil tempted her "day and night" and helped her do "so many bad things" that she could not begin to describe them all. She also admitted that she had often participated in satanic dances, sometimes taking her daughter along. In fact, historians have uncovered no evidence that satanic rituals actually took place, despite the fact that a few groups did try to practice magic or used ceremonies to deal with health problems, which may have provided a slim foundation to the fears and self-accusations about Satanism.

The more common kind of accusation involved beliefs that demonstrable misfortunes emanated from someone's practice of witchcraft. Thus a cow gets sick, or a baby dies, and a group is led to wonder if an unpopular neighbor, most likely an older woman with a sharp tongue, had caused these occurrences by applying devilish incantations. Accusations of this sort came mainly from ordinary men and women in the community, even though the legal framework for prosecutions was provided by society's elite. Many sixteenth- and seventeenth-century people firmly believed that their world was haunted by evil spirits, who worked their spells through the agency of particular individuals. The accusations were not made lightheartedly, nor did they usually come from a single complaint alone. Suspicion and fear built gradually in a village or neighborhood, and often a decade or more of mounting anxiety would be necessary before an outright accusation emerged. In this sense, the actual witchcraft trials were the mere tip of a larger iceberg, as they summed up larger and more longstanding fears.

Causes of the Hysteria

Belief in the power of the devil and witches was not new. Christians and pre-Christians in the West had long felt that there was an evil world beyond the world of the senses that was quite real. Both Catholics and Protestants continued these beliefs in the sixteenth and the seventeenth centuries. Hosts of popular practices, such as making the sign of the cross, or wearing charms, were designed to keep evil spirits at bay.

But the hysteria itself was new, for medieval people had not found it necessary to accuse others of witchcraft so commonly, or to develop a whole legal system designed to ferret out the satanic enemy. Signs of new fear had begun to develop before the Reformation. In 1484 Pope Innocent VIII issued a proclamation:

> That . . . many persons of both sexes . . . have abandoned themselves
> to devils . . . and by . . . incantations, spells, and conjurations . . .
> have slain infants yet in the mother's womb, . . . have blasted the pro-
> duce of the earth. . . . [They] afflict and torment men and women
> . . . as well as animals . . . with terrible and piteous pains . . . hinder
> men from performing the sexual act and women from conceiving . . .
> [and] over and above this they blasphemously renounce that Faith
> which is theirs by the Sacrament of Baptism.

What caused the new level of fear that rumbled over Western society for virtually two centuries? Obviously, to modern eyes, there was a new level of irrationality abroad, which caused people to believe what their eyes had not seen, or to attribute ordinary misfortunes to some higher agency. But dismissing witchcraft hysteria as irrational does not advance understanding. Nor does it help much to note that some witches were accused because of the individual psychoses of their accusers, or because of a desire for attention, or because of a hope to get rid of an annoying neighbor, though all these factors were sometimes present. A new level of tension had developed, a tension that caused not only the accusers but the many others who shared their fears and participated in the trials— and indeed those "witches" themselves who voluntarily confessed—to believe so deeply in the satanic threat.

Historians have not reached full agreement on what caused the overall

80

TWO
*The Winds of
Change: Religion
and Economics in
the Sixteenth and
Early Seventeenth
Centuries*

hysteria. But they do agree about what the contributing factors were. First, of course, were new religious uncertainties. Where the Catholic church seemed corrupt and distracted from its spiritual mission, people might wonder whether Satan's minions were gaining ground. When religious unity itself was disrupted, and where Protestants, though firmly convinced of their faith, might still suffer from the loss of traditional rituals and ceremonies that had so long kept evil spirits at bay, hysteria was particularly likely. Protestantism and many Catholic reforms helped to demystify the ordinary world and debunk popular superstitious practices. But people's beliefs did not change so rapidly, and the resultant gap led to a new level of fear. Areas where the Catholic Church remained strong and where the attention of authorities was directed to rooting out heresy saw little witchcraft hysteria.

New uncertainties about traditional medical practices added to the confusions that engendered witchcraft. Thanks to the spread of literacy to a growing minority, even ordinary people knew that customary explanations of disease and traditional remedies were now disputed. Physicians themselves, robbed of Galenic confidence by new, often conflicting means of diagnosis and treatment, often attributed diseases or symptoms to the devil's work. Patients who were confused about what remedies to apply or dismayed when remedies did not work might do the same. Some physicians increasingly attacked other practitioners, such as old village women who had long earned a bit of money by advising infertile women or by offering drugs or charms to assure the health of a newborn; these people might be seen as the devil's workers as well.

The new anxieties about the poor, and the new problems of poverty, definitely contributed to the hysteria. As property owners became more afraid of the poor people in their midst, and more reluctant to offer traditional charity, they often symbolically transformed individual poor people into the devil's agents. Furthermore, the poor themselves often had to seek extra money by selling charms and magical remedies. Here is the reason that so many elderly people were accused: Old people, and particularly older women who lacked property, faced growing distress in western society. Many were abandoned by younger family members, or pressed to retire without adequate means. Older women could rarely remarry once their husbands died, yet they might have few resources of their own. Even if a younger child were willing to help, the elderly often resented the loss of independence this entailed. In other words, some older people actually did try to earn money and a perverse kind of respect by acting as witches, using potions and uttering curses, and they too aroused wider fears because of the new anxieties about the poor and propertyless. Not only were the elderly particularly likely to be accused. It was in this period that the image of the witch as a haggard crone first emerged, for in previous periods witches were more likely to be seen as young, even lovely.

Changes in family ideals also added to the brew of hysteria. As families grew closer and women's roles were increasingly described by their family functions alone, the woman without family (who had never married or who was widowed and alone) became increasingly isolated, frightening, and possibly frightened. The witchcraft trials expressed a new belief in women's proper domesticity (although this domesticity could provide important satisfactions to the women involved). The trials helped enforce this newly rigid standard, as women were encouraged to understand that their safest path was the family path, and as older women learned that a passive, uncomplaining attitude was their safest course. The witchcraft hysteria thus served to enforce new values, just as it also responded to new uncertainties about the validity of popular beliefs and traditions.

Ultimately the witchcraft hysteria passed. There had been skeptics all along, and their number increased. By the middle part of the seventeenth century, magistrates became increasingly unwilling to accept evidence of witchcraft, and finally, though more slowly, popular belief in the phenomenon declined as well. This ending of witchcraft beliefs was as important as the hysteria itself, but it was completed mainly in the next period of Western history. During the sixteenth and early seventeenth centuries, witchcraft fears reflected a vital, difficult transition period in Western society, in which old beliefs and economic practices were increasingly uprooted, but in which a fully acceptable new outlook or social structure had yet to emerge.

Conclusion

The decades in which Western Europe was gaining new power in the wider world, showing an aggressive confidence and a new mastery of military technology, were decades of confusion and tension, from 1500 to 1648. Vital new structures were beginning to emerge, most clearly in the beginnings of proletarianization—a social pattern still vital in the modern West—and in hints of new beliefs concerning family, economic motives, and the control of spontaneous emotionality. But people at the time had no such perception, no sense of marching confidently or uniformly toward a new modern world. Governments and religious leaders faced new challenges, and the patchwork of wars and civil wars revealed the problems of maintaining order. Ordinary people faced challenge as well. The poor suffered most intensely, as a new gap opened up between owners and nonowners. Propertied peasants and artisans also encountered unwanted tensions, even as their standard of living improved. The threat of poverty hovered over them too, if only because uncertainties of support in illness or old age increased. More generally, the partial disruption of established community ties, popular recreations, and beliefs raised questions about alternatives. Some found solace in religious faith, old or new, and gained strength from new opportunities in popular religious music, family life, or economic gain. But disruptions had outraced new certainties. This is why so many ordinary people stood ready to protest or to lash out at mysterious forces of evil.

THREE

NATION-STATES AND THE SCIENTIFIC REVOLUTION: THE SEVENTEENTH CENTURY TO THE 1730s

1564–1642	Galileo
1610–1643	Louis XIII king of France
1624–1642	Richelieu chief minister
1630–1720	General population stability
1640	Frederick William, Great Elector of Prussia
1643–1715	Louis XIV king of France
1650ff	Development of mercantilist policies and theory
1662	Royal Society founded in England
1664	French Academy of Sciences founded
1667–1713	Louis XIV's wars
1680sff	Spread of the potato as a European crop
1682–1699	Habsburgs drive Turks from Hungary
1685	Revocation of Edict of Nantes (France)
1687	Newton's *Principia*
1688–1689	Glorious Revolution in England
1689	Declaration of Rights, political writings of John Locke
1689–1725	Peter the Great in Russia
1700–1721	Wars with Sweden
1703	Foundation of St. Petersburg
1721	Treaty of Nystadt
1694–1778	Voltaire; development of Enlightenment thought
1701	Prussian ruler takes title of king
1707	Union of England and Scotland as Great Britain
1713	Treaty of Utrecht
1733	Invention of flying shuttle loom
1740	Frederick the Great becomes king of Prussia

CHAPTER

THREE

NATION-STATES, SCIENCE, AND THE COMMON PEOPLE:

1648–1730

DURING THE SEVENTEENTH CENTURY, and particularly after 1648, several important new ingredients were added to the framework of Western society. Governments began to change in form and function, and in key countries what is called the nation–state took clear shape. Thus a change in political operation was added to the ongoing changes in social structure and popular mentalities to create a framework for Western life that in some respects continues to the present day. Equally important during this time was a revolution in science. At the most sophisticated levels of intellectual inquiry, a new belief system was generated by the 1680s and 1690s that deemphasized religious understanding in favor of scientific procedures and rationalistic assumptions. With these two changes, political and scientific, the "modern mind" was born.

The key developments in politics and science began among the elite of Western society. Strong nation-states acted *on* the ordinary people, far more than they reacted *to* popular political interests. Similarly, scientific discoveries were the fruits of educated genius, not of ordinary unschooled thought; although these discoveries began to be popularized, their most obvious audience remained a leisured, informed elite. Thus gaps between elite culture and popular culture widened in many respects. At the same time, some of the hardships of ordinary life seemed to ease. A decline in the birth rate reflected and promoted greater social stability. Proletarianization continued, but gradually and without the shock effects of the late sixteenth and early seventeenth centuries—and without as

83

much popular unrest. (Proletarianization is discussed on pages 68–70.) Although upheavals among the masses of Western society were less dramatic than before—and less dramatic than they were to become after about 1730—there were quiet changes of great importance. Family life continued to evolve toward greater domesticity and new patterns of child care. New popular beliefs began to take hold that suggested an outlook that bore some relationship to the scientific assumptions of the intellectual elite. The new beliefs accounted for, among other things, the end of the witchcraft hysteria.

The later seventeenth century also saw the extension of the Western orbit. Regions in eastern Europe drew into closer contact with western Europe. Colonization in the Americas created new trade contacts as well. Latin America emerged as a region with its own flavor, but in close economic and partial cultural dependence on the West. Colonies in North America actually extended Western civilization to a new frontier. The geography of Western civilization thus became more complex as Western civilization extended outright to England's North American colonies and other new relationships took shape with other parts of the world. This meant that the West's world role continued to change and that Western history itself began to transcend western European boundaries.

This chapter focuses on developments in Western society (now beginning to include parts of North America) from roughly 1648 to 1730. It also examines the forerunners of new forms of statehood and the scientific discoveries earlier in the seventeenth century, and it discusses trends that continued after 1730. The central focus on a roughly eighty-year period puts primary attention on the new nation-state system and the scientific revolution. It also captures a somewhat quieter interlude in the doings of ordinary people, between the often agonizing chaos of the early seventeenth century and a new series of disruptions that would begin to take shape during the second third of the eighteenth century.

The Emergence of the Nation-State

During the seventeenth century the nation-state unseated feudal monarchy as the characteristic political form of leading countries in western Europe. Some features of the nation-state spread as well to parts of eastern Europe in a process that drew the two regions closer together politically and diplomatically. Not all of western Europe yet participated in the new political form; Germany and Italy remained patchworks of regional states, while in Austria a new Habsburg monarchy produced a more centralized government but not a nation-state. There were, furthermore, two kinds of nation-states created in the seventeenth century; the absolutist monarchy and the parliamentary monarchy. But before we can understand these important differentiations, we must first get a sense of the form itself.

Nation-states differed from the characteristic political structures in many other societies. During the seventeenth century, the Middle East, and part of southeastern Europe, was organized in the vast Ottoman Empire, which ruled over diverse peoples with a mixture of centralized bureaucratic and military apparatus and considerable tolerance for local variations. Much of India lay in the hands of another diverse empire, the Mughal, which embraced a number of religions and many language groups. Western Europe had long since jettisoned any real possibility of this kind of overarching political unity. Instead, the nation-state involved a rough relationship between a specific cultural area, defined in terms of common language and historical experience, and its government. Thus the nation-state of France embraced most people who spoke French, and not many who did not. The resulting cohesion between the specific cultural area and the government was a source of strength and intensity for the nation-state form.

The nation-state also resulted from the triumph of the central state over feudal political units. Members of the aristocracy remained politically important but served increasingly as agents of the central state, or as representatives in a parliament, rather than as wielders of independent power. With power more centralized than in previous periods, the state could make more direct contacts with its ordinary subjects, rather than working through feudal intermediaries. Moreover, it could extend its functions. The nation-state did not become fully modern in the seventeenth century, but it definitely moved in that direction, in terms of bureaucratic organization and its growing ability to reach out to its subjects.

The Historical Precedent

Many earlier developments had prepared for the emergence of the nation-state. Renaissance political ideas had already produced a rhetoric in defense of the central ruler, untrammeled by feudal restraints and obligations. The destruction of Christian unity in the sixteenth century by the Reformation and the Counter-Reformation reduced the power of the Catholic church to limit central monarchs. And the chaos produced by religious wars (discussed in Chapter 2) created an atmosphere in which stronger state authority would be welcomed. Even earlier, during the twelveth and thirteenth centuries, feudal monarchs had developed the rudiments of a professional bureaucracy and army, plus some independent taxing power. But it was not until the seventeenth century that all these diverse antecedents coalesced to generate a really new kind of state.

France: The Absolutist Form

The classic nation-state of the seventeenth century was France, which also became the most powerful single country in western Europe. In concentrating sovereign power in the hands of the kings, the French produced the absolutist version of the nation-state. This version proved to be the most popular political form in the period—particularly for kings and their advisors. And the French case, aside from being most important in a power-politics sense, provides the clearest illustration of the aims and workings of the nation-state, and what about it was new.

Absolute monarchy and a full nation-state in France began to emerge with the end of the religious wars. During the early seventeenth century kings and their advisors reduced the influence of the aristocracy by using nonnobles as bureaucrats, refusing to call together the national parliament, the Estates-General, in which the aristocracy served as one of three branches, or estates, and attacking the military power of the class. Government functions expanded through an active road-building program, and foreign policy became more venturesome. Direct taxation also expanded, though limited financial resources remained a problem. Most important, agents of the central government were sent to the provinces, to replace local aristocratic rule in the administration of justice and finance.

SETTING THE STAGE FOR FRANCE'S ABSOLUTISM

Two men, a king and a chief minister, worked to increase royal power with particular effectiveness during the first half of the seventeenth century. The king, Henry IV, was one of the most popular rulers in French history—the only king whose statue would not be destroyed in the great antimonarchical revolution of the 1790s. The minister was a cardinal of the Catholic church, Richelieu, who served Henry's son, Louis XIII.

Henry IV, initially a Protestant, converted to Catholicism to gain the French throne, saying that "Paris is worth a mass." He proceeded to enact the Edict of Nantes in 1598, temporarily introducing toleration of Protestants and permanently ending the religious wars. His popularity benefited greatly from widespread desires for greater stability. He also reduced the most severe taxes on the peasantry, showing sincere interest in their hard economic life; in their stead, he established fees for some office-holding. Henry directly attacked aristocratic influence, using some advisors drawn from the middle class who depended for their income on royal favor. It was under Henry also that an ambitious road-building program began, and the government also sponsored foreign trading companies.

Richelieu effectively ruled France during most of the reign of Henry's successor, Louis XIII. This cunning statesman worked to reduce all groups and institutions to the authority of the French king. The nobility was his chief target. Richelieu insisted on quick executions for any nobles accused of treason; more durably, his armies used explosives to blow up many privately held castles. Richelieu also attacked Protestants, who held several armed towns. On the positive side, Richelieu greatly expanded royal authority by sending *intendants*, or royal officials, to all districts of the realm. Because they owed their position strictly to the central government, they were not tempted to set up an independent power base. Here was a clear bureaucratic alternative to feudalism. Finally, Richelieu guided a clever and active foreign policy, including France's involvement against the Habsburgs in the Thirty Years' War.

On the death of King Louis XIII, the nobility made a last try for a restoration of their power—a clear sign that they recognized the new kind of state that was emerging. Their rebellion was called "the Fronde" (named after the slings street urchins used to pelt carriages with stones and mud). Popular discontent against high taxes added to this period of unrest, which extended from 1648 to 1660 while the new king, Louis XIV, was still a boy. But when Louis came into his own, steeled by his uncertain childhood, he proceeded to complete the construction of the

The park of Versailles palace exemplified the rationalist's insistence on orderly discipline over nature. Versailles was the center of Louis XIV's splendor and power, and an impressive setting in which to manipulate his nobles.

absolutist version of the nation-state. A majestic if sensual monarch, Louis really believed his famous slogan, "I am the state."

Extending his predecessors' initiatives, Louis's absolutism involved an attack on previously powerful institutions. Louis maintained the policy of ignoring the medieval Estates-General, which had once been called upon to discuss taxation measures; he simply did not convene the body, which did not meet from the early seventeenth century until the French Revolution in 1789. The nobility was further defanged by Louis's luxurious court life, which induced many nobles to leave their local estates for the sumptuous new palace at Versailles, where they became enmeshed in a detailed social etiquette, vying for such privileges as watching the king eat, dress, and even defecate. Royal spies kept tabs on the noble guests, further emasculating them. And Louis chose key advisors from nonnoble ranks, seeking bureaucrats who would owe their power only to him. Finally, Louis sought increasing control over religion, again in the belief that the king should control every major institution in his realm. He supported the Catholic church but also chose its bishops and shaped its policies, forming a clergy that was partially independent from papal control. Louis also revoked the Edict of Nantes, denying tolerance to Protestants. This was bad policy, as many talented Protestant businessmen and artisans left the country rather than convert; but it made sense in an atmosphere of absolutism and it reflected a coherent nation-state concept in which the government should organize some cultural cohesion in its territories.

Louis's absolutism was not primarily an attack on old sources of power; rather, it involved a serious extension of state functions. Louis's main goal was the expansion of French territory, which he pursued through an aggressive foreign policy and a series of wars. A key tool of this policy was the development of a modern army, completely free from dependence on the feudal loyalties of the nobility. The French army became fully professional, recruited and paid by the state. The government organized its own supplies for its troops, rather than allowing them to simply live off the countryside. It regularized discipline and promotion, standardized weapons and uniforms, and organized medical care, building great hospitals for wounded veterans. This greatly enhanced the military power of the state, which was a factor in Louis's initially successful foreign policy but also a major force in France's internal politics. Although military service still called forth only 1 percent of the French population, more people served in the army than before; and the military was also available for the repression of popular unrest.

Louis and his ministers also increased the state's responsibility for the economy. They saw this as a vital tool for conducting foreign policy because economic organization would be used to compete with the economies of rival powers and could enhance the tax-paying potential of the French people. Louis's chief economic minister, the merchant's son Jean Baptiste Colbert, sought to increase French production and trade and to reduce dependence on outside imports. He used government funds to subsidize production of cloth, rugs, and armaments. Colbert regulated the quality of artisanal manufacturing and enacted high tariffs to protect

LOUIS XIV'S WARS

The wars led by Louis XIV, and the coalitions formed against him, dominated Europe's diplomatic history in the late seventeenth and early eighteenth centuries. These conflicts were the main events in international affairs following the Thirty Years' War, and they symbolized France's new position as the leading single power in Europe. The wars also expressed Louis's own chief goals, and the king spent more policy time planning his diplomacy and his campaigns than he devoted to any other effort. Aided by his professionalized armies, he long proved to be an opportunistic strategist, often catching his opponents off guard.

Louis justified many of his wars by dynastic claims, which involved arguments over rights to inherit certain territory; but these rationalizations barely masked a naked expansionism. In 1667 Louis first moved to the north, taking over provinces from the Spanish Netherlands, including the commercial town of Lille. Later Louis attacked Holland, and despite Dutch resistance did manage to gain some additional northern territory. Emboldened by these successes, Louis turned on the divided German states, taking over the province of Lorraine in the 1680s. Louis's armies laid waste to many castles in western Germany, thus assuring France's new eastern borders. This was the highpoint of Louis's power, however. New wars in the 1690s brought no new territory. The ruler of Holland, William of Orange, became king of England in 1689, and he organized a still larger alliance against the French king: key German states and the German emperor, plus Spain and Sweden, were pulled into the alliance, which fought Louis to a standstill. Then after 1701 Louis claimed the right to name his grandson king of Spain, which would have upset the European balance of power completely. Again an alliance went to work, augmented by English and Dutch competition with France in American and Asian colonial ventures. This time the French forces lost key battles. Peace finally came in 1713, in the Treaty of Utrecht; Louis's grandson did gain the Spanish throne but with a promise of independence from France, and both France and Spain turned over key territories to Britain, including Gilbraltar, at the mouth of the Mediterranean, and portions of eastern Canada. The Spanish Netherlands were released to Austria, as a further barrier to French expansion.

The Treaty of Utrecht was a major gain for the principle of balance of power in Europe, through which ambitious states were prevented from gaining ascendancy. By the same token it was a major setback for Louis XIV, whose wars had cost vast sums and disrupted French trade without adding significant new territory after 1684.

French industry. He encouraged the development of French colonies, particularly in Canada, and built a large merchant fleet. He supported internal trade by improving the roads and, particularly, by abolishing internal tolls and tariffs that had restricted movement of goods within the country itself; thus France became a national market for the first time. Yet Colbert's policies did not prod France into greater economic prosperity: some of his measures restricted individual initiative, and most of his efforts were aimed at increasing tax revenue, which in turn cut into living standards. But Colbert's policies did signal a new willingness and ability of the state to take on economic responsibilities, if only for its own interest—a key sign of the greater activism of the nation-state.

Finally, the French monarchy increased its patronage of the arts and literature, carrying on earlier Renaissance traditions. Louis's court at his Versailles palace, near Paris, became the center for dramatic productions, orchestral works, and paintings. In all branches of art Louis encouraged a sumptuous classicism, in which themes and styles from antiquity conveyed a sense of balance and order. Versailles itself was a typical product of this classicism: ornate, but severely geometrical, its expansive formal gardens showing man's power to discipline nature into precise regularity. The French monarchy did more than encourage artists and set tastes; it also established institutions to monitor and regularize the French language, producing dictionaries that set a linguistic standard at a time when other languages, such as English, were evolving more haphazardly.

Louis XIV's absolutism was hardly an unqualified success. Slow transportation and communication still limited the effective power of governments to reach outlying areas. Villages, local landlords, and churches still had great authority, despite the important growth of the central state and its functions. The heavy expenses of the new state—particularly its wars, but also the ambitious palace-building programs and court life—forced new taxation on the peasantry, which brought bitter discontent. The government was also tempted to sell public offices for cash, which reduced its control over its own bureaucracy and the efficiency of judges and tax collectors as well. Louis's wars, which early on added to French territory, increasingly brought alliances of weaker European states against him, forcing defeat and compromise. At Louis's death in 1715, the French government was bankrupt and unpopular, and its failure to recover in subsequent decades would eventually bring on outright revolution. Yet even in failure this was a new state: its power drew attention to the *government* as the source of discontent.

The Spread of the French Model in Europe

French-style absolutism spread widely in Europe. Many kings were eager to develop more efficient governments and to augment their own power. Spanish kings, after the new Bourbon dynasty ascended the throne in 1713, tried to develop a more efficient bureaucracy and improve the functioning of the state, and although their efforts won limited success, they did yield some change. Various regional German kings also copied elements of the absolutist model, including lavish palace-building in imitation of Versailles.

But the most important cases of absolutism outside of France arose in central and eastern Europe; they were linked to the rise of new or reconstituted states in the overall European power structure. Prussian, Austrian, and Russian rulers produced important statements of absolutist rule by the end of the seventeenth century, and indeed all three would continue to rely on absolutist principles well into the nineteenth century. Yet although absolutism thrived in eastern Europe—not only by imitating France but also as a result of repressive political traditions, particularly in Russia—it did not produce the same advance toward the nation-state evident in France, because of differences in basic social conditions. France had a larger merchant class and a freer peasantry than did eastern Europe, where the power of landlords over serfs limited the impact of the state on ordinary people. The rise of new states in eastern Europe was an important development in its own right, in reshaping Europe's list of great powers. It also illustrates (and frankly complicates) the fine distinctions between *absolutism*, which describes a monarch's relations with other power sources, and the more elusive *nation-state*, which describes a government's relations with its subjects.

The Rise of Eastern Europe

Prussia and the Habsburgs

Prussia was a regional kingdom in eastern Germany, initially the product of the conquest by Germanic knights of various Slavic peoples including the western Poles. In the sixteenth century a ruling house developed in the region, under the Hohenzollern family; the ruler and many of his subjects early converted to Lutheranism. Well into the seventeenth century the Hohenzollerns governed scattered territories, including a few small holdings in western Germany; they owed allegiance for some territories to the Holy Roman Empire, for others to the kings of Poland. A new Hohenzollern ruler came to power in 1640: Frederick William, called "the Great Elector." His efforts in the last stage of the Thirty Years' War won Prussia new territory, and he was able to organize a permanent army. Later diplomatic and military maneuverings won him recognition as a sovereign in his realm, and not simply a feudal lord.

Frederick William constructed the bases of Prussian absolutism not only by his careful reliance on a well-trained army, but by his policies of encouraging trade and economic development, including better agriculture. He played the Prussian nobles against each other, without depriving them of control over their own manorial estates. He insisted on religious tolerance, so that Calvinists and Jews as well as Lutherans flourished. Frederick William's successors continued the development of a strong monarchy and army. Cultural patronage increased, and Berlin came to be known as a leading intellectual center in northern Europe. In 1701 Prussia's ruler finally gained recognition as king. Subsequent decades saw the monarchy concentrate on building up the standing army, not for aggression or use so much as for defense and as an instrument for diplomatic maneuvering. The king also gave careful attention to the efficiency of the bureaucracy, and again to the promotion of handicraft industry, trade, and agriculture. He improved the direct collection of taxes, along with the revenue base, and he founded schools and examinations for state administrators. In the 1720s the king even established an elementary school system, with the idea (not yet fully feasible in practice) of making some education compulsory for everyone. Prussia was a prime example of the ways an efficient absolutist monarch could extend the functions of the state and its contact with ordinary people.

Prussia by the 1730s was still a second-rank state. But its absolutism was in most ways more solidly based than that of France, if only because its kings were careful not to engage in constant warfare or to overburden the state's treasury. As a result, military and bureaucratic efficiency and the importance of the state in economic and cultural life were far better and more durably established than in France, which was one reason that Prussian absolutism faced no outright revolutionary challenge until 1848.

Absolutism in Austria took a slightly different path. The Habsburg rulers of Austria had long relied heavily on their position as Holy Roman Emperors. But this office offered powers more nominal than real, particularly after Germany became religiously divided and so cruelly buffeted by the Thirty Years' War. Holy Roman Emperors did not really control most regional units, including rising upstarts such as Prussia. Gradually during the seventeenth century, therefore, the Habsburgs built their own dynasty in lands mainly outside the Holy Roman Empire. Toward the

This engraving, taken from a Prussian military manual of the seventeenth century, demonstrates the proper way for soldiers to drill. The professionalization of the military, which included new discipline and regular uniforms, was a fundamental feature of the seventeenth century.

end of the seventeenth century, they were spurred by a new threat from the Turkish Ottoman Empire. A new series of Ottoman rulers tried to recapture the military success of their fifteenth- and sixteenth-century predecessors, with Hungary and the German states the logical target. The threatened people appealed for aid to the Habsburg king, whose generals managed to defeat the Turks in key battles during the 1660s and again in the 1680s, when the Turks for a time beseiged the city of Vienna. Austria followed up its victories by taking over Hungary and also south Slavic lands (in what is now Yugoslavia), which were joined to holdings in Austria proper and in Bohemia. The Turkish threat never revived, and the Habsburgs were left with a large kingdom with a host of varied nationalities—Germans, Magyars (Hungarians), and various Slavic peoples. This was no national monarchy, and the Habsburgs never managed to develop the array of functions or the efficient bureaucracies that the Prussian or French kings could boast. Far more administration was left in the hands of the great aristocrats, who were mainly German or Magyar, than was the case in the genuine nation-states of the absolutist type. But the dominance of the Habsburgs at the center of their diverse holdings, unchallenged by any national parliament or other formal restraint, and the monarchy's growing wealth and military strength seemed to fit the new state into the absolutist pattern in some respects, just as the Habsburg empire clearly fit into the new roster of European great powers.

Russia's Peter the Great

Russia was the final case of absolutism, although it too differed from the French model in several important ways. Russia's tsars had emerged from their battles against the Tartars claiming great power—they needed no foreign example to inspire them to believe that they alone were sovereign in their land. As Russia continued to expand in the sixteenth and seventeenth centuries, particularly in central Asia and to the east, across the Ural mountains into Siberia, the tsars were able to trade land for service from their nobility. The Russian pattern involved nobles' control over great estates, with the serfs farming the land, in return for military and bureaucratic obligations to the tsars. Unlike western Europe, where feudal traditions had called for some voice for the aristocracy in political affairs, Russian nobles, though locally powerful, were officially under imperial control. Ivan IV, who ruled from 1533 to 1584 and was justly known as "Ivan the Terrible" because of his cruel treatment of any nobles suspected of disloyalty, played a major role in the extension of tsarist power. Noble resistance flickered once, early in the seventeenth century, when the tsarist family died out with no recognized heir. But in 1613, after a brief "time of troubles," a new family, the Romanovs, was selected to rule. Their dynasty would survive until the revolution of 1917. Gradually, during the seventeenth century, Romanov rulers regained primary power for the tsars over the service nobility, who in turn regulated the conditions for the serfs. Russia also resumed its policy of military expansion, moving against the Ottoman Empire in central Asia and southeastern Europe, and against Poland and Sweden in east-central Europe. Tsarist power was enhanced, finally, by a series of reform measures imposed on the Orthodox church against various errors that had been introduced during the Tartar period. Believers who resisted the reforms were exiled to Siberia and elsewhere, where they helped extend Russian power over its newly won territories; and the independence of the church itself was seriously reduced.

In 1689 Peter I, known later as "Peter the Great," ascended to the throne. A quick learner, energetic, Peter was also cruel and domineering, a giant of a man at six feet eight inches of height. Peter built on his predecessors' desire for absolute power, and he extended their interest in winning Russian entry into the ranks of European great powers. For this purpose, as well as to enhance more traditional expansionist interests in central Asia against the Turks, Peter resolved that the government must sponsor a series of changes in Russia's economy and society. Traveling to the West, working incognito as a craftsman at times, Peter learned of the craft skills and scientific gains that were transforming this part of Europe. Back home, after putting down a military revolt with great cruelty—he personally decapitated its leaders—Peter began his reform pro-

Peter the Great taxed beards as an obstacle to Russia's progress; as a result, beards became a luxury, and those who paid the tax rather than shave had to wear a beard medal. This cartoon shows Peter (right) as a barber.

gram, the first example of an attempt at "Westernization" by a state with a different, though in this case related, culture.

Peter tried to spur education for the Russian elite. He insisted that nobles learn some mathematics or be prevented from marrying. He required nobles to adopt Western-style dress, and he forced them to cut off their oriental-type beards, shaped in fashions established under the Tartars. These changes, of course, were mainly cosmetic, but they were intended to shake up established habits and open Russia's leaders to Western culture; they also demonstrated and furthered the tsar's power over his nobility. More important were Peter's reforms of the Russian military. He built a navy with the aid of Western experts, and reorganized the army along Prussian lines, with clear chains of command. He also built factories to supply weapons, and he encouraged Russian mining and metallurgical industries that would provide the needed materials for these new arsenals. Peter reorganized the bureaucracy, with more specialization of its function, creating clearer hierarchy. Peter also established a secret police to check on bureaucratic performance. The power of the nobles and the church diminished further as Peter ran the church as a department of the government, extended toleration to some other religions, and used talented commoners along with aristocrats in his state service.

PETER THE GREAT'S WARS

Peter the Great's predecessors had already taken much of the Ukraine from the Ottoman Empire. Peter launched new wars in 1695 and 1696, to gain territory around the Black Sea, with some eventual success. But his attention turned northward, and he made peace with the Turks in 1700. His target was Sweden, still a great regional power in the Baltic though fading from the military position it had enjoyed in the Thirty Years' War. The Swedish king initially held his own against Peter's army, but Swedish forces bogged down in Poland. Peter began building cities and naval bases on Russia's Baltic coast and was able to defeat the Swedish forces in 1709. The Great Northern War finally ended in 1721 with the Treaty of Nystadt, which gave Russia control of a number of Baltic states and islands. Sweden was reduced to second-rate status, and Russia's new role as a great power in European affairs, enhanced by possession of ice-free ports on the Baltic, was confirmed. Poland, still an important kingdom but loosely governed by councils of nobles rather than a strong monarch, did not directly suffer from this new arrangement, but its power was also eclipsed by Russia's rapid rise. The smaller east European states, or those that did not convert to forceful absolutism, were beginning to lose ground, not only in the north, where Russia and Prussia now vied for leading roles, but farther south as well, where the ancient kingdoms of Bohemia and Hungary had fallen under Habsburg control.

As a token of his power, and a gesture toward his desire to make Russia a great European power, Peter established a new capital on the Baltic, far away from the previous center in Moscow. He modestly named the new city St. Petersburg, and in it he and his successors sponsored an elaborate cultural life based mainly on Western fashions, including the ballet, a patterned dance form first developed in France. Ballet was symbolic of the orderly cultural forms that absolutists preferred and was taken over as a staple of the new Russian high art.

Eastern European Absolutism and the Classic Nation-State Model

The rise of new or revived states in eastern Europe showed the power and pervasiveness of absolutist government forms in the seventeenth and early eighteenth centuries. Yet none of the three ascending monarchies—Prussia, Austria, and Russia—was exactly a nation-state in the

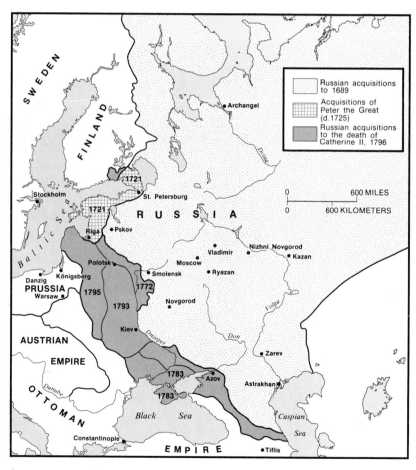

THE EXPANSION OF RUSSIA IN EUROPE AND THE MOVE TOWARD CENTRAL ASIA
Russia's overland acquisition rivaled the colonial growth of Western nations, and they have proved more durable.

French (or Spanish or English) sense. Prussia came closest, but fell short because it governed only a region, not a whole culture area—this was a dilemma that would be faced and resolved in the nineteenth century. The Habsburg empire, though powerful and newly important, simply did not have national characteristics, because of the multitude of cultures it embraced—German, Hungarian, and Slavic. Here too was a theme that would have important repercussions in the future, as multinational empires faced the challenge of national sentiment. Russia also ruled many cultures, including Muslims in central Asia and numerous Asiatic tribes in Siberia, as well as a variety of Slavs and others in its European holdings. There was a majority Russian culture, however, which gave the growing empire some national characteristics. But Russian absolutism was built over a rigid system of serfdom, in which noble landlords, though subservient to the tsar in national politics, politically and economically dominated their peasantry. The central monarchy had virtually no direct contact with peasants, except in the traditional functions of tax collector and military recruiter. Peter the Great's Westernization measures left or-

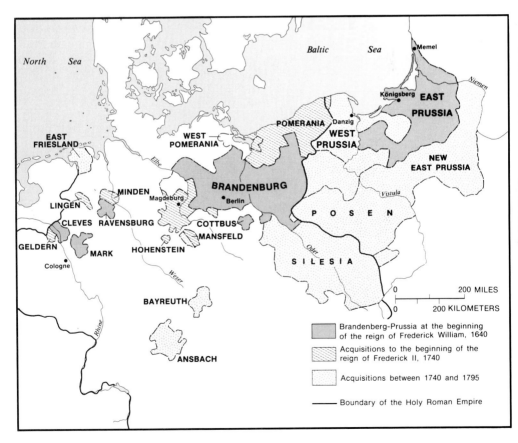

THE EXPANSION OF PRUSSIA
Prussia moved toward center stage in Germany and central Europe by successful use of war and a strong sense of what expansions were feasible.

dinary people untouched—or hostile to the foreign manners and French-
ified styles of the great lords. The government's economic programs,
though significant in developing a heavy industrial base for armaments
production, had virtually no impact on the agricultural masses, whose
methods remained traditional and whose standard of living, far lower
than that of the Western peasantry, was if anything worsened by the
government's growing tax demands. Russian tsardom and Habsburg rule
were legitimately absolutist, in that the power of the nobility to defy the
central state was limited; in this they shared qualities with the French
monarchy. But they were not quite nation-states, not only because of
their diverse cultures but also because the government did not reach
ordinary people directly. For most peasants, effective power—in the Russian case, growing power—lay in the hands of landlords who controlled
a share of all produce plus regular work service, and who ran the courts
of law and prevented freedom of movement.

The rise of eastern European absolutism created new political contacts
between east and west in Europe. Russia joined the Habsburgs, France,
and England as key players in Europe's diplomatic games, and Prussia
became a legitimate claimant as well. But Europe's political map remained
complex, if only because military or bureaucratic change did not erase
cultural and social gaps. Divisions between absolutist states and absolutist
nation-states would continue to affect European history into the nineteenth and twentieth centuries.

The Parliamentary Variant

One final complexity emerged in this same late-seventeenth century
era: the rise of a parliamentary form of nation-state in England and the
Netherlands. A considerable amount of political theory also arose in jus-
tification of this form. The Netherlands, freed from Spanish control in
the early seventeenth century, developed a federal system of government, in which each state had a local legislature elected by the aristocratic and merchant classes, with a federal body, drawn from state
representatives, electing a national executive. Although the executive was
selected from the noble Orange family, this was not a monarchy, much
less a centralized, absolutist form. And although Holland was small, its
far-flung merchant activities, its colonies, particularly in southeast Asia,
and its service as Europe's banking center, gave Dutch institutions a power
and prestige that they might otherwise have lacked. Dutch politics were
also noteworthy for their religious tolerance, despite the existence of a
Calvinist state church.

The Glorious Revolution

The English parliamentary form developed out of the civil wars of the
seventeenth century. Renewed attempts by Stuart monarchs to limit parliamentary power and enhance the position of Catholicism had brought
the so-called Glorious Revolution of 1688, in which the Dutch executive, William of Orange, and his Stuart wife were invited to take over

the English throne. A new parliament was elected in 1689 and formally extended the monarchy to William and Mary—an important step that symbolized Parliament's supremacy in being able to offer the Crown, rather than the king's supremacy in calling and dismissing parliaments. The new rulers accepted a declaration of rights that deprived the Crown of the right to suspend laws, tax without parliamentary consent, or maintain a standing army in time of peace. The companion Toleration Act extended limited tolerance—freedom of worship but not equality of political rights or rights to attend universities—to non-Anglican Protestants.

After the Glorious Revolution, subsequent British monarchs united England and Scotland. Parliaments met regularly, and monarchs and their ministers worked to create a viable majority so that the king's and Parliament's wishes could coincide. Elections to Parliament were vigorously contested, and a suggestion of a two-party system emerged; the Tory party professing greater loyalty to the monarch, Whigs to the principles of parliamentary rule. In fact, however, quests for office normally overrode principle. The percentage of people eligible to vote was tiny; women were excluded, and the small number of male voters was so dominated by the land-owning gentry and a few merchants that elections were often corrupt, with votes purchased by eager aspirants. English politics stabilized nevertheless after many decades of turmoil, and a real balance between Crown and Parliament was achieved. Although hardly a modern parliamentary system, if only because of the limited electorate, this was nevertheless a marked contrast to the absolutist system. The English bureaucracy was small, the army almost nonexistent in peacetime, the role of the Crown in setting the cultural tone decidedly limited.

England and Holland as Nation-States

Yet England and Holland were nation-states in their own ways. First, government functions expanded in a few respects, although not so widely as in absolutism. Second, there was a desire to promote economic development. England and Holland continued to support the great merchant companies, giving them special charters and legal privileges. Many of these companies, in turn, set up colonial administrations in places such as India or Indonesia, partially separate from, though again supported by, the actual national governments. Economic policy also involved tariff measures designed to promote national well-being. Early in the eighteenth century, England levied high taxes on cotton goods imported from India to protect a fledgling cotton industry at home. More generally, England and Holland tried, as did Colbert's France, to limit manufacturing activities in their colonies. They saw the colonies as sources of raw materials and of foods such as sugar, and as markets for products manufactured at home and carried in the ships of the mother country.

Thus nation-states, whether absolutist or parliamentary, adhered to the economic policies known as *mercantilism*. The mercantilist approach held that a nation should guide economic policy to maximize production and trade in the nation's own hands, while limiting the rights of colonies and nonnational outsiders. Even in the late twentieth century, and long after specific mercantilist ideas were discredited, nation-states in the West and elsewhere perpetuated a sense of responsibility for economic trends, and a desire to promote national self-interest above all, inherited from the mercantilist impulses of the first nation-states.

100

THREE
Nation-States,
Science, and the
Common People:
1648–1730

The parliamentary nation-states also acted according to some sense of popular political voice or sentiment. To be sure, most people did not vote directly; however, there was a belief generally that the parliaments spoke for national interests, and not just the interests of the elite group of those who could vote. And although this idea of a national representation was vague and embodied much wishful thinking, it was true that ordinary people could and did petition parliaments about grievances— thus suggesting that they too felt some attachment to the institutions of government. Just as the growing functions of the state in absolutist France drew new attention to the national government, so did this tenuous sense of popular involvement in the parliamentary states.

The Theoretical Basis of Parliamentary Monarchy   The most cogent political theory of the period confirmed this linkage between parliamentary monarchy and a nation's people. There was some theoretical support for absolutist monarchy, particularly during the seventeenth century. French and some English apologists wrote in defense of the "divine right of kings," arguing that monarchs were anointed by God. Earlier arguments about supreme royal power based on precedents in Roman law were still invoked. During the chaos of the English civil wars, Thomas Hobbes wrote a more original defense of strong monarchy, claiming that without it human nature would lead only to brutal anarchy; people should give up their rights to a powerful king in literal self-defense.

But the more significant line of political theory sketched during the seventeenth century urged that government authority sprang in some sense from the people themselves and was therefore ultimately controlled by them. Several Dutch and Swedish writers, building on a Protestant background of belief in the ultimate spiritual equality of all men, argued that arbitrary government was wrong and that people owed absolute loyalty to no ruler. In England the philosopher John Locke amplified these themes. He urged that people have rights to religious freedom that no government could legitimately abridge, so long as their religion was not immoral. In his *Two Treatises on Civil Government* (1689), Locke set about to justify and formalize the principles of the Glorious Revolution. Government stems not from divine right but from the will of the people, he wrote, and if it violates this will or tramples normal liberties, the people can legitimately overturn it. Locke argued that people were good by nature and would therefore agree only to a government that supported their independence. People had natural rights—to life, liberty, and property—that no government could violate legitimately. Locke did not suggest that governments should give everyone the vote, and his concern for property revealed his attachment to upper- and middle-class position. The proletariat was effectively excluded, as were women at all levels. But

Locke's language powerfully supported not only the parliamentary system, but also further demands for direct political participation.

Locke's views spread widely, not only in England but also in France and other parts of western Europe. By the early eighteenth century, it was becoming increasingly hard to defend governments, in theory, on any basis other than their embodiment of popular will or at least the common good. Even absolutist rulers, such as Frederick the Great in Prussia, began to avoid pure-power claims in favor of arguments that the monarchy best served the public interest and was compatible with the protection of some individual rights. However misleading such rhetoric might have been in terms of the actual wielding of power, the idea of a new linkage between a state and its people—one of the core ingredients of the nation-state impulse—was further enhanced.

Into the later eighteenth century and beyond, Europe remained profoundly divided politically. The collapse of feudalism as a basic political principle had yielded no single system. Parliamentary monarchies maintained the idea of restraint on government power. Absolutist regimes concentrated on the centralization and expansion of government functions. Rising eastern European monarchies developed their own versions of absolutism, only partially reproducing the form created in the nation-states of the West. Divisions in political structure within western Europe would be partially resolved only after 1850; divisions between western and eastern Europe have not been resolved to this day.

The New Politics of Absolutism and Changes in the Wider Society

As we have seen, during this period governments of successful states—of whatever form—were expanding their functions, generally taking a greater role in economic policy and, in the absolutist regimes, beginning to move into areas of welfare and education as well. On the other hand, governments that could not expand their range of operations, and improve their bureaucratic organization in the process, were doomed to decline—feudal Poland is one example—unless, like England, they could produce a new kind of parliament that would focus some popular loyalty. In either case, both absolutist and parliament regimes, particularly in western Europe, were escaping purely aristocratic rule. And in England, Holland, France, Prussia, and to an extent Spain, national monarchies were winning new attention as centers of political interest and expectation.

The new government functions and the attachments associated with the blossoming nation-states of western Europe add up to a considerable shift in the basic conditions of life. This is why the decades of the emergence of French or Prussian absolutism or British parliamentary rule draw so much attention to politics. For despite many previous strides toward centralization by European monarchies, it was at this point, in the later seventeenth century, that the localized political structures of feudal days finally gave way to central authorities, who had new and more efficient procedures, a new list of functions, and a new claim on people's loyalty.

102

THREE
Nation-States,
Science, and the
Common People:
1648–1730

The Extent and Depth of Change

Historian Charles Tilly has argued that the rise of the nation-state constitutes one of two really "big changes" in modern Western history to which people had to adjust. (His other "big change" is the shift in economic and social structure leading to new divisions between people with property and the growing number without.) There were in fact a few more major changes than these—including the shift in popular outlook associated with new family values, growing literacy and religious changes, that began to form in the sixteenth century and, later on, basic transformations in technology. But there is little question that the rise of the nation-state, whether absolutist or parliamentary, constitutes one of the great dividing lines between modern and "traditional" western Europe.

This is most obviously true at the level of elite life. The rise of the nation-state meant a new role for aristocrats, now tied to functions in the central state rather than operating as semi-independent regional authorities. It meant service as army officers in a clear hierarchy, for example, rather than operating as feudal military lords. It also meant new mechanisms and motives for wars and for diplomatic maneuvers. But the nation-state had its serious impact on ordinary people. As were the other major changes just mentioned, this impact was gradual, extending through the eighteenth and nineteenth centuries, rather than suddenly appearing around 1700. Additionally, the changes the new nation-states wrought were pervasive, particularly under absolutism. More people were recruited for military service, for example. Pressures to pay taxes grew, due to more efficient bureaucracies or to parliaments now giving sanction to tax levies; in the absolutist states, tax rates tended to rise as well. State agents began to collect statistics about ordinary people—for example, about their numbers and family status—as part of government recordkeeping and planning. Regulation of some economic activity and welfare institutions signaled other ways that the state had new contacts with ordinary life. During the eighteenth century, for example, French and Spanish governments established hospitals to receive abandoned children, so that in essence people increasingly turned over children they could not care for to the state rather than to church, private individuals, or the wilderness. Furthermore, the growth of the nation-state gradually began to redirect political loyalties and attention, as more and more people came to see the central government (monarch or parliament) as responsible for preventing certain wrongs and for maintaining certain standards. Thus they appealed increasingly to the nation-state for aid in times of famine, as in Louis XIV's France, or for more direct political rights, as in the renewed agitation for a more democratic voting system in England in the 1760s.

People who lived on the long borders of the nation-states experienced social changes directly. National borders divided many peasant communities. New state efficiency and functions increasingly made these borders not just mere paper lines, but real separators—not, to be sure, with a full array of guards and a physical barrier, but with noticeable enforcement of distinctive laws and commercial practices. People on either side of the divides experienced different laws and economic patterns and were drawn into different orbits of loyalty or resentment.

The Speed of Change

As with all the great changes set in motion in early modern Europe, including growing commercialism, the new social structure, and the shifts in popular mentality, the rise of the nation-state around 1700 only began a long process of change. Government contacts with ordinary people in 1750, though greater than in 1650, were hardly as extensive as they would become a century later. Local identity, and the political importance of regional aristocrats, still loomed large. Indeed, political culture changed no more uniformly or rapidly than did beliefs about witches, or commercial patterns. Political change was also complicated because, unlike the new levels of commercialism or literacy, it did not so obviously make Western civilization unique—even as it altered Western patterns from the West's own previous norms. European governments were in part paralleling procedures that more established civilizations, such as China, had developed long before—for example, providing explicit training for bureaucrats or government-run supply lines for armies. Even in this comparative respect, European political systems were gaining efficiency by the eighteenth century, a time when other states, such as the Ottoman, Mughal, and Chinese empires, were facing new problems in maintaining effective central controls. Furthermore, the nation-state form, insofar as it involved more than heightened efficiency, was not a mere replica of orderly governments elsewhere. Its close linkage of state, language, and culture group—in contrast to the more diverse peoples and looser administration in the Ottoman Empire, for example—helped produce an unusual intensity in the political beliefs attached to this state form. Europe's division into nation-states, rather than a development of a single dominant empire, obviously assured a pattern of fierce internal rivalry. The diversity of Europe's nation-state forms in this period, between absolutism and parliamentarism, also provided a certain flexibility to Western civilization as a whole—a flexibility that would mark the nation-state's response to subsequent challenge and change.

Thus, although hardly unique in all respects, the European nation-state formed a basic new ingredient in Western life, along with new levels of commercial contacts, the social division between those with property and those without; new popular beliefs, and new technologies. Not only did it contribute to transforming life in the West itself, but it also served as a key ingredient of the Western model for other societies around the world. Indeed, in our own century in the new nations of Africa and Asia, the nation-state has been copied more eagerly than any other aspect of Western society, including the constitutional form of government itself.

The Scientific Revolution

104

THREE
*Nation-States,
Science, and the
Common People:
1648–1730*

During the same decades in the later seventeenth century in which European politics were being transformed, science burst into unprecedented prominence in Western culture. This development had scant link with political change. Absolutist governments sponsored some scientific work—Prussian kings, for example, subsidized the mathematician Leibnitz in Berlin. Many states helped found scientific academies that aided in the transmission of knowledge. The tolerant political atmosphere in Holland and England contributed even more to the encouragement of science. Overall, however, politics left a clearer mark in other aspects of European culture in the late seventeenth century than on science. Monarchs such as Louis XIV patronized classical styles in drama and literature that appealed to their sense of orderliness and grandeur. Their architectural tastes, which involved luxuriously ornamented classical styles for churches and palaces, had the same basis. But although the late seventeenth and early eighteenth centuries were productive periods in Western art and literature, the great developments were in science and its larger implications for philosophical outlook. A French historian, Paul Hazard, has labeled the 1680s the point at which the "modern mind" was born among leading intellectuals, and he makes a good case. This means, in turn, that of the various ingredients of "modernity" in Western civilization, science took firm shape earliest. The changes in popular outlook, commerce, and nation-state politics that had developed during or before this period were gradual and uneven in their impact. Louis XIV, though no traditionalist, was also not a modern ruler, nor was John Locke exactly modern in the way he reasoned about political rights. But by the 1680s there were scientists and intellectual popularizers who thought much the same way that their counterparts think today. This section explores the seventeenth-century scientific revolution and then tries to answer the following questions: What does this change have to do with other developments in politics, the economy, and popular mentality? When did the various changes of the modern Western world link up, and in what fashion?

The scientific revolution was European in scope. Basic discoveries emanated from Italy and Denmark, from England and Poland. The revolution's impact was also Western-wide in recasting the West's intellectual life, much as Christianity had been a millenium before. It must be realized that, even as Western civilization was divided politically into better-defined nation-states, its common cultural foundation, now defined in terms of a scientific worldview in addition to the Christian heritage, was as solid as ever.

Western civilization, like other cultures, had advanced scientific inquiry before 1600. Already Western thinkers had recaptured Greek assumptions about the importance of relating human rationality to the larger order of physical nature. This Western tradition had not produced more *knowledge* than scientific traditions in India or China, but it did encourage a more theoretical bent. The Renaissance's encouragement of the re-evaluation of ancient learning, found in isolated cases such as the Copernican challenge to Hellenistic theories and an ongoing tradition of empirical work on optics and anatomy, also prepared the way for the seventeenth-century explosion. Technological improvements, such as better navigation devices, may also have helped set the stage by stimulating new thinking about, and a more general interest in, how nature works. Specific improvements in instrumentation during the first half of the seventeenth century played an immense role: the telescope, the thermometer, the barometer, the microscope, and other devices linked craftsmanship to basic scientific discoveries. Finally, ongoing improvements in mathematics, such as the development by René Descartes of analytical geometry in 1637, encouraged and reflected the new torrent of scientific work.

The Focus of Scientific Thought: Physics and Astronomy

Scientific advance proceeded on many fronts during the seventeenth century. A self-trained Dutch microscopist, Anton van Leeuwenhoek, described one-celled organisms, or protozoa, which he called his "little animals." More important still, in biology, was the work of the English physician John Harvey, who demonstrated the circular movement of the blood in animals, with the heart as its "central pumping station." This discovery corrected basic misimpressions in the anatomical tradition in-

PROSPECTVS INTRA CAMERAM STELLATAM

The new instruments and organization of science: the Royal Observatory at Greenwich, England.

herited from ancient times. Still other research focused on the movement of gasses, and there was some advance in the understanding of key chemical elements.

106

THREE
Nation-States,
Science, and the
Common People:
1648–1730

But pride of place in the seventeenth century scientific revolution went to discoveries in physics and astronomy. These built on the renewed attention given to the work of Copernicus, which had challenged the hold of tradition and also raised important questions about the motion and attraction of physical bodies (see also pages 61–63). From the 1590s on, new observations piled up data about the movement of planets, as it was discovered that their orbits were elliptical and not neatly circular as Copernicus had assumed; these observations also confirmed the "heliocentric" view of the universe. New planets and other bodies were discovered. The astronomer Edmond Halley, in 1680, predicted that the brilliant comet that bears his name would reappear in 1758—which it did, greatly enhancing popular faith in scientific acumen.

But observation alone was not the core of the new science; theory was equally important. By studying newly discovered pendulums and also other patterns of motion, both in nature and in experimental settings, the Italian scientist Galileo disproved ancient Greek theories about motion and gravity and began to sketch out the modern ideas of the principles of gravity and acceleration. Galileo was aware of his own importance, writing of "this heaven, this earth, this universe, which I, by marvelous discoveries and clear demonstrations, have enlarged a thousand times beyond the belief of the wise men of bygone ages."

It was Isaac Newton, with the publication of his *Principia* in 1687, who drew the various observations and theories together into a neat framework of natural laws. All motion, argued Newton, proceeds according to three simple principles: a body in motion maintains uniform momentum in a straight line unless impelled to change by outside forces; changes in rates of motion are proportional to the outside force; and to every action there is always opposed an equal reaction. Newton further described the forces of gravity in great mathematical detail and showed that the whole universe responded to these forces that among other things explained the planetary orbits. Knowledge of gravity and realization that it was a uniform force—part of the orderly uniformity of nature—allowed precise calculation of tides and improvements in map-making, in gunnery, and in a host of other practical areas. Newton's laws, and the kind of universe they suggested, held sway for over two hundred years. They were found to be oversimple and in some respects inaccurate only in our own century.

Newton and other scientists not only advanced knowledge; they also formalized scientific procedures. Newton urged that all scientists observe four precepts: the laws governing the physical world are simple; these laws are consistent; they are absolute, applying not only to experimental settings but also to planetary bodies we cannot fully observe; and they can be established by combining induction (that is, observation and experiment) and deduction (that is, reasoning out a general law from these particular cases and then applying it to the whole category of cases, whether directly observed or not). This approach amalgamated two con-

THE CATHOLIC RESPONSE TO
NEW SCIENTIFIC THOUGHT

One sign of the novelty of the scientific revolution lay in the opposition it initially aroused. The Catholic church, still smarting from
Protestant defections and rigorous in its watchfulness for subversive
ideas, struck back at the attacks on Ptolemaic theory, which held
that the earth was the center of the universe. For the Counter-
Reformation church, this notion of earth as center seemed to confirm God's creation and special attention to humanity. More
generally, church officials perceived—correctly—that criticisms of
tradition in science might easily translate into more sweeping blasts
at convention and at belief based on faith. So they moved, insisting
that Galileo retract his defense of Copernicus. The Inquisition found
the view that the sun was at the center of the universe, "mad,
philosophically false and wholly heretical, being contrary to Holy
Writ." Galileo was arrested in 1633, his attacks on traditional scientific views placed on the Index (discussed on page 47).

In fact, although Galileo was threatened with torture, he spent
his brief period of imprisonment in a luxurious five-room apartment. His punishment consisted chiefly of reciting penitential psalms,
and he was allowed to have his daughter, a nun, do the actual
reciting. But there was a period of conflict, a genuine effort to
intimidate the new scientists, who generally responded with cock-
sure defenses of their own intellectual prowess. And the new science could not be stopped. The Jesuit order itself continued to
teach Copernican theory. Interestingly, Catholicism was not un-
done by the new science; in fact, it did not depend on such literal
rendering of tradition. Thus sincere devotion not just to Catholic
piety but to theology persisted. But the seventeenth century did
see a shift of primary intellectual interest and creativity away from
the religious realm, and by the century's end many Catholic thinkers recognized that they were on the defensive, pleading in vain
against the passion for new secular learning.

trasting arguments developed earlier in the seventeenth century, which
continued to strain against each other in some instances. In 1620, Francis
Bacon had urged a science advancing steadily on the basis of repeated
experiments and direct accumulation of data. He also anticipated a link
between science and technology, arguing that progress in knowledge
would lead to better methods of agriculture and manufacturing. A French
school arose in partial opposition, based on the work of René Descartes
from 1637 onward. Descartes valued rational, mathematical deduction
over experiment. He felt that close logical reasoning could destroy error,
and he urged that all traditional beliefs be subjected to this kind of scru-
tiny. (To be on the safe side, however, he proved the existence of God
and then largely ignored this bow to religious convention.) For Des-

108

THREE
Nation-States,
Science, and the
Common People:
1648–1730

cartes, careful, logical steps related human thought to the external laws of the universe.

The different priorities of rationalism and empiricism would continue to affect Western intellectual endeavor from the seventeenth century onward, not only in science but also in social science. Successful scientists in fact borrowed from both approaches, Newtonian-fashion; even to interested nonscientists both approaches seemed complementary in their ability to generate new knowledge separate from reliance on tradition alone, and in their suggestion of a new pattern of progress in human understanding of the physical environment.

The new science had one other vital feature: it focused on how things worked in this world rather than on God and first causes. It involved, in other words, a shift in attention away from the staples of traditional theology, concerned with creation and with the nature of divinity, to the actual workings of nature that could be so elegantly and simply captured by the scientific approach. Thus Newton, though extremely interested in religion in other work, separated his science from concerns about why things occurred as they did—which he confined to the category of "occult qualities." Thus John Locke, writing of the human ability to know, separated our impressive capacity to grasp what we need to function well through our own learning capacity from an irrelevant inability to explain many classic theological issues, including what caused the universe in the first place. Scientific reasoning yielded all the knowledge humanity required, and a separate category of faith was unnecessary. The fact that most philosophers, such as Locke himself, were also scientists helped anchor the scientific approach at the core of knowledge; compartmentalization into various specialities, or into separate realms for religion, art, and science, was anathema to the leading intellectuals of the age.

The Scientific Outlook and Its Spread

The scientific revolution was not confined to formal intellectuals alone. It was transmitted to a wider reading public in a variety of ways, from the middle of the seventeenth century onward. Scientific academies sprang up across Europe—like the British Royal Society, designed in 1662 to promote "Physico-Mathematical Experimental Learning" and specifically excluding concern for "Divinity, Metaphysics, Moralls, Politicks, Grammar, Rhetorick, or Logick." The French Academy of Science followed in 1664, backed by Louis XIV and Colbert; Berlin's group, also supported by the state, was set up in 1700, St. Petersburg's in 1725. (The first American equivalent, the American Philosophical Society, was founded only a few decades later.) The societies encouraged outright research, but they also sponsored discussions that involved many nonscientists, mainly but not exclusively from aristocratic ranks. Their journals spread news of scientific discoveries to an ever wider audience, including businessmen and professional people. Furthermore, even more outright popularizers wrote pamphlets and gave lectures to elite groups on the wonders of the new science and the method it embraced. Thus the scientific rev-

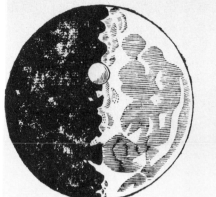
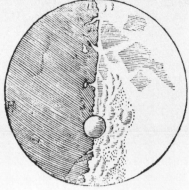

An example of "scientific publicity": Galileo's pictures of the moon in 1610, drawn from the view through his telescope, were the first to be published.

olution quickly spilled over into a wider intellectual climate, shaping or influencing attitudes well beyond the ranks of creative thinkers.

Before 1700 the scientific revolution spilled over in another sense, by affecting a wider range of intellectual concerns than the strictly scientific. Belief in the consistency of nature's laws, for example, brought direct challenges to traditional concepts of miracles. Pierre Bayle, a writer whose work was influenced by his French Protestant background as well as by his scientific enthusiasm, attacked miracles as incredible interruptions of scientific regularities. He claimed that most miracles had been fabricated by power-hungry priests. Among leading intellectuals, ideas of human nature began to shift away from Christian beliefs in original sin—in this case, a Protestant staple as much as a Catholic one—and toward an emphasis on human goodness and rationality. John Locke held that people were blank slates at birth, with no fundamental evils built into their personalities but rather with the capacity to learn virtue as well as knowledge from their own experiences as molded by what amounted to innate common sense.

Full development of a science-derived view of man and society awaited the next phase of European history, as the movement known as the Enlightenment took shape after 1730. But by 1700 it was already clear that science promoted new ideas about a host of conventional subjects quite apart from physical nature itself. The scientific revolution pulled together impulses previously scattered through the Renaissance and the Reformation, such as skepticism or a desire for some alternative to the Christian belief structure. Writers such as Bayle, as well as some (though not all) of the scientific pioneers, saw God not as an active regulator of nature or human life, but as a remote, artisanlike creator who set the machine of nature in motion, which could then function on its own and be understood without reference to faith or any of the other trappings of Christianity. This mechanistic concept, which allowed a God as an "engine-cranker" but not a hovering presence, was ultimately known as *deism*, and would blossom further during the Enlightenment; but it was clearly laid out during the scientific revolution itself.

110

THREE
*Nation-States,
Science, and the
Common People:
1648–1730*

Science was not alone in causing a rethinking of Christian conventions in the seventeenth century. Knowledge of other cultures, derived from growing contacts with Asia, also convinced some intellectuals to question the absolute veracity of Catholic and Protestant claims. But the scientific revolution seemed to its supporters solid evidence not just of problems with literal Christianity, but also of the existence of a valid alternative: the ability to rely on human reason to grasp what was a rational universe. Scientific discoveries seemed a tribute to man's power,—and evidence that, freed from superstition, still greater progress might be possible in the future.

By 1700, for the first time some intellectuals were ready to claim that innovation in the form of new thinking, rather than precedent, was the key to wisdom. Renaissance thinkers had occasionally hinted at this in their disdain for medieval scholarship but they had been restrained by their own reliance on classical learning. Now the mood shifted, and not only in science itself or simply with confident iconoclasts such as Galileo or Descartes. Around 1700, a "quarrel between ancients and moderns" broke out in literature that pitted attachment to past styles and the great classics against a growing belief that, here too, innovation was best. And so, with the new science as its centerpiece, Europe's intellectual underpinnings began to shift decisively.

The "Popularization" of the Scientific Outlook The scientific revolution, its "popularization" and its wider implications for religious or literary thought, remained, of course, largely provinces of the elite. Although enthusiasm for the new discoveries ran high, it by no means touched all literate people in western Europe, much less the illiterate majority. Some people shared religious objections to the new learning; others found it irrelevant. For still others, even if they were excited by specific findings, these findings did not alter their larger outlook. There is no evidence of significant penetration of new scientific ideas to most ordinary merchants or artisans before 1730, much less the peasant masses. Indeed, many historians have suggested that science helped drive a larger wedge between elite and popular belief than had prevailed during earlier centuries, when a common religious outlook, and even considerable shared belief in certain kinds of magic and ritual, united commoners and their social superiors.

Certainly the beliefs promoted by the scientific revolution provided a firmer basis for those in power to judge and regulate popular outlook. This showed clearly in the decline of witchcraft trials by the later 17th century. Magistrates in Catholic and Protestant regions alike became more and more reluctant to regard witchcraft as a serious possibility and therefore to try to punish people for its practice. This skepticism was not entirely new; even during the height of the witchcraft hysteria, earlier in the seventeenth century, some writers had urged that witchcraft did not exist, that its manifestations had natural explanations. But now this skepticism was much more widely shared by responsible officials, and the idea that nature was regular in pattern and thus scientifically explainable, rather than punctuated by irregular demonic interventions against good health or sanity, helped create this wider mood. Therefore, the witchcraft trials came to a virtual end, with only isolated exceptions after 1700. Yet *popular* belief in witchcraft did not abate so slowly. Ordinary people might not be able to take their anxieties about witches to an unsympathetic court—for the new confidence among the elite in an alternative way to explain behavior was unshakeable—but they could still hold on to their belief in an enchanted environment of which witches, charms, and rituals remained very much a part.

Such differences in outlook between the elite and the common people are not, however, the final word on the impact of the scientific revolution on the wider patterns of popular thought; active literacy and an awareness of the new science among members of the higher classes did not contrast totally with slower-moving popular attitudes. For although specific knowledge of the new science spread gradually, popular outlook was already in flux and was by no means closed to new ways of thinking about the environment. By 1700 there were some signs that the new intellectual horizons and the extended boundaries of belief of quite ordinary folk in Western society were beginning to merge. The result was that ordinary people did more than simply pull back from their folk beliefs; they also reduced the number of vantage points from which they viewed the operations of nature. People who in the early seventeenth century might attribute disease to a witch, or to the astrological configurations of the stars, or to worms, or to bad habits, or to contact with other sick people, were now beginning to question some of these options. Ordinary people did not yet accept wholeheartedly the view, current among the scientific-minded, that nature operates according to one particular order, but they began moving in this direction and away from their traditional eclecticism.

Conditions of the Common People

A Period of Quiet

The dramatic shifts in politics and intellectual life in the decades after 1650 were not matched by comparable upheavals among ordinary artisans and peasants. On the surface this was a relatively quiet period for the common people; the risings of the previous century had died down, in part because people deliberately tried to win greater stability and recapture traditions that had been under challenge. Some of the changes that did occur—for popular life was by no means static in the later seventeenth century—involved trends that had already begun, such as the gap between the conditions among property owners and those of the nonowning proletarians.

As we see in this section, the contrast between considerable social stability and the great shifts in political and intellectual direction, discussed earlier in this chapter, helps explain the signs of a new gap between elites and commoners. It also raises the prospect that vigorous elite groups were positioning themselves to force further changes on a

112

THREE
*Nation-States,
Science, and the
Common People:
1648—1730*

reluctant populace—that these elites were becoming a dynamic force over a sluggish, passive populace. Political leaders spurred by the new motives and mechanisms of the nation-state, and intellectual pundits or technological innovators buoyed by confidence in the new science, would press new laws, ideas, and procedures on ordinary people after 1700—and ordinary people undoubtedly often would have preferred to remain with their own tried-and-true ways of life. But here too, the balance between the elite and the masses was complicated, for although the surface of popular life regained some calm, there were undercurrents of significant new departures on this level as well.

Western Europe's population stabilized for several decades after 1650, following considerable, and unsettling, previous growth. Deaths matched or exceeded births until well into the eighteenth century, as the following table on the ten-year average birth rates for Nottingham, England, suggests:

Year	Baptism	Burials	Child Burials
1703–1712	206.7	220.3	119.1
1713–1722	261.0	277.2	143.9
1723–1732	326.9	397.5	206.3
1733–1742	359.6	429.6	227.9
1743–1752	382.9	342.4	170.9

SOURCE: Based on J. D. Chambers, "Population Change in a Provincial Town: Nottingham 1700–1800," in D. V. Glass and D. E. C. Eversley, *Population in History.* Chicago: Aldine Publishing Company, 1965, p. 352.

This stabilization was not the result of a massive increase in death rates. These rates *remained* high, particularly for infants, though not unprecedentedly so; various epidemics attacked the population, but nothing on the order of the catastrophic plagues of the later Middle Ages. Rather, population stability was regained by more careful implementation of the smaller European-style family, which used marriage age and rate to regulate births per average family. People began to marry later, and there was a large minority who never married at all, particularly among the propertyless proletarians, whose care in avoiding either marriage or at least many children was striking. These two groups kept the birth rate low enough to avoid any major population surge. In the more stable environment provided by European-style families, rates of illegitimate births, which were never very high, also dropped, suggesting again a fairly conscious community strategy of protecting established property relationships by averting the burden of too many children.

Stabilization also affected work and leisure patterns. With rare exceptions, work styles did not change much. Most people continued to work in or around the home, relying on family labor plus an occasional outsider who was treated in part as a family member. Although production for the market continued to increase, as growth of cities provided outlets for agricultural sales and exports of manufactured goods rose, most people also continued to provide for most of their own requirements, rather than relying on the market for basic necessities. Traditional recreations also continued, again with rare exceptions. The festival remained the centerpiece of popular leisure, spiced with customary games and folk dances. Earlier attacks on popular leisure as involving unseemly or immoral behavior abated somewhat, though they would resume after 1800. Most landlords continued to tolerate popular rural festivals, even though they mocked authority and involved minor disorderliness; indeed, landlords and artisan masters often participated in dancing and singing, and they sponsored some of the feasts, if only in their own self-interest. As one observer noted, regarding harvest feasts:

> These rural entertainments and usages . . . are commonly insisted upon by the reapers as customary things, and a part of their due for the toils of harvest, and complied with by their masters perhaps more through regards of interest, than inclination. For should they refuse them the pleasures of this much expected time, this festal night, the youth especially, of both sexes, would decline serving them for the future, and employ their labours for others, who would promise them the rustic joys of the harvest supper, mirth, and music, dance, and song.

The stabilization of population size, which produced a need to woo available labor, contributed to this attitude on the part of rural and urban employers.

In some Protestant areas ordinary people managed to create new festivals around secular, even patriotic themes, to replace some of the saints' days that had been eliminated earlier. Protestant regions still offered less leisure time than did Catholic, but there were signs of new popular creativity. In England, the dashing of a plot from the pre–Civil War period, masterminded by one Guy Fawkes, became a major national celebration. Officially it was in behalf of Parliament and Protestantism, but in fact Guy Fawkes Day was an occasion for bonfires and youth antics.

Outright protest leveled off somewhat compared to the tumultuous decades before 1650. There were periodic riots to protest new levels of taxation or poor harvests. Peasants and townsmen in Louis XIV's France frequently attacked grain convoys during times of bad harvest, on grounds that the government should relieve their area before shipping food elsewhere (particularly to Paris). These protests sometimes suggested a new inclination to look to the central monarchy for solutions to problems, a logical outgrowth of the turn to the nation-state. But the amount of unrest was not striking, and significant new protest methods or demands were not generated between 1650 and 1750. This fact does not suggest some uniform popular contentment, but the reasonably satisfactory results of the people's own efforts to stabilize their lot by reducing pressure on property and by protecting valued traditions in daily life.

The Rise in Material Comfort and Technology

In various ways, then, the eighty years or so after 1650 constituted a period of quiescence in popular life in western Europe, between two periods of great storm and stress, that of the earlier popular revolts (discussed in Chapter 2) and the revolutions in population and industry that began to surge after 1730.

114

THREE
*Nation-States,
Science, and the
Common People:
1648–1730*

But there were ongoing pressures for change among the common people as well. Earlier trends, based on growing trade and rising prosperity (at least for those with property), continued. Around 1700 ordinary Europeans became accustomed to buying coffee, tea, and sugar—all processed foods imported from the Americas, Africa, or Asia—to supplement their basic diets. Here was an early, if modest, sign of new consumerism. This change fed other developments in family life. Women in many households began to pay more attention to domestic routine. With use of coffee and tea came more elaborate utensils, such as teapots, and more elaborate rituals associates with meals. Cookbooks were written, essentially for the first time, that focused on home cooking, for daily family enjoyment, rather than on community festival dishes. In a growing number of households all family members were supposed to sit down together for meals. This meant a growing equality among family members; women no longer simply served and children were included in the conversation. It also meant a partial redefinition of women's roles, as they gained new rights and duties as arbiters of household ceremony (at the expense of some of their more basic work functions). This redefinition of the family, already underway with improved furnishings in the sixteenth century, was not sudden or complete, but it marked a growing reliance on family functions and a partial separation between the family and the wider community. The many men who growled about the new daintiness at home, and those who periodically fled the new domesticity for a local tavern, were among the people who noticed a change.

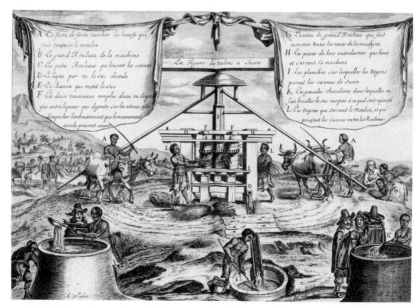

A sugar mill in St. Dominique, Antilles, West Indies.

Growing affluence also began to expand the role of leisure, despite the prevailing traditionalism. The first circus in Western history was launched in France in the late seventeenth century. Here was a sign that more ordinary people had some money to spend for amusements, and might be interested in seeing more wondrous and more "professional" entertainment than the occasional fair jugglers and amateur streetcorner efforts yielded. This theme would widen greatly in the next century and a half of Western popular history.

More important at the time were continued innovations in technology. Again, these innovations did not overwhelm established patterns, but they set the stage for much more dramatic developments in the later eighteenth century. First, by 1700 European technology had become the finest in the world in virtually all areas of manufacturing. This had been largely true a century before, but further gains in textile procedures eliminated most remaining gaps. This gave Europe an advantage in its economic dealings with other areas. Western Europe enhanced its position as the dominant partner in most world trade, providing processed or manufactured goods in exchange for the raw materials, foods, or slave labor of other parts of the world. This position, plus the fact that a disproportionate amount of world trade was carried in European ships, gave Europe the lion's share of world trading profits, as most other societies relied on their own cheap labor to mine the materials or farm the crops they traded for European products. Only China and Japan retained self-contained economic systems that could resist European superiority, which they retained into the nineteenth century. Elsewhere, Europe's technology increasingly supplemented daring trading activities, which brought new wealth and capital to European merchants and some artisans in turn.

The second set of technological innovations relates to the first but had even more novel implications: Several new inventions promised major improvements in per-worker productivity, just as the opportunity to sell manufactured goods grew with Europe's expanding prosperity and its worldwide shipping network. For example, in 1733 the Englishman James Kay invented the flying shuttle for weaving looms. This device automatically carried threads across the grain of a loom, so that a weaver only had to attach the fibers in one direction, while pumping the loom with his feet. As a result an adult weaver, with one child as assistant, could do as much work as two adults could before. The invention was intended for the domestic manufacturing system, in which weaving was carried on in the home. It did not compel a dramatic reorganization of work. But it did suggest a new level of inventiveness and an ongoing interest in adjusting manufacturing to growing market opportunities, which would have far more sweeping consequences in later decades. Another English device was the Newcomen steam engine, designed to pump water from mine shafts; this allowed the sinking of deeper shafts. England was running out of available wood for fuel and turned increasingly to coal; hence the new interest in mining and a device which, much modified, would soon have still more revolutionary consequences.

Finally, fundamental improvements began to be introduced into European agriculture. The center of this innovation was Holland, where increasing wealth and a substantial population pressed against limited land. The Dutch developed new procedures for reclaiming land from the sea using systems of dikes and canals, and they also pioneered drainage techniques that were of interest elsewhere. They also experimented with crops that would add nitrogen to the soil, allowing annual use of land rather than the traditional periods of fallow that had been needed to replenish the soil's fertility.

Although the Dutch developments were dramatic, and would be copied elsewhere in the eighteenth century, important changes began to take shape elsewhere in the types of crops grown. An increasing number of peasants began to experiment with the potato as a supplement to standard grain crops. A product of the New World, the potato had long been resisted as a dangerous innovation, not mentioned in the Bible, possibly a cause of plague. But growing knowledge of this tuber, plus the encouragement of enthusiasts such as the French noble Parmentier, promoted new use in the seventeenth century. Cooked potatoes began to be sold by Paris street vendors in the 1680s—the prototypes for the renowned French fry. Apart from service as an early urban fast food, the potato was an immensely productive crop, yielding more calories per acre than any European grain. Its growing use, and also the cultivation of a number of new beans also imported from the New World, would add to Europe's food supply. Along with Dutch technical improvements, the newly adopted crops brought the first major gains in Western agriculture since the Middle Ages. They foreshadowed a larger interest in improving food yields that would have even greater impact after 1730.

An Evolution in Popular Outlook

Along with technological shifts, there were continuing signs of change in the outlook of many common people. These resulted from the ongoing influence of previous developments, plus new factors. Protestantism and various forms of reformed Catholicism continued to influence many people to think in new ways about their environment, their families, and themselves as individuals. Literacy also continued to grow. By the late seventeenth century, daily news sheets and outright newspapers made their appearance in many western European cities, providing unprecedented amounts of information and opinion for a reading public. Postal services were also established on a regular basis, one of the results of more centralized government. This, too, increased the flow of information. Finally, the movement of people increased as well. Growing levels of trade brought more rural people into contact with urbanites. The influence of great cities such as London, Amsterdam, and Paris increased, spreading urban ideas to people who nevertheless remained firmly rural. Even in the countryside, mobility increased in some places, as some village families failed or moved, and others came in to take their place. Along with knowledge brought from overseas trade, this new mobility was a source of fresh ideas and challenge to settled habits of thought.

116

THREE
*Nation-States,
Science, and the
Common People:
1648–1730*

Demystification and the Increasing Importance of Family and Self The changes in popular mentalities followed directions sketched by the later sixteenth century (discussed in Chapter 2). A growing number of Europeans viewed their environment in nonmagical terms. That is, they saw nature as a force to be categorized and manipulated, not approached through enchanted tools or magical rituals. This "demystification of the world" owed something to reformed religious thought, and to the popularization of the new scientific and medical ideas. This demystification also owed something to the growing confidence with which some Europeans began to plan and organize their lives. Fewer misfortunes were now viewed simply as a matter of chance or evil spirits. Lost property, for example, was now a problem to be solved by information exchange, as news sheets carried notices and advertisements: magical procedures to "divine" where a valued item had disappeared became less necessary. Insurance companies were founded to protect against other disasters. Used in fourteenth-century Italy, insurance against shipping and other disasters spread northward by the late sixteenth century and became commonplace for large merchants by 1720.

This evolution of outlook—toward the environment, toward rationalism, and away from magic—proceeded in advance of major technological gains. The new mentality preceded major technological change, and probably helped cause it, only to be reinforced by the change once it took place. For example, people began reducing their credence in magic as an approach to disease even before actual cures improved. They began thinking about how to manage fire losses through insurance before new major developments in firefighting techniques arose. Willingness to use new crops, or consider new agricultural or manufacturing methods, also reflected the new manner of thought, not just on the part of individual inventors, such as Kay or Newcomen, but on the part of ordinary peasants who took a chance on the once-feared potato.

The family and the self focused other aspects of the new thinking. Religious reform continued to encourage attention to the family and a new effort at emotional warmth. Catholic family manuals, by the early eighteenth century, echoed themes earlier voiced by Protestants: spouses should love each other; they owed their children love as well as legitimately demanding respect; all family members should try to restrain their anger to promote the desired harmony. A new interest in young children began to take shape. Children began to be seen more as individuals to love, less as animal creatures to be endured until they were old enough to work. After 1700 increasing numbers of western Europeans began to abandon the practice of swaddling their children, or wrapping them in cloth for protection and to make child care easier, in favor of watching them but allowing greater freedom of movement. Here was another in the list of women's household duties, but it had significant implications both for the level of parental affection now encouraged toward infants, and for the personalities of the children themselves. Coincidentally with such attitudes, writers such as John Locke began exploring theories of human nature. Locke claimed that infants were born essentially good,

118

THREE
*Nation-States,
Science, and the
Common People:
1648–1730*

that discipline should be restrained and supportive, that parents should understand the importance of educating their improvable progeny. These ideas fit in with actual changes in parental practice and encouraged further change in the treatment of children and the emotional atmosphere of the family as a whole.

Finally, many relatively ordinary Europeans, particularly literate Protestants, began to express a new sense of self, in which the individual self could be identified, attended to, and seen as something other than the creature of God or chance. The new identification of self was reflected in the practice of diary-keeping, among a minority of men and women in property-owning families. The new sense of the self as actor, and not simply as something acted on, caused the growing interest in seeing individuals improve themselves, by restraining some natural emotional impulses, and in general demonstrating that they had some control over their lot.

The changes in the Western mentality, focusing on environment, family, and self, obviously overlapped one another. A belief that the environment could be controlled encouraged the new belief that individuals could control themselves and seek more intense contacts with other family members. Peasant families in Ireland in the eighteenth century began giving names to their infants at birth, rather than waiting to name them until they had reached the age of two and had demonstrated that they were not destined to an early death. This shift reflected new ties of affection between parents and children and also a belief that infant death was no longer an inevitable product of an uncontrollable environment.

The changes in popular mentality also paralleled many developments among the elite. The theme of greater control over the natural and social environment was reflected not only in the ordinary businessman buying insurance, but also in the new bureaucracies of the nation-state or the new claims of the scientists. New popular beliefs reduced the gap between the elite outlook, newly stimulated by knowledge of the scientific revolution, and the outlook shared by many ordinary people. Some of the scientific findings directly influenced some common folk—encouraging them to abandon magical explanations and the mania for witchcraft, for example—just as changes in ordinary beliefs probably encouraged scientific work.

But the shift in popular mentalities was no neat package. Certain parts of western Europe—particularly Protestant Britain and Holland—were more affected than others. Certain groups among the ordinary people were more fully transformed than others. City dwellers dropped the magical approach more readily than did country people. The ordinary people were themselves divided, along lines historians have yet fully to define, between those whose mentalities had been largely reshaped, and those who continued, though with less support than before, to use magical devices and beliefs. This division persists to some extent to the present day, as witchly covens and other remnants of the magical world still dot the Western landscape, but it was far more important in 1700. Moreover, individuals themselves might be divided in their own approach, particularly before 1730. They might abandon a search for witches but still adhere to lesser forms of magical ritual in an effort, for example, to counter disease. They might display a modern intensity in their love for their family but show a more traditional approach to their environment; thus one English diarist of the seventeenth century, devoted to his young children, took virtually no precautions to protect them against accidents, which he saw as God's will. Needless to say, he led a rather traumatic life as a result.

At virtually all levels, the period between 1650 and 1730 was an unusual time of transition. New political forms took clear shape, but their popular impact remained muted. The scientific revolution created a new intellectual framework, while supporting some trends in popular beliefs as well. But the larger impact of this transition had yet to be felt. The less dramatic developments in technology, family life, and popular mentality also helped shape future changes, but they were partly masked by the surface stability of ordinary life. The more dynamic decades after 1730, discussed in Chapter 4, would contrast with the tone of this transitional period, bustling though this had been in terms of political maneuvering and war; but these dynamic decades were themselves prepared by the complex forces, popular as well as elite, of the same turn-of-the-century era.

The Expansion of the West

One final form of change took place before 1730: the boundaries of Western civilization expanded due to international trade and colonization, as the West continued to improve its standing among world-class civilizations. In fact, new colonial acquisitions were added to the continuing growth of the West's merchant power. The Dutch solidified their hold on key ports and spice plantations in the Indonesian islands during the seventeenth century. They also wielded influence on the island of Taiwan and alone maintained limited trading rights in Japan after the Japanese government, early in the seventeenth century, closed off other Western economic and missionary contacts. Britain and France, in addition to expanding their explorations and settlements in North America, set up port-city colonies on the eastern coast of India. The decline of the leading Indian government, the Mughal empire, allowed European merchants to gain increasing inroads in India, and from port colonies British and French trading companies formed regional political alliances with various Indian princes.

Western influence in parts of Africa grew more extensive. Britain, France, and several other countries set up port colonies along the Atlantic coast, while Holland established a larger settlement on Africa's southern tip, initially intending it as a supply base for ships sailing to Asia. Dutch farmers, called Boers, fanned out around the port city of Capetown, taking some Africans as slave laborers; here was the origin of the unusually extensive white involvement with southern Africa that continues to this day. But the biggest white impact on Africa during the seventeenth century came not through outright colonization but through the West African slave trade. The Portuguese in their territory of Angola, as well

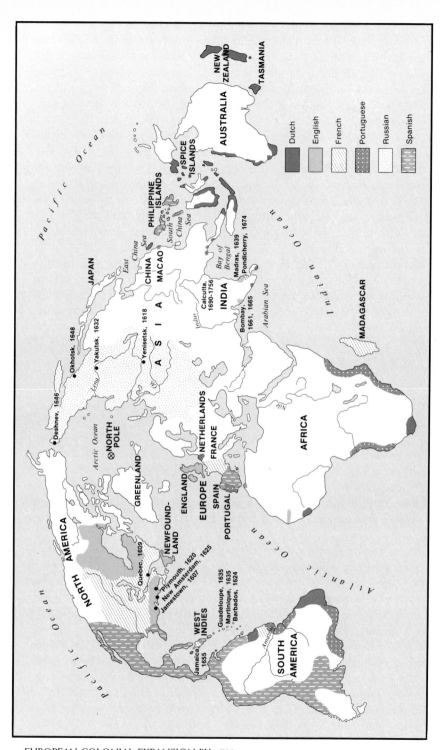

EUROPEAN COLONIAL EXPANSION BY 1700.
Western nations competed for gains in coastal areas, where seapower counted.
Penetration in the Americas, and Russia's advance in northern Asia, went further
still.

as the Dutch, British, and French farther north, made contacts with African rulers and merchants who traded slaves for European products, including guns. The slaves were then sent to European holdings in North and South America, with handsome profits made by the shippers in the process. During the seventeenth and eighteenth centuries as many as thirty million Africans may have been sent westward, in the largest and most brutal forced movement of human beings in world history. Africa's own population structure and economy suffered greatly from this exodus, even as individual African slave traders benefited along with the European buyers.

With Africa particularly, and with various parts of southern Asia to an extent, western Europe shaped a new world economic pattern from the sixteenth through the eighteenth centuries, which has survived in part even into recent times. Western Europe's superior technology and shipping linked various parts of the world in new but highly unequal economic contacts, with Europe reaping the major profits from sales of processed goods while other parts of the world supplied products based on cheap, sometimes forced labor. While this dominant–dependent relationship affected all regions involved, it did not extend Western cultural, or even political influence, on a massive scale at this point. European holdings in Asia and Africa were small, for the most part, based mainly on coastal settlements for the very good reason that Europe's main superiority in weapons lay in ship's artillery, not in the armaments of land forces.

A more extensive set of contacts developed with two key regions in the world. The expanding Russian empire, as we have seen earlier in this chapter, deliberately copied Western military institutions and some cultural and educational styles. This prompted greater interaction between the two main areas of Europe, east and west, than ever before, and without question brought new similarities between the two regions as well. Not only outright imitation, but the activities of Western merchants also helped forge new links. Russia was not converted into an outright economic dependency of western Europe, thanks in part to new metallurgical and mining enterprises set up by Peter the Great. But Russia did supply furs and grain to the West based on cheap serf labor, and it imported manufactured goods in turn. There could be no pretense that the two parts of Europe, east and west, were operating as equals in a single economy. The tightening rigor of Russian serfdom and the lack of significant urban culture also differentiated the two parts of Europe, with areas such as Prussia or Hungary, open to fuller Western influence but also dominated by serf-holding estates, falling somewhat in between. Overall, eastern Europe did not become a full part of Western civilization, maintaining important values and institutions of its own even as it fit increasingly into a common diplomatic framework and interacted more extensively at many levels.

Another somewhat separate society with a special relationship to Western civilization developed in Latin America, really from the sixteenth century onward but with increasing clarity in the seventeenth and eighteenth centuries. Spanish conquest and missionary efforts (or Portuguese efforts, in the case of Brazil) deliberately obliterated the formal cultures and po-

122

THREE
*Nation-States,
Science, and the
Common People:
1648–1730*

litical institutions of the great American Indian civilizations in Central America and the Andes. Diseases brought by the Europeans, such as measles and smallpox, which killed off over 80 percent of the Indian population, worked to the same effect. Latin America took shape as a amalgam of Spanish and Portuguese values, including a fervent Catholicism, lingering Indian cultures that still operated at a village level, and the institutions of colonial rule. Spain and Portugal discouraged independent political activity in their vast holdings by sending out governors from the home countries; even people of pure European origin born in the Americas had little voice. At the same time, the Latin American economy took shape as clear dependencies of the mother countries. The colonies provided precious metals, sugar, and tobacco, based either on slave labor or on semifree peasant work on large estates owned by people of European origin. Most sophisticated manufactured products and artistic luxuries were imported from Europe. The result was another culture enmeshed with the West but not exactly Western, particularly in political and economic styles.

In the English colonies along the east coast of North America, however, a somewhat different pattern took shape. Settlement began soon after 1600, and by the late eighteenth century some three million people of European origin, plus several hundred thousand African slaves, had forced a bustling new society on a harsh new land. Here, colonists developed active local political institutions. Though limited by English economic regulations, substantial trade and manufacture developed. Printing presses were early established, in contrast to the limitations on intellectual life imposed by Spanish colonial administrations, and this helped colonists maintain contact with European cultural activities including scientific discoveries. Furthermore, North American Indians had developed less sophisticated cultures than their Central and South American counterparts, and they were less numerous; these facts, along with a pervasive English racism that discouraged intermarriage, kept the white population more separate than in Latin America where *mestizos*, or people of mixed white–Indian ancestry, constituted the largest demographic group by the eighteenth century.

The North American colonies were not, of course, mere replicas of Europe. Southern colonies exported tobacco and sugar based on the labor of slaves imported from Africa. The existence of slavery and a plantation aristocracy resembled parts of Latin America in some ways, more than western Europe itself. The experience of dealing with Indians and the pressures of the frontier also shaped the character of the American colonists in distinctive ways. So did the absence of a formal titled aristocracy and a sophisticated artistic culture.

Yet the society that developed in the British North American colonies, and to some extent the colonies populated by the French in Canada, remained close to western European forms in many basic ways. North Americans eagerly followed developments in English political theory. They easily assimilated new techniques developed in western Europe. Even when they altered traditional European patterns, they often moved in directions in which Europeans themselves were proceeding. American colonists, for example, stressed the importance of close family ties and affectionate treatment of children. They quickly abandoned the European practice of swaddling, preferring to care for young children more directly. The North Americans' labor shortage and the absence of pressure on available land encouraged the new outlook toward children, while the strangeness of their environment promoted the new reliance on family. But a development of this sort, although it made the American family distinctive, in essence anticipated European trends—it did not defy them. Similarly, literacy in America developed faster than it had in Europe, spurred by fervent Protestantism; but again, although literacy rates differed, the patterns of thought did not.

The North American colonies emerged, then, as an extension of Western civilization, though with some special features and problems, and with an ability to take a lead in familial and social innovations because of abundant natural resources and the absence of some traditional constraints. Unlike other parts of the world, even areas fully as important to western Europe in diplomatic and economic terms, North America would long remain part of an essentially Western orbit, sharing values and institutions and experiencing similar kinds of changes at roughly similar times. In 1730, to be sure, this geographical extension of the West mattered little to the centers of European society, for whom the colonies were useful but subordinate economic assets, the colonists considered at best unsophisticated children of nature. In the long run, however, the extension of the geographical range of Western civilization was arguably as important as the rise of Western economic influence in the rest of the world.

Conclusion

The period from 1650 to 1730 saw an unusual mixture of obvious and subsurface developments in Western history. The ringmasters, operating in a blaze of light, were the new absolute monarchs and parliamentary leaders, plus the pioneers in the new science. They were abetted by scores of active, if more anonymous, bureaucrats, publicists, and international merchants. Their efforts began to reshape not just the formal arenas of politics and culture, but larger patterns of behavior and habits of mind.

Political and cultural innovation depended on the relative social stability of the period; protest or confusion at the level of the earlier seventeenth century might well have stopped the monarchs short, and kept the scientists isolated from wider intellectual currents. But society continued to evolve as well. The humble peasants who decided to take a risk on a new crop, the artisans who experimented with a new manufacturing technique, the parents who decided to behave a little differently toward their infants—all were preparing, along with the political and intellectual leaders, a period of renewed and creative ferment in Western life. Joining them were the Europeans working in the wider world, either extending new economic influence—to the West's benefit, if not usually to the benefit of the home society—or planting essentially European roots in the fertile soil of North America. These people, too, were shaping the West's emergence into a new social framework.

FOUR

POPULATION UPHEAVAL, THE ENLIGHTENMENT, AND THE AGE OF REVOLUTION, 1730–1815

1715	Louis XV king of France
1730–1800	Rapid growth of population; spread of the potato, domestic manufacturing
1730 ff	New enclosure movement in Britain
1730–1790	Development of Enlightenment t thought
1736	Beginnings of Methodism in Britain.
1738	"War of Jenkins' Ear" between Britain and Spain
1740–1748	War of Austrian Succession
1740–86	Frederick the Great reigns in Prussia
1756–1763	Seven Years' War (French and Indian Wars in North America)
1763	Treaty of Paris
1760s	Popular political agitation in Britain
1762–1796	Catherine the Great reigns in Russia
1773–1775	Pugachev peasant revolt
1762	Rousseau's *The Social Contract*
1769–1782	James Watt develops steam engine
1770s–1780s	Herder's "Romantic" philosophy
1772	First partition of Poland
1774–1786	Louis XVI king of France

1774–1776	Abortive efforts at French fiscal reform
1775	First volume of the French encyclopedia
1775–1783	American War of Independence
1787	U.S. Constitution; ratified 1788
1776	Adam Smith's *Wealth of Nations*
1780–1790	Joseph II Hapsburg emperor
1780s ff	Rise in illegitimacy rates, "sexual revolution"
1787	Assembly of Notables in France
1789	French Revolution
1789–1791	Liberal phase; Constituent Assembly
1792	War with Austria and Prussia
1793–1794	Radical (Jacobin) phase
1795–1799	Directory
1790	Beginning of birth-rate decline in the United States
1792	Mary Wollstonecraft's feminist *Vindication of the Rights of Women*
1795	Third partition of Poland
1799–1814	Napoleon rules France
1801	End of Second Coalition wars against France
1803–1807	Third Coalition wars
1812	Napoleon's invasion of Russia
1813–1814	Fourth Coalition
1815	Congress and Treaty of Vienna

CHAPTER
FOUR

THE WESTERN WORLD IN REVOLUTION, 1730–1815

THE EIGHTY YEARS following 1730 constituted a decisive period in Western history, with the clearest drama reserved for the decades after 1776. During the period as a whole, the scientific revolution was amplified and the outlook engendered by science spread to social and political theory in the intellectual currents of the Enlightenment. More striking was the upheaval of Europe's population structure, as rapid demographic growth challenged traditional social and economic forms. New tensions and new dynamism alike were spawned by the unprecedented population spurt. Yet although rising population disrupted society, it also encouraged developments already in the works, including proletarianization, changes in popular mentality, and growing reliance on market relationships. Finally, both intellectual ferment and social upheaval led to the beginnings of a long period of recurrent revolution, starting with the American War of Independence and blossoming with the great French rising of 1789. These early revolutions opened the way for additional social and economic changes, as well as further political unrest.

The theme of change and transition is a staple of historical inquiry. We have seen that virtually every half-century in Western history after 1500 (and indeed the same would hold true before) ushered in important new trends. Yet significant continuities persisted as well, particularly in the peasant world that described the lives of most people, but also in the organization and functions of elite institutions such as the monarchies. After 1730, earlier patterns of change picked up speed. For example, popular mentalities and family forms shifted decisively, as evidenced by the decline of religious practice in certain areas and transformations in the ways children were raised. The rate of proletarianization, formerly a minority current, now crescendoed; the percentage of propertyless workers greatly expanded, and many others became worried about their own possible fall in status. Furthermore, changes that previously had been confined to their own spheres began to interact. Popular beliefs now included new ideas about politics, which meant new pressures and expectations for the nation-state. More widespread commercialization brought demands that the state intervene in favor of old economic values—or free the economy for commerce more completely. The addition of a major new disruptive force, rapid population growth, fueled farther-reaching breaks with older institutions and forms of behavior. Meanwhile, continuities persisted from the past, especially because outside Britain a final ingredient—the technological (industrial) revolution—had yet to be fully integrated with the other impulses toward change. Nevertheless, what had earlier been a series of important but incomplete alterations in Western life now verged on outright turmoil.

These changes embraced not only western Europe but also the English colonies of North America. The export of Western civilization to North America was evidenced in the impact American events—notably, the War of Independence in 1776—now had on Europe. It was also evidenced, at a deeper level, in the similar trends that began to transform life, in politics, science, and family patterns, on both sides of the North Atlantic.

The Western world by 1815 was operating within an increasingly novel framework, in terms of the direction of economic and political development as well as formal culture. The emergence of this framework would have been impossible without the various changes that had occurred in the early modern centuries. The West's response to new ideas and new social stress built upon earlier changes provoked by Protestantism, the price revolution, and the rise of the nation-state. Nor was Europe totally transformed by 1815; most Westerners were still peasants, the majority were still illiterate, many had only the haziest notions of new political rights. But the decades that had yielded the beginnings of the first industrial revolution, the first clearly modern political revolution, and the first modern rebellion against colonialism, had clearly left their mark. Traditional institutions were much more obviously on the defensive by 1815 than they had been in 1730—not only monarchies and established churches, but also parents who looked to customary prerogatives over their children.

Rapid Population Growth and Its Effects

The clearest, earliest new ingredient in the Western brew after 1730 was the rapid growth of population. This was not fully perceived at the time, and indeed many historians have long treated the eighteenth century in terms of rather minor political shifts, prior to the great revolutionary outburst later in the century, plus the obvious intellectual glitter of the Enlightenment. But it was ordinary people doing the most ordinary things—having sex and starting babies, dying or trying not to die—who most directly broke the social calm, initially at a time when political developments ranged from fairly stable to fairly boring. Yet such was the complex linkage of causation in Western history that population growth was due in part to earlier shifts in statecraft and ideology.

The facts of the population upheaval can be simply stated: between about 1750 and 1800 the number of western Europeans increased between 50 percent and 100 percent, depending on the region. France, the West's largest country, experienced growth at the low end—but this still meant ten million more French people in 1789 than there had been a century before. The populations of Britain and Prussia virtually doubled. The dates at which the population surge began varied from country to country—for example, in Britain population growth began around 1730, in France a bit earlier, and in Prussia slightly later. But the theme of a serious population revolution, concentrated in the second half of the eighteenth century, applied to the whole of western Europe. North America also experienced a significant population increase, although its population growth had also occurred earlier as a result of a high birth rate stimulated by abundant land, and was supplemented by ongoing immigration from Britain and Africa. By the mid-eighteenth century, North American population growth was beginning to cause problems of crowding, prodding some settlers to move across the Appalachian mountains and creating in the older centers some of the same strains that western Europe was experiencing.

Throughout Western society, population growth rates began to ease by 1800. On average, by 1790 Americans began to cut their birth rate, and the French did the same; other parts of western Europe followed suit early in the nineteenth century. But population growth in absolute numbers continued on the basis of the previous increase because there were more people available to have children even as birth rates dropped. The impact of the population revolution, then, extended well into the nineteenth century.

Causes of the Population Surge

What caused this unprecedented surge? New ideas, including scientific ideas, may have played some role. Experiments in the early eighteenth century led to the discovery that vaccines against smallpox could be prepared from cowpox, and in some areas, particularly in England, vaccinations against this traditional killer reached into the general population. In another translation of the growing belief that the environment could be understood and controlled—an inheritance of the scientific revolution—groups of aristocrats across Europe, from England to Russia, formed societies to discuss improvements in agricultural technology. A few landlords translated talk to action by introducing new seed drills and drainage procedures that did improve food yields. On the whole, however, formal, planned action in medicine or estate management played little role in setting off the West's new population bomb or sustaining its early stages.

By contrast, new actions by governments loomed larger. Several states carried the absolutist belief in encouraging economic growth to the end of increasing state resources by urging tangible agricultural improvements. By the mid-eighteenth century, the Prussian monarchy was active in promoting the potato among its peasant subjects. More generally, greater government attention to roads and canals, by facilitating the transport of foods and other goods, helped sustain the population. On another front, more efficient governments also tightened their supervision of movements across national borders. Particularly crucial in this regard was the new power of the Habsburg monarchy in Austria. The traditional route of devastating plagues into western Europe had run from the Middle East through the Balkans. Now, the Habsburg government more carefully regulated people and animals moving into central and western Europe from the east.

Along with the new role of governments came a certain amount of sheer chance. Major plagues virtually disappeared in Europe between about 1730 and the 1830s (when the plague cycle resumed with a major cholera epidemic that also devastated North America). Although government controls played some role here, the key factor was a temporary cessation in the virulence of plague germs, as Westerners had developed immunities to specific plague diseases. These relatively brief interruptions in plague cycles had occurred before in world history, but this particular interruption, because of its conjunction with other factors, had especially dramatic effects in the West. Some improvements in sanitation in certain Western cities, and improvements in infant care, with the abandonment of unhygienic swaddling of infants, may have added to the effect.

But the biggest cause of the new population surge involved the new food crops, particularly the potato, whose adoption had begun in previous decades but whose impact was felt primarily from the 1730s onward. Encouraged by governments and some agricultural reformers, peasants from Ireland through Prussia (though not yet in eastern Europe) began to rely on the potato because it eased the hardships of relying on small plots of land, and particularly the amount of infant death due to malnutrition. Was a new popular mentality involved in this conversion? Certainly the potato improved a landowning family's control over its environment, notably by reducing the possibility of local famines. Its use might also have expressed a new attachment to children, a greater reluctance to see them die—although this attachment may have been the result more than the cause of the new food supply.

The Immediate Effects of the Population Explosion

Whatever the precise mix of motives, the new crops—not only the potato, but also new varieties of beans and, in southern Europe, use of American corn to feed animals—had effects more revolutionary than the peasant-planters intended. Infant deaths declined; instead of the traditional pattern of 40 percent to 50 percent infant mortality, western European families by the late eighteenth century were experiencing only about 30 percent mortality. This change automatically increased the size of the population. It also stimulated the gross birth rate, as more people lived to reach child-bearing age. These twin effects—the outright reduction in death rates among the young and the resultant increase in available parents—explain most of the population revolution itself. It is possible that a slight rise in the birth rate per average woman also occurred in the eighteenth century as sexual activity increased, particularly among the propertyless poor; improved nutrition may have helped spur sexual appetites and encourage a drop in the age of puberty. But outright increase in per-capita birth rates was at most secondary to the twin effects of declining death rates just mentioned.

And the result, the Western population explosion, had sweeping impact of its own. In the most general terms, rapid population growth simultaneously promoted new stress and new creativity. The first effect was the most predictable: rapid population growth *always* places new pressure on existing resources—for example, access to land or to established offices in governments or churches that do not expand their usefulness or services as rapidly as the population expands. This pressure in turn causes hardship and discontent, and the signs of this were abundant in the Western world during the later eighteenth century. Indeed, this aspect of the population growth helped trigger the sweeping wave of revolutions that extended from the late eighteenth century until 1848–49.

The second effect of the growing population, new creativity, is also understandable, though less assured. Growing population *can* encourage some individuals to think about new ways of doing things, to take advantage of the new market opportunities produced by growing numbers, or simply to provide for self and family in a less predictable environment. Many parents, at various levels of society, were faced with a concrete problem as the number of children who survived infancy surpassed traditional expectations. How could they provide for their growing brood? Some parents had no answer, with the result that growing numbers of children did not inherit the support their parents had had—a clear source of tension for individuals and the wider society. Many parents tried to respond defensively, by insisting on whatever place in society they had previously maintained. Thus aristocrats tried to eliminate the rise of merchants into noble ranks in countries such as France, breaking with an earlier flexibility; and they tried to monopolize high church offices for their younger sons. Thus artisan masters tried to assure established spots in their trades for their own children, blocking the mobility of other journeymen. These ploys might work for the families in power, but they contributed to tensions in the wider society. Finally, parents might think of new ways to provide suitably for their children. Businessmen might expand their operations, considering new techniques in the process. Peasants might contemplate the use of new tools or other measures to improve their productivity still further. These were the most creative responses resulting from the population surge, and the ones that translated the population revolution into more sweeping economic change. These were the responses, also, that prevented a renewed increase in death rates that would reverse the tide of population growth, as had occurred in western Europe as recently as the later Middle Ages.

Increased Proletarianization   Both in its harsh and in its creative consequences, the population revolution moved several of the key trends of early modern Western history into higher gear. Proletarianization, though already in the works, obviously increased in pace. In countryside and city alike, more and more people were denied access to the land or to other producing property apart from simple tools.

In rural areas, a growing number of peasants fell into the category of landless or near-landless, possessing a garden plot but not enough land to sustain life; they had to hope they could sell their labor. Many peasant families, faced with numerous surviving children, divided and subdivided their plots so extensively that their descendants were eventually proletarianized. In regions where primogeniture existed—where inheritance went to the oldest son—the landless proletariat, composed of younger children who had grown up without property, increased even faster. Adding to the pressure was the zeal of some landlords and more substantial peasants to increase their own holdings, to provide for their families more securely, and to take advantage of new opportunities to sell agricultural produce on the market. Landlords—including some merchants, who bought estates as commercial and prestige investments, as

The rural proletariat. Many landowners of the eighteenth century charged peasants invented dues that left them, when combined with their growing numbers, mired in poverty. J. J. Boisieu, *Peasants Begging* (1780).

well as established aristocrats—frequently pressed peasant smallholders to sell out entirely. This process of displacing peasant ownership went still further in England, where a new wave of legal enclosures heightened the hold of large estates. The enclosure movement, as in the previous round of enclosure during the sixteenth century (see Chapter 2), involved powerful landlords prompting parliament to rule that all property in their area had to be enclosed by fences or hedges. Most peasants could not afford this measure, and so they had to sell out. Many continued to work as tenants, overseers, or laborers on the newly enlarged estates; some even did well in the exchange. But the new estates could not employ all the rising population of the countryside, and the result was a growing band of people with no effective access to, much less ownership of, the land. Finally, even in peasant-dominated regions, such as much of France, a minority of peasant families who could afford to keep their land pressed the resources of their poorer brethren: They too might try to buy out smaller landholders. They also increasingly attacked village traditions such as the common lands, on which poorer peasants had long relied for subsistence, trying to divide these lands into private property, which they could acquire and exploit for market production. The peasant world, in other words, was increasingly divided between owning and nonowning families, again hastening the process of proletarianization that had begun two centuries before.

Rural proletarianization inevitably affected the cities, as many landless laborers moved into the cities in hopes of finding work or charity. This process, familiar in many developing nations today, created a growing urban proletariat. The insistence of guild masters on trying to monopolize shop ownership for their own children exacerbated this process, as not only unskilled urban workers but also many trained craftsmen could no longer expect to rise to property ownership during their lifetimes, becoming permanent wage laborers instead. Thus key urban and rural social groups, artisans and peasants alike, were increasingly divided between those who owned and the growing numbers who did not.

The Commercialization of Western Europe   The population explosion not only hastened proletarianization but increased the commercialization of European society. Indeed, the two processes went hand in hand. Spurred both by new numbers of people who could provide markets for goods, and new numbers of available laborers desperately needing work, Europeans in many economic sectors began to seize on market opportunities. Landlords and substantial peasants produced more food for the market, which included the growing cities. Grain merchants began to handle more of this trade, displacing localized trade for grain among acquaintances; more and more urban people relied on unknown traders for their basic food supply, rather than a more familiar community network around the town. Artisans, long familiar with the need to sell their goods, began to look for wider sales. But the most striking commercial result of the population revolution during the eighteenth century involved the rapid expansion of the domestic manufacturing or "putting out" system. Hundreds of thousands of rural workers in western Europe and the American colo-

A family team produces thread in a cottage, a scene of domestic manufacturing.

nies were enrolled in the production of thread, cloth, and metal products for sale in the often far-flung markets. The system was not new; its extent was. As before, domestic manufacturing allowed laborers to operate within the familiar confines of a household. Workers might buy raw materials from an urban sales outlet, produce the manufactured product, and then travel to town to sell, thus preserving substantial independence. More commonly, urban merchants sent their own agents into the countryside to distribute the raw materials and deliver orders, specifying what designs they wanted in cloth, for example, and then to pick up the product when it was completed. This version of domestic manufacturing was more fully capitalistic, in that merchants invested in the materials and had considerable power to dictate methods of work and timetables. Even here, however, workers normally operated within a familiar family economy, using other family members as assistants, and they typically owned their simple machines.

But the spread of domestic manufacturing brought many rural proletarians or semiproletarians—not a mere handful—into the orbit of market production. Whole villages converted to domestic manufacturing, using agriculture only to supplement their basic work. Thousands of men and women grew accustomed to dealing with strangers, handling money, and operating, however loosely, under the directions of merchants and their traveling foremen. Furthermore, they experienced growing pressures to be more diligent and to use their time more wisely. Merchants in the "putting out" system grew increasingly impatient with uncertain production schedules and irregular products. They pressed workers to become more reliable, using fines and other disciplinary measures as goads. Some merchants also encouraged technological change, urging workers to adopt the more efficient flying shuttle looms for cloth production, or introducing, after the 1760s, more automatic spindles for the manual production of thread.

Changes in Outlook

Child-rearing The population revolution and its most immediate effects, proletarianization and the heightened role of a market economy and capitalism, also spurred further changes in popular mentalities. Reconsideration of the treatment of children, already embodied in trends such as the abandonment of swaddling, received new attention, in part because child death became somewhat less common and so attachment to individual children grew less risky. Upper-class people, including aristocrats, expressed more emotional involvement with their children, and lavished more care on dressing them as individuals and as children rather than miniature adults. A new industry of educational book and toy production sprang up, symptomatic of the new desire to let children express themselves and learn, but also demonstrating a new interest in making sure that childhood was a time of supervised improvement. Many families in western Europe and North America began to move away from traditional physical discipline and "scare tactics," urging instead a gentler treatment that would build an individual conscience and sense of guilt rather than instill obedience through fear and shame. Infanticide declined. More and more families who could not care for their children tried to place them with state-run charitable institutions; the children were still quite likely to die from disease, neglect, and hunger, but the effect was not as traumatic or direct. Thus at various levels of society, a new view of children, and new methods of treatment, came into being. This view allowed the expression of greater emotional attachment and also, in certain sectors, a belief that children must be guided and improved to face a changing adult world.

Changes in child-rearing built on earlier trends associated with the new focus on affectionate family life, which had developed in the sixteenth and seventeenth centuries. It was at this point, however, that clear efforts to treat children with more individual attention widely altered normal family practices. Writings and sermons about the family began to insist that parents restrain anger and harshness toward children. This did not mean that all parents had behaved angrily before, or now became uniformly benign, but it did involve new pressures for parental restraint. The naming of children began to change. By the mid-eighteenth century peasants in Ireland named their babies, rather than waiting until they were older and surer of survival. Names less often duplicated those of the parents, another sign that children were seen as separate individuals.

Some child-rearing changes varied with social class. New educational toys were for the aristocracy and the middle class, not the masses. Nor was change always spontaneous on the part of parents. Children themselves, in the lower classes especially, could now defy parental authority more easily, when they had no prospect of inheriting land anyway. Nor, finally, was change clearly "good." New attention to children meant new

In a new outlook, common after 1730, the focus was on children in a loving family.

efforts at control, greater supervision toward developing conscience and
guilts. New affection, in this sense, could be double-edged, providing
more demanding standards for children to live up to. Becoming an adult
was in some senses growing more difficult, as adulthood now involved
greater dealings with strangers and more control of emotions such as
anger; the greater separation between the worlds of child and adult could
increase pressures on children. For all the complexities and social differentiations, however, there was a general upheaval in the relations between parents and children, which had important potential consequences
across Western society.

Notions of Self, Sexual Relations, and Marriage A new sense of individualism may also have developed, spurred by the decline of traditional community constraints and the growing opportunity for individual wage-earning. Changes in childrearing may also have prompted a growing awareness of the self. Illustrations of a new popular individualism are varied, though they coexist with older values. For example, male servants began to show a new taste for independence, in the households of the wealthy. Despite an uncertain job market, men displayed an increasing disdain for domestic service, or a desire to use service as a stepping stone to other work, because of the personalized dependency service involved; the ranks of household servants (outside the slaveholding areas of the American South) began to be filled increasingly by women. Furthermore, those who did work as servants, began after 1750 to demand a money wage instead of simply board and room; this shift gave them somewhat greater independence from their masters, while also reducing the tight bonds of familylike loyalty that previously surrounded service.

In some areas of behavior, a new individualism applied to women as well as men. This was particularly true in matters relating to marriage choices and the initiation of sexual activity. In the upper classes, young women who objected to a suitor on grounds of a lack of romantic spark could now prevent some parentally arranged matches, because parents accepted the importance of love in marriage. Female sexuality was more complicated. In the lower classes, consisting of the growing urban and rural proletariat, sex before marriage increased. This reflected new pressures on young women, when declining parental authority and uncertain livelihoods opened new possibilities of sexual exploitation. But some women may also have enjoyed new freedom in sexual relations, finding sexual activity a more important form of personal expression that had been true in the earlier atmosphere of more controlled courtship.

It is certainly possible that sex, for young men and young women alike, began to loom larger as a personal expression from the late eighteenth century onward, particularly for the proletariat and for youth. Something of a sexual revolution occurred, which launched a pattern of heightened sexuality that would continue, with many complexities, into the later twentieth century. Without question, parental controls over older children declined in many groups. Where parents could not promise to pass on property, because they had none themselves or too little to give to younger children, their ability to dictate children's behavior declined. Parents' voice in the arrangement of marriages diminished, as just mentioned. Even in the propertied classes, parental attention to children's wishes, including their sense of whether a prospective spouse was lovable, increased as beliefs in the emotional importance of marriage continued to expand. Within the proletariat, the decline of parental controls was visible also in the growing rate of illegitimate births. Throughout the Western world, from about 1780 until about 1870, the number of children born to unwed mothers, as a percentage of all children born, began to rise dramatically. More and more young people were engaging in sex before marriage than had been the case in traditional Western society. The spread of the market economy facilitated wider contacts than before, which may have stimulated sexual appetites and certainly provided more occasions for sexual encounters. The fact that many young people could no longer plan on inheriting land, and might be able to earn enough money to support themselves in their later teens by wages in domestic manufacturing, undoubtedly encouraged earlier indulgence in sexual impulse in both city and countryside. Was sex becoming more important as an expression of personal identity and pleasure? Or were young people in the proletariat, and particularly young women, simply confused by social change, so that they expected marriage to result from sex but were often disappointed? The question cannot be answered with certainty. What is clear is that changes in basic behaviors, such as sexual conduct, showed the decline of traditional social constraints and the rise of interests that would continue to be important in modern Western society. A young Bavarian woman early in the nineteenth century, when asked why she had given birth to three illegitimate children, answered simply: "It's okay to have babies, the king has okayed it." Here was expressed a belief that traditional rules were changing—for laws about illegitimacy did become less harsh: and possibly people gained some pleasure in the new permissiveness.

The Seeds of Consumerism   Although the population revolution caused unquestionable confusion and hardship, it did facilitate some new opportunities for enjoyment. Growing production for the market and involvement in a money economy brought some villagers as well as urbanites a chance to buy more colorful clothing—another sign of a new interest in personal expression?—and to pay for professional entertainment at local festivals. There were hints here of a new consumer outlook that would define pleasure less in terms of the repetition of customary activities and more in terms of variety, novelty, and stylishness.

Certainly the idea of earning money took on new attractiveness—not a new motivation, surely, but one previously confined to a smaller minority. New England farmers, around 1800, worried about the commercial values they saw spreading around them, warning against "letting money carry your mind from things of more importance." But there was a growing belief also, as the market economy spread in this region, that "the love of wealth seems natural to all mankind, and very few have sufficient of this world to content them." Popular reading in the North American colonies included urgings toward maximum use of time—"early to bed, early to rise"—in the interests of individual gain. The spreading use of pocket watches in much of the Western world showed a new time consciousness, which was also suggestive of new work values and personal discipline.

Thus the population revolution speeded and channeled a number of trends previously germinating in Western society, ranging from social structure to personal codes and beliefs. Change remained tentative, however. Many people worried about new popular habits in dress and sex, and many quarreled with the growing signs of market motives. Change also remained unevenly spread across Europe. Certain social groups refrained from new behaviors, Growing sexual license was confined mainly to the poorer groups, while propertied people treasured their contrasting respectability. Proletarian women suffered from economic change more than men. Their economic alternatives were more fragile, especially when new techniques began to cut into the less-skilled (and female) manufacturing jobs such as spinning. Gender differences showed in the growing flood of women into domestic service. Finally, some regions participated actively in domestic manufacturing and more commercial agriculture, whereas other villages remained devoted to a more traditional subsistence approach. Uneven change produced many opportunities for clash and conflict.

Protoindustrialization

The economic and social developments that led up to the population revolution or followed from it during the middle decades of the eighteenth century or even beyond have justly caught the attention of many historians in recent years. They have labeled the extension of commercial forms, including the spread of manufacturing, plus the related shifts in outlook and social structure *protoindustrialization*—that is, a major departure from the standards of traditional agricultural societies that was not quite a full industrial breakthrough, if only because of the lack of relevant technology. Protoindustrialization not only reflected great changes in Western society but also prepared further change by readying merchants, workers, and various institutions for the advent of industrialization itself. By 1815, far more people in western Europe and North America were involved in protoindustrial transformations than in the more dramatic factory settings of the dawning machine age. These transformations were difficult enough, though they did not pull most people entirely away from accustomed rural or household settings. Thus they allowed protests in the name of older values, and attempts by workers to regain more accustomed community ties. But, at least in western European history, protoindustrialization proved to be only a way-station—in some other parts of the world the process halted here—and although the stirrings of outright industrialization had their major impact after 1815, they also form part of the story of upheavals from the later eighteenth century, as the next section makes clear.

The First Industrial Revolution: England and Scotland

The Fertile Conditions for Innovation

The build-up of manufacturing and the availability of laborers desperate for new forms of work contributed to the final economic reaction to the social changes of the eighteenth century: the application of radical new technologies to manufacturing, and an industrial revolution that began in Britain and spread to other countries. In addition to the general factors prompting economic change discussed in previous sections, Britain benefited from unusual supplies of natural resources. Wood was running short as a result of centuries of settlement and the exploitation of timber for construction and fuel, and this shortage encouraged experiments with new uses of coal as an alternate fuel. Britain had coal in abundance, and also a network of rivers and an accessible coastline that allowed the movement of heavy minerals without major innovations in transportation. In some places, indeed, the British found iron and coal in virtually the same region, which obviously encouraged use of these two staples of early industrialization: coal as ready fuel for the iron smelters.

Britain was also unusually rich in capital, as a result of its far-flung trading activities. British banks, reorganized toward greater centralization during the eighteenth century, aided in economic change not so much by direct investment as in providing a reliable financial network. The same world trading position that aided British prosperity also provided unusual market prospects, as British merchants could see trading opportunities not only at home but in the Americas, India, and elsewhere.

Three other essential ingredients for industrialization in Britain were agricultural improvements, the inventive craftsmen, and an entrepreneurial spirit. The enclosure movement of the eighteenth century combined with an unusual interest on the part of British aristocrats in agricultural improvements and commercial success, to produce a growing food supply essential to support an urban manufacturing labor force. Building on Dutch precedent, British agricultural leaders urged greater use of nitrogen-fixing crops such as alfalfa and turnips. Seed drills and other inventions encouraged greater farm productivity. Drainage improvements opened new land, while stockbreeders produced more meat through breeding innovations. Thus market agriculture went further and involved greater innovation in Britain than in most other countries of Europe during the eighteenth century. The British were also willing to import some essential supplements to their own food supply in exchange for manufacturing

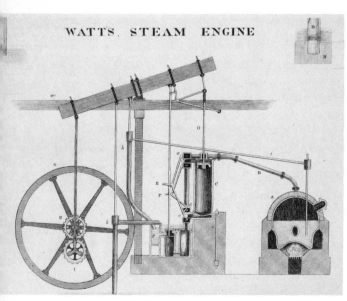

The first steam engine was invented by James Watt.

exports. Thus by 1800 Britain imported considerable amounts of grain from eastern Europe.

Because of their unusual inventiveness, artisans played a special role in British economic change. Most of the key innovations in early industrialization stemmed from the minds and hands of British craftsmen, who hoped at first simply to improve manual manufacturing techniques but ultimately transformed industrial technology. Market opportunities stimulated invention, as did a growing belief in the feasibility and importance of improving on established techniques. British artisans were freer from traditional guild restrictions on innovation than were their counterparts on the Continent, where the guilds, often backed by state laws, continued to discourage new methods. Individual British craftsmen (and in a smaller number of cases, French and American artisans as well) were thus encouraged to tinker with machines with the intent to improve them. From these improvements, in turn, came key inventions in spinning and weaving, as well as the all-important steam engine.

Finally, the special entrepreneurial spirit among British businessmen of the period was a less tangible aspect of early industrial change than new inventions or raw materials, but it was unquestionably essential. It required courage and zeal to take the risks of investing in new equipment and translating inventions into practical production systems. Ironically, most artisan-inventors proved inept as actual businessmen, and their systems (and the resulting profits) were taken over by the more outright entrepreneurs. Britain had a rather small government bent on scant regulation of internal economic activity, an aristocracy slightly less hostile to the business world than its continental analogues, and of course an extensive merchant tradition; therefore, Britain produced more than its share of entrepreneurs during the late eighteenth century. The anomalous position of Protestant religious minorities may also have played a role in this situation, as groups such as the Quakers, tolerated religiously but barred from political life, pushed for business success in compensation.

Early British Industrialization and Its Effects

Britain's special mix of favorable economic and social elements produced a special result. Inventions in textile manufacturing multiplied from 1733 onward, yielding more and more automatic processes to speed hand-driven production. "Spinning jennies," which automatically twisted fibers to make thread, formed a key step in this process. Then, around 1770, the Scottish artisan James Watt, whose firm produced scientific equipment for the University of Glasgow, invented a new kind of steam engine that could be adapted not just to pumping, but to manufacturing in general. With this invention, the age of fossil fuels, and the substitution of their power for that provided by humans and animals, really began. During the 1770s transmission devices, involving gear systems that would translate the power of engines or water wheels to producing machines, were elaborated.

By the 1780s British manufacturers were in a position to revolutionize certain sectors of textile production. Cotton spinning was the first branch to be fully transformed. Cotton, a durable fiber, was easier to mechanize than wool or linen, and spinning equipment was more adaptable to mechanization than was weaving. The fact that most domestic cotton spinners, unlike weavers, were women, and regarded as less economically central to their families' livelihood than men, may also have facilitated this concentration; women could be more readily exploited without damaging the economic base of family life. But the central feature that made the application of steam or water power to cotton spinning worthwhile was its incredible productive power: a single worker, tending an early mechanized "jenny," could produce as much as could a hundred manual workers.

Less dramatic but still impressive results attended other technological transformations in the late eighteenth and early nineteenth centuries. British metalworking began to use coal rather than charcoal for smelting and refining; in addition to saving on the scarce wood essential for the production of charcoal, the use of coal allowed larger smelting furnaces and encouraged growing production of iron. Wool spinning and cotton weaving were also partially mechanized, again with a substantial increase in output. Steam engines were applied to some sugar-refining operations. Coal mining—essential now as never before as a source of fuel—witnessed no transformations in techniques at the pitface, where the coal was actually chopped out. But pumping equipment continued to improve, allowing deeper shafts; and wooden or metal rails facilitated movement of coal from the mines' depths, in carts pulled by children or horses.

The new techniques were supplemented by a further increase in manufacturing labor. Coal output soared, above all because tens of thousands of new workers entered the mines. Mechanized thread production encouraged employment of many more hand weavers to produce cloth. Early mechanization helped produce available labor. Hundreds of thousands of domestic spinners, for example, were thrown out of work by the machines, and whereas some simply suffered growing poverty others were able to find employment either in the factories or as domestic weavers or metalworkers.

British industrialization by 1815 remained in its early stages, applicable to selected branches of production rather than the economy as a whole. Even its early stages, however, had a vital impact. Growing output spurred British efforts to find markets abroad. Salesmen poured onto the European continent, pressed their wares in Latin America and elsewhere. Their impact could threaten traditional forms of production, particularly in textiles, even where no industrialization had occurred, thus adding to the unsettling impact of population growth. German textiles, for example, were hard hit by British pressure. Growing output and rising sales added to Britain's prosperity, giving the nation new military and diplomatic leverage that it put to good use in the wars of the early nineteenth century and in expanding its empire in Africa and Asia.

At home, early industrialization added to the complexity of the British social structure. The new group of manufacturers, sometimes boastful of their success, sometimes apologetic for their association with grimy machines, pressed into the established middle class, ultimately adding to the power and confidence of this class but also creating tensions between older merchants and professionals and the industrial upstarts. A new breed of factory or mine workers emerged within the proletariat. Like other proletarians, they lacked property and had to count on the sale of their labor, relied on the work and earnings of women and children as well as men, and often lacked much voice in setting the characteristics of their own work. But the *conditions* of industrial work differed in important respects from those of more traditional labor. Factories were essential because water or steam power could not be transmitted over any distance; work had to be located near the source of their power. Thus factories separated work from the home, grouping workers, often strangers to each other, in the tens or sometimes even hundreds. Moreover, the new factories were unprecedentedly noisy and dangerous, and the speed of the machines' operations forced a rapid pace and coordination of work, which could take a psychological as well as physical toll. Factories also subjected workers to the explicit direction of others—owners or foremen—as few traditional rural or urban jobs had done before. Most industrial workers faced these new conditions amid conditions of long hours and low pay. The cost of new machines, despite their productivity, convinced most factory owners that workers should be exploited extensively lest the investment be lost. Although a few workers—those who made and installed the machines, for example—won superior conditions through their special skills and responsibility, the lot of most workers in the new setting was grim. Here was another aspect of industrialization with important potential for the future.

As Chapter 5 will make clear, the full impact of industrialization, even in Britain, would be realized primarily after 1815. It was at this point, too, that other Western nations would join in the industrialization process, making it the leading theme of the mid-nineteenth century. During these decades industrialization would become the West's most successful response to the pressures of population growth and its social consequences. Britain's first industrial steps were in part the product of special circumstances; nevertheless, they were the culminating examples in this period of the West's ability to change in response to the intense demographic pressures of the eighteenth century. For many of the workers involved, however, these steps were the latest examples of the inability of British proletarians to resist change in these same pressured circumstances.

The Realm of Ideas: The Enlightenment

During much of the eighteenth century, from the vantage point at least of Europe's elites, the tone of society was set not by anything so messy as birth rates or new inventions, but by a new world of ideas, in what was dubbed the Age of Enlightenment. Intellectual developments during this period, although more refined than the subsurface movements of the Western economy, were nevertheless unsettling, and they eventually conjoined with social change to produce new political movements and to further alter the belief systems of many ordinary people.

Background and Characteristics

The Enlightenment began to take shape in the early part of the eighteenth century. In most respects, it picked up where the scientific revolution, the initial popularization of that earlier movement, and the political theories of writers such as John Locke left off. Enlightenment writers believed fervently in the power of science and the scientific method. They used and further popularized Newtonian physics to demonstrate how orderly and benign nature was, and to praise the powers of human reason. Locke was also an Enlightenment favorite, and many eighteenth-century political theories returned to his emphasis on the essential goodness of humankind, to the need for political systems that would respect human liberty and key rights, including religious freedom, and to the idea that some essential sovereignty, or basic political power, rested with the people. Enlightenment writers also built on Locke's theories of knowledge, stressing again human rationality and the power to learn, and the absence of innate evil or sin.

Just as earlier Christianity had done, especially in the *Summas* of the late Middle Ages, the Enlightenment produced or extended a basic world view of humankind and the universe that could be shared by hosts of people besides intellectuals. Unlike Christianity, their world view was centered in *this* life, not the next: People are basically good; they can devise improvements over traditional ways of doing things; the scientific approach seeks fuller understanding of nature and of social life; progress and change are possible and desirable; and the focus of human attention is properly on life in this world. The central idea of the Enlightenment, that human nature is good and improvable, clearly arose from the implications of the scientific revolution, even as it clashed with traditional beliefs in the innate sinfulness of humankind.

The Enlightenment was not simply a continuation of seventeenth-century intellectual themes. First, the Enlightenment had a different and more sweeping geographical base. The scientific revolution, of course, had drawn its inspiration from thinkers in most parts of western Europe, but the application of ideas of rationalism or political change had been more narrowly confined, particularly to Britain and Holland. The Enlightenment's principal base was in France, where its tenets inevitably clashed with the weakened absolutism of Louis XIV's successors and also with the Catholic church. In other words, France gave the Enlightenment a more critical, even oppositional, role than the scientific revolution had had. It also guaranteed greater attention to the Enlightenment, for France remained the cultural beacon of the Western world. French Enlightenment thinkers, called *philosophes,* held the attention of Prussia and Italy that the more remote English had not won. And although the Enlightenment centered in France, it also described a wide orbit even aside from French influence. A German Enlightenment took shape on its own. Not only Italy but also Spain was affected. North Americans, with their links to England, continued their work in science and political theory and also, by the later eighteenth century, directly connected with French revolutionary thought. Russia and Latin America were more lightly affected, Russia because the government feared the potential for political opposition, Latin America because Spanish and Portuguese rulers, and Catholic officials, limited intellectual contacts; but these areas, too, were partially drawn into the Enlightenment's range.

The Range of Enlightenment Inquiry

In addition to having a larger geographical base than did previous scientific currents, the Enlightenment extended earlier thinking, particularly in the political and social spheres. Some seventeenth-century figures had suggested a deistic approach to religion—that is, a belief that traditional religion was largely superstitious and that God was essentially a clockmaker who set up the orderliness of nature and then left things alone. Many philosophers expanded on this deism, attacking the powers of priests, "blind" prayer, and what they viewed as superstition. Some even cast deism aside in favor of outright, sometimes strident atheism. Many Enlightenment thinkers similarly extended the idea of the essential goodness of humankind. Whereas Locke had stressed the need for sympathetic discipline and education of children, late-Enlightenment writers such as Jean-Jacques Rousseau argued that children are so naturally good that they essentially require no discipline at all, but should be left free to develop their natural impulses. A number of educational theories followed, some still periodically in vogue in the twentieth century, that argued for a permissive atmosphere at home and school.

The idea of progress underwent similar radicalization. Scientific writers and literary advocates of the modern over the ancient had begun to build the concept that human society could improve in this world at a fairly steady pace. In some cases, Enlightenment thinkers made this impulse far more formal. Toward the end of the eighteenth century, the French politician and writer Condorcet sketched a systematic statement of human progress—in knowledge, in political organization, in ethical conduct—concluding that in the future even human biology might improve. Various Enlightenment thinkers applied this more sweeping concept of progress to a host of institutional sectors—prisons and hospitals, as well as government forms—in the belief that rational human planning could inevitably improve on traditional practices, that the natural state of mankind was to move toward perfection. Enlightenment scientists, such as the French biologist Buffon, also took seriously the idea of physical progress, launching investigations of ways to improve longevity, with the claim that the natural human life span should be at least 120 years. To be sure, Enlightenment enthusiasm for progress ran into problems. The French writer Voltaire, devastated by news of an earthquake in Lisbon that took many lives, wrote a bitter poem questioning human control over destiny. Voltaire, Condorcet, and others who looked at history wondered how the Middle Ages could have occurred—for in their eyes, a relatively progressive ancient world had been followed by a more su-

VOLTAIRE: A PHILOSOPHE CAMPAIGNS AGAINST INJUSTICE

Voltaire, the most widely published of the *philosophes* with a huge shelf of essays, plays, and stories to his credit, began his career with a certain amount of caution, eager for patronage from France's king as well as lively sales of his work. Among other literary accomplishments, he translated Locke and wrote admiringly of English politics. He composed a number of literary works, publicized Newtonian physics, and wrote an intelligent, innovative history of Louis XIV. But Voltaire also was drawn into an increasingly active critique of French political life. His particular target was religious pomposity and intolerance, and he called the Catholic church an infamous institution for its efforts to ban Enlightenment publications.

Voltaire was also actively concerned with mistreatment of individuals. In 1762, a Protestant merchant in Toulouse, Jean Calas, was found guilty of killing his son, a prospective convert to Catholicism. Calas was broken on a device called the wheel, dying courageously despite the appalling torture. Informed of the affair by another Protestant merchant, Voltaire came to believe that Calas had been the victim of religious prejudice and suffered a gross miscarriage of justice, convicted not because he was guilty but because he was Protestant. Voltaire rallied his friends and a larger French public opinion toward the rehabilitation of Calas's good name, pouring out countless letters and pamphlets. Three years into his campaign Voltaire won: Calas was vindicated, and both church and state—the perpetrators of the injustice—were brought into further disrepute. Voltaire went on to take up other cases, sincerely convinced that freedom of opinion must be defended, and eager to attack those institutions that toyed with the dignity of man. Voltaire himself, living on an estate that sprawled into Switzerland, easily escaped direct attack from the French authorities.

Voltaire's belief in freedom is summed up in the famous phrase, "I disagree with everything you say but will defend to the death your right to say it." It is only coincidental that, insofar as can be determined, Voltaire never actually wrote the slogan itself, despite the long tradition that would attribute it to him.

perstitious period under Christianity, before the strand of progress resumed with the Renaissance. But they tended to explain away the Middle Ages as due to the plots of evil priests, and were not shaken in their basic faith.

The Enlightenment's tendency to radicalize earlier views applied most definitely to political theory. Whereas Locke had written cautiously of popular sovereignty, granting the people a right to revolt but suggesting no regular means of transmitting popular voice, many Enlightenment writers urged some degree of outright democracy. Even more daring extensions followed. If all men are basically good, as Enlightenment writers generally believed, then they should have not only political but also material rights, some French political theorists argued in the 1780s. Thus the Enlightenment generated early statements of socialism, arguing against inequalities established through private property. Again basing their arguments on fundamental human goodness, some writers held further that if men had rights, so might women—despite the firm belief by many *philosophes*, including Rousseau, in male superiority. Toward the end of the Enlightenment, Mary Wollstonecraft in England and several French writers urged a feminist case, stating that equality for women in law and in political voice followed from the essential worth of all people.

The Enlightenment thus extended the range of argument, begun in the aftermath of the scientific revolution, in many different directions, setting up at least the early stages of many political causes that still burn brightly in the Western world. The Enlightenment also extended the application of the scientific method, if in somewhat adapted form, by developing the foundations of the modern social scientific approach: If nature could be grasped through rational procedures—observation and generalization—why could not human nature and the functioning of human societies be understood in this way? Various French writers combined knowledge of history and of societies other than their own with a quest for general models to develop and explain major patterns of political behavior, asking such questions as why some societies have strong monarchies, whereas others have republics or despotic governments. Most of these writers went on to state what the best government was, stressing the importance of a rule of rational law and a balance of powers within the state, but their work constituted a form of political science as well as political theory. Other scholars, also particularly in France, offered a combination of theory and observation about human behavior, setting up the beginnings of formal psychological study. Most striking was the emergence of the first modern statement of economics. A mid-eighteenth century school of French theorists tried to elaborate some general principles of economic behavior and the generation of wealth in opposition to the statist orientation of mercantilism. But it was the Scottish economist Adam Smith, issuing his *Wealth of Nations* in 1776, who really founded economics as a social science. Smith offered general laws of economic behavior, starting from the premise that individuals can best pursue their own self-interest and that the operation of individual behaviors, freely competing without government intervention, will yield maximum social good in the form of the greatest output and the highest quality at the lowest possible price. Smith's ideas, which remained fundamental to the *laissez-faire* school of economics as against reliance on government intervention, were classic Enlightenment fare: People are rational and social behavior operates according to understandable general principles. But his *approach*, which combined observation of actual economic behavior with a desire to set up rational models, was just as important in shaping a framework for the study of economics as a discipline.

Extension of inquiry into social behavior brought Enlightenment theorists into other specific fields as well. The Italian economist Cesare Beccaria argued for a fundamental rethinking of penology. The typically harsh punishments of the time—torture, banishment, death for minor offenses—followed from erroneous beliefs about human evil. Criminals were thought to be inherently bad, unrepentant, and a scourge on society, and thus to be shown no mercy. Moreover, Beccaria found that punishments were capriciously applied. In contrast, he believed that since human nature is improvable, criminals should be rehabilitated, not treated to cruel acts of vengeance. English writers planned model prisons in something like this spirit, with the same faith that rational arrangements could revolutionize the treatment of criminals and undo the effects of more primitive traditions. Other Enlightenment writers attacked the inhumanity of slavery, the follies of war, the pettiness of customary school discipline. For given a sincere devotion to humanitarianism, rational reform, and progress, those in the Enlightenment believed there was no aspect of human affairs that could not be improved.

Finally, the Enlightenment helped the efforts of seventeenth-century writers to reach a wider audience. Leading figures were eager for readers, and with improvements in literacy, prosperity, and publishers' ability to market books, some Enlightenment thinkers, such as Voltaire, were able to make a rich living as publicists. Through their efforts, a far wider audience than ever before learned of new scientific findings as well as the theories of the Enlightenment itself. French Enlightenment leaders produced a massive encyclopedia, designed for wide sales, giving up-to-date views on all aspects of science and social science, while also showing unusual interest in technology. The British *Encyclopaedia Britannica* followed later in the eighteenth century.

For the Enlightenment, not as original as the seventeenth-century scientific revolution, nonetheless offered a full worldview, capable of application to virtually all realms of human thought. In this respect, it rivaled a religious faith; indeed, not only Enlightenment leaders but also many followers seized on new beliefs in rationality and progress with an almost religious intensity. Small wonder then that the Enlightenment could generate an encyclopedic approach to knowledge, similar in scope, though far different in nature, to the great *Summas* of the late Middle Ages, when thinkers also believed that they had the keys to all basic truth.

The Enlightenment and Broader Intellectual Life

The power and conviction of Enlightenment thinkers carried over into many facets of intellectual life besides philosophy and social science. Work in the natural sciences easily reflected Enlightenment values while further enhancing the prestige of the Enlightenment approach. The eighteenth and early nineteenth centuries did not see fundamental breakthroughs in scientific theory, but there was a growing body of empirical work—that is, detailed observations of phenomena—and some key findings in specific areas. In chemistry, for example, the French researcher Lavoisier discovered oxygen and its basic functions, ending a long debate over the nature of fire. Biologists piled up discoveries of new plant and animal species; in this regard, researchers in North America contributed mightily to Western knowledge. Biology also benefited from the new classification system developed by the Swede Carolus Linnaeus, which organized life into a hierarchy of groupings from species up to phyla. Here was a powerful use of the growing belief that nature was essentially orderly. Some biologists also began to wonder about the history of nature, speculating that nature was not a constant but rather a set of processes, in which some types change to meet different circumstances. Here was the origin of the ultimate idea of evolution, developed more fully in the mid-nineteenth century; and it fit neatly, at this point, with Enlightenment beliefs in progress. Indeed, one French biologist argued that species added traits in direct adaptation to circumstances, so that change and improvement were inseparably linked—this view proved oversimple at best, but it fit the temper of the times.

The Enlightenment also had considerable impact on the arts. The most fashionable painters stressed carefully controlled scenes and portraits, while architects maintained a devotion to classical styles. These patterns harmonized with Enlightenment delight in restraint and rational order, and also its enthusiasm for carefully selected features of the ancient world. Still more revealing were the styles of gardening popular particularly on the continent of Europe, where geometric designs of trimmed hedges and flower beds showed the mastery of man's planning over nature's haphazard impulses. In literature Enlightenment writers stressed the essay form, along with some rather stiff drama and poetry designed to teach clear philosophical lessons. The preference for the essay obviously reflected a desire to use writing to instruct and to encourage reasoned

The stiff regularity of classicism marked the arts in the Enlightenment. *Aeneas at Delos* (1672) by Claude Lorraine influenced the growing practice of landscape gardening.

debate, along with a delight in polemics and satire against what the essayists saw as hidebound superstition.

The Enlightenment's dominance over cultural life was not absolute, however, and other trends in the eighteenth century, though on the whole subordinate to the splendors of the *philosophes*, were significant in their own right. In the first place, consensus within the Enlightenment was not complete, and toward the end of the eighteenth century Enlightenment premises were used to attack some of its own conclusions. All along, of course, *philosophes* had disagreed vigorously over specific issues. Some, for example, insisted that a constitutional, parliamentary government was the only suitable politcal form, whereas others found merit in a reform-minded, "enlightened" absolutism. Rousseau was far more democratic and less coolly rational than was Voltaire. He also evinced a distrust of too much sophisticated civilization, praising the simple life, in contrast to the enjoyment of wealth and urban pleasures that Voltaire and other *philosophes* promoted. But the arguments that arose after 1780 went further than this. A number of theorists, particularly in England and Germany, argued that there was no scientific way to prove that progress was inevitable or that human behavior could be grasped through a few basic generalizations. The idea that political constitutions could be based on ideas of "natural rights" came under particular fire. Since before John Locke, and into the Enlightenment, political theorists had argued that people had certain natural rights that did not have to be justified or proved. The American Declaration of Independence, in 1776, referring to "self-evident truths," repeated this basic approach. But the rationalist skeptics argued that nature provided no demonstrable first principles in politics, and that faith, rather than reason, formed the basis of such claims. Increasingly, in fact, theorists turned to other kinds of arguments, as the tidy Enlightenment package began to unravel a bit. In England, for example, a school of utilitarians arose who claimed that political arrangements should be determined by whether they were useful to the greatest number of people. For the most part utilitarians advocated the same kinds of measures that the *philosophes* had, such as prison reform and religious freedom, but their philosophical base moved away from Enlightenment staples.

New Forms of Piety

More important still, during the eighteenth century itself, were cultural expressions outside the Enlightenment orbit altogether. Religious writing remained lively, even though formal theologians, in countries such as France, now felt on the defensive. Until the 1830s, more sermons and religious tracts were printed than any other literary form in the Western world. Here was clear indication of a divided culture, in which the new ways of thought had yet to win clear preeminence. More revealing still was the rise of new forms of popular piety during the century of the Enlightenment, in which Protestant preachers challenged established churches but in the name of a purer vision of God's power and the awesome quality of salvation and damnation, not in the name of rationalism.

In Germany, early in the eighteenth century, a Pietist movement arose within the Lutheran church, designed, as its name suggested, to inject a greater personal piety into religious life. Pietists urged active Bible study, individual religious contemplation, efforts to taste some mystical union with God, all spurred by powerful preaching and music, and by upright conduct. The Pietists attacked the Lutheran establishment for what they claimed was its hollow orthodoxy, which relied on formal belief rather than impassioned faith. Some small Pietist sections split off from Lutheranism, a few migrating to North America where they formed tight-knit communities, some of which, like the Amish in Pennsylvania, survive to this day. In England, a Methodist movement began under the brothers John and Charles Wesley. Their target was the formalism of the Anglican church, which they hoped to infuse with a "religion of love, joy, peace, having its seat in the heart; in the inmost soul." As in Germany, reform efforts did not win the established church, so that the Wesleys were forced to form their own denomination, the Methodists. They won great success in preaching to the rural and urban working classes in England, during the time of great social upheaval, and their preachers also gained many converts in the frontier areas of colonial North America. Although socially conservative, Methodist leaders attracted many ordinary people by their distance from the fashionable religions of the upper classes, their emphasis on personal dignity and morality, and their eloquent preaching. Finally, influenced by Pietism, Calvinist leaders in the American colonies sponsored a Great Awakening during the eighteenth century that crossed denominational lines, from New England to the South. Great Awakening preachers urged the power of individuals to win salvation through their own enthusiastic piety, attacking the dry doctrine emanating from the established pulpits.

The new religious currents within Western Protestantism were far different from the rationalistic promptings of the Enlightenment. But they also had some elements in common with the larger intellectual movement. They too suggested some human equality—in this case, the equal chance of all believers, including the poor, to win salvation. They too played down more traditional Christian beliefs in original sin and a world filled with evil. Their world too was orderly and beneficent, so that an individual could count on being able to reorganize his or her religious life once the decision to do so was made. Religious reformers stressed the importance of humanitarianism, as Enlightenment theorists did—for example, often attacking the existence of slavery in the Americas and the slave trade from Africa. They were active in founding schools, eager for widespread literacy so that the Bible would be available to all, though not for the more elaborate scientific learning of the *philosophes*.

Sentimentality and the Romantic Impulse

Just as religious revivalism implicitly countered one Enlightenment blind spot—its hostility to spiritual passion—so a final cultural current of the eighteenth century seized on another: the limitations of the Enlightenment attachment to cool, restrained artistic styles. A growing group of novelists arose in the eighteenth century, particularly in France and England. As the name implies, the novel was a new literary form in the West, and it featured outright storytelling rather than poetry or drama. The power and popularity of the novel depended on Europe's growing literacy, for people no longer needed their stories read or performed aloud but could enjoy the private entertainment reading a novel provided. The popular novelists, addressing a large readership in the middle and upper classes, emphasized a distinctive tone as well as a new format. Their stock in trade was sentimentality; their stories dealt with romantic love, the heartsounds of courtship and unrequited passion. Many of their heroes and heroines died young, and readers were urged to invest premature death with a new, tearful grief.

During most of the eighteenth century the sentimental novelists, who enjoyed great popularity, hardly challenged the Enlightenment pinnacles of intellectual life. They were storytellers, tear-jerkers—the precursors of the modern soap opera. They had no overall intellectual program. Nor did they completely contradict the Enlightenment view of the world; they too stressed youth—though a youth of yearning and frustration, not one of educational promise. The sentimental novelists did, however, see the essence of human nature differently from the *philosophes*, in stressing that emotion was its key; in this they served as somewhat secular counterparts to the religious revivalists, who also emphasized the importance of properly directed passion. Although these novelists did not directly challenge the Enlightenment, by the end of the eighteenth century and particularly after 1800, the current of sentimentality broadened into a wider, distinctly anti-Enlightenment cultural movement known, appropriately enough, as Romanticism. German writers such as Goethe, though by no means hostile to rational endeavor, praised the importance of soulful experience. Goethe's novel *The Sorrows of Young Werther*, written in the 1790s about a tragic life ending in suicide, caused a tremendous outpouring of vicarious tears, the popularity of morbid sensibilities, and a brief new popularity for dramatic suicide among German adolescents. In a more serious work, Goethe's *Faust* deliberately renounced rational study for intuitive experience: "Gray and ashen, my friend, is every science. And only the golden tree of life is green." English poets took up a similar theme; William Wordsworth wrote:

> One impulse from a vernal wood
> May teach you more of man,
> Of moral evil and of good,
> Than all the sages can.

The Romantic impulse, which would have its fullest impact after 1815, praised a spontaneous nature, not the disciplined, scientifically dissected nature of the Enlightenment. It revived interest in the Middle Ages, in some cases out of sincere religious conviction but more commonly from a desire to promote alternatives to structured, classical styles and Enlightenment devotion to the rational mind. Romantics would also counter Enlightenment enthusiasm for the sameness and orderliness of human nature with a new devotion to profound differences in popular cultures and national spirits. Here German writers took a distinct lead, beginning with Johann Herder, the father of German romanticism, in the 1770s. For Herder, knowledge of society came from instinct and history, not from rationalistic, social science calculations. Each people had its own soul, which could not be captured in formulas about human reason or the equality of all men. A national culture such as that of Germany evolved historically, like a living plant. Its distinctive spirit was not the same as those of the cultures of other nations, and it could be perceived, ultimately, only through sympathetic intuition and shared emotion.

Early Romanticism, clearly building in the decades around 1800, sketched an alternative vision of man and society to that of the Enlightenment. The vision was less fully expounded, because of its nature; more had to be left to the reader, precisely because the purpose was not to lay out a uniform rational model. But there was no question that despite the brief supremacy of the Enlightenment vision, Western culture would remain disunited, caught by an eddy of contradictory currents. Key elements of the Enlightenment would persist, but a rival approach, stressing emotion, aesthetic perception and a search for a larger spiritual force—in God, nation, or some other entity—would persist as well.

Yet the cultural division that opened up in the wake of the Enlightenment's heyday—often causing bitter dispute and certainly inhibiting coherence in overall intellectual output—should not obscure the one basic point that the Enlightenment, religious revivalism, and early Romanticism shared in common: They were all untraditional. Although traditional thinking was still dominant among many established church leaders—including much of the Catholic hierarchy—and in many schools and universities, it was unquestionably in retreat as far as creative intellectuals were concerned. Romantics talked of new styles just as Enlightenment leaders wrote of new ideas. Revivalists defended religion, to be sure, but by asking for new kinds of popular piety, not old doctrines. Thus the scientific revolution and the Enlightenment had not created a single path for Western culture, but they had decisively obliterated the path of intellectual tradition. The thirst for novelty became as ingrained in Western cultural life as the *fact* of novelty was becoming in the social and economic experience of Western people.

Popular Mentality

The coincidence between two domains of rapid change, the social-economic and the cultural, was not accidental. Enlightenment thought did not cause new sexual behavior, but it certainly contributed to an atmosphere in which some people could think about the validity of new secular enjoyments. Early Romanticism did not cause new attention to emotional attachments to spouse and children within the family, but it certainly gave a certain seal of approval to the growing interest in romantic love; in fact the popularity of romantic stories almost surely resulted in part from the prior existence of new romantic interests on the part of ordinary people. Stories of love winning out against great odds, or unrestrained grief when a beloved child died, were models of similar shifts in *actual* emotional standards, helping to confirm them in turn. Certainly religious revivalism, the most directly popular movement of the various intellectual currents of the eighteenth century, resulted in part from the new needs of a common people experiencing rapid change, eager to find spiritual outlets independent of established channels and a confirmation of individual dignity in God's sight.

Rising Literacy and the Popularization of Ideas

Few of the intellectual innovators came from the ranks of the most ordinary people; to put the case simply, few of them were of rural origin. But the fact that a growing number of writers came from middle-class ranks rather than the aristocracy—Rousseau even boasted proudly of his artisan origins—and the fact that sales of books to a wide readership began to replace court patronage as the key source of intellectual support, gave the new intellectual currents, including the Enlightenment, real contact with popular beliefs beyond the interest that both the *philosophes* and the early Romantics professed to take in ordinary people. The middle-class background of these writers was a basis for interaction between the changes in formal culture and the ongoing evolution of popular mentality.

Growing literacy and eager publishers contributed to the popular impact of the new intellectual movements. Aristocrats and priests were drawn to fashionable salons in France, where Enlightenment ideas were widely discussed and iconoclasts-in-principle, such as Rousseau, were trotted out for public pampering. At a slightly lower social level, coffeehouses, spreading as the brew itself became popular based on imports from Latin America and Asia, served as forums for excited discussion of Enlightenment political and scientific ideas. A host of "improvement" societies—landlords concerned with agricultural change, businessmen eager to promote new knowledge both to win social prestige and to bolster their own commitment to technological change—provided yet another forum for discussion and the dissemination of Enlightenment work particularly. Clearly, some contact with the new ideas did not always depend on active literacy, as there were many adepts eager to read some of the most striking discourses aloud to interested but less well educated audiences. Through direct reading or by other means, most urbanites in western Europe and North America, including artisans as well as businessmen, gained access to portions of the new thinking, apart from the somewhat separate current of popular religious revivals. How far the ideas gained notice in the countryside is harder to fathom, but growing travel and market contacts opened some rural channels as well.

In fact the new ideas, particularly at this point the thinking of the Enlightenment, did contribute to some changes in popular outlook. For example, before 1780 most North Americans, if they lied about their age, claimed to be older than they actually were, because in traditional society age added dignity and respectability. But after 1820—that is, after a period of transition that was several decades old—Americans who lied about their age did so downward, claiming to be *younger* than they actually were. (This pattern has persisted to this day.) Clearly youth gained new prestige, at least in theory. This change owed something to economic shifts that gave new importance to young people who could learn new methods; it owed something to politics, for the American revolution had put a younger leadership in charge and called attention to the virtues of a "young" republic. But new ideas played a role as well. The Enlightenment's emphasis on learning, its attacks on received wisdom, combined with Romantic delight in the passions of the young to turn age-group prestige on its head, downplaying the inherent virtues of age and playing up the promise of youth. This shift was passing into popular thinking at many levels of society. Even efforts to look older, such as wearing powdered wigs, were cast aside.

Consequent Changes in Mentality

Even though it cannot be charted with absolute precision, the popularization of new ideas, particularly those emanating from the Enlightenment, influenced actual popular mentalities in two, possibly three, directions. First, a growing number of people gained the idea that they had new political rights. In one of the first steps in the French revolution of 1789, representatives of the French middle classes, who were drawn primarily from the ranks of lawyers and other professionals but included some business interests, insisted that they should have more votes than the representatives of the aristocracy and the clergy. Their reason was that votes should bear some relationship to numbers, not to station; besides, the aristocracy did not really earn its position through hard work, as proper people should, but rather won it through inheritance. Possibly middle-class people would have sought new political power simply because of the growing size and wealth of the class, caused by commercial advance, but the fact was that Enlightenment ideas shaped the new demands. Even earlier, in the 1760s, many urban artisans in Britain formed political organizations seeking wider political representation, appealing to ideas about a fundamental equality among men and an ideological hostility to a political system still based largely on privilege. Artisanal agitation for greater democracy would resume in Britain in the 1790s. A variety of people, then, many of them profoundly shaken by the economic and demographic upheavals of the eighteenth century, learned directly from new political theory both about the evils of the existing order and about what kind of governmental structure should be installed in its stead.

Enlightenment ideas had some impact also on the politics of the family. As more people came to believe in basic human goodness and rationality, they were encouraged to rethink hierarchical relationships at home, granting somewhat more voice to women and children. This occurred despite the strongly patriarchal tone of many leading *philosophes*. Egalitarian political beliefs (or egalitarian thinking in the new religious movements) thus conjoined with changes in emotional standards to enhance the reshaping of family relationships. Some of these changes would also spill over into law. Although in the quarter-century after 1789 the legislation of the French revolution and Napoleon did little for women's rights, it protected children in some new ways. Particularly revealing was the official outlawing of primogeniture, by which the eldest won the entire inheritance, in the name of greater family equality.

The second direction in which the popularization of new ideas influenced popular mentalities involved demystification. Awareness of Enlightenment ideas clearly contributed to the long process of demystifying the natural and social environment. This process was already underway, as we saw in Chapter 3, and other factors—including commercialism and the decline of traditional community ties—contributed during the eighteenth century. But it was striking, nevertheless, that in eighteenth-century France a large number of adult males, in the cities but also in some rural regions, abandoned their formal religion. They did not simply turn against the clergy, which was an old impulse; they stopped actively believing that religion of any sort was particularly valid or significant. Popular dechristianization went further in France at this point than elsewhere, and it was by no means a majority current even there; but it foreshadowed more widespread abandonment of active Christianity prompted by the existence of an alternative, Enlightenment-derived view of the world. Smaller traditional rituals might yield to new ideas without outright dechristianization. German artisanal guilds after 1800, for example, began to abandon beliefs that had once helped bind them together. During the eighteenth century and before, many guilds maintained elaborate ceremonies to "cleanse" new journeymen of their subordinate, deviant status and make them into full-fledged men. Initiation rites included beatings, changes of costume, and shaving off charcoal "beards" to symbolize attainment of pure manhood. After about 1800 artisans simply stopped believing that people needed to be cleansed of impurities, for there were no mystical forces at work in the transmission of skills; thus initiation ceremonies turned into simple banquets, pleasant enough but lacking the intensity or binding power of the earlier symbols.

Third, the spread of Enlightenment ideas may have encouraged some wider beliefs in the possibility and desirability of progress. New businessmen, proud of their social ascent in any event, began trumpeting a more general belief that, with growing knowledge combined with improved technology, human life could change for the better. James Watt's commercial partner in developing steam engine production, Robert Bolton, was active in a variety of local booster societies in the 1780s in which these views were widely enunciated. Some changes in the outlook toward death, taking shape by the turn of the century, also reflected some new hope for progress. Fatalism toward death began a long process of decline, as some people turned away from acceptance of inevitability, cushioned by religious solace, once disease had reached an acute stage, and toward a new sense that death—particularly the death of children—was an inappropriate disruption of nature's beneficent order. Here was a cause of the growing outpouring of grief surrounding death, a cause also of new interest in improving the physical treatment of children in order to make death less likely.

Popular mentality did not simply and universally convert to Enlightenment ideology; traditional values and new currents such as the religious revivals complicated the change. Additionally, some regions in the West were more open to new ideas, some still relatively closed; some social classes, and those in urban areas, accepted Enlightenment thought, while others, including rural people, did not. There were also differences between men and women in their openness to new ideas. But generally the effervescence of formal culture did have a wider impact, contributing most obviously to new political ideas at the popular level, but influencing other attitudes as well.

Eighteenth-Century Politics

Western society after 1730 was thus shaped by two distinct but partially overlapping tides: the upheaval in ordinary economic life, spurred by demographic pressure, and the upheaval of established styles and ideas. Not surprisingly, by the end of the century political institutions would also be swept by these currents.

Yet the middle decades of the eighteenth century were decidedly undramatic in the political sphere. The crescendo that would lead to a half-century of revolution took time to build. After the agitation of the seventeenth century, for example, English politics settled down to something like routine. Whig and Tory politicians alternated in power, often skillful in their abilities to form and maintain parliamentary majorities. Elections, still confined to a small, largely land-owning voting pool, continued to be peppered with corruption. Voltaire noted the comment of one successful member of the English parliament who threatened that if he did not receive a bribe he would be forced to vote according to his conscience. Most parliamentary laws reflected not only the self-interest of members, but a keen desire to please the monied classes. Thus Parliament banned the import of cotton cloth, to favor industry, and it passed the enclosure acts that helped throw the rural world into turmoil in the interest of landlords. This system, to be sure, hardly kept pace with the growth of political awareness among the English common people, which was why a series of political riots disrupted in the 1760s. Nor was there a firm boundary line between royal and parliamentary authority; under George III, efforts to increase the king's power occasioned new dispute at home, as well as contributing mightily to the revolt of the American colonies after 1775. With these important exceptions, the course of British politics ran relatively smoothly, if unglamorously.

Trends in France were more troubling. Surrounded by the structures of earlier absolutism, the eighteenth-century French monarchy was never able to achieve the confidence and authority that Louis XIV had wielded in his glory days. The two kings who ruled after 1715, Louis XV and XVI, were personally ineffective. Financial problems loomed even larger than personal defects at the top. Louis XIV had bled his rich country severely, and under his more modest successors state expenditures still ran high. Efforts to increase taxation pressed the peasantry, while privileged groups—the aristocracy and the church—remained largely exempt. Recurrent efforts to reform the taxation system foundered against the resistance of those who stood to lose by change, and no monarch had the power to reorder French society. The absolutist system was further weakened by a growing tendency to sell bureaucratic offices rather than leave them open to talent. The French state remained powerful because France was powerful, but a growing sense of uneasiness marked the French political scene.

Enlightened Despots

More dynamic political developments occurred in northern and central Europe, under the banners of a modification of absolutist policies called "enlightened despotism." Enlightened despots were to some extent absolutists wearing a new public relations guise. They maintained the power trappings of absolutism, seeking strong centralized bureaucracies and showing no interest in traditional parliamentary institutions. They also eagerly sought ways to extend government functions, in the economy but also in the realm of culture. But their list of functions, and their justifications for assuming these functions, departed from absolutist patterns, reflecting the impact of Enlightenment ideas. (Several enlightened despots, in fact, eagerly patronized individual *philosophes*.) Enlightened despots thus worked not to promote a single church under royal authority, in the Louis XIV pattern, but rather to encourage religious freedom. They argued for government intervention in the economy, in essentially a mercantilist pattern, not in terms of generating revenues for the government's war machine but in terms of improving conditions for the people.

Enlightened despotism took clear shape in several countries. The Swedish monarch in the later eighteenth century reduced aristocratic power, but then he proceeded to encourage freedom of worship, a more extensive grain trade, and a program of elementary education. Enlightened despotism spread also to the Habsburg realm, particularly in the later eighteenth century. Maria Theresa, Habsburg empress during the first part of the century, worked to consolidate loyalty to the royal house, particularly from the Hungarian nobility. Her son, Joseph II, adopted a more clearly enlightened bent, attacking tradition at virtually every front. He established full religious toleration, including rights for Jews, while placing new controls over the Catholic church. He set up a state school system, while rationalizing the law codes and establishing the principle of equality in the court system regardless of social class. He also worked to abolish serfdom, which in part constituted an attack on the powers of aristocrats but which also reflected a sincere interest in creating more equitable social conditions.

Joseph's program was too ambitious, particularly in imposing centralized, German-dominated controls over his ethnically diverse empire. After the king's death following a decade of rule, most of the reforms were pulled back, allowing landlords and the Catholic church to resume much of their older authority. But Joseph stands as the leading example of what enlightened despotism could produce, in the form of rationalized state procedures designed for the common good, when carried to extremes.

The classic enlightened despot, in terms of intentions and results, was Frederick the Great of Prussia, who ruled from 1740 to 1786. Frederick contributed directly to political theory, arguing that the true origin of sovereign power lay with the people who established authority in order to maintain clear and equitable law; thus a prince could not himself violate good order. But Frederick carefully defined his idea of the general good not directly in terms of the people's interests, but in terms of the good of the state, which of course the king represented: "The prince is to the nation he governs, what the head is to the man; it is his duty to see, think, and act for the whole community, that he may procure it every advantage of which it is capable."

As a ruler, Frederick regularized and codified the laws, reducing the severity of punishments including torture. He allowed freedom of religion, although he regulated the press. He worked hard to improve the Prussian economy. He sponsored the draining of swamps, the use of new plows, and the planting of the potato, all in the interest of better agriculture. In true mercantilist style, he regulated trade and promoted state-run industries, while reducing internal barriers to the movement of goods. Frederick maintained his absolutist predecessors' support of a strong, well-organized army and a vigorous foreign policy. And although he improved the conditions of serfs on royal estates, he shunned any attack on the privileges of private landlords—thus demonstrating how monarchs continued to limit their interest in modifying existing social arrangements.

A hint of enlightened despotism reached Russia under the rule of Catherine the Great (1762–1796). Enthusiastic about the *philosophes*, Catherine displayed the enlightened passion for regularizing law codes by setting up a commission to investigate the prospects in the Russian context. But in fact, eager to maintain the full power of the tsarist autocracy, Catherine actually implemented nothing in this area. She did increase the power of the crown to supervise nobles who directed local governments, but she also maintained the Russian tradition of conciliating this same group by giving them absolute power over their serfs—even the right to execute them for crimes. She brutally suppressed peasant risings, including the Pugachev rebellion, which responded to conditions imposed on Russia's majority. Catherine's enlightenment mainly enhanced the influence of French styles in the Russian upper classes; it had far less to do with actual politics than was the case in western and central Europe.

And in fact the impact of enlightened despotism anywhere, except in Joseph II's reform efforts, must not be exaggerated. Despotism easily outweighed enlightenment, as eighteenth-century kings continued to repress most free political expressions while attempting to continue the trend of enhancing the crown's power. At most, enlightened despots realized that their goal of a strong state and a powerful army was best served by promoting a prosperous populace, one that could afford more taxes and that would have more children. But the goals of state aggrandizement remained foremost. France and England continued to try to expand their colonies, which brought them into frequent conflict; Catherine in Russia

EIGHTEENTH-CENTURY WARS

The major wars of eighteenth-century Europe had a patterned quality reminiscent of other aspects of the Enlightenment. They were conducted by well-drilled troops and in most cases they caused relatively little bloodshed; there was no great passion in these battles. But the wars maintained the trajectory of earlier absolutism in seeking to use military force to expand state power and territory. The states already gaining in strength grew stronger.

The wars of the mid-eighteenth century did not rival the conflicts around 1700 in extent—the campaigns of Louis XIV, discussed on page 89, and the Great Northern War between Russia and Sweden, discussed on page 95—although in some ways their scope expanded. Britain and Spain conducted a brief war in 1738—the "War of Jenkins' Ear," named for an injury inflicted on a British seaman—as Britain tried to gain trading access to Spanish colonies in South America. A more general war erupted in 1740, as a new Prussian king—Frederick the Great—tried to make his mark by attacking the new Habsburg empress. The War of Austrian Succession dragged on for eight years, with Prussia gaining the territory of Silesia and the Habsburgs winning an alliance with England to prevent further gains. Then, eager to regain Silesia, the Habsburgs allied with France in 1756. Simultaneously France and England warred both in North America and India, each hoping for colonial supremacy; and as part of this worldwide fight England supported Prussia. Thus the Seven Years' War (known in North America as the French and Indian Wars) began. Prussia had to fight for its life, as even Russia joined the fray; but Frederick the Great prevented territorial loss. England got the better of France, taking over key Canadian provinces and also the frontier across the Appalachians; the British also pushed the French out of serious contention for control of India. England was now Europe's colonial leader without question. The British East India Company, through a combination of alliance with regional princes and direct controls, increasingly dominated India, winning huge trading advances and a yearly payment in gold for administrative expenses. In North America, Britain's new supremacy led to tighter colonial policies that would help trigger revolution. In Europe itself, a balance of power seemed clearly at work, with England distracting France, and Prussia, Russia, and Austria all sharing influence in the central and eastern parts of the continent.

worked to gain new territory around the Black Sea, from the Ottoman empire, and territory in Asia—and Russian explorers moved into Alaska in the 1780s. Prussia and Austria warred twice for the sake of additional territory in eastern Europe, and in 1772 Prussia, Austria, and Russia combined to share a good part of Poland among them. Military expansion thus remained a chief political goal, and clearly the Enlightenment had no impact in that regard.

The American and French Revolutions

The placid politics of the eighteenth century was shattered by a series of revolutions that took shape in the 1770s and 1780s. In retrospect it seems almost inevitable that the disparity between rapid social and intellectual change, and business-as-usual politics only slightly tempered by reform rhetoric, would prove to be a combustible mixture. But the surge of revolution was not simply an attack on sluggish political institutions by those caught up in change—although this it was in part. Revolution also followed from complex conflicts among those involved in change—not only forces of innovation pitted against recalcitrant traditional privilege, but also groups that saw in revolution a way to arrest social change and return to treasured older values.

The revolutionary era that opened at the end of the eighteenth century was to touch the whole of Western society and would spill over into other parts of the world as well. Only a few countries as yet experienced actual revolution, however. Parliamentary forms helped shelter Britain and Holland, although new waves of agitation arose; the parliamentary form was sufficiently flexible to channel some of the new grievances short of revolution. Countries with particularly efficient monarchies, such as Prussia, were also exempt; however, they had to introduce further change from above in order to keep pace with the new revolutionary regimes.

The American War of Independence

American tensions with Britain set the revolutionary ball rolling, though the American colonies engaged more in a war for independence than a revolution in the classic sense. (For the revolutionary model of France, see especially page 162.) After Britain's victories in the Seven Years' War, the colonial administration sought to tighten controls over American society while also raising taxes to pay for increased governmental costs. The new approach stimulated widespread American resentment. The spread of new political ideas, along with more traditional attachment to considerable independence in local policy, gave force to the colonists' objections. Surely, the emerging colonial leaders thought, a people should not be taxed unless it also participated in government. Thus in developing new political demands, American colonial leaders were confirming their participation in Western, particularly Protestant and Enlightenment, culture. They were also reflecting, however, some of the new tensions of eighteenth-century social life—tensions that produced growing crowding and competition along the Eastern seaboard, accompanied by heightened commercial activity that could cause discontent among some of those wedded to more traditional habits while spurring others to seek new rights to correspond to their new wealth. In this regard too, Britain was a convenient target. When the British tried to discourage colonial trade and manufacture, in favor of British priorities, they directly harmed many urban colonial interests. When they sought to regulate the lands west of the Appalachians, they offended still more colonists who looked to the west as an outlet for growing population pressure.

To seek greater freedom from British control, all but one of the colonial legislatures sent delegates to the Continental Congress in 1774. War broke out in 1775, in Massachusetts, and a second congress set up a new army under the Virginia planter George Washington. Radicals pressed for an outright proclamation of independence, and the colonists appealed for aid from France in their war. On July 4, 1776, the Declaration of Independence was issued, using Enlightenment terminology for an appeal to the rights of all people to set up their own governments and to protect their "life, liberty, and pursuit of happiness." War dragged on for several years, but British strategic errors, the stubborn persistence of those colonists bent on national freedom, and French help after 1778 gradually turned the tide. Britain held its own in the conflict with France in other parts of the world, but on the eastern seaboard the colonists won out by 1781. After a few more years of confusion, a new national constitution was drawn up in 1787, proclaiming the United States a federal republic based strongly on Enlightenment principles. Particularly noteworthy was a strong Bill of Rights protecting various individual freedoms, and a system of checks and balances between state and federal governments and among branches of the federal government to prevent abusive authority and to assure representation to many voting citizens.

The establishment of the new American republic was in some ways a peripheral event in the Western history of the period—although the later development and expansion of the United States would catapult it into quite a different role. In 1800 the republic was still small and far away, insofar as most people in western Europe were concerned. Leaders of the republic, suspicious of "old world" entanglements, pursued a rather isolated path; despite strong trade links with Europe, the new United States would play no significant diplomatic role for many decades, as it concentrated on domestic affairs and its own westward expansion. Nevertheless, the American revolution had its own larger impact. Renewed war with England, in aid of the Americans as well as its own expansionist goals, had cost the French monarchy heavily, prompting new awareness among the French of the need to reform the tax structure; this awareness helped lead to internal developments that brought on revolution. More generally, the American republic long stood as proof that Enlightenment ideals could be successfully translated into politics, and that revolution might indeed work well. The existence of a regime with no monarch and no legal aristocracy, with widespread freedom of religion, with equality of citizens (though not, of course, of slaves or women) under the law, and with voting rights for many propertied men, stimulated the demand for similar gains in Europe. The United States would in this sense serve as a revolutionary beacon for several decades, and its existence fired up many agitators in France.

The Causes of the French Revolution

By the 1780s it was becoming clear that something had to give in France. Absolutism was ineffective, but its reform inevitably called the privileges of aristocrats and the Catholic church into question—these two segments of society paid no direct taxes while controlling a sizable minority of the arable land. Church and aristocracy did not simply resist reform efforts, however; both had some grievances of their own against absolutist controls. Individual aristocrats, like the Marquis de Lafayette, who had fought in the American revolution, actually embraced Enlightenment thought, as did some clergy. More common was a desire to revive aristocratic power, including the right to be heard in government. Thus quarrels between the privileged groups and the monarchy shaped the events that led up to revolution. The king, Louis XVI, called an Assembly of Notables in 1787 to try to persuade church and aristocracy to consent to some direct taxes in the face of a soaring national debt, but the effort failed when aristocratic leaders insisted that rights of representation must be offered in exchange. So, in 1788, the monarchy called for a meeting of the Estates-General, the medieval body that had been suppressed by absolute rulers since 1614.

With this call, the floodgates of discontent were opened, for there was no possibility of returning to feudal monarchy. Huge popular grievances had taken shape against church and aristocracy alike, which formed the first two of the three traditional Estates. Peasants resented lingering remnants of serfdom—the taxes and work services that many still owed to their landlords, along with prohibitions of hunting and other restrictions. They and other groups attacked church tithes and the luxurious lifestyle of the upper clergy. These basic grievances were spurred by Enlightenment attacks on religious obscurantism and aristocratic idleness and frivolity. Some people, indeed, wanted direct voice in government through a new kind of elected parliament. Finally, tensions produced by overpopulation and growing commercialism contributed to the storm of discontent, as propertied and propertyless alike felt threatened by change. A series of bad harvests, and resulting unemployment and high food prices in 1787–88, assured revolution.

The ingredients of the 1789 conflagration indeed provide something of a classical model of revolutionary causation. Fundamental social change shakes established patterns, causing both discontent and new expectations; yet change is not yet substantial enough to eliminate people's ability to rely on traditional community structures and values in order to mount action. New ideas shape and stimulate discontent for many groups; a severe economic crisis helps trigger revolt. Finally, the existing regime grows weak and divided, lacking the will to repress unrest wholeheartedly while also lacking the ability to lead in serious reform.

The Outburst in 1789   The first revolutionary moves occurred as the Estates General prepared to meet. The Third Estate, representing the nonnoble, nonclergy majority, had forced in advance a decision allowing them to have twice as many delegates as each of the two other estates. Then, when the assembly convened in June, these delegates insisted that the whole meeting sit and vote as a single body. The intent here was clear: the old medieval institution should be converted into the beginnings of a modern parliament, representing the whole people—or at least those with enough property to vote in the Third Estate—rather than the traditional privileged orders. After some hesitation, the king gave in and the National Assembly was formed, with support from a minority of nobles and clergy allowing the Third Estate representatives to plan a new, formal constitution for France. On July 14, Parisian artisans and others stormed a royal prison, the Bastille, to free what they assumed were hordes of political prisoners. They found few, but the event symbolized the end of traditional French government. More serious were rural riots that spread in the later summer, as peasants attacked their landlords and destroyed records of manorial obligations. Within a few months, the combination of widespread popular rioting and parliamentary leadership did what the storming of the Bastille symbolized: it altered the bases of Old Regime politics and society.

The Revolution's Liberal Phase   The Constituent Assembly, as the reconstituted parliament came to be called, governed the Revolution for two years. It created the underpinnings of a liberal society in France by a series of key measures. First, responding to rural unrest, the Assembly ended aristocratic privilege and manorialism. Adult males were to be equal under the law, all government jobs were to be open to competition rather than inheritance or purchase, and the remnants of serfdom were abolished. Second, the privileges of the church were attacked. Full religious freedom was proclaimed, as against previous church attacks on other religions or its efforts at censorship. Furthermore, the revolutionary government took over church property, providing payment to the church out of tax revenues. This measure was partly an act of financial desperation from a government still strapped for funds, but it also reflected a desire to control the church, rather than simply free it, on grounds that the institution was too powerful to be trusted. Finally, the Assembly issued a new constitution. Even during the tumultuous summer of 1789, a Declaration of the Rights of Man and the Citizen had proclaimed fundamental protections for individual freedom along with property rights. The later 1791 constitution followed up by creating a strong parliament to limit the king, based on a voting system in which about half of all adult males—those with some property—would be able to participate. Guarantees of rights, a constitution and a strong elected legislature, abolition of the traditional privileges of groups—such was the liberal (but not democratic) framework erected by the Revolution's first phase.

Yet the Revolution did not end in 1791; the liberal measures inevitably created powerful enemies. Not only many church officials, including the pope, but also many loyal French Catholics were turned against the Revolution by its attack on Catholic autonomy. Many aristocrats fled France and sought to rouse foreign opposition to the revolutionary threat. Many urban artisans were appalled by the Revolution's attack on the guild system; for true to the belief that all privilege must go, the Constituent Assembly had abolished these institutions as well, and then firmed up the protection of private property by forbidding other associations of workingmen. Serious economic instability, with rapidly rising prices, added to popular unrest. Moreover, foreign monarchs threatened revolutionary France; in defense of the French king, causing a French declaration of war on Austria and Prussia in 1792.

The Radical Phase   The result of all these pressures was a further radicalization within France of the regime, and an effort to increase the authority of the central government against internal and external attack.

A cartoon (1794) against the Terror and its leader Robespierre. The artist stresses the mechanical gruesomeness of the guillotine, which is watched over by a symbol of the Revolution (upper left), and points out that more victims came from the ranks of common people than from those of the privileged.

Liberal leaders were discredited, often accused of sympathizing with treasonous churchmen, and the Jacobin party arose bent on destroying the monarchy altogether. Military defeats in eastern France added fuel to the radical fire, as did domestic counterrevolutionary risings plus an ill-advised effort by the royal family to escape the country. Well-organized Jacobins took over the government, proclaiming France a republic and executing the king and queen under the blade of the guillotine, a newly invented device for capital punishment designed, in best rational fashion, to minimize pain. Two years of radical experiment followed, directed by the Jacobins. Traditional weights and measures were replaced by the sensible decimal systems. The control of the central government over local administrations was increased, aided by the destruction of traditional, provincial units of government that might have promoted regional loyalties. Summary courts tried a host of real or imagined enemies of the Revolution, focusing on wealthy businessmen as well as aristocrats and clergy. Several thousand people died in the Reign of Terror, which blackened the reputation of the Revolution but actually proved mild by twentieth-century standards of bloodshed.

The radical phase of the Revolution was not unrestrained. Although a few groups arose urging attacks on private property in the name of social justice, Jacobin leaders were firm in their devotion to basic business interests and attacked socialist groups as well as more conservative opponents. The principal durable achievement of the radical phase, aside from the imagery of violent rhetoric it promoted, was to resume the construction of a strong national state. Not only centralized administration, but also concerted efforts to win national loyalty and a new program of mass military recruitment moved in this direction. Now that traditional privilege had been overthrown, revolutionary leaders urged a tighter direct link between individual and state; widespread military conscription was one manifestation of this link:

> Young men shall go forth to battle; married men shall forge weapons
> and transport munitions; women shall make tents and clothing, and shall
> serve in hospitals; . . . and old men shall be brought to public places
> to arouse the courage of soldiers and preach the hatred of kings and the
> unity of the Republic.

Under radical leadership, revolutionary armies began to win success against France's conservative neighbors, and British and German armies were driven from French territories. But as the external threat eased, the Jacobin rule with all its tensions could not be supported, and the radical leadership was overthrown. Four years of conservative consolidation followed, to 1799, in which moderate leadership worked to dampen disorder and restore financial stability. But the moderates maintained an active foreign policy, winning Belgium from Austria and taking regions in western Germany and northern Italy. The combination of revolutionary zeal, the practical advantages of wider military recruitment, and new, talented leadership allowed France greater gains than in the age of Louis XIV. But these gains also roused more serious foreign resistance, particularly from Great Britain. The needs of war, along with recurrent domestic unrest, prompted a final revolutionary shift of power as the military general Napoleon Bonaparte took over the French government, essentially as dictator, in 1799.

The Napoleonic Phase   Napoleon was to rule for fifteen years, in the last phase of the great revolutionary era. His regime mixed monarchical and revolutionary elements. Napoleon hoped to establish a family dynasty; he even created a new honorific aristocracy. But he submitted key government measures to popular vote, offering people a simple yes-or-no choice in plebiscites, thus foreshadowing techniques used by modern dictatorships to legitimate their rule. Napoleon retained parliamentary forms but deprived them of power, and a strong secret police regulated political behavior. Yet Napoleon maintained male equality under the law in a series of sweeping law codes. He tried to conciliate Catholic opinion while retaining full freedom of religion. He promoted state-run education, particularly at the secondary and university levels, thus extending the functions of the state and assuring centralized control of the training of future bureaucrats. These measures along with improvements in the central administration and the tax system, helped solidify key revolutionary gains.

But Napoleon's most consistent goal was territorial expansion. He annexed many neighboring territories directly to France and set up satellite kingdoms in Holland, parts of Germany and Italy, and for a time Spain and Poland. His ambitions roused a series of coalitions designed to prevent French domination and restore a balance of power. But disunity among the allies and Napoleon's own brilliant generalship—particularly his use of mobile artillery and quick marches of troops—fed French success for many years. Britain remained indomitable, and Napoleonic efforts to challenge the British navy and the British economy both failed. But Prussia and Austria were crushed on several occasions, and skillful diplomacy diverted Russia for a time. Only after 1810 did Napoleon clearly overreach himself. He was bothered by guerrilla resistance to his forces in Spain, and his attempts to regulate the continental economy to exclude English goods stirred enmity elsewhere. Russia turned hostile again, and Napoleon's grand attempt to invade that country in 1812 failed miserably against Russian retreats toward the interior and a harsh winter. A new alliance including Britain, Prussia, Russia, and Austria formed in 1813, and Paris fell the following year, Napoleon going into exile. Napoleon's dramatic return in 1815 caused a new flurry of excitement, but his dreams were decisively dashed in the battle of Waterloo.

Yet neither France nor Europe could be put back together in the old style, even as a quarter-century of revolution and war draw to a close. The victorious allies met in Vienna to draw up the peace. They sensibly did not try to punish France beyond endurance, hoping to involve the nation in a postwar balance of power rather than launching a campaign of revenge. Thus France kept its 1792 boundaries, which included several gains in the north and east. To buffer France, Holland and Belgium were united, and new or enlarged regional states were set up in western Germany and northern Italy; there was no attempt to revive the old patchwork of small units. Prussia won new territory in western Germany, and Austria ruled two northern Italian provinces. Poland, which Napoleon had briefly revived, was divided once again, with Russia gaining the lion's share. Britain was rewarded for its efforts by a host of new colonies—it gained southern Africa from the Dutch, key islands in the Mediterranean and the Indian Ocean, and new West Indian holdings. Thus the Treaty of Vienna confirmed the continued gains of Europe's great powers.

Monarchy was restored in France, with Louis XVI's brother, Louis XVIII, coming to the throne. But here, and in most of the territories surrounding France such as the Low Countries and western Germany, revolutionary legislation introduced by French administrators, including Napoleon,

THE EUROPEAN POWERS AND THE FRENCH REVOLUTION

As the French Revolution began to turn radical, established monarchs elsewhere became actively hostile. In Britain Edmund Burke, a conservative statesman, railed against the idea that sweeping change could be introduced without chaos. Russia's Catherine the Great abandoned all pretense of sympathy with Enlightenment ideas, tightening the censorship over political writings both domestic and foreign. Prussia and Austria sent troops to France's borders, and these moves stimulated the French declaration of war in 1792. But the conservative powers were divided, and as eager for their own territorial gains as for defense of monarchy in France. Indeed Russia, Prussia, and Austria used the distraction provided by the French Revolution to partition Poland twice more, finally eliminating the nation altogether. French gains, however, prompted a second alliance effort at the end of the 1790s, which pushed France back in Italy. Britain was France's most consistent opponent, less because of principle than because of a particular fear of any dominant continental power that, through control of the Low Countries, might threaten invasion—and revolutionary and Napoleonic France easily qualified as this kind of threat.

Yet the Second Coalition failed, as Russia withdrew and Napoleon defeated Austria in 1801. Napoleon's hold in Italy and western Germany was confirmed through treaties, and the Holy Roman Empire—that network of tiny German states vaguely overseen by the Habsburgs—was dismantled once and for all. Yet France's continued agitation, not only in Germany but also in West Indies and Louisiana, roused Britain, Austria, and Prussia once again, in the Third Coalition (1803–1807). Napoleon's campaigns against this alliance brought some of his greatest victories but also the loss of his navy to Britain in the Battle of Trafalgar. The continental monarchies were defeated, and Napoleon for a time occupied both Berlin and Vienna. Then came a flirtation with Russia that turned sour, as Russia refused to obey Napoleon's orders to isolate Britain and grew fearful of French power. A resultant invasion of Russia in the winter of 1812 brought Napoleon to a scorched and empty Moscow, set ablaze to deny provisions to French troops, and the final, Fourth Coalition that finally tumbled the upstart emperor.

was largely retained. The Catholic church did not regain its lands. Manorialism and the guilds were not restored, and equality under the law remained largely operative. Parliaments and constitutions persisted, though their range was somewhat reduced in favor of stronger monarchies. Thus a large zone of western Europe beyond French borders maintained the destruction of essential features of the old regime, even as a more conservative atmosphere followed the Vienna settlement. And even outside this zone the revolutionary turmoil had left a mark. To match the power of France's armies, several governments had tried to reach out to their subjects in new ways, appealing for loyalty, improving administrative

THE CONGRESS OF VIENNA

The diplomats who met to settle the disruptions of the French Revolution and Napoleon ably represented the great powers of old-regime Europe. Britain sent the aristocratic foreign secretary Lord Castlereagh, eager to protect his nation's supremacy on the seas while constructing an effective new balance of power in Europe—Britain's by then traditional twin goals. Habsburg Austria was led by Prince Metternich, also eager for balance of power but anxious as well to secure conservative political principles against the revolutionary tide. Russian and Prussian rulers acted directly, eager for national gains. And France was allowed its own representative, the clever statesman Talleyrand, who had been a bishop before the revolution but had served every revolutionary government after 1789. Talleyrand had been Napoleon's foreign secretary until 1807.

The diplomats at Vienna, though undeniably self-interested, were in many ways surprisingly sensible. Unlike later war-settlers, they were not bent on massive revenge. Nor did they bind themselves to fixed slogans—though Alexander, tsar of Russia, did a bit of posturing in stimulating a religiously inspired (and hollow) Holy Alliance among the three conservative monarchies of central and eastern Europe. The Treaty of Vienna admirably took into account irreversible developments—such as the destruction of many features of the Old Regime in France and the disappearance of countless small states in Italy and Germany—and tried to give all the major powers some satisfaction. Certainly no one emerged from Vienna demanding immediate redress, and in fact Europe was to avoid another all-out war, or even a clash on the level of the two mid-eighteenth century wars, for ninety-nine years, until the First World War. Yet in a larger sense, Vienna did not stabilize Europe. The treaty did not prevent new surges of liberal and nationalist sentiment, which would not only promote revolution but would remake Europe's territorial map. As Chapter 5 shows, it certainly did not prevent continued economic and social change that was fully as subversive of the status quo as Napoleon's great armies had been.

efficiency, and extending the range of military conscription. Prussia, particularly, resumed its tradition of monarchy-inspired reform. Serfdom was abolished, though landlords retained great powers; state-run schools expanded; and the government managed to organize armies of unprecedented size. Thus even in nations that did not directly experience revolution, the needs of government efficiency, redefined by the successes of revolutionary France in mobilizing popular energies, jostled against traditional social arrangements.

Finally, the French Revolution had stirred passions throughout western Europe that no clever treaty arrangements or moderate constitutions could fully restrain. Although the Revolution's violence stood as proof to some of the need for conservative restraints, revolutionary gains stimulated political expectations among many common people. During the 1790s British artisans resumed their quest for voting rights, although their effort was finally repressed in the name of the war effort. In 1815 far more Europeans were aware of the desirability of constitutions, bills of rights, and a voice in government than they had been during the eighteenth century. The Revolution had also stimulated considerable popular nationalism. Within France, appeals to revolutionary loyalty and the achievement of a regime that seemed to emanate from the people, plus the attack on traditional regional and group affiliations, had spurred a new excitement for a glorious France. French invasions, combined with the loosening of some older ties to localities and churches, spurred nationalism in Germany, Italy, and Spain—a force that had not been appeased by the arrangements of 1815.

Conclusion

The age of the French Revolution both closed and opened periods of decisive change in European history. The Revolution itself followed from widespread social and cultural upheaval. It built on the growth of the nation-state and changes in popular mentalities that included new political ideas and a waning of traditional religious fervor. Napoleon himself has been characterized as the last and greatest enlightened despot, and although this description does not fully capture his boundless ambitions, it does characterize his reform goals well; and this too suggests that the revolutionary period was the dramatic end to a period of Europe's history.

But the French Revolution also launched new pressures for change. The expectations it promoted would bring new agitation, in the 1820s and 1830s, toward more liberal and nationalistic regimes. The Revolution also opened the way for further economic change. Revolutionary leaders, drawn disproportionately from business and professional ranks and persuaded by mainstream Enlightenment beliefs in the importance of economic progress founded on private property, attacked a number of key impediments to innovation, and most specifically to the industrial revolution. The full abolition of manorialism created a more mobile labor force that could move to industrial jobs without the restraint of traditional obligations. The attack on guilds, and the prohibition in theory of other worker combinations, aided technological innovation and the control of labor alike. Rationalized currencies and new commercial law codes also favored business activity. Equality under the law enhanced the enthusiasm for economic gain, at least among businessmen, because traditional status categories were now less sacrosanct. The revolutionary era itself saw little fundamental economic change, though production for the wars solidified British industry; recurrent chaos was no friend to consistent development. But the Revolution, in ending the old social order in France and its continental neighbors, proved to be a vital precondition of a new level of economic change after 1815, as the industrial revolution became not just a British specialty, but a phenomenon that spanned the West. Here, clearly, the Revolution helped open a new era, in a society crowded by new population levels, new ideas and a growing market

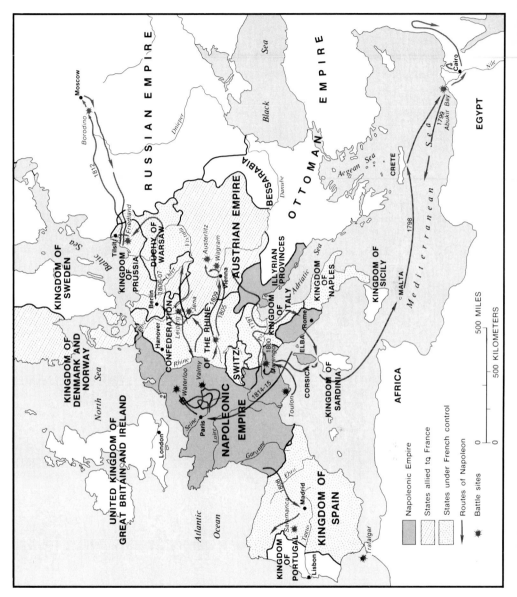

NAPOLEON'S EUROPE IN 1812 AT THE HEIGHT OF THE EMPIRE
The map shows the various zones of revolutionary influence radiating out from
France, and the reshuffling of traditional boundaries.

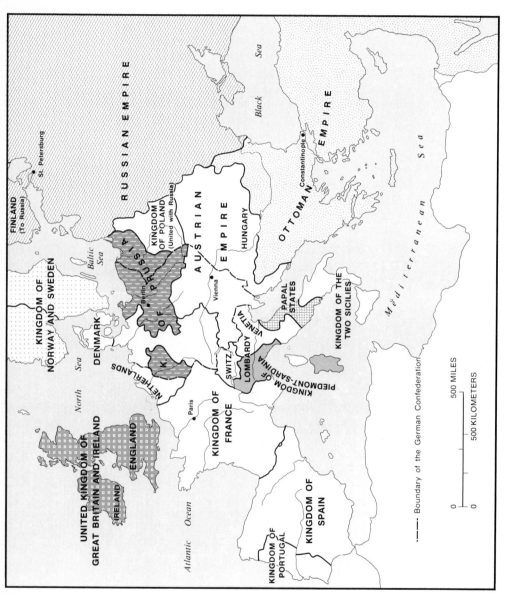

EUROPE IN 1815, AFTER THE VIENNA SETTLEMENT.
Napoleon's Europe was disciplined, with new restraints on France, while other
states gained new territory. Balance of Power, rather than pure tradition or new
nationalism, prevailed.

economy but not, until after 1815, opened fully to the most challenging new technologies and methods of organizing work.

More generally, key developments after 1730—culminated, of course, by the quarter-century of revolution—showed how the various strands of change in Western society began to interlace. Spurred by massive population growth and the continued expansion of a market economy, new kinds of social inequalities now divided Western society profoundly; centered on the gap between propertied and propertyless, in city and countryside alike. Gender divisions at points enhanced these social divisions, as unequal economic opportunities for men and for women differentiated their roles and earnings alike. Changes in mentalities fed by intellectual movements such as the Enlightenment and early Romanticism, in some ways enhanced the new inequalities. Propertied people, increasingly literate, had ideas different from those of many proletarians; they were more open to scientific findings and more convinced of the importance of sexual respectability. But new ideas also cut across social lines, giving various groups new notions of individuality and political rights. At the same time, the growth of state power increasingly focused political attention on the central government, and where this government could no longer defend itself, as in France, the result was revolution. Yet with revolution came further extensions of state power, as the nation-state continued to gain in impact over ordinary people through new direct taxes, new laws that framed aspects even of family life, and new levels of military recruitment. Family politics was changing as well, particularly through the new constraints on parental authority, and this related to shifts in the class structure, in mentalities, and in more formal political life.

Important features of life in the West, to be sure, still reflected more traditional patterns. Most people, still peasants, worked much as their ancestors had. Even here, however, new crops, higher population, and new market pressures promised further change. An age of revolution, not only in politics but in ideas and even sexuality, reflected the juncture of new institutions and new beliefs in Western life.

Although there were still great and humble people alike in Western society, all social levels had been profoundly shaken, both in personal and public life, by these tides of change. The great now had to think about new political threats and the challenge of new commercial habits. The humble had to adjust to a life without property, and to a new set of family and community values. New ideas aided adaptation to change in some respects, but they also weakened traditional supports such as established religion. Small wonder that, around 1815, various elements in Western society groped for ways to arrest change. Conservative leaders at the Congress of Vienna, as well as ordinary workers who protested industrial equipment or commercial practices, were aware that an older society had been profoundly shaken. As Chapter 5 makes clear, events would soon prove that innovation could only increase, as the trends of change in modern Western history continued their work.

FIVE

THE DECADES OF THE INDUSTRIAL REVOLUTION AND POLITICAL CHANGE, 1815–1870

1769 ff	New spinning machines invented
1769–1782	James Watt develops workable steam engine
1780 ff	Industrial revolution in Britain
1830 ff	Industrialization in Belgium, the United States, France
1840 ff	Industrialization in Germany
1788	First steam boat
1800 ff	Development of interchangeable parts in machine manufacture
1811–1825	Development of the railroad
1829	First commercial railroad line
1815–1848	Height of Romanticism
1815	Formation of Holy Alliance; Metternich system in central Europe; elaboration of conservative policies
1820	Revolutions in Spain, southern Italy
1821 ff	Greek revolution
1830	Revolution in France, Belgium, parts of Germany and Italy
1832	Great Reform Bill in Britain
1833	First extensive child-labor law (Britain)
1844	British law regulating women's working hours
1833	New primary education law (Guizot law) in France
1834 ff	Development of department stores
1837	Invention of the telegraph
1847	Karl Marx's *Communist Manifesto*
1848	Revolutions in France, Austria, Hungary, Italy, Germany
1848	Culmination of Chartism in Britain

1851	Louis Napoleon (Napoleon II) takes full power in France
1852	Proclamation of the Second Empire
1851–1861	Cavour prime minister in Piedmont
1854–1856	Crimean War
1856	Invention of Bessemer converter
1858–1861	Unification of Italy
1858	Piedmont alliance with France
1859	War with Austria; 1861 Kingdom of Italy proclaimed
1866, 1871	Acquisition of Venice, Rome
1859	J. S. Mill, *On Liberty*, classic statement of liberalism; Charles Darwin, *Origin of the Species*
1861	Emancipation of serfs in Russia
1861–1865	U.S. Civil War
1861	Morrill Act encourages higher education
1862	Bismarck chief minister of Prussia
1864–1871	Unification of Germany
1864	War with Denmark
1866	Seven Weeks' War with Austria
1867	North Germany Confederation formed
1870–1871	Franco-Prussian War; German Empire proclaimed
1867	Syllabus of Errors
1867	*Ausgleich* in Habsburg monarchy
1867	British suffrage reform
1867	Publication of Marx's *Kapital*
1870–1871	Fall of Louis Napoleon in Europe; Third Republic begins in France

FIVE

THE INDUSTRIALIZATION OF THE WEST, 1815–1870

BY THE CRITERIA OF 1870, the Europe of 1815, and indeed even the United States, would have seemed quite traditional. The majority of the population remained illiterate. Cities, although growing, were small; only a few centers contained over 100,000 people. The bulk of the population, urban and rural, still worked in or around the home in close association with other family members. Of course political revolutions had left their mark in the establishment of considerable equality under the law, as against the aristocratic principle of privilege at birth, and in the attack on traditional institutions such as church and guild. But even revolutions seldom change as much as they appear to do. The French aristocracy, for example, although weakened by the French Revolution, still served as a powerful social class that was politically influential and controlled many productive landed estates despite the abolition of outright manorialism. The Catholic church dominated most primary education, and the hold of religion ran strong for many French people. In some ways, as we have seen, the Revolution furthered trends of government centralization and the focus on the national state, rather than producing a fully novel political structure. The still-new United States stood as a fresher political creation, but here too older themes, including the persistence of slavery, qualified political change.

By 1870, in contrast, cities were vast agglomerations. Work was increasingly separated from home and family. Schooling was a common if not yet universal experience for children. In most Western countries parliamentary systems had been installed, and in many countries most adult men could vote. Above all, much of Western society had moved from a

173

stage of protoindustrialization, in which new commercial forms and manufacturing compromised with older work habits and organization, to outright industrialization. The age of the smoke-belching factory had arrived, and with it came a host of changes in personal, political, and military life.

174

FIVE
The
Industrialization of
the West, 1815–
1870

As we have noted before, change in modern Western history is a slippery theme to pinpoint. The decades before 1815 had profoundly altered European and North American life through revolution, population upheaval, new ideas, and new popular beliefs. The West in 1815 was in no sense really traditional if measured, for example, by the criteria of the sixteenth century or the criteria of most other societies in the world in the early nineteenth century. Changes that occurred in the eighteenth century, and even before, were by no means superficial. Indeed, their scope and depth serve as explanations for the continued transformation of the West through outright industrialization. As the world's industrial pioneer, lacking models to imitate, the West required profound preindustrial shifts as goad and guide. What happened after 1815, in the period of the full-fledged industrial revolution, built on earlier changes even as new strains and opportunities were added.

What happened in the first two-thirds of the nineteenth century was the addition of major technological change to the other factors already reshaping Western society. Technology had played a role in earlier trends, but now it seized center stage. Technological change also propelled other trends, giving them greater intensity. Thus commercialization and the expansion of the state took on new elements, while earlier shifts in popular outlook, family values, and women's roles were given new impetus and definition.

Yet change remains an elusive subject, even as it constitutes the historian's essential focus. The decades of industrial revolution, from 1815 to 1870, did not alter everything; certain regions, groups, and behaviors remained stubbornly aloof. The West of 1870—still largely rural even though rural habits no longer set the social tone—combined change with important continuities. Furthermore, some key changes during the industrial revolution period itself proved temporary. Leisure habits, for example, moved further away from traditional forms but did not become clearly modern; they would have to be revolutionized once again after 1870. Political leaders, too, tried to stake out a society that would be liberal without being democratic, and this was a waystation that would also be swept away later. Thus to give an accurate picture of life after 1815, not only the continued hold of tradition but also some special flavor of early industrialization must be captured, rather than simply a headlong rush toward what today we would label "modern."

Technology Takes Command

The Spread of Industrialization

The spread of steam engines and other new devices, plus more widespread factory organization of industry beyond British boundaries, began in earnest after about 1820. A certain number of British businessmen and skilled workers set up shop in places such as Belgium, France, and the New England states, helping to introduce new procedures in mining and metallurgy and new textile operations. By the 1830s, for example, over 20,000 skilled British workers were employed in France, where they set up textile equipment and served as chief operatives in coke-based iron smelting in return for unusually high wages—despite their disdain for French eating habits and for the absence of good British beer. More important still were local entrepreneurs who copied British machine design, displaying almost as much risk-taking zeal as the British pioneers themselves. British law forbade direct export of machine designs until the 1840s, so early New England and Continental industrialists resorted to unusual devices—such as rowing disassembled machines across the English Channel in disguised fishing boats.

By the 1820s factory-based cotton- and wool-spinning, using both steam engines and water power, and some mechanized weaving, were solidly ensconced in France and Belgium, as well as in Massachusetts and Rhode Island in the United States. New forms of ironwork, an expansion of coal-mining labor, plus some use of steam engines in sugar refining, printing, and other processes spread rapidly as well. German industrialization took off slightly later, delayed in part because of a lack of capital, in part because British imports of machine-produced textiles long held back this sector of German manufacturing. By the 1840s, however, German metallurgy and mining began to expand on the basis of new meth-

This engraving from a drawing of English spinning mules in 1835 hints at how the scale, noise, and dangers of industrial labor contrast with traditional forms of work. Factory conditions would intensify as industrialization continued.

176

FIVE
The
Industrialization of
the West, 1815–
1870

ods, fed by a growing market for railroad equipment; and there was some textile mechanization as well. By this point, indeed, the centers of Western industrialization were beginning to concentrate in areas of rich natural resources—particularly along major coal seams, because coal was the most expensive industrial ingredient to transport. This concentration favored Britain, which was rich in coal, but also Belgium, northern France, the Ruhr valley in western Germany, plus the Great Lakes region in the United States.

Industrialization outside this core zone proceeded somewhat more slowly. Regions within individual nations—much of France, for example, or the American South—developed only scattered factories before 1870, in part because they lacked extensive resources in coal and iron. Regional factory centers developed in northern Italy, northeastern Spain, and parts of Austria, but the larger national units, including segments of the Habsburg domain such as Hungary, did not yet launch serious industrialization. Even Holland, although it was highly commercial, did not develop an extensive factory network before 1870. Outright industrialization was sufficiently widespread, its impact felt even beyond the factory centers, that it is accurate to designate the decades after 1815 as the conversion point of Western society to an industrial economy.

As the industrial revolution spread, it varied from one country to the next, even aside from outright laggards such as southern and southeastern Europe. For example, although France began industrialization relatively early, it proceeded at a slower pace there than in Germany; much of the French manufacturing sector continued to depend on artisanal production but put increasing pressure on the artisans to cut into their traditional methods, which included long apprenticeships and artistic embellishments, in order to heighten productivity. German industrialization relied more on heavy industry and big companies than was the case farther west; it also allowed a greater role for the state. Prussia and other regional states increased their economic underwriting of industrial development, for example, by sponsoring most railroad development, in part to compensate for a lack of capital in private hands. Governments in Germany and France after 1850 actively encouraged large investment banks as well, which built up funds for lending to industry while also promoting the formation of large business units that controlled substantial shares of such sectors as iron and steel or chemicals production. Differences in the pace, focus, and organization of industrialization had more than economic impact; they affected changes in the power balance among European nations and the way labor movements were formed.

Industrialization and Technological Change

The general spread of industrialization also had important effects across much of Western society. One clear effect was the growing role of technological change in shaping work and a wide range of other social activities. Spreading industrialization automatically involved technological change, of course. By 1850 important groups of workers on the European continent and in the United States, as well as in Britain, were dealing

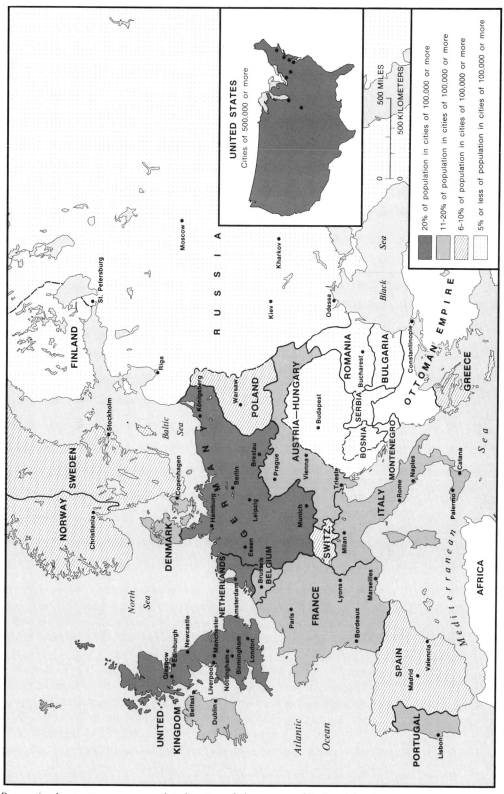

Rates of urbanization are a good indication of the extent of industrialization in nineteenth-century Western countries. Urbanization rates around 1900 show what parts of the West had moved first or fastest toward industrialization: Germany, England, and the United States.

178

FIVE
*The
Industrialization of
the West, 1815–
1870*

with steam-driven textile equipment, coke-fired smelting ovens, and so on. But the industrial revolution did not consist simply of a one-shot technological transformation. Innovation was not constant, but it was *recurrent*, so that workers and managers in virtually every mechanized sector had to deal with periodic modifications in the way they operated. In textiles, for example, early equipment had involved considerable skill and strength on the part of master spinners, who were assisted by child workers who tied broken threads on the machine and did other, often dangerous, supplementary tasks. By the 1830s, however, textile machinery was becoming more sophisticated. Individual workers supervised a larger number of looms or spindles, which functioned more automatically than before. Skill requirements tended to fall, but the number of jobs for children also declined. Coal mining also witnessed important periodic changes. Initially the principal new technological input into mining was the steam-driven pump, which allowed deeper shafts; otherwise the work was little altered. By the early nineteenth century, however, wooden, then metal rails were laid in many mines, which allowed horse-drawn wagons to move coal out of the pits; and soon steam engines were applied to these in turn.

Metallurgy and machine building witnessed still more important nineteenth-century transformations, not only in industrially emerging areas but also in established centers such as Britain. Invention of the Bessemer converter, in 1856, allowed the construction of larger blast furnaces for smelting iron ore; it also permitted the automatic reintroduction of elements such as carbon in order to make steel. Many difficult but highly skilled jobs were eliminated by these new procedures. A group of workers called puddlers, for example, who had stirred molten metals in the early coke-fired furnaces, laboring in great heat but commanding high salaries, were now rendered obsolete. With the Bessemer converter and other furnaces, steel began to replace iron as industrialization's basic metal product. Similarly, in machine building, early construction efforts had been essentially artisanal, as each steam engine or mechanical spinning jenny was crafted separately. That meant that each part had to be crafted with the tolerances and fit of a single machine in mind. Early in the nineteenth century, however, the American Eli Whitney invented the principle of interchangeable parts, initially for the manufacture of rifles; a part for one machine could now replace the same part for any machine like it. This allowed standardized manufacture of machinery, greatly increasing productivity and ease of repair. Machine building remained a highly skilled sector until well after 1870, but it embraced rapid technological change.

Furthermore, new and often power-driven technologies extended steadily beyond the initial factory industries. By the 1830s roller processes could turn out newspapers and other printed material at far faster rates, in greater quantities, and at lower cost than any previous printing procedure had allowed. By the 1840s mechanization could be applied to higher-quality textile fibers such as linen and silk, although these industries continued a relative decline in the face of cheaper, brightly colored cottons. Mechanization began to spread into the manufacture of clothing after 1850, with the invention of the sewing machine. Before long, even private homes were touched by this particular facet of technological innovation, as housewives turned to new equipment to facilitate their work. Mechanization spread also to agriculture. Before 1850 technological change remained fairly modest in this area. Seed drills increased productivity, and so did the growing use of heavy scythes, rather than smaller sickles, for harvesting. After 1850 American inventors introduced large reaping and threshing machines, drawn by horses; these were ideal for the extensive holdings of many American farmers and pushed American productivity in grains well above European levels. Agriculture also relied increasingly on chemical fertilizers, developed from the 1830s onward, particularly in German laboratories. Along with growing production of dyes and explosives, manufacture of fertilizers spurred a growing chemicals industry in the final decades of the early industrial period.

The application of new technology to transportation and communication had still more revolutionary implications. Transportation problems became increasingly pressing during early industrialization, for with growing production seeking wider markets the movement of goods in bulk became crucial. Communication needs rose also, to link far-flung business operations. Britain, France, and parts of the United States responded initially with road- and canal-building programs, including such American projects as the Erie Canal, which linked the agricultural hinterland with the Atlantic seaboard. Experiments with steam shipping began soon after 1800, and steam-powered ships soon plied major riverways. Steam engines and iron-hulled vessels soon entered oceanic transport as well, greatly increasing the volume of goods that could be carried and ultimately improving speeds. Needs for better land transport were met by the invention of the steam-powered railroad engine. Originally developed for commercial lines in Britain during the 1820s, the first intercity line was opened between Liverpool and Manchester in 1830. During the 1830s local lines spread in most Western countries, and plans were set for more ambitious, national networks, which were in turn completed by 1870. Finally, the invention of the telegraph proved a successful first response to new communication demands, allowing faster exchange of news and commercial information than ever before.

Technological Change and the Changing Face of Society

Well before 1870, most people in Western society had been directly touched by technological change. Only a minority directly worked on, or managed, the new machines, although this minority steadily expanded in size. But far more people experienced the excitement and fear of the railroads, with their awe-inspiring belches of steam and sparks. Far more recognized that a prospect of technological transformation awaited them in the future, even if it had not yet arrived. Thus the fears of artisans, even in unmechanized crafts, increasingly focused on the downgrading of skill and artistry that machines seemed to imply. Painters, novelists,

A new environment of coal and smoke: a view of Sheffield, England, in 1858.

and a host of ordinary folk worried about the ugliness, the "defilement" of natural beauty, generated by monster factories and their grimy, noise-battered operators.

For persistent technological change, rooted in the revolutionary implications of applying fossil-fuel power to a growing list of activities, increased the ability of technology to shape society. All societies are defined in part by technology; equipment always plays a major role in determining how people work, how many resources are available to individuals and to institutions such as the state. In this sense the determining role of technology during industrialization was not entirely novel. But industrialization after 1815 did more than set up a technological framework. By adding the principle of recurrent innovation, it brought this framework to the fore, made it a more active force in people's lives than ever before, in such a short span of time. And so the combination of new technology and persistent change was added to the list of fundamental factors—new mentalities, the rise of the nation-state, the development of a new capitalistic social structure resting on widespread proletarianization—that were reshaping Western society.

The Worker   In the 1830s a French textile manufacturer established the practice of decorating the week's most productive mechanical loom with a garland of flowers. It was a silly gesture in a way—one imagines that the flowers did not last long—but a gesture that revealed a new sense of priorities, in which equipment might seem more important than the humans who operated it. Recurrently, since the early 19th century, Westerners in various ways have wondered if they were running the machine, or if the machine were running them.

Certainly many early industrial workers wondered. The spread of factories involved increasing numbers of workers in carefully coordinated, fast-paced jobs. Owners and managers felt a conscious need to reshape traditional work habits to the demands of the machines. This meant forcing workers to show up on time—for a whole crew must be present for machines to run effectively. Hence systemized factory rules stipulated fines for tardiness; factory whistles warned workers that the gates were about to close. On the job, workers had to become accustomed to faster motions and a more unremitting pace. The ubiquitous shop rules stipulated that workers were not to sing, or chatter, or wander about—the traditional mixture of leisure and work had to give way to machine-driven intensity. And, during this early industrial period, the new discipline combined with long, twelve- to fourteen-hour days, as owners judged that they could not relax traditional work stints lest they fail to pay off their expensive equipment. Workers did not, to be sure, allow themselves to be totally trapped by machine-dominated standards. Factory workers frequently took unauthorized absences, or changed jobs, or simply refused to labor at the expected pace. These recourses, which revealed a desire to maintain some sense of traditional work rhythms and individual control, eased the factory environment, but clearly did not break the new grip of machines in any fundamental way. And although factory workers were most directly ensnared in machine-driven work, other producers—including the still-growing force of urban artisans—encountered related pressures to speed things up, particularly when they faced direct competition from machine-made products.

In the new industrial nations and on their fringes, agriculture faced active pressures to change its work systems to meet new market demand and also to provide tax funds for growing states. Industrialization obviously depended on increased food production. Some of this increase resulted from new technologies; some resulted from new pressures on coerced labor, such as the serfs of eastern Europe or slaves in the cotton-growing regions of the American South. Most generally, however, higher food production resulted from efforts to develop new commercial incentives for individual farmers and to speed up their work and that of the growing force of paid agricultural laborers. More food to sell meant more money to pay rising taxes and to buy new products, such as cotton clothes, available in rural markets. Less dramatic than factory transformations, the commercialization of agriculture and the rising pressures placed on rural, proletarian labor, both male and female, were an important part of nineteenth-century history.

Family Life and the Role of Women   In countryside and city alike, but particularly in the growing urban areas, the new technologies and work systems impinged on family life. Machine-driven work was located outside the home, for with rare exceptions the new equipment was too bulky, the new power sources too concentrated to permit household labor. Households continued to accomplish some production, but home work was increasingly hard-pressed or blatantly supplementary to the efforts of the main wage-earners or profit-makers. Here was a revolution-

182

FIVE
*The
Industrialization of
the West, 1815–
1870*

ary change in family life, as production was removed as a direct family function. Families were sometimes rejoined in machine labor, particularly in the earliest stages of industrialization. Children thus often worked with fathers and uncles, and in the textile factories mothers were sometimes employed. But the strangeness and intensity of machine work, combined with the real need to have some family members available for shopping, housework, and the like—plus the general belief that men's production responsibilities were greater than women's anyway—forced increasing division between work and family as well. Young children were not particularly useful in machine-driven work, and working families and humanitarian reformers increasingly urged that they be banned. Child labor laws, beginning in the 1830s in most industrial countries, gradually limited the use of children under twelve in the new settings. Women's work was also limited by some laws; for example, a British enactment in 1844 restricted women to ten-hour days in the factories. These measures, which limited the use of women in key manufacturing jobs, plus the more basic separation between work and home, altered family structures by giving men more pure work commitments, women more daily family control plus, in the working class, a host of low-paying jobs, such as laundry work, that could be done in the home. Men became more removed from domesticity than ever before, while women's production functions became more peripheral. This change, in turn, encouraged many Westerners to view the family as a haven from the dirty world of machine-driven work—a view that piled new expectations on the family as a source of comfort and as a deliberate retreat from the dominant forces of machine-made reality. This idealization affected the middle class most clearly, but it gradually spread to the better-paid workers as well. The impact of technology thus heightened previous trends to see home and family in sentimental, romantic terms.

The dilemmas industrialization posed for women were abundantly illustrated in the campaigns to limit women's hours of work. Middle-class men simply assumed that the place for proper women was in the home. Working-class men were also eager to monopolize skilled jobs in the factories, and they were truly concerned about the threat to what they viewed as a suitable sexual environment for "their" women. Therefore, they too supported special limits on women's work. Some working women agreed, if only because of the huge practical burdens in combining long working hours with domestic chores. But other women cited the equally practical difficulties of earning a living with shorter hours, and many resented the deterioration of their work skills that shorter hours allowed. Yet, barred from the leading, male-dominated protest groups such as nascent labor unions, they found little means of voicing their position. Thus at various social levels factories and industrial technology greatly furthered the linkage of women's lives with the domestic sphere.

The Machine-Driven Economy   Changing technology reshaped far more than private life. The nature of economic crises shifted, although unhappily the fact of economic crisis itself did not. Old-style economic crises involved a harvest failure that drove up food prices while reducing pur-

A slum in Staithes, Yorkshire, England, typical of working-class housing and
living conditions during industrialization.

chases of manufactured goods. The last such crisis in Western history
occurred in 1846–47. With improvements in agricultural output and particularly with speedy transportation that could import food into food-
short regions, the classic agricultural slump would never recur in the
Western world except as a direct consequence of war. But the machine-
driven economy had its own vulnerabilities. Steadily expanding production did not always find a ready market, for purchasing power was still
limited and miscalculations about output or investment levels endemic.
Rash investment, in equipment or other items that did not quickly pay
off, could trigger bank failures, which in turn would weaken demand for
industrial goods, undermine pay and employment levels, and create a
misery only slightly less great than that produced by agricultural failures.
Short industrial crises of the new type occurred in 1837 across the Western world, and again in 1856–57.

184

FIVE
The
Industrialization of
the West, 1815–
1870

In happier times, the new productive technology began to reshape consumer habits. Growing output required new kinds of commercial outlets. Formal stores spread to the countryside, as peasants and farmers purchased more of the goods they needed. In the cities the giant department store responded to the new need for mass consumption. Paris was the retail pioneer in the 1830s; its stores displayed wide varieties of goods and depended on high-volume sales for their success.

The Cities   New technologies altered city life in other ways. Factory work, plus continued rises in rural populations and improvements in the food supply, naturally fed the growth of cities. The peak rate of city growth in many Western countries occurred between 1820 and 1870; in 1850, half of Britain's population was urban, the first time this balance had occurred in any large society in human history. Growing cities brought hosts of hardships, as housing and sanitary facilities initially failed to keep pace. But new technology provided some restraints to the sharpest miseries. Wider use of machine-made clothing facilitated laundering and personal cleanliness. Bedding and eating utensils also improved; forks, for example, replaced communal utensils or fingers in the working classes for the first time around 1830. After the 1830s, more active urban governments joined public health reformers in the development of new sewer pipes and street paving to attack the worst urban sanitary problems. On another front, the spread of gas lighting, initially confined to wealthy sections of the cities, also reduced some traditional dangers in urban life. The cities produced by the first waves of industrial technology were not gardens of delight, but technology helped confront some pressures that might otherwise have overwhelmed the urbanization process. And for those with extra money, technology in the form of commuter rail lines also allowed escape from the most miserable sections of the cities in a new, class-segregated pattern of urban life. Quite simply, middle-class people and some skilled workers moved out of the city centers to the outskirts and suburbs, where they could mingle with their own kind. By 1850 the growth of suburbs began to approximate the growth of core cities.

The State and International Relations   Of course technological change stretched to encompass the aims and workings of the state itself. Governments could use rails and telegraphs, plus growing tax revenues fed by industrial expansion, to increase the presence of the nation-state. Trains could move troops rapidly, while the factory output of guns and uniforms created larger, better-armed forces than ever before. For example, the American Civil War (1861–1865) confronted a fierce-fighting but largely rural army of the South with the sheer numbers and firepower of an industrialized force from the North in what was, technologically, the first essentially modern war. European observers, led by the Germans, were quick to pick up some of the lessons, and the impact of changing technology on warfare, and by extension on diplomacy, grew steadily from the 1860s onward, first in Europe and then around the world.

Indeed, for some decades an unprecedented technological gap opened between the West—already supreme in armaments and ships—and the rest of the world, where industrialization had yet to penetrate. Steam-driven ships allowed Westerners to move on African river rapids where no people had been able to navigate before. The sheer growth of Western output virtually impelled Westerners to seek new controls over non-Western markets, and before 1870 there was no non-Western response in terms of efforts to match the technological surge. Technology, then, more than any other single factor, reshaped the West's position in the world—not forever, but for a crucial century.

An Ambivalent Response

Within the West itself, the impact of technological change—indeed, the growing recognition of this as a new factor shaping society—drew ambivalent response. Some people wished the machines would go away. Artists of the Romantic period responded to the new machine age with nostalgic pictures of a machine-free countryside—their way of saying that the world was turning sour. Small groups of workers attacked machines directly, first in Britain after 1810. These Luddite movements, named after a mythical leader invoked by the British "machine-breakers," expressed widespread fear among traditional producers, but they did not come close to succeeding and their movement soon lapsed. At the other extreme were entrepreneurs who touted machines as panaceas: Whatever was technologically feasible was progressive and hence good. A major exposition at London's Crystal Palace in 1851, held in a glass-and-iron dome itself a testament to the new technology, featured the latest in technological genius, and it drew millions of admiring visitors. Many world's fairs and local exhibits would follow in the same vein. Probably most Westerners found themselves caught in the middle—sincerely admiring technological results that seemed clearly beneficent but shocked by the pace, noise, and dirt of new technologies in other respects. However ambivalent the response, it seemed increasingly clear that technological change had picked up a momentum of its own, not only in industry but in military life and, soon, even in the world of leisure. Many people might have agreed with the French industrialist, anxious about keeping up with the latest new methods, who lamented, "Progress cannot be stopped, unfortunately, but its results are not always progressive." Indeed, many Westerners might echo a similar sentiment even in the later twentieth century, as technological change, for example in medicine, continues to excite and unsettle. This sense that technological change was inevitable and unpreventable was not the least of the effects of the early industrial period on the Western mentality.

Machines, Society, and Protest

The technological changes that sat at the core of the West's industrial revolution greatly heightened earlier trends in Western society toward commercialization and proletarianization. These two trends, more than technology itself, spurred a passionate outpouring of protest that was comparable to the risings two centuries before, when accepted social structures first came under systematic attack.

186

FIVE
The
Industrialization of
the West, 1815–
1870

The Pressures of Commercialization

Commercialization—that is, production for money and for sales on the market, with concomitant reliance on the market for other needed goods— had of course increased fairly steadily in Western history since the sixteenth century. The protoindustrialization of the eighteenth century had brought still larger numbers of people into market relationships. Yet in 1815 large pockets of people remained somewhat remote from the market mentality. They still thought in terms of dealing with people they knew, rather than with strangers; of valuing free time and community contacts more than maximum earnings; of taking pride in skills or the satisfaction of land ownership that could not be measured entirely in terms of earnings and losses. Industrialization and related developments after 1815 challenged these remnants of precommercial values, and the result was serious strain.

Industrial factories obviously depended on the idea of workers laboring for a money wage, owners and managers seeking to maximize their profits (or at least to seek reliable high profits). But industrialization also prompted a wider commercialization outside the factory gates. Peasants and farmers were pressed to produce more food for sale, and to use their earnings to buy manufactured products on the market. Small-town businessmen, often comfortable with modest earnings that gave them a secure, middling place in local society, now witnessed the rise of large industrial and commercial fortunes, which seemed to threaten their own stable social role. Some undoubtedly viewed this as a challenge, to figure out new ways to earn more; others saw such changes as a threat. Urban artisans were particularly hard-hit by the new levels of commercialization. Before 1870, few were displaced outright by new machines. Construction workers, jewelers, furniture makers, and the like did not yet face powered equipment that could do their work. But they did see artisan masters, concerned about their own social status, attempt even more fully to monopolize shop ownership for themselves and for their children. It became virtually impossible to rise from journeyman to master except through inheritance. Craft workers also saw growing pressures to produce more, to cut the attention they paid to training apprentices in the full range of traditional skills, to work faster and in larger groups.

Overall, then, new industrial technology, by greatly increasing the output of goods and by causing the wider dissemination of goods, brought new levels of market pressure—or market opportunity—to most occupational sectors. The result, even where considerable adaptation to earlier market levels had occurred, was anxious stress.

For example, the reactions of factory workers to the pace and pressure of their work clearly revealed preference for older economic values. Many workers continued to expect employers to provide not just a wage, but support in hard times in the form of commodities to tide over sickness and layoffs. And although many employers did offer more than a money wage, they tended to think less in terms of mutual support and more in terms of a tidy, predictable market arrangement in which a wage was the measurement of what a worker was worth and in which low pay resulted either from uncontrollable forces of supply and demand or the laziness of individual workers. Factory owners were supported in their view by most reigning economic theory, which, building on Adam Smith, held that any attempt to interfere with market forces—for example, by providing much charity—would be detrimental to the market. Workers and owners also disagreed about the importance of earning as much as possible. Many workers thought in terms of a controlled output of effort, and their big concern, if they could assure their subsistence, was to have enough leisure time. Hence highly paid workers often took extra days off rather than maximize their earnings as employers expected. Here was another simmering dispute between older values and new.

Peasants had their own troubles with commercialization. They continued to see ambitious neighbors trying to buy up additional lands, or to take over common lands, in the interest of market production. They were cajoled and tempted by shopkeepers peddling new industrial goods. They were also pressed to pay higher levels of taxes—in money, not handiwork or agricultural goods. Many governments raised their tax rates after 1815. With manorialism abolished in places such as France and parts of Germany, governments felt it was legitimate to raise direct taxes to the state. They also needed higher revenues in part to pay for state-sponsored industrial developments such as the building of railroads. But higher money taxes forced peasants to try to produce more for sale, and many peasants—with small holdings, with a desire to maintain tradition, and with considerable ignorance about the most advanced agricultural methods—simply could not respond.

The pressures of commercialization did not hit the lower classes alone. Many middle class people felt the pinch. The comfortable small-town middle class generated increasing laments about the unbridled wealth of factory and department-store owners. Even some factory owners resisted the implications of the market mentality. A couple content with a modest weaving setup in northern France, for example, held stability and the chance to keep a direct eye on all operations far more important than huge profits. When their son brought in big new machines from England to create a "monster" factory, with a managerial staff to direct various production phases, the parents refused to set foot in it, terming the enterprise "immoral." Still another middle-class group, the older professionals in law or medicine, regarded the rise of market habits and big-business fortunes with dismay. Their stock in trade had been close personal relations with "clients" or "patients"—not customers, thank you, lest their activities smack of money-grubbing shops. But now money-grubbing was king, and the older professionals had to work hard to adapt. Most sought an alternative to market competition by building strong professional

188

FIVE
*The
Industrialization of
the West, 1815–
1870*

associations that could regulate the licensing of members. The claim was that special knowledge—of law, of medical science—conferred special privilege, and that the numbers and credentials of practitioners should be controlled. This professionalization process was partly successful, but it left many professionals uncomfortable and some poor and disgruntled, still.

But after 1815 it was the artisan class that most loudly reacted to the new levels of commercialization in Western society. This group had a firm sense of traditional values and considerable cohesion, the key ingredients for coherent reaction. Many artisans harked back to guild values, particularly where the guilds were still in existence or of recent memory, such as in Germany. Artisans wanted protection from machines and from the competition of new immigrants to the cities, but they also sometimes envisaged a precommercial world, in which work was satisfying in and of itself, in which group values predominated over individual interest. Many artisans, including some who were uncomfortable with commercialization, made personal adjustments to the commercial world, obtaining better education, seeking to branch out into shopkeeping, or even entering factories as privileged, highly-paid operators. But the clash between artisanal and commercial values rang through the Western world through the middle decades of the nineteenth century.

Proletarianization and Growing Poverty

As before, proletarianization was closely linked to commercialization, and without question technology heightened the division between those with and those without producing property. By 1850 Western society was roughly evenly divided between families that had property (or reasonable expectation of it when older) and families that had nothing except a few tools and rather more consumer items. And the trends suggested that proletarianization would increase still further in future. The rural world, increasingly commercialized, gave advantage to those with reasonably sized plots that could produce more than a family needed and that could employ some landless laborers. Peasants with substantial property and owners of larger estates alike continually pressed marginal owners to sell out entirely. Continued population growth, based on the surge of the second half of the eighteenth century and despite a reduction in the per-capita birth rate, added to pressures on the land. Furthermore, propertied people were now markedly more successful than most propertyless in restraining their birth rates. Poor workers usually had more children than shop owners or factory managers—a reverse of the traditional ratio, in which the poor had been more cautious in demographic behavior than the wealthier groups. (However, the very rich still often had large families.) Propertyless people, lacking access to inheritance, had less reason for restraint than most people had had in the traditional Western world. They could also sometimes benefit, or hope to benefit, by child labor. And they used sexual activity as an outlet for pleasure in ways that "respectable" owners, more conscious of their need to protect property by limiting family size, were reluctant to admit. So the proletarian practice of having large families served to increase the size of the proletariat in relation to that of the middle class.

Machines also played a new role in increased proletarianization. Production from the new factories progressively cut down flourishing rural manufacturing industries, forcing spinners and weavers to abandon their looms and often their cottages—their only property, in other words—and become outright proletarians. Here was the most dreadful direct impact of industrialization, a condition made more hopeless still because it was often ignored. Rural poverty remained hidden from view and might be clothed in nostalgic assumptions about the superior joys of life in the countryside. Gradually, machine competition would squeeze some categories of urban craftsmen as well, adding to the commercialization pressures that converted many journeymen into permanent wage earners, or proletarians.

The increased pace of proletarianization during the industrial revolution was conjoined to the growing urbanization of the same proletariat. A substantial group of propertyless agricultural workers remained behind in the rural areas; but with better agricultural methods and improved transport of food, plus the decline of domestic manufacturing, the rural resources for the proletariat were now limited. So the proletariat not only grew but increasingly moved to the cities, becoming more visible—and more menacing—in the process. Not only the new factory-working class, propertyless all, but also the new army of female domestic servants working in middle-class homes made the urban population proletarian in its majority. Not all these proletarians, particularly in the cities, were desperately poor, however. A minority of servants and a larger percentage of factory workers could earn wages above subsistence. But the rise of the urban proletariat was confusing in a society that still associated worth with ownership. Not only middle-class people, who often fled the proletariat toward the suburbs, but also artisans and workers who feared or resented proletarian status, viewed the heightening of this long-standing social trend with intense dismay.

Indeed, proletarianization was heightened not only by the growth of the propertyless classes, but also by the growing self-consciousness of the property-owning, urban middle classes. Opportunities to exercise a profession, on the basis of advanced education, or to open a business—a factory, a small shop—proliferated during the early industrial decades. Middle-class status did not exempt a family from serious worries, including anxieties about many trends in modern society. But on the whole, growing wealth and numbers helped feed a rising confidence. Middle-class people believed that they had earned their station in life, unlike older social elements that had relied on privilege at birth. They believed that their values of hard work, rationality, and sexual restraint made for a worthy life. Middle-class people might themselves find reason to protest, particularly when they wanted to win political rights to match their new economic position. But they tended to see a big gulf between themselves and the irresponsible, dangerous proletariat. Their public efforts to criticize and moralize workers only sharpened the grievances of proletarians.

190

FIVE
*The
Industrialization of
the West, 1815–
1870*

New machines and work patterns, new commercialization, the rising tide of the proletariat, the ascending of the middle class—here were ingredients aplenty for a new wave of popular protest. There were other ingredients as well after 1815. The French Revolution had spawned more political aspirations than it had met. Many business people wanted a new voice in government and new policies that would favor industry and some individual freedoms. Many groups sought governments that would express nationalist sentiments—particularly in Italy and Germany, where national unity did not exist, but also in places such as France, where the Revolution had spurred a belief that governments should be both glorious and responsible to the nation's people. In other words, an array of political demands helped promote discontent even aside from the basic social grievances. New ideologies and well-led political movements worked for liberal goals—constitutions, protection of rights—or democratic or nationalist goals. Furthermore, most European governments after 1815 reacted to the ending of the French revolutionary era with a new, repressive conservatism, which involved the use of troops to break up demonstrations, police spies to ferret out agitators, and firm laws against freedoms of the press or assembly. This new repression eventually heightened the tide of protest, but it could hamper effective protest organization as well.

The key protest groups after 1815 came from various sources. Rural protest was greatest where middling peasants felt trapped by growing commercialization and continued pressure from landlords, which included in some cases remnants of manorial obligations including labor service. Agricultural laborers rose in a few instances, as in England in the 1830s, when they attacked new harvesting equipment and low pay. Middle-class elements also played a role in protests; students were often active in espousing one or more of the new ideologies. They also expressed disdain for repressive governments and concern about the new directions of the economy. Factory workers joined protests on some occasions, though their newness to the city, their confusion, and in certain cases their contentment with wages reduced their impact. Artisans formed the most consistent protest group, relying on strong grievances, some exposure to new political demands, and solid organizational tradition. For the most part the leading protesters at this point were male; women's confinement to home work and domesticity kept them farther away from the mainstream of protest than had been true in previous centuries. But along with some support for labor unrest, a small current of feminist protest began to emanate from middle-class women who were impatient with domestic confinement and inequality of rights; and this helped feed the protest surge as well.

The protests took many forms. In Britain factory workers and artisans alike organized periodic trade union movements, sometimes hoping to take over the whole of industry and organize it on a basis of producer cooperatives rather than profit-seeking management. Unions were illegal, and the more sweeping movements ultimately failed. But strong local organizations, backed by strikes, could sometimes win improved wages and other conditions. British artisans and rural and urban workers also backed the massive Chartist movement in the 1830s and 1840s, which periodically used huge petition drives and some outright riots to seek a voice in government, support for better education, and some restraint on technological and commercial change. The last Chartist protest crested in 1848, briefly creating a seemingly revolutionary atmosphere though ultimately producing no major change.

Strikes and riots became endemic in countries other than Britain as early industrialization took hold. Although the phenomenon was not new, bread riots punctuated European history between 1815 and 1848, as any bad harvest triggered price increases that brought immense hardship and also complaints about the "gouging" practices of merchants. Tax collectors were another popular target, as were groups of new workers, or workers from a different region or nationality, on whom job insecurities could be vented. New immigration to the United States brought important clashes among different groups of Irish workers and between the Irish and the native born, spawned in part because of the reshuffling of economic and social structures. And there was a steady increase in strike activity in most cases as well. Huge strikes in the silk industry of Lyons, France, in 1831 and 1833 sought a minimum wage for the whole area, as artisans sought to combat growing commercialization by a return to the protective devices of the guild tradition.

At another level, crime rates increased in most Western societies during early industrialization, in the countryside as well as the city. Particular crimes were a response to particular hardships, of course, especially during periods of bad harvest; they also followed from the weakening of community structures as many young people migrated to new regions and to the cities. But the general rise in crime undoubtedly reflected broader social concerns as well, and it served as part of the drumbeat of unrest in this tense period of Western history.

Protest during the early industrial period, especially that which involved direct action and violence, mixed the reactions of misery and desperation with a firm belief that a proper economy and society should be organized according to values that the new forces of commerce and industry were violating. The risings from 1815 to 1850, in fact, constituted the last great outbreak of protest specifically in the name of an older moral economy, in which group welfare was held to be above independent profit making and the new direction of work by formal management. At the same time, popular protest brought up new issues as well, as protesters sought new political rights—the Lyons silk workers, for example, wanted a democratic republic to replace the monarchy—and new goals such as widespread education. Popular protest also used traditional values not simply to seek restoration of old production forms, but also to blast the grasping, money-hungry motives of the rising business elite; and these criticisms often survived into later protest periods, even as the full range of traditional values faded somewhat.

192

FIVE
*The
Industrialization of
the West, 1815–
1870*

THE REVOLUTIONS OF 1848

The February 1848 revolution in France culminated a long campaign against the narrow, corrupt monarchy that had taken power in 1830. In that year King Louis Philippe had accepted a slightly larger electorate and had briefly granted other liberal reforms, including some limits on the power of the Catholic church. But he increasingly manipulated parliament and attacked all signs of popular unrest. A new liberal movement took shape in the 1840s, seeking to extend the vote and, possibly, to install a republic.

The actual revolution was made by discontented artisans, in Paris and elsewhere, who forced the king to flee. A new republic was set up that would last until 1851. But it turned increasingly conservative, attacking artisanal organizations and other radicals, and finally yielded to a new empire established by the great Napoleon's nephew, Louis Napoleon, who soon styled himself Napoleon III.

As news of the February rising spread, artisans and students spurred revolts in Vienna and Berlin. Here the old regimes were not toppled, but they did retreat. Revolutionaries met to draw up new constitutions for Austria; and in Germany a congress of nationalists met to seek German unity. Risings in other Habsburg territories, particularly Hungary, complicated the picture, as Austrian nationalists hesitated between defending the empire and attacking the emperor. Both the Habsburg and the German risings were also complicated by divisions between middle-class liberals and artisans who were hostile to modern business forms. With these divisions preventing unity, monarchs were able gradually to beat down the revolutionary sectors one by one, while also winning peasant support through the abolition of manorialism.

Revolution in Italy featured nationalist attacks on the Austrian-ruled provinces in the north, but also more popular risings, including a republican surge in Rome against papal control. It took bitter fighting by troops from the Habsburg monarchy and, in Rome, from newly conservative France to put this revolt down.

In general, the revolutions of 1848, although more sweeping than the rising of 1789 in France, had far less direct effect, and they were put down far more easily. There were several reasons for the different outcome. The new, complicating factor was nationalism,

Revolutionary Attempts and Failures   Popular protest in the form of strikes and riots played a vital role in the revolutionary waves that swept over many parts of western Europe after 1815. Important revolts occurred in Spain and southern Italy in 1820, and soon after a nationalist rising began in Greece against control by the Ottoman Empire. The revolutionary movement in western Europe resumed more specifically in 1830. Prefaced by bad harvests and an increasingly clumsy monarchy, artisans, spurred by middle-class liberals, took to the streets in Paris in

LE SALUT PUBLIC.

Periodicals such as the French poet Baudelaire's *Le Salut Public* encouraged popular protest during the Paris rising of 1848. In this vignette for that paper by the French artist Gustav Courbet, heroic workers are depicted as armed with bayonets and on the barricades. The banner reads, "Voice of God, Voice of the people."

which often divided revolutionaries from different ethnic groups or distracted them from other purposes, such as protesting for individual rights or controlling the executive branch by a strong parliament. Additionally, many of the governments that were attacked, such as that of Prussia, were far less debilitated than the Old Regime monarchy of France had been. The overarching fact that diluted the effectiveness of these revolutions was that middle-class political leaders, who tended quickly to take charge in the name of liberal and nationalist goals, grew much more quickly afraid of the force of popular protest, which now seemed so menacing and so hostile to the kind of business economy that the leaders themselves espoused.

July, hoping for sweeping reforms; in fact they won only a different royal house and a slightly more liberal regime. The current of revolt in 1830 spread to Belgium and also several states in Germany and Italy; in all these cases nationalist demands mixed with popular and liberal themes. Only in Belgium, however, where a separate nation formed free from Dutch control, was there any concrete result.

The most sweeping set of revolutions occurred in 1848, again triggered by a revolt in Paris. The French monarchy was toppled for good,

194

FIVE
*The
Industrialization of
the West, 1815–
1870*

pressed by liberal politicians and artisan street fighters. Revolution spread to Berlin and other parts of Germany, to Italy, and to Vienna and Budapest. Goals of the revolutionaries varied, but in each case the core revolt followed from intense popular reactions both to the specific problem of a new food crisis—harvests had failed tragically in 1846 and 1847—and the larger issues of a commercial economy that seemed, in popular eyes, to be out of control.

The revolutionary quality of much popular unrest was not, of course, uniform throughout Western society. England, though faced with the final Chartist surge in 1848, avoided outright revolution. Earlier political reforms, which had granted the vote to most business and professional people, and a wider belief that the political system offered some flexibility helped fend off revolution, despite widespread popular grievance. The United States was even less troubled. Here, even more clearly, a flexible political system, reformed during the presidency of Andrew Jackson in the 1830s by extensions of the vote and establishment of a secret ballot, made revolution irrelevant. Levels of popular unrest were also somewhat limited, despite widespread rioting on occasion. Many American workers enjoyed relatively good wages. They felt they were part of the social order, not pitted against a hostile owning class; thus many grievances were handled by negotiation. Growing tensions over the issue of slavery also helped distract from other unrest. Social peace in the United States was neither complete nor permanent, but the nation did stand somewhat apart from European currents of protest until later in the nineteenth century.

In Europe, the failure of most popular uprisings was as important as the surge of protest itself. The sweeping demands of artisans in the name of an older moral economy were largely ignored. More modest strikes, for improvements in wages, might succeed, and some artisans learned from this that a moderate set of goals was more appropriate. Peasants had somewhat greater success. Peasant risings against remaining manorial obligations played an important role in the revolutions of 1848 in the Habsburg lands, and in parts of Italy and Germany. And the peasants won; central governments, eager to separate peasants from the body of revolutionaries and aware that manorialism had seen its day, ended the system fully. This was an important change that many peasants applauded. The result, ironically, was to subject peasants more fully than before to the rigors of the commercial economy through rising direct taxes; in many areas, such as Hungary and southern Italy, the hold of large landowners remained as strong as ever. Yet, with the important exception of the end to manorialism popular grievances were largely unheeded—as they had been two centuries before, in a comparable wave of unrest. Parisian artisans in 1848 briefly won a set of government-sponsored workshops designed to relieve unemployment and, some hoped, to usher in a new organization to the manufacturing economy. But as soon as conservative forces recovered from the revolutionary onset, they attacked the workshops and their craft defenders during what is called the bloody June Days—and the workshops disappeared. Similarly, artisan meetings in Germany and in Vienna were attacked by a combination of established armies and frightened middle-class liberals, with the result that serious social reform was stillborn.

The failure of the revolutions of 1848 terminated a major phase in the reactions to industrialization. Indeed, with rare though important exceptions in the aftermath of wars, the phenomenon of revolution itself ended in the West with 1848. Attacked by renewed police repression, subdued by failure, many workers turned to other methods and sometimes to more modest goals. In Britain, for example, a cautious artisan union movement arose in the wake of Chartist defeat, careful to stick to nonpolitical goals and to use respectable methods, careful also to separate the interests of skilled workers, who had solid bargaining power, from the mass of the proletariat. Similar craft unionism arose on the continent and in the United States. Another telling factor against popular revolution was the end of recurrent famines. Crop failures might still occur, but after 1847 railroad and shipping facilities prevented famines or even catastrophic price increases of the sort that had triggered the most sweeping popular movements in the West since the later Middle Ages. Finally, in a larger sense, the traditional goals that could be held up against commercialization and technological change began to seem increasingly remote. Guilds and villages were by now so fully transformed, in some cases obliterated, that protest in the name of their values, however idealized, no longer made much sense.

This did not mean that popular protest was over for good. New protest goals were gradually constructed, involving less direct appeal to the past and more effort at winning new rights in the name of progressive justice. Even older grievances continued to simmer, sometimes poorly articulated, sometimes cropping up in a host of superficially novel movements such as socialism or fascism. Although the protest current would begin again, particularly after 1870, the failure of the surge through 1848 left the forces embodied in industrialization essentially triumphant. A long era of recurrent popular struggle against the principles of a market economy, proletarianization, and now rapidly changing technology had ended.

Politics during the Industrial Revolution: The Extension of the Nation-State

The tensions of the industrial revolution put great strain on existing state forms, but in the long run they served to strengthen the nation-state. During the decades after 1815, the key issues revolved around the constitutional structure of the state—in almost all cases still, the monarchy. Here was where the political currents engendered by Enlightenment ideas and the French Revolution of 1789—the new array of political -isms—clashed most obviously. Internal debate, among other things, drew attention away from lively diplomacy until after 1850. But a number of governments also became aware of new social and economic issues—what to do to respond to England's industrial example, for instance, or how to handle new forms or levels of popular unrest. These issues, less dramatic than constitutional crises, nevertheless also forged political change.

Furthermore, the prior growth of the nation-state, including its redefinition in the French Revolution, plus industrialization helped create new political beliefs. Political commitments of all kinds began to enter popular mentalities. More people than before judged that they needed and deserved a voice in political affairs and that they should have a political ideology that would shape the state to their own interest; here was a key source of conflicting political doctrines that ranged from conservatism to socialism. Even women's reform movements tended to turn toward the state to demand new laws or political rights that would correct injustices in the family or at work. Many grievances created by industrialization took political forms. Furthermore, industrialization, by weakening ties to traditional communities and older loyalties such as religion, opened many people to an emotional need to participate in new, often intense beliefs; this falling-away of local loyalties was most clearly one source of nationalism, which served special interests—for example, middle-class desires for promotion of national industry—but which also roused passions. Emotional as well as rational satisfaction could be found in liberal or socialist beliefs as well.

The Flourishing of Political Debate

The rise of new political loyalties focused attention on the form of government but also affected the definition of the functions of the nation-state. Clashes over government form emerged quickly after 1815; indeed, they extended debates that had already surfaced during the French revolutionary period. Exponents of *conservatism* argued that changes in political and social structure were generally to be avoided. In theory, said leaders such as Austria's Prince Metternich, change might occur, but it must be evolutionary, not abrupt or planned, and it should be in close, organic linkage with past forms. In practice conservatives urged careful government supervision of all political activities, including newspapers and university teaching; close alliance between the state and the established church, in the interest of promoting religious values; and firm support for the monarchy. For about ten years after 1815, this conservative mood dominated policies in most European countries, including Britain. It was most intense in the Habsburg lands and leading German states.

Against the conservative view were arrayed liberalism, radicalism, and nationalism. Liberals sought substantial civil rights, including religious freedom. They wanted a constitution and a meaningful parliament to modify monarchical power. Many liberals were interested in governmental promotion of education, for liberals believed deeply that people were rational and that change and progress occurred most logically through greater knowledge. Early nineteenth-century liberals tended to attack government intervention in the economy, arguing, *laissez-faire* fashion, that individual interest was a better guide to economic progress than state action. But many liberals saw pragmatic reasons for some government effort—building railroads, or using protective tariffs to encourage

196

FIVE
*The
Industrialization of
the West, 1815–
1870*

DIPLOMACY AFTER 1815

Exhausted by a quarter-century of war, the European great powers initially sought to use diplomacy to counter internal unrest. Thus they held conferences several times into the early 1820s to authorize intervention against rebellions in Italy and Spain. As Britain and France became more liberal, these collective efforts faltered, though such conferences helped recognize Greek and later Belgian independence. A hint of French–British rivalry resumed after 1830, but there were no major incidents. Britain, still expanding its colonial empire, also took a lead in trying to restrain Russian appetites in the Middle East, helping to settle several conflicts between Russia and the Ottoman Empire; both Britain and France preferred a weak Ottoman Empire to a strong Russian hand in this region. After the 1848 revolutions France, under Napoleon III, cast about for a more glorious foreign policy. This brought French interest in opposing a new Russian move in the Middle East. France and Britain allied to oppose a Russian advance in the Black Sea region, in 1854, ultimately winning this distant conflict, called the Crimean War. France also allied with Italy in 1858 against Austria, and the French helped set up a short-lived European regime in Mexico in the 1860s, when the United States was distracted by the Civil War. But it was only the unification efforts of Italy and Germany (see page 200) from 1858 to 1871 that brought more active diplomatic concerns back to center stage in Western history.

native industry; so this was not an area of unwavering principle. Radicals differed from liberals mainly by seeking wider political rights. Liberals typically wanted the vote restricted to men with substantial property, on the grounds that such people alone had a sufficiently mature stake in society to vote responsibly. Radicals, on the other hand, wanted wider popular representation, and some urged outright democracy. Radicals also had some interest in governmental measures to aid the poor. Nationalists, finally, urged attention to links between government and a wider nationalist purpose. They were particularly active in Germany and Italy, where simply obtaining national unity remained an issue, and in Habsburg lands, where many different nationalities competed. Most nationalists were also liberals or radicals, hoping that a proud national state would also modify the increasingly rigid structures of old-regime monarchies.

Underlying the clashes among these various views, of course, were the wider social changes of the early industrial decades. The leading political actors were aristocrats and middle-class professionals and businessmen. They did not represent the masses, and except for the radicals they did not, for the most part, directly appeal to them. Before 1848 even nationalists had a largely middle-class constituency. But the political debate drew strength from the changing social balance. Liberals and nationalists were arguing for changes that would, in essence, give the middle class a greater political role (national unity was an appealing goal for business because it implied wider markets) to correspond to its growth and economic gains. And both liberals and nationalists were able to use still more widespread grievances on occasion. Thus French liberals, concerned about press freedoms and the like, could call out artisans, some of whom shared liberal goals but who had a wider agenda, in the 1830 revolution; some of the same cooperation occurred in the earliest phases of the 1848 risings.

198

FIVE
The
Industrialization of
the West, 1815–
1870

Governments' Responses to Political Debate

The initially conservative reactions of the established European governments after 1815 quickly began to change to two types of response. The countries in which absolute monarchy had been most firmly and successfully entrenched conceded little before 1848, whereas countries with a stronger parliamentary tradition (now including France, whose parliamentary tradition had been revived and updated through the experience of the Revolution) began to seek new kinds of compromise.

Not suprisingly, the leading early compromiser was Great Britain. Already a parliamentary monarchy with a growing urban middle class, Britain also faced renewed lower-class pressure for political rights during the later 1820s. In response, while avoiding democracy, Britain moved toward a liberal redefinition of the older parliamentary forms. In 1832 Parliament passed the Great Reform Bill, which gave the vote to most property-owning people, thus achieving the liberal goals of the day and moving Parliament further from its medieval base as the representative of privileged groups alone. During the 1830s the reformed Parliament proceeded to pass tariff legislation favoring middle-class interests; tariffs on grains were repealed, thus facilitating food imports and easing pressures on the wages owners paid to workers. Religious liberty was extended to Catholics and Jews. City governments received new powers, and middle-class groups increasingly took over control of urban centers, using local governments to improve physical facilities. The British government, in sum, became more relevant to the needs of a changing society.

Increasingly liberal regimes spread also to Scandinavia, to some of the regional governments in western Germany, and to the Low Countries, including Belgium after the 1830 revolution. Powers of parliament were increased and governments became more sensitive to the interests of the business community. Unlike Britain, which proceeded through reform of tradition rather than through the drafting of a new constitution, most of the liberalized continental states issued formal documents that specified the powers of parliament and monarch and assured rights, including religious freedom, to individual citizens. For a time after the revolution of 1830, France also moved toward the liberal camp, in extending its parliament's power, limiting the educational monopoly and political privileges of the Catholic church, and extending the vote to a slightly larger group of the wealthiest property owners and professionals.

In contrast, the Habsburg monarchy, Prussia, and most of the Italian states remained unyielding in their rejection of reform. The Spanish monarchy underwent some periods of liberal ministries, but there was no durable change in Spain's political structure. The Prussian government in the 1840s did revive a medieval kind of parliament, or Diet, and introduced a few other reforms to please the business groups. But for the most part the atmosphere of repression persisted. The Habsburgs especially claimed a particular role in putting down unrest, not only in their own domains but in other parts of Europe (such as Spain in the 1820s), lest radical contagion spread.

The revolutions of 1848 obviously expressed the pent-up discontents that had built in those parts of Europe where compromise with liberalism remained incomplete (as in France) or had yet to be attempted. Important agitation spread to Scandinavia, furthering political change but without outright revolution: the power of parliament in Denmark, in particular, was formally increased. A similar development occurred in Holland, where the parliamentary upper house, previously appointed by the king, was turned over to representatives of provincial governments and the national ministry was made responsible to parliament rather than the monarchy.

But the revolutions' failure seemed to leave conservatism triumphant in the core areas of central Europe. And although France briefly established a democratic republic, the creation of a new imperial government in 1851 actually turned the tide against liberal and radical politics for a full decade. The regime of Napoleon III featured an active political police, a purely rubber-stamp parliament, and new concessions to the Catholic church. The church itself turned more fully against political change as a result of the revolutions, which had seen the pope chased from Rome for a time by republican forces. The church busily shored up monarchical regimes in Austria and Spain, and it bitterly fought nationalist currents in Italy itself. In 1867 the pope, selected before 1848 as a possible compromiser, issued the Syllabus of Errors, which condemned liberal political goals, including the idea that individuals should have freedom of conscience, root and branch.

Although it was unquestionably a major defeat for liberalism, the failure of 1848 was not complete. Liberal leaders in Germany and Italy learned that outright revolution did not work, but they did not abandon their cause and, in working for more piecemeal change, began to gain new influence. A new breed of conservatives came to power in several countries bent on salvaging the essentials of the old order, including a strong monarchy and a state capable of withstanding popular unrest, but through compromise with selected aspects of liberalism rather than down-the-line resistance. Thus in the Habsburg monarchy a new rationalizing spirit took hold, bent on reducing the local governing powers of aristocrats in favor of a new-style, efficient (and largely German) bureaucracy. Thus the small state of Piedmont, in northwestern Italy, granted some new power to parliament and began to sponsor railroads and other measures pleasing to business, in the interest of showing that monarchy need not be tied to an unchanging status quo. Thus too Prussia in 1850 issued a new constitution granting some liberties to all citizens and setting up a parliament whose lower house was elected by universal suffrage but with men divided according to wealth so that the richest 15 percent of the population controlled two-thirds of the seats. This was a modest gesture in some ways, though it would survive in Prussia until 1918. But it did allow election of a growing number of liberal politicians capable of pressing the government on matters of taxation and military spending. The results of 1848, in sum, furthered the kinds of compromise with new politics that had occurred earlier in nations with a richer parliamentary tradition.

200

FIVE
*The
Industrialization of
the West, 1815–
1870*

Nationalism and Political Compromise

The key political force with which conservative leaders now came to terms was not liberalism but nationalism, and in adopting nationalism the monarchies won widespread acceptance of the continued limitations on liberalism in government structure. Nationalism obviously fed the interest in developing strong nation-states, which had begun in the seventeenth century. It supported further state development in established nations such as France, but above all it helped motivate areas with cohesive cultures but divided political units to join the camp of other unified nation-states.

Italy was the first to do so. The Piedmontese state, led by its able prime minister, Count Camillo di Cavour, began to espouse the case of national unity. By a series of diplomatic maneuvers Piedmont won a French alliance against Austria and in an 1858–1859 war drove Austria from the province of Lombardy, which was yielded to Piedmont. Nationalist risings then occurred in central Italy, and a small force of nationalists under the flamboyant revolutionary Garibaldi attacked the southern kingdom of Naples. These areas too were joined to the Piedmontese—now Italian—monarchy. The resultant new regime had a parliament based on very limited suffrage, with the monarchy rather than parliament in ultimate control of the ministers. Personal freedoms were extended and the power of the Catholic church curtailed, but the government continued periodically to censor the press and attack dissident political groups including socialists.

Inspired in part by the Italian example, flexible conservative leaders in Prussia, headed by Otto von Bismarck, began to undertake a similar sponsorship of nationalism. The goal was to unite Germany under Prussia and to use successful nationalism to defuse the most intense liberal and radical pressure. During the 1860s the goal was achieved. In a series of carefully calculated wars—with Denmark over German-speaking provinces, with Austria over the issues of a Prussian-dominated union of north German states, and then with France, which had so long opposed a united Germany to its east—the Prussians combined alliances with outright conquest in creating a single nation that embraced most German speakers outside of Austria and Bohemia. The provinces of Alsace and Lorraine were seized from France in the treaty of 1871 as part of this process. Prussian victories followed from Bismarck's careful diplomatic planning, which kept Russia and Britain friendly, and from the strong, well-disciplined Prussian army, which had recently become adept at using technologies such as the railroad in moving troops rapidly.

The structure of the new German empire involved another of those compromises fully pleasing to neither conservatives nor liberals but acceptable to elements of both camps. A national parliament was created, based on outright universal suffrage for men. But its upper house was composed of delegates chosen by state governments; because Prussia was the largest state and its parliament was skewed to favor the wealthy voters, conservative dominance of this body was assured. Furthermore, appointment of ministers lay in the hands of the emperor (formerly the king of Prussia). And although religious freedom was extended to Jews and increased freedom of the press and other liberties were granted, the government periodically intervened against dissident groups.

The Habsburg monarchy developed its own brand of compromise politics. With a host of nationalities living within its borders, the government was far less able to use nationalism to solidify its rule. Efforts at Germanization in the 1850s, as the central government sent German-speaking bureaucrats to all corners to replace decentralized manorial rule, had roused new discontents among Hungarian and Slavic leaders. Then the startling loss of the Seven Weeks' War with Prussia in 1866 forced a new approach: to conciliate Hungarians as well as ethnic Germans. A settlement in 1867, called the *Ausgleich*, granted substantial autonomy to Hungary, which set up a limited parliament and enforced the dominance of ethnic Hungarians (Magyars) over the large Slavic minorities. In Austria a slightly more active parliament was created that allowed extensive liberal voice, and religious liberties were extended to Jews. The result again ignored Slavic aspirations but pleased most German-speaking liberals.

By 1870 a politics of compromise had produced striking changes in the political structure of western Europe. Parliaments existed everywhere, with real powers though in some cases lacking ultimate sovereignty. Even democracy was moving forward, although less uniformly. A new reform in Britain, under conservative auspices, extended the vote to most male urban workers in 1867. Liberals and conservatives in most countries had found a political system that both could accept—although minorities in each camp held out for greater purity. Debates over constitutional structure were by no means over in the West, and in France a process of settlement still awaited the 1870s after Napoleon III's empire collapsed under the force of German arms. But the debates were now less shrill, as some middle ground had been discovered and as key political groups moved away from the battles of principle common before 1848 to a more pragmatic stance. The powerful force of nationalist loyalty helped cement the new arrangements. Once linked to liberalism but now more widely shared, nationalism could be used to appeal for loyalty to the state to woo conservatives who would rather not have had anything to do with parliamentary politics, or to sway liberals who might otherwise have sought firmer protections for civil rights or parliamentary sovereignty. Although the role of nationalism in sealing approval for the new

202

FIVE
*The
Industrialization of
the West, 1815–
1870*

THE UNIFICATIONS OF ITALY AND GERMANY

The essence of Italian unification involved a pragmatic coalition between nationalist leaders, who had learned they could not win by revolution or radicalism alone, and the expansionist leaders of Piedmont. The sponsorship by Count Camillo di Cavour, Piedmont's prime minister, of industrialization and liberal reform in the 1850s aided the combination; so did clever diplomacy. Cavour joined in the congress called in 1856 to settle the Crimean War, raising the issue of Austria's occupation of northern Italy. He then played on Napoleon III's dreams of an active, revolutionary diplomacy to win French help in 1858; this move, combined with carefully staged revolts, finally created a unified Italian state. Austria continued to hold the province of Venetia, but Italian alliance with Prussia in 1866 ended this anomaly. The final gap was closed in 1870, while France was distracted by Prussia. Italian troops took over the papal city of Rome and made it the nation's capital.

Otto von Bismarck, who became Prussia's chief minister in 1862, had more to work with than did Cavour, given Prussia's strong

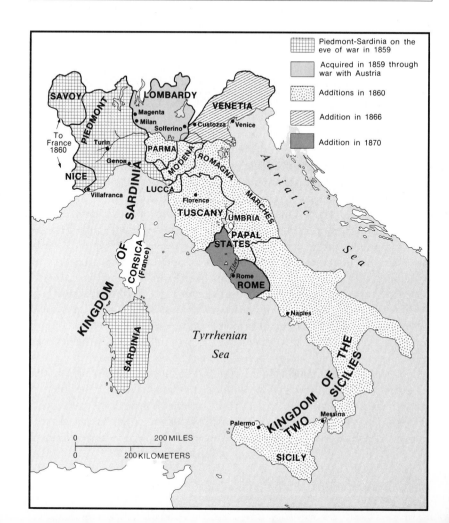

military tradition; but he also had more obvious potential opponents, given the region's central location. Bismarck was probably less interested in nationalism per se than Cavour was, but eager to expand Prussia and to play off diplomatic success against internal political unrest. Carefully conciliating Russia by assisting against a Polish rising in 1863, Bismarck used a minor dispute with Denmark over the provinces of Schleswig–Holstein to mount a "German" war, which had the added advantage of being easy to win. He then picked a fight over these same provinces with Austria, again making sure that Russia and France would stand aside. Against every expectation of a difficult struggle as in the eighteenth-century Prussian–Habsburg wars, Prussia won in an easy seven weeks. Bismarck took nothing from Austria, preventing lasting enmity, but used victory to organize a Prussian-dominated north German state. The final independent south German states, including powerful Bavaria, were brought into the fold after Bismarck cleverly picked a war with France by making it seem that Napoleon III had threatened Prussian honor. Prussian troops easily moved through France, though a long seige was needed to subdue Paris. The peace took France's eastern provinces and a large indemnity, and the new German empire was proclaimed in January, 1871, in the palace of Versailles.

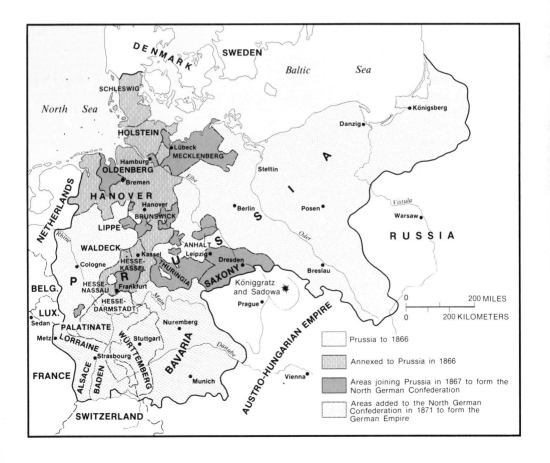

204

FIVE
The
Industrialization of
the West, 1815–
1870

political structure was most obvious in Germany, it operated in Britain and France as well. Almost everywhere in western and central Europe during the 1860s, a system had been constructed that gave moderate liberal and conservative political parties legal room to maneuver, to compete for votes, and to vent opinions in the public press.

The United States had been largely exempt from the kinds of political debate that so dominated western Europe between 1815 and 1870. The structure of the new nation was already liberal, with a mixture of federal and state governments, division of powers among the three branches of government, and fundamental power resting in the electorate. After some debate early in the nineteenth century, both major political parties accepted the constitutional structure. In the 1820s voting rights were extended for white males in many states. The result was that American politics was typically dominated by consensus—far more even than in Great Britain—with all major political groups operating from a central liberal core. Nineteenth-century American politics often roused great passion, and splinter movements sometimes raised divisive issues such as fear of immigrants, but basic political values were far more widely shared than in western Europe. The United States faced its own political crisis, however, in the growing dispute about slavery and the relationships of state governments—particularly Southern state governments—to the federal Union. Growing efforts to undermine Southern slavery led to secession of the Confederacy from the Union in 1861. Essentially in the name of nationalism, the federal government resisted and, after four years of bitter warfare, prevailed in holding the Union together and in abolishing slavery outright. The result, in the 1870s, was an American version of political compromise, in which national unity and legal equality for all were recognized but state governments were allowed to impose new kinds of racial discrimination in fact. On this basis the process of consensus politics in the United States would resume.

In various ways, then, most Western nations had grappled with the problem of devising a political system less rigid than in the past, in which diverse political views could be expressed without overwhelming governmental stability. After bitter battles ranging from revolution to civil war, successful compromises were struck. Although there were still important distinctions between those nations where liberal institutions triumphed and those, such as Germany, where essential power still rested with kings and their largely aristocratic advisors, one result was that Western nations became more similar in political structure than at any time since the rise of absolutism.

The Changing Functions of the State

During these decades of great political controversy, a subordinate theme involved the further growth in the functions of the nation-state. Strict liberalism argued for a reduction in the state's role, but briefly in only two countries—Britain and Norway—did state activities actually shrink. For the industrial revolution called for new state outreach, facilitated in turn by improved transportation and communication. Most Western governments did reduce certain traditional efforts, such as enforcing a state church or the details of guild restrictions; this change was part of the compromise with liberalism. But most governments assumed new economic roles, such as supporting the development of railroads and other elements of the infrastructure essential to urban, industrial societies. Public works projects expanded. Most governments also stepped up their educational efforts. France in 1833 authorized local governments to set up primary schools for both boys and girls, and although schooling was not yet a requirement and the Catholic church retained considerable involvement in education, a network of state-run, secular schools did spread. Outside the South, American state governments were also active in establishing school systems through the high school level, in some cases requiring attendance until age twelve. In the 1860s the federal government authorized the use of land to set up state universities, in a further illustration of this new government role. Welfare activities represented a third area of growing activity, along with education and promotion of economic growth. Most national governments (in the United States, the states) passed laws regulating child labor and setting other protective limits. Local governments, particularly after 1850, became increasingly involved with housing and sanitary inspection, and the construction of parks, paved roads, and other amenities.

On another front the military efforts of many governments expanded. During the 1850s and 1860s, Prussia set up peacetime military conscription, one of the bases for that nation's great victories in the unification effort. During the Civil War the United States more temporarily extended the power of government to regulate citizens for military ends by drafting recruits, imposing an income tax, and extending the federal power to requisition supplies such as guns or uniforms.

A final area of new government activity involved policing and the control of deviance. Before the industrial revolution most policing had rested in the hands of private groups of citizens who served on city watch committees. With city growth and rising crime, and even more rapidly increasing fears of crime, these relatively informal methods seemed inadequate. Hence the British government, in the 1820s, set up a professional police force in London and other centers—the agents known as "bobbies" after the founder Robert Peel. American cities such as New York did the same shortly thereafter, as did Germany after 1848. Coupled with these new police measures was continued revision of the punishments for crime, reducing physical punishments and executions, and making those that occurred private rather than public occasions, while expanding state prisons. The net result was a substantial expansion of government involvement in the repression of crime and the treatment of criminals. Governments also began to take over the care of the insane, setting up asylums that replaced more informal, community mechanisms. In sum, the role of the state in defining and maintaining order and normalcy increased notably, even as efforts were launched by humanitarians to make prisons and asylums into effective and humane centers of rehabilitation.

National states, in sum, were becoming more active, branching out in new ways, and gaining new contacts with and powers over individual citizens.

Industrialization both facilitated and demanded new state activities. At the same time, governments proved adept at gaining a portion of the growing prosperity produced by industrialization—just as they had done during the sixteenth-century trend toward commercialization; new tax resources facilitated state expansion as well. Once the fundamental disputes over government form were resolved, by 1870, this aspect of the political response to industrial society—the further expansion of the hold of the nation-state—would become even more apparent.

206

FIVE
The
Industrialization of
the West, 1815–
1870

Culture and Popular Mentalities

The same decades that saw the industrial revolution, new social unrest, and important shifts in Western political and military structure also saw vital changes in the way Westerners thought. These changes affected both formal intellectual life and popular outlook. Although they were dramatic departures from past patterns in some respects, they also built on previous trends that had been reshaping Western culture for some time; in this they resembled the trends in social and political structure that also embellished earlier themes such as proletarianization or nation-state roles.

The Full Expanse of Romanticism

Intellectual life after 1815 resonated to debates already prepared by the Enlightenment and its critics, but it also responded to political conflicts and to the crude forces of industrialization. The Romantic current that had begun in the eighteenth century, expressed primarily in sentimental novels, blossomed between 1815 and 1848, using not only novels but poetry, theater, painting and sculpture, and philosophical treatise as outlets. Romantics had several messages. They remained hostile to what they saw as the sterile rationalism of the Enlightenment tradition. They wanted spontaneity, variety, emotion. They were also hostile to classical styles, and this was perhaps even more revolutionary. Romantic theorists such as Victor Hugo held that there should be no set rules for style, in theater or in art. Romantics attacked the long hold of aesthetic canons some of which derived from ancient Greece. And although their own styles seem tame in comparison with more recent artistic examples, the Romantics did experiment with new verse forms, with new theatrical arrangements, with new uses of color in painting, and very definitely with new musical styles. This passion for stylistic innovation could relate to the desire for emotional expression, both in artist and in audience, but it could also take on a life of its own, as art became increasingly associated with change itself. And although Romantic productions won wide attention—popular novels in the Romantic motif, for example, gained substantial readership—many people began to prefer "classical styles" to more modern, less predictable innovations, thus opening a gap between culture producers and culture consumers that remains, to an extent, to this day.

The political implications of Romanticism were varied. Some Romantic theorists, particularly in Germany, wrote of the importance of the state as an abstract concept with a transcendant reality of its own. Romantic interest in history and religion could also support such conservatism. But Romantic passion and individualism led as well to defense of individual freedom, and a concern for folklore led some Romantics to democratic sentiments. Romantic liberals and radicals played important roles in the revolutions of the early nineteenth century, and the failure of the 1848 revolution—which in France had been headed by the Romantic writer Lamartine—actually helped close the Romantic era generally.

There followed, before 1870, a more mixed artistic period. Some artists turned to realism, using novels and paintings to portray grim social scenes. Charles Dickens, for example, whose writings spanned from the early 1830s to 1870, attacked the hardships of industrial life and the precarious treatment of the poor in a variety of widely read novels. But another group of artists, particularly in France, moved more exclusively to stylistic innovation. Poets such as Charles Baudelaire turned against any link with politics and against the materialism of their industrializing society, holding that art should express the emotions of the artist regardless of impact. In their personal lives and in their writing, many of these "artists for art's sake" defied convention and tried, through symbolic imagery rather than established forms and even established word use, to pour forth their souls. Art became an increasingly complex, individualized response to an increasingly complex but organized society.

Science and Social Science

The artistic outpouring between 1815 and 1870, itself diverse, stood largely apart from the equally lively heritage of the Enlightenment. One facet of this heritage involved continuing research in science. Experiments in electricity and magnetism advanced physics. A number of new chemical elements were discovered; research laboratories, particularly in Germany, linked science to technological advance more directly than ever before, as chemists such as Justus Liebig and Louis Pasteur produced new fertilizers, brewing procedures, and the like. Pasteur's germ theory brought a new round of scientific advance to medicine, in which there were also important breakthroughs in the study of anatomy and pathology. Outright scientific advance and the common association between science and material progress both confirmed the broad intellectual vision of the Enlightenment.

The same held true in social science, although here there was more partisan debate over results. Centers for the collection of statistical data about society arose, much as the various institutes for scientific research had; in both areas it was assumed that more abundant data would yield significant understanding. Social science was also marked, however, by diverse theorizing based on assumptions about human rationality. Liberals sought to prove the need for personal freedom by showing its utility; thus John Stuart Mill, in England, touted freedom on the grounds of its encouragement to advancing knowledge and improved defense of truths already known. Liberal economists tried to show the adverse effects of government intervention on maximum output, although unlike Adam Smith some of them were so pessimistic about problems such as poverty that economics under their leadership was dubbed the "gloomy science." Overall, although the specifics and tone of the inquiry changed from what they had been during the Enlightenment, the assumption that rationalistic generalizations could capture how society functioned continued to be fundamental in the social sciences.

Many of the most important developments in science and social science theory occurred after 1850. In 1859 Charles Darwin published his *Origin of the Species*, establishing a full theory of evolution for the first time. In unifying masses of diverse data, his work was as fundamental to biology as Newton's had been to physics. Darwin was trying to reconcile evidence of change and disappearance, or new appearance, in various species. He argued that species evolved through the struggle for existence, with those possessing the characteristics most fitted for survival passing on these qualities. Over time—Darwin tended to assume gradual change—this process could exterminate whole categories of organisms and create others. In this view, humans were evolutionary results of change among the apes—and not surprisingly the image of man descending from monkey quickly caught the public fancy, producing irate outcries from Christian groups, particularly Protestants, who saw yet another challenge to religious beliefs about human creation in the name of science. Darwin did not in fact have a full grasp of evolutionary mechanisms, and the wider implications of his theory, plus considerable misuse by racists and nationalists bent on showing the superiority of their particular groups, generated continued controversy. But in demonstrating anew the power of science both to shatter previous convention and to draw together and explain a host of specific empirical findings, Darwin extended scientific dynamism.

Karl Marx, writing in the same period and hoping actually to dedicate the first volume of his theoretical work, *Das Kapital*, to Darwin, believed he could combine science and history toward the production of a bold new political program. Marx, of German–Jewish origin and working for the most part in London, believed that all human activity was fundamentally determined by the means of production—the technology and the group that controlled it. All history was based on a constant struggle among social classes defined by their relationship to the means of production. Thus in the past the business class, or bourgeoisie, struggled with the aristocracy that controlled landed wealth. But this struggle was now yielding to a new conflict between the victorious bourgeoisie and the desperate proletariat, ever growing and ever poorer through the march of factory industry. This new clash, like the old, would generate revolution. But the proletarian revolution would yield not to new class struggle, but to a proletarian dictatorship that would wipe away all traces of class. Then the state itself would "wither away," and people would produce peacefully and in full freedom. Marx was by no means the first post-Enlightenment socialist. Many other theorists had argued against the injustice of private property and had urged the formation of cooperative, utopian communities. But Marx poured scorn on the utopians, arguing that they had not founded their beliefs on historical law and had ignored the need for revolutionary clash.

Marx's theories won growing attention as a new socialist movement formed in the 1860s, but their main practical impact came after 1870. Marxism also represented an important extension of social scientific thinking, in its ambitious attempt to capture historical change and its assertion that forces like technology or ownership might affect societies in fundamental ways apart from formal ideas or leadership goals. These insights would be taken over by many social scientists, including non-Marxists.

Although new developments in science and social science extended the basic Enlightenment heritage, they also complicated it. Darwin showed the power of observation and theory—the scientific method—but he also downplayed humans as special, rational creatures. Marx offered an Enlightenment vision of the human future—progressive, peaceful, free—but he showed people now trapped by historical forces that they could not control, impelled often to violence to achieve change. Clearly, the Enlightenment vision was becoming more complex, even as belief in dispassionate scientific methods remained firm.

The Rise of the Middle Class

Developments in popular culture added new twists to a framework already taking shape before industrialization, as did those in science and art. Knowledge of popularized science and political ideas became increasingly widespread. Growing literacy, which passed the 60 percent mark almost everywhere in the West by 1870, continued its work in spreading ideas and reshaping traditional thought.

The middle classes of the West—business people, prosperous farmers, professionals—took an increasing lead in shaping public opinion, particularly those opinions expressed in the most widely read books, journals, and newspapers. The middle class conveyed a clear view of the world, one that reflected changes in popular beliefs that had developed earlier but was reinforced by the presumed lessons of industrialization. Religion, for example, played a role in the middle-class view of things, but it should be a liberalized religion that stressed progress and goodness, deemphasizing the old themes of hellfire and damnation. In many ways the middle-class mentality translated basic Enlightenment concepts ranging from the power of science and technology to the importance of education into wider, daily life.

The middle class increasingly believed that the key approach to the problem of disease, for example, was through medical doctors. Diseases should be manageable, and the road to progress lay through science. Doctors, for their part, encouraged this reaction by linking their treatments with scientific knowledge—although in fact there were few out-

210

FIVE
The
Industrialization of
the West, 1815–
1870

right improvements in therapy in this period. Medical knowledge about pathology did improve, and doctors increasingly shifted toward examination of bodies and away from mere discussion of symptoms in dealing with a patient. Thus classification of disease became more precise even if treatment might not change greatly, and this represented another important step in the conversion to a "scientific" approach to disease. Not only through consultation but also in reading doctor-authored advice columns, the Western middle class by 1850 was imbibing the belief that many diseases could and should be prevented through proper care and diligent personal discipline. The result of this new view was still anxiety—middle-class parents worried greatly about the health of children, for example. But the worry was focused not on lack of control or on magic, but on defining what the most up-to-date science demanded.

Along with advancing popular beliefs in science, the new middle-class outlook also furthered the intense family ethic that had been building for several centuries. The middle-class family itself saw increasing division in roles between men and women, as work moved outside the home. Many early factory owners initially used their wives as accounts managers but cut this practice when prosperity arrived. Most middle-class women as well as men made a virtue of the separation of home from the competitive world of work, and of the new domination of the home by women. Women were expected to learn sensible management skills in caring for the home, and they were felt to exacting standards of cleanliness. But beyond practical tasks, women were felt to be a civilizing, moralizing influence, capable of restraint of bad passion. As "angels in the house," women were supposed to be ideally suited to provide solace after a day's work and above all were expected to provide proper moral guidance for children in a culture that, almost of necessity, focused growing attention on mothers as guardians of the young. Family and especially women thus became invested with deep, almost spiritual qualities. The results for women were frankly ambiguous; the dominant view held that women were too weak and irrational to undertake wide public roles but granted them effective superiority as moral, familial agents. The results for the family were ambiguous as well. The middle class undoubtedly was sincere in idealizing the family. It extended earlier trends of investing marriage and parent–child relationships with love. But it also placed new burdens on the family, now called to live up to demanding expectations not only to provide nurturing affection but also to avoid significant anger as well.

Intense hopes rested on children, who were held to be fundamentally good—innocents capable of improvement if treated well. The middle class felt great obligations to children, expressed in massive outlays for education, marriage, and business arrangements, and also in newly deep grief should a child die. Harsh practices that might disrupt childish innocence were increasingly attacked, extending the desire to guide rather than discipline children, to instill a sometimes guilt-ridden conscience rather than mere conformity to authority. But this valuation of the child was a burden as well. Children were subjected to considerable supervision, instilled early on with the idea that they had the obligation to make something of themselves in an achievement-oriented environment.

This English photograph from 1865 reflects the idealization of women common among members of the middle class of the time.

The Middle-class Worldview   Armed with beliefs in individual capacity, science, progress, and the family, the middle class had an overall worldview, an informal framework for interpreting life, supplemented usually by liberal political commitments and optimistic religion. There were dissenters within the class itself, of course, who held to a more traditional religious outlook, a more pessimistic view of human nature, and a more static concept of society. Even mainstream middle-class opinion was sometimes contradictory, on one hand preaching individual responsibility to achieve, for example, while on the other urging the lower classes to stay in their place. But despite inconsistencies, the middle-class view was reasonably comprehensive, and it was preached with a passion, through the new schools and magazine and newspaper outlets that the class dominated—preached to children, to the government and the aristocracy, and to the lower classes.

The reshaping of popular mentalities that had begun three centuries before solidified into a middle-class outlook, complete with its own substantial opinion-shaping power. For the middle class was impatient, even appalled, at continued evidence of more traditional beliefs. It urged science, thrift, strong family ties on everyone. But its larger missionary campaign focused on three apparently diverse but in fact interrelated facets of popular life—poverty, social deviance, and leisure habits. Thus it extended the earlier tensions between enduring popular values and an elite "civilizing" mission now made more powerful by the success, numbers, and outreach of the middle class itself.

212

FIVE
The
Industrialization of
the West, 1815–
1870

First, poverty and deviance received a more intense moral criticism than ever before. The middle-class ethic set work as a chief human good, open to everyone and assured of successful result. He who was poor, the strictest argument ran, had only himself to blame: He had not worked properly. Middle-class stories and newspaper articles delighted in citing, and exaggerating, cases of individuals who had risen through their own labor, or who had maintained a respectable family even amid personal hardship, through the ever-ready habit of diligent work. Many liberal economists trumpeted this theme: Any effort to aid the poor, as through traditional charity, save in encouraging better work zeal, would be counterproductive, in that the poor would become addicted to aid, labor less well, and perhaps have more children, and they would therefore emerge worse off then before. This notion was implanted in nineteenth-century policy, as Britain and other countries tightened relief requirements for the poor to try to squeeze out the able-bodied. Charity did not cease, and the middle class did not consistently adopt the harsh approach to poverty. But there was an enduring change in tone that could affect the self-image of the poor themselves, making them believe that their misfortunes might indeed be their fault.

The same attitude carried over into definitions of and approaches to deviance, again building on themes established some centuries earlier but now taken further given the solidity of middle-class beliefs. Middle-class reformers sincerely hoped that criminals or the insane could be rehabilitated, but they also insisted on segregation until this process was completed. Hence, there was a new enthusiasm both for lighter physical punishments—fewer death penalties, for example—and for the construction of huge prisons and asylums where deviants would be taught proper work habits and isolated from the social mainstream. Since a disproportionate number of the institutionalized were drawn from the poorer classes—the American asylums by 1860, for example, contained a large number of Irish immigrants—this desire to avoid contamination with those who could not function effectively bore heavily on the poor as well.

The ascendant middle class, joined by aristocratic elements, also mounted a new war against popular leisure habits. This was a crucial element in renewed attack on popular tradition. Middle-class ideas about appropriate leisure related closely to the intense ethics of work and family. Leisure was good when it improved capacity to work and strengthened family ties; hence middle-class families devoted great attention to reading uplifting stories, attending lectures, and encouraging children's games that would build character. As in the approach to deviance, this view of leisure was not rigorously consistent. Middle-class people also patronized art and theater in order to display new wealth and gain access to cultural preserves previously monopolized by the aristocracy. Middle-class patronage indeed allowed increasing professionalization among mu-

New styles of punishment were instituted in the large, impersonal prisons of the nineteenth century, where uniformity of behavior was thought to be a key to prisoners' reform. Inmates march in lockstep into the dining room at New York State's Sing Sing Prison.

sicians and actors, improving the quality of performance, just as it supported the growing publishing industry. But the middle class did display some real anxiety about purely frivolous leisure. This outlook, along with the labor needs of early factory industry, brought direct confrontation with popular tradition.

The attack on leisure customs had many targets, many of them leisure habits fundamental to popular life in earlier centuries. Employers of labor, particularly in the factories, tried to reduce the alternation between work and play on the job by banning singing and gossiping. Humanitarian groups and many local governments attacked amusements such as bear-baiting based on apparent cruelty to animals. Festival habits came in for special disapproval. Long festival periods reduced work time; they dissipated energy; they threatened to mass rowdy crowds that might disturb order; they displayed in general a group enthusiasm and lack of restraint that many middle-class people found profoundly alien. The festival tradition was hard for ordinary people—even rural people—to maintain fully in a period of massive migration, given disruption of the community ties on which particular rituals had depended. But the new, official attack was even more devastating. Middle-class leaders did more than preach against exuberant leisure behavior; they also guided newly formed urban police forces to stamp it out. One estimate held that half of police time was devoted to enforcing rules against popular leisure. Some efforts failed, to be sure. Repeated attempts to limit working-class drinking proved impossible fully to enforce, as the tavern became the leading leisure center in the growing cities. But popular leisure forms that had depended on larger, public, groups, such as the festivals, did begin to wither. And they were not fully replaced in the early industrial period, a bleak time for leisure in the Western world. Gradually a few professional performance activities, such as circuses that had been launched a bit before, spread to fill part of the void. But although these performances brought excitement to large crowds, they depended on less participation, more passive spectatorship, than the leisure tradition that was now fading away.

214

FIVE
The
Industrialization of
the West, 1815–
1870

Finally, the middle class attempted to impose tighter restrictions on aspects of personal behavior, particularly on its own members. It was trying to rigorously socialize its own children, but it also extended the goal of restraint in the advice it offered to the working class and in its hostile judgments of worker behavior that did not seem up to standard.

Sexual restraint was a key goal. Middle-class people were eager to limit their birth rates, to protect access to inherited property and education—both costly items that could be dissipated through having too many children—and to assure ample maternal attention to each child born. Therefore the middle class, throughout the Western world, led in the downward movement of the birth rate—a trend that began even before 1815 in the United States and France, and soon developed elsewhere. In this period limiting births depended mainly on limiting sexual activity: preventing sexual intercourse before marriage (since marriage usually occurred rather late, particularly for men); urging limits to sex within marriage; and, more tentatively, attempting milder restraints such as *coitus interruptus* or the use of new birth control devices that developed—technology again—after the vulcanization of rubber in the 1840s. But limits on sexual activity could no longer be imposed by community sanctions, because communities were too loose, at least in the cities, and the desire for individual and family privacy too great. Nor was religion quite as effective as before. So the middle class attacked head-on, blasting uninhibited sex, urging that unbridled passion was a sign of bad character and would lead not only to unwanted social consequences, but to serious health problems. Masturbation, for example, might bring blindness, insanity, or acne—a diverse list of consequences, but all undesirable. The middle-class sexual ethic did not preclude sincere sexual passion, particularly in marriage. It also did not prevent young men from using professional prostitutes, a growing group in the cities, or other unsanctioned outlets—for the ethic bore particularly heavily on middle-class women, held to be the guardians of purity. But in creating new limits or at least new guilts and tensions about sexual expression, the ethic of restraint had some effect on most middle-class people.

The campaign for restraint extended to other bodily functions. A growing passion for cleanliness was a logical response to fears about urban pollution and contagion, but the middle class carried the passion to great lengths. The installation of bathtubs, made possible by plumbing improvements available toward 1850, placed soap as a new god in middle-class life—as the saying went, next to God himself. Toilet training also became more rigorous, and middle-class children were taught the filth and foulness of human excrement much more fully than before. Here too technology entered the picture, as indoor flush toilets began to be installed in middle-class homes, allowing more rapid disposition of human wastes than ever before.

Finally, the middle class urged careful emotional control. Their image of the public world was one of careful rational calculation, in which emotion should have no place. Families provided contrast, allowing expression of feelings such as love, nostalgia, or grief. But even here certain emotions must be held in check; anger, for example, was a new taboo, and men were also urged to keep back fear and weeping.

Middle-class values thus extended the long Western effort toward personal control of more spontaneous impulses. The campaign can be variously interpreted as an unfortunate repression or as much-needed civilizing; but there is no question of its importance. And although middle-class control standards applied particularly to the class itself, it also entered into the attack on "vulgar" popular recreations, into efforts to discipline worker behavior on the job, and into attacks on many workers and peasants as virtually an inferior species because of their inability to wash regularly, restrain their language, and avoid violence. The divide between "respectable" and "unrespectable" people ran deep in early industrial society—in the minds of both groups. It translated into more precise social terms the earlier divisions of popular mentality into more "controlled" and more "traditional" camps.

The Workers' Reaction   But middle-class values were not entirely alien to workers and peasants, even aside from the impact of work regulations and police restrictions. Middle-class sponsorship of uplifting tracts and speeches had some effect. Many workers and artisans, eager to adapt to the new economic system, agreed that personal restraint, sobriety, and hard work were important virtues. Although removed from middle-class idealization of women's purities, workers also saw important needs for family cohesion, and women staked out vital roles in this process. Although working-class women held jobs during their teens, most of them quit work outside the home upon marriage. Even when working, more urban women held servant jobs in middle-class homes than anything else, because of the link between this work and domestic skills; servanthood gave many working-class women some taste of middle-class values, which they might then apply to their own families later on—no small means of transmission. Working-class wives took on new parenting functions, winning respect for motherhood in this class too; they also organized relationships with other kin, as the working-class family in its own way became more female-centered. In sum, workers did not entirely disagree with middle-class assessments of family life and women's role in shaping it, even though their family habits were not identical in areas such as birth rates or marriage age. Increasingly literate, many workers also agreed that scientific findings had dispelled many older beliefs about health and nature. Often uncomfortable in luxurious urban churches and dismayed at the support many church leaders gave to the rich and to repressive governments, many workers in fact moved further from religious practice than ever before—further, indeed, than the middle class. This shift opened workers to new beliefs and political loyalties, many of which urged a broadly scientific framework, commitment to progress on earth, a new understanding of individual freedom. Popular mentalities, in other words, were changing in some directions that paralleled the middle-class pattern—this was not surprising because attitudes had been shifting similarly in previous centuries. Most workers and most members of the middle class still differed in outlook, but the division was not total. Building on past change, the shock effects of urbanization and new technology inevitably challenged previous habits of thought still further, though without entirely uniform results.

216

FIVE
The
Industrialization of
the West, 1815–
1870

Unity in Cultural Change

The distance between formal intellectual life and popular culture in the decades of industrial revolution was obvious. Major discoveries such as evolutionary theory still caught widespread attention, but much scientific and statistical social scientific work was becoming increasingly specialized and recondite. The gap between artistic innovation and public preference for more settled styles was great as well.

Yet there were important links among the various facets of early industrial culture. Both popular mentality and intellectual activity were marked by important divisions. Family values with their emphasis on emotional depth were kept separate from cool, rational behavior in public (at least according to middle-class principles), a division that paralleled the dichotomy of impulsive art versus rationalistic science in formal intellectual life. Not surprisingly, the prevailing imagery suggested that men were adept at science, women more avid for arts—another dichotomy within popular values. More striking still was the high degree of innovation that characterized both high-culture and popular sectors. Given rapid political and technological change, Western people might have sought comfort from a highly traditional culture—as seems to be the case in parts of the developing world today, where economic change is cushioned by careful reference to the cultural past. Nostalgic impulses abounded in the West—in the effort to invoke family values, or the Romantic concern with religion and medieval styles. But the past invoked was not, for the most part, really traditional. Romantics did not attach themselves to traditional Christianity, as both the emphases and role of religion continued to change. The middle-class family was highly untraditional in its stress on emotional goals and its allocation of novel roles to men, women, and children. The fact was that changes previously launched at all cultural levels could not be stopped, and the industrial revolution on the whole heightened the need to innovate in many areas of life. Culture might still serve as refuge from broader forces of change, but it too was moving away from traditional reference points.

The West and the World

Colonialism

The decades of industrial revolution were inward-looking for much of Western society. Energies poured into factories and cities, into political tension and response. Attention to diplomacy outside the Western orbit was limited as a result. On paper at least, earlier colonialism actually receded. Between 1810 and the 1820s, most Latin American nations won independence from Spain and Portugal, taking advantage of the distraction of the Napoleonic wars and also Britain's control of the seas and its desire to open the area to its own trade. Most Latin American countries attempted liberal, nationalist constitutions, but many soon converted to an authoritarian political form—thus developing a somewhat different political pattern from that prevailing in the West during the same period, though with some similar ideological ingredients.

Although formal European expansion remained limited between 1815 and 1870 compared to the end-of-the-century surge still to come, the new technologies and growing output involved in industrialization inevitably increased the West's role in the world. Britain and Holland regularized their control of India and Indonesia, respectively, moving from colonial exploitation to full government. The introduction of more efficient bureaucracies and the beginnings of rail and steamship lines played a vital role in this process.

Western zeal for trade pushed open the Chinese and then the Japanese markets. Western merchants encouraged opium imports to China from British-controlled India, and when the Chinese government resisted they simply forced it to back down in a series of Opium Wars in the 1830s and 1840s. American and then British fleets visited Japan in the 1850s, and under threat of bombardment compelled the Japanese to open their doors to Western merchants. Western trade with Latin America also expanded, limiting the region's economic independence even as political freedom had been won. Industrial imports cut into local manufacturing and encouraged further concentration on the production of food and raw materials—sugar, rubber, tin, tobacco, and the like, which depended largely on low-cost labor and which only precariously covered the costs of industrial imports.

And there was outright acquisition of territory. To defend India, Britain pushed out to neighboring territories such as Burma. France extended explorations in Africa and in the 1860s began to send missionaries and administrators to Indochina. Still more important at this stage was the steady westward expansion of the United States. Wars against Indian groups and against Mexico gave the United States increasing control of the trans-Mississippi West. And although frontier conditions had their own flavor, the pioneer period yielded soon to the fuller imposition of United States–style Western civilization. Indeed, frontier settlements themselves sedulously installed not only political institutions in the liberal-democratic tradition of the larger nation, but also more personal values such as a tendency to exalt women as civilizing forces.

Eastern Europe

Finally, the surging strength of Western society had a new impact on eastern Europe. The example of the French revolution and nationalism spread to the Balkans, as merchants and others led a new struggle against Ottoman control. A Serbian revolt during the Napoleonic period had won some autonomy for this region. The Greek revolution of the 1820s gained outright independence. A Romanian rising during 1848 brought again some autonomy, which would soon lead to nationhood. The European section of the Ottoman empire was breaking up, inspired in part by Western ideas and by the growing military and diplomatic power of states such as Britain and France, who along with Russia could pressure the Ottomans to make concessions.

218

FIVE
The
Industrialization of
the West, 1815–
1870

Western cultural forms spread widely to eastern Europe, accelerating the contacts established earlier. Poles and Russians participated actively in the European community of music and art. Romanticism, with its invocation of popular traditions and folklore, had a great appeal to eastern European intellectuals, encouraging them to develop a cultural nationalism of their own. Russian novelists and poets borrowed heavily from Romanticism, adding special concerns about Russian values and a plea that the Russian soul not be swallowed by complete Westernization.

In politics, however, eastern Europe stood apart. No serious liberal movements arose in Russia, except for a brief flurry among young army officers who led a revolt in 1825. The Russian government remained firmly autocratic, extending the controls of the secret police and avoiding any of the concessions made by Western conservatives. Socially, also, Russia and much of the rest of eastern Europe remained distinct. There was little urbanization or new manufacturing development. Noble landlords tried to take advantage of Western markets for grain by increasing the labor service of their serfs. Social structure thus remained traditional and in some ways increasingly rigid, contrasting with the dynamic social patterns of the West.

Such contrasts created tensions in eastern Europe. Russian leaders were quite aware that Westerners found their nation backward. They might respond by criticizing the materialism and factory exploitation of the West, but they sensed that, in sheer power terms if nothing else, Russia was lagging behind. Then came the Crimean War of 1854, the result of another round of Russia expansionism at Ottoman expense. Britain and France, fighting far from home, used their industrial strength and new transport facilities to mount an effort that defeated Russia literally in its own backyard. Here was proof positive that Russia needed to change, and probably to attempt again, as in the days of Peter the Great, a partial Westernization.

The first concrete result of this new belief, shared by a new tsar, Alexander II, and many of his ministers, was the Emancipation of the Serfs in 1861. By this decree, serfs no longer owed labor service or other obligations directly to the nobles. And they received a good bit of land—unlike American slaves freed two years later. But nobles were allowed to retain some of the most fertile land. Former serfs, furthermore, were obliged to pay redemption payments to the state, which were used in turn to reimburse the landlords for the property they had lost; the tsarist government, clearly, had no desire to overturn the noble-dominated social structure. Villages were required to supervise peasant payments, and former serfs were not free to leave their villages or, in some cases, to introduce improvements on their land without village authorization. The Emancipation was designed to loosen restrictions on Russian labor, reduce serfs' discontent, and provide greater justice and vigor alike to Russian society. But it did not create a fully free peasant population eager and able to introduce more modern agriculture; and it actually spurred growing discontent because of the restrictions imposed. Russian rural society remained different from that of the West. But Emancipation did assure further change. New local government institutions had to be established to replace manorial courts, and Alexander II remained committed to other reforms designed to enhance Russia's economic and military strength. Russia thus remained in a special relationship with the West, particularly susceptible to the new signs of Western dynamism and eager to keep pace without becoming fully Western.

Conclusion

The decades of the industrial revolution, so filled with dramatic technological, political, and social change, obviously opened the way for further developments in the future. Decades after 1870 would see dramatic shifts in the West's relationship with the wider world, along with additional adjustments to new political forms and the new techniques of work. But the industrial revolution period had also brought some lingering themes in Western history to a certain culmination. Proletarianization, for example, long a vital undercurrent, now became a fact of life for most Westerners. Most men and women had to adjust work patterns, family life and child care to the fact that their lives would always depend on those who owned the capital and defined the jobs. Proletarian status would extend still further after 1870, but it was already by this point a fundamental feature of social structure. The undermining of traditional leisure and other features of popular mentality had again taken on new contours with industrialization, as new technology and the sheer uprooting of masses of people from their rural communities speeded the process of reshaping popular outlook, which had long been underway.

Changes in outlook and even shifts in social structure are never easy to pinpoint, for they inevitably extend over long periods of time. Certainly important resentments about proletarianization lingered after 1870, as did elements of earlier outlook. Nevertheless, it is accurate to see the decades of industrial revolution as not only resulting from but in some senses closing a long process of erosion of traditional social forms. One sign of this was the tendency after 1850 for protest to face away from direct appeals for the restoration of past values, real or imagined, and toward demands for new goals that could facilitate adjustment to the new world of commerce and industry. Workers stopped asking directly for guild communities or their equivalent and began to talk of democratic and socialist rights more stridently. Older themes still intertwined with protest, but the explicit attempt to resurrect the past was less visible in the aftermath of the failure of the revolutions of 1848.

But if the decades of industrial revolution brought certain trends to fruition, they did not fully answer questions about what kind of society would be shaped on their foundation. Traditions of popular leisure, and certain enthusiasms long associated with them, might be things of the past, but what new patterns would rise in their stead? How would social and political structures react to the advent of fully proletarianized masses? The industrial revolution promised recurrent technological change and expanding markets, but it did not predict the more intimate dimensions of modern society. As Chapter 6 will make clear, developments after 1870 would begin to flesh out the nature of a modern, industrial West in greater detail, freer than ever before from the hand of tradition.

SIX

MASS SOCIETY AND IMPERIALISM, 1870–1914

1863 First national football (soccer) association in Britain

1867 British North America Act sets up Confederation of Canada

1869 Territory of Wyoming grants vote to women

1870 ff Rapid development of white-collar jobs

1870 ff Spread of compulsory primary education

1875 Gotha program unifies German Socialist party

1875–1879 Formation of the basic institutions of the Third Republic in France

1876 Formation of baseball's National League in the United States

1877 End of post–Civil War Reconstruction in the United States

1878 Berlin Congress settles some disputes in Balkans, opens the door to more imperialism in Africa and the Mediterranean

1878 Anti-Socialist laws in Germany

1879 German-Habsburg (Dual Monarchy) alliance

1880 ff Bicycle craze, one of first great consumer fads

1881 Assassination of Alexander II in Russia; beginning of greater conservatism

1881 Three Emperors' Alliance (Germany, Habsburg Monarchy, Russia)

1882 Triple Alliance (Germany, Habsburg Monarchy, Italy)

1882 Compulsory education law in France

1883–1889 Social insurance laws in Germany

1884 Legalization of trade unions in France

1884 Expansion of suffrage in Britain, covering most adult males

1890 Bismarck fired (Germany)

1890 ff Development of major socialist and syndicalist movements in France

1894 French trade union confederation adopts principle of revolutionary general strike

1890 ff Industrialization of Russia

1891 First Franco-Russian agreement

1893–1894 Formal defensive alliance, France and Russia

1891 Pope Leo XIII issues *Rerum novarum*, updating the Catholic position on social issues

1894–1906 Dreyfus affair in France

1901–1905 Separation of church and state in France

1896 Italian army defeated in Ethiopia (Battle of Adua)

1898 Germany begins major naval development program

1894ff Rapid expansion of European imperialism in China

1899 ff Revision controversies in Socialist movement

1899–1902 Boer War in South Africa

1900 ff Rise of feminist suffrage agitation in Britain and the United States

1902 Formation of British Labour party

1904 *Entente Cordiale* between Britain and France

1904–1905 Russo-Japanese war

1905 Revolution in Russia

1907 Sweden and Norway grant vote to most adult women

1907 Triple Entente (France, Russia, Britain)

1909 Austria annexes Bosnia-Herzogovina

1911 National Insurance Act in Britain, a major extension of social insurance

1911–1912 Major wave of industrial strikes in Britain

1912 First Balkan War

1913 Second Balkan War

1914 Assassination of Austrian Archduke Ferdinand at Sarajevo; World War I

1914–1915 Denmark grants women's suffrage

CHAPTER
SIX

THE EMERGENCE OF
MASS SOCIETY,
1870–1914

WESTERN EUROPE AND THE UNITED STATES built on the beginnings of the industrial revolution in many ways after 1870. Larger factories with faster equipment increased the pace of economic change, as did the spread of new techniques to other branches of production. While industrialization now began in two non-Western centers, Russia and Japan, the West's economic preeminence grew worldwide. The West's appetite for conquest also grew; these were the classic decades of imperialism, as the United States joined western European nations in devouring huge territories in Africa and Asia to form vast colonial empires. Imperialism and economic competition ironically ended by increasing tensions on the home front, as Europe stepped up its armaments and its diplomatic entanglements in a spiral that resulted in World War I.

Within Western society, the overriding theme of the turn-of-the-century period was the emergence of new forms of mass expression. Proletarianization continued, now affecting middle-class ranks as the formation of small businesses stagnated and increasing numbers of middle-class people took paid but propertyless employment as managers and clerks. But for many groups proletarian status was less novel and confusing than before; it was instead a situation to build from, rather than a disorienting deterioration. With urban and industrial conditions less bewildering than before, with wage earnings improving slightly and providing a modest margin above subsistence for many proletarians, the masses became a new force. Mass cultural outlets and products for consumption sought their patronage, as new forms of popular culture took shape. Trade unions and political parties gave many proletarians new voice and bargaining

221

power, modifying the shape of the political system. Mass conscription changed the nature of military life, as did new weaponry, and both became the stockpiles for the bloody onslaughts of modern warfare.

Mass society meant more than new forms of expression for ordinary people, however. It also meant the development of organizations geared to the manipulation and control of large numbers of people. Big business learned more effective methods of discipline. Governments learned how to appeal to mass loyalties such as surging nationalism. The mass press and professional sports promoters learned how to win wide attention. Clearly, the rise of the masses was an interactive process in which the masses were acting as well as being acted upon. A key question, not fully answered by 1914, was who was controlling whom.

The Social Structure of Mass Society

The Elite

The rise of the masses was shaped by important changes in the social structure of Western society. At the top, a partially new upper class pulled away from its earlier middle-class roots. In the early industrial period, the rise of middle-class values and political voice had not unseated the aristocracy in western Europe, although it had placed the class more on the defensive.

In the later nineteenth century, aristocrats became more willing to compromise, socially as well as politically, with the wealthiest group of merchants and industrialists, and they found most of this elite only too eager for alliance. The most prestigious schools, once attacked by middle-class reformers for their elitism and outdated program, now adjusted their curricula slightly by adding some modern history, modern language, and science, and they opened their doors to the wealthy; the result was a new educated upper class drawn primarily from a mixture of the aristocracy and the upper middle class. Big businessmen tended to shift also from adamant liberalism in politics to a growing desire to put down popular unrest and protect landed estates, coal, and steel. In Germany, a famous 1892 tariff resulted from a direct alliance of big business with aristocratic conservatives that offered coverage both for estate-produced grain and for steel. Government bureaucracies and military hierarchies also increasingly mixed aristocrats and men of big-business origin. As marriages between members of these two groups increased, daughters of tycoons gained titles and aristocratic heirs gained wealth. The continued aristocratic element showed that privilege of birth was not dead as an element of the European social structure; but money spoke even louder in undergirding the social pinnacles, for without question the trend of the highest social structures in Western industrial society was toward a basis in wealth rather than birth. And "big money" was more visible after 1870 than ever before.

The emergence of a new upper-class alliance rested heavily on the growth of larger business organizations. Most Western countries liberalized their rules on the forming of corporations. Corporations, in turn,

Conspicuous consumption by the new upper class: dining on horseback at Sherry's Ballroom in New York in 1903.

rising in the hundreds each year, permitted big business to amass more capital than ever before by relying on funds drawn from hundreds of investors. Large banks, investing in industry, added to the concentration of wealth and power. Large business concerns often acquired huge shares of major industries. For example, the German chemical industry and the United States steel industry were controlled by a small number of giant firms. Big business also extended its reach vertically, as steel companies gained control of iron and coal mines at one end of the production process, and the manufacture of equipment and armaments at the other. Not all industries were as firmly entrenched in big-business structures as was heavy industry; some new branches, such as automobile production for a decade or so after 1900, began on the basis of small concerns. But big business was a growing reality, shaping a new class of plutocrats—the robber barons—in the United States as well as in Europe. And a new, enriched, and showy upper class focused attention on the division between the powerful and the masses. The upper class would draw the attention of the masses to their need to use force of numbers to compensate for the new force of wealth and inherited prestige.

A genuine middle class remained beneath the levels of the elite, and it was by no means subsumed in some undifferentiated mass society; but the articulation of a distinct middle-class voice became somewhat more difficult against the new polarization between the immensely rich and the numerous poor.

The Urban Working Class

"The masses" themselves were a product of the long process of proletarianization, but also of further changes that made conditions among various groups of proletarians more similar than had been the case before. In the cities, for example, the differences between craft and industrial workers lessened after 1870, although they by no means disappeared. The earlier trends among artisanal journeymen that reduced their chances for mobility continued; although the dream of success continued to an extent, few journeymen now had the opportunity to rise to become masters or employers on their own. Guilds, which had been abolished throughout the Western world except as informal social groups in a few places such as Germany, no longer protected apprenticeship or skill qualifications, and there were many complaints that young workers were poorly trained. Indeed, the children of many journeymen left the craft in favor of factory or office work, preferring higher earnings and more secure employment to the faded glory of the craft skill. Above all, technological change cut into the artisanal tradition. Development after 1870 of electrical and then internal combustion engines allowed the application of machine power to scattered work sites—thus bringing artisans into the industrial fold even when they were not literally placed in a factory setting. By the 1890s, for example, most bakers used mechanical kneading machines, which reduced the customary skill component; and they also faced competition from some giant merchanized bakeries, which could turn out large quantities of processed bread or cakes. Printers, already accustomed to some mechanization, now encountered automatic typesetting machines that could be operated by semiskilled workers. They had to choose between accepting the new machines, with their lesser skill requirements, and facing growing unemployment—no choice at all, in fact. Construction workers found their jobs changed by the use of factory-made metal beams, structural cement, and machine-powered saws and loading devices. Again, skill requirements tended to fall, and work crews expanded in size, which further reduced the artisanal element.

After 1870 many artisans faced and made basic choices about how they viewed their jobs and their status. Without abandoning some special sense of their craft, they increasingly recognized their position as wage-laborers and their lack of fundamental control over their job conditions. This did not mean that they delighted in the transition, but they did tend to make it. Printers, for example, after considering frontal attack on the automatic composing machines, almost uniformly decided that they could accept the machines, even though the work became duller, in return for shorter hours and higher pay. Another revealing shift involved a growing desire to separate work and home life. Artisans increasingly fought against lingering traditions of being housed and fed by employers. These traditions made sense when a journeyman was preparing to become a master, but they now seemed galling restrictions on freedom when wage-earning status was permanent. In sum, artisans increasingly saw themselves as part of the larger proletariat, if a superior part, as had in fact been the case for some time.

Factory workers and miners, their numbers still growing, now formed the most numerous part of the urban proletariat. They too encountered some newly homogenizing forces. The sheer passage of time had allowed segments of the working class who had been new to their jobs and the city in 1860 to feel part of a larger group by 1900. Many rubber products workers in Bezons, a town near Paris, came from the province of Brittany. At first an isolated enclave in the town, by 1900 they, or more commonly their children, had intermarried with local people and had moved into a variety of skill levels rather than being confined to the lowest ranks. They had also become less fervently Catholic, again merging by 1900 with the local working-class culture. There still were new entrants to the factory labor force, to be sure. Polish workers who moved into the German Ruhr Valley to take jobs as miners and steelworkers—and even more pointedly, the large numbers of southern and eastern European immigrants to the labor force in the United States—did not mix smoothly with the "native" working class. On the whole, however, several generations of urban experience had reduced some of the divisions between worker groups. The years had also softened the sheer disruptive effect of the urban, factory experience itself. In most Western cities crime rates stabilized or rose more slowly after 1870 than they had in the early industrial revolution. Rising illegitimacy rates also stabilized, suggesting that working-class family culture had regained authority. In the British working class, for example, although sexual intercourse was a standard part of courtship, intense pressure could be put on a man to marry if he "got a girl in trouble." Finally, technology played a role in reducing some differences within the factory working class. A new wave of machines transformed factory industry around 1900 that at once reduced highly skilled work and brought more common laborers into semiskilled ranks. These new laborers were not elaborately trained but were expected to learn some limited processes thoroughly. In machine building, for example, new automatic riveting and cutting machines created a growing number of specialized semiskilled jobs, as the number of common haulers and the number of machine designers both declined. Thus on a variety of fronts, more and more factory workers could recognize each other.

White-collar Workers

The masses were also augmented by a still more novel development in the occupational structure of the Western nations: A host of white-collar jobs arose after 1870. The needs of big business organizations, growing governments and expanding commercial outlets created a virtually new social group—a propertyless, salaried lower middle class—to handle paperwork and sales. Britain had 7,000 female secretaries in 1881, and 90,000 by 1901. By 1900 almost 5 percent of the French labor force worked in government white-collar jobs as secretaries and lower-level technical personnel. Here was the most rapidly growing group in Western society,

Emerging patterns of work in the new mass society included women in previously all-male secretarial jobs in large business offices.

embracing not only office workers but bank tellers, telephone operators, and department store salespeople. Many were drawn from lower-class groups that had previously been more isolated. The ranks of female domestic servants, for example, began to stabilize or drop gradually, as lower-class women gained better education and also a greater desire for freedom from the petty tyrannies of bourgeois housewifery. To such women office work could seem genuinely liberating. A smaller number of working-class men moved into white-collar ranks as a step up the mobility ladder, as did some former peasants. There were also entrants from the propertied middle class as well; shopkeepers who found competition from larger stores increasingly difficult might fall into this new office proletariat.

The new white-collar class was no mere extension of the urban working class into an office setting. White-collar work was often routine, and it increasingly involved new, rapid technologies such as typewriters and cash registers. But white-collar workers depended on literacy for their jobs; they could dress rather like other middle-class people. Their work involved more emotional than physical strain, and no outright danger. Often they gained or maintained other middle-class values, such as esteem for education and a desire for further upward mobility. Paid by a monthly salary rather than an hourly wage, often receiving benefits such as retirement pensions, and separated from ordinary workers, the white-collar force was encouraged to maintain a distinctive outlook than would keep it distant from the classic proletariat. The differentiation was significant, as white-collar workers were typically more conservative politically, less likely to unionize, than were factory hands or artisans. Yet there were similarities as well: their common urban, propertyless status and their experience of working in groups (unlike, for example, most domestic servants). Certainly mass culture depended heavily on white-collar tastes and participation.

The Rural Segments

Finally, the masses were redefined in part by changes in the rural world. Here, even more than when discussing white-collar workers, there is need for caution: peasants, sharecroppers, and agricultural laborers did *not* become part of a single working class, because their work habits and residence still kept them somewhat separate from urban experiences. Furthermore, many peasants and small farmers, by retaining property ownership, had resources that the actual proletariat, including rural workers, lacked. Nevertheless, groups in the rural world experienced some changes toward a common outlook with other elements of "the masses."

Developments after 1870 brought Western peasants into fuller contact with market agriculture than ever before, and this meant more dealings with urban tradesmen and more possibilities of exchanging ideas with city-dwellers. Improved oceanic steamshipping plus the development of canning and refrigeration for food increasingly opened western Europe to agricultural competition from the United States, Canada, Argentina, Australia, and New Zealand. These newer lands used more sophisticated agricultural equipment on larger holdings than most European farmers could venture. The result was new downward pressure on food prices and on rural earnings. To counter this peasants had a number of options. They could seek tariff protection, often uniting with large landlords, even aristocrats, in this venture. They could seek access to new methods and new equipment. Peasants in France and elsewhere began to use new fertilizers, seeds, and farm machinery in the later nineteenth century, moving further than ever from reliance on tradition as a guide to work. This openness to innovation meant increased interest in education and technology—and an increasing similarity between farm work and the work habits of the urban masses. Finally, peasants in many areas pulled away from production of grains in favor of concentration on market products in which they would have a more obvious advantage, if only because of their greater proximity to large cities. Thus Dutch and Danish farmers converted with great success to dairy goods production, forming cooperatives to pool resources for processing and marketing the result. Co-operatives could buy equipment such as cream separators that individual peasants could not afford.

Peasants, in other words, were exposed to forces that partially weaned them from individual or purely village control over work. They were opened to some of the same new technologies and new organizational forms that were affecting the urban masses, and their sense of separateness from urban life declined somewhat. Furthermore, the decades after 1870 brought peasants under the sway of compulsory, state-run educational systems and widespread military service—new forces that deliberately attacked local attachments and again brought peasants into contact with other segments of mass society. They also exposed peasants to some of the same discipline that urban workers received. Schools, for example, vigorously attacked traditional peasant manners; French rural education deliberately intended to "soften the savagery and harshness natural to peasants," "to modify the habits of bodily hygiene and cleanliness, social and domestic manners, and the way of looking at things and judging them." Many school programs attacked the very language that peasants used, in favor of a uniform national speech. French education ministers sought to root out minority languages such as Breton and Provençal, with considerable success; German schools did the same to Polish. The result was twofold: younger peasants could understand speakers and advertisements from other parts of the country, while their hold on their own tradition was severely weakened.

Despite these efforts European peasants, and also many small American farmers such as the black freed slaves who worked assiduously after Emancipation to acquire small plots of land in the South, were still removed from urban mass conditions in many ways. Their attachment to the land and to largely self-directed work set them apart (though some agricultural laborers, working in large gangs, were exceptions here). Rural standards of living lagged behind urban, as housing stock and other amenities were often old and run-down. There were fewer resources and less leisure time to spare for new enjoyments, the best of which could only be found in cities and towns. But the new forces in the countryside did bring many peasants and laborers to share in some of the important features of the larger mass society: in strong nationalist loyalties, in new protest movements, and in new forms of political action.

The rise of the masses thus involved some partially unifying forces across various sectors of the proletariat or near-proletariat. These forces exposed the masses to common experiences, such as national school systems. They also exposed them to technological change and to a fuller realization that their work was now dependent on market forces beyond their own control. Artisans who learned to think of themselves as sellers of labor rather than privileged possessors of skill, peasants who learned to think of farming as a market venture and not an enshrinement of family and village traditions, were subject to some similar, often disconcerting, lessons.

Material Conditions among the Masses

A final ingredient of the "rise of the masses," most prominent among workers and the clerical lower middle class, involved improved material conditions. Intense material hardship still burdened the proletariat. Not only unskilled factory workers but many clerks earned very low pay for long hours of work. Clerks were further burdened by the need to afford "respectable" clothing for their jobs. Severe economic slumps punctuated the proletarian experience, although they were no longer accompanied by rising food prices. The mid-1870s and the mid-1890s witnessed falling wages and rising unemployment, and there were two shorter crises after 1900.

Yet material life did improve overall, without becoming either luxurious or reliable. Real wages went up, aided by a drop in most consumer prices, including the cost of food, until after 1900. By 1900 it was estimated in Britain that only a third of the population regularly hovered on the brink of want—a huge figure, to be sure, but far smaller than ever before. Most proletarians, by this same calculation, now had some margin above bare subsistence—with which they could afford slightly better housing, more clothes, a daily newspaper, some new leisure expenses. French workers by 1900, for example, were spending 60 percent of their income on food, rather than 75 percent as in 1870—and they were getting more food in the bargain. The general improvement in wages was enhanced by better birth control in all sectors of the proletariat. Though working-class families were still larger than families in the middle class, the rate of decline in size was now the same. Workers mainly relied on abstinence from sexual activity or *coitus interruptus* but were sometimes familiar as well with artificial birth-control devices. They now realized that children were costs, not assets in a modern society, and they reduced their outlays accordingly. Finally, material life was improved by the general amelioration of the cities. Now that the rate of urban growth was slowing, city governments found it easier to catch up with street paving, park building, sanitary inspection and other basic health-protection measures.

One raw but vital index of the improvement in proletarian life was the fact that cities after 1870 showed more births than deaths—really for the first time ever in the Western urban experience. Furthermore, between 1880 and 1920 a veritable revolution occurred in infant mortality. Improved urban hygiene, better housing and diet (protein consumption rose rapidly among the proletariat), plus more available medical advice and new products for infant feeding led to dramatic improvements in this traditional high-mortality sector. Death rates among infants in the United States dropped almost 17 percent per decade during this period, falling to under 10 percent by 1920; changes in western Europe were almost as dramatic.

Along with improved material conditions, the masses began to enjoy increased leisure time, again particularly in the cities. Employers began to realize that the intense pace of industrial work made the maintenance of traditional twelve- or fourteen-hour days unrealistic. Workers themselves came to the same conclusion even more fiercely, seeking lower hours as a compensation for the driving pace of work and for lack of control over job conditions, as well as a basis for richer family life and leisure opportunities. A mixture of strikes and labor agitation, some government initiatives (as in laws that reduced coal miners' hours to ten or even eight), and reconsideration of working hours by employers gave increasing numbers of workers some daily margin between work and sleep. Variations remained considerable, but by 1900 a large number of workers enjoyed ten-hour days, particularly in the big cities; and there was an increasing move as well to grant Saturday afternoons off, in what was known as the "English weekend." A few annual holidays also began to surface, although large blocks of vacation time were still to come for most urban proletarians.

So the rise of the masses followed from growing numbers of people sharing some similar proletarian circumstances, facing a market economy with little more than their labor to sell; it also followed from improved, if still constrained, resources in time and money. These were the social preconditions for the rise of a mass *society;* the following section examines the mass *culture* that resulted.

Mass Culture

Signs of the new position of the masses abounded. The media were transformed, for example, by the rise of new mass-distribution newspapers. A new popular journalism took hold everywhere, leading to papers selling a million or more copies a day in the largest cities such as London, Paris, New York, and Berlin. The mass press depended on the technological improvements in printing, but it also depended on a newly available readership sufficiently literate to enjoy newspapers, sufficiently well-heeled to buy them (and perhaps to buy the myriad products they advertised), and sufficiently similar in its interests to read the same three or four major papers per city.

The mass press had several basic characteristics. It offered a fairly simple vocabulary combined with screaming headlines and lots of pictures. It focused on entertainment, downplaying the political content and abundant editorializing of earlier middle-class journalism. There were serious political newspapers available to the working class, particularly through socialist presses, but generally they did not draw the readership of the big commercial ventures. Mass papers featured dramatic stories of crime or war, the latter often leavened with intense patriotism. Special features appealed to women's interests or sports fans. Venturesome editors, particularly in the United States, even organized their own activities to create sensational news; for example, the reporter Stanley was sent to find the famous Scottish missionary David Livingstone in Africa. American papers also innovated by introducing regular comic sections, again with a desire to entertain.

Mass culture also affected the traditions of urban theater, building on earlier trends that had seen increasing emphasis on professional entertainment for a passive, if enthusiastic audience. Popular music halls, called vaudeville in the United States, drew young workers and clerks in large numbers. The first music hall in London had been built in 1849, to provide skits and music for a lower-class audience; it held 100 people. By 1856 it was being rebuilt to house 1,500 people, and by the 1880s there were 500 halls in London, the largest entertaining an average audience of 45,000 per night! As one worker told a government commission, music halls had become "the great entertainment of the working man and his family."

Indeed, this new mass theater offered a celebration of the small pleasures of proletarian life—a glass of beer, a good meal, a day by the seaside, the pleasures of courtship, and the amusing tribulations of later family life. The outlook was hedonistic, approving of fun—as an English popular song put it, "A little bit of what you fancy does you good." Jokes, often poking fun at working conditions as well as family life—mothers-in-law were a common target—helped relieve normal tensions. Music halls offered escapism while remaining rooted in the realities of life. In the United States, working-class theater was enlivened also by special ethnic traditions, again mixing some traditional sense of identity with a new entertainment form directed at a mass audience. After 1900 popular theater was increasingly supplemented by technologically more novel entertainments, including fast-flipped photographs, which were the forerunners of motion pictures.

The force of the masses spilled over into other entertainments as well. Railroad companies began organizing group excursions on holidays to seaside resorts and elsewhere. Large troupes of urban workers, often dressed in their Sunday finery, would thus sun themselves on beaches—typically unable to swim, for this skill would spread widely to the masses only after 1920. Amusement parks attracted masses of people to view side-shows and encounter the thrills of new mechanized rides such as the Ferris wheel.

What was happening, obviously, was a revival of leisure under the auspices of the new mass culture. Rather than the traditional festivals and the alternations of work and leisure characteristic of older community-based recreation, the masses now had increasingly standardized offerings, consumed in large audiences. The normal day became divided among work, leisure, and sleep, and although leisure for many workers—particularly after youth—consisted mainly of a nap, a pipe, and a pint of beer, the association of daily leisure with some kind of "fun" or distraction increased. Many people indeed hailed the new entertainments as a novel achievement of industrial civilization. Thus in the United States President James Garfield declared in 1890, "We may divide the whole struggle of the human race into two chapters: first the fight to get leisure; and then the second fight of civilization—what shall we do with leisure when we get it?" In fact, although the leisure forms were new, the phenomenon itself was not, and in a real sense the rise of mass recreations followed from the decline of traditional forms earlier in the nineteenth century.

Not surprisingly, the new recreations reproduced many of the themes of the old, even though they involved quite different settings and timing. They provided opportunities for courtship—taking a girl to the music hall or one of the fancier dance halls or saloons was a common courtship activity, just as using the excitement of a festival had once been—and other distractions for the energies of youth. The new recreations pro-

The new leisure spirit was spread through the middle and working classes by companies eager to profit from the increases in workers' free time, and advertising helped develop the new ideals of the good life. This poster featured a standard middle-class family choosing a resort from a suburban London subway station.

vided some community contacts as well. Mass leisure by definition lacked the intimacy of village celebrations, but neighborhood bars and music halls could provide a sense of neighborhood spirit.

Yet there were new features as well, quite apart from specific forms. Middle-class groups and reformers such as church and settlement-house workers continued their drive to make popular leisure "respectable," to give it an uplifting purpose. They discouraged rowdy behavior and excessive drinking, and although they by no means conquered mass leisure, the advocates of respectability did have some impact. Mass leisure also reflected some of the influences of industrial forms of work, even as it provided some escape or distraction. A fascination with speed and with setting records marked much new entertainment, and of course the professionalization of performance converted leisure into an "industry" of its own.

No mass outlet so readily expressed the complexities of the late-nineteenth-century leisure revolution so perfectly as the rise of team sports, beginning in England and spreading quickly to the United States and western Europe (and indeed soon around the world). Sports were not new, of course; games and matches had always been part of the popular entertainment tradition. But late-nineteenth-century sports, although they built on earlier games, were different. They, like so much of industrial life, were organized with newly fixed rules and umpires to enforce them. The rough-and-tumble spontaneity of earlier games was curbed to an extent. Sports were seen, further, not simply as distraction but as "good training" for people to learn military virtues, teamwork, and individual prowess. More than most mass leisure interests, sports won approval from the middle class as well, because of their improvement feature. Finally, the leading sports were quickly professionalized. Professional soccer, football, and rugby teams in Britain, and baseball teams in the United States, began to surface in the 1860s and 1870s. Promoted by commercial impresarios, some of the teams were housed in giant new stadiums that drew mass attendance which was facilitated by the growing urban streetcar network. Professional teams could rouse great enthusiasm from their fans, allowing some outpouring of community loyalty in otherwise anonymous cities. They could even express some of the class tensions that traditional protest once transmitted. Thus working-class teams in England played more viciously than the upper-class amateur teams with which they competed, becoming, according to the amateurs, "a byword for money-grubbing, tricks, sensational displays and utter rottenness."

Mass leisure, expressed in sensationalized newspapers and other reading matter such as "westerns," amusement parks, and sports, had a number of common features. It attracted unprecedented numbers of people to some rather standardized interests. Although making some bows to the theme of leisure-as-improvement, it stressed distraction and fun; young working women, as well as men, explicitly sought entertainment after routinized work days. Further, entertainment was largely secular. Much mass leisure cut directly into church attendance, as Sundays were increasingly converted to days of play rather than, or in addition to, prayer and worship. The masses were not religiously uniform, but generally the force of religion declined still further, particularly among urban workers. Almost uniquely, the working class in the United States retained considerable religious loyalty. (Religion also gained ground in Ireland as a rallying point against Protestant British rule and a solace to devastating population declines.) American religion served as a vital loyalty in otherwise strange circumstances, particularly to the many immigrant workers

who remained attached to Catholicism. American religion, constitution-
ally separate from the state, was also less tainted than was religion in
Europe by links to conservative politics. But with this important American exception, mass religion declined—even as churches throughout the
West began to wake up to the age of the masses toward the end of the
nineteenth century, organizing settlement houses, youth groups, and other
large-scale activities. Under a new pope, Leo XIII, the Catholic church
even turned away from adamant conservativism, expressing sympathy with
welfare reform efforts in the 1890s even though still suspicious of modern
political forms and hostile to socialism. But for the most part these initiatives were too little and too late in Europe, as workers turned to new
loyalties, including the newfound pleasures of mass culture. Secularism,
then, gained ground as leisure and religion were largely separated.

Finally, mass culture was highly organized, operated on commercial
principles by large business concerns. It was indeed the expression of a
manipulated consumerism, arranged in part by advertisers and others who
guided the masses in the spending of newfound funds. The mass press,
the sports teams, the amusement parks—these were large business operations concerned with catering to mass taste but also with organizing it
to a profit. Was the new mass leisure—standardized, rather anonymous,
organized from above—less satisfying than the traditional forms, now
irretrievably lost, had been in the earlier centuries? Did it flow from mass
needs and enthusiasms, or was it imposed in the vacuum created by the
earlier attacks on tradition? Certainly mass culture had immediate critics,
who saw the rise of mass taste as the incarnation of debased values and
shallow pleasure seeking. This criticism was important, in turning some
intellectuals and others against what they saw as the reigning values of
their society. But it was not necessarily correct, for the pleasure the
masses took in their new cultural outlets suggested more than passive
response to manipulation. Yet questions remain, precisely because the
leisure forms, if not their meaning, were so new to the masses themselves, and so commonly sold to them rather than created directly by
them. Clearly, the new leisure forms added a vital dimension to mass
life; but did they substitute for what had been lost earlier?

Mass Protest

The rise of the masses involved new forms and levels of protest, as
well as a new leisure culture. The rate of protest incidents rose steadily
after 1870, as did membership in protest or potential protest organizations such as trade unions and socialist political parties. At the same time
the forms of protest shifted, away from riot and revolution toward strikes
and electoral action; and the goals of protest changed as well, moving
increasingly toward demands for new conditions or rights, away from
attempts to revive past values. The working class, including artisans but
now embracing most manufacturing segments, spearheaded this transformation of protest, but other groups were involved as well, including
agricultural laborers and some clerks.

Conditions of mass protest were altered by changes in basic law. Most

Western countries legalized trade unions, while the vote spread more widely than ever before. Thus many protest actions were possible in part within the law, although police repression figured in many union meetings and strike activities and in some countries, notably Germany in the 1880s and Italy in the 1890s, attempts were made to outlaw socialist appeals.

But legal change did not alone account for mass protest. The fact that many segments of the masses had grown more accustomed to urban, industrial life improved chances of staging protests as well, for some of the rawest disorientation yielded to firmer goals and community structures. It was significant that crime rates stabilized after 1870, suggesting that purely individual reactions to distress were no longer the main option for many laborers. Families who had weathered several generations of factory life now realized that their situation was permanent, and not some fleeting horror that might allow a later return to the countryside; they could set about formulating demands to improve their lot.

Grounds for Activism

There were grievances aplenty. Improvements in wages were not uniform, and setbacks due to economic recessions were frequent. Furthermore, attracted by new goods and entertainments, many segments of the masses now were developing higher material expectations. Thus an effort to restore, maintain, or advance material conditions played a mighty role in the new protest surge.

Changes in work systems swelled the chorus. Not only artisans but also factory workers encountered new technologies and a faster pace of work. New systems of management deprived growing numbers of workers of any voice in their daily assignments. By 1900, led by the United States, many Western factories began to introduce work systems determined by efficiency engineers, who sought to organize each basic motion on the job in the interests of removing chance and individual initiative. Clerks, for their part, faced new equipment and the competition of growing numbers of employees, including women; many feared that their status was deteriorating as their jobs became more routine and more highly supervised. Some elements of the masses sought to improve their job situation directly; others wanted shorter hours to limit the work experience, or higher pay to compensate for distasteful changes on the shop floor.

Finally, elements of the masses sought new ways to exercise some power over their lives. They sought a voice in the companies where they were employed, if only because day-to-day latitude in determining job conditions was increasingly preempted by corporate bureaucracies. Thus trade unions typically pressed for formal inclusion in the determination of wages and hours, through some kind of collective bargaining arrangements. The masses also insisted on political rights. Where the vote had not yet been extended to all adult males, important protest movements resulted. In Belgium in the 1890s, in Italy and Austria after 1900, strikes and other agitation attacked limited suffrage systems and usually won new rights. More generally, the masses used their growing consciousness of power to press governments to offer some protection against the worst disasters of life: state aid in dealing with crises of illness or old age, and protection against particularly abusive employers in the form of state inspection of work places and rules to guide safety measures.

Strikes, Unions, and Political Action

The triple concerns about standard of living, work, and power spurred a wide array of mass initiatives. Strike rates soared steadily beyond all previous levels. Now committed to lives of working for others, growing numbers of craftsmen, factory workers, and rural laborers used the withdrawal of work as their chief method of direct action; although riots continued on occasion, they declined as a protest form. In 1892, French workers struck 261 times against 500 companies; most of the efforts were still small and local, and only 50,000 workers were involved. By 1906, the peak French strike year before 1914, 1,309 strikes brought 438,000 participants out for varying durations. British strike rates were higher still; here a massive wave of agitation involved over two million workers between 1909 and 1913 alone. Most strikes still featured action against individual companies, but many groups of workers—including printers, miners, railway men, and dockworkers—now were able to mount nationwide or regional strikes that could bring operations to a standstill. Many workers also became increasingly sophisticated in the organization and timing of their effort, assembling strike funds to tide themselves through weeks of unemployment, formulating careful demands and indentifying bargaining agents, and avoiding efforts in slump periods when employers would have little reason to yield. The largest strikes focused on improved pay and reduced hours, but strikes could also express the desire to gain bargaining recognition, insistence on new attention from government, or acute personal tensions with individual managers or foremen. A number of important strike efforts revealed particular concern for worker dignity. Thus British workers lashed out against required medical checkups by company-appointed doctors, claiming that they were "pushed and poked like pieces of mutton" or against dismissals regarded as unfair.

Unionization was the second prong of mass protest. Here too, rates climbed above all previous levels and grew fairly steadily; here too, the form of action changed. Trade unions based on small groups of skilled workers persisted, and often proved highly effective. But increasingly unions grouped on a national basis, so that policy and action could be coordinated across regional lines. Furthermore, unions in individual trades often combined to form more general federations, such as the American Federation of Labor (AFL), the British Trades Union Congress, or the French and Italian General Confederations of Labor. These organizations sought to agitate for workers' rights with government, to provide aid to member organizations during strike periods, and in general to use the power of the organized masses to the fullest. Additionally, some of the new confederations were ideologically motivated in origin. The German federation was closely linked to the Socialist party, and the French and

The rise of trade unions saw workers protesting, but also often appealing for respectability. This design appeared on the membership certificate of the skilled Amalgamated Society of Engineers in Britain in 1851.

Italian groups espoused a syndicalist ideology that urged direct action, outside the political sphere, to win ultimate worker control of the means of production. Finally, increasing numbers of unions were set up on industrial rather than skill lines. These industrial unions grouped unskilled as well as skilled workers and fought for improvement of general conditions in industries such as coal mining or textiles. The inclusion of common laborers in the union movement was a key development, particularly noteworthy in sectors such as dockwork and the merchant marine, where masses of unskilled, sometimes transient workers had previously been at the mercy of employers' dictates.

Unions were not simply protest vehicles; many also organized benefit funds and social activities. But union members and the wider public viewed the union movement primarily in terms of its "combat" role. And the size of the new union movement inevitably called attention to the new potential for civil action of the masses. British unions collectively had a million and a half unionized workers by 1906. These figures constituted only a minority of the proletariat, to be sure. Few clerks participated, and other categories, including rural laborers and women workers, lagged somewhat. The "protesting masses" were disproportionately urban, skilled, and male. But the union movement unquestionably organized a larger segment of the proletariat than ever before.

Finally, the masses sought new outlets in political action. There was no single political voice among the masses. Many clerks sought respectability by voting for established conservative or liberal parties. A smaller number of clerks expressed concern about their marginal status in the middle classes by espousing extreme nationalism or anti-Semitism, seeing in these causes a way to attack the power of both big business and organized labor without uniting with the working class. Anti-Semitic parties and street demonstrations, attracting clerks and shopkeepers particularly, were important symptoms of lower-middle-class unease in France, Germany, and Austria in the 1890s; in Vienna, a conservative anti-Semitic political party, the Christian Socialists, won control of the city government. Developments of this sort obviously prevented any unified political stance among the masses.

Even workers were hardly united in their political affiliations. Some groups remained attached to liberal movements; British textile workers, in contrast, formed a tight bond with the Conservative party, which carefully granted some legislative benefits, such as regulation of work time, when in power. But the most important expression of mass politics after 1870 was unquestionably the rising socialist movement, which drew growing support from urban workers, some rural laborers and small peasants, and a minority of discontented middle-class professional people.

Germany led the way. New socialist parties formed in the 1860s, as Bismarck granted wider voting rights; by the 1870s the main socialist strands had agreed on an essentially Marxist doctrine, calling for ultimate revolution and proletarian control. The party was far quicker than its liberal or conservative brethren in realizing the conditions of mass political action. It developed a tight organization and a substantial staff, capable of reaching out not only for electioneering but also to attract and retain members in off-years. Newspapers, educational efforts, and social activities supplemented the political message. By the 1880s the German party was clearly winning working-class support away from the liberal movement, despite the antisocialist laws Bismarck established to stem the tide. By 1900 the German party was a major political force, gaining about two million votes in key elections and a large segment of the parliamentary deputies. By 1913 the German party was polling four million votes in national elections, and was the largest single political force in the nation. Socialist parties in Austria, Scandinavia, and the Low Countries won similar success, while socialism in France and Italy, though troubled by weaker organization and more factional divisions, also gained ground steadily. France had over one hundred socialist deputies in its parliament by 1913. British socialism grew more slowly, and with less attention to formal ideology whether Marxist or otherwise. The Labour party was formed in the 1890s and long lagged behind the Liberal party in winning working-class votes. Still, by 1913 the Labour party was a significant third force. Finally, socialist parties in most countries not only won important national visibility—in France in 1899 they had even joined the government as a minority party, winning control of the Ministry of Labor as a reward—but also captured many city governments where they could increase welfare benefits and improve the regulation of urban and factory conditions for their constituents.

In another sign of the somewhat unusual character of American political life, the socialist surge partially bypassed the United States. American workers participated strongly in strike activity, mounting several large, often violent efforts against well-entrenched employers who frequently called in private police and state national guards in reprisal. American workers were active unionizers as well, with the moderate, craft-oriented AFL rivaled by the industrial unions in the International Workers of the World (the IWW or "Wobblies"). But although a significant Socialist party took shape before 1914, it remained a small minority current. Rapid immigration retarded socialist organizing by creating internal disputes and language barriers in the American working class. The power of religion and the strong urgings toward Americanization, defined among other things as antisocialist, also played a role. But most American workers were also convinced that the political process was relatively open to them already; this fact, plus the American tradition of a federal government system with rather restricted functions, helped keep socialism down. Yet even in the United States the political impulse surged periodically—for example, in the Populist movement of the 1880s, which joined many rural workers and small farmers, black as well as white, in attacks on big business.

Although the rise of mass protest was by no means uniform from one country to the next and although it definitely did not unite the whole of the masses in one common cause, it was a fundamental new ingredient in Western life after 1870. Strikes and unions partially reshaped industrial conditions, helping to induce wage increases and reductions in hours. Even more clearly, the rise of socialism altered the political structure of most Western countries, reducing the force of the liberal movement and prompting governments to consider new measures to keep the working classes content. The old debates between conservatives and liberals about political form were still vigorous but now took a back seat to even more vigorous discussions of what was called "the social question"—which meant what to do about the conditions of the masses and their newfound political muscle.

Although the rise of mass protest was unquestionably significant, it also carried within it some important ambiguities. It was by no means clear how much the masses actively wanted. Clearly, the groups involved in strikes and unions sought immediate gains, but at times they also pointed to more basic restructuring of work and management. Syndicalism, for example—the ideology that won many trade unionists in France, Italy, and elsewhere—helped guide vigorous efforts for lower working hours, but it also stood for ultimate revolution through a general strike. The leading socialist parties on the Continent, Marxist in principle, insisted on their devotion to a new society. But in fact they applied most of their energies to working within the electoral system and to gaining welfare legislation or fuller political rights. Most Marxist parties, in fact, encountered by 1900 a growing crisis over a new doctrine called *revisionism*. Revisionists argued that literal revolution was neither necessary nor possible: reform was preferable, and socialists should seek allies with other parties and with segments outside the working class toward this end. Most Marxist parties, led by the German giant, rejected revisionism in theory but accepted it in practice.

The simple fact was that although mass protest was vital and, to ruling groups, often threatening, it did not have clear revolutionary potential in the West. Resentment against loss of workplace power and tradition ran high in many groups, but it jostled with the desire to win new gains from the system. Socialist revisionism resulted in part from the socialist leaders' knowledge that they could win elections and form alliance with other parties, but it also followed from the desire of many ordinary voters not to jeopardize the chance for higher wages and reform laws with too much talk of a golden revolutionary age to come. A German worker put it this way:

> You know, I never read a social democratic book and rarely a newspaper. I used not to occupy myself with politics at all. But since I got married and have five eaters at home I have to do it. But I think my own thoughts. I do not go in for red ties, big round hats and other similar things. . . . We really do not want to become like the rich and refined people. There will always have to be rich and poor. We would not think of altering that. But we want a better and more just organization at the factory and in the state. I openly express what I think about that, even though it might not be pleasant. But I do nothing illegal.

No revolution occurred in the West between 1870 and 1914—nor any serious revolutionary effort. A small, discontented minority acted openly, often relying on anarchist notions of destroying the state altogether; the result was periodic political assassination (like that of the American president William P. McKinley in 1901) or other terrorism. But mass protest in the industrial West worked mainly to extend the boundaries of the existing political and economic system, not to overturn it by force. The result was change—less than many reform-minded workers wanted, but not a return to the more revolutionary context of the earlier nineteenth century.

Women and Mass Society

The rise of mass culture and protest forms involved new public roles for women. In one basic sense women's conditions did not change greatly between 1870 and 1914: they were still in the main expected to focus on domestic roles and to avoid any lifelong career commitment. Although the nature of women's work altered somewhat, with the growth of clerical and secretarial opportunities and the stagnation of domestic service, the percentage of women in the labor force increased only marginally. Most factory work and the crafts were still dominated by men, as was the bulk of the formal labor movement. Some young women worked in textile factories and elsewhere, providing a vital period of independent (if low) earnings; and married women in the working class continued to carry out low-paid production in the home. Production work was rarely, however, a primary commitment beyond a brief stage of life. Most married women did not work outside the home, and even part-time production opportunities within the home, if still vital, were declining. New jobs in school teaching and nursing did allow a growing number of middle-class young women to work respectably before marriage—thus imitating working-class patterns of temporary involvement in the labor force. And a few important pioneers entered more durable professional careers. Both in western Europe and in the United States, a small number of women pressed through medical and law schools after 1870, becoming lifelong professionals. But the norm remained different; marriage and motherhood did not mix with full-time work. And the rate of marriage reached an all-time high, with over 90 percent of all women marrying by the age forty—a sign of the value of this institution in women's lives, but a symptom also of a lack of viable alternatives.

Other aspects of women's conditions were less stagnant. Educational levels improved steadily—more rapidly indeed than those of men, simply because women started from a lower base of years of schooling and so benefited more by the extension of primary-school facilities and requirements. Although the domestic focus remained vital, many women in fact found less to do around the house, due to the combination of falling birth rates and increased schooling—there were fewer children to take care of and less to do for them, after infancy, given the impingement of other institutions on the family. Recreational opportunities took up some of the slack. Although the new mass leisure was in general resolutely masculine, other outlets brought women a new sense of public freedom. Middle-class women began to play games such as tennis. Bicycles allowed women new mobility. Working-class girls and secretaries avidly patronized some of the new entertainment centers, including amusement parks. Women's costumes changed, reflecting new roles in leisure and as consumers. Fashions became less concealing and confining, a prerequisite of activities such as bicycling. Many women, in sum, developed an active sense that their share in mass culture gave them new opportunities—including the chance to shock old-fashioned diehards who wanted women tightlaced and secluded from independent public roles.

Women also increased their involvement in various reform causes, from the 1870s onward (and even earlier in the United States) again a sign of branching out from strictly familial functions. Many middle-class women signed up in associations to provide better education for the poor, or to control drinking, or to promote missionary work (women, particularly in Protestant regions, were decidedly more active in religious affairs than were men by the later nineteenth century). Many individual women from various social classes also played an active role in socialist and trade union ventures, seeing in these causes a means of improving women's conditions generally. A number of leading German socialists were women.

The decades around the turn of the century also saw a growing wave of feminist protest, which used many of the techniques of mass action— huge petitions, marches, and some controlled violence. Feminist movements surfaced in most Western countries; they were strongest in Britain, the United States, and Scandinavia. Feminists' demands were varied; many sought new legal protection for women to control property, and legal reform did move increasingly in the direction of greater equality of family rights including custody over children in cases of divorce. Other feminists worked for a reduction in educational barriers, particularly in the most prestigious universities. By 1900, feminist movements in most countries focused increasingly on the right to vote as the key to other gains. Feminists argued in terms of democratic theory, while also using earlier beliefs about gender, to urge that women, being morally purer than men, might in fact improve the art of government.

Feminist movements drew particularly heavily from middle-class women, whose educational levels were highest and who were burdened by fewer day-to-day family and work functions. Other groups were drawn in to an extent, and major feminist demonstrations certainly took on the full quality of mass protest. Suffragettes, as they were called in the English-speaking countries, frequently disrupted transportation facilities by lying down on tram tracks, and used other tactics to dramatize their cause. In Britain, particularly, the combination of feminist and working-class unrest after 1900 seemed to threaten the very stability of the state.

A number of American states, headed by Wyoming in 1869, and several Scandinavian countries extended the vote, and women gained local voting rights in Britain; however, few suffrage goals were won before 1914. Clearly, whatever the degree of success, a new "women's issue" was an integral part of mass society, involving not only protest but also a wider array of behavioral changes. Rising divorce rates, particularly in the United States, often initiated by women, showed a new desire for independence as well. Domesticity had not been replaced by a new set of standards for women in the age of the masses, but a variety of women questioned its sanctity.

The Organized Society

The rise of the masses included more than a new popular culture and massive protest movements. It also involved the growth of organizations designed to deal with the masses and to control them. In response to mass pressures, organizations in some ways became more flexible. Businessmen and employers' associations, for example, learned that a strike could often be resolved or even prevented by granting a wage raise, and they preferred a compromise on this issue to basic concessions on decision-making power or work rules. This helps explain why wage strikes were the most common form—they proved easiest to win—but also why management retained essential controls. Aristocratic politicians learned that to win success in a mass society they had to campaign directly among the people, stifling their well-bred distaste at this kind of involvement with the political process; but they also found that the right kind of slogans, including fervent nationalism, could win substantial support on occasion. Businessmen learned that they had to advertise attractive and inexpensive products, but they also found that they could win masses to a consumer culture in which the desire to buy increased steadily. Mass society, in other words, was a two-way street, with both organizational response and the capacity to manipulate the masses from the top as vital constituents to match the new visibility and self-consciousness of the masses themselves.

The power of organization to deal with mass demands increased on many fronts. The effort to strengthen work discipline was a developing facet of this more mature period of industrial development. During the decades of the industrial revolution, efforts to discipline the labor force had been decentralized. Factory owners issued shop rules, and middle-class propagandists preached work zeal, but day-to-day direction was left in the hands of foremen or even master workers, whose approach varied greatly depending on personal whim. As the size of factories and other work units increased after 1870, a more bureaucratic style developed. Workers were still preached at, though less fervently than before; and shop rules were still issued, now for clerks as well as blue-collar labor. But primary reliance shifted to formal work standards prepared and enforced by the managerial bureaucracy. *Industrial engineering*, first developed in the United States, involved charting the motions of individual operatives and then setting up pay systems and coordinated chains of workers to enforce optimum efficiency. Not only individual workers but also foremen lost much discretionary power in this process. Under the new system, workers did not convert uniformly to mindless work habits. They resisted through strikes but also by simply changing jobs or by slowing up the pace of their work. But the disciplined nature of work did become more pronounced. The introduction of assembly-line methods in automobile manufacture, shortly before 1914, carried the discipline effort still further, as belts carried products past the lines of workers and each operative was expected to repeat a limited set of motions over and over again. Organizational mandates bore somewhat less heavily on clerks, but even here standardization was attempted by such devices as lessons on how to smile at the angriest customers.

The organization of the masses proceeded off the job as well. An advertising industry sprang up to stimulate and guide consumer choices. Mass leisure outlets such as organized sports showed the power of big business to channel popular taste. Leisure interests such as sports served a direct disciplinary function as well, by teaching adherence to rules, specialization according to team position, and coordination of individual talent with a team effort. Spontaneous play, so important in much of the popular leisure tradition, was in some ways reduced, as certain kinds of leisure became serious business. Even travel became more organized, as companies such as American Express and the British Thomas Cook's set up itineraries and other arrangements for eager but inexperienced middle-class tourists. Protest itself became increasingly organized, as we have seen. Trade-union and socialist party bureaucracies often took on a life of their own, and not surprisingly, by the 1900s, there were protests directed against this faceless leadership as well as the more common big-business targets.

The rise of organizations to control and manipulate large numbers of people depended on structural changes in the nature of organization itself. Big business, of course, developed on the basis of corporate finance. The use of widely sold stocks, issued on the basis of limited liability to each shareholder as provided by the new laws that authorized corporations of the modern type, and of bank finance allowed unprecedented accumulations of capital, facilitating the formation of companies far larger than the family enterprises typical of the early industrial decades. Businessmen supplemented the giant corporations with intercorporate agreements on labor, supply, and pricing policies. The United States government, particularly devoted to free-enterprise beliefs, attempted to modify these agreements by laws against monopoly and restraint of trade, but the process of coordination continued. In Europe—particularly in countries such as Germany, where heavy industry was emphasized—cartels among leading firms not only guided major industries but also strongly influenced government policy in matters ranging from tariffs to armaments purchasing. Pressure groups such as Germany's Navy League, formed from a combination of military leaders and shipbuilding industrialists, profoundly affected policy through a combination of public propaganda and pressure on key government figures. These groups helped generate developments that had basic impact on the course of European diplomacy, such as Germany's entry into naval-building competition with Britain. Big organization clearly might build on mass support, such as the industrial trade unions, but it could also function autonomously in shaping the course of events.

The rise of large, powerful organizations depended on the development of a new bureaucratic impulse. In business, the image and reality of the independent entrepreneur began to fade, in favor of managerial hierarchies capable of administering extensive operations. Britain, more adept at the entrepreneurial style than at more impersonal organization, began to decline in business dynamism, increasingly challenged by Germany, the United States, and to an extent France, where cultures friendlier to formal organization existed. Even in Britain bureaucratic styles became increasingly dominant. A key reason for the rise of team sports, particularly in schools, was their presumed role in socializing the young for the coordinated effort required in turn-of-the-century bureaucracies. In business itself, rules for recruitment and promotion became increas-

ingly standardized as middle-class managers abandoned, though sometimes reluctantly, more traditional aspirations to set up their own
operations. Beneath the managerial ranks, of course, hordes of white-
collared clerks scrambled to organize the paper flow that expanding
bureaucracies generated.

The Organized State

The theme of expanding organization, and its use to shape the nature of
mass society, unquestionably extended to the national state. Government
bureaucracies burgeoned everywhere, with new groups of inspectors,
teachers, statisticians, and planners. All Western governments in the 1870s
and 1880s introduced civil service procedures for key government personnel. They sought a bureaucracy recruited on the basis of tested ability, rather than birth or influence; indeed, civil service examinations did
open government service to a minority of talented people of lower-class
origin. Civil service rules were also designed to insulate the bureaucracy
from corrupt or personalized treatment, in favor of standardized behavior. The same impulse resulted in efforts to rationalize government operations in the name of impartial efficiency; police forces, for example,
were reformed in many countries to reduce the latitude of individual
officers (and also the possibility for corruption), in favor of more uniform, "professional" standards. In the United States the Progressive
movement after 1900 attacked personalized patronage systems in many
city governments, in favor of more impartial recruitment and more orderly behaviors.

The power of government to regulate increased immensely between
1870 and 1914. Urban conditions seemed to require a growing array of
enforceable rules. Codes were issued for building styles and for safety
and sanitary features. Food processing and marketing were monitored in
the interests of hygiene. So were public bath houses and the activities of
beggars and vagrants. Passports and border controls marked national
boundaries, which meant that international travel and shipping were enmeshed in bureaucratic procedures as never before. Health practices were
regulated. Influenced by professional medical associations, many governments stepped up the long campaign against unofficial medical treatments. They attacked the use of midwives at births, in favor of formal
(usually male) obstetrical care. A number of inoculations were now required in most countries. Sex came in for new regulation as well. Many
governments, reluctantly convinced that prostitution could not be eliminated, tried to confine it to fixed "red light" districts, in the belief that
at least the evil could be monitored and contained. And in some countries or cities, prostitutes themselves were required to register and receive
periodic health examinations.

The regulatory impulse expanded the range of the law, making some
activities criminal that had once been reluctantly tolerated. Beginning
somewhat before 1870, many American states outlawed abortions, previously considered a private matter but now increasingly attacked as immoral and also dangerous to the propagation of "superior" native-born

whites. Throughout Western society after 1870 regulation of youth behavior tightened up. New codes of juvenile delinquency criminalized many activities, such as minor vandalism, that had once been part of accepted youth culture. Overall, Western countries displayed increasingly demanding standards of public order—with the ironic result that crime rates often seemed to rise, not because of outright increase but because so many new categories and offenders were identified.

Governments applied their new regulatory power to the field of taxation. Large bureaucracies and growing functions required ample revenues, and although generally rising prosperity helped, new means of taxation were essential. Around 1900 most government in the Western world established regular income taxes to supplement more traditional levies on real property and sales. Initial tax rates were low and collection was spotty, but the very ability to reach into individual income showed the new power of governments to discipline personal behavior through standardized rules and bureaucratic staff work.

The Results of Government Regulation

The rise of public and private bureaucracies and the related heightening of the role of formal organizations in individual life was clearly a vital aspect of the kind of mass society that was developing in the Western world after 1870. The activities of organized bureaucracies built on earlier trends. Regulation in the name of professional medicine, for example, had been a recurrent theme since the sixteenth century, as doctors sought state backing for their version of how to treat disease. Much of the new regulation seems virtually inevitable, as the Western world became increasingly urbanized and crowded; traditionally populous societies such as China had introduced a bureaucratic atmosphere far earlier. Regulation also followed from the decline of more traditional community structures, such as guilds, that had once monitored individual behavior.

Much of the regulatory activity was clearly beneficial. Health rates improved dramatically throughout the Western world after 1880, and although private efforts played some role, the provision of public facilities, including hospitals and advice centers, plus the network of sanitary regulations, had undeniable impact. Any single measure generated debate, yet virtually no political current in the West, except for fringe movements such as anarchism, thoroughly opposed the expansion of public and private bureaucracies. Liberals, once champions of small government, increasingly shifted toward pragmatic approval of regulatory reforms, partly to woo voters who found traditional liberal causes somewhat remote, partly because middle-class people themselves saw a need for protections against unrestrained business activity. American Progressives, English Liberals, and German National Liberals all encouraged important new government initiatives. Socialists were even more comfortable with the basic impulse to regulate at least capitalist excesses in the interest of mass welfare. Most conservative groups encouraged discipline in the interests of good order, military strength, and political stability. The fact that all major currents agreed on the need for extension of government organization, if not on its purposes and targets, showed the strength of the new trends.

Yet the expansion of the bureaucratic state had drawbacks as well as advantages, just as any major historical development has had. Personal freedom was constricted in important ways, even as the value of individual self-expression remained high in theory. Many people found themselves trapped between a culture that encouraged individual rather than community decisions—in marriage or career choice, for example—while reducing latitudes for choice through the force of public and private regulations. As the masses rose in the West, they also became more disciplined, less disorderly, and perhaps less spontaneous. The family may also have been constrained (or improved) by the rise of larger organizations including the state, as choices once left to family decision—about how to train one's children, or whether to beat one's wife—were increasingly intruded upon.

Without question, the expansion of organized bureaucracies, with their new resources and functions, ushered in a new chapter in the long history of the Western nation-state. National governments exercised far greater powers than ever before, and they played a vital role in counterbalancing the rise of the masses.

Politics and the State in the Mass Society

Key constitutional issues in most Western nations were settled by the 1870s or before. No major changes occurred in German political structure between 1871 and 1914, although there were periodic demands by liberals and socialists for greater parliamentary power. Britain expanded the suffrage again in 1884 to include most male workers nationwide; in 1911 it scaled down the power of the House of Lords, to create undisputed sovereignty for the elected House of Commons. More serious political disputes erupted where universal suffrage for men came more slowly. Italy's grant of democracy in 1912 was a belated but genuinely radical step after many decades of high property qualifications and an accordingly restricted electorate. There were a few countries, such as Spain, where constitutional issues were more open, and periods of constitutional monarchy alternated with more authoritarian rule; Spain, still largely agricultural and with a strong anarchist movement, was also one of the only Western nations in which revolutionary pressures still challenged the political fabric. Finally, the Habsburg monarchy, now divided between Austrian and Hungarian sections for domestic rule, was seriously threatened by the demands of Slavic nationalists, which added to the more conventional pressures by socialists and other groups. Unwilling to grant major concessions to the Slavic minorities, the Habsburg regime faced growing instability, particularly after 1900.

For the most part, however, political structure in the West after 1870 involved fine tuning, not fundamental dispute. Even France, so long buffeted among different political options, settled down to a parliamentary republic. The French had grown increasingly restive under Napoleon III's empire during the 1860s, and when it lost to Bismarck's German coalition the regime simply collapsed. There followed some years of confusion when royalists hoped to establish a new monarchy, but a democratically elected parliament in fact ruled and gradually, by the later 1870s, established its own sovereignty. This Third Republic was to endure until another German victory, in 1940 in World War II, and it won at least lukewarm support from most French people.

The resolution of key issues about the nature of political regimes, in France and elsewhere, did not end dispute between liberals and conservatives. In most countries liberal parties still represented middle-class interests against the rural and upper-class predelictions of conservatives. Liberals distrusted the military, and conservatives distrusted too much secular education—there were ample grounds for dispute over issues of this sort. A major dispute divided conservative republicans (and other conservatives still uncomfortable with the very idea of a republic) from radicals in France in the 1890s, when the army falsely accused a Jewish

---

FRANCE'S THIRD REPUBLIC

The first parliament elected in 1871, after Napoleon III's downfall, was monarchist in majority, partly because the peasantry, frightened by the war, turned to local landlords who once elected strove for a new king. But the royalists could not agree on what king to choose—a Bourbon family member or an Orléanist; and while they dithered during the 1870s, parliament ruled in fact. Able republicans such as Léon Gambetta campaigned vigorously for the idea that France should return to the ideals of the liberal phase of the French revolution, offering political rights but a conservative social policy—and no king. Gradually, by-elections converted parliament to the republican side, as peasant voters agreed that liberal politics did not have to bring social disarray. The new republic, which emerged gradually and without a formal constitution, had a figurehead president, with parliament selecting the prime minister.

The resulting regime lived up to its promise of social caution, as France lagged well behind other Western nations in developing welfare measures or other reforms to benefit urban workers. The regime was also superficially unstable with frequent changes of ministry. But in fact most parliamentary parties supported the political structure itself, and the upper bureaucracy remained stable even when ministries changed hands. Hence France steered a fairly even course, despite a few major crises, until 1914. It worked effectively to strengthen its military and to develop a protective alliance system against the hated German enemy. It also spread a secular school system that promoted loyalty to France and republic alike, meanwhile building canals and local railroads to improve economic performance. The Third Republic, seldom loved, functioned longer than its more dramatic predecessors.

army captain, Alfred Dreyfus, of spying for the Germans. When the baselessness of the accusation was brought out, radicals urged a new attack on conservative forces such as the army and the Catholic church. Indeed, radicals finally forced a church–state separation between 1901 and 1905 that removed all Catholic influence from most French education while forcing the church to rely on the contributions of its own members rather than on tax funds.

There were political quarrels in other countries as well. German liberals supported Bismarck in an attack on the Catholic church there in the 1870s because of fears of foreign loyalties that might weaken the new German state. Republicans and Democrats in the United States feuded vigorously over the treatment of the defeated South until the late 1870s. For the most part, however, liberal–conservative dispute cooled considerably as both groups accepted the existing political structure and both also gained new fears about the force of socialism. At many points liberal and conservative parties did little more than label factions that argued over which politicians should have which jobs—the result of the decline of divisive issues within the political arena. Italy, indeed, produced a political phenomenon known as *transformismo*, or transformism, in which deputies, no matter what liberal or conservative platforms they campaigned upon, were transformed once in Rome into carbon copies of each other, squabbling over political spoils.

The decline of political issues and the often hollow disputes within parliaments turned some groups against the political process outright. Radical conservative leaders arose in a number of countries to attack parliaments as weak and corrupt. Often they joined critiques of mass society and a virulent anti-Semitism that blamed Jews for ills of the modern world ranging from trade unionism to capitalist profit-mongering. These rightist groups, working outside the political system, had little impact before 1914, but their potential for serious trouble would be abundantly revealed soon thereafter.

The more serious political force before World War I was of course socialism. With socialist parties on the rise and working-class pressure visible in strikes and unions, and finally with conventional liberal–conservative disputes ebbing, government policy-making turned increasingly to the question of responding to, and restraining, the masses.

One impulse, expanding state functions beyond previous limits, involved enactment of limited social insurance measures, designed to offer segments of the urban working class some state-run protection against accident, illness, and old age. This in principle was a major step away from reliance on local community and family for such protection, or against punitive almshouse measures for the very poor. Bismarck pioneered the new approach, as part of his attempt to beat down the Social Democratic party in the 1880s. The German insurance measures were widely copied during the 1890s by Austria, Holland, and the Scandinavian countries. Britain entered the welfare field slightly later, led by Liberals eager to retain working-class support. A major social insurance measure passed Parliament in 1911 offered some protection against unemployment for a small number of workers. France and Italy organized more voluntary schemes, while several American states added their names to the list as well.

Welfare measures remained limited in scope and benefit levels before 1914. They certainly did not stem the tide of socialism. But they did represent a significant redefinition of what the state might do for the mass of its citizenry, particularly when combined with the increasing regulation of working hours and other urban conditions.

Still more significant, in the decades after 1870, was the extension of mass education in state-run systems. During this period, almost all Western governments undertook a commitment to offer at least primary education to all citizens, male and female; they thus greatly enhanced earlier trends of spreading literacy and numeracy. Furthermore, the new education was not optional; compulsory education laws extended through age twelve almost everywhere by 1890, with the southern states of the United States belatedly joining the parade soon after 1900.

Motives for mass education were mixed. Liberals had long advocated education as the key to personal and social betterment; this impulse remained—enhanced, in places like France and Italy, by a desire to replace Catholic education with more secular values. Conservatives increasingly accepted education in the interests of better military recruitment and training in social discipline. Most schools, for example, carefully stressed the duties of women to provide a secure home and sound moral values to men, in an attempt to encourage traditional family life. Various proponents saw education as a key to industrial advance; an educated work force, capable of sending its ablest members on to secondary school and university, would provide the most skilled work and the highest-quality bureaucracy. Characteristically, the United States went furthest in encouraging social mobility through education by expanding access to secondary school and by setting up state-sponsored (land-grant) universities that charged little or no tuition. European postprimary education remained a more elite option, though even here there were experiments with new secondary curricula that would be more relevant than the classical strand for the children of clerks and artisans.

But the key motive for mass education was political. With voting now a widespread right, the nation-state needed to assure an educated citizenry capable of reading, thinking, and choosing. Because voting opened the doors to potential radicalism, the nation-state needed direct contact with citizens at an impressionable age to persuade them of the glories of the nation itself and the fervent obligations of patriotism. For the new mass schools were training grounds in nationalism, bringing a new or at least enhanced loyalty to the masses as they lost attachments to local regions and sometimes to the traditional force of religion. Schools pushed nationalism hard, stressing the wonders of the national language (and attacking minority languages and dialects); presenting a carefully slanted view of the nation's history (as in the United States's textbook claim that it had never started but also never lost a war—both untrue even before 1900); and denigrating traditions of other nations.

Mass schooling of course had many effects. By encouraging literacy it promoted mass culture and also some of the new forms of protest, which depended on the ability to read tracts and instructions. The definition of childhood shifted increasingly away from productive functions, toward the duty to be educated—a shift that might well be confusing to various family members. But the most obvious impact was nationalistic. Though mass schooling did not create nations of docile citizens, it did create unprecedented loyalty to the nation itself. Politicians would learn that they would ignore this nationalist fervor at their peril; and governments freely played on the loyalty, even using it to persuade union leaders, on occasion, to abandon strike demands in favor of maintaining the nation's strength.

The expansion of education as a contact between government and citizen was compounded by the extension of mass peacetime military conscription after 1870. Prussia's great war record in the 1860s revealed the benefits of a large pool of trained soldiers, even on reserve. So France, Austria, and other continental nations rushed in with similar programs, requiring a year or more of service. Military recruits, normally assigned outside their home region deliberately to break local ties, also were open to new loyalties: to the military itself and to the nation it served.

The state-fostered spread of nationalism represented a desire to win active allegiance, not mere calm, from its citizenry—a marked departure from traditional political strategies and another sign of what change the rise of the nation-state, combined with the new visibility of the industrial masses, had begotten. Nationalist fervor was of course uneven. Middle-class people and clerks more commonly celebrated nationalist occasions than did workers. Socialist leaders indeed characteristically argued against nationalism, in the name of class solidarity across boundaries. But workers, too, bought popular newspapers, which fed nationalist slogans to an avid readership, commending all possible signs of national achievement and lamenting the slightest setback or dishonor. And workers proved open to more general enthusiasms for wars fought in the nation's name, including the tragic war—World War I—that was to break out in 1914.

Yet the promotion of nationalism as a means of cementing a basic social order in the age of the masses, although demonstrably effective, was a double-edged weapon: It brought loyalty, yet it also put pressure on the state to feed the same nationalist appetite. One of the main functions of the state, in this period of Western history, became the production of diplomatic glory and military success—not a new goal, to be sure, but now enhanced by the desire to nourish nationalist passions and distract from potential unrest at home. And as the next section discusses, it was this same area of war and diplomacy that would ultimately undo the precarious consensus reached after 1870 in politics and society, and would indeed threaten the position of the West itself.

Diplomatic Alliances and the Imperialist Climax

Diplomatic tensions increased markedly in Europe and indeed around the world from the 1860s onward. Nation-states in the West had long been competitive and expansionist. By 1870 this tradition was amplified by the new industrial resources at the service of these states and by the new crowding of the European map. German and Italian unification (discussed in Chapter 5) removed vacuums of power that had cushioned great-power rivalries since the fifteenth century, so that direct confrontations were more likely. Germany was a great power in its own right, and Italy sought to be; these factors also created new tensions. The unifications had left France badly aggrieved, because of humiliating defeat and loss of territory, and Russia belatedly nervous about her newly potent neighbor.

Bismarck, by far the cleverest diplomatic maneuverer in the 1870s and 1880s, sought to stabilize Germany's gains through a system of protective alliances. This was an important innovation in European diplomacy; most previous alliances had been formed against threatening aggressors and near a war setting. Bismarck's alliances were intended to prevent further conflict, and they worked well for a time; but their long-term effect was to reduce the flexibility of international relations in the West.

Bismarck's desire was to isolate France to prevent a reprisal attack toward regaining the lost provinces of Alsace-Lorraine. By 1882 Germany had forged alliances with Italy and the Habsburgs, on the basis of promises of mutual aid against outside attack; to this Triple Alliance Bismarck joined a separate understanding with Russia. Because Germany also cultivated friendly relations with Britain, which however remained aloof from formal ties, France was effectively alone. Germany became the linchpin of a network of promises to keep the peace.

This system came partially unglued in 1890, when Bismarck, its mastermind, was forced out of office by an ambitious new emperor, William II. William and other advisors urged that the Russian alliance be dropped because it conflicted with German obligations to Austria-Hungary, and this was done. France quickly began to woo Russia, now a free agent and obviously relevant to France's desire to escape isolation and to press Germany on two sides. Despite the incongruity of a radical republic allying with Europe's most autocratic monarch, the alliance jelled in 1893, again on the basis of promises of mutual defense. The European alignments now became more even, but more potentially menacing with all the great powers except Britain ensnared in hostile entanglements.

Imperialist Impulses

The reckoning of the opposing alliances was delayed, however, by the West's new involvement in an explosion of imperialist acquisitions. In part because of heightened tensions within Europe, the great powers after 1870 exhibited an unprecedented thirst for colonies abroad, particularly in Africa and Asia.

In Asia, France completed the takeover of Indochina in the 1800s and Britain, eager to protect India, gained Burma as a buffer state in 1886. France, Britain, Germany, and the United States all vied for Pacific Oceania, with Germany and the United States dividing control of Samoa and France developing Tahiti. In the Spanish-American War in 1898, the United States also took over the Philippines, plus gaining Puerto

THE ORIGINS OF THE ALLIANCE SYSTEM: TROUBLES IN THE BALKANS

The first sign of diplomatic trouble following the Italian and German unifications stemmed from revolts in the Balkans during the mid-1870s, which indeed became Europe's most vulnerable area for the next several decades. Riots against Turkish rule broke out in several spots, and two small Balkan countries, Serbia and Montenegro, followed up by declaring war on the Ottoman Empire. Russia joined in by 1877, seeking both to protect Slavic "brethren" and to implement the longstanding policy of winning new territory at Turkey's expense. Easy victories against the weak Ottoman regime resulted in a large Bulgarian state, closely linked to Russia, and new Russian holdings on the Black Sea. Neither Austria-Hungary, also interested in this region, nor Britain, concerned that no power dominate the Middle East and so threaten India, could accept this result. Bismarck, anxious for peace, called a Congress of Berlin to settle the issue. The result was a smaller Bulgaria, new territory for Serbia, full independence to Serbia, Montenegro, and Romania, and Austrian administration over the Slavic territories of Bosnia-Herzogovina. Britain was given the island of Cyprus, increasing its power in the eastern Mediterranean. And France was encouraged to take over Tunisia. Almost everyone, in other words, got something, and the overall European sense that it could take outside territories at will was obviously enhanced. Bismarck alone played "honest broker," seeking only peace and declaring that united Germany was a satisfied power.

But the potential for trouble, particularly between Austria-Hungary and Russia as rivals for influence in the unstable Balkans, remained great. This is why Bismarck worked to ally with both countries and to persuade each to minimize their differences with the other. Alliance with Italy, offended by France's move in Tunisia, was simply a bonus for Bismarck's system. The system itself encouraged various powers, including Germany, to look for territorial gains outside Europe, rather than challenge the tightly woven alliance structure directly.

Rico and other territories in the West Indies. China itself, the greatest traditional state of all, was also put up for bidding. The Chinese lost a war to industrializing Japan in 1894, and this clear sign of weakness opened the new scramble. Russia, Britain, France, and Germany won long-term leases on key Chinese ports and surrounding territories, with the Chinese powerless to resist. A Chinese rebellion against Western encroachments, the Boxer Rebellion of 1899, was easily put down by a handful of troops from various European countries and the United States.

The dismemberment of Africa was even more thorough. Portugal expanded its effective control of Angola and Mozambique. The king of

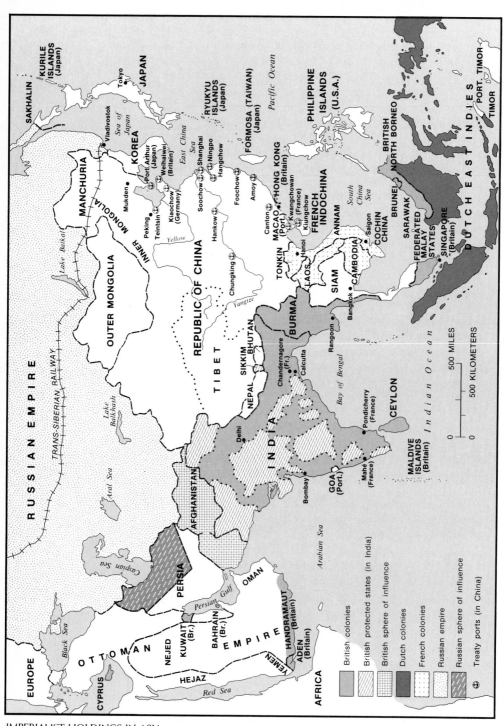

IMPERIALIST HOLDINGS IN ASIA
The United States and Japan join Europe's scramble before 1914.

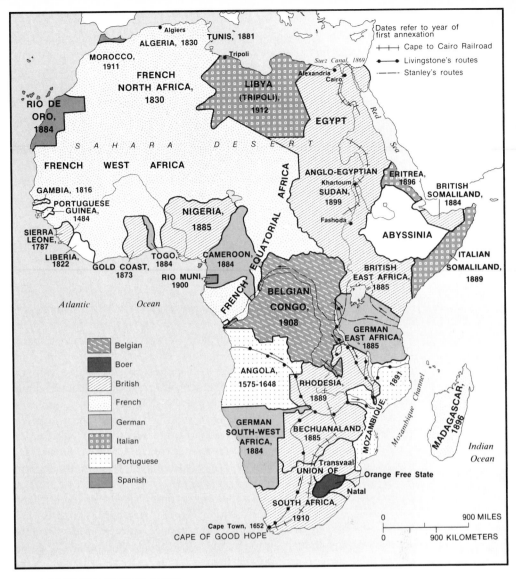

THE DISMEMBERMENT OF AFRICA
The holdings of the European powers by 1914.

Belgium took over the Congo, Germany gained new colonies in southern Africa, while France developed a huge string of colonies running from west to east below the Sahara desert. Britain had already taken over administration of Egypt in the 1860s, which involved control of the new Suez Canal, a vital route to India. Now the British expanded holdings in West Africa while also pushing northward from South Africa in the east-central part of the vast continent. Finally, in addition to the seizures of Egypt and Tunisia (plus French conquest of Algeria earlier in the century), North Africa was swallowed up through French occupation of Morocco and Italian administration of Tripoli shortly before 1914. By that date, only Ethiopia remained entirely independent in the whole of Africa, having defeated an Italian force in 1896. The rest of the continent, like much of Asia, was now part of the European imperial system. Important chunks of the Middle East were colonized as well, when Britain administered coastal states on the eastern part of the Arabian peninsula while, along with Russia, exercising strong influence in Persia and Afghanistan.

During the decades of imperialism, finally, growing immigration and political reform created unified, autonomous nations within the British empire, in Canada, Australia, and New Zealand. Not new acquisitions, these areas differed from the outright colonies by participating directly in Western institutions, values, and trends. They established parliamentary systems with mass political parties, increased wealth through industrialization or commercial agriculture, and reproduced Western family patterns that included a strong emphasis on virtuous domesticity for women.

The outburst of new, worldwide imperialism resulted from a number of factors. Fundamental was the new world power balance, which gave the West unusual advantage over most other parts of the world. Steam ships allowed Europeans to sail up African rivers, which always before had resisted human navigation. Repeating rifles and early machine guns allowed small forces to defeat vast land armies. In addition to technology, improvements in European bureaucracies permitted effective administration of large territories once they were conquered. Not only new colonies but also older holdings, such as British India, were now effectively run by groups of European administrators at the top, who supervised court systems, railway and postal networks, as well as defense and police, supplemented often by local leadership or bureaucrats at more junior levels.

Technological and administrative opportunity, however, did not have to translate into the imperialist surge. Power advantages, which is what the West enjoyed at this point, do not necessarily lead to sweeping aggression, and indeed although the West had long displayed colonial interests, it had never indulged them so widely. In actually motivating the new imperialism, four factors within the West interacted.

First, a number of people saw the empire as a vital means of personal profit and expression. Businessmen wanted to control new mining ventures, where profits could be higher than at home. Missionaries, ironically faced with a more secular society at home, spread the gospel to "heathen" abroad. Nationalists, eager to see their countries share the symbols of power already established by Britain and France, staked out patriotic claims. Aristocrats, uncomfortable in the businesslike atmosphere of their own nations, might bask in the prestige of serving as colonial overlords. And simple adventurers, hostile to organized mass society, exulted in the excitement of the bush. A host of people, in sum, gained various kinds of satisfaction not only in serving the new empires, but in staking claims in the first place, which they then cajoled their governments to implement.

With the rising in the advertising of consumer goods, businesses began to recognize the effectiveness of aligning their products with appeals to patriotism and imperial might. This British advertisement from 1909 was set in India, one of Britain's principal colonies.

The second factor in the motivation for colonial expansion was that a number of Westerners still saw colonies as a vital economic resource. Expanding industrialization brought new economic competition for markets and materials. In some cases policymakers also worried about continued population growth, hoping for colonies that would allow location of residents without loss to the nation's strength. But the big arguments were directed toward assuring markets for industrial goods and, in return, locking up supplies of materials that would feed growing production—arguments that echoed earlier mercantilist beliefs but that took on new force in an age of heightened rivalry and realistic understanding of how easily industrial production could outstrip buying power at home. The general economic motives were largely inaccurate—many colonies cost more than they brought in; sales to other industrial nations exceeded those to the underdeveloped areas of empire. But this does not mean that the arguments made no sense as a motive, particularly when supplemented by profits available to individual businessmen.

The third impetus for colonial expansion was that imperialism followed from established national diplomatic rivalries. Germany wanted colonies to emulate and restrain Britain; Britain expanded, almost willy-nilly, to respond to German gains. France used imperialism in Indochina, Tunisia, and sub-Saharan Africa to compensate for national disgrace in the Franco-Prussian war, even though some nationalists argued that no amount of colonial territory could compensate for the needed revenge on Germany. Italy, like Germany, sought colonies to establish great-power status, but the Italians were less consistently successful than other colonial powers. Once involved in the colonial game, the arguments for further acquisition became compelling. Britain acquired Egypt and the Suez Canal to prevent French control of a vital route to India. France moved on Morocco to protect its Algerian colony. And so it went. Given Europe's huge power advantage over the rest of the world at this point, rivalry games explain more of the imperialist thrust than any other single factor.

But the fourth motivating factor for continued colonialism was the ingredient of mass nationalism. Mass nationalism did not *cause* imperialism, but it certainly supported it and was fed by it. The mass press trumpeted imperialist victories, poured scorn on any setbacks. Europeans and Americans were treated to lavish stories of exotic places, conde-scending accounts of "native" ways that only superior Western civiliza-tion could rectify. Imperialism, with its frequent, usually easy and successful, wars and its comforting assurance of Western cultural suprem-acy, undoubtedly resonated among many people. Lower-middle-class clerks, particularly, found in imperialism a respectable and exciting sup-plement to often humdrum work lives, but the enthusiasm reached many workers as well—despite the fact that socialist parties generally opposed the imperialist surge. Crises in the imperialist strategies, as when British and French forces met in the Sudan in 1898, drew big crowds into the streets to urge their governments toward firm resolve. British recruitment efforts, during a battle with the Dutch Boer settlers in South Africa, won widespread patriotic response from many workers. Imperialism thus gained mass backing and also seemed, in the eyes of policymakers, a useful means of distracting from social conflicts at home.

Imperialist expansion was by definition finite, however. By 1900 most available territories had been devoured; further additions ran against es-tablished great-power interests. Germany thus encouraged the Boers against Britain, because German colonies in Africa would be threatened by a firmer British hold. France's acquisition of Morocco roused much greater opposition than earlier expansion had done, for with little territory left each new move seemed more momentous.

The imperialist surge thus slowed down after 1900. It had produced three major consequences. First, Westerners controlled a much wider array of people than ever before, which meant that world developments became more closely intertwined with Western patterns. Africa and Asia did not Westernize in response to imperialism, but they unquestionably changed, for the new imperialism was a major episode in modern world history.

Nationalism and symbols of military prowess could be "packaged" for internal consumption, furthering many business and national interests. This postcard was issued when the German emperor launched a new warship, the S. S. *Imperator.*

The second consequence was that imperialism heightened the West's domination of world commerce. Not all colonies were paying propositions, for nationalist rivalries prompted some takeovers of rather barren territory. But imperialism overall heightened Western ability to convert many parts of the world into raw-materials producers for Western consumers and markets for Western-manufactured goods. Imperial controls were not in fact essential for this economic relationship, as Latin America, now mainly independent politically, fell into the same network; but imperialism expressed and abetted the relationship in other regions. Ultimately this relationship made the West dependent on world economic conditions as well as the reverse, but in the short run the Western ability to sell more expensive processed goods, in return for materials and foods produced by cheap labor, was the most striking point.

Finally, imperialism ultimately served to heat up rivalries among the Western nation-states themselves. The United States, long isolated, was drawn into international disputes and conferences because of its new imperialist stakes, even though it did not participate in the alliance system. More generally appetites whetted by imperialism turned back to Europe itself when the phase of easy expansion had ended, making power politics within Europe more dangerous than before. And new rivalries resulted. Most important was growing British–German tension. As Germany developed an empire and a navy to match Britain's, while also maintaining its powerful continental position and increasing its industrial strength, Britain became increasingly nervous. Although the British won the Boer War (1899–1902), they were hard-pressed and came to realize how vulnerable they were in standing alone. So they began to seek allies, forming a new pact with Japan and then, in 1904, developing a loose link—the *Entente Cordiale*—with France. Old and new enmities between Britain and France were buried in the interest of opposing German strength. Military negotiations followed, and in 1907 the French facilitated a British–Russian understanding as well. Thus the old Triple Alliance was now opposed by a Triple Entente, as imperialist rivalries among Britain, France, and Russia were subsumed into greater concerns about preserving a balance of power within Europe.

Growing European tension, plus the imperialist disputes, fed growing armaments, which were also supported by big business in the interests of sales of heavy industrial goods. Although Russia, concerned about the impact of buying armaments on its precarious budget, sponsored some disarmament talks, the race to extend periods of military service and build more gigantic navies dominated the years after 1900. Britain introduced a new naval weapon, the battleship, which Germany quickly copied. All efforts to stop this particular rivalry failed, as Britain sought outright naval superiority while Germany insisted on a naval role sufficient not to match, but to distract Britain in case of war.

What was happening, after 1900, was an escalation of nation-state rivalry to a new and dangerous flashpoint. Just as Germany's growing strength provoked Britain and made the French still more anxious about their powerful neighbor than before, countermeasures roused insecurity in Germany. With the Triple Entente Germany faced the prospect of a two-front war, against France in the west and Russia in the east, with Britain trying to rule the seas. Germany's allies, a beleaguered Austria-Hungary and a weak and unreliable Italy, were small comfort in this new alignment.

At the same time, the habit of using dynamic, aggressive foreign policy to distract from internal pressures—the pressures that resulted from the rise of mass protest—complicated diplomatic reactions still further. Massive strike movements, the steady increase of socialist voting strength, and in some cases militant feminism as well convinced many statesmen that they could not afford an appearance of weakness on the foreign policy front. It was even tempting to believe that a "good war" might smooth over internal tensions, by calling the masses to a clear patriotic duty—a thought particularly prominent among German military planners, but not absent in Britain and France. The tensions of mass society, in other words, and the habit of looking to nationalism as a key means of social control, exacerbated nation-state rivalries.

Finally, the tense alliance system that had emerged by 1907 made the industrial leaders of the West increasingly dependent on far less stable nations to the east. As the next section makes clear, Austria-Hungary, wracked by nationalities conflicts, and Russia, beset by even more fundamental social fissures, were both essential to the alliance system and visibly vulnerable. Leaders in these nations, but also their respective German and French/British allies, came to believe not only that no further setbacks could be accepted in foreign policy, but that positive new gains were essential to knit an unraveling social fabric.

Eastern Europe

The decades in which mass society arose in the West, on the basis of maturing industrial economies, saw even more fundamental social and political changes in eastern Europe. Rapid population growth produced growing land hunger and urbanization in Russia, Hungary, and the Balkans—as well as a soaring emigration to North America. Agricultural technology lagged and rural conditions remained desperately poor. The continued prominence of large estates in much of eastern Europe, including parts of Russia, provided an obvious target for rural discontent. In Russia grievances about the redemption payments and other restrictions that had resulted from the Emancipation of the Serfs in 1861 further fanned the flames.

Eastern Europe was also troubled by a multitude of unresolved nationalist issues. The new, small nations in the Balkans were unsatisfied; they wanted more territory, and they wanted to link with fellow Slavs in other lands. Serbia thus sought Serbian-speaking territories controlled by other Balkan states and by Austria-Hungary. Russia faced growing self-consciousness among minority nationalities including Jews, Ukrainians, and Poles. The country responded by vigorous, often violent attacks, killing many Jews and trying to force other nationalities into a Russian mold. In Austria-Hungary not only southern Slavs, such as the Serbs, but also other Slavic groups led by the Czechs, pressed for some autonomy, if not independence. Nationalism, which had been a unifying force in places such as Germany, in the East threatened a welter of new rivalries and divisions.

Russia (including Russian Poland) added yet another ingredient to the unstable brew by launching an ambitious program of industrialization. Efforts to industrialize followed from the reform effort that had begun with the Emancipation, for the tsarist regime realized that it must begin to match the economic strength of the West or decline as a great power. Extensive railroad building, capped by the Trans-Siberian line stretching across the vast country, encouraged factory industry, and by the 1890s extensive mechanization was transforming textile and metallurgical production. Government sponsorship, and foreign investment from the Western nations, spurred many, often huge factory complexes. Cities grew rapidly, and a new working class took shape. Conditions remained poor, however, and in combination with the unfamiliar pace of factory work spurred recurrent worker unrest. Strikes, unions, and a growing socialist movement marked this development. One segment of the socialist movement, in turn, was fervently Marxist, advocating violent revolution and arguing that the importation of industrialization and capitalism into Russia made a proletarian rising possible even in these early stages of economic change. Under Nikolai Lenin, an able theorist and organizer, the Bolshevik, or Majority, wing of the Marxist movement developed tightly knit groups of workers capable of surviving extensive police repression.

For along with the various discontents and pressures in Russia came renewed tsarist autocracy from 1881 onward. Alexander II's reformist spirit, which had carried through the 1870s with the creation of local government assemblies, new law codes, and military adjustments, ended with the tsar's assassination by anarchists in 1881. Then the government clamped down again, refusing to accept political change, extending new police powers, lashing out at Jews and other minorities. These autocratic policies did not prevent recurrent peasant unrest and worker protest, in a country where periodic famines, the most basic of all reasons for popular risings, added to other popular grievances. Many students and businessmen also sought change, from sweeping anarchist attacks on government of all sorts to more timid liberal programs. But the new tsar, Nicholas II, and his advisors resisted, arguing among other things that Russia must not fall into the trap of Westernization, with its scorn for proper authority and its social disintegration.

Then an economic recession in the early 1900s was followed by an abortive war with Japan from 1904 to 1905. The Japanese, frightened by Russia's expansion into northern Chinese provinces and eager to seize Korea on their own, surprised the world by besting the Russian forces, aided by the empire's difficulty in transporting troops to the Asian theater. Defeat led in turn to the 1905 revolution in Russia. Massive general strikes by workers combined with two years of classic peasant rebellion, in which estate records were seized and land taken over. The tsar responded by granting extensive concessions. Peasant redemption payments were cancelled and a series of reforms encouraged a group of ambitious peasants to gain more land and convert more fully to market agriculture. A parliament, or *Duma*, was established. But here the reform spirit was truncated as soon as order was restored. The parliament became little more than a rubber stamp, and socialist parties were outlawed. Repression returned, and any chance for a liberal approach to Russian politics ended. Although the peasantry did calm, worker unrest actually increased, and renewed revolution became increasingly likely.

Toward World War I

The strains of eastern Europe rebounded on Europe's general diplomatic system. Russia, blocked from further Asian conquests because of Japan's new power, turned back to the Balkans and its "little Slavic brothers" for new foreign-policy adventures. The Balkans drew Austria-Hungary also, because of the desire to attack South Slavic nationalism and prevent any enlargement of aggressive new nations such as Serbia. So Russia and Austria-Hungary veered toward a collision course, and their respective allies, eager to defend what were clearly shaky regimes, backed them without great question.

Tensions mounted in a series of Balkan crises from 1907 onward. In that year Austria annexed Bosnia-Herzegovina outright—the territories it had administered since 1878. This was a fearful blow to Serbian pride, which held that these regions were nationalist domain. Russia was unable to act but yearned for compensation in the region to cover its humiliation by Japan. In 1912 the Russians helped several Balkan states join in

NEW EFFORTS FOR PEACE

Europe's great powers were not unaware of the dangers of growing nationalism, the tight alliance system, and the flammable rivalries in eastern Europe. A series of international initiatives in the later nineteenth century sought to counter some of these pressures. Agreements to coordinate postal service, for example, led to an International Postal Congress in Switzerland in 1874, to facilitate global mails. Less formal meetings of various powers tried to deal with rebellions and atrocities in the Middle East, such as an Ottoman massacre of Armenian dissidents, though few concrete steps resulted. Other conferences, often based in Switzerland, treated rules for international shipping and for weights and measures.

In 1898 the Russian tsar proposed a major extension of the international regulatory movement, and during the following year the first International Peace Conference met at the Hague, Holland, attended by twenty-six nations. Russia hoped to cut the burden of its armaments expense, though it masked its understandable motive in higher-blown rhetoric. The other great powers resisted any real disarmament, but a series of measures were approved to define the laws of war; for example, gas warfare was outlawed and better treatment of prisoners was detailed. An international arbitration court was established to facilitate the peaceful resolution of international disputes. But the most serious tensions continued unabated, and most of the rules of war were to be violated just fifteen years later. A second International Peace Conference, in 1907, saw serious British efforts to limit naval armaments, but these were blocked by German fears that Britain was trying to legislate its permanent domination of the seas. Again, only some agreements on the rules of war resulted. Recurrently in the next few years, conferences tried to take up the growing naval buildups, and Britain also negotiated independently with Germany on the subject, all to no avail. Germany continued to expand its navy, whereas Britain was too fearful to acquiesce to Germany's demand that it pull away from France and Russia. The idea of serious international negotiation for peace was launched, but its impact remained hollow.

a new attack on the Ottoman empire, with all the allies hoping to take over Macedonia. The Balkan nations won the war but then quarreled over the spoils. This led to a Second Balkan War, in 1913, in which Bulgaria attacked Serbia and Greece, with Turkey and Romania, hoping for spoils of their own, joining in against Bulgaria. Yet this war only created further bitterness, in what was clearly becoming a hopeless diplomatic mess. Serbia, though a winner, still wanted to attack Austria-Hungary, while Austria-Hungary was deeply concerned about the Serbian victories.

Then, in 1914, the Austrian Archduke Ferdinand was assassinated by a Serbian nationalist. This, for Austria-Hungary, was the last straw: Serbia had to be attacked. Germany supported Austria, partly out of loyalty to a weak ally and partly because some leaders believed that world war was inevitable and sooner was better than later, because both France and Russia were in early stages of military reforms that would strengthen them in the long run. Russia refused to let Austria bully Serbia, lest it lose all Balkan influence; and France vowed to support Russia come what might. When Austria declared war on Serbia on July 28, Russia declared a general mobilization—because Russian procedures were slow, it believed it had to prepare. Mobilization frightened Germany, whose strategy called for a quick defeat of France before turning to Russia; so Germany declared war on both allies on August 1. Britain hesitated, hoping for peace, but in fact it was heavily committed to France and then was frightened and offended by Germany's invasion of Belgium, which was part of Germany's plan to knock France out quickly by pouring in from the north as well as the east. Britain entered the fray on August 4. After a century of considerable peace in Europe, the nation-states had once again launched a general war. But this one, fed by the new powers of the state, by new nationalist passions, and by the devastating armaments produced by industrialization, would have far more awesome consequences, as Chapter 7 makes clear, than any previous struggle.

Conclusion: The Moods of Mass Society

The establishment of mass society, involving new forms of mass expression and new kinds of organizations to deal with mass populations, provoked diverse reactions from different groups, sometimes indeed from the same individual. Many features of the new society seemed obviously good. Material conditions, health levels, educational attainments were improving at an unprecedented rate, and there were few who would deny that this was progress. Newspapers, both middle-class and mass, at the turn of the century heralded the achievements of the nineteenth century and looked forward with optimism to the twentieth century to come. Although elements of the masses might disagree with the progressive vision, pointing to dislocations and to the constraints at work, the leading mass movements also carried optimistic seeds. Socialists pointed to a brighter future; nationalists rejoiced in the new strengths of their society.

Yet mass society had its critics. A variety of artists and writers lamented the decline of good taste, arguing for aesthetic expressions that the masses could not comprehend. Social and behavioral scientists developed new fascination for exploring the irrational elements of the human consciousness and of mass behavior. Crowd psychologists such as Gustav le Bon in France emphasized the passions of mob action, while a variety of researchers from the United States to Russia followed up on Darwinism by studying the animal components of human reactions. Elements of both art and science, in other words, responded to mass society with a new interest in disorder and crude vigor. A number of political theorists turned to the need for new, decisive leadership to discipline mass impulses and escape the divisions and corruption of the parliamentary state. The vision of patterned, rational progress became less clear than before on the intellectual front.

Clearly also, much established leadership greeted mass society with mixed feelings. Devices such as mass education responded creatively to the new posture of ordinary people, reshaping important elements of popular life and outlook. But the masses were not tamed by these devices, and whether realistically or not many statesmen and members of the big-business and aristocratic elite were running scared after 1900, uncertain what combination of further reform, police pressure, and diplomatic adventure could succeed in keeping the masses in their place. The rise of the masses in no sense caused World War I. Specific nation-state entanglements and the special problems of eastern Europe played an obvious role. But the tensions of dealing with the masses in a Western society unwilling to jettison social and political hierarchy played a role as well, in leading toward a war that, as the first fully mass and industrial conflict, severely crippled the civilization that produced it.

Ironically, however, the outset of World War I was greeted with the same optimism that had heralded the onset of the twentieth century. Troops departed for the front almost gaily, their departure hailed by enthusiastic civilians who draped their trains with flowers. The whole affair would be over by Christmas, everyone thought. Ordinary troops and strategic planners alike counted on swift, decisive strokes that would bring greater glory to the nation, a taste of invigorating action for a society that too often seemed routine and constrained. The hopes were misplaced, as mass warfare proved to be a grinding, bloody affair. But the initial mood showed the confidence, and also the need for release of energy, that the first decades of mass society had created.

SEVEN

WESTERN SOCIETY AND WORLD WARS: 1914–1945

1914	World War I
1915	Submarine warfare
1917	Entry of the United States: Russia withdraws
1918	War ends; Germany surrenders; German emperor flees
1919	Versailles Peace Conference; major treaties; League of Nations established
1919	Formation of Weimar Republic in Germany
1917	Russian revolution
1918–1920	Civil war in Russia
1919	Women's suffrage granted in the United States and Weimar Germany
1919–1939	Isolationism in the United States
1919–1921	Division of Ireland; independence of the Irish Republic
1920–1921	Postwar economic depression
1921	Lenin's New Economic Policy
1923	End of inflation in Germany
1923	Hitler's Beer Hall *Putsch*
1924	Lenin's death
1924	Treaty of Locarno
1926	British general strike
1927	Triumph of Stalin in Russia
1928	First Soviet Five-Year Plan; collectivization in agriculture
1931–1932	Widespread famine in the Soviet Union
1928	Vote granted to women in Britain
1929	Beginning of the Great Depression
1932–1933	Trough of the Depression
1932	Peak Nazi vote in German free elections
1933	Hitler takes power
1933	New Deal launched in the United States
1935	Hitler begins German rearmament
1935	Italy invades Ethiopia
1936	Hitler violates Versailles treaty by remilitarizing the Rhineland
1936–1939	Spanish civil war
1939	Franco's forces victorious
1936	Popular Front government in France
1938	German *Anschluss* with Austria; Munich conference
1938–1939	Great purges in the Soviet Union
1939	German–Soviet pact
1939	Outbreak of World War II
1940	Fall of France
1942	United States–British advance in North Africa; Soviet advance begins after seizure of Stalingrad
1944	Allied invasion of France (D-Day)
1940 ff	Holocaust against Jews
1940 ff	Massive entry of women into the labor force
1945	Atomic bomb dropped on Japan
1945	End of World War II; Yalta and Potsdam conferences; Hitler commits suicide

CHAPTER
SEVEN

TOTAL WARS AND INTERWAR DISCONTENT

THE THREE DECADES THAT OPENED with World War I and closed with the end of World War II were dominated by events of unusual magnitude. The wars themselves pervaded the lives of two generations. Adding to their impact was the Bolshevik Revolution which seized Russia in 1917 and shook Western politics and diplomacy as well, and the Great Depression, which opened in 1929.

History often alternates between periods in which the shape of society is determined by basic processes such as political forms, demographic behavior, or social structure, and periods in which events take a leading role. The contrast is partly artificial, of course; basic forces shape events and are shaped by them, whereas events cannot be understood apart from the larger context. But the simple fact is that some periods, such as 1870–1914, are marked not by earthshaking events so much as by clusters of smaller events, "headline-grabbers" in their own year that largely illustrate more basic forces such as imperialism or the rise of socialism. In contrast, the era of the world wars must be understood first in terms of what happened at the event level. Occurrences such as war and revolution set the tone of Western society even during superficially calmer, more "normal" periods such as the mid-1920s. The events clearly marked the consciousness of those involved. Many people, particularly in the upper classes and intellectuals groups, saw World War I as a decisive turning point, after which nothing could be the same. Their belief may have been exaggerated, but it was very real to them and governed their own political and cultural activity during their mature lives.

The era of the world wars, from 1914 to 1945, was an unhappy and confused chapter in Western history. Few decades in the history of any society have seen so much blind violence, so many political extremes, so much fundamental, often paralyzing division. This was not, fortunately, the final chapter in Western history, although to some who lived through the period it seemed so. One of the challenges of coming to terms with these decades of war and confusion is to figure out how durable was the mark they left on the Western society that emerged after 1945.

Even during the war years and the interwar decades, events were not all-powerful in their shaping of society; many basic processes continued trajectories set in the previous period. Birth rates continued to drop as family life was redefined to include fewer children. Business organization and mass politics gained fuller definition. The nation-state expressed its power through war and continued to expand during the interwar years. Yet this new period brought structural change as well, linked to the big events. Communism and fascism were important additions to the political spectrum, with effects that would inform the postwar period as well. Even more important was the slippage of western Europe in the world at large, as imperialism reached a final high point and then began to recede. The rise of the United States to a role of world power represented new strength for Western society but it also brought new tensions on both sides of the Atlantic. The arduous but impressive development of a new Soviet society—more isolated from the West than was the Russia of the later tsars—and the growing strength of Japan were additional forces reshaping the West's position in the world. After examining the shocking events that gave special character to the decades after 1914, we return to consider what was changing, and what was not changing, in the basic features of the West.

World War I

The First World War expressed many previous tensions in European society; in no sense did it spring forth as an accident or an isolated event, as Chapter 6 made clear. But the war also had a causal force of its own, altering the course of eastern European history decisively and that of Western history substantially. Although seeds of postwar troubles did exist prior to 1914, as Chapter 6 explained, many of the horrors of the 1920s and 1930s, including the severity of the Depression and the rise of German Nazism, probably would not have occurred without the war's prod.

For World War I was a bloody, dreadful affair, almost as bad for some of the Entente states who "won" as for some of the losers. Initial hopes for a quick and glorious national victory were soon dashed, and disillusionment—the shattering of optimistic beliefs—was not the least of the war's results. Never before had so many lives been lost for so little result, as battle fronts hardened, with every minor alteration costing the lives of tens of thousands of men and an even larger number of maimed casualties.

The Fields of Battle

France thrust briefly into Germany in the late summer of 1914, but on the western front, the German conquest of Belgium and advance through northern France were the big news. For a brief moment, as French forces pulled back in panic from their own offensive, it looked as though German hopes for a quick Western settlement might be met. But France rallied, aided by British reinforcements and by heroic civilian support, including a famous troop convoy organized by Parisian cabdrivers. Soon northern France was pockmarked with trenches, from which little advance was possible. The awesome technology of modern war was revealed in all its power, as devastating artillery, barbed-wire fences, and soon the use of poison gas defined the deadening stalemate. By 1916 stagnation on the western front had turned into nightmare as the Germans lost 850,000 men in the single year on this front alone, the French 700,000, the British 410,000—without any appreciable change in the lines of battle. A German novelist later described life in the rat-infested trenches:

> The front is a cage in which we must await fearfully whatever may happen. We lie under the network of arching shells and live in a suspense of uncertainty. Over us Chance hovers.

Another trench-warfare situation, only slightly more fluid, developed after 1915 between Austria-Hungary and Italy. Italy had stayed out of

Seeing the remains of the carnage produced by Britain's Somme offensive of 1916 moved the English poet Siegfried Sassoon to write, "I am staring at a sunlit picture of Hell."

the war initially, despite its official membership in the Triple Alliance. It was actively wooed by France and Britain, who promised huge potential gains at Austria's expense and also in the Middle East—a crucial sop to Italy's frustrated dreams of empire. So Italy came in on the side of the Entente but was unable to make great headway against its Habsburg opponents.

Other fronts were slightly more mobile, although they too took huge tolls in lives. Germany fought off a Russian offensive but had to aid Austria-Hungary, which was outclassed by Russian troops. Most of the eastern front fighting took place in the western portions of Russia, with some momentous battles. Fighting also spread to the Balkans, where Austria crushed Serbia and the other small states aligned variously in hopes of local advantage. The Ottoman Empire joined the Germans, swayed

THE MAIN FRONTS IN WORLD WAR II.
The stalemate on the western front contrasted with a greater flux in Russia and the Balkans.

by a long tradition of relying on German military advice; this won a Western attack on Gallipoli and Western-encouraged Arab risings against Turkish control in the Middle East.

War spread also to the seas. Britain successfully bottled up the bulk of the German surface fleet, but the German introduction of submarine warfare severely troubled British naval activity and merchant vessels as well. German attacks on American ships bringing people and supplies to Britain was the most important single cause of the United States's entry into the war in 1917.

Minor warfare affected other parts of the world. Small imperialist forces battled around Germany's African holdings. Japan entered the war on the Entente side in the interest of seizing German islands in the Pacific, which it did with characteristic efficiency. World involvement in the European fighting was still more significant. Britain used many troops from India, France many from Africa. Commonwealth countries such as Australia and Canada poured men and resources into the British war effort. The United States's involvement, which came after years of hesitation in the interests of a traditional hands-off stance toward European squabbles, brought America's growing power into the world arena decisively. American supplies and, to a lesser extent, fresh troops, helped turn the tide against a weary Germany after 1917, as the western front finally crumbled and the Germans were slowly pushed back into their own land.

More important at the time than the international context was the intensity of involvement among the combatants. The conscripted and professional soldiers of the mass armies were most heavily engaged, of course, and even those who survived would long be marked by physical and psychological scars including, often, a resentment against civilian authorities, politicians above all, who could not have known what the horror of war was. Yet civilian commitment was itself considerable, as each nation-state showed its power of mobilization to the fullest. Governments increasingly organized the major sectors of the economy to ration resources and production and to prevent crippling labor disputes. Whole industrial sectors, such as railroads in the United States, were administered outright by the state. Within government, the executive branch increasingly took over from parliament—particularly in Germany, where by 1917 a top general virtually ran the country. Governments also leaned heavily on public opinion. Dissent was censored, dissenters arrested. Newspapers and other media were manipulated to create the most favorable public opinion possible. Thus the British (and through them, the Americans) were regaled with exaggerated stories of German violence, while Germans were carefully shielded from military setbacks after 1917 so that many did not know they were losing until the end actually came. The power of governments to command resources and also beliefs and passions made this truly the first total war.

The war in essence speeded up many developments visible in the previous period. The power of organization increased, particularly through the new interventions of governments. To keep the social peace, socialists and trade unions were given new recognition, serving on governing

This recruitment poster of 1916 from the British Ministry of Munitions exemplifies propaganda for continuing the war.

boards for industry and the like; but by the same token many labor leaders also became more involved in the existing system, which heightened revolutionary discontent among a minority of workers and others. Women's participation in the labor force increased greatly, although this proved to be a fragile trend as men recaptured many jobs at the war's end. At the same time, the war brought material shortages, even outright famine, to many people in the belligerent nations, while imposing great tensions on soldiers and civilians alike. These hardships, plus feverish hopes for a better world after war had ended, brought a revolutionary or nearly-revolutionary mood to many European nations after four years of struggle.

The Legacy of the First World War

The catastrophe finally ended in 1918. Germany had won its eastern front battle the previous year, when revolution in Russia finally forced a settlement granting huge territories to Germany. But agitation against Germany in these areas, plus a growing crisis in Austria-Hungary because of nationalist unrest, prevented total concentration on the western front, where the United States supplement was just beginning to arrive. As its troops were pushed back from France, Germany began to face increasing domestic unrest, while in Austria-Hungary minority nationalities rioted outright. The war may have been prolonged through most of 1918 by Allied insistence on the Central Powers' unconditional surrender. Nationalist doctrine, convinced of the total justice of one's own cause, had led to new inflexibility in wartime negotiations, for victors wanted a passive opponent to dispose of as they pleased. The German government held out until defeat and domestic agitation prevented any hope of solace, and then abdicated in part to avoid the taint of dealing with the Allies. Empire and monarchy fell together in Germany, and it was left to a Socialist-led civilian republic to pick up the pieces.

Settlement of the war was difficult, even with the military apparatus of Germany temporarily dismantled or underground. Diplomats of the victorious nations convened at Versailles, near Paris, where they debated the fate of much of the world, with Russia, Germany, and indeed most of the world unrepresented. France was bent on revenge against Germany and assurance that Germany would be so weakened that it could not attack a third time. It got its lost provinces back, but not the security it yearned for. Italy wanted new territory in abundance; it received some, but not enough and emerged unsatisfied as well. The United States, led by President Woodrow Wilson, espoused great ideals, hoping for just settlement of all nationalities issues and a new League of Nations to deal with future disputes and to make war unnecessary. But ideals were hard to put into practice amid the welter of conflicting interests, and opinion back home prevented the United States from taking a consistently active role; the nation did not even join the League that its representatives had devised. American isolationism contributed to French and British fears for the future, in a peacetime that was badly born.

The big losers at Versailles were of course Germany and Austria-Hungary. The latter empire collapsed entirely, as nationalist groups carved out the new nations of Czechoslovakia and Hungary, plus Yugoslavia as an enlarged south Slavic state, leaving a somewhat fragile Germanic Austria, cut off from its traditional markets, as one of many small countries in a weakened region of Europe. Germany lost Alsace-Lorraine, plus territory to a revived Polish state in the east. It was also blamed for causing the war and faced huge reparation payments to the Allies, particularly France and Belgium. The level of military forces was limited, and the region west of the Rhine was supposed to remain demilitarized entirely. These various impositions created huge discontent in Germany, with many leaders vowing revenge on France as the leader of the punitive peacemakers. The impositions also burdened the new republic with an initial impression of nationalist betrayal; many Germans, startled by unexpected loss, linked republican leaders to a sellout of national honor. Yet however distasteful the peace was, Germany lacked the power in 1919 to resist. Russia, ignored as a communist pariah after its revolution in 1917, was also cut back through the creation of additional small states in eastern Europe at its expense—Poland, of course, but also several Baltic republics. Here too was potential for future trouble.

The Versailles peace settlement thus set up important, though not inevitable, preconditions for future diplomatic strife, by creating new categories of discontented great powers; insecure or disappointed victors; and a new series of small states in various parts of eastern Europe that might tempt future expansionists.

The legacy of World War I involved more, however, than a difficult diplomatic heritage. The war had devastated Europe's economy and society. More than ten million people had died, meaning that almost every European family had a death to mourn. The loss of young men was an economic as well as a psychological blow, for these men were the potential cream of the upcoming labor force and leadership groups. Loss of men also hampered the European birth rate, for families that might have formed now could not start. Massive destruction of industrial property and agricultural land temporarily dislocated many economies, leading to a period of postwar instability that ended only in 1923. More serious than these largely reparable setbacks was an imbalance produced by the methods of financing the war. Most combatant regimes had borrowed heavily, unwilling to raise taxes too much lest civilian morale be destroyed. Even during the last years of war, despite government restrictions, prices began to rise because of the inflationary impact of increased government spending and money supply. And after the war, in many countries inflation soared. Although some groups could profit from rapidly rising prices, many people with fixed savings were nearly wiped out, while others, such as many farmers, were encouraged to unwise borrowing that would later leave them strapped for funds. In various ways, then, the war introduced basic dislocations that promised, and later produced, further trouble.

The war also reduced western Europe's economic standing in the world. So many resources had been plowed into war that Western nations had dissolved investments abroad. The United States, as a result, turned from debtor to creditor nation for the first time since the industrial revolution had begun; the era of strong American partnership in the Western economy essentially took off from the First World War. Eager American and Japanese businessmen also captured many European markets in world trade. Western Europe was by no means removed from a dominant position in the world economy, but it was set back and forced, from this point onward, to share. The war also stimulated nationalist grievance against Western imperialism. The Versailles peace settlement and related treaties did allow Britain and France to take over most German colonies, and also to establish administrations in the Arab portions of the former Ottoman Empire (which now collapsed, yielding a vigorously nationalistic but smaller Turkish nation). But these new holdings were officially League of Nations mandates, not outright colonies, which implied efforts to move toward greater autonomy. Wartime slogans of nationalism and self-determination were not lost on Arab, or Indian, or African ears, and the growth of internal opposition to European rule in Asia and Africa increased steadily after the First World War.

Finally, within the West itself, the war left a cultural legacy of confusion and bitterness. Returning veterans felt unappreciated and misunder-

After World War I, inflation in Germany became so severe that money could be worth more as kindling than as currency. This housewife uses it to light her stove.

stood; they formed veterans' groups that later became an important political force. Violence increased, in political clashes and also rising crime—a legacy of wartime pressures. Many people felt cheated by the grand promises of wartime governments that now, clearly, had been betrayed. Americans, whose contact with the war had been brief, responded by a frantic desire to return to "normalcy," including diplomatic isolation. Europeans also responded with new suspicions of former allies, but they added frequent distaste for parliamentary politicians as well, who seemed mendacious or ineffective. Workers resented the profits many businessmen had made in the war, leading to new strikes and political confrontations. The upper classes, too, were newly insecure; they had lost many of their own younger generation, for in trench warfare young officers were the most likely to be killed. They also were bewildered by the brutality that had emerged from the polished, progressive world they thought they inhabited before 1914. New levels of popular grievance combined with hesitant or defensive leadership to produce many of the problems of the postwar period.

There were only a few somewhat positive notes to come from the war's end. The constitution of the new German republic—called the Weimar Republic after its initial capital—was an admirably liberal and democratic document, in a society that had long vaunted principles of political authority. Germany, Britain, and the United States responded to postwar enthusiasm and prewar pressures by granting women the right to vote; previous feminist arguments plus women's war-work contribution tipped the scales. And although women did not gain major economic change, after a wartime period of new work roles and independent earnings, the tide of feminist protest receded for a time. Changes of this sort were significant but hardly matched the tremendous disequilibrium that the war had produced.

The Russian Revolution

The replacement of tsarist government by Communist government in Russia through the 1917 revolution was an event of great moment, closely linked to the war and adding to its unsettling effects in some aspects of the wider European society.

Revolution of some sort may have been inevitable in Russia, given a government unyielding in its resistance to political reform and a variety of groups, based particularly in and around the working class, bent on challenging the existing order. The failure to grant real political voice to the masses after the 1905 revolt guaranteed great tension. Whatever the degree of inevitability, World War I unquestionably strained Russian society beyond the breaking point. Although the Russian army was not overwhelmed by German forces, it lost more than it won. Furthermore, maintaining the military effort with an economy that was still largely agricultural was a tremendous burden, leading to privation and food shortage at home. During 1916 the rate of strikes and bread riots increased, for prices had risen almost 700 percent. In March 1917 new strikes broke out in St. Petersburg and gradually assumed revolutionary proportions, as troops joined the strikers and even gave them weapons. A council, called a *soviet*, was formed and took control of the city, arresting the government ministers.

Initially the new national government was headed by liberals, bent on providing a constitutional regime with free elections. Unfortunately these same liberals, intensely devoted to the democratic ideals shared by France and Britain, also felt obliged to continue the war effort, so as not to let the Allies down. This decision triggered further popular protest, as worker groups seized most city governments and the peasantry began to stir. In November 1917 (October by the Russian calendar) the liberal government was swept away and the Bolshevik party, headed by V. I. Lenin, took charge. Although only a minority even of the urban workers were Bolsheviks, with other Marxist and Social Revolutionary groups far larger, Lenin had a determination, and the Bolsheviks had a tightly-knit organization, that soon prevailed. A democratically elected parliament, with its majority from the rural-based Social Revolutionary party, was disbanded and the Bolsheviks took over the government outright.

Actually governing, however, was another matter. A variety of forces opposed the new regime. Although the tsar and his family were executed, former army officers organized civil war in many parts of the country. Foreign intervention against the radical new regime was more briefly a problem, as Britain, France, the United States, and Japan all sent troops in an abortive effort to wield some influence. Years of revolution and civil war caused renewed economic hardship, which prompted some working-class risings against the Bolshevik regime; and efforts to control the land and its produce for the benefit of urban supporters antagonized many peasants. In the face of these forces, Lenin himself recognized the need for flexibility. Although he was adamant in refusing any voice to political opposition, in 1921 he did promulgate a New Economic Policy, which allowed peasants and small business people to run their operations free of state control. State ministries continued to direct the leading industrial sectors, in the interests of ridding Russia of capitalism, but Lenin's compromise was sufficient to improve the economic climate. Bolshevik or Red armies, with a new officer corps recruited from below, also gained a firmer hold, and after considerable bloodshed on all sides, the new regime stabilized by 1921, its constitution calling the revolutionary nation the Union of Soviet Socialist Republics.

The 1917 revolution was a crucial watershed in Russian history. Although political authoritarianism returned, and indeed was enhanced as the Bolsheviks built up the political police and clamped down on dissidence, other key features of the old regime were quickly torn down. Landlords existed no longer. The government quickly showed its devotion to mass education, as literacy rose rapidly. A more wholehearted commitment to industrialization showed quickly as well, for the socialist state could not be built without greater wealth; and the independence of the communist system could not be defended by an economy notably weaker than that of the West. Finally, throughout most of the 1920s an experimental tone enlivened various other facets of Soviet society. Worker councils were widely consulted over policy issues and often affected government decisions. Women were given direct political voice, and family law was often debated and revised. By the late 1920s, under Stalin's grip, this open atmosphere ended, as for example a conservative family law code was introduced. But the experimental period helped draw many groups into enthusiasm for the new regime and served to jostle old habits in a number of spheres.

The revolution also had dramatic impact on Western society. The process of building a new state and focusing energy on internal development reduced the Soviet Union's voice in European affairs for many years. This added to the novelty of the diplomatic climate and, ultimately, to German attempts at new influence in eastern Europe. For with the rest of eastern Europe divided among weak and jealous new nations, the temporary eclipse of Russia was an obviously destabilizing factor.

The revolution was also terrifying or exhilarating to the West, depending on one's social vantage point. Many Russian leaders confidently expected the Western proletariat to join their revolution. Brief postwar communist uprisings did take place in parts of Germany and in Hungary. The Bolsheviks, their capital now in Moscow, took command of a new international communist movement, which replaced older socialist cooperation. Most Western labor movements split by 1921, a majority re-

RUSSIA'S REVOLUTIONARY LEADERSHIP

V. I. Lenin emerged as the central figure of the early Bolshevik Revolution, providing a stable if authoritarian hand at a point when many revolutions founder amid internal and external opposition. An able organizer and inspiring leader, Lenin had a firm sense of the basic revolutionary goals: to construct a dictatorship that would remove all traces of the old order and usher in a socialist utopia. He had no doubt that Russia, despite its economic lag behind the West, was ripe for this kind of restructuring. But he was sufficiently flexible to meet new crises with compromises such as his New Economic Policy of 1921, which freed the livelihoods of many people from state control. Grouped with Lenin were a number of other key leaders, responsible for such sectors as the secret police and international communist agitation. As Commissar for War, Leon Trotsky emerged as second in command, vital in organizing the new Red Army and masterminding its success in the civil war against various forces of the old regime.

Soviet leadership was challenged when Lenin fell ill in 1922 and then died in 1924. A power struggle ensued, which by 1929 resulted in the victory of Joseph Stalin, a former worker and prerevolutionary Communist who had an unerring instinct for political opportunity. Stalin initially allied with other leaders to block the flamboyant Trotsky from becoming dictator and then used key bureaucratic positions in the Communist party to advance his own cause. As the Party spread its control over key institutions of government, the military and state-run industries and unions, Stalin, as General Secretary, moved forward accordingly. Not the theorist Lenin had been, Stalin nevertheless was successful in advocating concentration on Russian development—"socialism in one country"—as opposed to Trotsky's more international interests. Gradually Stalin built up loyal leaders in various branches of government and the Party, so that he was able to crush all opponents. By 1929 Stalin was in a position to advance his central goals of taking over the agricultural sector and forcing a rapid industrialization that would make the Soviet Union a major economic and military power.

maining socialist, but an active, often aggressive minority forming communist parties and labor movements. Leftist politics thus became more complicated, with the communists far more genuinely interested in revolutionary agitation than in mere electoral politics—more than most socialists had been for some time. But the revolution, and the rise of a small but unmistakable Western communist movement, also frightened many business and political leaders. In the United States and elsewhere a "Red scare" developed during the 1920s that branded any radical movement subversive. "Red scare" tactics helped eliminate even socialism as a serious political current in the United States. Socialism remained vigorous in western Europe, but fears of communism added new divisiveness to the political process and convinced some leaders that vigorous action, even some kind of conservative authoritarianism, might be necessary if the Bolshevist menace began to gain ground. The Russian Revolution, in sum, set in motion both a long-term social transformation and, in the shorter term, added to the new political and diplomatic anxieties of the West.

"Normalcy" and Depression

The Years before the Great Depression

The next link in the chain of major events came with the economic depression of 1929, called the Great Depression. The impact of the First World War on the European economy had led to several rocky years into the early 1920s. War-induced inflation was a particular problem in Germany, as prices soared daily and ordinary purchases required huge quantities of currency. Forceful government action finally resolved this crisis in 1923, but only by a massive devaluation of the mark, which did nothing to restore lost savings. More generally, a sharp, brief recession in 1920–1921 had reflected other postwar dislocations, though by 1922–1923 production levels had regained or surpassed prewar levels. Great Britain, an industrial pioneer that was already victim of a loss of dynamism before the war, recovered more slowly, in part because of its unusually great dependence on an export market now open to wider competition. The British did not suffer inflation, but they did see key traditional sectors stagnate—textiles facing new rivalry from countries such as Japan, coal mining lagging as imported petroleum began to dominate the energy field. One result was a bitter series of labor conflicts, as miners, particularly, resisted unemployment and declining wages.

Structural problems affected other areas of Europe besides Britain and lasted well beyond the predictable readjustments to peacetime. Farmers throughout much of the Western world faced almost chronic overproduction of food and resulting low prices. Food production had soared in response to wartime needs, and then during postwar inflation many farmers, both in western Europe and in North America, borrowed heavily to buy new equipment, overconfident that their good markets would be sustained. But rising European production combined with large imports from the Americas sent prices down, which made debts harder to repay. One response was continued flight from the countryside, as urbanization continued. But remaining farmers were hard pressed, and they were also unable to sustain high demand for manufactured goods.

Another market weakness lay in many of the regions that produced raw materials or specialty crops such as coffee for Western consumers. Production of these goods tended to rise more rapidly than demand, leading here too to low prices and weak markets for industrial exports. The small nations of eastern Europe, which produced mainly food, also slumped. Most failed to introduce significant land reform, and the large estate owners and peasants alike were resistant to technological change.

Furthermore, tariff barriers set up by the intensely nationalistic new nations complicated economic growth. Much of eastern Europe—except for Russia, which now separated itself from world markets in favor of concentrating on internally funded development—was in a slump by the mid-1920s. This slump was potentially dangerous for the industrial West, because it lessened purchases of manufactured goods by the eastern European market.

But despite continued danger signals, the Western economy seemed to bounce back in the mid-1920s, contributing to a general but short-lived euphoria that extended to politics and popular culture. Manufacturing production increased steadily once wartime damage was repaired, a sign of the resiliency of most of the industrial nations. Wages rose as well, and profits for many investors and corporate directors soared. The mid-1920s saw a peak of upper-class affluence, including a new spate of mansion building on both sides of the Atlantic and a frenzied night life for the idly young and rich—including new public freedom for women to smoke, drink, and patronize the growing network of nightclubs. But except in the depressed industries, it was not a bad period in which to be a wage earner. Consumer opportunities rose with new devices such as the radio, popularized cosmetics for women, and new artificial fabrics such as nylon, which incidentally helped reduce competition from Japanese silk textiles.

Greased by the affluence of the mid-decade, political tensions eased. Conservative governments easily retained control in Britain and the United States, although the British did need to beat back a bitter general labor strike centered in the coal mines in 1926. France elected a left-leaning government in 1924, but it made no big social experiments and a more conservative coalition took the helm by 1928, providing France's strongest leadership of the entire decade. The real political showcase was Weimar Germany. This new republic had been governed by moderate socialists in its early days, leaders who were willing to sacrifice major social reform for consolidation of the new constitution. But the early years had been marked by violent protest both from the left—communists and others—and from rightist groups who wanted authoritarian leadership rather than the parliamentary regime. Street violence was common. One extremist leader, Adolph Hitler, even attempted a *coup d'etat* in Bavaria, though it was easily put down. After 1924 extremist agitation died down. Hitler's Nazi party nearly vanished, and more mainstream conservative groups, still suspicious of the republic, nonetheless cooperated with the electoral process. Germany's mid-decade leader, Gustav Stresemann, was himself a conservative, but he was eager to make the republic work.

Finally, greater political calm encouraged an easing of diplomatic tensions. The immediate post-Versailles years had been difficult for international relations. Germany frequently fell behind in its reparations payments, in part because they were regarded as unfair, in part because they were simply too high to manage easily. France at one point moved troops into the Ruhr industrial region to enforce the punitive peace settlement. But the French did not really have the stomach for a difficult occupation, which was greeted by widespread German unrest. The French wanted

Holeproof Hosiery

HOLEPROOF is the hosiery of lustrous beauty and fine texture that wears so well. It is not surprising, therefore, that it is selected by many people who can afford to pay far more for their hose, but who prefer the Holeproof combination of style and serviceability at such reasonable prices.

Obtainable in Pure Silk, Silk Faced, and Lusterized Lisle styles for men, women and children in the season's popular colors. If your dealer cannot supply you, write for price list and illustrated booklet.

HOLEPROOF HOSIERY COMPANY, Milwaukee, Wisconsin
Holeproof Hosiery Company of Canada, Limited, London, Ontario © H. H. Co.

The West's renewed affluence in the mid-1920s exposed middle-class consumers to a widening range of goods and services previously available only to the wealthy.

peace, and France concentrated increasingly on building a defensive chain of forts, the Maginot line, designed to prevent a World War I–type German invasion; the fact that this line was technologically out of date, given the new potential of tank warfare, occurred to only a few. The Germans, for their part, wanted reentry into the regular diplomatic system. Stresemann agreed, in pacts known as the Treaty of Locarno, to accept the Versailles settlement in the west—that is, to recognize Germany's new boundaries with France and Belgium—and to negotiate in the east. In return, Germany was admitted to the League of Nations. Related negotiations rearranged its reparations payments. It looked briefly as though postwar tensions might be resolved. Optimism ran so high that two diplomats from the United States and France, Kellogg and Briand, negotiated a statement, the Pact of Paris or the Kellogg-Briand Pact, outlawing war; rhetoric being cheap, many other countries signed also.

In retrospect it is easy to see how fragile the good feelings of the mid-1920s were. Key German groups remained suspicious of the republic. The army, secretly building forces that had been outlawed by Versailles, was virtually an independent entity. Even the conciliator Stresemann refused to accept the whole status quo, keeping open the question of Germany's borders with Poland and Czechoslovakia. France had proven that it was unable to maintain a tough line against Germany, but now it fell back on frankly inadequate countermeasures. In addition to the ostrich-like Maginot line, the French concluded a series of alliances with the small eastern European states, intended to press Germany as the former alliance with Russia had done. But the small states were no Russian equivalent, and it was not clear whether these alliances were more than provocations, particularly as the eastern states, most of them turning into authoritarian-nationalist regimes, quarreled so bitterly with each other. In fact, France depended increasingly on German good will. Without strong leadership, Britain grew suspicious of France, while the United States—although an active and often overenthusiastic investor in Europe—maintained its isolationist stance, except for hollowly optimistic gestures such as the Kellogg-Briand pact.

Furthermore, key states were pulling away from the European mainstream. The Soviet Union was busy consolidating its new regime, particularly after Lenin's death; only after a few years did a new leader, Joseph Stalin, triumph, and Stalin was particularly uninterested in the larger world, arguing that Russia's task was to build its own socialist society. Italy had been taken over by a new fascist regime headed by Benito Mussolini. Italy had emerged extremely disappointed from World War I. With the new system of universal suffrage for men, Italian leaders found it impossible to return to the prewar system of political compromise. Large Socialist and Communist parties clashed with a new Catholic party after the war, and when worker and peasant unrest greeted the economic recession of 1920–1921, the Italian upper classes feared outright revolution. Into this situation stepped the small Fascist group, named for the Italian *fascismo* from the Latin *fasces*, or "bundles" of rods—used as a party symbol and copied from ancient Rome. The Fascists preached nationalism and a principle of authoritarian rule; in fact, fascism provided protection for the large landowners in the south and the big industrialists in the north. In 1922 the Italian king agreed to the formation of a Fascist government, which proceeded, over the next several years, to eliminate all major opposition. The parliamentary regime was dismantled, major parties outlawed, a number of leaders killed. With power achieved, Mussolini proceeded cautiously during the rest of the decade, making agreements with major existing institutions such as the Catholic church. Nationalist bombast was not translated into adventurous diplomacy. But Fascist Italy stood as a major exception to the democratic systems of the postwar West, and to many troubled Westerners an attractive alternative as well.

Even the popular culture of the 1920s showed some potential weaknesses. There was a frenzy in the passion for enjoyment, the fascination with passing fads such as trans-Atlantic flights, glamorous film stars, and lurid crimes, all of which preoccupations may have been intended to conceal darker fears. The United States, more affluent than ever before, turned its back on a long-standing tradition by passing laws virtually eliminating immigration, a sign of the fear of contagion from "baser" peoples and also a sign of trade-union anxiety about protecting jobs. More generally still, the continued drop in the birth rates of most Western nations, after brief postwar recovery, may have signaled popular insecurities about the future as well as a desire to enjoy now; although it also reflected the huge loss of young men during the war years. Countries such as France, where birth rates fell to levels barely adequate to sustain population size, certainly worried about the weakness that demographic stagnation portended, but worries produced no answers.

The Crash of 1929

None of the fears or the pleasure-seeking of the 1920s would have mattered in the long run had economic conditions remained encouraging; but this was not to be. The Great Depression, which began in 1929, with advance signs such as growing unemployment a year before, posed massive new problems that the political and diplomatic systems of the 1920s were incapable of handling. The good years of the mid-decade were soon a nostalgic memory. And the mood of the 1920s, in distracting leaders from serious attention to structural problems such as agriculture and in encouraging often excessive speculation in foreign investments, land deals, and corporate mergers, contributed, along with the wartime heritage, to the economic collapse itself.

The collapse occurred in October 1929, when the New York stock market crashed. Stock values tumbled, as investors quickly lost confidence in issues that had been pushed ridiculously high. United States banks, which had depended heavily on their stock investments, rapidly echoed the financial crisis, and many institutions failed, dragging their depositors along with them. Even before this collapse, Americans had begun to call back earlier loans to Europe. Yet the European credit structure depended extensively on American loans, which had fueled some of the industrial expansion but also less productive investments such as German reparations payments and the construction of fancy town halls and other amenities. In Europe as in the United States, many commercial enterprises existed on the basis not of real production power but of continued speculation. When one piece of the speculative spiral was withdrawn, the whole edifice quickly collapsed. Key bank failures in Austria and Germany followed the American crises. Throughout most of the industrial West, investment funds dried up as creditors collapsed or tried to pull in their horns.

With investment receding, industrial production quickly began to fall, beginning in the industries that produced capital goods and extending quickly to consumer products fields. Falling production—levels dropped by as much as a third by 1932—meant falling employment and lower wages, which in turn withdrew still more demand from the economy and led to further hardship. The existing weakness of some markets, such as the farm sector or the nonindustrial world, was exacerbated as demand for foods and minerals plummeted. New and appalling problems developed among workers, now out of jobs or suffering from short time and reduced pay, and the middle classes as well. The Depression, in sum, fed on itself, growing steadily worse from 1929 to 1933. Even countries initially less hard hit, such as France and Italy, saw themselves drawn into the vortex by 1931.

In itself, the Great Depression was not entirely unprecedented. Previous periods had seen slumps triggered by bank failures and overspeculation, yielding several years of falling production, unemployment, and real hardship. But the intensity of the Great Depression had no precedent in the brief history of industrial societies. Its duration was also unprecedented; in many countries full recovery came only after a decade, and only with the forced production schedules provoked by World War II. The Depression was also more marked than its antecedents because it came on the heels of so much other distress—the economic hardships of war, the catastrophic inflation of the 1920s—and because it caught most governments utterly unprepared to cope.

The Initial Response   The Depression provoked three initial reactions from governments in the West, all of them counterproductive. First, it prompted a tendency to scale back economic programs in which the state was involved. Government tax revenues dropped drastically along with all other economic indicators in the early Depression. Yet most established leaders were eager to prove themselves fiscally responsible—to conciliate property owners, who traditionally resisted tax increases; to avoid inflationary pressure, the bugaboo of the previous decade though absolutely the reverse of the real problems of the Depression itself when demand and prices fell rather than rose; and out of sheer unfamiliarity with complex economic issues. The French parliament, for example, boasted only two deputies who had ever taken a formal economics course. Weak, largely conservative leadership, in sum, prevented vigorous response to the Depression's onset. Governments actually fired personnel, adding to unemployment, and scaled back relief measures, adding to misery, in the interests of misplaced fiscal rectitude.

With initial government responses feeble and unhelpful, the Depression almost inevitably fostered heightened political division, even polarization, this was the second political response. Communist movements grew, reaching large proportions in Germany by 1932 (where the party won 17 percent of the vote) and gaining new visibility even in Britain and the United States. Movements on the far right grew as well. Again in the United States groups such as Father Coughlin's National Union for Social Justice arose, advocating a combination of welfare measures and authoritarian politics. Existing authoritarian movements in Europe expanded and became more violent in street demonstrations, while new groups arose bent on disrupting the political process and attacking the left. Political polarization, with its concomitant reduction of centrist forces in many countries, made coherent economic policy still more difficult, as any move in one direction would prompt response from groups advocating opposite interests. In Germany, coalition governments became harder to form, their lifespan increasingly brief, their positive policies, even as the Depression deepened, still more wanting.

Third, the Depression, although an international economic crisis, provoked largely nationalist responses. Tariff barriers, already dangerously high, were raised further in a desperate effort to protect home industries even at the expenses of flourishing trade. Nation-states manipulated their currencies for the short-run advantage, regardless of longer-range consequences. France, even before it was badly hit, refused to help the beleaguered German republic, insisting on continued reparation payments, which Germany could no longer meet and which further discredited the republican regime. The United States pressed European governments to pay the war debts they owed, even though this too became impossible, and refused to participate in international financial stabilization while the war-debts issue was unresolved. For four years, at almost every level, most Western governments seemed helpless as well as narrowly selfish in their response to an economic disaster that grew steadily worse.

The Social Cost of the Depression   The Depression was more, of course, than an economic and political event. It reached into countless lives, creating hardship and tension that would be recalled even as the crisis itself eased. Loss of earnings, loss of work, or simply fears that loss would come could devastate people at all social levels. The suicides of ruined investors in New York were paralleled by the vagrants' camps and begging that spread among displaced workers. The statistics were grim: up to a third of all blue-collar workers lost their jobs for prolonged periods. White-collar unemployment, though not quite as severe, was also unparalleled. In Germany 600,000 of four million white-collar workers had lost their jobs by 1931. Graduating students could not find work, or had to resort to jobs they regarded as insecure or demeaning. Figures of six million overall unemployed in Germany, 22 percent of the labor force in Britain, were statistics of stark misery and despair. Families were disrupted, as men felt emasculated at their inability to provide and women and children were disgusted at authority figures whose authority was now hollow. In some cases wives and mothers found it easier to gain jobs in a low-wage economy than their husbands did, and although this development had some promise in terms of new opportunities for women, it could also be confusing for standard family roles. And again, the agony and personal disruption of the Depression was no short shock; for many it was desperately prolonged, with renewed recession around 1937 and with unemployment still averaging 10 percent or more in many countries by 1939.

Just as World War I had been, the Depression was an event that blatantly contradicted the optimistic assumptions of the later nineteenth century. To many, it showed the fragility of any idea of progress, any belief that Western civilization was becoming more humane. To still more it challenged the notion that standard Western governments—the parliamentary democracies—were able to control their own destinies. And because it was a second catastrophic event within a generation, the Depression led to even more extreme results than the war itself had done—more bizarre experiments, more paralysis in the face of deepening despair.

As it did elsewhere, the Depression helped reaffirm the distinctions between Britain's upper and lower classes. The poorer, local boys on the right eye two students from Eton waiting outside the cricket grounds in London in 1937, site of the Eton vs. Harrow match.

Nazism and the Reactions of the 1930s

The most concrete product of the Depression, in terms of general and immediate impact on Western society, was the rise of the Nazi regime in Germany—another event in the jigsaw puzzle of interwar confusion. Other developments, in the form of more constructive reactions to the Depression, paralleled the Nazi rise, but they were for a time overshadowed by the swastika-emblazoned monster.

Adolf Hitler came to power in 1933. A World War I veteran, a passionate nationalist and anti-Semite, Hitler had struggled for years to find the political power that would match his intense personal drive and his inchoate feelings about Germany's destiny. As Italy's Benito Mussolini and other fascists in many countries were doing, Hitler espoused the vaguest of political ideologies—a sign, some would argue, of the poverty of the twentieth-century political theory after the richness of the two preceding centuries. Hitler's National Socialism, for which "Nazism" was the abbreviation, stressed the importance of power and nationalism. According to Nazis and other fascists, people needed authority, plus devotion to a higher cause. Liberal values corrupted true politics by stressing individual interests and by ignoring the beauties of irrational force. Socialism was a corruption as well, because it divided the nation into hostile class camps. Nazism promised a new social unity that would attack both the evils of socialism and communism, and the exploitation and selfishness of capitalism. Fascist theorists were vague about the programs to be established instead, but a corporatist approach was stressed that would link people in groups and in turn tie the groups to the authority of the state. Nazi *nationalist* ideas were clearer: Germany had a special destiny; it should reverse the humiliations of Versailles and expand to seek *Lebensraum*, or "living room," against the inferior Slavic peoples of the East. More than most other fascist movements, Hitler's Nazism also stressed racial purity within the nation, attacking Jews for introducing capitalism, socialism, and alien-inferior principles of art and culture.

287

Nazism and the
Reactions of the
1930s

The Nazi Movement before the War

Nazism had won brief notice in the years immediately after World War I, when many discontented veterans—among them Hitler himself—sought to readjust to peacetime. It then faded with Hitler briefly jailed, at which time he wrote the bombastic *Mein Kampf*, or "my struggle," which spelled out his nationalist and anti-Semitic vision and his worship of a powerful state headed in turn by a powerful *Führer*, or leader. Renewed nationalist discontent later in the 1920s, but particularly the economic problems that led to the Depression, gave Nazism a new lease on life. Vote totals increased with every election between 1928 and 1932. Money poured in from big businessmen and landlords who were mostly not Nazi but saw the movement as a device that could be used to manipulate the government and as a vital protection against growing communist and socialist strength. Membership in Nazi groups increased as well, for Nazism provided powerful group bonds and served as a channel for Hitler's dramatic speechmaking abilities. Nazi groups, in turn, identified by their brown shirts and the swastika on their arm bands, not only propagandized for their cause, but also sowed disruption by breaking up opposition political meetings, beating up candidates, and in general illustrating their claim that a parliamentary regime could not keep order.

Nazism picked up support—sometimes fervent support—from a variety of groups. Although the movement was a product of the confusions of defeat and economic dislocation, it played on earlier strands in German society. Anti-Semitism went far back in western European history. The presence of a large Jewish minority in Germany, which became increasingly visible in business and politics after the legal freedom they had won in the 1870s, caused some Germans to focus on Jews even more than before, as rivals and as symbols of what was wrong with modern society. Germany also boasted a tradition of strong government and powerful army, going back to early Prussian absolutism, and an unusually sharp division between the private sphere of individual and family life and acceptance of public discipline. Key elements of German culture, then, although in no sense inevitably leading to Nazism without the tremendous dislocations of the war and the 1920s, helped the movement to catch on.

Still more important was the movement's service to a variety of groups. Craftsmen seized on a Nazi pledge to revive older work groups and to limit the excesses of industrial capitalism. Peasants listened to orators praise folk culture and the virtues of the village and small farm. Small-town businessmen and urban shopkeepers heard attacks on department stores and other rivals. Women heard praise for their domestic roles. Antifeminists, women as well as men, harked to the Nazi belief that women should be homebodies and breeders of children. Nazism, in sum, appealed particularly to elements in various groups that had particular reverence for tradition and also, usually, some specific economic griev-ances as a result of inflation and then the Depression. These were also groups unusually drawn to nationalist slogans, eager to identify once more with a dynamic state, and particularly hostile to socialism and commu-nism. Nazism could also win other support, even from workers who might tire of socialist or communist promises and try a different bandwagon for a time. But the movement's disproportionate attraction rested in groups buffeted first by the general forces of economic and social change in industrial, parliamentary Germany, and then by the specific problems of the interwar period.

Nazism has also been explained—was explained, by fearful observers at the time—as a product of the new mass age. Certainly the Nazis stressed the mass, with their organized parades and the promise of group security against individual isolation. Certainly important elements of the masses, and not only in Germany, looked for alternatives to ineffective parliamentary systems during the interwar crises. Certainly Nazism re-vealed the limits of mass commitment to liberal values. But Nazism in no sense won the entire mass of Germans. It did relatively poorly in the working class, and at its electoral height (in 1932) polled only 37 percent of the total vote—a vast figure, to be sure, but hardly an indication of some sort of uniform mass delusion. Although there were some links between Nazism and mass society, the impact of particular German ten-sions and (even outside Germany) the tremendous dislocations caused by war and economic collapse explain most of the Nazis' popular surge.

But Nazism did not come to power on popular strength alone; in fact, the party's vote totals were beginning to decline in 1933. Nor was Hitler willing to venture outright revolution. His earlier failed coup attempt, his respect for the army, and his realization that the police power of the modern state made actual revolt more difficult than before, all argued for a superficially legal acquisition of power. His chance came when the Weimar republic proved increasingly unable to form stable coalition gov-ernments, and a number of conservative leaders, wrongly convinced that they could control Hitler, helped arrange a Nazi cabinet, backed by some of the powerful elite interests eager to attack the growing power of the leftist parties. Thus through a "legal revolution" Hitler became chancellor early in 1933.

The Nazis in Power

Once installed, Hitler's instinct for power—the most consistent thread in the whole Nazi phenomenon—took full command. During 1933 and 1934 the Führer systematically eliminated potential political rivals. Com-munist and Socialist and finally all opposition parties were outlawed, with many leaders sent to concentration camps. The trade union movement was decapitated as well, with state-run unions taking its place. Hitler also purged his own party, eliminating Nazi leaders who had hoped for serious social reform. Hitler increased German centralization, replacing state governments—some of them, such as Prussia, centers of anti-Nazi strength—with new, smaller districts that could be run by loyal agents sent from Berlin. Key ministries, many filled with traditional elite figures, were partially purged or were kept in check by rival agencies set up under strict Nazi control. Even the army, vital but somewhat suspect as a center of conservative rather than Nazi values, was paralleled by Nazi military forces such as the Storm troopers. Schools and universities were also purged, professors and teachers with liberal or humanist sentiments fired, giving new opportunities to loyal Nazis—many of whom had been frustrated by barriers to mobility in traditional Germany. Within the state, in sum, Nazism at once centralized power under the Führer and produced radical shifts in personnel.

Hitler and his ministers also, true to their doctrine, sought a new relationship between state and society. In principle, all established institutions were to be leveled beneath the power of the state. Thus Nazism not only replaced trade unions with loyal, party-led organizations designed to pacify workers through group activities. It also attacked independent Protestant leaders, seeking to make churches effective agents of the state and to promote Nazi racial doctrines; Jewish-looking Christ figures were replaced by blonde, Aryan images. (The Catholic church was less directly attacked, as Hitler had a healthy respect for papal authority; but the church prudently avoided confrontation with the new regime.) By attacking key nongovernment institutions, and also manipulating public opinion through strident propaganda and state-run media, Hitler established a classic totalitarian government in Germany in which, in principle, no competition with the state was allowed. A powerful, brutal political police, the Gestapo, capped this system, making opposition difficult and dangerous. And Hitler skillfully whipped up mass hysteria against foreign enemies, real or imagined, and particularly against the Jews, whose rights were progressively reduced and who became subject to widespread villification and attack.

The Nazi regime did not directly undertake a social revolution, for its focus remained on political power. Government-sponsored public works and armaments production quickly reduced unemployment, though they did not restore pre-Depression wage levels. Attacks on traditional institutions and elites gave individuals new chances at personal mobility, as more lower-class people, and women, entered universities, and as unskilled workers gained new technical training. But, aside from gestures to folk costumes and guilds, Hitler did not fulfill his earlier promises of remaking Germany in a traditional image. He did not support peasant farms, but rather subsidized the landlords' large estates. He encouraged big business, because of its previous support and because it was essential in building a stronger German economy and potential war effort; he eliminated the independent labor movement, which played a vital role in this process. Government planners guided the economy to an extent, but there were few restrictions placed on private enterprise, and profit-taking, now shared by luxury-loving Nazi leaders, went unchecked. Ironically, although Nazism helped bring Germany out of the Depression and encouraged further industrialization at the expense of more traditional interests, the regime did not maximize economic efficiency, a failure that would prove telling when Hitler launched a new total war.

The Nazi regime by no means won active loyalty from all Germans. Workers, for example, though attracted by full employment, remained lukewarm to the movement. But the regime won sufficient support, and made opposition sufficiently hazardous, that there was little formal protest. Here was one area, as Stalinist Russia was also demonstrating, where totalitarian states really worked. By eliminating alternate leadership channels, by providing some popular measures, by active propaganda with full use of intrusive media such as films and radio, and above all by a diligent political police, determined totalitarian regimes, backed by the resources and facilities of an industrial society, can normally be dislodged only by war. That, at least, was the lesson of Hitler's Germany, where only a handful of formal attacks on Hitler were attempted until 1944, and most of these easily nipped in the bud.

Nazi Germany thus produced a power state, bent on radical political change not social revolution. It was a state devoted also to a powerful new military role. Whatever his vagueness on social policy, Hitler was sincerely committed to reversing Germany's losses at Versailles, though he had no rigid master plan for new conquest. Quickly, after his seizure of power, Hitler suspended all reparation payments, walked out of a disarmament conference and withdrew from the League of Nations. In 1935 Hitler announced German rearmament, and in 1936 he brought military forces into the Rhineland—both moves in violation of the Versailles treaty. When these challenges were greeted with verbal dismay by the other European powers, but nothing more serious, Hitler was poised for a further buildup of German strength and further diplomatic adventures that would ultimately lead to World War II. Nazism, which had glorified war as an expression of human and national purpose, which downgraded intellectual life in favor of military training in the schools, came to depend on a diet of expansion that finally roused a weary France and Britain to fight back.

The International Reactions to the Nazi Buildup

The rise of Nazism in Germany, and the clear threat a rearmed German state posed to European peace, added new complexity for governments elsewhere in the West already hard pressed to deal with the ongoing Depression. In several countries Nazism and the Depression also encouraged larger, more violent movements on the radical Right, which polarized the political process still further. Although no French Hitler emerged, there were many aspirants, as authoritarian political parties, eager to use street violence to supplement campaigns, gained serious strength for many of the same reasons (aside from Hitler's appeal to Germanness) that had spurred Nazism.

291

*Nazism and the
Reactions of the
1930s*

This poster urges German citizens to purchase the inexpensive, government-subsidized radio receiver shown: "All Germany listens to the Führer on the people's radio set." Indeed, for all Western governments in World War II, radio became a powerful means of spreading news and propaganda quickly and convincingly.

The key Western powers responded feebly to the new threats, though they did begin to grapple more constructively with the issue of economic crisis. France and Britain remained weakly led during most of the 1930s. In Britain Conservative ministers ruled, but they were increasingly troubled by a rising Labour party vote, viewed as more menacing than the traditional second party, the Liberals, had been. Britain faced no serious internal Fascist or Communist threat, for parliamentary habits remained deep-rooted; but it did display growing political division as liberalism fell back to small, third-party status. France revealed even more crippling political paralysis. Here too, liberal centrist groups lost votes, as Socialist and Communist vote-getting improved on the Left, and Conservative and Fascist groups vied for support on the Right. Any strong measures taken to please one faction roused new hostility in the other camp so that, with rare exceptions, French ministers, like their British counterparts, found it safest to venture very little.

Nevertheless, there was some constructive action. The British government introduced more flexible currency policies and improved unemployment assistance. The British economy itself revived, sparked by growing production of automobiles, appliances, and even a modest television industry—though this revival did not end massive unemployment and widespread discontent. In France a Popular Front government formed in 1936, led by Socialists but with liberal and Communist support. The government was bent on pushing back the Fascist menace and relieving economic distress. Workers prodded this last impulse by a massive series of sit-down strikes. The government did nationalize certain industries, while reducing the hours of work per week and extending annual vacations to workers in hopes of relieving unemployment. Most of these measures were ineffective, however, and some, by increasing production costs, were actually harmful in the short run. Furthermore, by 1938 the Popular Front had lost its parliamentary majority, as Communists withdrew support of a merely reformist program and as liberals moved toward a more conservative stance. A new coalition government, with little positive program, took the helm.

Political paralysis in France and Britain had obvious foreign-policy implications. Few governments in either country were forceful enough to take diplomatic initiatives. Major political parties disagreed about the foreign threat. Many British conservatives saw Soviet Russia as their chief enemy; few liked Hitler, but many found him palatable when compared to Stalin. In contrast, Labour leaders supported elements of the Soviet experiment while excoriating Nazism. The dilemma in France was starker still. Outright Fascists swallowed anti-German traditions of French nationalism in favor of Hitler's policies, and the Popular Front parties vainly tried to develop an anti-Nazi alliance that might embrace the Soviet Union.

Outside the obvious great-power orbit, the 1930s brought some more varied reactions. Italy, firmly Fascist, became increasingly adventurous in foreign policy, attacking Ethiopia in 1935 to avenge an old imperialist setback. Italian adventurism was spurred by the example of Hitler, who both terrified and fascinated Mussolini and who ultimately drew an Italian alliance. Italy suffered from the Depression, but government economic programs mitigated the pressure.

The Soviet Union, building a separate economy with few links to world trade, avoided direct setbacks from the Depression. Industrialization proceeded rapidly under five-year plans formed and implemented by the state. Peasant agriculture was converted to a system of collective farms, amid great resistance. But, although agricultural productivity remained a massive problem, Soviet economic progress during the 1930s was undeniable. It permitted an extensive system of welfare benefits to workers, which cushioned some of the pressures of rapid change. Stalin's authority remained firm at the top, even though the leader himself, fearful of new opposition within Communist party and army ranks, conducted massive purges between 1936 and 1938.

Finally, several parliamentary democracies demonstrated new vigor. Scandinavian governments, taken over by large but moderate socialist parties, began constructing elaborate welfare programs and government economic planning, which quickly reduced the impact of the Depression. Tax-supported medical care systems, pensions, and unemployment insurance cushioned various hardships and also provided vital buying power to the lower classes, which in turn spurred the economy. Somewhat less successfully, the United States, under the presidency of Franklin Roosevelt from 1933 onward, launched a New Deal that developed for the first time a significant national welfare program, headed by the social security system to aid the elderly and unemployed. Roosevelt's various experiments at government-sponsored economic measures did not fully end the Depression, but they brought important new development to certain regions through measures such as rural electrification. The New Deal did launch a new United States welfare commitment, however, and also convinced most Americans that government was responsive to national issues. Thus the United States, like Scandinavia, avoided the doldrums that infected Britain and France though even the United States, carefully preserving an isolationist foreign policy, remained timid on the diplomatic front.

World War II

Nazi aggressiveness, Allied weakness, Soviet isolation, and suspiciousness were the elements that brought war steadily closer during the later 1930s. In 1936 civil war engulfed Spain. In 1931 a republic had succeeded a period of authoritarian rule. Conservative landowners, churchmen, and officers opposed this republic, joined by a small Fascist movement. An army rebellion led by General Francisco Franco brought outright warfare. Franco quickly picked up military support from the fascist regimes of Italy and Germany, both eager to flex their muscles and gain military training in such fields as bombing civilian targets. The republican forces drew substantial volunteer support from the democratic countries, but they won precious little official aid. The French Popular Front offered some initial backing, but then pulled back because of internal dispute—the polarization syndrome mentioned earlier—and British coolness. Only the Soviet Union consistently aided the republican side, which lost the war in 1939; Soviet experience taught Russian leaders that democracies were not to be trusted.

In 1938 Hitler proclaimed a long-sought union—*Anschluss*—with Austria as a fellow German nation. Western powers complained and denounced but did nothing. In the same year Hitler marched into a German-speaking part of Czechoslovakia. War threatened, but a conference at Munich convinced French and British leaders that Hitler might be satisfied with acquiescence; so Czechoslovakia was dismembered, the western (Sudeten) region turned over to Germany, as the British prime minister, Neville Chamberlain, duped by Hitler's apparent eagerness to compromise, proclaimed that his appeasement had won "peace in our time." ("Our time" turned out to be slightly over a year.) Emboldened by Western weakness, in March 1939 Hitler took over all of Czechoslovakia and began to press Poland for territorial concessions. He also concluded an agreement with the Soviet Union, which was not ready for war with Germany and had despaired of Western resolve. The Soviets also coveted parts of Poland, the Baltic states, and Finland for their own, and when Hitler invaded Poland, Russia launched its own war to undo the Versailles settlement. Hitler attacked Poland on September 1, 1939, not necessarily expecting general war but clearly prepared to risk it; and Britain and France, now convinced that nothing short of war would stop the Nazis, made their own declaration in response.

The early years of World War II carried key trends of the 1930s toward even deeper tragedy. Germany seemed unstoppable and the Western democracies, which had done little to prepare (though Britain had launched some vital development of its air force), suffered accordingly. German strategy focused on the *Blitzkrieg*, or "lightning war," involving rapid movement of troops, tanks, and mechanized carriers. With this the Germans crushed Poland, and then after a brief lull pushed, early in 1940, into Denmark and Norway. The next target was Holland, Belgium, and France, with invasion prepared by massive bombardments of civilian targets. Rotterdam, for example, was flattened at the cost of 40,000 lives.

German dynamism was matched, again as in the 1930s, by Allied weakness. France fell surprisingly quickly, partly because the French were unprepared for war and reliant on an outdated defensive strategy based on the Maginot line, partly because French troops were quickly demoralized after such long stagnation within their own society. By the summer of 1940 most of France lay in German hands, while a semifascist collaborative regime, based in the city of Vichy, ruled the remainder. Only Britain stood apart, able to withstand Hitler's air offensive, able indeed to win the contest for its skies known as the Battle of Britain. Imaginative air force tactics combined with solid new leadership, under a coalition government headed by Winston Churchill, and iron resolve on the part of British citizens to resist the devastating air raids. Hitler's hopes for a British collapse were dashed.

In 1940 Germany controlled the bulk of the European continent. It aided its ally, Italy, in a conquest of Yugoslavia and Greece. It moved into North Africa to press British and French holdings. Conquered territories were forced to supply materials, troops, and compulsory slave labor to the German war machine. Hitler also stepped up his campaign against the Jews, aiming at a "final solution" that meant mass slaughter, and not only in Germany but the tribute territories as well. Even as Germany ground out its war effort, it forced six million Jews from all parts of Europe into concentration camps and gas chambers. The Holocaust stands as the deepest descent of Western civilization after 1940.

The balance in the war still began to shift slightly, however, in 1941. Blocked from invasion of Britain, Hitler turned toward the tempting target of Russia, viewed as an inferior Slavic state in Nazi racial ideology. Germany's attack began in June, all pretense of alliance abandoned, and the Germans easily penetrated into central Russia. Yet the Soviet forces, while giving ground amid massive loss of life, did not collapse. They moved back, and Soviet industry was relocated eastward as well. As with Napoleon's invasion attempt over a century before, weather also came to the Russians' aid, as a harsh winter caught the Germans, who had counted on another quick victory, off guard. As in Britain, civilian morale in

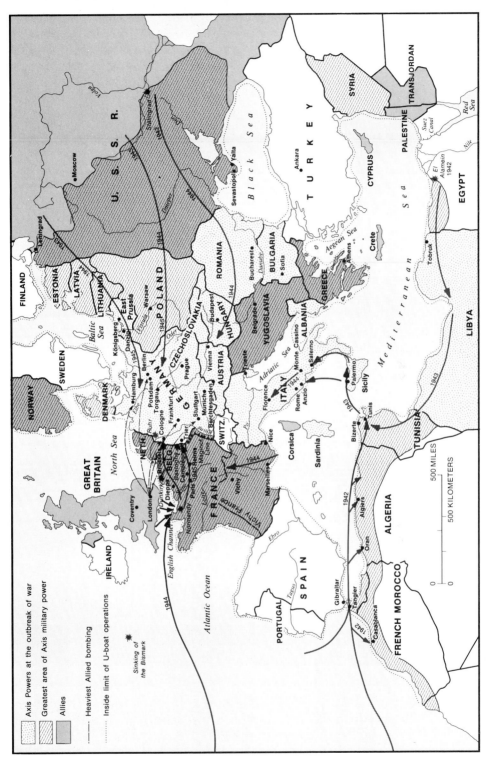

EUROPE AND NORTH AFRICA IN WORLD WAR II.
Massive Axis gains slowly gave way to pushes from the east, south, and west.

Russia greatly aided the war effort, and although German forces continued to advance through 1942, the knockout blow eluded them. The invasion attempt also stretched German resources very thin, revealing how ill-prepared Hitler's economy was for a long-haul effort, even how inefficient it was in many aspects of war production.

The American Entry into the War

Late 1941 also brought the United States's entry into the war, spurred initially by the attack on Pearl Harbor by the Japanese, who were loosely allied with the Germans but operating in fact against German wishes. United States leadership had already supported Britain with loans and supplies, and now eagerly used the occasion to enter war in Europe as well as Asia against what seemed a clear threat to Western democracy, perhaps to Western civilization itself. American involvement, delayed because of lack of full prior preparation, began to make itself felt in 1942, when American and British forces challenged the Germans in North Africa. The Soviet Union, in the same year, pushed back an intensive German seige of the city of Stalingrad, which if successful might have opened the way to the Ural mountains and Russia's new industrial heartland. Over a third of the German force surrendered, and the Red armies began a gradual push westward that would take them past their own borders, through eastern Europe and, by 1945, deep into Germany itself. In the meantime, British and American forces moved into the Italian peninsula from North Africa, ousting Mussolini, while also bombing German industrial and civilian targets. Then in 1944 the Allies invaded France, again pushing the Germans back with the aid of French forces hostile to fascism. Amid bitter fighting—Hitler decided to resist as fiercely as possible, goaded in part by Allied insistence that Germany surrender without conditions—the Anglo-American forces gradually pushed into western Germany. In late April 1945, Russian and American troops met on the Elbe River. On April 30 Hitler committed suicide in his Berlin bunker, and in the following month German military commanders surrendered their country to the victorious invaders.

Within months after this the war in the Pacific also ended. This conflict had become primarily a duel between Japan and the United States, but British and Chinese forces were also engaged and, after the European theater of operations closed, the Soviet Union turned its attention eastward as well. Japan's surrender was precipitated by American use of atomic bombs on two cities, Hiroshima and Nagasaki, climaxing several years during which the Japanese had been pushed back from their holdings in the Pacific islands and on the Asian mainland.

The End of the War and After

World War II, like its predecessor, was a total war. Under government direction, Britain bent all its resources to the war effort, actually creating a far more effective war economy than did Germany under Nazism. The war also made the United States by far the most productive industrial nation in the world. It was organized less rigorously than Britain was, but its war materials, provided not only to its own forces but to those of allies including the Soviet Union, constituted a tremendous Allied advantage. The Soviet Union, devastated by Germany's invasion and then its destructive retreat, saw its standard of living drop below the levels of its Civil War years, but it held on, aided by the prior tradition of state economic control. For all combatants the war consumed vast resources. Invasions and bombings had knocked out transportation facilities and factories all over Europe, and agricultural production was also distorted; here were guarantees of peacetime reconstruction problems.

The war also engaged mass opinion. In contrast to World War I, there were few popular illusions about war, and in this sense less potential disillusionment. But German occupation brought despair as well as state-inspired terror to many in the West, while massive loss of life, civilian as well as military, added to the tensions for those that survived. And if the grinding terror of trench warfare was largely avoided, thanks to the new technology of airplanes and tanks, the war brought more devastating bombs, rockets directed by Germans against British cities, and, though applied only against Japan, the awesome destructive power of nuclear weaponry.

Yet the war also produced some sparks of hope. Britain found, at least temporarily, a sense of purpose it had long lacked. The government blended Conservative and Labour politicians to organize more effective services, including food supply, for the poor than ever before. And it began planning for more extensive welfare programs after the war, to reward a working-class population that had been highly supportive of the war effort. The United States found war-inspired production—and the consequent boost in jobs—a solution to the plague of the Depression and increased its productive capacities. In occupied countries, small but dedicated Resistance movements arose against Nazi forces and against domestic collaborators. Resistance activity reduced the sense of impotence that many Frenchmen had felt during the 1930s. In France and elsewhere, resistance movements brought a new, young leadership to the fore, including Communists who, once Germany attacked Russia, were among the most resolute opponents of German rule. Resistance movements also formulated hopes for the future, issuing statements pledging not only defeat of Hitler, but also plans for European revival that would reduce the potential for depression or nationalist warfare. A "resistance spirit" thus emerged that, although by no means fully implemented after 1945, helped guide a surprising Western revival, a multi-faceted attack on an old diplomatic and political order that had proved bankrupt to prevent the German onslaught.

The war dramatically changed Europe's diplomatic map. Wartime leaders from the United States, Britain, and the Soviet Union (joined at times by General Charles de Gaulle, the leader of French Resistance forces operating from Britain) met periodically from 1943 onward to discuss how to organize peace once it was won. The leaders agreed that Germany must surrender completely and that Nazism and other fascist regimes must go. They also discussed a new international organization, the United Nations, to replace the League of Nations that had so obviously failed to prevent interwar aggression and war itself. At a key meeting in Yalta, in 1945, when German defeat was imminent, the Allies focused on the war against Japan, in which the United States sought Soviet assistance, and particularly on the disposition of eastern Europe. It was clear that the network of weak states in this region had to be modified. It was also clear, at least to Stalin, that the Soviet Union deserved to regain territories lost in the Versailles treaty and ought to dominate independent nations in this region as a buffer against further German aggression. Agreements were reached that in essence assured Soviet influence over new regimes in countries such as Poland, and Western influence over areas such as Greece and Italy. Germany, it was agreed, would be divided into occupation zones, with the Russians holding the east sector (including part of Berlin), the Western powers (later including France) the remaining territory and also parts of Berlin. Yet by the time of a final conference, three months later at Potsdam in defeated Germany in 1945, it was clear that the erstwhile allies were beginning to split apart, with the United States increasingly hostile to Soviet dominance of eastern Europe and also eager to sustain occupied Germany, against a Soviet desire to confiscate as many goods and factories as possible.

The war ended amid massive problems of economic dislocation, compounded by huge movements of people—returning from forced labor and prison camps, fleeing Soviet occupation in eastern Germany, or (the case among half a million surviving Jews) seeking escape toward the promised nation of Israel. It ended also amid a new and menacing confrontation between the two giants whose armies now occupied much of Europe itself: the United States and the Soviet Union. Britain remained an active force, but it was so exhausted by the war effort that it could no longer sustain an equal role. The war had tossed up two new superpowers, economically and militarily more powerful than the former European great powers, one newly armed with atomic weapons—used against Japan in 1945—the other soon to be armed equivalently. With the internal economies of the European countries barely functioning because of wartime destruction, and with diplomatic initiative increasingly passing outside western Europe itself, many observers wondered whether the heartland of Western civilization could ever revive.

Themes 1914–1945: Europe and the World

The spiral of events that opened with World War I unquestionably dominated Western history through 1945. Each major event seemed to lead almost inexorably to the next, and each new tragedy made further problems more likely. The severity of the Depression and the problems of coping with it stemmed from World War I; that war and the Depression combined triggered, and may indeed largely explain, Nazism; Nazism plus wider confusions led directly to World War II. The tragic skein was tightly wound.

The dominance of events, however, should not obscure the larger processes at work, some of them intensifications of earlier trends, some more novel. The most clearly new general theme—unless one accords pride of place to the innovations of fascism—involved Europe's altered position in the world. One historian, Geoffrey Barraclough, has even described the twentieth century in terms of a major new stage in the whole history of the world, precisely because of the shifts away from the centuries-long pattern of rising Western power.

Declining Birth Rate

The West's altered position had several facets, many of them complex. Western nations were certainly losing ground to the rest of the world demographically during the first half of the twentieth century. The West's demographic transition continued with a vengance between the wars. Many European countries were barely reproducing themselves, as the Depression added a new motive to restrict family size to the ongoing effort to limit birth rates in order to assure the family's standard of living and provide opportunities for the children born. Particularly in the middle classes, the use of birth control devices became increasingly common; their use was generally founded on women's power or responsibility to protect themselves against unwanted pregnancies. Religious scruples about separating sex from procreation remained, but increasingly even loyal Catholics, especially in countries such as the United States, began to rely on new forms of contraception, while overall public opinion shifted decisively in favor of the legitimacy of birth control. Most of the non-Western world, however, remained in quite a different demographic orbit. Population growth increased in Asia, Africa, and Latin America, as improved sanitation and more assured transport of foods reduced death rates and guaranteed that more people would survive childhood to become parents in turn. Japan, for example, was adding a million people a year to its population during the 1930s, even amid the severe impact of the Depression in that country. The West's share of world population began to sink steadily.

The West's new demographic position had advantages as well as shortcomings. Slower population growth made it easier for societies, as well as individual families, to assure relatively high standards of living. Even amid the poverty of the Depression, few Western people died outright from starvation, as misery, although undeniable, became a somewhat relative concept in industrialized society. But the West's demographic lag did have some adverse effects or adverse potential. Other parts of the world—Japan in the 1930s, for example—might turn against Western dominance, seeking Western-held territory to relieve their population pressures and take advantage of the sparser populations of the West. Population pressure unquestionably helped build up new resentments within the Western colonies, adding to the problems of maintaining colonial controls. In a few cases, significant immigration began to impinge on the West from outside its civilization. In the 1920s France, for example, began to receive a large number of North African immigrants who were eager to take over low-paying jobs that offered better rewards than did opportunities in their homelands. The West's relative demographic retreat was certainly noted with concern in some quarters, given the undeniable potential that its white civilization could be overwhelmed by the growing numbers of non-Western, non-Caucasian peoples throughout the world. In the United States, eugenics groups arose to argue that means should be found to encourage birth control outside the West, while new laws against immigration were designed to protect established positions against the same new non-Western numbers.

Nationalism Outside Europe

Nationalism, building both on local sentiments against foreigners and on outright imitation of Western nationalist values, increased in many parts of the non-Western world. The first pan-African congress met in 1919 to plan strategies to achieve African independence from Western dominance. Arab nationalism gained even more rapidly. The collapse of the Ottoman Empire and Western encouragement of Arab forces during World War I accelerated Arab insistence on self-rule. Arab nationalist groups were active in all the Western-administered mandate territories in the Middle East during the 1920s and 1930s, and the sentiment spread to colonies in North Africa. Indian nationalist sentiment against British rule, already brewing in the later nineteenth century, took a decisive new turn after World War I under the leadership of Mahatma Gandhi. Gandhi managed to combine the desire for political freedom of India's elite with more popular resentments against British controls. He was able to direct huge, largely peaceful demonstrations against imperialist administration, counting on British reluctance to shoot down hundreds of thousands of unarmed Indians. British efforts to repress, by some clumsy violence and through arrests of leaders such as Gandhi, only drew more attention to the nationalist cause. Gandhi's well-publicized fasts in jail made it impossible to imprison him indefinitely; if he were to die of starvation while in jail, he would be a martyr to a victorious cause. Britain began in fact to grant increasing roles to Indian politicians and bureaucrats, and although ultimate power remained in British hands until 1947—indeed, control of India through martial law was viewed as essential against the Japanese threat in World War II—it was clear by the 1930s that Britain's ruling days might be numbered. New nationalism also surfaced in Latin America, where technically independent states chafed against Western economic dominance, particularly that of the United States. A Mexican revolution in 1911 reduced foreign control of lands and oil resources in that country. During the 1930s, as the Depression hit Latin American economies hard, nationalist regimes in Brazil and then Argentina tried to impose new limits on outside economic intervention. In various ways, and with varying degrees of effectiveness, the world was beginning to rebel against Western imperialism.

The force of the rebellion was unevenly distributed, to be sure. Western influence was definitely pushed back in East Asia. A Chinese revolution in 1912, accomplished in the name of some Western political values against the traditional rule of an emperor as Son of Heaven, in fact pushed against Western holdings in the various treaty ports. Once World War I stretched Western resources, and as new threats arose which made it desirable to conciliate the new Chinese government, most European governments abandoned the bulk of their treaty rights early in the 1920s. Although Britain retained Hong Kong, Portugal held Macao, and Western economic and cultural influence, particularly that of the United States, remained strong in China, European administrative controls receded. Along with the dramatic rise of Japan, this spelled a significant reduction of the Western surge in this region.

The Western role remained stronger in the Middle East, India, and Southeast Asia; however, increasing concessions to nationalism were necessary. In the Middle East both France and Britain either granted or promised independence to several nations during the 1930s, including Syria, Lebanon, and Egypt. In the 1930s also, the United States promised independence to the Philippines. World War II then further weakened the Western hold in many of these areas. The Japanese conquered French Indochina, parts of British Malaya and Dutch Indonesia. German advances challenged colonies in the Middle East and North Africa. In many cases Western administration returned after the war; in Southeast Asia, particularly, there was real hope that the Japanese interruption could be forgotten, especially since Japanese control had hardly been popular. But the dramatic evidence that Western imperialism could be dislodged, and by an Asian people, spurred further nationalist agitation and guerrilla attacks, and within a few years after 1945 formal European imperialism in most of southern Asia had ended.

European imperialism was less shaken in Africa; strong colonial controls were newer here. Most Europeans were convinced of African inferiority, and they felt that a long period—indeed, an indefinite period—of civilizing domination might be needed before Africa was ready to attain independence. Thus even Europe's willingness to concede to nationalism elsewhere in the world did not lead to belief that changes were needed in Africa. Western-dominated educational systems, mining concerns, and other classic expressions of imperialist rule indeed took deeper root during the 1920s. African nationalism was slow to respond, despite some important initial gestures. European holdings in Africa bore no relationship to traditional African political units, which made it difficult to solidify reactions. African leaders, still reeling from the late-nineteenth-century Western onslaught, faced complicated decisions about whether to work within their new territorial framework—arguing that each colony should be a nation—or to strive for more traditional patterns, or even to seek an elusive overall African program. In this context, vigorous anti-imperialist movements, as opposed to periodic popular rioting over economic issues, were insignificant between the wars. World War II brought some new factors into play. Several French colonies served as centers for resistance to the Vichy regime, and African leaders hoped for greater autonomy in return for their loyalty. Even with this, aside from powerful intellectual tracts in the name of African culture, serious new agitation against Western imperialism awaited the 1950s.

Throughout much of the world, furthermore, Western economic influence proved harder to dislodge than outright imperialism. The fact was that the West continued to predominate as a potential market for the export of goods most of the rest of the world produced. The West could buy coffee, rubber, and tropical fruits at unprecedented levels. It also continued to dominate most banking and shipping operations on a worldwide basis, while providing most of the manufactured goods dependent on industrial technology. There were, to be sure, some compensatory developments. India began to build its own steel industry, and in the 1930s Brazil established new factory centers. But these developments were outweighed by continued European and American penetration of economies from Latin America to southern Asia. Britain and France converted a number of African colonies to cash-crop production of items such as peanuts and cocoa. Both colonies and Latin American nations increased their output of export crops, tending to drive down the prices to the benefit of the European markets. Increased exploitation of the vast oil resources of the Middle East remained largely in the hands of European and American combines, which helped explain why oil prices remained low, and why many (though not all) of the profits were siphoned back to the West. In no clear way, then, was Western dominance of much of the world being displaced economically, even as Western controls, and the hardship brought about by the Depression, prompted new outcries.

The continued economic rise of Japan, however, did show that Western economic muscle was no longer unchallenged. Japanese industrialization had begun during the later nineteenth century as a unique national response to Western insistence on new trading rights. While using Western advisors and carefully studying political as well as technical and military patterns in Europe and the United States, the Japanese had stayed out of the imperialist orbit and had in fact launched some imperialism of their own during the 1890s. By the 1930s Japan had further developed its factory industry. Although not yet the technical and economic equal of the West, the Japanese were competitive, particularly in the textile field. Heavily dependent on exports to pay for needed raw materials in a resource-poor country, the Japanese proved to be able rivals for Western business in the Asian markets. For the first time since the fifteenth century, Western economic advance was now paralleled by the vigor of another society.

The pattern of Western advance in the world was also disrupted by the revolution in Russia. The Bolshevik regime was not a direct military rival to the West until after World War II, but it definitely pulled Russia further away from Western influences than its tsarist predecessor had done during the eighteenth and nineteenth centuries. Russian Marxism derived from Enlightenment ideology, as Marx had built on it in his writings in Germany and Britain during the nineteenth century—its emphasis on scientific outlook and training, secularism, and industrial advance all paralleled roughly similar developments in the West. But Russia was far less open than before to Western cultural models, and its economy was deliberately built apart from Western-dominated world patterns. Although the Soviet regime faced tremendous economic problems, it was successful in demonstrating that a separate industrial society could be constructed.

In a variety of ways, then, the West was beginning to encounter new resistance and new rivalry in its world role. Two bitter internal fights—the world wars—obviously made the West more vulnerable. But quite possibly in the long run Western supremacy could not have remained unchallenged even without its internal decay, as the peoples of Asia and the southern hemisphere mixed some Western techniques and ideas such as nationalism with their own traditions and pushed for a more independent voice.

Changes in the West's world role were compounded by the shift in the balance of power within the civilization toward the United States. American economic might outstripped that of western Europe by 1918; its military strength did the same by 1945. Most Americans believed that their society represented an extension of key Western values, while improving on specifically European patterns by being more democratic, more politically stable, less prone to devastating warfare. To many Europeans, however, the rise of the United States constituted yet another sign of Western decline. The American giant seemed too uncultured, too crass in its devotion to economic gain, too naive in its use of political power really to represent the West satisfactorily. In fact, the rise of the United States can be seen as a major qualification to the other symptoms of a declining West, for the new giant shared actively in the Western tradition. Nevertheless, the shift of power across the Atlantic did represent change, and it was another sign to western Europeans of their waning military muscle. The new position of the United States was therefore troubling and confusing to people on both sides of the Atlantic—to Americans accustomed to isolation and to Europeans who once called the West's shots.

Many Europeans indeed argued that the West was declining irretrievably. In the pessimistic aftermath of World War I, a book by the German historian Oswald Spengler, starkly called *The Decline of the West*, won popularity. To Spengler, democracy and party politics, plus devotion to the trivial values of consumerism, betokened a Western decline comparable to that of ancient Rome—and many people agreed. Western decline was not so clear, however, even after the exhaustion of World War II. The war did hasten the loosening of imperialist controls, combining new nationalist pressures with the declining ability of western Europe to sustain colonial administrations; within two decades after 1945, decolonization would strip most European empires throughout the world. Along with the postwar dominance of two superpowers, both looming over a weaker and divided Europe, decolonization set the seal on a massive loss of western-European world power. But whether this ongoing process of relative decline was also a sign of internal decay was open to question, as the West—even aside from the United States—was to display surprising signs of renewal. The relative eclipse, however, was important in its own right—it was an interruption of centuries-long trends and a defiance of the West's self-satisfied confidence in its own superior values. Here too reactions were inevitable, as Chapter 9 makes clear, and would shape Western history even as the tensions of postwar decolonization eased.

The Internal Dynamics of the West:
Mass Society Evolves

The relative decline of the West in the world, cushioned to an extent by the rise of the United States, represented a break in patterns. But beneath the discouraging cycle of events of the period of the two wars, basic internal trends in most ways built upon earlier developments. Technological change continued, for example. Few new basic processes were developed, in contrast to the later nineteenth century (or, as things turned out, to the post–World War II era). But great imagination was applied to developing new consumer products, such as cheap but fashionable artificial fibers, a variety of home appliances, and television (whose technical foundations were laid in the 1930s).

The Proliferation of the Consumer Culture

Mass culture greatly extended its range between the wars. Dependent on considerable prosperity, its high point came in the 1920s, but many of the new forms continued into the 1930s. Professional sports teams and entertaining mass newspapers extended their popularity. Newspapers, supplemented now by movie newsreels and by radio, were inventive in digging up diverting human-interest stories. Major crimes, such as those associated with the Prohibition era in the United States, received great attention. Efforts to find the Loch Ness monster, or tracking Lindbergh's pioneer solo flight across the Atlantic, were headline-grabbers also. Nudist movements and other currents that, although unusual, seemed to relate to a pleasure-seeking society, received considerable play. In sports, boxing reached a peak of popularity in the interwar years, and cycling and auto racing were added to the list of major attractions. Professional football lumbered into the American sports scene in the 1920s. Gambling on sports results increased, another sign that older values of hard work and severity were yielding. Perhaps the most important new development in mass culture was the advent of the film, which underwent a series of technological transformations after the herky-jerky, silent motion pictures of the World War I years. Like earlier outlets of mass culture, films tended to appeal to a fairly standardized taste. Important artistic films were made, of course, particularly in European (including Russian) studios, but the rise of the movie was rooted in wider popular appeal. Movies were entertaining. They drew audiences to scenes of luxury, romance, passion, and physical beauty that few people encountered in real life. Even off the screen, film stars reached a level of idolization never before accorded to entertainers, in Western or any other civilization, and rarely accorded even to political or religious heroes in past eras. Lavishly paid, the top stars were also permitted a defiance of conventional moral standards, as their avidly reported private lives became almost as entertaining as their professional performances.

Mass culture, indeed, could even suggest a new belief system, in which the vicarious pursuit of pleasure, the thrill achieved from watching movies or sports events, replaced earlier religious or political enthusiasm. Women, having won the vote in many countries, seemed in many cases to concentrate on a new freedom as consumers, turning away from intense feminist commitments except in a few cases. Exciting new dance styles, the short skirts and boyish look of the flapper era, a new license to smoke and drink in public, convinced many young women that a new age of freedom had dawned. Even older women showed new interest in seeking expressive pleasures. Authors of sexual advice manuals found themselves besieged, between the wars, with queries from married women about how to achieve orgasm, demonstrating not only a new frankness about sexuality but also suggesting a new level of sexual expectation.

The hold of mass consumer culture should not be exaggerated, of course. Many people remained too poor to participate in it actively. British health officials in the 1930s were startled to find that working-class teenagers were on average two inches shorter than their middle- and upper-class counterparts. This physical difference, not necessarily new, resulted from a nutritional gap, and amply revealed the continued gulf that proletarianization had sustained in consumer standards. (This particular difference also had military implications in the ability of undernourished, generally lower-class troops to sustain a battle—a key reason that the British government tackled nutritional deficiencies during World War II.)

The consumer culture affected each country differently. Moreover, it proliferated more rapidly in the United States than in Europe. The United States had been spared the worst pressures of World War I. It lacked well-established upper-class canons of taste and during the 1920s it was more affluent. So America became a mass-culture pioneer, with "Hollywood" serving as a synonym for popular movies. United States exports of movies, dance crazes, popular music derived at least loosely from jazz (America's only native art form), and even newsstand reading materials, such as the western or the tough-guy detective novel, profoundly influenced European mass cultural taste, while also creating images of the United States as a society in which great luxury, sexual abandon, and gangsterism swirled in a confusing mix.

Even in the United States, however, mass culture hardly converted everyone to a life of pleasure-seeking. Many new fads, such as the nightclubs that sprang up from Los Angeles to Berlin, were for the idle rich, not for the masses. Rural people, though drawn into some contact with movies and, particularly, radio, shared at most irregularly in urban delights. And many people carefully separated cultural escapism from what they knew full well were their real-world concerns and values. Mass consumer culture certainly did not prevent the continued growth and diversification of mass political movements and some other protest forms. New consumer hopes and expectations indeed made the Depression an even worse shock than it might otherwise have been, contributing to protest voting that insisted on some redress. Nevertheless, the continued surge of mass culture did suggest some interesting new tensions: between the growing interest in play and a continued commitment to hard work, between escapism and other forms of action. Many groups, certainly, from intellectuals to young working women eager to use their spending money for fun, seemed bent on consciously defying what they saw as the unduly restrictive standards of the nineteenth-century West. Although Western society still labeled more extreme statements of sensual indulgence as pornography, there were growing attacks on the presumed repressiveness of "Victorian" values.

The further rise of mass culture and its interest in defying older standards of respectability led to some fascinating confrontations in the interwar period. In 1919 the United States, center of commercial productions for mass culture, also attempted to extend nineteenth-century campaigns to moralize popular habits by enacting Prohibition, which prohibited the public sale and consumption of alcohol. The experiment had mixed results. Working-class drinking habits were genuinely altered, as the reformers had intended, with the decline of the neighborhood bar. But the growing middle class, including women as well as men, was drawn increasingly to defiance of the new restrictions, so that in this group drinking levels, and the acceptability of drinking as a social convention, actually rose. Prohibition was cast aside as a failure in 1933. Germany in the mid-1920s was another mass cultural center, whereas Berlin became a haven for unconventional artists. These taste changes, however, served as one of the campaign issues for Nazism, which as a mass movement of another sort professed a desire to return to sexual purity and more traditional cultural forms. The rise of new popular-cultural standards, in sum, produced new anxieties as well as new opportunities, even before the Depression forced a more solemn mood.

The Extended Reach of Corporations and the State

In technology and popular culture as also in demography, the interwar decades thus involved a continuation of earlier trends but with some interesting new twists. The same holds true for the development of formal organizations and the nation-state. Giant corporations grew still larger in the giddy years of the 1920s, when investment money seemed plentiful. Mergers, often across national boundaries, were the order of the day. The organization of work also built on earlier trends. Assembly-line production, first introduced in United States automobile manufacturing, became increasingly standard. Soviet industrialization, attempting rapid progress without a large skilled labor pool, introduced many of these procedures as well. The production of masses of goods, such as cars, involved still further routinization of work for the mass of workers. Increasing attention was devoted to arrangements that could further speed and smooth the work process. Industrial engineers experimented with the use of music to increase efficiency. In many jobs, the closer the worker came to machinelike performance, moving steadily at the task without either disruption or creative spark, the happier the bosses were.

Just as business organizations had done with their far-flung mergers and their greater control over work procedures, the nation-state reached out further than before during the war years and in the interwar decades. Indeed the powers of wartime governments, in both world conflicts, exceeded anything ever before dreamed of in the Western political tradition. Governments could now, at least when justified by the special dangers of war, direct huge sectors of the economy, regulate the flow of capital and resources, control job choices, draft hundreds of thousands of people, and censor and manipulate news almost at will. It was the power of wartime government—specifically the German government under military leadership in 1917—that drew Lenin's attention and provided a model for the state he sought to create as an instrument for remaking Russian society.

Hitler's Germany also drew on the example of the First World War in using the state to intrude not only into the economy, but into churches and family organizations. To be sure, Hitler's state was less monolithic than it appeared: It paid careful attention to the wishes of businessmen and landlords; it was careful not to antagonize middle-class opinion by regulating the supply of servants, even in a desperate wartime economy; it even allowed German workers to rise in skill levels—at points when the real needs were for semi-skilled hands. The Nazi state, in other words, responded to interest groups; it did not simply impose order from above. But the power and influence of the German state did grow during the Nazi period. It sought to remake German character by replacing traditional educational goals with more militaristic, sports-centered (and less cerebral) activities. Somewhat ironically, it helped to break down the hold of purely traditional elite groups, allowing greater mobility and new channels for access to power. By partially bypassing the aristocracy, the old bureaucracy, and the military leadership, the Nazi state helped open Germany to further change—although this became clear only once the regime itself had been overturned.

Even in peacetime Western nation-states expanded. School systems grew. It was in the 1930s that high school attendance began to be seriously enforced in the United States. Reactions to the Depression, even when initially timid, brought more government economic regulation—for example, laws restricting the operations of banks, in the interest of greater financial stability—and new welfare efforts. These developments, and further planning that took place during World War II, suggested the emergence of a full-blown welfare state, as the most recent product of the nation-state's long evolution toward fuller contact with its citizenry.

The Political Rise of Proletarian Groups

Finally, the phenomenon of proletarianization continued between the wars. Nazism implicitly promised to reverse the growing displacement of small businessmen and artisans by promising to restore guilds and battle the "Jewish" department store owners, but in fact it continued the erosion of small-propertied classes in favor of a larger working class and white-collar labor force. In Germany and elsewhere, the number of peasants and small farmers continued to decline. The United States saw a massive movement, during and after World War I, of southern black workers who abandoned small plots of land or sharecropping arrangements in the hope of winning manufacturing jobs in the north. Here was another sign that the pattern of working directly under supervision, for wage payments, was becoming ever more common.

As before, of course, the proletariat was no single mass. Women continued to have different roles from men, as more extensive employment during World War I quickly yielded to a renewed domestic focus. White-collar versus blue-collar divisions remained intense, producing political conflicts in countries such as France and Germany when white-collar preference for conservative response clashed with blue-collar interest in socialism or communism.

The interwar years did demonstrate, however, a common proletarian tendency for greater political involvement. Even peasants became newly articulate, seeking out groups that would represent their interests, and not those of landlords; many peasant movements had some fascist overtones. Other kinds of protest action became more difficult following World War I. Employers, often backed by government force, took a tougher line toward strikes, and although important strike action continued, the sheer number of walkouts declined. Union membership also suffered from counterattacks by employers, and the increased failure of strikes took its toll. Additionally, these developments pushed the masses toward greater reliance on political action. By the 1930s major strike and union efforts often combined with politics. A surge of industrial unionism in the United States, involving a new labor federation—the Congress of Industrial Organization (CIO)—followed from New Deal legislation protecting workers' rights to organize. French workers struck massively as part of the installation of the Popular Front government. The masses, in sum, were looking increasingly to the state, and to political movements—the Socialists, the Communists, the American New Deal Democrats—that would represent their interests in the state.

This political surge finally brought the masses into new conflicts with the elite, which on the whole sought to defend its own vested political positions. Yet in many Western countries the quality of leadership by the elite was declining between the wars. Decimated by World War I, relying on an education that provided little economic or technical expertise, many segments of the Western elite were also increasingly bent on using politics to defend their larger social and economic position. Businesses freely called for state aid against strikes—as in the British General Strike of 1926, when the government helped organize replacement services. Landlords, producing inefficiently, sought state subsidies and tariff protections—a key goal of Junker aristocrats in Germany. Elite rigidities combined with the new political pressures from segments of the proletariat produced the growing polarization of many Western nations, and also the success of fascist political currents that could conciliate the elites while diverting a segment of the masses.

Conclusion

The heightened clash between mass pressures and elite defensiveness, particularly when the Depression replaced consumer culture with new poverty and uncertainty, brings us back to the tragic sequences of events that dominated so much of Western history between 1914 and 1945. Even trends such as proletarianization took on a new color in these decades, producing greater tension, greater political distortion. The openness of masses of people to standardized cultural fare, perhaps a bit frivolous in the 1920s, turned to high drama when the fare was dished out by skilled Nazi propagandists. Basic trends in modern Western history, manageable if not always beneficent before 1914, seemed dangerously awry, as the movement from war to Depression to war and the Holocaust slaughters abundantly demonstrated. It was not clear, in 1945, how new directions could be found, how the cycle of events could be broken through, how the division between the proletariat and the elite could either be reversed or differently managed. It was not clear, indeed, whether the shattered pieces of Western society could be picked up at all.

EIGHT

LANDMARKS IN THE DEVELOPMENT OF IDEAS AND BELIEFS, 1870–1950

1865	Mendel's discovery of genetic principles
1870 ff	Spread of compulsory mass education
1870–1890	Impressionism in art
1881	Pasteur discovers the principle of immunization against disease; rise of the germ theory
1887	Daimler introduces the first successful automobile
1889	Edison develops the motion picture
1895	Freud begins work on psychoanalysis
1895	Discovery of the X ray
1900	Max Planck's quantum theory
1900–1920	Classics of modern sociology: Weber, Durkheim
1900 ff	Rise of cubism
1905–1916	Einstein's development of the theory of relativity
1910–1916	Development of IQ tests
1914	Mother's Day proclaimed (United States)
1916 ff	Dadaist movement in art
1919	First experiment in nuclear reaction (Ernest Rutherford)
1921 ff	Spread of cosmetics, radio, Hollywood films
1923 ff	Expansion of industrial psychology and efforts to control the emotional environment of work
1923 ff	Development of sulfa drugs
1926 ff	Development of Keynesian economics
1927	First transmission of television signals
1928	Heisenberg synthesis on the behavior of atomic particles
1944	First edition of Dr. Spock's child-care manual

EIGHT

THE CULTURE OF MASS SOCIETY, 1870–1950

DISCUSSION OF WESTERN HISTORY FROM 1870 through World War II in the two previous chapters has focused on structural developments and on events. The impact of technological change, the expansion of bureaucratic organization and the nation-state, the development of a modern social structure—these features, along with the skein of events after World War II, have commanded our attention.

We turn now, covering much the same period of time, to the issue of how people thought and perceived. This involves examining the major intellectual and artistic developments of what was a busy period in Western cultural life; it also involves looking closely at the evolution of popular outlook or mentality. Of course developments in both these spheres interacted with the structures of modern society—we have already seen how mass culture was expressed in new forms of leisure and political debate. We have also touched on both mass outlook and intellectual reactions in dealing with political events such as the rise of fascism. This chapter, however, seeks to look at outlook and values directly, to try to reconstruct the mentality of modern Western society—the ways people thought about self, nature, and passion—as previous chapters did for the early modern centuries.

Historians have spent more time studying the transformation of Western mentalities in the early modern centuries, from 1500 to 1800, than with more recent shifts. Trends in more modern mentalities are difficult to plot, for two reasons. First, although important changes have occurred in the modern period, they lack the full sweep of the earlier transformation; earlier shifts, such as secularization or the redefinition of the family or the discovery of a new sense of self, continued to take hold in many respects. Between the late nineteenth century and the mid-twentieth century, then, we are dealing with modifications and new directions within a framework established before—not with a largely new framework, as in previous periods. Second, the earlier transformations saw important relationships between popular outlook and more formal intellectual developments, particularly as summed up in the Enlightenment. This relationship was not entirely easy, as many workers and peasants sought to maintain older values only to find their outlets restricted by upper-class and official reactions. Nevertheless, concepts such as the demystification of nature and the decline of magic operated at the level of high ideas as well as the level of ordinary beliefs. In the period from 1870 to 1950, the relationship between intellectual life and popular mentality became more complex. Intellectuals became more specialized, often deliberately obscurantist; and they often attacked mass ignorance and bad taste. New divisions arose between experts and common people. Thus it becomes harder—but not impossible—to assemble an overview that will cover belief systems at all levels of Western society.

This chapter, then, explores a particular, if extensive, topic, without repeating the larger history of the decades covered. The purpose is to explore themes downplayed in recent chapters, to renew attention to intellectual life and popular mentality. The assumption, already stated in terms of other facets of the Western experience, is that after 1870 a new "construction job" was necessary on the beliefs and mentalities of Western society, the industrial revolution having completed the substantial destruction of traditional mentalities—including deep and extensive religious belief as opposed to more cursory, mainly-on-Sunday religious feeling—although devout belief did survive in some groups. The question before us now is, What is the modern Western mind?

Two basic tensions loom in exploring this topic. The first, already noted but requiring a deeper look here, involves the relationship between formal intellectual activity and ordinary thought. Intellectuals separated themselves in many ways from the reach of ordinary people after 1870, as they developed recondite jargon and specialized fiercely, used mathematics or abstract style rather than ordinary language and representation. By no means is intellectual history and the history of mentalities synonymous in the modern West. Yet, we will argue, there may be some relationships—for example, in the ways both intellectuals and ordinary folk tried to overstep some of the restrictions of daily life in industrial society. The second tension, visible in formal intellectual life but particularly in popular mentalities, involves a conflict between heightened discipline and new spontaneity or impulse. It is indeed by recognizing this tension that students of modern history can reconcile the apparently disparate aspects of mentality in the period.

Intellectual Life: Science

The backbone of Western intellectual activity after 1870 continued to be science, which maintained its claim to offer basic explanations of the physical and human environment and to add incrementally to the store of knowledge. To many Westerners, and not only intellectuals, science was the counterpart of industrial advance, confirming man's ability to grasp and control physical nature. Its seemingly regular and measurable advance—in new knowledge of distant galaxies, for example—also contrasted with the more erratic fluctuations of artistic styles and perceptions.

Breakthroughs in the Physical Sciences

In biology, although no breakthroughs rivalled Darwin's evolutionary theory, fundamental discoveries were offered, many of which had real or potential medical or agricultural applications. Work on the germ theory of disease was further elaborated, as scientists learned how to prepare pure cultures or bacteria for experimental study. Not only sterilization procedures but also inoculations advanced steadily. Biologists and psychologists alike proceeded on Darwinian foundations to examine animal behaviors and human reactions that could be best understood through their evolutionary function. Emotions were analyzed, both through facial expressions and bodily changes, as mechanisms that would spur fight or flight in an individual in a crisis situation. The Russian scientist Pavlov explored the conditioned reflex in people and animals, showing that dogs, for example, could be trained to salivate when they heard a bell, if for a time the bell sound was linked to the presentation of food. Other biologists and doctors studied hormones and tissues, showing the role of complex chemicals and glands in the human body; some medical applications, dealing for example with certain processes of aging, were forthcoming. Still more basic was the discovery, by Gregor Mendel, a Moravian monk, of the principles of genetics, a finding that began to win attention around 1900. Working with peas and other vegetables, geneticists demonstrated how hereditary properties were transmitted. This new understanding greatly enhanced evolutionary theory, which had previously been rather vague about how natural selection actually operated in transmitting qualities from one generation to the next. Genetics also had practical application in the development of improved strains of seeds and livestock.

New fields of research opened up outside biology. William Roentgen and Pierre and Marie Curie initiated the study of radiation and X rays, showing how rays were emitted by rare substances such as radium and actinium. Practical applications were quickly made available, as the use of X rays greatly improved medical diagnosis. (Roentgen, the X ray pioneer, died of cancer incurred during his experiments, in what might have been taken as a stronger warning about some of the drawbacks of the new techniques.)

Striking theoretical advances were made in the field of physics. During the late nineteenth and early twentieth centuries, physicists from a number of nations improved their understanding of the behavior of electricity and particularly probed the nature of the atom, which had already been established as the smallest basic unit of each chemical element. The physicists proved that the atom itself was composed of electrical particles, some with positive and others with negative charges, all revolving about each other at enormous speed and with vast force. These findings demonstrated the power and sophistication of scientific thought, and also steady improvement in laboratory equipment, even though they painted a far more abstract and difficult universe than the law-abiding nature proposed by Isaac Newton. Furthermore, basic Newtonian laws were themselves qualified by the next findings. Laws of motion, for example, were not as regular as Newton had posited, nor were they as fixed. Shortly after 1900 the physicist and mathematician Albert Einstein demonstrated that such fundamental categories as time, space, and mass were merely relative, depending on the vantage point of the observer. Weight thus varied with gravity; light varied with time, which now became a fourth dimension (along with height, breadth, and depth) in all measurements. Einstein's complex mathematical theories were the subject of wide dispute, particularly since many could not easily be proved by observation or experiment. But later work on atomic physics and improved observation of the behavior of planetary bodies and systems outside the solar system largely confirmed Einstein's findings. In 1928 the German physicist Werner Heisenberg pulled together considerable prior research on the structure of the atom and proposed that instead of seeing the behavior of subatomic particles such as electrons as minute replications of a Newtonian system, atomic particles must also be seen as "indeterminate." That is, because physicists had to work with instruments that were moving relative to the subatomic movements being studied, they could not measure the position of electrons without distorting their speed. Thus the atomic world was not fully regular or predictable except in terms of statistical probabilities. The simple, mechanistic world of Newton (discussed in Chapter 3) was further collapsing; but with a combination of advanced mathematics and intuition, this world could still be grasped, and indeed Newtonian concepts still worked much of the time. This meant that, even as physics became steadily more complicated and abstract, and far too difficult for most interested laymen to grasp directly, the *authority* of science—its ability to coherently explain the universe and to predict future discoveries reliably—remained for the most part unquestioned.

As science had often demonstrated, one set of scientific findings produced still others. The revolution in physics in the early twentieth century prepared the way for new findings, between 1920 and 1950, in the study of crystals, solid-state physics, the behavior of high-energy particles, and the living cell. Particularly important was work in the 1940s that combined physics, chemistry, and biology in grasping the structure of the basic genetic materials in living things. Scientists in Britain and the United States (surging now to new prominence in basic research) charted the "double helix" shape of deoxribonucleic acid, or DNA, the fundamental protein element of genetic material. This finding in turn permitted new understanding of how genetic traits were transmitted and, by the 1960s, would also produce new industrial and medical applications as living tissues could be synthesized from inorganic matter.

The dynamism of science had a number of implications, particularly after 1900. Actual scientific research became increasingly recondite, open only to handfuls of highly trained specialists. In this sense the gap between elite understanding and popular culture widened further than ever before. Intelligent laymen had been able to follow scientific arguments and debates not only in the age of Newton, but also through the mid-nineteenth-century decades in which Darwinian theories won wide attention. This possibility was now largely closed as catchy terms such as relativity won media attention, but a real grasp of the concepts involved was reserved for the top scientists themselves. At the same time, scientific research became increasingly expensive, confined to industrial research laboratories and, particularly, the largest universities in western Europe and the United States. Science became professionalized more fully than before, as amateur dabbling proved impossible. Most scientists themselves concentrated on small subdisciplines; with a few brilliant exceptions research involved small accretions of knowledge through experiment and observation, which cumulatively added vast stores of data but which rarely produced dramatic theoretical breakthroughs. Cost and specialization also brought the practice of science increasingly under the

POST-NEWTONIAN PHYSICS: ANOTHER REVOLUTION

The probing of subatomic particles followed from the accidental discovery of the X ray in 1895. Physicists found that when X rays were passed through a gas, they dislodged tiny electrically charged particles that left traces on a photographic plate, and this in turn suggested that these electrical particles must be components of the atoms of gas—components later named electrons. Thus was a whole new world of atomic physics opened up. Also, around 1900, a German scientist, Max Planck, developed a theory to explain why energy did not flow continuously, as mechanistic assumptions would predict, but in periodic packets of energy, or quanta. This quantum theory explained the otherwise arbitrary movement of electrons around the proton of an atom—but it also suggested considerable randomness foreign to Newtonian assumptions.

Einstein's theory of relativity was consistent with these new and complex findings. Einstein sought to explain experiments that showed that the velocity of light was constant no matter in what direction it was emitted. These findings meant that either the earth was not moving, or the universe was not uniform. The theory of relativity, elaborated between 1905 and 1916, showed that time and space were not absolutes. The behavior of light could be explained only through a hypothesis of curved space, with space and time relative to each other and forming a single continuum. The relativity theory won great acclaim in 1919 when the British Royal Astronomical Society proved, during a solar eclipse, that light rays were indeed curved when they passed through the sun's magnetic field.

purview of basic policy decisions about what research should and should not be funded. Scientists were often constrained to work on projects that could be justified in terms of practical pay-off in industry, medicine, or war. The classic case involved the recruitment during World War II of physicists, in Germany on one side, the United States and Britain on the other, to develop atomic weaponry. The theoretical principles of these physicists had already been worked out through the discoveries of the behavior of subatomic particles and relativity theory. Science, which had earlier encountered strong moral objections because of its impact on religious views, now generated moral dilemmas through its practical effects on how people could manipulate nature and how they could kill each other.

Yet the important changes in the position and results of scientific research did not generally affect widespread popular faith in the scientific approach. The fact that science on the frontiers was less comprehensible than before counted for less than the success of science in developing new knowledge and producing new products. The atomic bomb roused widespread fears, but science was more commonly lauded for its development of new and productive seeds for agriculture, or the host of new medical products that appeared as the result of chemical and biological research from the 1920s onward. Most notably, sulfa drugs and then penicillin and other antibiotics began to eliminate the more serious respiratory diseases, long the most potent killers of people in childhood and old age. Results of this sort reconfirmed the link between science and progress, despite new complexities, new admissions of the relativity rather than mechanistic certainty of basic findings, and new moral dilemmas.

The Social Sciences

The prestige of the scientific approach was reflected, as before, in the adaptation of scientific methods of empiricism and theory-building by social scientists. Sociology, the study of the behavior of people in groups, became a recognized university discipline after about 1870. Sociological research accumulated increasing amounts of data about political behavior, suicide, divorce, and crime. Major theoretical formulations developed as well. In France around 1900, Emile Durkheim examined the alienating effects of urban, industrial culture, explaining phenomena such as suicide in these terms. A "Chicago school" of sociologists followed in the 1920s with a mixture of theoretical claims and data collections designed to demonstrate the impact of urban alienation on crime rates and other indices of maladaptation. A somewhat different theoretical approach was pursued by the German sociologist Max Weber, who blended history and sociology in developing models of bureaucratic behavior and the evolution of capitalist personalities and value systems.

Anthropology, the study of human beings, also won increasing recognition as a distinct discipline with research on primitive cultures. The emphasis here was on empiricism, with field workers amassing vital new materials on various tribal societies, including American Indians, and on artifacts and archeological remains; but there was some theory building also, concerning the classification of religious belief systems and the historical evolution of human values.

Economics, the study of money and value, won even more attention. Following from Adam Smith, economics had long been a field dominated by rationalistic theorizing and the development of *laissez-faire* arguments about the operation of untrammeled market forces. Or, following Karl Marx, economists had disputed *laissez-faire* models with a historical, but also highly theoretical, picture of class dominance and class struggle. By the later nineteenth century, particularly in Britain and the United States, a somewhat different approach emerged that blended theory with empiricism. Economists began to collect masses of statistical data and develop middle-level theories about economic behavior—for example, the patterns of economic cycles—on these bases. Statements of economic principle remained, of course, as economists might still line up in a *laissez-faire* camp, opposing most government intervention, or as Marxists might preach the class struggle as a means of understanding and of political action alike. But economics became increasingly linked to less sweeping theories, and more to practical advice about how the economy could actually be managed. During the Great Depression, a British economist, John Maynard Keynes, already noted for his accurate criticisms of prior economic policies, developed an approach that urged government activism and increased spending to compensate for economic slumps, matched by relatively decreased spending and accumulation of revenues during prosperous times. Keynesian economics found many adherents in government circles, as in the American New Deal administration, and this in turn solidified the discipline as an essentially scientific basis for policy formation.

Headed by economics, in sum, the social sciences by the twentieth century were generating a mixture of massive data sets, both impressionistic and statistical; theoretical formulations; and concrete policy suggestions about how to deal with crime, or business cycles, or inadequate parents. Although basic theories in the social sciences typically lacked the prestige or sweeping acceptance of their analogues in science—human society proved harder to capture in mathematical models than physical nature was—both social scientists and many members of the wider public assumed that the increasingly influential army of economists and sociologists were essentially scientists and deserved somewhat comparable authority in their fields.

Psychology, the study of the mind, also made increasingly powerful claims on public attention as a means of scientific understanding of people in groups and as individuals. Researchers in France, Germany, and the United States, from the late 1800s onward, developed new mechanisms to test individual intelligence and aptitudes. Use of intelligence quotient, or I.Q., tests and other batteries took hold increasingly in school systems as a means of assigning students to different tracks, and in the military service from World War I onward. This success helped produce the subfield of industrial psychology, particularly in the United States, which developed additional testing procedures to assist businesses

The first mass use of group intelligence testing took place in World War I using American recruits.

in personnel selection and studied as well contexts that would improve the performance of existing employees. Here too, a combination of data collection and theories about human motivation or intelligence—middle-level theories about how people behave in specific settings—had wide impact on government and corporate policy, which in turn won for social and behavioral scientists a new influence over how people actually lived.

Freud's Theories of Personality   Psychological theory, however, was dominated during the first half of the twentieth century not by the work of cognitive and industrial psychologists, but by the personality theories of Sigmund Freud, extended and partially disputed by subsequent analysts. Freud was an empiricist of sorts, and he was alert to the notion that ultimately the human mind could be understood through grasp of biological and chemical processes (avenues of discovery that would open up much later). His own work, however, rested on individual case studies he encountered during his treatment of emotionally disturbed people through the procedure he dubbed psychoanalysis—and on the fascinating theoretical structure he built on these case studies. Freud insisted that a large reach of the human mind harbored unconscious instincts and impulses, which vitally affected behavior even though largely unnoticed by the individual involved. The mind also contained conscious mechanisms including a conscience, or superego. But the balance among the various elements was fragile, and too much repression of the unconscious could lead to severe mental disturbance:

> We come to the conclusion, from working with hysterical patients and other neurotics, that they have not fully succeeded in repressing the idea to which the incompatible wish is attached. They have, indeed, driven it out of consciousness and out of memory, and apparently saved themselves a great amount of psychic pain, *but in the unconscious the suppressed wish still exists*, only waiting for its chance to become active, and finally succeeds in sending into consciousness, instead of the repressed idea, a disguised and unrecognizable surrogate-creation . . . to which the same painful sensations associate themselves that the patient thought he was rid of through his repression.

Although Freud's "discovery" of the human unconscious urged attention to individual conflicts in treating actual patients, it did not present a human nature that was random in its essence. Not only were all personalities constructed of the same basic ingredients—the unconscious or id, the ego, and the superego—but also all people encountered the same fundamental conflicts in growing up. Children, for example, naturally love their opposite-sex parent so intensely that they often wish the death of their same-sex parent as a rival; but their conscious minds quickly learn that this sexual jealousy is not acceptable, so they repress their basic desires. Most people work out the resultant conscious-unconscious conflicts sufficiently well to emerge mentally healthy, but in some people that harmony does not coalesce, producing the symptoms, such as hysterical illness, of mental derangement. As had happened to physics under the impact of relativity theories, psychology in Freudian terms became vastly more complex, preoccupied with childhood crises, dreams, and unintended behaviors, but it continued to yield basic models and rules. Freudian psychology thus stood as another sign of man's increasing capacity for scientific understanding—in this case, of his own complex self (and his own self's complexes).

As the other sciences had done, Freudian psychology yielded a host of practical results. Freud himself not only theorized about the irrational, but he developed through psychoanalysis a procedure to deal with it when it got out of hand. Lengthy individual discussions with disturbed patients were designed, quite simply, to bring the repressed, unconscious impulse back into the conscious level, where it could be handled in such a way that the unintended behavior—such as a psychosomatic illness—would disappear:

> If this repressed material is once more made part of the conscious mental functions—a process which supposes the overcoming of considerable resistance—the psychic conflict which then arises, the same which the patient wished to avoid, is made capable of a happier termination, under the guidance of the physician, than is offered by repression.

Popularized Freudian psychology, or other theories that stressed the importance of unconscious drives or impulses, had impact aside from the psychoanalytic approach. Many experts began to urge a less repressive approach to sexuality, for example, arguing that "Victorian" or "Puritanical" habits caused needless mental suffering. Most expert advice to parents by the 1920s thus urged that masturbation was not the horror that nineteenth-century experts had held, but rather a natural expression of impulse whose repression could cause far more problems than its toleration. Similarly, aggression between children was now seen as natural, something to be regulated but not totally repressed and certainly not the sign of some appalling failure on the part of parent or child. The message of psychology was that people have instincts that they can and should learn to manage, but that cannot be turned off through sudden repression save at great cost. Particularly after 1940, and especially in the United States, popularizations of some basic Freudian notions lent a new air of scientific validity to child-rearing advice—while changing the nature of some of the advice as well.

Science in Society: Relativism and Cultural Despair

The rise of the social sciences and psychology had many other features that paralleled the natural sciences. They emphasized specialization in a growing array of disciplines. In contrast to Enlightenment patterns, it was no longer possible to claim general intellectual expertise. The specialized disciplines centered on university faculties, as universities became increasingly important centers of research, sources of specialist training, and guardians of the scientific faith. They produced bewildering amounts of data and theory, making it hard (though somewhat less hard than in the physical sciences) for a lay public to keep up or to understand. Yet, even more directly than the sciences, the social sciences produced policy decisions, institutions of policy study, and authoritative advice that had wide impact on how ordinary people lived—particularly when these ordinary people wanted to think of their lives as organized on the basis of science and reason rather than tradition or whimsy.

Leading discoveries both in science and social science also had a double-edged effect on wider intellectual life after 1900; that is, they also contributed to a new mood of pessimism and cultural despair, which had already been building among some artists and thinkers in the later nineteenth century. The intellectual questions thus become: If natural phenomena can be understood only relatively or in terms of probability, is nature indeed a benign machine, harmonious with human reason, as Enlightenment thought had once argued? If the human personality is not driven by reason, but by fearsome instinct, is there any cause to believe in human progress? If, as anthropologists contended, human values thought normal in the West were totally different among, say, the Pueblo Indians, was there any way to argue that one set of beliefs is better or more natural than another? Particularly in the somber mood of post–World War I Europe, when intellectuals had ample cause to question the stability of their own society, concepts or tag-words borrowed from the sciences gave legitimacy to new doubts, new arguments against liberal optimism, new commitments to religious or artistic movements that made no pretense of rationality. Some of this cultural despair even contributed to support for fascist movements, where irrationality and violence were made positive virtues.

The mood of cultural despair, and its partial basis in the new complexities discovered in the universe and in human nature, did not pass entirely in the 1920s and 1930s; elements would continue to affect Western intellectual life after 1950. But the more durable impact of the new science and social science was to confirm the essential validity of the scientific approach and the idea that human reason could grasp the essential features of how the universe worked. Science might become more complex, and the simplicities of the Newtonian universe did fade from view, but scientists could still be relied upon for knowledge and progress. Social scientists, pointing to new complexities in human behavior, nevertheless continued to argue that the social environment could be understood through rational inquiry and that understanding could produce better policy. Freudianism, often interpreted by the cultural pessimists as exalting irrational impulse, in fact was profoundly rationalistic at base. For though it discovered a more complex human nature than Enlightenment optimists had assumed, it continued to argue that reason could control. Psychoanalysis consisted essentially of assisting reason, now called the conscious mind, to gain more explicit control over impulse—an updated version of Enlightenment belief.

So although developments in science and social science contributed to an important cultural mood between the wars, they did not shake some of the essentials of the belief system that had emerged, two centuries before, with the Enlightenment itself. Certainly the confidence of the various specialist scientists was not shaken, as they continued their blend of observation, experimentation, and theory to produce new knowledge.

Philosophy and Theology

A key sign of the continued gains of scientific and social-scientific approaches showed in the relative decline of traditional philosophy and, on the whole, of theology as well. There were, quite simply, no new philosophical breakthroughs in the West after 1870, in the sense of anyone persuasively creating vast, all-embracing systems of thought. With science now dominant in understanding nature and human nature, purely abstract systems lost ground. A significant cluster of philosophers arose in Europe in the later nineteenth and early twentieth centuries to trumpet alternatives to dominant rationalistic assumptions. The German Friedrich Nietzsche elaborated a combination of mystical visions and philosophical slogans in arguing against humanitarian values. Nietzsche preached a philosophy of strength, in which a race of supermen could rise above morals for the sake of a will to power. Other philosophers advanced ideas about irrational impulses dominating life or about some mysterious elementary force, uncapturable by science, that guided nature and life alike. This philosophical stance would feed into the mood of cultural despair in the interwar years, but it was hardly a full philosophical system. Other philosophers, particularly in the United States, urged a more frankly pragmatic approach that would bypass any search for basic truths in favor of discussions of what was practical. And many academic philosophers, finally, turned to scientific study of linguistics or mathematics, rather than pursuing an overarching philosophical framework.

The decline of formal philosophy was marked in the area of political theory. Although various thinkers continued to work in nineteenth-century theoretical traditions such as liberalism or Marxism, making important specific contributions, there were no really novel departures aside from the largely antitheoretical current of fascism. Politics increasingly seemed a sphere not for the philosopher, but for the trained political scientist or economist who could talk about how systems worked and how they could be made to work better.

Theology fared somewhat less badly than did traditional philosophy. Spurred by reform-minded popes in the later nineteenth century, Catholic theology revived, using principles derived from Thomas Aquinas to talk about the reconciliation of science and faith. A number of Catholic writers also took up social problems, arguing that reforms guided by Christian principles could correct the evils of capitalism without accepting a socialist alternative. Protestant thought revived as well after the bitter battles against Darwinism in the 1860s and 1870s. Some Protestant leaders took up a social gospel, urging practical changes as the best service to God. The Salvation Army, founded in Britain in 1878, expressed the new Protestant social mission. More sweeping Protestant theology in the twentieth century, spearheaded by German thinkers, many of whom later settled in the United States, argued for a return to basic Christian traditions, which included an understanding of human sin as opposed to facile rationalistic optimism. These developments were important in showing the continued vitality of older currents of Western thought and the undeniable diversity of Western intellectual life. But theology did not regain a leading intellectual position, either in the schools or in the wider cultural sphere. Some of the religious thought, particularly when focused on social action rather than theological basics, actually conceded much of the intellectual terrain to the scientific approach. Christian leaders who stressed religion's role in aiding the poor or spearheading some nonsocialist trade unions might thus focus on earthly pragmatism rather than on the spiritual, supernatural framework that had traditionally strengthened the faith.

The Arts

Scientific work did not dominate all facets of intellectual life. Developments in the arts suggested a different, though not always entirely unrelated, vision. Something like two cultures had developed in Western intellectual life—the scientific and the aesthetic—with relatively little mutual interaction or appreciation. Although the scientific culture undoubtedly won the widest acclaim, the artistic culture demonstrated great vitality on its own and maintained important influence over a wide public.

The twin keys to most Western art between 1870 and 1950 (and indeed to a considerable extent thereafter) involved related commitments to develop innovative styles rather than rely on past standards, and to use art to convey an intensely personal, often highly emotional reality. Artists built on the earlier Romantic defiance of fixed stylistic canons, but they became far more daring in their own innovations than Romantic painters and writers had been. The intentional innovations of modern artists complicated simple characterizations of style, as true now as then; there was far less agreement on style than had been true of earlier Gothic or classical ages. The term "modern" was frequently applied to art after 1870, but the modern style often represented little more than a common interest in defying tradition.

Painting and Sculpture

Deliberate efforts to shock established tastes were particularly prominent between 1870 and 1914. During these decades the most stylish paint-ers—the ones whose works were displayed in established salons and who made a fashionable living from the patronage of the wealthy—worked mainly on classical and Romantic themes. The painters who actually set the tone for the art that has been remembered from this period, in con-trast, forged their own styles, worked often in considerable poverty and obscurity, and mounted their own exhibitions in defiance of the art schools and the major exhibitions. The first new dominant trend in painting,

Approaches to painting near the turn of the century included the pointillist style, in which the canvas was carefully dotted with multicolored paint, producing a unified effect of light, color, and form when seen at a distance. Georges Seurat, *Sunday Afternoon on the Island of La Grande Jatte* (1884–1886).

based in France but with practitioners from many countries including the United States, was impressionism. Impressionists, intoxicated with the qualities of light and color, worked to convey the visual essence of scenes and people, not their literal qualities. Impressionists reacted in part against the rise of photography, which increasingly took over the task of literal representation and which became the most pervasive visual art as far as ordinary people were concerned. Impressionists were also influenced by advancing scientific knowledge in optics and chemistry, believing that careful use of color could promote a deeper insight into visual reality than "realism" could accomplish. Early impressionists, such as Edouard Manet, shocked the artistic public with their initial displays, but they were actually rather timid compared to later masters such as Claude Monet, who created misty, evocative, sometimes nearly unrecognizable landscapes. By the 1890s, impressionism itself yielded to new visions. Paul Gauguin, painting first in the south of France and then in Tahiti, introduced greater form and dimension into painting, employing vivid colors, while still avoiding literal representation. The half-mad Dutch painter Vincent van Gogh filled canvas after canvas with brilliantly burning suns and fields of grain, emanating an almost overwhelming luminosity amid thick brush strokes. Henri de Toulouse-Lautrec, in the same period, painted music-hall scenes, evoking personalities with an almost cartoonlike style. After 1900 a number of painters began experimenting with geometrical shapes in order to convey a scene without direct representation. This style, ultimately led by Pablo Picasso, a Spaniard who worked mainly in France, developed into cubism.

By the 1900s, the world of painting was characterized by a bewildering array of styles and increasing abstraction. Russian and German painters splashed brilliant daubs of color on canvas, supplementing with different shapes and line strokes. Recognizable figures might intrude, with objects, animals, or portions of human form scattered about, but the intent was an increasingly personal vision, as opposed to a realistic scene; painters were trying to capture motion, or energy, or mood, not a fixed entity. Sculptors began working in similar modes, with masters such as Auguste Rodin moving increasingly away from conventional figures toward evocations and, after 1900, entirely nonrepresentational shapes that would elicit subjective responses from the viewer.

Music and Literature

Music also broke away from established canons; composers such as Arnold Schoenberg and Igor Stravinsky began using atonal scales and clashing rhythms instead of the conventional harmonies of the great Romantic composers.

Literature revealed some similar tendencies. Important realistic novelists continued to wield great influence. German author Thomas Mann focused on scenes from his own society, chronicling, for example, the decline and fall of a merchant family in Hamburg. A powerful group of Russian novelists, including Fyodor Dostoyevski and Leo Tolstoy, also painted word portraits of their society and often followed a clear plot line as well as characterizations of personalities. On the whole, even the realist school focused increasingly on mood, social setting, and the emotional life of individuals, rather than on a host of events and exciting actions. But their commitment to conveying an identifiable reality remained clear. Among other writers, however, the use of words to defy convention and express personal moods and feelings became predominant. Poets and playwrights in France and Britain, including Stephane Mallarmé and Oscar Wilde, deliberately shocked through their choice of unconventional themes and images. They also experimented with new verse forms, avoiding conventional rhyme and meter and sometimes accepted punctuation. A new type of novel, in the stream-of-consciousness style, arose after 1900. James Joyce, in Ireland, wrote powerful, jumbled sentences with little or no plot, to convey mood and to appeal to the subjective impressions of his readers. Use of profanity and explicit sexual imagery was part of this process. Somewhat more sedate was Marcel Proust in France, who was nevertheless also concerned with using his scenes not to tell a story or convey objective conditions, but to evoke the senses and provoke flashes of memory.

The Messages of Modernism

The work in art, sculpture, music, and literature from 1870 to 1950 was extremely diverse, really by definition of what "modern" meant. Not all leading practitioners were self-conscious innovators, and the innovators themselves disagreed widely about what forms were most appropriate. Yet from this diversity came a set of common messages. First, there is no single, agreed-upon artistic reality. Reality depends on the mood and the emotions of both artist and viewer. Second, the essence of things revolves around impressions. These impressions are not always harmonious or pure. They must include smells, discordance, sex, the energy and grinding quality of a machine age. A group of artists and writers based in Italy, called the Futurists, proclaimed the mission of art to be the use of abstraction to describe the clashes and frenzy of modern life. Third, the viewer or reader must be appealed to not primarily in terms of rationality, but through subjective responses that involve unconscious feelings, hidden urges, and fears. Art is not a matter of orderly rules even for its audience. In this spirit playwrights, such as Luigi Pirandello in Italy, wrote dramas deliberately defying conventional stagecraft and avoiding clear plot, to appeal for greater, inherently diverse audience participation and response.

The spirit of innovation and defiance spread also to architecture, although here, since buildings are functional, the abstract and subjective elements were less noticeable. A modern building style developed, one of the three great, distinctive architectural styles—along with classical and Gothic—that Western civilization has ever produced. Modern architects abandoned the eighteenth- and nineteenth-century habit of copying past styles—whether medieval, Byzantine, or classical—to generate something new. They benefited from novel building materials, including structural steel and poured concrete. Their products ranged from the skyscraper, first pioneered in Chicago, to the use of multilevel, linear designs for homes and small offices, to new circular motifs in the design of other small buildings. The modern style spread also to furniture design, where previously most artistic effort had focused on recapturing the traditional styles of the eighteenth-century aristocracy or the forms of older craft art. Modern furniture emphasized simple but daring lines and often vivid colors; representational patterns on furniture declined in use, at the level of the most artistic efforts. Here were symptoms of the passion for new styles, but also some links to the functional world of industry and the consumer public.

The various currents of modern art continued full force between the world wars. Indeed, stylistic innovation became ever more varied and daring. Many paintings became completely abstract as even cubism was abandoned, after the early 1930s, in favor of geometrical shapes—the chartlike constructions of Piet Modrian—or blobs of color or the distorted figures of Picasso in the 1930s. Music moved still further from conventional melody and harmony, trying to convey emotion directly and proud of clashing, discordant sounds. Artists continued to seek a truth, but it was clearly not a standardized truth open to rational debate. The importance of unconscious drives and the messy nature of modern society both precluded a tidy, standardized statement. What was left was subjective impulse; or some sort of elemental process too complex and murky to capture except by art; or some social horror, like the mass bloodshed of the Spanish Civil War that Picasso tried to capture with the vivid, painful figures of his painting *Guernica*. Or perhaps it was simply the deadly monotony of dehumanized modern life suggested by the poem "Preludes" by the Anglo-American T. S. Eliot:

> The morning comes to consciousness
> Of faint stale smells of beer
> From the sawdust-trampled street
> With all its muddy feet that press
> To early coffee-stands.
> With the other masquerades
> That time resumes,
> One thinks of all the hands
> That are raising dingy shades
> In a thousand furnished rooms.

Modern artistic and literary styles roused great controversy, as they were intended to do. Many artists unquestionably delighted in tweaking the public nose, blasting the conventionality of mass taste. Modern art was in part a reaction against the presumed boredom and tawdriness of life in an industrialized, mass-consumer society, an attempt to show the contrast between artistic vision and ordinary perceptions. For its part, the art-consuming public was indeed duly shocked by many modern-art productions. Many critics long held out against the renunciation of established values, the deliberate experimentalism. For one commentator who admitted, for example, that innovations in musical composition such as Schoenberg's twelve-tone scale "do say something," there were far more waiting to pounce:

This complete upsetting of all traditional values, this disdain of all previously accepted melodic and harmonic relationships, suggests to me, not so much courage and sincerity, as an inflated arrogance of mind that can only be described as megalomania—a dreary wilderness of cacophony that somehow contrives to be pedantic and hysterical at the same time.

Hostility to modern art, visible in countless cartoons about meaningless squiggles hung on museum walls, even had political ramifications. Nazi ideologues blasted modern art as un-German and urged a return to realistic aesthetics. Interestingly, the Soviet regime in Russia also condemned modern art as part of its new suspicions of Western culture, disliking the freedom and irrationality of the new genres. Soviet "socialist realism" emphasized heroic, muscled figures of soldiers and workers, building a predictably better world.

For their part, artists refused to concede to public pressures: their vision was their own, with art serving for the sake of art. Paul Klee, a painter of largely abstract works, defended the primacy of the artist's creative powers over either "objective" reality or popular taste by imagining a dialogue with a tiresome layman who "always looks for his favorite subject" in a picture:

> Layman: "But that isn't a bit like uncle." The artist, if his nerve is disciplined, thinks to himself: "To Hell with uncle. I must get on with my creation. This new brick is a little too heavy and to my mind puts too much weight on the left. I must add a good-sized counterweight to the right to restore the equilibrium."

In sum, as Klee insisted, the artist "must distort, for therein is nature reborn." For, despite wide varieties among avant-garde styles, the dominant mission remained the expression of heightened feeling and emotion, a nonrational link between artist and viewer (or reader or listener).

Outreach to a Wider Audience

Despite the apparent gap between high art and popular taste, which threatened constantly to widen as artists became increasingly abstract, piling one new approach on another for the sake of personal innovation, there was an increased harmony between artistic mood and public mood in the 1920s and 1930s. The pessimism induced by World War I and other dislocations found some echo in artistic work that, while not always gloomy, did emphasize a world bounded by no set controls. Putting the case simply, as artists stressed the nonrational, they found an audience among people whose faith in the rationality of their society was declining. Surrealist painters, for example, developing in the interwar decades, portrayed grotesque imaginary landscapes in which highly realistic details were placed out of any normal context or connection. Their intent was at once playful and disturbing, and although it by no means won uniform public approval—many people aware of art at all still expected it to look "nice"—the brooding mood they evoked, threatening some unnamed disaster, fit the tone of these difficult decades.

Furthermore, modern art styles increasingly reached public consciousness through a wider range of mediums. Designers of buildings and fur-

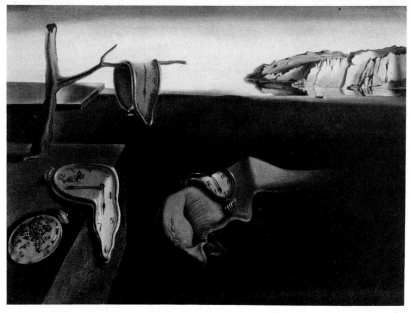

Salvador Dali's *The Persistence of Memory* (1931) well exemplifies the dreamscapes of surrealist painting.

niture required some public acceptance if their models were to be built. Unlike painters, who might survive on an audience of artists alone, architects needed contracts if their buildings were to go up. They were vividly aware of engineering opportunities and the demands of function, as well as the new artistic impulse to innovate. Groups of modern designers such as the influential Bauhaus school in Weimar Germany heightened their interaction with actual patrons and consumers. They did not win the day for modern architecture completely; one of Nazism's targets was the sleek-lined building styles, which they labeled "Mediterranean" or "Jewish," preferring traditional Germanic peaked roofs and, for official buildings, a heavy-handed classicism. Bauhaus designers, accordingly, largely left Germany after Hitler's takeover, many coming to the United States. But contacts with a wider public did develop, and many artists, convinced of a social mission and not just eager to attack popular bad taste, worked hard to make contacts even with a working-class audience.

Playwrights and artistic filmmakers also reached for a new audience between the wars. Politically radical authors such as Bertolt Brecht combined new theater forms with a desire to portray popular suffering and to attack capitalist controls; furthermore, Brecht wanted workers to see his efforts. Filmmakers in France, Germany, and Russia, hardly rivaling the commercial products of Hollywood in sheer numbers of viewers, wanted innovative art to uplift. They were often disappointed, finding the masses unduly conformist and controlled by escapist story-telling. As Klee said, artists were still "seeking a people." A wide gap remained between the burst of artistic creativity and what most people expected from art—if indeed they had any expectations at all. But the gap was less complete than when the modern art movement had begun in the nineteenth century, and among artists the mood of defiance of social reality declined as well.

The Two Cultures

Artistic and literary work on the one hand and science and social science on the other increasingly overlapped between the wars. Artists who studied optics, functional modern architects concerned with engineering advances, and musicians who combined musical and mathematical theory in developing new tonalities directly blended scientific and technical advance with their own work. They did not see art as uniformly antithetical to science.

For their part, new scientific interest in ideas of relativity and intuition, and particularly the new emphasis on the irrational in human nature, brought the findings of science closer to the concerns of artists. Freudian psychology was in part a scientific translation of the views artists had been emphasizing for some time about the primacy of emotion and irrational impulse in the human personality.

Yet two almost unbridgeable gaps remained between most artists and most scientists, however much selective borrowing of terms and concepts occurred. First, scientists remained wedded to the basic method developed in the scientific revolution of the seventeenth century. Data collection combined with rationalistic theory-building provided truth about nature and society alike. Artists, in contrast, relied on their own impulse, their subjective perception, to guide their music, painting, or literary effort, and they depended on emotional rather than rationalistic audience response.

The second gap involved social position and professional context. Science was now enshrined as a public value. Although individual scientists might lament their lack of funding, particularly if their work was viewed as too theoretical, too devoid of practical implications, the fact was that most scientists were employed at publicly supported institutions, at business corporations and particularly at universities. The modern artist, in contrast, typically remained more marginal. University employment was possible, but there artists had to contend both with the rising prestige of science, which diverted potential support, and the traditionalism of many academic humanists, who thought they should defend older styles, not embrace new. In essence, modern art was not accepted as the only kind of art, and art in general saw its claim on public support lessened by the growing confidence in science and technology. For social as well as theoretical reasons, then, art and science remained largely apart. This meant, in turn, that modern Western high culture was rooted in some fundamental complexities, even disharmonies. Quite apart from traditional residues such as theology, there was no single modern value system from which the various branches of intellectual endeavor neatly flowed.

Mentality During Early Industrialization

Popular mentalities, or the ways people thought about their world and themselves, had been changing extensively for several centuries before the blossoming of Western industrial society. Indeed, these earlier shifts in outlook helped explain why the industrialization process got started, and why it had produced some of the effects that marked the nineteenth and early twentieth centuries—such as the emphasis on family warmth as a contrast to the colder world of economic life. In previous chapters we have identified several major themes underlying a host of specific changes, including greater literacy. First, a growing number of people had increased their emphasis on rationality and regularity in viewing their natural and social environment; their way of seeing and interpreting the world had been "demystified" in the sense that the emphasis on arbitrary forces and unseen spirits—witches, Satan, or simply blind chance—was curtailed. Demystification sometimes included a reduction of religious fervor, and a growing number of ordinary people did turn from formal Christianity in the eighteenth and nineteenth centuries; but it also sometimes involved a reorientation of religion itself. During the nineteenth century many middle-class Protestants in the United States and western Europe believed firmly in God and a church, but also believed that God was benign, the sponsor of a well-ordered and largely predictable nature, and a sure rewarder of good living through a heavenly afterlife. Complications such as hell and damnation were played down in this revision of the Protestant mainstream.

Along with demystification had come the redefinition of family life and a clearer concept of the self. Family underwent a clearer separation from the larger community, and the economic functions of family were supplemented by a new concern with emotional intensity and an almost religious invocation of the family as the bearer of purity and virtue in a complex world. New definitions of the self were generated by a growing belief in reason as a key ingredient of individual identity, plus a growing ability to see the self as an independent actor in life—not simply as something acted upon, or merged with larger entities. The newly discovered self also emanated from a growing interest in defining appropriate expressions—and restraining inappropriate expressions—for individual identities. Simultaneous emphasis on the self and on family could become complicated, for the first implied individualism, the second intense familial bonds that meant unselfishly subsuming one's individualism for the good of all. But the two concepts could be reconciled if, for example, the family was seen as a freely-formed unit among individuals and a place where self-expression was possible. The idea, increasingly current from the eighteenth century onward, that proper families should be launched through two individuals "falling in love" was exactly this kind of reconciliation, at least in theory, between self and family identity. New emphases on family and self both derived from the decline of traditional community bonds and structures, as guilds disappeared and vil-

Defining for immigrants the American way of life was undertaken by a stereoscope view-card company in its series depicting how a model American family spent its day. Note that breakfast was served in the kitchen and included packaged cereal.

lages and neighborhoods waned as distinct social entities. The weakening of community structures, with their ability at once to enforce rules and safely embrace spontaneity, was a vital change in the context of modern Western outlook.

Thus the earlier changes in popular outlook had a clearly constructive side, involving the formation of new values and not simply the loss of old—although the new values were not necessarily better than those they replaced. At the same time, however, the evolution of popular mentalities through the early industrial revolution also had a negative, or destructive side, as various elite groups, and then the larger early-industrial middle class, tried to impose new values on the masses and to limit traditional cultural outlets. Doctors railed against popular medical practices and informal practitioners, increasingly urging that there was but one, "scientific" way to deal with health problems. Beliefs in witches, or ideas that suicides resulted from direct intervention of the devil, were banned from court proceedings. The beliefs might continue, but by the eighteenth century it was no longer possible to accuse someone of witchcraft, or to insist that the body of a suicide be mutilated to prevent Satan's minions from gaining ground. The rowdiness and emotional spontaneity of festivals was attacked, first during the period of the Reformation and the Catholic Counter-Reformation, then with even greater success during the early industrial decades. New popular beliefs did arise alongside these efforts, but at the same time the elite-sponsored war on many fronts against the traditional outlook makes it unclear how many people really found a new set of values and how many were simply inhibited in their expression of old ones.

For example, in Germany in the late nineteenth century, a fairly old working-class woman was urged to go to a doctor to deal with some health problems. She adamantly refused, arguing that a few herbal remedies would suffice and that anyway the force that determined health was God's will—when God wanted her, she would go. Science and rationality had no sway against this kind of partially fatalistic traditionalism; they simply made it harder to articulate.

It is possible, indeed, that the confusion of industrialization, which had heightened the elite attack on older popular habits, actually altered the evolution of outlook for some common people. In a world filled with strange techniques and uncontrollable forces of change, it was hard to believe in regularity and control. Many workers, urged by middle-class reformers to save money for hard times, simply refused—partly of course because they had in the best of circumstances little money to save, but partly because the future seemed so incalculable. Any effort now might be swept away later. Workers who considered their old age would often talk of having no idea what would happen to them, short of death—"we'll go where the wind blows us." This was because old age, for new proletarians, became a more uncertain state than it had been in pre-industrial times, when one might hope to have a bit of property to rely on.

The forces that had built up through the early industrial revolution were thus complex. The erosion or partial repression of older values was not fully matched by clear new lines of belief. By 1870, indeed, it often seemed that different social groups were engaged in a virtual cultural war, with middle-class opinion-shapers, largely converted to the ideas of science, benignly intense families, and controllable selves, attacking a proletariat eager to retain older expressions such as festivals, or simply confused in their new setting, or resolutely clinging to beliefs, such as fatalism in health, that had lost their fuller traditional context.

The Pressures for Self-improvement and the Rise of Expertise

Not surprisingly, then, as a more fully modern mentality took shape after 1870, it embodied a number of complex currents. The elite and middle-class efforts to reshape popular beliefs unquestionably continued. The new mass education system worked hard not only to instill nationalism, but also to teach new habits of cleanliness—people can exercise useful control over their own bodies—or ideals of loving parenthood. Schools and also other agencies pushed healthful, sane recreations, such as reg-

Socializing youth to "sound" values was a goal of the British Boy Scouts, which undertook community service work at every opportunity. This photograph was taken during the summer holiday of 1923 at Waterloo Station in London.

ulated team sports, over presumably more violent popular (particularly teenage) habits. Britain contributed the scouting movement, which spread widely in North America as well. Scouting was designed to instill in urban youth values that some leaders feared were being lost: bravery, courtesy, honesty, and teamwork. In the United States and elsewhere, playground and settlement-house movements tried to provide sensible outlets for young people, while also teaching good personal virtues and family habits. French school curricula promoted ideals of hard work and good discipline for men, with strong warnings about drunkenness; girls were told to provide a sound moral example and a well-ordered home life. Private companies contributed their voice as well. The Ford Motor Company, near Detroit, even established what it called a "Sociology Department" to Americanize immigrant labor—which meant teaching punctuality, good treatment of children, habits of saving, and a warm family atmosphere.

Expert pressure to reshape mass values was taken up by government agencies besides the schools. For example, social workers visited parents who had problem children, or who seemed to abuse their children. Clinics worked to teach not only hygiene, but also appropriate affection and stimulation for the young. Clinics for children dealt with severe mental disorders, and also many cases of what was still termed sexual misbehavior, but they also worked on more subtle issues such as boys who seemed lacking in "spunk" or, on the other hand, unable to curb anger in dealing with authorities.

Finally, there were abundant pamphlets, books, and magazine articles by experts—real or self-appointed—telling people how to raise children, how to gain a more pleasing personality, how to marry right. In the United States during the 1920s and 1930s, Dale Carnegie addressed millions of people on how to become a winning salesman. Marriage counselors claimed to have reduced mate selection and good husband–wife relations to a science, urging for example that people marry only within their own religion, or that no argument be allowed to extend past bedtime. By 1949 over 500 United States colleges had courses on marriage, in which the latest wisdom was freely dispensed. Child-rearing pamphlets became a big business. In the 1940s Dr. Benjamin Spock wrote his commonsense manual, *Baby and Child Care*, which was to become the most widely selling book in the Western world aside from the Bible. Expert writers also continued to define proper homemaking, household budgets, and standards of hygiene, working extensively through wives and mothers who were supposed to translate appropriate values to individual families.

Expert advice and guidance varied widely. Indeed, expertise in some areas gained a certain faddish quality, as one generation seemed deliberately to attack the wisdom of its predecessor. Thus mothers were told, around 1900, that toilet training, thumb sucking, and other such childish habits should be tolerated in a relaxed atmosphere; but the next generation, by the 1920s, was sternly warned that too much affection was harmful and that children should be treated as though they were well-regulated machines, with bad habits directed away. Dr. Spock returned to urge that rigid standards were silly.

The Message of the Experts   Even with its faddish features, however, expert advice and other forms of intervention had some common ingredients. First, they were for the most part scientific. Even religiously based settlement houses increasingly claimed the mantle of science as well as God. The claim was that there were ways to study behavior or habits and to produce scientifically valid rules to gain better results. Second, the experts argued, directly or implicitly, that they could help eliminate chance in human upbringing and family relations. Marriage counselling, for example, was designed to take the guesswork out of mate selection. Finally, the new levels of expertise were designed to supplement or replace previous, more traditional authority. Many experts argued that families and communities had become so weak that people needed to be told how to manage their lives.

Experts generally urged that people adopt certain key traits. They should be self-controlled. They should have individual personalities and not simply replicate parental models by force of habit. They should expect progress: the world can get better if people will only improve themselves, and personal effort will be rewarded. The experts envisaged a fundamental orderliness to the environment, such that a salesman, for example, who tried harder would surely win more sales. Family values received great attention, for an affectionate, orderly family continued to be seen as a wellspring of virtue. Thus in general terms, expert advice and intervention painted a middle-class, Enlightenment-style world, in which reason could understand and control, and families had conventional values. Here was a clear sign, in fact, that rationalist values persisted in the popular sphere, just as they did, amid new complexity, in science and social science. An American expert, Dale Carnegie, who assured his audience that if they controlled their emotions and produced a pleasing personality they would be assured of high sales and growing wealth, was translating the older idea that people could determine their own destiny into the twentieth-century economic context.

The Mass Response to Expertise   The existence of a host of sources of expertise does not mean that expertise had predictable or uniform impact. Much advice was directed to middle-class people who used it mainly to reinforce established habits. Readers of women's magazines or members of chambers of commerce who heard a Dale Carnegie lecture, might find specific hints novel, but not the general tenor.

"Sports builds character" was a lesson taught to boys from an early age—a lesson that helped them choose their idols. A British World War I hero, bombardier Billy Wells, judges a track meet at Streatham Hill College in 1926.

Advice continued to vary, also, depending on social class, gender, and (in the United States particularly) race. Experts assumed that the middle class was already on the right track, but they could continue to disparage more popular impulses among immigrants and the working class for being too violent or sexually promiscuous. Experts also preached somewhat different personalities, as well as roles, for women and men. The male was expected to develop values, including aggressiveness, appropriate for work in a competitive world, whereas women were urged toward greater gentleness and affection. Public schools, translating expert opinion, thus often banned competitive sports for women, while sending boys to soccer or football fields to learn what struggle was all about. Because people are individuals, the complexities of expert advice, as it was tailored to gender roles or social structure, were not always easy to follow.

Furthermore, advice received was not necessarily taken. Marriage counselors often urged that mates be chosen dispassionately, for love could be a misleading emotion; but there is no sign that popular opinion, still wedded to visions of romance, really accepted this argument. Parents might read child-rearing advice and even claim they were affected by it, but disciplinary habits changed more slowly than this fashionable awareness might suggest. Furthermore, many social workers who actually dealt with poorer families tempered their advice to meet existing standards, rather than purveying middle-class standards alone.

Whether or not experts were heeded, their variety and their very existence were significant, on two counts: they reached out to groups that initially preferred other, more traditional values, and they reflected a felt need for precisely the kind of authority they offered.

The Enforcement of Expert Opinion   As in earlier periods in modern Western history, expert advice was not simply offered; it also related to some clear enforcement mechanisms. Parents who might have found their teenage children's behavior acceptable, when they skipped school and engaged in minor vandalism, might be told, from the 1890s onward, that they faced a delinquency problem. Increasingly rigorous definitions of juvenile delinquency, designed to produce controlled, property-respecting, school-attending adolescents, placed a large number of working-class youth, particularly males, in new contacts with police and courts, in both Western Europe and the United States. Even if their parents did not share the official judgment of their children, believing, as popular tradition maintained, that some restrained wildness was a normal part of growing up, they could not but realize that they had a problem on their hands that might require some rethinking of family relations and child-rearing. Another case of the enforcement side of advice involved medical care around 1900. Doctors in many Western countries developed growing political power in the later nineteenth century, forming substantial professional associations that urged governments to regulate medical practice in their favor. They could point, of course, to significant new knowledge of disease, hygiene, and some new therapies (including improved surgical techniques) in their favor. The result was heightened pressure on a number of traditional practitioners, now prevented by law from claiming medical authority or presuming to practice medicine. The yellow-pages listing for quacks disappeared from the New York telephone directory after the 1880s. Midwives were forbidden to deliver babies, at least on their own, in a number of European and American areas around 1900. These changes hit hard at customary worker and peasant health practices, and also at the authority of women. Workers—among them the many immigrants who continued to prefer midwives in the United States—might not have reassessed their medical beliefs on their own initiative, toward firmer faith in the importance of science and the capacity for progress in controlling bodily ills; but now they had to alter their behavior, as expert promptings and new voluntary clinics were supplemented by the heavy hand of the law in squeezing out traditional alternatives.

But compulsion from above was only part of the story. Changes in popular life, prior shifts in outlook, and the impact of expert advice itself all combined to produce a new willingness to consider alternative ways of thinking and to seek guidance in the process. Use of (male) doctors and hospitals began to increase not only because of attacks on other options, but because ordinary people themselves began to seek progress and greater scientific reliability in dealing with health. Their judgments may not always have been right—although with improving sanitation, going to a doctor did make increasingly good sense; and hospitals began to shed their traditional reputation as places in which to die, as new procedures helped cut infant and maternal deaths in difficult deliveries, and new surgery aided accident victims and attacked tumors. The fact was that many people did jettison both their fatalism toward health and the even more pervasive eclecticism among various options, in turning toward medical advice as primary authority. Traditional home remedies and superstitions remained, and outright charlatans could still create a stir, but popular belief evolved increasingly toward the notion that every health problem had its scientific remedy.

Compulsory reinforcement of values, such as the new rigor toward juvenile behavior, was not the only story in the child-rearing field either. Schools, publications, informal contacts with middle-class families (such as through female domestic service), even trade union leaders helped open many workers to an understanding that some changes in the treatment of children might be a good thing. This openness, in turn, had two effects, particularly from the 1920s onward. First, working-class parents joined their middle-class counterparts in an eagerness at least to read about current advice. Second, class gaps in the approach to children began to close, as working-class parents adopted new concerns about avoiding too-frequent spankings, urging at least adequate school habits, and promoting greater self-control. Class distinctions in the treatment of children were not obliterated, and great variety remained among individuals within a single social group, but the expertise did have some impact and not only because it was forced on an unwilling audience.

The pressure of official standards of belief thus remained a vital factor in the evolution of mentalities after 1870. The standards, eagerly preached and in some cases actively enforced, built toward further reliance on rationality and science, plus an individualism based on self-control and shaped also by strong family values. The result was not a mindless uniformity of outlook, but a growing recognition that traditions might be further rethought, that the experts might usefully be listened to.

Continued Secularization and the Rise of New Beliefs

The process of secularization of outlook continued; in fact it picked up speed after 1870. Religious practice and at least fervent religious belief dropped in a number of groups. The British working class, previously affected by the rise of Methodism, now moved away from this alternative to established religion, but in the direction of no strong religious preference of any sort. Dechristianization gained further ground in France, among not only workers but peasants as well. The process went further in some regions than others, and further among men than among women. In some cases, isolated areas were simultaneously jolted out of traditional religion and into a host of new beliefs and practices. For example, a mining village in central France, long conventionally pious, was visited by Socialist leaders during the course of a strike in the 1890s. Within five years the village saw church attendance plummet and the Socialist vote soar, while the birth rate decreased radically as the result of a new belief in the possibility of controlling this aspect of the family environment. In yet another case, religious practice declined notably among German peasants after 1920, spurred not only by the general forces of secularization but by the bitter experience of World War I.

The loss of religion was not uniform. Even in groups such as the British working class, fervent attachments remained for a minority. Middle-class people were more likely to remain at least nominally religious than were working-class people, although their religion was sometimes transformed by a declining attachment to traditional doctrines of hell or original sin. Urban people were more likely to lose religion than were rural folk. Ireland continued to buck the general European trend, as the hold of Catholicism (and in northern Ireland, Protestantism) if anything increased. The United States remained considerably more attached to religion than did most of western Europe; religion served as a point of identity to many workers, including Catholic immigrants, and the separation of church and state, plus the absence of strong socialism, placed religion in a distinctive political context. In the United States belief became more secular also, as advice literature shifted from the hands of ministers to scientific experts; but for most Americans, secularism still conjoined with some real religious interest.

Alongside or in place of religion, a number of belief systems arose and competed for attention in popular outlook. Socialism provided a framework for some, and it could be embraced with a religious fervor: Marxism, particularly, provided a sacred doctrine, a host of martyrs, and a goal of heaven on earth. Nationalism was another growing secular loyalty; like socialism, it could provide a cognitive framework for people's lives, and it could spur deep emotion as well. Less formally, beliefs in science supplemented or replaced religion at key points.

One reason for religious decline both in the eighteenth century and after Darwin was an impression in some quarters that, at least as traditionally stated, Christianity was simply wrong. Science did not answer all of religion's questions, particularly about the origins of things or about ethics, but it did explain an apparently increasing array of natural and human phenomena with great confidence in its own accuracy. Consumer values may also have worked to displace religious interest, as people became more fascinated with gadgets, more interested in material enjoyment, and had greater expectation of higher living standards.

Growing secularization, even when formal religious practice persisted, was no mere matter of abstract loyalties—to nation more than to church, or to socialist future more than to heavenly afterlife. Rather, secularism showed in some basic features of the modern experience of being human in the West. Attitudes toward death began to change. This had not been a static concept earlier in the West. Medieval fascination with the physical horrors of death had yielded from the Renaissance onward to greater concern with individual death and salvation. During the Enlightenment scientific interest in preventing early death increased at the theoretical level; and there were signs of growing grief, expressed in increasingly elaborate funeral practices, when death did occur. But what began to develop by the later nineteenth century was a growing desire to distance death, rather than to assimilate it as part of normal experience. Cemetaries began to be placed farther from normal residence. Partly this reflected concerns about sanitation and the sheer pressure of urban crowding. But the result was to make the monuments of death far less visible than they had been before. The growing use of hospitals meant that death began to occur less often in or around the home, more often in unfamiliar medical settings; and the agents of society most concerned with death began to shift from priests and pastors to medical personnel, whose training was designed to fight death rather than to accept it. Death, in sum, was being secularized, its mysterious qualities downplayed or ignored in favor of combat through medicine or, when combat failed, considerable public reticence. Even elaborate expressions of grief became less fashionable, as death was not supposed to interrupt the regular course of human activities; handling grief became more a personal than a social issue, and in many ways it grew increasingly difficult as a result. The modern outlook turned away from death, made it in some senses a new taboo. Revealingly, children were now carefully shielded from participation in death rituals, and euphemisms arose to circumvent dealing with death in children's presence. Death of course did become far less common in key groups during this same period, particularly among children; in this limited but important sense, the phenomenon came under greater control. But the effort to push death aside when it did occur, by segregating the dying into hospitals, reducing formal mourning and distancing cemetaries, suggested that the modern Western mentality not only secularized death but also faced real problems handling the ultimate unmanageability of this aspect of the human condition.

Family and Children

Family and Children   The changing outlook toward death illustrates the modern desire to assure substantial control over the environment wherever possible. This had long been part of the effort to demystify, but with growing confidence in science, and some improvements in resources, the attitude spread more widely. Parents turned to child-rearing advice in the hope that following formulas would assure satisfactory personalities in their offspring. The use of insurance, launched in the seventeenth century as part of greater security for business, now spread to individuals. During the early nineteenth century, burial insurance was the only commonly adopted form of personal insurance, as people sought sufficient funds to assure avoidance of a degrading burial in a common pit. But after 1870 life insurance became a widespread commodity, in the interest of family security (and especially the protection of widows) against untimely demise. Growing demand for pensions, and eventually pressure for government assurance against the impact of disasters such as long-term unemployment or unsecured old age, formed part of this common pattern: with proper systems, along with some personal foresight, the worst buffetings of chance could be countered.

The idea of the natural and social environment as rationally understandable and regulable was not intended, however, to deprive life of spice in a secular or only sporadically religious context. For ballast there remained the family, still the object of great reverence—indeed viewed by some as a personal equivalent of religion in providing outlet for passion and securing goals beyond the self. The romantic ideal of marriage, established earlier, maintained its bright flame and may have spread to a wider array of social groups than before. Certainly various innovations reflected the exacting emotional goals of modern marriage; for example, divorce laws in many countries, particularly those of predominantly Protestant culture, began taking emotional incompatibilities into account, by introducing justifications such as "mental cruelty" and withholding of affection. A proper marriage, in other words, should not only avoid violence and provide economic subsistence; it should avoid undue anger and offer some emotional warmth. Standards of this sort may have made marriage actually more complex, as disappointment could surface more readily; rising emotional expectations helped cause rising divorce rates. At the same time, insistence on positive emotional satisfaction in marriage reflected how a growing number of people thought about families.

Emotional attachment to children also increased after 1870. With children far less likely to die, and with the decline in the birth rate encouraging greater attention to individual children, it was small wonder that the redefinition of children continued. Parents and children alike were expected to give and receive love. The new emotional expectations concerning children made individual youngsters more valuable to families than they had been in earlier periods when they actually contributed to family income.

The overall imagery of the family was reflected in the spread of new holidays such as Mothers' Day, first enacted in the United States in 1916, and in proud proclamations such as the expert judgment that hailed the dawn of the twentieth century as the "century of the child." More concretely, steadily rising marriage rates showed the actual popularity of—indeed dependence on—an institution that was evolving increasingly away from predominantly economic uses and toward social and emotional roles. Despite the phenomenon of divorce, the family had never been more popular in the modern centuries of the Western experience. By the early twentieth century, with over 90 percent of the population marrying by age forty, the incidence of matrimony was about as high as it could get. Although some rhetoric about the family smacked of hyperbole, and although there was much worried comment about the fragility of the family in modern society, it was clear that beliefs in having a family described very real popular hopes and values. There was of course an important tension here, for the very experts who preached emotionally warm families also expressed doubts that families, unaided, could accomplish their functions. At the popular level too, worry about the family accompanied the continuing redefinition of its role.

Family ideals in part preserved the division established earlier, during the industrial revolution, between a private, intimate world and the larger environment where regularity and restraint held sway. This was not an easy division to sustain, particularly for married workers or even schoolchildren who shuttled back and forth between the two spheres daily. But the idealization of the private family had all the more meaning for being difficult to maintain, and many a worker or clerk who had a troubled family life insisted that familial values formed the underlying meaning of his existence.

The Self Family ideals also jostled against the concomitant belief in individual identity. Families were seen as voluntary groupings of individuals, not as superordinate entities; intense bonds of affection were supposed to tie people together as a family without forcing them to lose their identity. Child-rearing advice and practice recognized the individual qualities of the young and urged inculcation of separate identities. Children were not seen as mirror images of parents, but rather as separate persons who owed loyalty to themselves as well as to family and ancestors. The common impulse to educate children separately from the family, and often to educate them better than their parents had been educated, showed the strength of the belief in individual destiny. The belief applied to the very young as well. Babies were treated as distinct creatures; indeed, the modern Western insistence on the importance of infancy and the need to begin to instill certain values early was quite different from patterns in most civilizations, where the separate identity of infants before the age of two was typically of scant concern. Western parents, in contrast, began to wonder if their children's personalities were not virtually formed by that age, and their concern for proper child care may have helped young children develop a sense of themselves as individuals.

Individuation was aided by the declining birth rate, which left more children in close contact with parents, or at least mothers. But parents advanced the process further by their choices and behavior. A key consumer choice of German working-class families in the later nineteenth century was to strive for separate bedrooms for children—separate at least from parents, and if possible from each other. Many parents claimed that this was a goal worth considerable overtime labor. Many factors went into this choice to add greater physical separation for family members, including imitation of middle-class respectability and a desire for sexual privacy; but the belief that individuals need "room to breathe and to be" was an important constituent. The practice of giving allowances to children was also launched in the later nineteenth century in several Western countries. This practice showed an intent to train children in financial responsibility and consumerism, but also a desire to encourage modest individualism in children's purchasing choices. Adolescence was defined in terms of the stress of further honing individual identity, as children began the painful but desirable process of separating themselves from the parental nest. One of the key reasons that the concept of adolescence became necessary in the later nineteenth century was to decrease the strains perceived in moving from loving family to fuller selfhood. By full adulthood the self should have become a standard point of reference, a clear basis for one's identity.

Strong belief in individual personality, however, was not intended to produce random self-indulgence. As during the seventeenth and eighteenth centuries, in defining the self attention to developing the individual was coupled with a belief that individuals could and should control their own characters, keeping subordinate any elements that might detract from self-command. From the later nineteenth century onward, concern for physical discipline increased, as good health became a matter of choice. Parents, of course, cared for the health of children with new intensity, and tried to teach children to maintain responsibility for their bodies. Schools and other agencies, plus a growing number of youth groups—the hiking clubs that sprang up in Germany around 1900 are an example—spread the message of physical fitness. Sickness was not invariably the product of individual failure, but the new emphasis on the virtues of health set something of a standard against which people without the proper discipline and control could be judged. Among women, the growing fashionableness of slender body forms, even as modes of dress became less restrictive, imposed another important discipline.

Efforts to achieve emotional control reached out in new directions as well. Salespeople and white-collar workers were told that they must shape their work personalities not as their own feelings dictated, but toward consistent pleasantness. Nasty customers and angry bosses should be handled with a smile. A veritable campaign against anger in the workplace began in the 1920s. It was motivated in part against the rising tide of unionization and strikes, but it also expressed the middle-class belief that work should be tempered by sweet reasonableness at all times. Foremen were thus retrained to reduce their angry confrontations with workers. They were taught how to receive grievances pleasantly and to make a worker repeat his or her complaints until he or she was embarrassed by the passion behind them and was often ready simply to drop the whole matter. "The angry man may himself be the chief victim of his emotion. It incapacitates him from dealing with his problems in a corrective way." Following from the new standards of the ideal work personality, many parents by the 1940s began to increase their attempts to remove any festering anger from children, teaching them that the emotion was unpleasant and counterproductive in any setting. Too much intense feeling of any sort might indeed be looked upon with suspicion in a world where the motto of human relations became, in the words of one American personnel advisor: "Impersonal, but friendly."

Thus a substantial segment of the modern mentality was built upon elements that had been developing since the seventeenth century in the West: a desire to regularize the environment; an emphasis on family virtues; a stress on the self, but coupled with injunctions of control and self-discipline. Particularly in the areas of environmental regularization and the related impulse to insist on personal restraint, the shifts in popular outlook after 1870 reached new levels. Much of the emphasis in popular outlook bore some relationship, as well, to the scientific approach in high culture, which also talked of regularities, if with new complexity, and the ultimate power of reason to control.

Toward a Glorification of Impulse: New Complexity in the Modern Mentality

As in high culture, the popular mentality of the late nineteenth and early twentieth centuries showed important tensions against the dominant themes just discussed. The high value placed on predictability and restraint did not rule uncontested. Most traditional forms of spontaneity had been repressed throughout the long campaign that culminated during the early industrial revolution. New forms of impulsiveness now began to surface, particularly in sexuality and certain leisure interests.

There were several reasons for the renewed complexity within the popular mentality. Some of the proscriptions against displays of emotion may simply have gone too far. Efforts to remove anger from the workplace, for example, were hampered by the bitter grievances that remained during the Depression years. Only after the 1950s, amid greater prosperity, would there be signs that the goal of controlling one's anger was once again a part of everyday life. Class differences also complicated any single standards. The working class, although increasingly influenced by middle-class goals, had different leisure and sexual traditions, and these remained quite visible as we will soon discover. Finally, the needs of a consumer economy pushed against some of the personality standards that had developed earlier in the middle class. Restraint of impulse, so desirable at work, was not so clear a merit for customers during a department-store sale or in an automobile salesroom. Advertisements urged indulgence, an enjoyment of excess, an identification of self with pleasure-seeking rather than self-control and predictability. This consumer-based factor also entered into the new tensions visible in popular outlook.

Sexuality was one of the areas in which the tensions of the emerging modern mentality became increasingly open. Restraint of sexual impulse had been a key element of middle-class values in the nineteenth century, with apparent scientific backing from doctors and other experts who warned of the social and individual damage that resulted from excess. The ethic of sexual restraint did not fully convert the lower classes, where avowal of sexual pleasure remained somewhat more open; and it did not fully describe actual middle-class sexuality either, where sexual expressionism could become an important part of marriage and an outlet for individual identity. In the later nineteenth century, the official emphasis on sexual restraint began to lessen. Doctors found that rigid restraint was not as salutary as once believed. Advertisers found that sexual connotations helped sell goods and free up other impulses. Music hall producers and, later, movie producers found that their audiences, middle-class as well as working-class, enjoyed a somewhat freer sexual atmosphere. And ordinary people, perhaps more frankly now in the middle class than elsewhere, began to rethink their own sexual standards, inclining toward an interest in less confinement, more personal pleasure and self-expression. The development was particularly marked among women. During the 1920s a British biologist, Marie Stopes, ashamed of her own sexual ignorance that had spoiled her pleasure in marriage, became something of a sexual guru, urging through books and newspaper articles the desirability of an open pursuit of pleasure as a woman's right. Her work unleashed a flood of letters from middle-class women who professed satisfaction with their own marriages but at the same time had a real desire for greater sexual pleasure, particularly the regular achievement of orgasm. "I have never had during our unions [intercourse with her husband] what you refer to as orgasm," wrote a Birmingham woman in 1928, "and I know many women do not seem to desire it, but I do." Correspondents wrote to Stopes over and over again of their realization of their "passionate" natures, and their desire (typically not fully realized) to enjoy this quality to its fullest. Stopes herself, like a growing number of widely read experts, freely fed this desire, writing as though each sexual encounter should produce some transcendant ecstasy. Describing women's sexual potential, for example, Stopes wrote:

> Welling up in her are the wonderful tides, scented and enriched by the myriad experiences of the human race from its ancient days of leisure and flower-wreathed love making, urging her to transport and to self-expression.

Not everyone became a convert to sexual bliss. Women remained more restricted in their sexual experiments than did men. But the sexual imagery of popular culture and the clear shift in the expectations of some groups did suggest a new interest that countered the earlier counsels of restraint. Sex was increasingly sought as an outlet for pleasure and as an expression of the self quite different from the carefully controlled personalities being recommended in other spheres. The simple fact was that by the 1920s sexual activity was increasingly divorced from procreation, as birth control devices and the rapidly declining birth rate meant that people either had to ignore sexual appetite or express it in terms of pleasure-seeking.

The new openness to impulse and spontaneity was not confined to bedrooms. The new popular leisure that emerged in the later nineteenth century, with its emphasis on physical prowess, record-breaking feats of speed or endurance, and large, enthusiastic crowds, also suggested the emergence of new forms of popular exuberance. Although the games of western Europe and the United States had a new orderliness in the form of rules and referees, they also encouraged the display of emotion and virtuosity, and they could serve as a release for powerful emotions even in a crowd of spectators. Here too, the restrained standards of the rational world were far from triumphant. People who felt too confined by the canons of restraint could seek release in the displays of energy in sports or the boisterous laughter of a music-hall crowd, just as those resistant to scientific standards could turn to the wilder aesthetic of modern art. Even the norms of predictability were defined. New gambling interests—in some cases, outright passions—reflected growing openness to chance. In Britain and elsewhere, gambling spread from horse racing to revived lotteries and team sports. Fascination with fears inspired by amusement park rides and horror shows was another sign of the new participation in impulsive experience.

One could participate in both the rational and the impulsive aspects

The amusement park attained great popularity among the masses as a cheap means of diversion from the drudgery of work. This is Steeplechase Park on Coney Island in New York.

of the popular culture. Those who learned subdued emotions at work, for example, could let out their anger in the crowd noise and the hatred of opponents at a ball game, or could express their yearnings for more spontaneous experience in watching the soaring performance of a top athlete.

To be sure, by no means was all leisure so expressive. Much of mass culture seemed contrived and tawdry, commercially manipulated, and anonymous compared to the intensities of older popular festivals. The spontaneous elements of Western culture, though reviving, may have had less free play than in centuries past—just as modern art, at the level of high culture, may not have gained the prestige accorded to science. Yet the outlets provided by modern leisure may have been more significant than some critics allowed. Though many aspects of popular life had changed, including the rhythms of work and the community context, some of the complexities characteristic of earlier popular mentalities did seem reborn in new guise. The discomfort felt by some observers who criticized new sexual passions or new leisure excitements was itself testimony to the tensions that had resurfaced—tensions felt not only between elite and lower classes, but within individuals at various levels of society.

Conclusion: The Levels of Culture

The gap between high and popular culture between 1870 and 1950 cannot be wiped away. Most people had a rooted faith in science but little grasp of what scientists were discovering, outside the realm of direct applications in technology. Similarly, most people had scant contact with modern art, relying on commercial art or the classical standards displayed in museums and reproductions. Members of the fashionable elite and ordinary people did not think alike. An elite–mass gap that had oscillated in modern Western history—widening in the seventeenth century, then closing somewhat during the Enlightenment and into the nineteenth century—now opened wider again.

But the real gap should not conceal some vital common themes among the various cultural levels. Both high and popular cultures were predominantly secular, but there were important religious currents still in play. Both tended to stress novelty. Neither built primarily on traditional justifications or on traditional frameworks, although they used trends that had begun development some centuries before. At the popular and high-culture levels alike, Westerners had decided that new intellectual and aesthetic frameworks were the means of confronting a changing world. This choice was not inevitable, and it may have caused tension as the standards of the "new" were not always clear; but the choice was generally consistent across seemingly incompatible reaches of culture. Related to innovation was a considerable penchant for fads: the newest scientific finding or art style was given great credit, just as the newest advice approach to family life or the newest consumer gimmick was embraced in the popular realm.

Both formal and popular cultures were also marked by a fascinating, seemingly endemic tension between controlled rationalism and a deliberate effort at nonrational spontaneity. Collectively, intellectuals and ordinary people both seemed to question, at least concurrently, whether order and regularity, pushed to new heights, or some almost-mad impulse best described their modern world. Art often seemed to be saying to science, in formal culture, that the image of a regular nature was all wrong, that the essence of reality consisted of impulse and, sometimes, gruesome horror. Similarly in popular culture, efforts to reduce the role of chance and to impose order and restraint were challenged by a new fascination with erotic elements and with emotional frenzy. The same person who strove to create orderliness in work and family life might seek a leisure that promised surprise and fear.

To some observers, of course, it seemed that controlled rationality was winning out in the modern mentality. There was no question that science overshadowed art in prestige, or that the emotional control needed for respectable work (a job or career) was officially rated higher than weekend spontaneity. But the spontaneous, aesthetic impulses would not go away, and their role, at high culture and popular levels, in many ways solidified after 1920, when the first shock effect of modern art and modern leisure had passed. The modern Western mentality seemed caught in a complex interchange that emerged in formal art and thought and in popular outlook alike. Although expressions of the interchange differed greatly, the essential similarity in the attempts to play off new spontaneity against themes of rational order suggested that Western culture was not as unintegrated, as divided between high art and mass taste, as many observers believed. The interplay between reason and impulse was complex, but it seemed vital to the modern mentality that took shape as Western society settled down, after 1870, to the task of defining what industrial life was all about.

NINE

WESTERN EUROPE, 1945–1980

1940 ff	Rise of women in total official labor force
1944–1962	The postwar baby boom
1944–1947	Coalition government in France under Charles de Gaulle; welfare state
1947	Communists expelled
1945 ff	Existentialist philosophy
1945	Labour party victory in Britain
1945–1947	Coalition government in Italy under de Gasperi
1947	Pakistan and India independence; beginning of worldwide decolonization
1947	The Marshall Plan
1947–1948	Berlin blockade; cold war takes shape
1948	West German government forms; economic stabilization and beginning of "economic miracle"
1949	New intellectual feminism; Simone de Beauvoir's *The Second Sex*
1949	Formation of NATO
1951	The Soviet Union develops atomic bomb
1955	Warsaw Pact
1956	Independence and neutrality of Austria

1956	France and Britain launch abortive attack against Egypt over Suez Canal
1958	European Economic Community (Common Market) formed
1958	Fifth Republic in France
1958–1963	Pope John XXIII
1962–1965	Vatican Council II updates aspects of Catholicism
1962	France concedes Algerian independence
1968	Massive student revolts in France and elsewhere
1969	Socialist party comes to power in Germany
1970 ff	Development of Eurocommunism
1973	First oil crisis
1973	Britain, Ireland, Denmark join Common Market
1974–1976	Spain, Portugal convert to liberal, parliamentary regimes
1975	Portugal concedes independence to its former African colonies
1979	Second oil crisis; economic downturn
1979	Margaret Thatcher becomes prime minister of Britain; partial attack on welfare state

CHAPTER
NINE

THE WEST IN A
CONTEMPORARY WORLD,
1945–1980

MORE THAN FORTY YEARS HAVE PASSED since the end of
World War II. This length of time alone, as well as the recency of the
postwar era, make this one of the obviously important periods of Western history—all the more compelling in that we must place our own
society within it. Moreover, the period is arguably of unusual significance in its own right because of the changes in diplomatic, political,
and social structure that occurred amid new constraints and a new eagerness for innovation. Although less marked by dramatic events than the
earlier decades of the twentieth century, the post–World War II decades
have at least as much place in defining what the West is all about—and
in redirecting some of the trends that seemed so overwhelming just a
quarter of a century before. Compared to the predominant tone of the
1920s and 1930s, with their spiral of uncontrollable events, Western society changed radically in character after 1945. Foreign policy interests
were redefined toward a reduction of nationalism and imperialism but
also a narrowing of western Europe's world role. Internally the functions
of the state were recast—with reference to earlier initiatives—as the "welfare
state" took shape. Economic renewal propelled the Western world to
new heights of prosperity, and it also entailed new social and organizational forms. Even family life seemed revolutionized, as throughout the
West married women entered the work force in large numbers for the
first time since the industrial revolution.

Thus the most obvious feature of Western history after 1945 was its
contrast with the previous period of war and disillusionment. But the
West also built on some of the underlying themes that had taken shape

earlier in the twentieth century, including the tensions of high culture and popular mentality. Here evolution predominated over sharp change, despite some talk of a new, "postmodern" personality coming to the fore, contrasting with the leading norms of the industrial age.

Postwar Western history must therefore balance innovation, and its attendant advantages and drawbacks, with the maintenance of some underlying themes established earlier. In fact the spheres overlapped. Economic planners were a new breed in the postwar Western world, helping to extend government functions and giving a new boost to economic growth. But their impulse to regularize and rationalize derived from earlier thinking, particularly among social-science experts. And the reaction they helped generate, including student protests in the late 1960s against undue materialism and constraint, related to earlier strains in the modern mentality as well.

This chapter covers western European history from the war's end until roughly 1980, reserving for the final chapter an assessment of developments in the 1980s and some larger issues of Europe's place in the world, patterns in eastern Europe, and the role of the United States in contemporary Western civilization.

The thirty-five years covered in this chapter involve three rather distinct subperiods. Until about 1949, sheer recovery from the war took up most of Europe's energies, though new political structures were established during this time and the cold war framework took shape as well, along with the first round of decolonization. Then during the 1950s and 1960s the character of the "New Europe" was more fully delineated as a result of rapidly rising prosperity. Finally, as will be treated in the last segment of this chapter, a new wave of protests in 1968 and new economic difficulties ushered in a different mood and different set of problems during the 1970s.

A Changing of the Guard

Postwar western Europe was shaped, of course, by the massive dislocations of the war years. Territories changed hands, particularly as Germany was split between a Russian-dominated Eastern zone and French–United States–British zones in the West. Millions of refugees wandered over the continent, fleeing from disbanded concentration camps or from the Russian occupation of eastern Europe, or simply trying to return home from military or labor service. Most of Europe's remaining Jewish population, half a million in all, ultimately emigrated to the new state of Israel. As these movements of people continued, refugee camps of various sorts dotted many nations. Economic damage, and the destruction of cities caused by bombings, provided other fearsome distractions. Transportation was impeded by the devastation of rail lines and bridges and the exhaustion of much rolling stock. Food was in short supply, and many people, such as miners in France, had to try to work despite inadequate nutrition. In occupied Germany, confusion and dislocation prompted massive inflation; currency was so worthless that American cigarettes were used as a medium of exchange.

Until 1948, the crudest kind of postwar recovery seemed western Europe's major challenge. There were those who thought that the continent had been rendered permanently enfeebled, doomed to economic dependency on more vigorous nations such as the United States. Even after 1948, the war's cost, in lives, goods, and morale, continued to shape European policies.

Yet wartime destruction was not the only legacy of a half-decade of turmoil. Indeed, despite a few additional years of intense suffering, some of the dislocations proved temporary. Most of the refugees who did not emigrate were integrated into their new surroundings. Although rebuilding took time, it turned out that much of the basic industrial capacity remained, and the opportunity to update equipment proved a vital boon to Europe's economy. Loss of life in Germany and eastern Europe had been appalling, but the war caused less demographic damage to France and Britain than the previous world war had done, and their comparatively light casualties also ultimately eased recovery.

Furthermore, the war served as an opportunity for a substantial shift in leadership in many of the major Western nations. Relatively few top personnel from the 1930s and early 1940s remained in power; this was true not only in government but also in private business. A younger leadership, with new ideas, surged to the fore. Many of the new leaders

Refugees streamed over Europe after World War II. The refugee issue resulted in large part from the massive removal of populations by the Nazis for forced labor, military service, and imprisonment, and also from reactions to new national boundaries after the war. In turn, refugees complicated postwar diplomatic and economic reconstruction.

had been active in 1930s renewal movements as young people eager to see more creative directions in their Depression-torn society. France, for example, benefited from some leaders who in the 1930s had organized in new Catholic action groups, seeking more imaginative social and economic policies. Many of these and other leaders in France, Italy, and the Low Countries had subsequently been active in Resistance movements, sharing the vague but powerful impulse to see a new Europe born from the ashes of the old.

Nations that had experienced fascist rule, including Vichy France, automatically required new leadership, since the old leaders were thoroughly discredited by their wartime policies. Many French and Italian fascists or sympathizers were tried for war crimes. Again, this pattern involved business as well as politics. The head of the Renault automobile company, for example, was dispossessed because of wartime collaboration, and the company was taken over by the government. Large numbers of German leaders were tried for war crimes or fled the country, leaving the way open for new leadership there as well. Because the Nazis themselves had cleared out much of the traditional elite from the bureaucracy and military as part of their own drive to power, Germany, somewhat ironically, became quite open to new blood. It was true that Germany's first postwar political leader, Konrad Adenauer, was no youngster, having served as mayor of Cologne under the Weimar Republic. But even his national role was unprecedented, as he was a Catholic; and he drew into his ministries many younger men, including liberals from the southwest.

A New Political Spectrum

Renewal of the Western leadership was symbolized and furthered by changes in political alignments. France and Italy were both ruled for several years by a coalition of parties that had been active in the Resistance to fascism. In France Charles de Gaulle, the wartime Resistance leader, directed a coalition cabinet composed of Communists, Socialists, and Catholic Liberals. The Italian coalition consisted of the same uneasy trinity—Communists, Socialists, and Christian Democrats. Similar coalitions formed in Belgium. Scandinavia, to be sure, remained in the hands of socialist parties, but these parties had already demonstrated considerable ability before the war. Spain and Portugal were still authoritarian systems. But Britain shifted gears in 1945, electing its first Labour majority. Voters judged that Labour was more likely to use government as an active agent for social welfare and housing reconstruction, and a large segment of the middle class temporarily switched allegiance from the Conservative party as a result.

These political shifts reflected several changes in the political spectrum that had prevailed between the wars. The far right was discredited, and outright fascist parties were outlawed in Germany. Neofascist movements survived in Italy and cropped up periodically in France, but they never gained the momentum of their prewar analogues. Mainstream conservatism now focused on Christian Democratic movements. Christian Democratic parties gained primacy in Italy and Germany, and they played a considerable role in France and the Low Countries. These parties had some precedent in earlier Catholic groups, such as the German Center party. But they were less narrowly confessional than their predecessors; the German party, in particular, made a point of including Protestants. They were more solidly committed to democratic and parliamentary regimes, and they were quite open to pragmatic social reforms. Finally, the power of socialist and communist movements grew in many countries. Britain's Labour party obviously won unprecedented success. Communist parties surged forward in France and Italy, benefiting from their active role in the Resistance movements, their solid organization, which allowed them to seize the principal trade union movements, and some active support from the Soviet Union.

With new political parties and a new political balance of power, the opening to new leadership was greatly enhanced. And on the whole, European politics swung somewhat to the left, away from defense of business and propertied interests alone.

Social Renewal

The changing of the guard in western Europe entailed new individuals, new ideas, or at least a desire for some alternatives to older policies, and new political currents. It also involved new underpinnings in the wider society. Some of the sources of leadership that had dominated western Europe since the later nineteenth century, declining in any event as a result of economic change, found in the war and its results something like final closure.

The aristocracy of western Europe, so long significant in politics despite the decline of agriculture and of legal protection of noble privilege, was virtually removed as a coherent political force. New taxation in Britain burdened the large estates, forcing many aristocrats to seek new lines of work. The German aristocracy was decapitated by Russian and communist takeover in the east, where the class had maintained its most solid roots. Estates were seized and the old Junker group finally dismantled. Individual aristocrats might still play a prominent role, and gentle birth did not necessarily serve as a handicap; but there was little advantage in aristocratic status, and most leaders who came from this class laid their claims on the basis of talent and expert training, not inherited privilege.

Much of the old big-business class was also displaced. Some old families died out. Government nationalizations, as in the Renault case mentioned earlier, took their toll. Although wartime collaboration did not destroy the Krupp industrial empire in Germany, it did help dislodge direct control by the Krupp family. A new breed of managers increasingly took over big business, both in the private sector and in newly nationalized enterprises. These managers, usually risen from a status lower in the middle class and expertly trained as engineers or economists, thought in somewhat different terms than the older family dynasties. They were more interested in long-range planning and in smooth social relations, less concerned with some of the traditional trappings of social prestige.

Even other sectors felt the breath of social renewal. In many villages old peasant notables, some of whom had collaborated during the war, were pushed aside by a younger generation often equipped with some Resistance experience and eager for a more vigorous agriculture and more assertive rural voice. In the confusion of the war's end, some older village leaders in France were even killed outright.

As a result of fascist attacks on traditions before World War II, the war itself, and wider social transformations, something of a leadership revolution occurred in Europe during the postwar period. Whereas the United States and the Soviet Union, where social change had been more substantial earlier in the century, retained the same people or types in power, western Europe experienced fundamental renewal. Furthermore, the new regimes quickly built in further changes in the recruitment process for the future. Educational systems were overhauled to place greater emphasis on technical expertise—science, engineering, economic planning—and to allow greater access from lower social groups. University attendance was subsidized by government scholarships, and tests were redesigned to improve the chances of people from worker or peasant backgrounds.

What Europe was aiming for, and partly achieved, was a "meritocracy," in which school training would be geared to the skills needed in later work life, including leadership functions; in which school access would depend on talent, not prior wealth or birth; and in which elite recruitment would result from the achievement displayed in school. The system proved far from perfect, particularly in that the lower classes did not fully engage in the new system. But there was new mobility from below, and combined with updated training this assured some reinforcement for the leadership renewal that had occurred at the war's end.

New leadership, not just at the top but at various organizational levels, explains much of the development of western Europe into the 1960s. Not only postwar recovery but also social and economic reform followed from the new personnel and their commitment to innovate. Changes within Europe's diplomatic structure brought about another key result. The new leaders had to acquiesce to a reduction of Europe's wider influence in the world, but the fact that they managed even this with relative grace was in a sense a tribute to their creativity. During the two decades after World War II, western Europe combined a massive loss of world power with substantial internal renewal—not an easy mixture to assimilate as we will see.

The Diplomatic Context of Postwar Europe

When World War II ended in 1945, few thought that the European puzzle pieces could be fit back together in any coherent fashion. There was no overarching plan of reconstruction similar to the one Woodrow Wilson had brought to Versailles in 1919. Germany, long the leading continental power for better or worse, was smashed far more thoroughly than before. France, under the de Gaulle government, clung tenuously to great-power status. Britain was exhausted. The United States, eager to get its troops home, nevertheless maintained influence and armed presence over wide stretches of western Europe, and the Soviet Union did the same in the east.

Furthermore, the war had culminated three decades of economic weakness and nationalist rivalry throughout western Europe, which had distracted the great powers from attending to the new forces developing outside their ranks. Not only United States and Soviet power but also Japanese economic and military might, along with forces of nationalism in various parts of the colonial world, might have called for a new unity among Western leaders, to preserve Europe's precarious advantage—but quite the contrary occurred. What happened after World War II translated the growing decline of western Europe into more specific forms than ever before, but in a sense it merely stated the obvious.

And what happened, in terms of the diplomatic reduction of western Europe, was summed up in two basic processes: decolonization and the cold war. The first process meant that European nations lost most of their colonial territories, as western Europe's ability to directly administer outside national boundaries crept to its lowest ebb in over four centuries. The second process meant that the erstwhile great powers of western Europe, like the smaller states of eastern Europe, were now folded into a military and diplomatic rivalry between two superpowers that they might hope to influence but could not control. Again for the first time in centuries, western European nations were literally outgunned by powers outside their region, as the world's most powerful diplomatic combinations escaped their grasp.

The Loss of Europe's Colonies

Decolonization was a momentous event for the European and non-European states alike, but its cause was hardly complex. Nationalist pressures had been building in many areas even before World War II. In the Middle East and India, some recognition of the need for ultimate independence had already been offered. Then came the disruption of the war, which taught many Asian and African leaders still more about the vulnerability of their colonial masters. Several colonial powers hoped to reassert the empire after the war, but they had neither the resources nor the will to undertake a prolonged struggle, and when new independence demands surfaced, most quickly gave in. Indeed, after some initial conflicts many countries tried to anticipate nationalist pressures by granting freedom before serious trouble could surface.

Most Asian colonies gained independence within a few years after 1945. Britain's Labour government was eager to free itself from colonial responsibility and expense in the interests not only of postwar recovery but of building a welfare state at home, so it granted independence to India and Pakistan in 1947. The British did invest in a prolonged and successful campaign against communist guerrillas in Malaya but otherwise removed themselves from Asia promptly. The Dutch returned to Indonesia after the Japanese occupation ended but they soon pulled back against a powerful nationalist surge—and they were encouraged also by the United

States, which fancied itself the champion of colonial peoples and was eager to win the friendship of new nationalists in the context of the cold war. France, stung by its earlier defeat at German hands, harbored greater hopes of maintaining its empire. It tried to hang on in Vietnam against massive and well-orchestrated guerrilla fighting, until a defeat and a peace conference in 1954 finally marked the abolition of the French colonial regime.

The end of colonialism in the Middle East and Africa came slightly harder. The British, unable to reach agreement among Muslim and Jewish forces in Palestine, held on until 1948 when Jewish leaders simply proclaimed the state of Israel. France, taught by Vietnam, conciliated nationalists in Tunisia, Morocco, and sub-Saharan Africa by timely withdrawals, although for a time it harbored hopes of continued, if reduced, administration in the nations below the Sahara. In Algeria, however, French policy was different. Here was France's earliest North African colony, long regarded (by the French) as part of France, and with a substantial European minority. The French military joined Algerian settlers in insisting on a war to the death against Algerian nationalists. Bitter fighting went on for years, with cruelty on both sides and the threat of outright civil war in France itself. Finally, in 1962, a new regime set up by Charles de Gaulle, initially installed in 1958 to reassure the colonialists, realized the hopelessness of the struggle and negotiated independence for Algeria.

Britain also faced problems in Africa. The British, taught by their experience in India, prepared independence for several West African nations smoothly enough, in a process that culminated in the late 1950s and early 1960s. But in eastern and southern Africa, minority European settlements made for political complications. In Rhodesia, a white minority government declared independence unilaterally in 1965, and only patient negotiation, aided by the British, led over a decade later to a regime run by the Africans themselves. South Africa, which not only declared independence but pulled out of the loose British Commonwealth, was another lingering colonial remnant of sorts, though not directly a European responsibility; Belgium abruptly abandoned control of the Congo in the early 1960s but then had to intervene several times to protect Western economic interests. Portugal, clinging stubbornly to its colonies under its authoritarian regime, quickly shifted to decolonization when a democratic, parliamentary system was installed in the mid-1970s.

And so, in two waves culminating in the final flurry of the 1970s, imperialist Europe pulled out of the rest of the world. A process that had begun with the construction of Spanish and Portuguese empires in the sixteenth century, then was amplified by British, French, and Dutch holdings in the seventeenth and eighteenth centuries, and was crowned by the wave of imperialist acquisitions in the late nineteenth century, was now reversed. European nations that even in the interwar period clung stubbornly to colonial authority, particularly in Africa and Southeast Asia, were now forced to change their tune. Only a handful of small holdings outside Europe remained—a few in the West Indies, French

Tahiti, and the British lease on Hong Kong, which was however negotiated to yield to Chinese control in the 1990s.

The process of decolonization was in many ways surprisingly smooth. With a few exceptions, notably France and Portugal, European countries did not try to hold on at the expense of political stability and economic advance at home. Their acceptance of national independence movements was hardly generous, often no more than acknowledging the inevitable; poor preparation within the former colonies by repressive European administrators led to many troubles in the new nations. But although decolonization signaled a great reduction of European power, it did not overwhelm the European economy, which indeed prospered mightily during the decolonization period in part by retaining market patterns that had operated in the imperialist era; and it did not distort European politics unduly. Most of the colonies abandoned did not boast large European settlements. A number of former administrators and estate owners returned to Britain, Holland, and certainly France, some of them bitter against what they regarded as national betrayal. The agony of the Algerian war in France brought more concrete political movements among military leaders and European settlers in Algeria, which threatened terrorist action against government concessions. But most Europeans did not seem greatly dismayed at the loss of empire, and certainly no large political movements arose to protest the trend. Only France suffered a change of regime, from a rather loose parliamentary republic to a more authoritarian parliamentary system, as a result of conflict over empire. And even in France, once the decision to yield was made, the political aftermath seemed to fade relatively quickly.

Cold War between East and West

The other ingredient of Europe's diplomatic framework, the cold war, was more insidious and certainly more durable in its influence on politics and society. The conflict between the United States and the Soviet Union, with most of Europe pressed to take sides, shaped up between 1945 and 1947. The last wartime meetings among the leaders of Britain, the United States, and the Soviet Union had rather vaguely staked out the dimensions of postwar Europe, but they were certainly open to varied interpretations. Russian troops by the war's end firmly occupied most eastern European countries, and within three years the Russians had installed communist regimes to their liking, while excluding opposition political movements. Thus an "eastern bloc" shaped up that included Poland, Czechoslovakia, Bulgaria, Romania, and Hungary. And Soviet boundaries themselves had pushed west, reversing the decisions of the post–World War I Versailles conference. The Baltic states disappeared while Poland lost territory to Russia, to be compensated from former German lands. Finally, Soviet occupation of the eastern zone of Germany itself gave Russia a base further toward the heart of Europe than the tsars had ever dreamed of.

Offended by Russia's heavy-handed manipulation of eastern Europe,

United States and British policymakers tried to counter. The new American president, Harry Truman, was less eager for smooth relations with the Soviets than Franklin Roosevelt had been; he was emboldened by the United States's development in 1945 of the atomic bomb. Britain's wartime leader, Winston Churchill, had long feared communist aggression; it was he, in 1947, who coined the phrase "iron curtain" to describe the division between free and repressed societies that he saw taking shape in Europe. But Britain frankly lacked the power to resist Soviet pressure, and under the Labour government it explicitly left the initiative to the United States.

The United States responded to Russia's power plays with vigor. It criticized Russian policies and denied Russian applications for reconstruction loans. It bolstered regimes in Iran, Turkey, and Greece that were under Soviet pressure. In Greece, particularly, Americans took over British resistance efforts to a powerful communist guerrilla campaign. Then, in 1947, the United States proclaimed its Marshall plan, a program of substantial loans that was designed to aid Western nations in rebuilding from the war's devastation. In Soviet eyes, the Marshall Plan was a vehicle for American economic dominance, and indeed there is little question that in addition to humanitarian motives the United States intended to beat back domestic communist movements in countries such as France and Italy by promoting economic growth.

The focal point of the cold war in these early years was Germany. Soviet policy in Germany initially concentrated on seizing goods and factories as reparation. The Western allies soon prevented Russian intervention in their own zones and turned to some rebuilding efforts in the interests of playing a modest "German card" against growing Soviet strength in the east. That is, although the West, led by the United States, did not intend to resurrect a powerful Germany, it soon began to think in terms of constructing a viable political and economic entity. Allied collaboration began to build a unified West Germany in 1946, and local, then more national political structures were established through elections. When in 1947 the West moved to promote German economic recovery by creating a stable currency, the Soviet Union responded by blockading the city of Berlin, the divided former capital that sat in the midst of the Russian zone. The United States responded with a massive airlift to keep the city supplied, and the crisis finally ended, in 1948, with two separate Germanies, East and West, beginning to take clear shape along a tense, heavily fortified frontier.

Cold war divisions spread from Germany to Europe more generally with the formation of two rival military alliances. The North Atlantic Treaty Organization (NATO) was formed in 1949, under United States leadership, to group most of the western European powers plus Canada in a defensive alliance against possible Soviet aggression. The NATO pact soon legitimated some rearmament of West Germany in the context of resistance to communism. It also legitimated the continued maintenance of a substantial United States military presence not only in Germany but also in other member nations. In response, the Soviet Union organized the Warsaw Pact among its eastern European satellites; and when, in 1951, the Soviets announced their own nuclear capability, the world—particularly, the European world—seemed indeed divided between two rival camps, each in turn dominated by its own superpower. Numerous American and Soviet military divisions were permanently stationed in Europe on either side of the cold war divide.

The cold war had a number of implications for western Europe. It brought new pressures from the United States on internal as well as foreign policy. Americans pressed, through the 1950s and beyond, for acceptance of German rearmament (though under some agreed-upon limits); it lobbied for higher military expenditures in its old allies France and Britain; it pressed for acceptance of American forces and weapons systems. The United States's wishes were not always met, but the Americans had vital negotiating leverage in the economic aid they offered (and might withdraw) and in the troops they stationed in Europe and the nuclear "umbrella" they developed (and might, in theory, also withdraw); the nuclear weapons seemed to offer the only realistic protection should the Soviet Union venture direct attack. The Soviets, for their part, influenced western Europe not only through perceived aggressive intent, but also by funding and supporting substantial communist movements in France and Italy, which in turn affected but did not overwhelm the political process.

The cold war did not maintain the intensity it reached in its early years. Centers of conflict shifted in part outside Europe, as Korea, then Vietnam, and recurrently the Middle East became flashpoints. A few European states, in special circumstances, managed to stay out of strict cold war alignment in any event. Sweden and Switzerland maintained traditions of neutrality; Finland, a capitalist democracy on Soviet borders, was neutral perforce. Austria, divided into occupation zones after the war, was released in 1956—in a period of lessening cold war dispute— on condition of neutrality; and Yugoslavia, though communist, pulled away increasingly from the Soviet camp. Finally, the main Western powers themselves, once launched on recovery, found increasing room to maneuver. After de Gaulle returned to power in 1958, France became more and more restive under what it viewed as Anglo-American dominance of NATO, and it finally withdrew its forces from the joint NATO command, requiring also that American troops leave French soil. In the 1970s Germany would open new negotiations with the Soviet Union and eastern bloc countries, toward increasing export opportunities and reducing diplomatic tension.

But the fact was that the cold war and the resultant alliance system continued to describe much of the framework of East–West relations in Europe. France might gain partial independence from NATO, but it did not withdraw entirely. Although tensions often receded after the highpoint of the late 1940s, fear of possible Soviet aggression remained; for this reason United States military presence was deemed essential by leading policymakers, if not the entire European public. Western Europe could no longer plan on defending itself against a major outside enemy. Although Great Britain and, after 1958, France developed small nuclear capabilities, they simply could not afford the massive stockpiles and

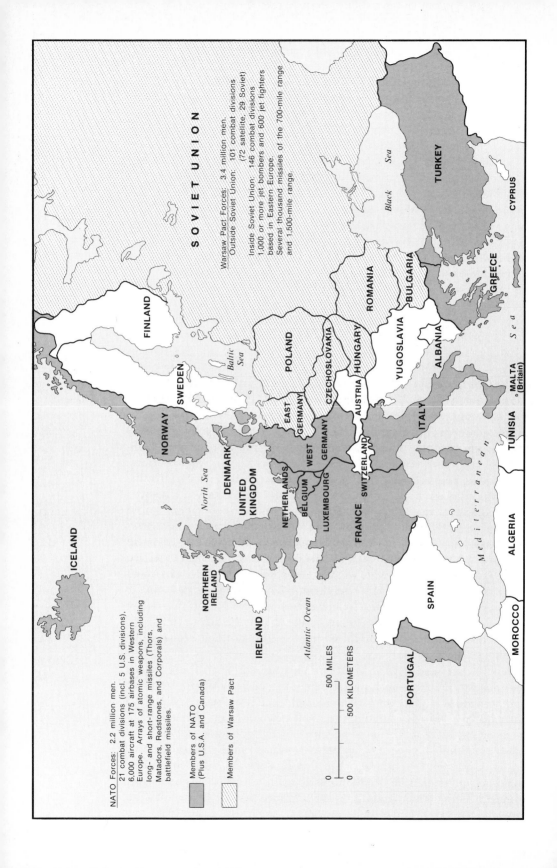

ICELAND

FINLAND

SOVIET UNION

NORWAY

SWEDEN

Baltic Sea

POLAND

ROMANIA

Black Sea

TURKEY

CYPRUS

GREECE

BULGARIA

YUGOSLAVIA

ALBANIA

Sea

DENMARK

EAST GERMANY

CZECHOSLOVAKIA

HUNGARY

AUSTRIA

ITALY

North Sea

UNITED KINGDOM

NETHERLANDS

BELGIUM WEST GERMANY

LUXEMBOURG

SWITZERLAND

FRANCE

Mediterranean Sea

MALTA (Britain)

TUNISIA

NORTHERN IRELAND

IRELAND

Atlantic Ocean

SPAIN

PORTUGAL

ALGERIA

MOROCCO

Warsaw Pact Forces: 3.4 million men.
Outside Soviet Union: 101 combat divisions
(72 satellite. 29 Soviet)
Inside Soviet Union: 146 combat divisions
1,000 or more jet bombers and 600 jet fighters
based in Eastern Europe.
Several thousand missiles of the 700-mile range
and 1,500-mile range.

NATO Forces: 2.2 million men.
21 combat divisions (incl. 5 U.S. divisions).
6,000 aircraft at 175 airbases in Western
Europe. Arrays of atomic weapons, including
long- and short-range missiles (Thors,
Matadors, Redstones, and Corporals) and
battlefield missiles.

Members of NATO
(Plus U.S.A. and Canada)

Members of Warsaw Pact

500 MILES

500 KILOMETERS

0
0

rocketry of the two superpowers. To some extent, indeed, Europeans ultimately grew rather comfortable in their reliance on United States protection. Not only during the lean postwar recovery years, but even after prosperity returned, European nations kept military budgets relatively modest, compared to United States or Soviet levels, and some leaders even boasted of setting a new pattern for a civilian, rather than military, political orientation. The argument was attractive, but it had as an undeniable corollary a degree of vulnerability to outside military and diplomatic pressures that had no precedent in modern European history.

The Formation of the European Economic Community

Its colonies lost, western Europe was forced to the undeniable and accurate realization that its world role had declined and its grandeur departed. The new diplomatic tensions of the cold war seized center stage but in part they bypassed European control in favor of the new, heavily armed superpowers, bringing also an undeniable recurrent fear that Europe might be held hostage in some future United States–Soviet exchange, a battleground or negotiating pawn without voice. This new and daunting diplomatic framework might have yielded a society in decline, so overwhelmed by foreign policy losses that new internal directions could not be seized. Conceivably, in the long run something like this may yet develop, for the new framework certainly has pronounced drawbacks. But in the postwar decades to date, and particularly during the 1950s and 1960s when decolonization and cold war were becoming established facts, western Europe seemed to respond to partial loss of world role with a heightened vigor at home.

Part of the response lay in the diplomatic realm, as western European countries resolved to put aside the internal divisions that had plagued the continent for centuries, and had culminated with such grim effect in the two world wars. Resistance leaders, and particularly Christian Democrats, wanted to reduce nationalist contest. Economic analysis urged greater European cooperation, rather than the narrow and self-defeating tariff wars of the 1930s. Policymakers in the United States pushed toward the same end; aid under the Marshall plan, ultimately over $15 billion in loans and grants, was attached to insistence on some international coordination of Western actions in relation to the economy. American and European leaders alike saw improved coordination as a vital Western response to Soviet initiatives in the cold war context. A variety of factors thus pushed toward a new internal structure for the states west of the communist bloc.

Early efforts at new integration in western Europe, born particularly of the Resistance spirit, proved overambitious. A Congress of Europe was established, but it held few powers and the strictly political effort collapsed. The same fate awaited an attempt at military integration, launched by France in 1950 as a means of permitting German armament without the threat of past nationalism. In theory, after all, a united western Europe could have gained military parity with the superpowers and recovered some of the diplomatic independence lost in the cold war. But as the cold war eased somewhat, France itself had second thoughts about such fundamental surrender of national independence, and Britain refused outright to participate. Military coordination among nations through NATO—not full integration—was the only option available.

Economic coordination, however, was another matter. Two farsighted French planners developed a scheme to coordinate heavy industry in France, Germany, Italy, and the Low Countries (Belgium, the Nether-

POSTWAR WEST GERMANY: BECOMING THE GOOD EUROPEAN

West German politics during the 1950s were dominated by the austere figure of Konrad Adenauer, the Christian Democratic leader, seconded by his able economics minister Ludwig Erhard. Authoritarian in temperament, Adenauer was able to work adequately with parliament, which in any event his party firmly controlled. He faced vigorous opposition from the Social Democratic party, but this party was somewhat hampered by its own issues of identity, as it renounced its Marxist past amid considerable internal debate. Adenauer was thus fairly free to build support for West Germany's new constitution and for a series of austerity measures deemed essential to rekindle economic growth. Into the early 1950s, German workers and their unions accepted low pay and high unemployment in the interests of amassing the capital needed to spark the nation's industrial machine.

Adenauer pulled German politics out of a traditional mold in a number of respects. He stressed private economic initiative rather than massive state planning or a vast new extension of an already substantial welfare apparatus. With little choice, given Allied occupation, he acquiesced in a reduced and greatly reformed military apparatus. Above all, he moved Germany's foreign policy decisively toward the West, building on West Germany's strong anti-communist mood and fears of another war. Throughout his administration Adenauer faced the anguishing problem of a divided Germany, compounded by millions of refugees from the East. He consistently paid lip service to the goal of reunification, but he prevented this issue from dominating the political process. Rather, his goal, enhanced by his Catholic, Rhineland background, was to gain new harmony with France and to tie Germany's future firmly to a Western alliance. This pushed Germany to the forefront of most steps toward greater European unity, including the Common Market. His motives included an understanding that playing the good European was the most profitable course for a Germany at this time, but he operated with far fewer reservations than had Gustav Stresemann in the 1920s; and his success in cooperation with French Europeanists helped prevent the growth of a revenge sentiment that had so marked Weimar Germany as well.

lands, and Luxembourg), which took effect in the early 1950s. Coordination in the atomic energy field soon followed. Then, in 1958, the European Economic Community (the Common Market) was launched among the same six member states. The Common Market reflected awareness of the competitive weakness of individual European nations, facing economic powerhouses such as the United States. Its conviction was that coordinating trade policies and creating a single market, Europe could develop the same economies of scale, the same giant international corporations that the American economy had generated. The Common Market not only reduced internal tariffs, finally removing them; it stipulated common agricultural and labor policies, common commercial law, a single tariff policy toward the outside world, and backed it all up by a substantial international bureaucracy based eventually in Brussels. Common Market success was such that several initial resisters—Britain, Ireland, and Denmark—later gained admittance. In the 1980s new democracies in Greece, Spain, and Portugal were also admitted.

The Common Market proved a success in two senses. Although it probably did not cause Europe's postwar economic surge, it certainly facilitated economic growth. Often divided among the national self-interests of member states—indeed virtually paralyzed on occasion—the Common Market nevertheless signaled the end to the kind of internal rivalries that had separated France and Germany, Britain and the Continent for so long. As western Europeans traveled and traded freely across national borders, a certain sense of their being European, in addition to their being French or Italian, began to arise as well.

Internal Politics: The Spread of Democracy and the Welfare State

Constitutional and Democratic Foundations among the Western European Nations

The striking new diplomatic initiatives were abundantly matched after 1945 by new political structures and definitions of government function within each country. Quite simply, parliamentary democracy became far more widely accepted and uniform in the western European constitutions than ever before, while the elaboration of the welfare state developed a new, and at least partly beneficent, set of relationships between government and citizen.

Most of the major Western states had to set up new constitutions following the turmoil of World War II. Britain maintained its existing structure, as did the Scandinavian governments; these countries had long operated under parliamentary, democratic systems. Elsewhere fascist or collaborationist regimes had been expelled, creating a political vacuum that had to be filled. Political reconstruction was aided by the fact that the discrediting of the far right removed, at least temporarily, characteristic conservative reluctance fully to accept liberal, democratic structures. The Christian Democrats and other leading conservative groups wholeheartedly embraced parliaments, civil liberties, and universal suffrage. Furthermore, although communist parties, to the left, were eager for social revolution in principle, in fact they cooperated in support of parliamentary structures. Most postwar politicians were also eager to set up regimes that would avoid some of the weaknesses that had characterized earlier ones such as Weimar Germany or Third Republic France.

With some guidance and constraint from Allied occupying forces, West Germany opted to become a federal democracy. Under this form, substantial administrative powers resided in the separate states. The central government of the Federal Republic of Germany boasted a two-house parliament, with the prime minister chosen by parliamentary majority. German leaders were careful to prevent loopholes by which an excessively strong executive might seize power, as had happened in the last days of Weimar. The abolition of outright fascist parties and, in 1956, the Communist party as well helped narrow the political spectrum to movements firmly in support of this liberal system. Other measures discouraged small, splinter parties that had often complicated coalition-building in Weimar times. Germany emerged with a much stronger democratic regime than it had ever before enjoyed, with two major parties—the Christian Democrats and the Social Democrats—and a smaller centrist grouping that played a role in certain coalition governments. Although the Christian Democrats held power for two decades, the Federal Republic of Germany later proved able to accept a change in party control, toward the Social Democrats, without disruption.

Italy, which had only briefly known a parliamentary regime combined with universal suffrage, quickly adopted the democratic republic system at the war's end; a referendum voted the end of the monarchy in 1946. Italy's political system was more centralized than that of West Germany, although provincial governments gained some strength, but the power of its parliament was greater. Unlike Germany at this point, Italy developed a proliferation of political parties. Christian Democrats were strongest, followed by the Communist party. Two socialist movements, a host of centrist groupings, and several small semifascist and monarchist movements on the right completed the array. Political divisions made for frequent shifts in parliamentary majorities, and Italian cabinets fell with great regularity. Despite this surface instability—and frequent, often passionate election campaigns—the structure of the Italian government was widely, if not always enthusiastically, accepted.

The French tried to set up a republic that would avoid some of the weaknesses of its Third Republic predecessor. Various voting systems were tried that might restrict small, splinter parties and improve party discipline, but they had limited effect. Christian Democrats and also the political partisans of de Gaulle hoped for a stronger executive, to counterbalance the power of parliament, but they were largely disappointed. France emerged with a Fourth Republic quite similar, in constitutional structure, to the Third, although women were now granted the vote. Interparty squabbling and frequent changes of ministries prompted de Gaulle to withdraw from politics in 1946. No single party commanded majority support and, as before the war, coalitions often proved fragile.

This instability was modified, however, by the fact that certain parties normally controlled key ministries from one government to another, providing considerable consistency from one year to the next. France's leadership toward European unity, for example, was facilitated by the fact that Christian Democrats controlled the foreign ministry most of the time.

It was true, however, that after the first postwar coalitions broke down, France had a difficult time forming stable ministries or developing daring policies. A key and decisive move in 1954 won agreement to ending the war in Indochina, but then the crisis of the Algerian war threatened to destroy the political process altogether. In the situation of near civil war, de Gaulle emerged from retirement and ushered in the only major regime change any of the postwar democracies experienced. The Fifth Republic, established in 1958, provided for direct election of a strong president. Parliament's control over the executive was thus broken, and the power of parliament declined overall. De Gaulle formed a political party that, in collaboration with more traditional conservatives, maintained majority control in parliament and presidency alike until 1981, lending unusual stability and a decidedly authoritarian tone to France's democracy.

The power of parliamentary democracy in postwar western Europe was extended in the 1970s when authoritarian regimes in Greece, Spain, and Portugal gave way to surprisingly open and effective systems. General Francisco Franco, Spain's dictator from its Civil War years, prepared a monarchy to replace him, but on his death the new king opted instead for a strong, liberal parliamentary system that won wide support. By 1980, in fact, the whole of western Europe operated under some version of liberal democracy, for the first time in history. And although small movements both on the right and on the left disputed the political system, and many people grumbled about ineffectiveness, the parliamentary regimes seemed to enjoy substantial approval.

The evolution of the communist movement in western Europe both reflected and promoted the solidification of democracy. Communism was not a major factor in British or Scandinavian politics, and because of cold war pressures it was removed from the West German repertoire as well. But in France and Italy, and later in Spain and Portugal, the movement drew great strength. French communists regularly polled between 18 percent and 25 percent of the vote, and the Italian party enjoyed a full third of electoral support. Communist movements stood for serious social change. They willingly used strikes to support political goals and were tempted on occasion to employ other disruptive tactics to discredit the existing political process. On the whole, however, communist leaders in the West opted for cooperation with the democratic political system, hoping to improve their vote totals within this system. The parties controlled a number of key provincial and city governments, giving them a real foothold in political power at this level. In the 1970s a movement known as Eurocommunism, with particular strength in Italy and Spain, committed Western communism even more fully to the political process rather than to literal revolution. Eurocommunists stressed their independence from the Soviet Union, agreed to maintain existing diplomatic commitments even to NATO—although with some hope of revising policies within this framework—and argued that they should be included in coalition ministries with other reform-minded parties. This communist evolution meant that, although the political left and the right might disagree on a host of vital issues, they agreed now that the constitutional structure itself was not only acceptable, but worth preserving—a marked contrast to the widespread attack on the parliamentary framework that had marked the interwar decades.

The Functions of the Welfare State

The politics of postwar Europe were marked by a redefinition of government functions at least as dramatic as the new clarification of constitutional issues. Resistance ideas and the shift leftward of the political spectrum helped explain the new activism of the state in economic policy and in welfare issues. Wartime planning in the British government had pointed to the need for new programs to reduce the impact of economic inequality and to reward the lower classes for their loyalty. Not surprisingly, the governments that emerged at the war's end, Britain's Labour party and the communist–socialist–Christian Democrat coalitions in France and Italy, quickly moved to set up a new government apparatus that would play a new role in economic planning and develop new social activities as well. By 1948 the basic nature of the modern welfare state had been established throughout western Europe, as not only the new regimes but also established reformists such as in Scandinavia extended a variety of government programs.

The welfare state elaborated a host of social insurance measures. Unemployment insurance was improved. Medical care was supported by state-funded insurance or, as in Britain where it became a centerpiece to the new Labour program, the basic health-care system was nationalized outright. State-run medical facilities have provided free care to the bulk of the British population from 1947 onward, although some small fees were later introduced. Family assistance was another category, not entirely new, that was now greatly expanded. All western European governments provided payments to families with several children, the amount increasing with family size. Because the poor now tended to have the largest families, family aid programs both encouraged population growth—of particular concern to countries such as France—and helped redistribute some income toward the neediest groups, drawn from general tax revenues. In the 1950s, a French worker family with low earnings and five children (admittedly an unusual brood by this point) could improve its income by as much as 40 percent through the family aid received. Governments also became more active in the housing field—a virtual necessity given wartime destruction and then postwar population growth. Britain embarked on an ambitious program of "council housing," providing many single-family units that deliberately mixed working-class and middle-class families in new neighborhoods. By the 1950s over a quarter of the British population was housed in structures built and run by the government.

British council housing was a major part of the new welfare state. This development, in the industrial city of Glasgow, provided new amenities but also imposed a new, impersonal sameness on the living space of the urban lower class.

The welfare state also took on new responsibilities in labor–management relations. Scandinavian regimes had earlier worked to promote trilateral bargaining, with government a participant along with unions and business. British Labour pinned great hopes on new worker–management councils in industries taken over by the state. France at various times experimented with mandatory "enterprise committees," designed to give worker representatives a voice in company policy decisions. In 1951 Germany launched supervisory boards in heavy industry with strong worker voice, and later experimented with "co-determination" schemes toward the same goal of reducing the gap between owners and proletarians in the decision-making process. Some of the programs won only modest success, as unions were suspicious of undue involvement and management kept serious issues off the collective table. But there was some change, and welfare states also extended regulations designed to protect workers in other respects. Not only health and safety, but also dismissal now became surrounded by state-enforced rules, requiring managers to justify their actions and submit to inspection rather than operating from their own initiative alone.

As the welfare state emerged in the postwar years, it was a compromise product. Its emphases varied from one nation to the next. It recognized a substantial private sector and tried to limit and cushion individual initiative rather than replacing it with state action alone as in the communist system. It provided aid for citizens at many income levels. Middle-class people might benefit from family assistance, and they certainly used state medical insurance. They also disproportionately benefited from the expanded educational systems and university scholarships that developed along with the welfare state. In other words, although the welfare state focused particularly on problems of workers and the poor, it won support from other groups by dealing with some of *their* special needs as well. Relatedly, although some aspects of the welfare state redistributed income, by using tax funds generated through graduated levies and giving them disproportionately to programs benefiting the poor, the welfare state did not generally make a huge dent on western Europe's unequal class system. In some countries income taxes were not steeply graduated—in other words, they did not tax the rich proportionally more than they taxed other groups. Furthermore, starting with France, a supplementary tax system was installed, beginning in the late 1950s, that was not graduated at all. This "value-added" tax system, which quickly spread through the Common Market and beyond, levied taxes on each stage of the production process, operating essentially as a super–sales tax ultimately paid by consumers. Here was a potent source of revenue that had little redistributive effect.

The welfare state was, in sum, an important new definition of government functions, but from a social standpoint it was hardly a revolutionary device. It cushioned citizens against big expenses and unusual hardships, rather than rearranging overall social structure. It did protect the purchasing power of the very poor against catastrophe, and it did contribute to improved health conditions generally. It also, of course, increased contacts between government and citizen, and it produced a host of new regulations that framed European life.

As a compromise system, the welfare state quickly drew a host of opponents on both left and right. Some conservatives and liberals lamented the decline of individual initiative, arguing that the state had become too powerful and cumbersome. Certain groups, such as British doctors at the outset of the nationalized health system, resented government controls over earnings and the very practice of medicine. On the left, many socialists and communists attacked the incompleteness of welfare practices, and particularly the continued role of private initiative and the persistence of substantial income differentials. Yet, despite such carping, the welfare state initially seemed to win wide acceptance. The British, for example, became quickly attached to their new health system, making it virtually impossible to revise the system in any substantial way. For the most part political debate centered around tinkering with the welfare state, not revolutionizing it in any particular direction. Socialist parties, when in power, extended welfare measures by improving their coverage and benefits. Conservative parties, for their part, often cut back a bit and promised more efficient administration. Into the 1970s, no major political movement attacked the new state root and branch.

The welfare state was undeniably expensive. It greatly expanded government bureaucracies, in addition to channeling tax monies to new purposes. By the 1950s, up to 25 percent of the gross national product of countries such as France or Holland was going to welfare purposes, and the figure tended to rise with time. As military expenses began to stabilize, welfare commitments became far and away the largest component of government budgets themselves. Here was a clear indication of the extent to which the western European state had altered its relationship to the wider society.

Nationalization and Central Planning

Parallel to the welfare state was an increased governmental role in economic policy. Most postwar governments nationalized some sectors of industry outright. France and Britain took over coal mines and railroads, and all or part of the steel industry was brought under state control as well. These were industries so basic to national prosperity that purely private direction was now regarded, by the political majority, as inappropriate. Not coincidentally, these were also industries that had been particularly productive of labor dispute. Government control of utilities, such as electricity, also increased.

Many of the nationalized industries proved effective. State-run rail systems were costly but efficient and helped reduce pressure for massive roadways of the sort that the United States government launched in the 1950s. At the same time nationalization did not prevent continued disputes between workers and managements particularly in sectors such as coal mining that were increasingly faced with competition from other products. Conservative parties, when in power, moved to denationalize some sectors, although as with the welfare state they did not undo postwar programs entirely. For their part socialist leaders typically pressed for further nationalization, and when a socialist party finally achieved new power in France, in 1981, a host of nationalizations followed.

Government economic policy went well beyond nationalization. All European countries set up new planning offices, responsible for developing multiyear economic projections and for setting goals and the means to meet them. By coordinating tax concessions and directing the flow of capital from state banks, government planners had genuine power to shape, although not directly to run, economic activity. Planning extended to agriculture as well as industry. Planning offices regulated crop sizes and encouraged consolidation of land for greater efficiency, and they could require farmers to participate in cooperatives that would improve marketing and purchasing procedures.

Planning involved European governments more directly than ever before in commitments to economic growth, full employment, and avoidance of damaging recessions. It was also aimed at improving the economic development of laggard regions. Italy thus tried to direct increasing industrialization toward the south, France toward the west, in both cases with partial success.

The new, active state was not a uniform agent throughout western Europe. West Germany, with a long tradition of government activity, changed least in that direction. Indeed, many Christian Democratic leaders were particularly committed to the workings of free enterprise and competition. France, building on its long tradition of political centralization, developed a powerful new state apparatus. Its *Office du plan*, or planning department, had unusually extensive powers to channel economic activities beyond the nationalized sector. Britain, just a century before western Europe's weakest government, now became heavily statist.

Despite important variations, the role of the state loomed unprecedentedly large throughout western Europe from the 1940s onward. A new breed of bureaucrat, often called a "technocrat" because of intense training in engineering or economics and because of a devotion to the power of national planning, came to the fore in the offices of the gov-

---

AFTER THE LABOUR GOVERNMENT IN BRITAIN

Labour's dramatic victory in the British elections of 1945, and its successful development of the nationalized health plan, widened social insurance and key nationalizations in industry but did not give the party a firm hold on the British electorate. The party demonstrated a growing tendency to split, under the impact of success, between moderates who wanted to hold onto middle-class voters, and radicals whose core appeal was to hard-line trade unionists. By 1950 the radicals wanted still further reforms—more nationalizations, attacks on upper-class private schools; the moderates wanted to run on the party's record as a welfare provider. Partly because of the split, partly because many of the voters in 1945 had been moved by the special circumstances of wartime disruption and housing damage to seek a new option, Labour lost the 1951 election decisively.

The Conservative party, now in power, benefited from a modest new economic prosperity through most of the 1950s. Britain was lagging behind the Continent economically, but it was gaining ground in absolute terms. International tensions also eased, as decolonization had been completed in most of Asia and as Britain came to terms with its second-rank diplomatic status. Conservative leaders indeed benefited from an easier relationship with American leaders, as they were able to play upon special ties. The Conservatives made no effort to undo the bulk of Labour's welfare program. They survived the one real crisis of the decade, a joint effort with France in 1956 to attack Egypt after the latter's takeover of the Suez Canal; this attack, joined by Israel, met firm United States and Soviet opposition and had to be called off, a clear sign of the end of British imperial might in the Middle East. Conservative leaders displayed excellent instincts at political maneuvering, a recollection of wartime heroics (particularly featuring the aging Winston Churchill), but no clear policy directions beyond maintaining the status quo. British politics remained relatively sedate, certainly uneventful beyond a few steamy personal scandals; the country, to judge by opinion polls, was reasonably happy; yet a sense of drift and decline, even as measured by neighboring continental states, was pervasive as well.

ernment. Some state initiatives undoubtedly reflected the potential over-zealousness of the new breed. Housing authorities forced workers out of old but comfortable slums into anonymous high-rise structures that, however elegant on paper, never felt right to those involved in actual residence. Peasants, no friend of distant central governments even before, often lamented heavyhanded requirements. Yet here too, as with the welfare state, no particularly coherent political disputes took shape, at least until the 1960s. The new state seemed to work well enough that it was difficult to attack categorically.

The fact was that big, contentious political issues were notable for their absence through most of Europe during the 1950s and 1960s, except for the polarizing experience of the Algerian war in France. Reformist governments of the immediate postwar years tended to give way to more conservative regimes during the 1950s. Labour, for example, lost the 1951 election in Britain and, even earlier, communists had been forced out of coalitions in France and Italy. But the conservative regimes were generally content to support the existing definition of state functions, with only *ad hoc* amendments, rather than trying to return to some earlier pattern. And when socialist or labor governments gained renewed access to power, as in Britain in the 1960s, they too, typically, had no dramatic new programs to offer. For better or worse, Europeans seemed to accept the state in its new social and economic role as well as in its constitutional structure. Political debates were often fierce, and partisan loyalties intense, but few sweeping issues were raised.

Economic Growth: An Affluent Europe

Political changes were intimately connected to the new economic patterns that took shape after immediate postwar reconstruction, in two respects. First, some of the new government measures contributed directly to economic growth, as they were intended to do. Planning helped, particularly when capital resources were scarce. France, poor in fuel resources, was able to build, through government sponsorship, an extensive network of nuclear power plants that eventually provided over 60 percent of its power needs. Welfare also helped European economies: putting new funds in the pockets of the poor stimulated consumer demand, which in turn spurred growth. Some government initiatives may well have retarded growth by using funds uneconomically or reducing incentive, and there is no way to argue that Europe's new state functions were *essential* to the economic growth that occurred. But there is also no denying that the new functions arose during (if they did not directly cause) one of the most rapid spurts of productivity and wealth in Europe's history.

Second, in the connection between the economy and the political affairs of the state influence also moved the other direction: from economic prosperity to political stability. Rising productivity and income made politics less contentious. The welfare state was relatively widely accepted in part because living standards were improving—it was possible to pay more in taxes and still have more disposable income, given rapid growth. Business people might fume about government red tape and bureaucratic interference, but their political response was restrained by the soaring profits they enjoyed. Workers might vote communist and mean their vote as a sincere protest against their continuing lack of voice and unequal status, but their protest was muted when they had a new car or motorbike to play with on the weekends. Indeed, communist activism visibly declined even when the vote did not, as workers devoted themselves to their new consumer passions. New wealth, in other words, greased the political process, helping to explain why deep political cleavage receded, even as the state was redefined and as Europe suffered through an immense diplomatic decline.

For there was no question that, by the mid-1950s, western Europe had entered a new economic phase. Agricultural production and productivity increased rapidly, as peasant farmers, backed and spurred by the technocrats, adopted new equipment and seeds. European agriculture was still less efficient than that of North America, which necessitated some hotly debated tariff barriers by the Common Market. But food production easily met European needs, often with some to spare for export. Retooled industries poured out textiles and metallurgical products. Expensive consumer products such as automobiles and appliances supported rapidly growing factories. Western Europe also remained a leading center of weapons production, trailing only the United States and the Soviet Union in exports.

Overall growth in gross national product surpassed the rates of any extended period since the industrial revolution began; it also surpassed the growth rates of the United States's economy during the 1950s and 1960s. The German economy, once some basic reconstruction and currency stabilization had occurred by 1948, took off at a 6 percent annual expansion during the 1950s; with few modest setbacks this pace continued into the early 1970s. France attained an 8 percent growth rate by the late 1950s, maintained almost this level during the 1960s, and returned to rates of over 7 percent annually by the early 1970s. By 1959 the Italian economy, a newcomer to the industrial big leagues, was expanding at an 11 percent annual rate. These were, admittedly, the clearest success stories. Scandinavian growth was substantial but more modest, and Britain, also expanding but clearly falling rapidly in rank among the European national economies, managed at best a 4 percent increase annually. Even this, however, contrasted markedly with the stagnation of the 1920s and early 1930s.

Growth rates of the sort common in western Europe, their impact heightened by the absence of major depressions, depended on rapid technological change. Europe's rising food production was achieved with a steadily shrinking agricultural labor force. France's peasant population, 16 percent of the labor force in the early 1950s, fell to 10 percent two decades later—but overall output was much higher than before. During the 1950s the industrial work force grew as part of factory expansion; but by the 1960s, despite rising production, the relative proportion of factory workers also began to drop. Workers in the service sector, filling functions as teachers, clerks, medical personnel, insurance and bank workers, and performers and other "leisure industry" personnel, rose rapidly in contrast. Europe, like the United States, began to convert technological advance into the provision of larger bureaucracies and service operations, without jeopardizing the expanding output of goods. In France, by 1968, half of all paid workers were in the service sector, and the proportion rose steadily thereafter.

The high rates of economic growth also assured relatively low unemployment after the immediate postwar dislocations passed. Certain regions suffered; old mining and factory centers, such as northern Britain or northern France, declined as the more active economic sectors located elsewhere. Southern Italy continued to trail the northern part of the country despite improvements. Britain, with slower development, had more nagging unemployment problems than other countries. Even so, during most of the 1950s and 1960s Britain averaged no more than 4 percent unemployment per year, whereas countries such as France and Germany, with rates of 2 percent to 3 percent a year, had about as low a level as a modern country can achieve except through blanket government guarantees of jobs for everyone. Indeed, many parts of the continent were labor-short and had to seek hundreds of thousands of workers from other areas—first from southern Europe, then, as this region too industrialized, from Africa, the Middle East, and parts of Asia.

The Fruits of Prosperity

Unprecedented economic growth plus low unemployment meant unprecedented improvements in incomes, even with the taxation necessary to sustain welfare programs. Whereas per-capita disposable income rose 117 percent in the United States between 1960 and 1973, it increased 258 percent in France, 312 percent in Germany, and 323 percent in Denmark. Scandinavia, Switzerland, and the Federal Republic of Germany indeed surpassed the United States in standards of living by the 1970s, while France, long an apparent laggard in modern economic development, pulled even. New spending money rapidly translated into huge increases in the purchase of durable consumer goods, as the tables below exemplify. By 1969 two of every ten people in Britain, Sweden, West Germany, and France owned an automobile. Ownership of television sets became virtually universal. France and other countries indulged in a mania for household appliances. Shopping malls and supermarkets, the agents of affluence and extensive but efficient shopping that had first developed in the United States, spread widely, at the expense of more traditional, specialist small shops. A West German concern in fact took over a key American grocery chain in the late 1970s, on grounds that Europeans now knew mass marketing as well as or better than the American consumer pioneers.

Europe's advancing prosperity also helped support a considerable natural population increase that began in the mid-1940s and extended until roughly 1962. Population generally spurts forward after a war, and many Europeans had also delayed births during the 1930s. The early phases of the European baby boom were thus understandable, even though they

Two Measures of Rising Consumer Prosperity in Europe, 1957 and 1965

Automobiles	1957	1965
France	3,476,000	7,842,000
Germany (Federal Republic)	2,456,288	8,103,600
Italy	1,051,004 (1956)	5,468,981
The Netherlands	375,676	1,272,890
Sweden	796,000	1,793,000

Televisions	1957	1965
France	683,000	6,489,000
Germany	798,586	11,379,000
Italy	367,000	6,044,542
The Netherlands	239,000	2,113,000
Sweden	75,817	2,110,584

Sources: Based on *The Europa Year Book 1959* (London: Europa Publications, 1959) and *The Europa Year Book 1967*, vol. 1 (London: Europa Publications, 1967).

reversed many decades of declining growth rates or, in countries such as France, outright stagnation. Government family aid measures and other features of the welfare state facilitated having children, which indeed was one of their purposes. Still, the baby boom was unexpected, particularly in the context of wartime dislocation and diplomatic decline. The boom suggested that many Europeans were gaining new confidence in their societies' future, as in fact they put rising incomes to use in part to afford a larger number of offspring. The baby boom in turn helped sustain economic growth by creating new product demands, although it also put serious pressure on facilities such as schools.

Europeans' use of rising income was not identical to the patterns of consumers in the world's other affluent area, the United States. The baby boom, for example, was less pronounced in Europe, suggesting that Europeans still held back slightly in their commitment to numerous children. Given smaller travel distances and better transit facilities, Europeans used less of their money on cars. They used more, in contrast, on high-quality foods, on welfare matters, and on leisure. Vacation time increased rapidly in Europe, reaching an average of three weeks a year (not counting special holidays) for most workers, and more for many in the middle class. This commitment to extensive leisure was not matched in the United States, save in growing rates of retirement at the end of working life.

Nevertheless, Europe had unquestionably developed a framework of affluent consumerism as fully as had the United States, with at least as much impact on basic social patterns and habits of thought. Advertising

The increases in income and vacation time in Europe during the 1960s and 1970s engendered a booming vacation industry. La Grande Motte, a tourist holiday development on the French Mediterranean coast, was a product of the 1960s.

was not quite as ubiquitous in Europe as across the Atlantic, particularly because most television channels were state-run and noncommercial. But promptings to buy, to smell good, to look right, to express one's personality in the latest car style, began quickly to describe European life. The frenzy to find good vacation spots was certainly intense. Literally millions of Germans poured annually into Italy and Spain, seeking the sun. Britons thronged to Spanish beaches. Europeans were bent on combining efficient work with indulgent leisure.

Western Europe's economic advance was not without some dark spots. At various points between 1950 and 1970, several European nations suffered balance-of-payments problems, as they imported more rapidly than they exported; this in turn forced some restrictions on activities abroad, when nations such as France and Britain tried to protect the value of their currency by limiting spending outside their borders. Inflation was another recurrent headache, when demand outstripped production. And inflation in the 1970s, affecting even the cautious Germans who were particularly eager to avoid this specter from the past, caused serious dislocation. Pockets of unemployment were troubling. Furthermore, many immigrant workers, from Turkey, North Africa, Pakistan, and the West Indies, suffered very low wages and unstable employment. These immigrants, euphemistically labeled "guest workers," were often residentially segregated and the object of considerable prejudice. They formed something of a separate labor force, confined for the most part to menial jobs and hardly benefiting from the prosperity of the society around them.

Many Europeans, even amid rapid growth, also worried about a continued disadvantage compared to the United States. In 1969 a French journalist, Jacques Servan-Schreiber, wrote *The American Challenge,* which quickly won wide and dismayed attention by arguing that Europeans had yet to match the strength, capital power, or technological sophistication of American corporations. The argument was hard to assess, because Europeans also had strengths—including balanced government budgets—that the United States could not match. It was true, however, that western Europe had not yet equaled the overall economic power of the United States and remained vulnerable to economic problems that the United States might, intentionally or not, export. By the 1970s rising Japanese competition was another very real concern.

Well into the 1970s, however, economic success—what the Germans modestly dubbed their "economic miracle"—was clearly the main story. Along with Europe's new political structure, economic expansion helped reshape social structure and the relations among social groups, and altered the nature of family life. Economic growth, in fact, helped compensate for apparent diplomatic decline, for even as colonies disappeared and as military might shrank, western Europe remained a major world force through its power to buy, produce, and sell.

European Society in the Decades of Affluence

Changes in economic and political structures hardly erased social boundaries in Europe, but they did ease a number of traditional tensions among social classes and they partially redefined the bases of social structure itself. Increasingly, power and prestige came not from ownership of property alone, but from levels of education, access to specialized knowledge and information, and decision-making power. Managers and bureaucrats, in other words, rather than owners of land and factories, stood at the top of the heap. With nationalization, aristocratic decline, and high taxes, outright ownership declined in importance, although the wealthiest 5 percent in most European countries continued to own a disproportionate amount of capital and property and held great power on this basis. Most middle-class people, however, were no longer defined primarily by possession, but rather by educational levels and position in a private or public bureaucracy. Workers were still propertyless, except increasingly as owners of substantial consumer property, but their lower social position followed less now from their propertylessness than from their relative lack of power in decisions about work or technology. The growing lower middle class of clerks and salespeople was similarly disadvantaged, and the boundary line between worker and white-collar employee grew increasingly fuzzy. Whether all this added up to a radically new social structure, or simply a substantial redefinition of the old capitalist–proletarian division, might be debated, but there was no question of significant change.

Europe's social lines were also blurred by unprecedented social mobility. The growth of the white-collar sector allowed many blue-collar workers to advance—over 30 percent of the French working class moved "up" in this sense in the two decades following the war. Mobility described the new movement from peasantry to townsman. It meant blue-collar workers insisting on taking only highly-skilled positions, leaving more menial and dangerous jobs to the immigrants. It meant a minority of people of worker or peasant backgrounds using new educational opportunities to enter universities and the managerial class. Britain, which made the most substantial strides here, saw 30 percent of its university student population emanate from working-class levels by the 1960s. But even in France, where mobility to the top was less substantial, a significant minority of the bureaucratic and political elite now came from below the middle class. For the first time since the industrial revolution began, in fact, rates of European mobility now matched those of the United States, particularly due to the opening of new channels of education.

The Changing Rural World

Rapid social change in Europe was also defined in the experience of individual social groups, for a definite class structure persisted despite new mobility and considerable redefinition.

The peasantry was one of the groups particularly affected by change, even aside from its rapid shrinkage. Agricultural workers in some countries, such as England, had long since jettisoned most of the features associated with the peasantry, as commercial agriculture and urban influence steadily cut into older traditions. Peasantries in places such as Denmark and Holland had adopted new organizational forms, through the strong cooperative movements, which pooled production or purchasing on the part of thousands of small proprietors, and a firm commitment to specialized commercial production. Nowhere in western Europe was a fully traditional peasantry extant by 1945, given changes in economy, demography, and outlook. Still, observers in the early 1950s had little difficulty identifying strong peasant remnants in the villages of France, Italy, and even West Germany: a commitment to separate rural values; strong village structures and a certain remoteness from the wider world; devotion to land, which could take precedence over maximizing profit.

By the 1970s much of this peasant world had disappeared; indeed, one French sociologist wrote simply of the "vanishing peasant." Signs of change abounded. Peasants became more actively concerned with their standards as consumers. Rising incomes made them avid for more, and television and other experiences increased awareness of urban advantages. Younger peasants grew more open than before to technological change, as tractors became a more important status symbol than land itself. Some peasants now preferred to use capital to acquire more equipment than to buy land, preferring to rent—an unprecedented recasting of their values toward commercial cost-to-benefit calculation. Village politics changed as well. Starting with the triumph of local resistance movements, many traditional local leaders or leading families were pushed aside by younger, more ambitious farmers. The spread of cooperatives and government agencies, some of them requiring participation in regional elections, gave peasants a wider political experience and reduced their reliance on personality as opposed to issue in political choice.

Changes in the rural world of western Europe produced a new potential for protest. Tractor-driving peasants, starting in the late 1960s, often blocked the traffic of city dwellers leaving on vacation, or demonstrated in administrative capitals including the seat of the Common Market, to insist on government protection of food prices and improvements in living standards. Although small in size, the active peasant voting bloc put strong pressure on government policies in France, Italy, and elsewhere. No longer swayed by political movements that advocated nostalgic rural values, as they had been earlier in the fascist period, and now focused clearly on calculated economic interests, western European peasants–turned–commercial farmers still left their mark on the wider society.

Farmers did not, to be sure, simply merge into an urban-defined social structure, even as their peasantlike characteristics declined. They still had slightly larger families than city people did and rated the number of children more important in defining family success. Their divorce rates were lower than urban levels. They were more likely to be religious than urban people were. Despite government efforts to promote land consolidation, they still clung to scattered small plots. And although their festivals were hollow echoes of older tradition—filled with urban band music and busloads of city tourists—they retained at least a vague sense of older habits. But the peasantry as such was truly gone, replaced by a small-farmer class in close contact with urban ways and values. This conversion culminated many centuries of change in rural life but took particularly dramatic form in the postwar decades.

An Affluent Working Class

Working-class traditions, though less hoary than those of peasants, were also attacked by political and economic changes from the 1950s onward. A minority of workers, as we have seen, were directly drawn into the mobility process, rising to white-collar status or sending their children into the university system. Far more workers improved their position while remaining in the working class. A full 54 percent of all French workers were skilled by 1968, and five years later the figure had risen to 66 percent. New technologies, which increased automation but also demanded higher skill levels for operators, helped account for this internal shift; so did the continuing arrival of foreign workers, who took up the less skilled jobs. Many workers, then, felt less blocked from improvement than they had earlier in the industrial revolution, and less separated from the wider society as well. Joined to this real and perceived gain was the general increase in affluence. Only a small minority of the working class—12 percent in Britain in 1963—fell at or near subsistence levels; much of this minority was elderly or foreign. For most workers, improved real wages meant new opportunities for better housing—which itself disrupted tradition by breaking up once-solid working-class neighborhoods; for durable consumer goods; for more elaborate leisure.

One clear victim of changes in working-class standards involved the recreational patterns workers had established from the nineteenth century onward. Neighborhood bars—pubs in England—clearly declined in number and patronage. The shift away from older residential cohesion was partly responsible. Television played a large role, as many workers went home after work, to enjoy what quickly became the favorite leisure outlet, rather than spending time drinking with workmates. This privatization of leisure marked a major redirection of working-class life. Other new or expanded recreations, such as gardening, tennis, or vacationing, took workers away from older group activities and toward individual or family initiatives. Class-conscious leisure by no means disappeared, but it did decline. A Danish union-owned brewery, which had long relied on working-class loyalty to sell its product, had to close its doors in the 1960s because workers no longer found solidarity a good reason to shun better-tasting beer made by capitalist firms, and they had the money to indulge their palates.

Some observers claimed that, because of greater affluence and the welfare state, along with less authoritarian structures on the job, workers were coming to resemble the middle class, in a process known as *embourgeoisement*. They pointed not only to overlaps in consumer and leisure behavior from class to class, but also to more shared family values. In truth, workers often reported an increased pleasure and emotion in their family life, and a decline of traditional role-playing as fathers became more interested in enjoying infants and adopting a friendly, rather than punitive, relationship with their offspring. Furthermore, there were some signs of reduction in class-conflict interests within the working class. Although votes for socialist and in some cases communist parties stayed high, though never commanding entire working-class support, most of these parties focused increasingly on reform and not revolution. Furthermore, many former working-class militants now devoted their time to new leisure interests, or to overtime work necessary to pay for a new car or a better apartment, effectively reducing their political commitments. Trade-union membership, rising into the 1950s, also stabilized and then began to drop relative to the size of the labor force.

Yet despite real change and a probable lessening of class-based hostilities, the working class did *not* merge with the middle class. Trends of a mass society in which consumer habits blurred class lines continued, but most working-class people insisted, with rueful pride, on their separate social status. Unlike the United States, where 85 percent of the population claimed to be in the middle class, most urban Britons or Frenchmen said they were working-class and (somewhat) proud of it. The label of "worker" was not hollow; workers, more than other urban groups, maintained an ambivalent outlook toward their jobs. Skilled workers retained strong pride, but they also typically believed that they were bossed around by incompetent managers. Semiskilled workers complained less about bosses but showed less indication that they expected or, normally, found pleasure in work at all, as opposed to the instrumental rewards—pay and benefits—they obtained. Most workers admitted to some satisfaction in work or reward—though a minority of up to 31 percent dissented according to opinion surveys in western Europe—but they also said that, had they to do it over again, they would choose another line of work. Modern work still seemed partially out of control, and the European working class saw no reason to come to terms with it entirely.

The same ambivalence showed in relations with the wider society. Although the bitterest class hostilities did decline, workers were quite aware that they were different from most people in the middle class. They provided far less encouragement than did middle-class people for their children to do well in school or to push into the upper, university-bound school tracks. They relied heavily on family, including extended kin, for their social contacts, rather than dealing socially with outsiders; in this sense the working class became, if anything, more isolated than before. And although certain forms of protest did moderate, the working class, or important segments of it, remained capable of passionate out-

Rioting by sports fans was a new source of violence in European society A fatal Brussels soccer riot in 1985 pitted British against Italian fans. Many ascribed this violence to emotional outbursts by deprived lower-class youths. However, theories of collective behavior provide wider explanations for the crowd's brutality.

burst. British workers produced several crescendos of strike activity, sometimes against union leadership as well as management. Workers in nationalized industries in several countries burst out against government-imposed wage restraints. German metalworkers, normally fairly docile, conducted an unprecedentedly bitter strike in the mid-1980s for more voice over conditions as well as better pay. There were other outbursts as well. Working-class youth frequently displayed a restiveness that could not be captured by conventional protest. Young workers were responsible for a growing wave of spectator violence at British soccer matches, for example, during the 1970s and beyond, expressing a sense of frustration at a life of routine and absent opportunity quite reminiscent of proletarian grievances in past times.

The Changing Face of the Middle Class

Changes in the middle class added a final element of complexity to Europe's postwar social picture. Some distracting traditionalist elements faded from view, as they had among farmers and workers, in the world of business and professional people. The older small shopkeepers were increasingly eclipsed, or became effectively the employees of large distributing companies. From the 1870s onward, this traditional lower middle class had often resented economic change in the form of large corporations and department stores, sometimes developing distinctive political attachments to anti-Semitic or outright fascist movements; now the class was far less visible. Small shopkeepers in France, to be sure, briefly supported a protest movement in the 1950s, and had enough influence to curb supermarkets by law in some center cities, but they had far less vitality than in the past. The new middle class was defined increasingly in terms of openness to education, agility on a bureaucratic ladder, and commitment to change. Suspicions against the consumer society also declined, as middle-class people fully embraced a leisure ethic for off-work hours. Fascination with vacations, participant sports, and an active, satisfying retirement blended with a commitment to hard work during business hours. Certain traditional distractions, such as long, leisurely lunch breaks, faded as an efficient work pattern, followed by expressive play, became the ideal. Expanding management opportunities and, particularly, the growth of educational facilities blended nicely with the middle-class value system. In a number of key respects, starting with the final demise of an effective aristocracy, western European life conformed to middle-class standards more fully than ever before.

Yet the development of the postwar middle class was not untroubled. Although most middle-class people accepted some version of the welfare state, many were concerned about levels of taxation and regulation. Some groups found their status sufficiently jeopardized to the point that they had to resort to forms of protest previously reserved for the outright proletariat. Thus doctors' strikes punctuated the social peace in countries such as Belgium and Italy, as medical professionals, now virtual employees of the welfare state, sought a new voice.

More important still was the growth of the white-collar sector. White-collar workers often reported higher job satisfaction than did factory hands; however, there was no question that many clerical and sales jobs became increasingly routinized and specialized. Personnel managers and office supervisors kept careful tabs on employees, while new office machinery made certain past skills—for example, rapid arithmetic ability—outmoded. In many cases white-collar salaries did not keep pace with the growth of factory pay, and the lines between middle- and working-class living standards increasingly blurred. Not entirely new, this issue of white-collar status became more widespread. Unionization developed more strongly than before among a number of white-collar groups, and strike movements were not unknown. British bank tellers, once a pillar of middle-class respectability, struck on several occasions. In the May, 1968, rising in France, many technicians and clerks joined a larger protest, and some observers felt that in these groups, growing in numbers but also increasingly frustrated, lay the social base for significant future unrest.

Avenues of Social Tension and Change

Europe's postwar social transformation thus produced a number of ambiguous signals. Social patterns seemed simplified in some respects, as certain traditions were stripped away. Peasants were less peasantlike and workers moved closer to middle-class standards in certain respects. Some social rigidities lessened. But a definite social hierarchy persisted, and new complexities moved in to replace the old. A clerical proletariat, though not identical to its factory counterpart, separated more clearly than before from the mainstream middle class. The new, immigrant subproletariat generated new social issues from the bottom of the social heap. Western European society seemed in many ways transitional, as some of the old divisions and conflicts, while still visible, became muted, and new fault lines had yet to become definitely articulated.

Crime   One sign of significant social change and tension lay in crime rates. Levels of violent crime and property crime alike tended to move up in postwar Europe. At first the dislocations and broken families of the war seemed to blame. Gangs of working-class youth in the 1950s, called "Teddy boys" in England or Halb-Stärke (half-strong) in Germany, often came from fatherless households. But the end of postwar dislocations, and significant social gains, did not reverse the crime trends. Forgeries and shopbreaking rose severalfold in the 1960s, and the murder rate nosed upward as well. European crime rates remained markedly lower than those in the United States, but they did generate increasing alarm. The chief constable of Liverpool, England, stated in 1981: "Crime is becoming a real threat to our way of life. If we cannot prevent this dreadful increase, or contain it, the freedom we have been accustomed to for so long will vanish." There was no easy explanation for crime increase among rising affluence. Youth problems, racial tensions, resentment at opportunities that failed to keep pace with expectations, sheer boredom amid routinized work and welfare regulations—all seemed involved. Crime trends expressed the rapid social change of postwar Europe and the complexity and dislocation that change involved.

The Family and the New Roles of Women   Along with shifts in social structure and the major social groups, European family life faced new pressures and opportunities. As with other social characteristics, change blended with some continuity; and new opportunities also bred some new problems.

Family ideals displayed particular continuity, with the middle class again articulating the clearest standards. Middle-class people expected family to provide an atmosphere of affection, even intense passion. Indeed, emphasis on motherhood roles and family warmth were staples of the popular media, particularly in the 1950s. Those in the middle class were sometimes disappointed, and women's expectations in this area were higher than men's. But far more middle-class people claimed to find joyful affection in family than did rural people. The urban working class increasingly shared middle-class ideals and frequently claimed to find loving companionship, if not torrid romance, in marriage. As a British worker put it, "A loving family is the finest thing; something to work for, to look to and to look after," or again, "That's my life, wife and children."

Urban families also expanded their functions as a leisure unit. Television, family vacations, and other activities associated family with the use of nonwork time more fully than ever before. Social contacts with wider kin were sustained by automobiles and telephones. Here was an area in which older family values blended with the new opportunities provided by higher earnings, shorter working lives, and more ample housing.

The clearest innovation in family life came through the new working patterns of women. World War II brought increased factory and clerical jobs for women, as the earlier world war had done. After a few years of downward adjustment, the trends continued. From the early 1950s onward, the number of working women rose steadily in western Europe, as it did in the United States. Women's earlier educational gains had improved their work qualifications; the growing number of service jobs created a need for additional workers—and women, long associated with clerical jobs and paid less than men, were ideal candidates. Many women also sought entry into the labor force as a means of adding to personal or family income, to afford some of the consumer items now becoming feasible but not yet easy to buy, or as a means of personal fulfillment in a society that associated worth with work and earnings. The growing employment of women, which by the 1970s brought the female percentage of the labor force up to 44 percent of the total in several countries, represented particularly the employment of *adult* women, most of them married and many with children. Teenage employment dropped, as more girls stayed in school; but longer-term work commitments rose steadily. This was not, to be sure, a full stride to job equality. Women's pay lagged behind men's. Most women were concentrated in clerical jobs, rather than spread through the occupational spectrum, despite a growing minority of middle-class women who were entering professional and management ranks. Clearly, however, the trends of the initial industrial revolution, to keep women and family separate from work outside the home, had yielded to a dramatic new pattern.

Other new rights for women accompanied this shift. Where women had lacked the vote before, as in France, they now got it; only Switzerland, of the West European nations, doggedly refused this concession at the national level. Gains in higher education were considerable, though again full equality remained elusive. Women constituted 23 percent of German university students in 1963, and under socialist governments in the 1970s the figure rose higher still. Preferred subjects, however, remained different from those of men, as most women stayed out of engineering, science (except medicine), and management. Family rights improved, at least in the judgment of most women's advocates. Access to divorce increased, which many observers viewed as particularly important to women. Long a bitterly partisan issue in Catholic Italy, for example, divorce was finally legalized in the 1960s. Abortion law eased, though more slowly in countries of Catholic background than in Britain or Scandinavia; it became increasingly easy for women to regulate their birth rate. Development of new birth-control methods, such as the contraceptive pill, introduced in 1960, plus growing knowledge and acceptability of birth control, decreased unwanted pregnancies. Sex and procreation became increasingly separate considerations. Although women continued to differ from men in sexual outlook and behavior—over twice as many French women as men, for example, hoped to link sex, marriage, and romantic love, according to 1960s polls—more women than before tended to define sex in terms of pleasure.

The various changes in the status of women had obvious impact on the family. When women worked and contributed to the family budget, their decision-making role in the family improved. Along with continued emphasis on the importance of familial affection, this change helped produce greater equality and a sense of companionship in husband–wife relations. By the 1950s many British workingmen noted that their wives had full rights: "Equal partners, we must agree together in everything." The man who claimed to be boss was viewed as an anachronism. To some observers the contemporary European family constituted effectively a new type, different both from the traditional and from the industrial model: in this "symmetrical family" both spouses worked outside the home, and contributed income, and both shared power and consumer satisfaction, as earnings were pooled for joint decisions about what to buy and what vacations to take.

New Definitions of the Family

Predictably, of course, changes in the family, including the roles of women, brought new issues as well as redefined ideals of companionship. Issue number one involved children. The increase in the European birth rate ended in the early 1960s, and a rapid decline ensued. By the 1970s some countries, led by Germany, had such a low birth rate that, were the trend to continue, by the twenty-first century they would not be able to reproduce themselves except perhaps by immigration. Women working and the desire to use income for high consumer standards mitigated against children, or very many children, particularly in the middle class, where birth rates were lowest. Those children born were increasingly sent, often at an early age, to day-care centers, one of the amenities provided by the European welfare state and particularly essential where new fears about population growth began to surface. European families had few hesitations about replacing maternal care with collective care, and parents often claimed that the result was preferable for children. At the same time, however, some observers worried that European society, and family life, were becoming indifferent to children in an eagerness for adult work and consumer achievements. In Germany a new word, *Kinderfeindlichkeit*, was coined to describe worries about outright hostility to children and to parental responsibilities. To be sure, many families still had children and embraced them in familial affection. There were continued, potentially fruitful changes in the redefinitions of parental styles. It was only in the late 1960s, for example, that German parents began seriously to modify older disciplinary styles toward children, in the interest of becoming more interactive, less authoritarian. Yet it was suggestive that the leading resort club founded in postwar Europe, Club Med, focused on single people and couples, not on families with children, although facilities for the latter were ultimately developed; in contrast, the leading American resort chain, the Disney complex, had a strong child-centered component early on and only gradually moved into more discrete adult activities. It was certainly true that children were built less solidly into the European definition of family success than had previously been the case, and less solidly than was true in the United States.

Family stability also opened new cracks. The European divorce rate went up massively after World War II, but then it declined and stabilized. Divorce rates remained well under United States levels, particularly in the 1950s, suggesting greater familial stability and even conservatism. But with pressures to readjust family roles, with women able to earn outside the family context, and with growing legal freedoms for women, men and women alike began to turn more readily to divorce. In 1961, 9 percent of all British marriages ended in divorce; by 1965 the figure was 16 percent and rising. By the late 1970s a third of all British marriages would end in divorce. Countries with a Catholic background saw greater stability, in some cases because of more restrictive divorce laws; but even there the rate inched upward. The decline of the peasantry facilitated rising divorce, as the strictest kinds of community traditions gave way to greater individualism. Just as earlier in the United States, divorce tended to feed itself; As divorce became more common, stigmas against it declined.

Finally, even aside from divorce, the changing roles of women raised questions about family definitions. Expectations lagged behind reality. Polls taken of German women in the 1960s indicated that a solid majority believed that mothers with children under 12 should stay home; yet in fact a solid majority of such mothers were working. Gaps of this sort, between ideals and practice, suggested that, like European society generally, the family was in a new transition, its end state far from clear.

The development of a new surge of feminist protest, although it reflected far wider concerns than family life alone, showed the strains caused by women's new activities and continued limitations. Growing divorce produced many cases of impoverished women combining work and child care. New work roles revealed the persistent earnings gap between men and women. More generally, many women sought supporting values and organizations as they tried to define new identities, less tied to the domestic roles and images of previous decades.

A new feminism began to take shape with the publication, in 1949, of *The Second Sex*, by the French intellectual Simone de Beauvoir. Echoed in the 1950s and 1960s by other works, in the United States even more than in western Europe, a new wave of women's rights agitation arose after three decades of relative calm. Just as the feminism of the late nineteenth and early twentieth centuries had done, the movement sought specific legal gains for women, particularly now in education and the workplace. Many European governments responded by assuring equal pay for equal work, though the new proclamations had little immediate impact. The new feminism differed from its predecessor, however, in more frankly confronting and disputing the image of woman that had arisen as part of the first adaptation to industrialization and even earlier. For several centuries, in fact, women had become more and more exclusively associated with home and were given standards deemed appropriate for domesticity. Although previous feminist movements had invoked equality, they had often accepted aspects of women's presumably special virtues. Feminists early in the twentieth century, for example, had often urged that women deserved the vote because they were more moral, peaceful, and motherly than men. The new feminism tended to emphasize a more literal equality that would play down special domestic roles and qualities; therefore, it promoted not only specific reforms but more basic redefinitions of what it meant to be male and female.

This new feminism did not win all women, even in the middle class, its most avid audience. It also did not cause some of the most sweeping practical changes that were taking place, as in the new work roles. But it did support the revolution in roles. From the later 1960s onward it pressed European governments for further change, raising issues that were hard to fit into established political contexts. And the new feminism expressed and promoted some unanswered questions about family functions. In a real sense, later twentieth-century feminism seemed to respond to the same desire for individuality and work identity in women that had earlier been urged on men, as part of the new mentality suitable for a commercialized economy. Family remained important in the evolving outlook of women, although some feminist leaders attacked the institution outright as hopelessly repressive. Even for many less ideological women, however, family goals were less important than they had been before.

Postwar Culture

The Arts and Intellectual Life: A Flagging of European Energies

The dynamism that western Europe displayed after World War II in redefining politics and the state and in spurring economic growth was not fully apparent in cultural life, particularly in the intellectual and artistic spheres. Important developments occurred but with a few important exceptions there were no new breakthroughs, no fundamental new visions. Prewar styles and themes persisted in the main, and although there were many able European practitioners no commanding figures emerged outside of quite specific fields. The partial cooling of European intellectual life raised interesting issues for those who judge that, ultimately, cultural creativity is the most accurate measurement of a society and its prospects. It is also possible that intellectual life reflected a channeling of creative energies in other directions, including those of mass culture, where Europe in fact displayed new spark.

One key factor in Europe's relative intellectual lag was a shift of focus toward the United States. Greater political stability in the United States during the 1930s and 1940s, plus Hitler's persecutions, had driven many prominent intellectuals to American shores, where they often remained even as western Europe revived. As American universities expanded, their greater wealth fueled more scientific research; what was called a "brain drain," based on dollar power, drew many leading European scientists to the United States even during the 1950s and 1960s. European science remained active, but the costliness of cutting-edge research produced a durable American advantage. Money also mattered in art, as American patronage became increasingly important and New York replaced Paris as the center of international styles.

Europeans did participate in some of the leading scientific advances of the postwar years. Francis Crick, of Cambridge University in England, shared with the American James Watson key credit for the discovery of the basic structure of the genetic building block deoxyribonucleic acid (DNA), which in turn opened the way for rapid advances in genetic knowledge and industries based on artificial synthesis of genetic materials. Europeans also participated in nuclear research, often through laboratories funded by Common Market or other inter-European agencies. European space research, slower to develop than Soviet or United States initiatives, nevertheless also produced noteworthy achievements by the 1970s, and again there were important commercial spinoffs in communications satellites and other activities. By the 1980s European space research in unmanned vehicles in some respects seemed more solidly based than that of the United States, where greater emphasis had been given to showy—and much more costly—manned space programs.

The European commitment to science thus did not flag. Scientific research everywhere consisted increasingly of largely incremental additions to the knowledge store, rather than sweeping breakthroughs of the Newtonian or Einsteinian sort. It remained true that the clear European leadership, a fact of scientific life since the sixteenth century, seemed to have passed.

Trends in the Arts

Developments in the arts maintained earlier twentieth-century themes quite clearly. Most artists continued to work in the "modern" modes set before World War I, which featured unconventional self-expression and a wide array of nonrepresentational techniques. The clearest change involved growing public acceptance of the modern styles, as the shock that had greeted earlier innovations disappeared and the public, even when preferring older styles displayed in museums or performed by symphony orchestras devoted to the classics, now seemed reconciled to the redefinition of artistic standards.

A number of earlier artists continued their activity into the 1960s. Pablo Picasso, churning out increasingly cartoonlike figures, was a fixture in modern art. Several Bauhaus-trained architects defined modern styles in public buildings, contributing to the aesthetics of contemporary European cities as they rebuilt them, and producing important modern statements in cities such as Berlin. In France, Le Corbusier designed a number of housing projects in glass, steel, and concrete. New names were added to the roster of leading modern artists. Bernard Buffet, in Paris, scored important successes with gaunt, partially abstract figures. The British sculptor Henry Moore produced rounded figures as well as outright abstractions that conveyed some of the horrors of wartime life and postwar dislocations. A new group of "pop" artists in the 1960s tried to bridge the gap between art and commercial mass culture by incorpo-

The prevalence of pop art in Europe in the 1960s was an example of the European search for new expression amid a burgeoning commercial economy faced with rising American influence in vanguard Western culture. Shown is a portion of the American James Rosenquist's *F-111* (1965).

rating cans and other products, comic strips, and advertisements into paintings, prints, and collages. As also held true in the realm of fully abstract painting, American artists increasingly took the lead.

Europeans retained clearer advantages in artistic films. Italian directors produced a number of gripping, realistic films in the late 1940s, portraying both urban and peasant life without frills. Italy, France, and Sweden became centers of experimental filmmaking again in the 1960s. Jean-Luc Godard and Michelangelo Antonioni portrayed the emptiness of urban life, while the Swedish director Ingmar Bergman produced a series of dark psychological dramas. Individual directors in Spain, Britain, and Germany also broke new ground, as Europeans remained more comfortable than Americans in producing films of high artistic merit, relatively free from commercial distractions.

Developments in literature, as in painting, generally continued prewar directions. A variety of French writers concocted the "new novel," which focused on concrete details and descriptions of surfaces and objects, without plot, character development, or a clear sense of the observer's identity. A variety of German novelists were more realistic, using the novel to satirize the frenzied commercial society around them. Heinrich Böll won the Nobel Prize for his *Group Portrait with Lady*, written in 1973, which followed fifty years of Cologne life in the twentieth century through the activities of a young woman.

In music, composers continued to search for new sounds to liberate themselves from conventional tone and harmony. New electronic techniques were added to earlier experimentation, as computers and synthesizers joined instrumentation developed in Europe in the 1930s. Another new trend was the use of silence and chance in "aleatory" music that performers improvised according to general instructions from the composer. The experience of American jazz, which was profoundly influential in Europe, contributed to this development. A number of European composers achieved solid reputations in atonal music and its growing variety of styles, although there remained a wider gap between avant-garde forms and public tastes in music than in most other artistic genres.

Modernism also continued to affect the theater. A Romanian and an Irishman, Eugene Ionesco and Samuel Beckett, both living in Paris and writing in French, were probably the most important postwar playwrights. Both eschewed clear plot and strove instead for symbolic impact. But realistic playwrights won attention also; in England, for example, John Osborne and others used the theater for strong political and social messages.

Overall, the arts reflected significant levels of activity but, in general, a substantial acceptance of stylistic statements developed as much as a century before. In several fields Europeans at least shared eminence with practitioners in the United States, in what was increasingly a transatlantic high culture.

The Social Sciences: Competing Specialties

Important but less than seminal developments occurred in philosophy and the social sciences. As had been the case since the later nineteenth century, little attention was directed toward formal political theory, although Marxist and neoliberal statements were issued. A school of existential philosophy emerged after World War II, centered in Paris but building on work by nineteenth-century German and Scandinavian thinkers. Existential thinkers argued for the fundamental meaninglessness of the physical universe and human existence, both based on random developments rather than any purposeful plan. The novelist Albert Camus emphasized passive acceptance of the insignificance of human action in the face of the blind, powerful workings of the universe. But Camus and others also wrote of the need for humans to construct their own meaning, and typically they argued for powerful political action in the name of the oppressed, of women and of social justice more generally. The existential school, with its pessimism but also its call to action, remained widely popular through the 1950s. In the 1960s, as part of student protest both in Europe and the United States, critical writings of Herbert Marcuse, a European based in California, became popular. Marcuse blasted the conventions of corporate capitalism with its many constraints and injustices, and urged a freeing of the human spirit from consumerist fetters.

Movements of this sort were significant in intellectual as well as political life. It remained true that no sweeping new philosophical vision developed, and that a certain faddishness crept into the movements that did catch on. A number of formal philosophers shied away from large ethical or metaphysical statements altogether, preferring to study the logic of individual statements.

Fragmentation also defined the social sciences, where no commanding figure arose to succeed the Marxes or Webers of previous generations, willing to posit fundamental social dynamics or sweeping theory. Many specific fields in the social sciences turned to massive data collections and pragmatic, detailed observations; in many of these, in turn, United States practitioners developed a decided advantage. Economics, in particular, became something of an American specialty in the post-Keynesian decades and focused on massive quantitative studies of economic cycles and money supplies.

Basic innovation and European leadership did conjoin in the structuralist movement in the social sciences and related literary criticism. Here the leading figure was the French anthropologist Claude Lévi-Strauss. Starting with field work among Indian tribes in Brazil, Lévi-Strauss set out to discover basic, common ingredients in thought processes among primitive peoples generally. By analyzing rituals and myths concerning food and other fundamental activities, Lévi-Strauss believed he could decipher and catalogue a limited number of standard thought processes applicable to all human societies, primitive or not, featuring the logic of pairing, determining opposites, and similar activities. There was a code, in other words, through which human structure could become known. Not only anthropologists but also literary critics, again led by French thinkers, turned increasingly to structuralism to find patterns independent of conscious intent and of historical change alike. By the 1980s French analysts were urging that works of literature, rather than being studied according to historical period, could be "deconstructed" in terms of their fundamental patterns. They claimed, relatedly, that conventional divisions between great literature and common writing might break down in this same process, as taste became less important than structural interpretation.

French intellectuals also contributed to a redefinition of historical study, building on innovations launched between the world wars. Social history, or the focus on changes in the lives of ordinary people, became increasingly the order of the day, giving a great spur to historical research throughout western Europe and the United States. Some French social historians were attracted to a structural approach that downplayed fundamental change, but others retained a lively interest in periodization and the discovery of basic alterations of human and social modes.

Sciences, arts, and social sciences evolved on the whole within the modern intellectual framework established in the more creative period of Western culture of the late nineteenth and early twentieth centuries. Characteristics continued to involve a high degree of specialization and, in many fields including some of the arts, considerable remoteness from ordinary audiences. No vision of a total culture was offered, or at least widely accepted. Scientists, such as some of the structuralists or social historians, occasionally tried to unite a use of scientific and impressionistic methods, or to discuss the deterministic versus socially generated features of the human environment, but most social scientists opted for detail rather than synthesis, while accepting topical divisions of thought— economics, or political science, or sociology—that made unified vision difficult. Finally, in what was perhaps the most important new development, Europeans also lost confidence in their own cultural superiority, as, particularly in science, some of the cutting edge was honed elsewhere.

Religion in a Secular Society

One other development in high culture reflected continuing—or more properly revived—European intellectual energies, although ironically it had ambiguous results. European churches joined other sectors of European society in vowing a postwar renewal. Protestant theologians, continuing strands that had emerged in the interwar decades, urged a return to some fundamental beliefs, including a concern with the pervasiveness of human sin; rationalism and an easy belief in humanitarian progress seemed too shallow, particularly after the Nazi experience.

Renewal of the Catholic church came in a number of forms. Shortly after the war a "worker-priest" movement arose in France, in which priests actively entered working-class life in order to develop an appropriately modern missionary field. The idea was to share worker conditions and concerns in order simultaneously to show the relevance of God's word. The movement enlisted great enthusiasm, though it was viewed askance by church leaders, particularly when it turned out that many priests converted to communism. However, the wider desire to update and popularize the Catholic message remained strong. A new pope, John XXIII

(1958–1963), called the first world Catholic council since 1870. This council, soon known as Vatican II, authorized the use of local languages rather than Latin in the mass, approved discussions with other Christian sects, and vested more power in national church councils. Pope John also stressed the need for Catholic efforts in behalf of social justice and peace. Later popes continued aspects of the updating program, particularly in traveling widely and improving the representation of Asian, Latin American, and African Catholics in church affairs.

The new signs of Christian revival did not, however, seriously reverse the secular tone of European culture, both at formal and popular levels. Church attendance continued to lag. Catholic leaders' insistence on traditional beliefs about issues such as women's rights and birth control limited the effects of their modernization program, and in fact several popes faced serious conflicts with more liberal European bishops and theologians, which in turn confirmed many Europeans in their distaste for formal religion. Christianity remained significant in European intellectual life, but on the margins. At the popular level, religion was now a minority current. The Catholic church, still European-based and -led, found its vibrant support now in Latin America and Africa, and to an extent the United States, not amid the skeptical tides of European society, where religion was at most just another of the various intellectual fragments operating in the postwar decades.

A Lively Popular Culture

Western Europe displayed more vitality in its popular culture than in formal intellectual life, which reflected the concentration on economic and social change. Here too, as in previous decades and as in high culture, United States influence was strong in what was in so many respects a common North Atlantic pattern. As European economies struggled to recover from the war, and as American military forces spread certain enthusiasms more widely than before, some observers indeed spoke of an American "Coca-cola-nization" of Europe. American soft drinks, blue-jeaned fashions, gum, and other artifacts became increasingly common. American films continued to wield substantial influence, although the lure of Hollywood declined somewhat. More important was the growing impact of American-made television series. American television, blessed with a wide market and revenues generated from advertising, was quite simply "slicker" than its European counterparts, and series such as the western drama "Bonanza" or the soap opera "Dallas," and many other shows, appeared regularly on European screens to define, for better or worse, an image of the United States for Europeans.

In contrast to the interwar decades, however, European popular culture had its own power, and it even began to influence the United States as well. The most celebrated figures of popular culture in the 1960s were unquestionably the Beatles, from the British port city of Liverpool. The Beatles, to be sure, adopted popular music styles of the United States, including jazz and early rock. But they added an authentic working-class touch in their scoffing at authority and hierarchy, and their celebration of impulsiveness as against traditional British reserve. They also expressed a good-natured desire to enjoy the pleasures of life, which is characteristic of modern Western popular culture regardless of national context. British popular music groups continued to set standards in the 1970s and had wide impact on western Europe more generally.

Other facets of popular culture displayed new vigor. Again in Britain, youth fashions, separate from the standards of the upper class, showed an ability to innovate and sometimes to shock. Unconventional uses of color and cut, as in "punk" hair styles of the later 1970s, bore some resemblance to the anticonventional tone of modern painting and sculpture.

Sexual culture also changed in western Europe, building on earlier trends that linked sex to a larger pleasure-seeking mentality characteristic of growing consumerism, and to a desire for personal expression. European films and television shows demonstrated more relaxed standards about sexual display than did their counterparts in the United States. In countries such as Britain, Holland, and Denmark, "sex shops" sold a wide array of erotic materials and products.

Like the United States, western Europe experienced important changes in actual sexual behavior starting around 1960, particularly among young people. Premarital sex became more common. The average age of first sexual intercourse began to go down. For a time, as a result, rates of illegitimate births began to rise once more, after a long period of stability

Punk styles flourished in London in the 1970s.

since 1870. But Europeans adjusted relatively easily to the new habits and began urging the use of birth control devices to teenagers; in contrast, reactions in the United States were more tentative and prudish, with the result that teenage ignorance of birth control measures remained more widespread. Expressive sexuality in western Europe was also evident in the growing number of nude bathing spots, again in interesting contrast to more hesitant initiatives in the United States. Although the association of modern popular culture with sexuality and body concern was not novel, the openness and diversity of expression unquestionably reached new levels and also demonstrated western Europe's new confidence in defining a vigorous, nontraditional mass culture of its own.

Cultural innovation, like social change, brought disturbance as well as enthusiasm. Although critics of changing tastes were less numerous and less political than between the wars—there was no counterpart to the Nazi attack on modern styles or women's fashions—there was concern about the disparity between formal intellectual life, where energies might be flagging, and the vibrancy of youth-oriented popular styles. Other observers wondered whether enthusiasms for new fashions and anti-establishment lyrics misleadingly distracted ordinary people in what was still a hierarchical society—but this, of course, was a complex subject that had emerged with the birth of modern popular culture itself.

Clouds on the Horizon of a Renewed Europe: 1968 and After

The clear theme of western European history in the 1950s and 1960s was renewal. Observers wrote persuasively of a "new Europe." Trends in leadership, in politics and intra-European diplomacy, in the economy, in social relations, and even in important aspects of culture all seemed to display new confidence and vigor, despite the reduced place of Europe in the wider world. By 1980, however, this tone had changed. Without denying important changes and solid trends—without ignoring, certainly, the contrast between postwar Europe and the "doldrums society" of the interwar years—assessment increasingly dealt with problems and uncertainties. The fact was that Europe's upward trajectory, although not reversed, was at least slowed from 1968 onward. The excitement of rebuilding waned. Leadership changed hands from those who had previously concentrated on making sure that Europe did not repeat past mistakes. Adenauer, de Gaulle, and the initial architects of the Common Market passed from the scene, and many questioned whether their successors had comparable vision or ability.

Student Protest and the Strike Movement

The first clear chink in the new Europe opened with the youth rebellions of the late 1960s. The spread of youth protest—primarily among secondary school and university students—was not simply a western European phenomenon. It affected the Americas, Africa, and eastern Europe as well. Young people in many societies may have come to believe that adults, from parents through teachers, had less to teach them than was once the case, as change had become so rapid. Student conditions certainly generated discontent, as had in fact often been the case in the past. The transition between childhood and adulthood could be painful, as students felt ready to contribute more and decide more than school systems allowed. International issues played a role; students in many countries were outraged at ongoing signs of imperialism, particularly in the United States's war against communist rebels and their allies in Vietnam. This issue triggered massive outbursts within the United States, where anxiety about the military draft supplemented ideological concerns, but it also fueled European unrest as well.

There were more specifically European issues. Students in the late 1960s faced extremely crowded schools and classrooms, as the late stages of the baby boom surged into outmoded facilities. The authoritarian character of European universities, which left students with little faculty contact, added to discontent. Many students also resented the failure of universities seriously to recruit from the lower classes. And some, more pragmatically, were fearful for their own futures; many student rebels came from disciplines such as history or sociology, where job prospects were uncertain. A large number of students also resented what they saw as sell-outs by their parents, many of whom had been politically radical in their own student days but now seemed comfortably ensconced in one of the prosperous bureaucracies.

Serious student protest burst forth in a number of European centers. German universities were disrupted by demonstrations and the formation of left-wing and even terrorist groups from 1967 to 1971. Italian students protested frequently, sometimes clashing with rightist organizations. Again, a small minority of students entered new political organizations to the left of the Communist party, and some began to experiment with terrorist violence. British universities, where faculty–student contact was more extensive, were less troubled, but there were significant protests at the London School of Economics. The most spectacular rising occurred at the University of Paris, in May 1968. A student protest movement against university careerism, whereby docile technocrats were trained to serve the established order, escalated into classroom sit-ins and overreactions by the police. By mid-May, the university quarter of Paris's Left Bank lay in student hands, with barricades established to block police attack. Campus seizures occurred in other university centers in France, in the wake of the Paris rising.

Student goals were varied. As in any major protest movement they included quite practical concerns about the adequacy of facilities amid rising enrollments, as well as sweeping ideological appeals. Student ideology was itself rather diffuse. Its targets were clear enough: the establishment, imperialism, big business. But many student leaders reacted more generally against the lures and deceptions of consumer society, scorning materialism and the success ethic of the middle class. And they also attacked the dominant rationalism and pragmatism of Western culture. In their stead, students appealed to spontaneity and action, with slogans such as "imagination has seized power," and "be realistic: demand the impossible." These student goals were sincerely felt, and they were also fascinating, as an ongoing reminder of the tension between restraint and release in modern Western popular culture—a tension that young people experienced perhaps most keenly. But there were drawbacks to the vagueness of the student appeals as well, for students had difficulty touching base with other protest groups, including more conventional radicals who operated in the rationalist tradition, and also failed to develop solid protest organizations beyond a very small-group level.

Nevertheless, the Paris student rising did trigger a wider social upheaval, in what almost turned into a revolutionary effort. Workers in France and elsewhere had become increasingly troubled, during the 1960s, by nagging inflation that often saw wages lag behind prices; by the end of the decade inflation was speeding up, conveying a sense of an economy out of control. High strike rates in many countries responded to this pressure. Workers were also troubled by routine and boring jobs. Better educated than ever before, many workers found assembly-line conditions demanding and monotonous. Trade unions often seemed unresponsive to concerns about work satisfaction, and government regulations were part of the problem. Many Swedish workers preferred to live off unemployment insurance rather than submit to bureaucratized boredom, at least until key companies began to modify assembly-line specialization with greater job variety. White-collar concerns about routinized jobs and inadequate mobility opportunities sometimes supplemented the anxieties of skilled factory workers.

During the Paris student rising in 1968, crowds clashed with police on the Boulevard St. Michel, protesting the cordoning off of the university and the order for its evacuation by occupying students.

These various labor grievances erupted after French students had taken the lead. Headed by workers in the most technologically advanced industries, such as automobiles, and by some white-collar technicians, a massive strike movement formed, ultimately spreading to ten million people. Student radicals eagerly sought contact with dissident workers, with some success. But union leaders, and also communist politicians, had no interest in the student demands and indeed feared the vague radicalism (and the middle-class backgrounds) of the university rebels. So most workers occupied their factories, in large part because their leaders wished to insulate them from the school risings, rather than setting up barricades of their own. And workers stressed pay and work quality demands, not the anticonsumerist rhetoric of the youth movement.

In this situation the government of Charles de Gaulle, initially caught unaware by the most significant social movement since the mid-1930s, was able to react. Workers were bought off by a huge raise. Elections in June gave de Gaulle a solid majority, as frightened Frenchmen, including many communists, sought to preserve their postwar gains against the disruption of a month of economic paralysis and against the uncongenial lifestyles of student radicals. The revolt was over.

However, youth protest had a number of durable aftereffects, despite the overt failure of the most sweeping movements. Consumer society was not reversed, but it was revealed as a more fragile construct than had often been imagined. University life was quietly revolutionized. Governments took specific student grievances quite seriously and began to give students and young faculty members much greater voice over university affairs. German universities became the most democratic in the world—at some cost, observers claimed, to the quality of technical training. Finally, although large student movements declined somewhat by the early 1970s, a mood of agitation persisted among some European youth—in contrast to the United States, where student rebellion virtually disappeared after 1973. And small radical groups, recruited mainly from former students, continued to affect European political life as they adopted terrorist tactics. Particularly in Italy and Germany, Red Brigades and similar organizations participated in bombings and kidnappings periodically through the 1970s, adding a new and troubling element to the European political scene. Overall, student disruptions did not fundamentally alter the course of modern European history, and in certain ways they led to creative responses by government and school authorities; but they did mark a mood of greater uncertainty than had characterized the Europe of the postwar "renaissance."

"The Decline of Europe"

The student–labor crisis was followed by new economic difficulties. In 1973 the nations on which Europe was dependent for oil, headed by the Organization of Petroleum-Exporting Countries (OPEC), cut production and raised prices, initially in response to a Middle Eastern war with Israel. Oil prices remained high through the 1970s and in fact rose again in a second energy crisis in 1979, triggered by a revolution in Iran. High energy prices in turn fed the inflationary pressures of the European economy, and also led to setbacks in manufacturing and employment levels. This crisis revealed more deep-seated problems, as European industries faced new, cheaper competition from East Asia and other areas. Key sectors, such as automobiles and steel, could no longer expand, and indeed some of the less efficient units could not even maintain existing production levels. During most of the 1970s the economic performance of western Europe remained adequate; only after the second oil crisis did full-scale recession intrude, with rising rates of unemployment. But it was clear that the easy growth of the postwar decades had ended. Furthermore, new kinds of economic problems surfaced: even as production grew more slowly, prices continued to rise, a simultaneous stagnation and inflation quickly if inelegantly dubbed as "stagflation." Efforts to spur investment to end the stagnation problems pressed prices up, while anti-inflationary measures made unemployment worse.

As in the face of student unrest, European governments and business leaders were not lacking in creative responses to the economic challenges. New conservation measures helped reduce dependence on imported oil. Several nations embarked on rapid development of nuclear energy production. Some of the more out-of-date branches of the steel industry were closed. European productivity rates continued to improve, more rapidly in fact than those of the United States. But in the tighter economic climate of the 1970s, responses to problems generated other problems. Closing inefficient plants spurred labor protest. Development of nuclear power created new environmentalist concerns. Neither socialist nor conservative leaders offered clear new directions, as opposed to piecemeal reactions.

Furthermore, European political initiatives during the 1970s seemed increasingly anemic. The vigorous postwar leadership had ended. De Gaulle resigned soon after the student unrest drew to a close, over a minor political issue—almost as though this last of the great Allied warhorses grew tired of keeping up. The new leaders of most Western countries, whether conservative or socialist, were rather cautious, content to be managers rather than visionaries. In some countries, such as Britain, economic tensions combined with political timidity produced a recurrent alternation of governments, with a Conservative majority succeeding Labour and then yielding in turn, as though voters were sure only that they did not want to retain the party in power. In Italy changes of government became more frequent amid high inflation and political terrorism. West German leadership in the 1970s, under the Social Democratic party for the first time since Weimar, did display greater initiative. The West Germans opened new contacts with eastern European nations, including the Soviet Union, while remaining attached to their alliances with NATO and the Common Market. The idea was to use West Germany as a key actor in reducing cold war tensions, while also improving chances for exports and for contacts with communist East Germany. The West German government also actively expanded welfare programs and extended educational opportunities. German welfare expenses increased dramatically. But in Germany too, by the late 1970s, as also in France, leadership became more and more cautious, preferring to react to events rather than to anticipate.

Some observers saw new political troubles brewing beneath this some-what uninspiring surface. Voter participation began to fall in western Europe, though it remained far higher than in the United States. Many people seemed less able than before to identify strongly with the leading political parties. The rise of small but active leftist movements showed disillusionment with communist and socialist leaders who had clearly re-nounced revolution—who indeed, in the France of 1968, had actively opposed worker unrest beyond the confines of a major strike. Some new issues, such as environmentalism and feminist demands for fuller rights for women, did not fit neatly into existing party alignments, causing some speculation that the political spectrum that had framed European politics for over thirty years was about to burst apart.

As the economy became more troubled and politics less imaginative, some observers reversed the optimistic scenarios that had described Eu-rope's postwar resurgence into the 1960s. Instead of hymns to a Euro-pean renaissance, books now bore such titles as *A Continent Adrift*, and by the early 1980s American magazines, eager to capitalize on any apparent trend, featured special articles on "The Decline of Europe." This pessi-mism was overdrawn, or at least premature. The 1970s produced a dif-ferent mood from that of the two previous decades in western Europe, but they hardly played a dirge. New economic difficulties did not de-stroy democratic regimes, as had been the case between the wars. The arrival of parliamentary democracy in Spain and Portugal, during these very years, suggested the vitality of what now seemed the standard Western political form. The 1970s also witnessed the development of Eurocom-munism, a sign of some flexible thinking on the part of key leaders on the left. Indeed, in 1980 many European leaders, such as the pragmatic socialist prime minister of Germany, professed greater doubts about the stability of their ally the United States than about the future of their own societies. After all, they noted, despite the general advent of new eco-nomic difficulties and slower growth, unemployment rates in the United States remained considerably higher than those of western Europe, while rates of saving, investment, and productivity growth were lower. Levels of crime and family disruption were far higher in the United States, suggesting problems of adjustment considerably greater than those of western Europe. American politics hardly seemed a model of stability, as the presidency changed parties with each election; and as to the quality of leadership, Europeans were prone to mutter about peanut farmers and movie actors who ended up as presidents.

It was not easy around 1980 to neatly characterize western Europe's condition and prospect. Was it more troubled than in the early 1960s? Yes. Was it on the verge of collapse? Not clearly. Was western Europe politically and economically weaker than the United States, or indeed most other societies in the world apart perhaps from Japan? Debatable at most. Developments during the 1980s would sharpen some of these questions and possibly suggest some more clearly pessimistic answers. They also raised some new questions about how to place recent Euro-pean history in the perspective of a larger past. But even at the end of the 1980s western Europe remained a society difficult to label, still swim-ming strongly in the currents of change.

TEN

POSTWAR EASTERN EUROPE AND THE WEST IN THE EARLY 1980S

1953	Death of Joseph Stalin
1956	Krushchev launches de-Staliniza-tion campaign
1956	Hungarian rising and its suppres-sion
1968	Czechoslovak rising and its suppression
1980 ff	Polish Solidarity agitation and its suppression
1980 ff	Reductions in welfare state out-lays in Western Europe and the United States
1980	The Reagan administration in the United States
1980 ff	Rise of new minority political parties in France, Germany, Brit-ain
1981	Socialists win French government; new nationalizations
1982	Christian Democrats regain power in West Germany

CHAPTER

TEN

THE CONTEMPORARY WEST IN TIME AND PLACE

THE RENEWAL OF WESTERN EUROPE after World War II, and the several changes in direction it has since undergone, raise a number of issues about defining the West in the world and placing postwar Western civilization in the continuum of its own past. After the war, Western society continued to relate closely to a number of other geographical areas. The divisions, but also the parallelisms with eastern Europe, now made less accessible culturally by communist regimes, remained vitally important, both from the analytical standpoint—toward determining how diverging traditions on a single continent continued to evolve—and in very real political terms, as people on both sides of the cold-war divide wondered about how to coexist. The complex relationship within the Western tradition between Europe and the United States also took on new dimensions, and these were also important from both theoretical and practical standpoints. Finally, although western Europe's role in the wider world undoubtedly declined, Europeans continued to wield considerable influence. Putting recent western European history in its proper geographical context is a vital part of bringing any analysis of the modern experience to a close.

The concluding task also involves further consideration of Europeans' conception of themselves. Many Westerners seemed to find Europe's adjustment to the postwar world, a fairly painless process. Just as Sweden, after exercising wide power in Germany and the Baltic regions in the seventeenth century, sank back after 1700 into second-rate power status without loss of internal vigor or morale, so may western Europeans prove able to build on domestic success even as their wider influence wanes.

But aggressive nationalism was by no means dead in western Europe. A brief war between Britain and Argentina in 1982 over the Falkland islands off the coast of Argentina revealed a surprisingly powerful—some said mindless—nostalgia for imperial power on the part of most Britons that led to a bitter, if brief, struggle over dubious real estate and to a decisive British victory. Thus Europeans may not be as calm about loss of power as some measurements suggest. Their nervousness about being caught between two superpowers surfaced frequently in various forms of anti-Americanism. Communist and, at times, socialist movements frequently protested American military and economic presence in Europe—from the late 1950s onward. More conservative observers usually accepted this presence but bemoaned American cultural impact, in the form of linguistic innovations, commercial styles, and television shows; the United States was a convenient target for attacks on mass taste in general. Conservative politicians, most notably Charles de Gaulle, sought further to develop a European power base separate from the United States, although with incomplete success. More popular anti-Americanism surfaced again, in the early 1980s, in powerful disarmament movements and new resentments against United States power and policy. A comfortable new place for Europe in the world, even after four decades of unusual peace, had yet to be defined.

The problem of placing the postwar West in terms of its past is another aim of this summary chapter. A number of leading themes, though very general ones, had run through European history from the sixteenth and seventeenth centuries onward—themes about economic and social structure, science, technology, political organization, and outlook. Where did the postwar West sit in relation to these themes? There were some signs that certain staples of the modern experience were being transformed. For example, could modern European traditions about the family survive the revolution in women's roles and values? For several centuries, women had been increasingly associated with domesticity in the West, first through the early modern emphasis on the affectionate family, then through the industrial revolution's attack on women's functions in economic production. With women returned to the labor force, some change in domestic ideals and pervasive women's imagery seemed inevitable, and this might lead to a new, "postmodern" pattern that would alter some durable modern trends. Were classical capitalism and the nation-state—two other longstanding forces in modern Western history—giving way to essentially new forms of welfare planning and inter-European collaboration? Was technology so changing the social structure, by redefining the proletariat from factory hands to office workers, that earlier formulas and divisions no longer applied? There were those who argued that western Europe (and the United States) had moved from preindustrial, to protoindustrial, to industrial forms and now, in at least as great a transformation, were pushing toward an unprecedented postindustrial form, not only in technology or occupational layers but in family life and personality traits as well.

As is true in locating the West in the geographical context of its loss of world power, the issues involved in placing it in relation to its past

The new power of popular sentiments for disarmament was based in part on massive protest marches such as this one in London's West End in 1981.

were not merely theoretical. Some observers argued that the West was changing so much in the postwar decades that its solidity, its buffering layers of tradition, were being fatally weakened. This argument, too, must be assessed.

Finally, of course, Western history refused to hold still. Developments after 1980, in a variety of spheres, suggested new vigor and new problems, and these too must be built into a final assessment of the West and its prospects. Western history provided no neat "1980s revolution," by which a historical account might dramatically end, for as in most previous decades change was a matter of incremental processes, not conclusive events. But the trajectories of this decade can be assessed and in fact related to the larger framework of time and place.

The West and the World

To most Africans or Asians (including the more technologically advanced Japanese), the West in the later twentieth century remained a fairly definable entity, bonded by shared values and institutions and based on many centuries of shared history. The West included the western European core, of course, but also the United States, Canada, Australia, and New Zealand. Beyond these, many other societies shared or tried to imitate Western patterns. Thus Western artistic styles, industrial forms, and even political institutions were no longer a Western monopoly. Nevertheless, there was a Western identity, composed of a distinctive combination of discrete characteristics. Thus India was a parliamentary democracy after 1947 but hardly Western in culture or economy; Japan was as industrialized as the West but possessed somewhat different values and institutions; eastern Europe continued to bear a special historical relationship to the West but was more fully separate in its political forms than before the war. For their part, many Westerners were conscious of common bonds across a wide geographical span. National pride still butted against the larger Western coherence, to be sure, and Westerners were particularly uncertain about how fully a common civilization embraced both western Europe and its noisy offspring across the North Atlantic.

Indeed western European developments from 1945 through the 1980s often called forth characterizations that placed this society on a middle ground, structurally as well as geographically, between United States capitalism and Soviet communism. For example, the Swedish welfare state has been described as a "middle way" between the more clear-cut forms to the west or the east. The terminology was frankly inexact, as the United States continued to resemble western European patterns more closely than did the Soviet Union. But the characterization is one example of the genuine problem of capturing the identity of western Europe amid those of other closely related societies.

Eastern and Western Europe

Eastern Europe, led militarily, economically, and politically by the Soviet Union, seemed to transform traditional distinctions from the West into clear-cut differences after World War II. A more autocratic political past loomed larger as communist regimes spread as far as East Germany—just as the Western nations were adopting or confirming parliamentary democracy. Longstanding rural differentiations, which had once contrasted Eastern serfdom with freer peasant conditions in the West, were now redefining into divisions between the collective farmers of the East and their commercially minded Western counterparts. Even as the worst tensions of the cold war, with its "iron curtain" rhetoric, receded after the 1950s, East and West seemed more firmly divided than ever before. At the same time, however, ongoing industrialization in eastern Europe brought new similarities to Western industrial patterns, particularly as new forms of management spread in Western capitalism; corporate managers in the West, no longer freelance entrepreneurs, were not totally different from the bureaucrats who directed state-run factories in eastern Europe. Also, eastern European politics were not monolithic, as the rigidities of the Stalinist decades gave way to somewhat greater flexibility. And eastern Europeans, often proud of their own social and political forms and eager to avoid strictly Western models, nevertheless remained attracted by much of what they knew of the West. This paradox, though no novelty, also continued to link the two parts of the European continent.

The Soviet Union   The Soviet Union had suffered severely during World War II; its traditional suspicion of the outside world and fear of further attack were confirmed by its devastation at the hands of the Nazis. Yet the war had not crippled the Soviet industrialization effort, and solid economic growth quickly resumed, with some help from equipment and designs brought in from Germany and other parts of eastern Europe. By 1950, indeed, the Russian industrialization process had in some senses been completed, as the giant nation passed the fifty percent urbanization mark with half its population in the cities. As it had before World War II, Russian industrialization operated under a radically different economic system from that of the West; state ownership of all factories and centralized planning of all economic and industrial growth took the place of the West's elaborate competitive market mechanisms; the emphasis on heavy industry, rather than consumer goods, also remained. Food production continued to be a trouble spot, as the collective farms (in which they had no individual ownership stake in the land) failed to motivate peasants to maximum effort. Attempts to defy the Russian climate by extending agriculture toward the north also diverted resources during the 1950s. Nevertheless, the Soviet economy supported gradual improvements in living standards and also a mighty military apparatus.

Soviet domination of eastern Europe, as established by 1948, was solidified not only by communist control over the apparatus of government but also by a formal military and economic alliance, the Warsaw Pact, and by the stationing of Russian troops in the various Eastern-bloc countries. Many features of the Soviet system were imposed, from one-party rule at the top to collectivization of agriculture and state-run industries at the bottom. Opposition political movements were crushed, often with considerable brutality, and occasional popular risings, as in East Germany, were firmly put down.

Soviet rigidity eased slightly, however, from 1953 onward, with the death of Stalin. No single leader gained power comparable to Stalin's, and the use of police repression also moderated somewhat. Committees that selected new leaders balanced various interest groups in the Soviet hierarchy—the army, the secret police, and the Communist party apparatus—and major initiatives were for the most part precluded as entrenched interests geared to defend their established prerogatives. In 1956 a new Russian leader, Nikita Khrushchev, attacked Stalin's dictatorial approach, blasting the late leader's crimes against opponents. This current of "de-Stalinization" roused great interest in the eastern European satellite states, eager to loosen Russian control. More liberal communist leaders arose in Hungary and Poland, seeking to create governments that, although communist, would allow greater diversity. In Poland the Russians accepted a new leader more popular with the Polish people; among other

Soviet tanks guard a Budapest intersection during the anti-Communist demonstrations that swept the city during the Hungarian revolt of 1956.

results, Poland was, alone of the East-bloc nations, allowed to halt agricultural collectivization in favor of peasant holdings. But a new regime in Hungary was brutally crushed by the Russian army, showing the limits of de-Stalinization. Within the Soviet Union itself, de-Stalinization produced a reduction of political trials and somewhat greater subtlety on the part of the political police. Massive purges and forced Siberian labor eased, although dissidents were still punished, often by enforced stints in insane asylums. Some cultural diversity was permitted, which among other things led to greater contacts with Western intellectuals and artists. But the apparatus of the state, including the one-party system, centralized economic planning, and propaganda control, remained intact.

Indeed, after the immediate de-Stalinization furor patterns in Russia remained unusually stable. Economic growth continued, but without dramatic breakthroughs and with persistent worries over sluggish productivity, unresponsive central planning and periodically inadequate harvests, the latter resulting in expensive grain purchases from Western nations. Khrushchev himself was eased from power in part because ambitious industrial and agricultural plans failed to yield promised results. Several subsequent leadership changes occurred, often with initial promises of major overhaul, particularly of the centralized planning system, but in fact established patterns persisted. By the same token, transitions from one leader to the next were handled smoothly, as committee decisions were respected even amid jockeying by ambitious aspirants.

In 1985 a new, reformist current developed in Soviet politics when Mikhail Gorbachev took over the leadership of the government. Gorbachev pressed for change on several fronts. He sought to improve the standing of the Soviet Union in Western eyes by allowing somewhat greater freedom for political dissent and by more open communication about conditions and even problems in Soviet society. He urged a reduction in nuclear armament, and in 1987 negotiated a new agreement with the United States that limited medium-range missiles in Europe. Internally, Gorbachev proclaimed a policy of *glasnost,* or "openness," which implied new freedom to comment and criticize. He pressed particularly for a reduction in bureaucratic inefficiency and unproductive labor in the Soviet economy, sketching more decentralized decision-making and the use of some market incentives to stimulate greater output. The sweep of Gorbachev's reforms, as opposed to an undeniable new tone in Soviet public relations, remained difficult to assess. Strong limits on political freedom remained, and it was unclear whether Gorbachev could cut through the centralized planning apparatus that controlled the main lines of the Soviet economy.

Soviet military development persisted, with growing strength in nuclear weaponry and rocket systems. The Soviets superpower position was dramatized by leadership in many manned space probes and by growing success in international athletic competitions, including the Olympic Games. The control of eastern Europe loosened slightly after the Hungarian revolt, for heavy-handed repressions cost considerable prestige, including disaffection among western European Communist parties and intellectuals. Eastern European governments were given a freer hand in economic policy—Hungary, for example, decentralized economic planning and improved consumer levels—and were allowed limited room to experiment with greater cultural freedom. Although interactions with Western political, business, and intellectual figures did not attain prewar levels in countries such as Poland, Hungary, and Czechoslovakia, there was renewed interchange, and a considerably greater sense of contact than prevailed in the Soviet Union itself. There was even an influx of Western tourists. In Romania, leadership combined a strong police state internally with new flexibility in foreign policy, occasionally even contradicting Soviet interests.

Severe limits remained in the smaller eastern European states, however, as Soviet leaders insisted not only on basic military control but also on substantial political conformity. An attempt to create a more liberal regime in Czechoslovakia, in 1968, brought Soviet army repression, and this historically most "Western" of the eastern European states constructed a strongly autocratic regime. Renewed agitation in Poland, in the late 1970s, featured strong Catholic opposition to communist rule, nationalist resentment of Russian authority, and worker rebellion against poor living standards and the official, communist-dominated trade union movement. Massive demonstrations did not bring outright Soviet intervention, but the situation was carefully monitored and the Polish army gradually ended disorder without major concessions. The Soviet Union also directly entered Afghanistan in the late 1970s, against Muslim movements that seemed to threaten disruption among a key Soviet minority— another sign that Soviet policy, although cautious in many ways, brooked no major shifts in what was, in effect, a new empire.

Typical of the overwhelmingly Catholic Poland, and the role of the Catholic church in protest there, a mass was celebrated at the entrance to the Gdansk shipyard, birthplace of the Solidarity trade union movement, in August 1980. Lech Walesa, a key figure in the movement, is at the far left.

Eastern Europe and the West: Affinities and Contrasts   Eastern European society was not, however, totally removed from Western patterns. Both parts of Europe enjoyed a common cultural fund. Classical music repertoires, ballet, and art derived from a shared tradition, and as cultural exchanges resumed after Stalin this aspect of "European-ness" proved genuinely meaningful. New trends also brought important convergences between East and West. Both societies became increasingly secular—although in the East this resulted from a forced march away from church influence and not simply the corroding effects of prosperity, science, and the like. The unusual power of Catholicism in Poland, a symbol of national resistance, contrasted with Christian decline in the West as well as the East. Aspects of social structure also revealed new similarities. Both East and West were now largely urban, though the rural percentage remained higher in the East. Major social groups emphasized the importance of limiting family size in order to raise its standards of living and in order to assure considerable attention to those children born. In eastern Europe a new managerial class, composed of Communist party leaders and directors of state-run enterprises, behaved similarly to its managerial counterpart in the West—a fact noted and lamented by disillusioned critics of eastern Europe's fading revolutionary zeal. Eastern managers proved jealous of guarding their positions and assuring their children's educational advantages, eager for new consumer items and vacations, interested in a close-knit, nuclear family. In eastern Europe most women worked, but this was increasingly true in the West as well; in both societies, despite communist propaganda to the contrary, full job equality was not achieved, and women continued to bear disproportionate family responsibilities.

In sum, shared traditions and the common dynamic of industrial society produced important commonalities between East and West, producing, as in previous modern centuries, significant overlap.

Yet the distinctions remained important as well. The absence of serious parliamentary forms and political opposition in eastern Europe was no hollow fact. Legislatures such as the supreme Soviet were elected by universal suffrage, but without real choice; and they largely rubber-stamped decisions already taken by the Communist party executive. Government functions were far more extensive than in the West, in directing a wider-ranging welfare operation—including state-run vacation resorts—in making basic allocation decisions for agriculture and industry, as well as in sustaining an elaborate political police and an official press.

For its part, although Soviet culture emphasized some heritage shared with the West, it remained profoundly suspicious of contemporary Western cultural forms. Modern art and music were largely anathema; more traditional Soviet styles, augmented by the passion for "socialist realism" that glorified heroic workers and soldiers in painting, sculpture, and story, were officially promoted. Suspicion of foreignness combined with a perceptive grasp of the nonrational implications of Western art to make Soviet authorities, eager to portray a progressive, rationally controllable environment, retreat from the West's influence. Limited contacts, and the somewhat fuller access of the smaller eastern European countries, reduced the cultural isolation of the Stalinist years and produced some small bows to modernism, but a real gulf remained. By eschewing elaborate attention to consumer interests, Soviet patterns of industrialization helped produce a distinctive society as well. Despite massive economic changes, the Soviet Union could still seem economically backward in Western eyes, given pervasive shortages and shoddy quality in the consumer goods sector. Nothing like the consumerist culture of the West was allowed to develop, not only because economic productivity could not yet sustain it but because, in Soviet eyes, it seemed misplaced effort: too shallowly materialistic, and too devoted to individual pleasure-seeking rather than social gain. It was also true that the race to develop atomic weapons and missile systems, between the United States and the Soviet Union, channeled a high proportion of Soviet production into the military sphere.

New Issues in Eastern Europe   Some of the ongoing differences between East and West in Europe also raised questions about the future of the communist regimes. Soviet planning, despite setbacks and inefficiencies, had produced a solid industrial economy. But there were doubts about its openness to further change. By the 1970s it was clear that the Soviet Union was lagging well behind the West in adopting new technologies such as the computer. Centralized planning was often wedded to routine and not pressed by market factors of supply and demand; therefore, it joined with the fears of an authoritarian state about too much innovation, particularly in the area of information-exchange technology. Some Westerners wondered whether eastern Europe was not locked into what was an increasingly outmoded industrial system by Western standards. Questions also arose about worker motivation. In the West, the routine jobs and intense discipline of modern work had been cushioned, at least to an extent, by growing consumer pleasures. In eastern Europe, although welfare systems provided security, consumer pleasures were scanty. By the 1970s, flagging rates of worker productivity, plus growing levels of alcoholism, suggested that motivation problems had become widespread. Yet a conversion to Western-style consumerism was profoundly foreign both to tradition and to the interests of an autocratic, militaristic state.

Real or potential problems in eastern Europe—and Russian authorities of course pointed vigorously to different sign of disruption in the West—did not reach the solid roots of the communist system, at least in the Soviet Union. With the reduction of Stalinist-style fears, with real gains in education, welfare, and living standards, and with real pride in Russia's new world prestige, most Soviet citizens showed no active desire for massive change, even aside from the absence of easy, legal outlets for protest and the restrictions on information among ordinary people concerning Western alternatives. Humor and traditional resignation helped cushion the rough spots and inefficiencies. There seemed little likelihood of a major shift in directions in eastern Europe—and so little likelihood of significant reduction of the distinctions that continued to divide East and West as societies, despite new reform interests of Soviet leaders in the late 1980s.

This continuing gulf had its own impact on western Europe. The fact of being different from eastern Europe was not new, although some of the forms of differentiation and certainly the precise geographical boundaries had changed. But being *militarily inferior* was a novel experience, and a troubling one. Some Westerners found advantages in the Soviet system, although with Eurocommunism and, in France, a notable reduction of communist strength, this overlap was declining by the 1980s. Other Western leaders, not at all communist, nevertheless looked to the stability of eastern Europe and to shared traditions as important facts that cold war alignments did not sufficiently account for. Thus West German leaders, particularly but not exclusively Social Democrats, worked toward more solid economic and cultural bridges with East Germany as a vital supplement to Western commitments, when the new *Ostpolitik* or "eastern policy" opened in the 1970s. Thus Charles de Gaulle, eager to free France from what he saw as excessive American and English influence, spoke nostalgically of a "Europe to the Urals"—a Europe that, despite internal differences, had sufficient commonalities to operate as a single diplomatic and cultural system against the overweening brashness of the New World.

The growing power of the Soviet system was a vital fact in shaping the postwar West and its prospects; the overlap between Eastern and Western systems and traditions continued to play a role in the self-definitions of both regions.

Western Europe and the United States

If eastern Europe became a distant relative to the West, not really familiar yet linked by memories of shared kinship, the United States turned into a neighboring cousin, independent and noisily successful but careful to visit frequently to make sure the family ties held firm. For most western Europeans the new power of the United States was a more visible, and therefore often more resented, innovation in the contemporary era than the evolution of the Soviet system. Yet it was not only the postwar alliance system that brought the United States closer to its western European progenitors. In a number of key respects changes in western Europe and the United States after the 1940s brought increasing cultural and social similarity, in a framework already closely aligned through shared Western institutions and values.

Convergences across the Atlantic   Convergence with the United States unquestionably describes many western European patterns through the 1970s, for most Western nations either imitated characteristics of the United States or spontaneously developed similar features. Convergence does not mean unity, of course; but there was little question that western Europe in the 1980s more closely resembled the United States than it had in the 1920s, when (compared to most of the rest of the world) the two societies had already seemed part of a common civilization.

Outright convergence described a host of social and political trends. Most obviously, changes in the western European class structure minimized some traditional differences between the two sides of the North Atlantic. The decline of the role of the aristocracy and the rise of a management-based upper class were features of both European and North American elites. As the European peasantry shrank in size and became more commercial in their outlook, they embraced some of the patterns, including the thirst for new technology, that had been established earlier among American farmers. Although the reduction of traditional working-class characteristics in Europe did not propel European workers to claim middle-class status as their blue-collar counterparts in the United States had done, it clearly closed the comparative gap to some extent. The general impact of affluence, with its concomitants in new family interests, new shopping styles, and new media influence, brought many Europeans closer to habits and values that had emerged a decade or more previously in the United States.

Political convergence was more approximate, as the hold of tradition continued to shape distinct patterns on the two sides of the ocean. Politics in the United States was more resolutely consensus-minded than that in Europe, and by European standards it leaned decidedly toward the right—particularly in the continuing absence of any significant socialism in the United States. The American two-party system had no exact analogues in Europe. Britain and Germany, to be sure, operated until the late 1970s with essentially three parties, a conservative and a socialist force, with a small liberal movement in between that was able on occasion to play a coalition role. But even in these cases the ideological and practical gaps between the two major political parties were far larger than those between American Republicans and Democrats, whose political goals in fact overlapped. Most European countries had more than three significant parties, as well as a still-larger range of views in the active political spectrum. American traditions of consensus politics, of substantial compromise and avoidance of strong ideological commitments, continued to mark its unusual political tradition. But as European politics mellowed, with increasingly pragmatic stances on the part of most major groups, there were greater similarities with American politics than had been the case between the wars. Indeed, by the later 1950s, some observers were noting a common decline of passion and an "end of ideology" in politics throughout Western society, and although most of these observers were American, and later developments such as student protest at least complicated their predictions, there did seem to be a new political calm on both sides of the Atlantic during much of the postwar period, compared to earlier turmoils. This calm was greased on both sides of the Atlantic by growing prosperity and new social mobility.

Parallel Trends in the United States and Western Europe   In addition to various areas of convergence—in which Europe usually developed its own approach to patterns set previously in the United States—a number of parallelisms shaped the two main branches of Western society from the late 1940s onward. That is, in some respects both western Europe and the United States changed in the same direction but independently. This was not new; earlier changes, such as the rise of science, industrialization, or the reduction in the birth rate, had developed separately in roughly similar ways and at roughly similar times in both places. But it was noteworthy that at least this operation continued. The baby boom was thus a trans-Atlantic phenomenon. It yielded a somewhat higher birth rate in the United States than in western Europe, based on greater American affluence and, perhaps, confidence immediately after the war; and it lasted about eighteen months longer in the United States. But it had very similar general features and a common result in producing new vigor as well as new intergenerational tensions. New sexual behavior, including more premarital sexual activity and, initially, rising illegitimacy rates, was another trans-Atlantic parallel, starting around 1960—another sign of common rhythms in Western life, even at quite intimate levels. On another front, both the United States and western Europe became open to a new wave of immigration by the 1950s and 1960s. Immigrants came from nonindustrial areas—from Latin America and parts of Asia in the case of the United States, and from Asia, Africa, and the West Indies

The new Europeans can be immigrant children from Africa and the Middle East. These students are in an orientation class for non-French-speaking immigrants in Paris in 1986.

for western Europe. Both sides of the Atlantic needed cheap, unskilled labor, and both places experienced the creation of new racial minority issues—in Europe as well as in the United States, where they had long been prominent. Another extremely important parallelism involved the new occupational and family structures resulting from the rise of the white-collar sector and the surge of women into the labor force—where North American and European developments were virtually identical.

Finally, of course, there was outright imitation. Leading consumer products spread easily and quickly through the Western world, whether their initial source was western Europe or the United States; artistic styles and scientific discoveries did the same. Although specifically American or European emphases in art or literature might still be identified, the leading themes of formal culture, and much popular culture as well, obviously spanned the Atlantic.

Four factors, then, created strong bonds in a trans-Atlantic Western society after World War II: the earlier shared heritage, outright mutual imitation, convergence, and parallelism. Because the second factor was in many ways stronger than ever before, it was possible to argue that despite local variations and some mutual antipathies, western Europe and the United States comprised a common Western culture more firmly than ever. Convergence made some observers believe that any lingering distinctions that existed in western Europe, such as some peasant remnants or a socialist tradition, would shrink still further as ongoing affluence and shifts in occupational structure worked their magic on some of the traditional European customs.

Differences between the United States and Western Europe   The United States and Western Europe had long formed part of a common basic civilization, sharing not only key traditions but also a common dynamic of change; nevertheless, there were new complications to balance against trends of convergence in the postwar decades.

The first complication was that the United States did not hold still while western Europe developed the trappings of an affluent society. It was probably true that western Europe changed more rapidly than the United States did through the 1970s, at least in terms of domestic social trends; Europe's higher economic growth rate both symbolized and helped cause this differential. But American society was hardly static. As Europe's peasantry vanished, becoming more like American commercial family farmers, the American family farm began to yield to new agribusiness combines that dominated hundreds of thousands of acres for commercial production. These combines bypassed family farmers in favor of employed labor. Here was one reason that American agricultural productivity remained higher than that of Europe, but it also marked a continuing differentiation between the rural worlds of the two sectors of Western civilization. The civil rights movement that developed in the later 1950s in the United States, which featured a massive push for new voting rights and fuller legal and social equality for blacks, had no counterpart in Europe, where new racial issues were just emerging. The civil rights movement helped fuel a more substantial American feminism as well as bringing some real change to American political life through the greater vigor and effectiveness of black voters.

Another key change in postwar United States ran almost opposite to trends in western Europe. As Europe settled down, more or less grudgingly, to a smaller world role and lessened military power, the United States developed growing world commitments. American involvement in the Korean and then the Vietnam wars, the American role in crises in the Middle East and other trouble spots, and the steady buildup of American military arsenals, had no real European counterpart at this point, as Europe accommodated militarily to a mainly regional rather than worldwide role. The larger sense, that the United States, against its previous traditions, was becoming increasingly militaristic, its economy and society increasingly shaped by factors of world-power politics, whereas western Europe, against its previous traditions, was becoming less militaristic, suggested the further ramifications of this important divergence in trends.

The second complication was that, in several key respects, western Europe chose to depart from American patterns not by remaining more traditional—as in harboring a less efficient agricultural sector—but by choosing a different style of innovation. That is, while converging with the United States in some key respects, western Europe was becoming a different kind of advanced industrial society in others. Three examples illustrate this point in the areas of education, welfare, and leisure.

First, when western European nations attacked outdated traditionalism in their educational system in the decades after World War II, they did not opt for an American standard. To be sure, they adopted a more technical curriculum, raised the minimum age at which one could leave school, and expanded higher educational facilities—all measures already present in the American system. But they did not incorporate team sports, various kinds of life-training courses, or abundant extracurricular activities into their schools—which meant that schools in Europe served a more strictly academic purpose, and had a lesser role in the community than did schools in the United States. The Europeans also continued to track students quite rigorously; that is, they segregated students based on academic standing and gave each group its own curricula and degrees. They tried to modify tracking that occurred too early, in order to recruit a wider social mix; but they did not adopt the American model of a largely common educational experience through the secondary level. Revealingly, West Germany did introduce an American-style high school (the *Gesamthochschule*) as one of four major secondary options, but it proved the least popular. In general, European secondary school students were tracked, as a result of examination results and teacher recommendations, into university preparatory, technical, or essentially apprenticeship programs by the age of fourteen or before. Furthermore, tracking occurred on the basis of achievement tests, in contrast to the strong American preference for aptitude testing. Europeans, in other words, built cumulatively on past educational records more than Americans did, allowing far fewer "second chances" to enter a more demanding curriculum; and educational performance bore a closer relationship to later career success than in the United States. Finally, whereas college enrollments in the United States continued to mushroom, passing fifty percent of the relevant age group by the early 1980s, Europeans confined a postsecondary education to a smaller minority, who were more rigorously screened through testing at age sixteen or seventeen. And the Europeans encouraged another minority of students, those with lower academic success, to drop out of school programs at fourteen or fifteen to undertake guided apprenticeship instead.

In sum, although Europeans transformed their educational system, they preserved a franker differentiation among students than did the more democratic United States. Both approaches produced roughly equal mobility. The European approach, however, tended to accentuate social boundaries, whereas the American approach, more expensive overall if only because of far larger college costs, may have encouraged more democratic intermingling—and also, perhaps, more frustrated career dreams.

Second, the Europeans produced a much fuller welfare state than did the United States. The New Deal of the 1930s had generated a strong Social Security program for old age and, to a lesser extent, for unemployment. This system was expanded after World War II to embrace more people and to provide higher benefits. In the 1960s, under President Lyndon Johnson, a new "Great Society" initiative added a host of government programs to aid the poor, plus a state-funded medical scheme for the poor and elderly (Medicaid and Medicare). But even with this important extension, largely stabilized during the economic doldrums of the 1970s, the United States remained noticeably apart from European patterns of state-sponsored medicine or medical insurance, family aid, and other measures. The American state, long less socially active than its European counterpart, thus changed in some similar directions but hardly closed the gap. It thus differed from Great Britain, which had also long boasted a small-government tradition but in the twentieth century became one of the more socially activist states in the West. Americans, more reliant on a rhetoric of individual initiative, more concerned with supplying opportunity—through roughly democratic education—than welfare, moved in a somewhat different political orbit from that of post-war Europeans. The contrasts of the two regions along the political spectrum of socialism mirrored this difference. So did greater American tolerance—by European standards—for relatively high unemployment or, in the early 1980s, rising rates of hunger. Despite shared trends and traditions, Americans did not move to a contemporary European definition of state responsibility. Even aside from the welfare apparatus, the United States remained the only Western nation without a formal economic planning mechanism.

Third, Europeans in some respects made a clearer adjustment to new leisure patterns than did Americans; perhaps Europeans were transmuting a tradition of aristocratic skepticism about the work ethic to a new, contemporary guise. European vacations, of a minimum of three to five weeks per year, had no overall United States counterpart. Some observers noted that American eagerness to retire—retirement ages declined notably in the United States from the 1940s onward—might have reflected Americans' wishes for a belated compensation for rather meager vacations during working life. The fact remained that formal leisure time in the United States prior to retirement increased only modestly after the late 1940s, whereas in Europe it veritably exploded. European governments, picking up on this trend in good welfare-state fashion, were by the 1970s setting up "ministries of free time" to help oversee and sustain this development, while American politicians remained, rhetorically at least, committed to the general proposition that work makes worth.

The final complication in the convergence of the values of the United States and western Europe was that, in some respects, Americans had become more traditional than their European counterparts. This was a nebulous difference that came in addition to new directions of change in the United States (as in the military field) and nonconvergent innovations in Europe (as in education and leisure). This sense of America's greater traditionalism was not the common belief—indeed, American tradition dictated that the United States be seen as the young, innovative pioneer *without* the fetters of tradition—and it was not uniformly true; but in some respects the proposition seemed valid. For example in the United States a vast majority professed religious belief and a near-majority attended some church regularly. Thus it was the most religious industrialized society in the world. Western Europe, where secularism made continued inroads, was obviously different, and this difference helped generate others. Death ceremonies in Europe, for example, changed more substantially than did those in the United States. On both sides of the Atlantic, death now mainly occurred outside the home, in a hospital, and was battled by medical personnel. But the United States retained relatively elaborate funeral practices when the fight against death was lost, whereas many Europeans, constrained by lack of space as well as encouraged by declining religion, chose comparatively unceremonious cremation.

In certain areas Americans also seemed to retain more traditional family values. They were less comfortable with day-care centers for children than were Europeans, for example while maintaining higher average birth rates in the first place. In other words, despite their higher divorce rate, Americans may have retained a more idealized family picture, including loving parents caring directly for small children. Even Americans who used day-care facilities tended to be slightly apologetic, trying to be sure that traditional "mother love" could be provided in new ways. This was in contrast to the Europeans who expressed relief at less contact with children and a belief that day-care was actually a boon for the young. Finally, Americans remained more openly nationalistic than did Europeans, if only because the United States's position of national power was less challenged. Nationalism remained a force in Europe, but it was qualified by some European loyalties and particularly by an embarrassed skepticism. American patriotism was challenged, to be sure, by the messy war in Vietnam, along with antiwar protests and the loss of the war itself to the communist forces; but it bounced back fairly quickly and rode high, as the saying went, during the flag-waving Reagan administrations of the 1980s. In sum, although Americans continued to flock to Europe in admiration of Europe's long historic-mindedness, the ironic possibility was that the hand of tradition was now more firmly visible in the United States.

Western Civilization and World Role   Americans and western Europeans, as cousins, had never been sure they were in exactly the same family, although they knew they were related. On the whole, this complexity persisted in the postwar period. Some earlier differences eased; others, as in the educational system, took new forms. New distinctions arose, most obviously in world power position but also in such unexpected areas as the sense of rootedness and custom. One could always analyze western Europe and the United States as separate societies, and it remained possible to do so after World War II. As before, however, more accurate analysis embraced both societies as part of a common Western orbit while noting the important distinctions and the possibility that, at some point, a more sweeping differentiation might result. Developments in the postwar United States, including its growing world role, did constitute an increasingly vital part of the modern history of Western society; but, because of America's distinctiveness new and old, it was not always characteristic of the West as a whole. Europeans sympathized with many American goals and indeed imitated a host of American fashions, while also worrying about some American habits they found strange and even dangerous; they were aware of some of the subtleties of this comparative relationship.

The "Western, but" position of the United States created one final complication in judging the position of the contemporary West: its position in the wider world. The decline of western Europe, which occurred as a result of decolonization and the rise of stronger military superpowers, was incontestable. Whether the West *as a whole* was declining depended obviously on judgments about the integral position of the United States, for the American rise compensated at least in part for the eclipse of Europe.

Even if the United States can be seen as taking up larger Western banners, however, the West still underwent a readjustment in world status. Because of competition with the Soviet Union and the political power of new nations, particularly in Asia, Western political influence has not rebounded from the loss of colonies. European nations retain strong political voice, particularly in parts of Africa: the United States speaks more loudly, and at times more effectively. But the West no longer runs the world, even in the partly superficial sense it could claim during the decades of imperialism. Relatedly, although it retains an edge over most other societies in military technology, it is no longer unchallenged in this area—even when the strength of the United States is included in the Western arsenal.

The United States and Western Europe combine in contributing to the decline of the West in two other ways. First, the Western birth rate, even with the baby boom, has lagged behind that of most of the rest of the world. Between 1975 and 1980, for example, although the population of the West increased by .4 percent, world population soared by 1.7 percent. Only the Soviet Union and Japan show a roughly similar relative decline since World War II. Prospects for the future suggested still greater slippage—perhaps an absolute decrease in native-born population in the West by the later twenty-first century, if birth rates continue to drop. This demographic lag in the West may be a strength, in preserving a high ratio of resources to people and so protecting environment and standard of living—although pessimists noted that the West's population, older than the world's average, might find its productivity hampered by a lack of youthful hands and minds. The demographic lag unquestionably leaves the West vulnerable to demographic pressure from other areas, as the immigration patterns of the last several decades have abundantly demonstrated. Demographic vitality was a key part of the West's rise, in the sixteenth century and again in the eighteenth and nineteenth centuries; it remains to be seen how much it will be missed.

The West's monopoly, long shared between western Europe and the United States, of a dominant position in the world economy has also ended. Japan now shares in the dominance and other challengers, such as South Korea, may soon step over the threshold. Western Europe's postwar economic resurgence, which allowed the region to regain significant economic power even as worldwide political controls lapsed, suggests that loss of monopoly status may not involve absolute decline. But again, as in politics, military technology, and demography, the West has had to adjust its economic standing in the world—and this adjustment will almost certainly continue in the future.

Finally, Western culture retains substantial influence in the world. Here the American role is most obvious, with the wide use of English and the common currency of American films and other media events. But European cultural influence also remains substantial, sometimes preferred to that from the United States if only because fewer power-politics strings may be attached. European teachers and technical advisors fill a substantial role particularly in Africa but also in China, Latin America, and elsewhere. European art and architecture, and its sports styles, remain widely emulated. Several individual countries, including France and West Germany, have devoted greater attention and resources to international economic and cultural assistance, again particularly though not exclusively in Africa, than have the United States or the Soviet Union. The sheer prestige of Western styles, then, plus ongoing attention to shaping development through advice, education, and cultural contacts, made the West still something of a standard-setter for all but the most isolated parts of the postwar world. Whether Western cultural strength would hold up against growing national pride in many areas, and against the competing economic and military muscle of several other societies, is open to question; some observers predict a resurgence of regional cultures, as the world continues its transition from outright Western dominance.

Overall, the West's decline remains a mixed and gradual process. By no means does it suggest an inevitable replacement by another dominant civilization or some absolute loss of vigor within the West itself. Aside from the military sphere, Western influence in the world involves Europe as well as the United States, and this influence has proved more resilient than the currents of anti-Westernism immediately after World War II indicated.

The West in the 1980s

The position of the West in the world, and more specific relationships between Europe and the United States, were not of course fixed entities. The 1980s brought important adjustments to the comparative position of the West, particularly in the form of new and vexing problems for western Europe. Several of the staple trends of the postwar decades, including a growing economic vitality that partially compensated for new military inferiority toward the two superpowers, were called into question.

A second oil crisis, stemming from the Iranian revolution of 1979, triggered the most burdensome economic recession western Europe had experienced since the postwar recovery period. Recession initially trapped the United States as well, bringing increased levels of unemployment into the early 1980s, but here a more pronounced recovery ensued.

The problem was not oil alone, although higher energy prices inevitably complicated manufacturing while tending to drive prices up in the characteristic "stagflation" pattern. Western European economies faced several other, related pressures. Competition from Japan and other nations hit hard, particularly in basic industrial sectors such as steel and automobiles that had been mainstays of the postwar boom. These pressures were felt keenly in the United States as well. But the United States displayed somewhat greater vigor in developing new production and service activities. There was increasing concern that western Europe, eager to defend established success, was slow in moving to new areas such as computers and genetic engineering products. The French government, for example, talked elaborately about computerization equipping even small villages with computer networks, but in fact tried to protect a laggard and inefficient domestic computer manufacturer rather than launching full-scale into international competition. Some Europeans also complained that economic problems at home were exacerbated by United States policies from the late 1970s onward. They noted that the United States was piling up a huge government debt, which helped fuel the American economy but also generated high interest rates, and these rates in turn attracted European capital to the American market and complicated new investment at home. European governments, more conservative fiscally, avoided new indebtedness and also tried to restrain inflation, but this limited their ability to stimulate new economic growth.

By the 1980s the economic problems of western Europe were not catastrophic. Modest economic growth continued. Most countries brought inflation under some control. Investment in research was maintained, and per-worker productivity actually increased more rapidly than in the United States. The French introduced more use of robots for manufacturing than American companies did. Average living standards rose, though more slowly than before. Overall, it was not absolute decline but loss of momentum and fears of further slippage in the future, especially against rising international competitors and the growing wave of new, sophisticated technologies that described Europe's new economic scene. It was not even certain that Europe was permanently falling behind the United States, for many observers warned that growing American deficits would imperil the American economy in the future. But Europe did face new anxieties, and high rates of unemployment through the first half of the 1980s—ranging up to 12 percent in some cases—brought economic difficulties home to millions of Europeans. Here, at least in the short run, Europe did slip behind American performance, after boasting a better employment record through most of the postwar period. American unemployment, quite high between 1979 and 1981, began to drop thereafter, toward rates of 7 percent to 8 percent.

The Shift to Political Conservatism

New economic pressures, and the growing concern about the future, produced some political reactions. It is noteworthy that, in contrast to the 1930s, the basic political regimes held firm. But there were new political currents, and a tendency to experiment with new solutions, in a number of countries.

In Germany, over a decade of Social Democratic rule ended in 1982 with a new Christian Democratic victory. The new leaders offered a largely pragmatic approach to the economic problems, rather than some sweeping alternative. They cut welfare payments to the unemployed and retirees by about 6 percent, without contesting the legitimacy of the welfare state. They actually maintained Social Democratic foreign policy, collaborating with the United States on new European armaments programs but also continuing contacts with East Germany. A new political force arose in Germany, in the form of the "Green" party, which advocated new attention to environmental issues, disarmament, and feminist programs. Led by former student radicals of the late 1960s, the Greens won over 10 percent of the vote in some state elections, and also put a new, leftist pressure on the Social Democrats. Whether they would prove to be a significant and durable political force was unclear, but their emergence suggested the arrival of new problems and new confusions on the political scene.

Scandinavian politics also shifted ground somewhat, in a process that actually began in the mid-1970s. For the first time in forty years, Social Democrats lost control of several governments to conservative coalitions, which cut back some welfare programs and tried to hold the line on tax increases. Even when back in power, socialist leaders had to focus on a prudent administration of welfare.

The political picture in Britain and the United States veered more sharply toward an aggressive conservatism. The British Conservative party, led by Margaret Thatcher, won major election victories in 1979, 1983, and 1987, as she became one of the most durable prime ministers in Britain's history. Her platform stressed not mere tinkering with the welfare state, but a substantial dismantling in favor of lower taxes and more private initiative. She also battled the power of trade unions, in hopes of making British workers more adaptable and productive. Actual new measures fell short of promises. The government budget was not cut substantially, as key welfare programs proved too popular to attack. Nationalized industries remained nationalized, although shares in some of the nationalized companies were sold on the private stock market. Government spending was more tightly controlled, but some measures, such as drastic reduction in support for higher education, seemed questionable in terms of Britain's economic future. Hard bargaining with unions did permit the closing of some unproductive coal mines, but Britain made no dramatic economic turnaround. Inflation dropped, but unemployment remained high.

Thatcher's new conservatism was aided by her popular and successful defense of the Falkland Islands against Argentina. It was also aided by a new division in the Labour party. Out of power, many Labourites veered leftward, calling for more nationalization, nuclear disarmament, and freedom from NATO. A more moderate group, eager for defense of the welfare state but not radical innovation, split away, forming a new Social Democratic group closely allied with the Liberal party. As in Germany, the political spectrum was changing under the impact of new problems and a new generation of voters who had experienced neither the Great Depression nor World War II and were impatient with some of the older political alignments. As in Germany also, however, it remained unclear how substantially British politics had altered. Thatcher's popularity was shakier after 1985, while new Labour leadership steered a more moderate course.

Conservative resurgence in the United States brought the election victories of Ronald Reagan in 1980 and 1984. Like Thatcher before him,

Reagan promised a scaling down of traditional welfare programs; like Thatcher, he did not tamper greatly with the largest and most popular programs, notably Social Security. Increased defense spending actually exploded government budgets, leading to unprecedented deficits. Nationalist rhetoric and some military skirmishes against small countries brought considerable popularity, and the rival Democratic party seemed hard-pressed to come up with popular policy alternatives to the Reagan approach.

Italy and France: Moves to the Left

Italy and France had long been headed by conservative politicians—the Christian Democrats in Italy, Charles de Gaulle's heirs in France. In these countries new politics meant a turn to the left. In Italy, energetic Eurocommunist leaders pressed for inclusion in the government, promising support for a pluralist democracy and firmly pledging independence from Soviet foreign policy. Christian Democratic leadership was on the decline, blamed for economic problems and instability, plus considerable corruption. Passage of laws legalizing divorce and then abortion, during the 1970s, showed how the Catholic hold over Italian voters was declining. But the alternative to Christian Democracy proved not to be the Communist party, whose popularity began to wane somewhat in the early 1980s, but rather new coalition governments constructed by socialist and other noncommunist leaders.

French politics witnessed a clearer shift. Aided by an alliance with the communists, who were however less firmly Eurocommunist than their Italian counterparts, the socialist party revived and won a smashing election victory in 1981. The new president, François Mitterand, quickly introduced extensive new nationalizations and a host of welfare measures, including a retirement age of fifty-five. But this dramatic program soon foundered on the problems of a stagnant economy and growing unemployment. By 1983 the socialists were focusing on reassurance of the business community, modernization of industry even at the cost of lost jobs, and cuts in welfare payments. Conservative parties, including the Gaullists, began to pick up renewed support, and an ominous new rightist movement, which attacked parliamentary politics and other signs of modernity, including women's rights, won up to 10 percent of voter support. New parliamentary elections in 1986 produced a small conservative majority and a Gaullist prime minister—the first time parliament and the presidency had been held by different parties under the Fifth Republic. Meanwhile the French Communist party went into a tailspin. Initially outclassed by the resurgent socialists, the communists seemed unable to find a successful platform, often appealing to working-class racism against immigrants; support for the party fell to a postwar low of 11 percent. As in other parts of Europe, French politics were changing, but in diverse directions.

Evaluating Political Trends

The extent of political change in the West was particularly unclear. American and British conservatism was redefined, at least for a time, but more in principle than in practice. One antiparliamentary movement arose, in France. The German Green party scoffed at the establishment and defied political conventions, for example, by wearing jeans to parliamentary sessions. But basic political alignments remained intact, and although many Americans and western Europeans were disillusioned with politics, there was no strong current attacking the democratic, parliamentary ideal. Conservatism of one sort or another held sway in northern Europe during most of the 1980s, and in the United States, whereas socialist governments or coalitions ruled in Greece, Spain, and Portugal as well as France and Italy. But growing conservative fortunes in France and a resurgent Labour party in Britain made it likely that these alignments, too, were only temporary as Western politics continued to operate within a fairly recognizable framework.

There were new issues, however, and what political change existed reflected this fact. The problem of adjusting to greater international competition and to the decline of some staple industries such as steel, posed acute political dilemmas. Should choice be left largely to market forces, as seemed the United States preference? Or should planners somehow find a rational way to phase out old sectors and develop new technologies—and if so, what new technologies would prove viable?

Stagnant economies put huge burdens on the apparatus of the welfare state. Rising unemployment automatically increased welfare costs, although less in the United States than in Europe because of the smaller scale of American programs. Furthermore, throughout the West the population was aging. Low birth rates combined with increased longevity to produce a rapid increase in the absolute numbers and the relative importance of those over sixty-five; indeed, the age group over eighty-five increased more rapidly, in percentage terms, than any other cohort. An aging population meant new expenses for medical care and for retirement. Here were new burdens on the welfare state even apart from the economic slowdown; with the slowdown, the prospect was for rising welfare costs won from a shrinking, or at best stable, revenue base.

Thus a key new political issue was whether the welfare state could be sustained. All governments, socialist or conservative, cut back benefit levels in the 1980s. Whether these pragmatic cuts would suffice, or whether more drastic measures were necessary, remained an open question. The welfare state, long assumed as a staple of postwar political life, now became once more a subject for agonized debate. Even in the United States, where welfare programs loomed less large, Social Security was reexamined; as one observer noted, "there were no easy votes" on Social Security issues anymore. Yet, despite some strident attacks on welfarism—including some new leftist criticism of the dulling restrictions and unequal treatment the welfare state imposed on working people—there was no clear alternative vision. The welfare state remained too popular, in its essentials, to dismantle. The question was whether piecemeal changes were enough, and whether durable economic advance could be spurred anew despite high welfare expenses and attendant high taxes or (in the United States) budget deficits. In answer to this question new uncertainty, not dramatic new developments, held center stage in the West in the later 1980s, along with questions about whether political responses, comfortably moderate on balance, had proved adequate.

Economic problems spilled over into intra-European relations. The European Economic Community was not powerful enough to address key issues with a collective voice. Individual nations, for example, struggled to secure oil imports from the Middle East, preventing an overall Common Market stance. With economic stagnation came some new infighting among member nations. France and Italy quarreled over wine imports. British and German payments to support Common Market farmers, disproportionately located in France and Italy, caused repeated crises, sometimes threatening the existence of the Community. As in other aspects of Western political life, the Common Market seemed to have lost its forward momentum. It functioned, but it no longer seemed a magic springboard toward a better future. Yet, again as with other political and economic trends, there were some modest positive developments. From 1979 onward a European parliament was directly elected by voters in the member nations, rather than being appointed from national parliaments. Europe-wide elections in turn promoted some new contacts among national political parties, even though the Community parliament had few powers other than debate. Admission of Greece and then Spain and Portugal showed Common Market commitment to support new democracies, even though the new members, less industrialized than other participants, threatened additional burdens. The Common Market functioned, improved in small ways, but no longer inspired.

Leading Issues by the Late 1980s

The larger international context for the West raised new problems as well. Although terrorism by Europeans themselves declined somewhat, in part thanks to improved policing, tensions in the Middle East spilled over into terrorist attacks on European soil, often directed at Israelis or Americans. Growing Soviet armament, in the later 1970s, threatened clear nuclear inferiority for western Europe, particularly through the installation of new Russian intermediate-range missiles equipped with multiple warheads. In response, NATO countries in 1979 called for the installation of new United States missiles. But this measure, gradually implemented, prompted a new wave of disarmament protest in many European countries, reviving antiwar and anti-American movements that had surfaced periodically since the late 1940s. Demonstrations and other agitation in Britain, Holland, and West Germany matched or exceeded any level since the cold war began. American missile installations proceeded, and by the later 1980s the disarmament movement had cooled somewhat. But its vigor suggested both the renewed level of western European insecurity, and some potential new conflicts of interest between the United States—in the 1980s increasingly blustery in foreign policy—and European states on the whole eager for greater conciliation of world tensions, whether with Arab nations or with the Soviet Union.

The 1980s brought no overwhelming catastrophe to the West. It did bring a new set of problems, based most obviously on what appeared to

Injured people being attended to after a Paris car bomb explosion in 1986. The threat of terrorism on European soil, as well as to Europeans and Americans abroad, gave rise to debates such as the need for security versus the preservation of individual liberties and loomed as one of the major issues confronting the West in the 1980s.

be durable economic pressures but reflecting also key social changes such as population aging. The sense of forward momentum that had described the West during at least portions of the 1950s and 1960s—in areas such as economic growth, American civil rights progress, new social mobility, the Common Market—had largely dissipated. Europeans, in particular, felt that a variety of conditions had once again escaped their control. Interest rates were set, essentially, by the United States government—an entity in which Europeans had no great confidence. The military environment, increasingly ominous, was established by Washington and Moscow; Europe had clearly been unable to recover political strength commensurate with its continued economic power or with its genuine intellectual vitality. The resultant sense of frustration—a marked contrast to growing American confidence in the 1980s—was inevitable.

Some observers argued that the problems ran deeper still, with more troubling portents for the future. Had Western people so constricted their outlook that they depended on the pleasures of consumerism for satisfaction? If so, what would happen if steady consumer gains became jeopardized, through a combination of international competition, domestic stagnation, and welfare expenses?

Western Europeans, some warned, had become so dangerously cut off from earlier beliefs—in church, in nation, in army, even in past—that they really had little else to look to except economic progress. Change had been so rapid, particularly since World War II, that older values had been knocked away. School curricula, updated to focus on producing a technically competent elite and labor force, gave scant attention to history or to a larger culture, beyond some rote memorization in the primary grades. Class loyalties, even fervent beliefs in movements such as communism, had been eroded by affluence and skepticism. With little but materialism to focus upon, Europeans were unusually vulnerable to the consequences not just of economic setback, but of lack of progress. Their political goals riveted on economic performance, and where this was wanting they might turn against the political system itself. Americans were not so clearly embraced by this argument, because of the wider array of traditional values available and because of the nation's greater power.

But there was a still wider debate about values that included Americans and western Europeans alike. Various analysts contended that changes in personality structure, rooted in looser or disrupted family ties, made Westerners increasingly incapable of decisive action, increasingly dependent on shallow, narcissistic satisfactions doled out by advertisers, media, and consumer-goods producers. Concerned about pleasing peer groups, people found strong, individual initiative increasingly difficult. Economic management became more timid, political debate and ethically

Western children of the 1940s and 1950s were the first generation to grow up with television, and with the consequent demands of the medium for their time and loyalty—to the disadvantage, some analysts have claimed, of traditional Western values.

motivated action more circumscribed. In the late 1970s moral critics wrote
of a deep malaise in American life, and the decline of healthy indignation
in the West as a whole.

These judgments were speculative. European politics in fact survived a
decade of increased economic difficulty, into the late 1980s, without
decisive collapse. American self-esteem, unquestionably shaky during the
1970s in the wake of the Vietnam War, seemed rekindled thereafter.
Polls in the 1970s had revealed an interesting disparity between American skepticism about overall progress in their society and continued confidence in personal improvement; but in the 1980s both areas registered
considerable confidence, whether well founded or not. The idea of some
new, fatally flawed Western value system or personality had yet to be
proved for either side of the Atlantic. Some social scientists did attempt
to measure creativity, in the form of rates of fundamental new inventions, claiming that western European activity had dangerously declined
while the United States was dropping off relative to East Asia. And the
more general lack of fundamental new intellectual or artistic visions in
the West in the later twentieth century might be taken as a foretaste of
some larger cultural sea-change. But again, measured by pragmatic tests
such as economic and technological power or political stability, the West,
and even western Europe alone, continued to do rather well by the later
1980s. If collapse was being prepared by some new and fatal moral flaws,
it had yet to break through.

Nevertheless, the idea of new, possibly troubling shifts in values, along
with the undeniable array of problems that faced the West toward the
end of the twentieth century, does raise a final set of questions, in terms
of placing contemporary Western history in the larger perspective of past
time. Was a fundamentally modern set of patterns, initiated several centuries back, being maintained? Or were the modern patterns, derived
from the scientific revolution and the Enlightenment, yielding to still
newer shapes as yet somewhat indeterminate? Those who argued that
the West had lost its key convictions or that Europe had cut itself off
from a meaningful past were contending, essentially, that the postwar
decades, along with earlier shocks, had jolted Western society out of
familiar modern trends and into a new, transitional status. Others, who
were far more optimistic in arguing that the West was moving toward an
unprecedented technological age, in which information production, for
example, would replace the production of goods as the key engine of
social and political structure, were nevertheless making the same case:
that the West was leaving the modern era and entering a transition to
some new, postmodern future.

The Contemporary West in Historical Perspective

With rejoicing or lament, a number of pundits saw the West by the
late twentieth century cut loose from its previous moorings. Among the
lamenters, a growing number of commentators began to contrast contemporary Western values and habits with those of the nineteenth century, that quintessentially modern era of the industrial revolution. The

industrial West featured strong families with active parents who instilled a sense of conscience into children, making them capable of significant work achievement, morally based protest, or both. The industrial West featured a devotion to work, an eagerness for competition. In contrast, the contemporary West was moving toward loose family structures, a high valuation of pleasure seeking, a preference for conformity over competitive achievement; in this West, characteristic "modern" values must be regarded with nostalgia, for these strengths have been irretrievably lost.

With rejoicing, a still larger number of forecasters began, from the 1960s onward, to use terms such as "postmodern" or, more commonly, "postindustrial" to describe a Western society that was beginning to become as different from industrial society as industrial society itself had been from agricultural. Two related features of contemporary life were singled out to support this view. First, important new technologies promised to facilitate manufacturing with lower labor use, or to revolutionize the generation and transmission of data. At the least, these technologies seemed to presage one of those technological upheavals that had dotted Western industrial history periodically since 1800; at the most, there were leaps forward to an outright shift in emphasis as substantial as the initial industrial revolution itself. Simply put, with robots doing more of the manufacturing work, and with computers revolutionizing the information field, the technological framework of the economy was shifting rapidly. Second, along with this shift—in fact predating the microchip computer—was the rapid rise of the service sector of the economy. Occupations were based more on information exchange—teaching, filing, transmitting, researching—and other, more diverse service categories including sales and leisure, and less on the sheer manipulation of goods than ever before. The relative decline of manufacturing jobs echoed the earlier decline of agriculture, as Western nations (and Japan) learned to produce growing quantities of goods of all sorts with a smaller production force.

Having defined a postindustrial society in terms of machines and jobs, one that contrasted at least in part with industrial patterns of the nineteenth and earlier twentieth centuries, some forecasters then went on to posit a more sweeping definition for postindustrial society. The postindustrial city was thus envisioned as a contrast to its industrial counterpart. Manufacturing would disperse, into the countryside and suburbs, because with computer controls centralized factories and offices would no longer be needed. Cities would become a focus for recreation and occasional meetings, and little else. Leisure time would logically expand, at least for the majority of the population; but pundits were often hard pressed to define what people would do with increased nonwork time except watch more television, play electronic games, and the like. Postindustrial families might find production returned to a familial setting, as computer-linked workstations were set up in households—it was sometimes unclear where the children would be. Social inequality might increase through a new form of proletarianization, as a minority who controlled information and really understood the new technology, and who worked quite hard, received huge rewards in contrast to the majority who merely transmitted data and services. On the other hand, a number of advocates claimed that, even for most ordinary people, computer-based work would become more pleasant and satisfying, responsive to individual interests and scheduling rather than dedicated to maintaining the assembly-line lockstep of the industrial workplace. Material standards would also improve, and consumer products could be more closely tailored to individual taste—again a blow for individualism against the mass dictates of classic industrial society. The shape of postindustrial society, and certainly its quality of life, were by no means entirely clear, but a variety of academics and publicists in the United States and Europe were convinced of its imminence.

There were some links, finally, between the visions of the postindustrial optimists, who argued that new technology was not only inevitable but would determine a better life, and those who worried about a massive deterioration of values central to the modern West. With a new, service-based occupational structure, and with new machines altering human interactions, it was perhaps logical that personality characteristics cherished in the past would now give way. When most people dealt not with goods but with ·people, and often worked in large management structures, competitiveness and intense achievement orientation would perhaps be less useful than personalities geared to smooth interactions with peers. Changes in values might of course be disturbing, particularly in a transitional period, and they would bring loss as well as gain, but if the idea of a profoundly novel postindustrial society was correct, it was hardly surprising that it would affect personal outlook and aspirations—mentality, in sum—as well as the more formal institutions of Western society.

The predictions of radical change in the West's near future were fascinating. Western intellectual life and popular beliefs had long been geared to a concern with the secular future and to a fascination with the progress possible through new knowledge and machines. In a sense many of the postindustrial forecasts simply advanced this modern intellectual tradition, finding a ready popular audience among ordinary readers who also believed, if somewhat nervously, that science and technology could generate a better future.

Whether the forecasts were accurate or not, however, was another matter. That change was occurring in Western society was undeniable—change had been a fundamental feature of Western life for centuries. What was debatable was the claim that Western society was moving out of modern framework, which had been constructed gradually since the sixteenth century, and into something substantially different. Such a transformation would surely occur at some point, but whether it was already happening, so soon after the industrial revolution itself had taken shape, was open to question. Many of the predictions related to changes that had not yet taken place or at least could not yet be proved. Thus the idea of a postindustrial family working around the home-based computer was a conceivable vision, but aside from a handful of well-publicized cases it did not describe actual trends in the later 1980s. Some of the claims about changes in the Western personality pointed to new patterns of mental disorder, away from the classic neuroses of the nineteenth century; but many authorities argued that neuroses were just as prevalent as before, disputing the idea of great disruptions in modern patterns. Forecasting itself was often questioned; studies showed that over 50 percent of all forecasts issued by Western experts since World War II had proved inaccurate.

Certainly some of the visions of a revolutionary new future suffered from interesting omissions. First, the impact on a postmodern future of population aging was not commonly assessed. Basic Western demography had not changed greatly in the twentieth century, except for the brief baby boom after World War II. Western families on average worked for population stability through the modern mechanisms of low birth rates combined with low child death rates. But the one change that did emerge, with particular clarity from the 1960s onward, was the increasing average age of Western people and the growth of old-age cohorts. This change was not typically figured into the more sweeping forecasts. Would aging *retard* technological change? Would it affect the way Western families functioned, even the way children were trained? The shaping of the modern West had included not only factors of technology, human organization, and outlook, but also basic population characteristics. Figuring these characteristics into a coherent vision of the future was no easy task. It was also doubtful, despite some comments on the changing shape of the postindustrial city, that Western people were facing a substantial change in residential patterns as had occurred with the earlier process of urbanization. The continued predominance of urban living, like the considerable stability of demographic behavior, might argue against the idea of fundamental upheaval in Western life.

Second, it was not clear that some of the technological changes taking shape would alter actual human conditions as drastically as some experts contended. Computerization, for instance, might well increase the standardization and organized coordination of work, extending trends that had taken shape with industrialization and the advent of mass society. New work controls would themselves constitute important change, but in established rather than novel directions.

Finally, many of the discussions of the West's postindustrial future did not take a larger international context into account, except perhaps to note that the West "must" revolutionize its technology to maintain a lead on the rest of the world. Whether the West could forge a radically new kind of society when its technological prowess was now shared by countries such as Japan was debatable. Whether the West and Japan together could forge such a new kind of society when most of the rest of the world was still struggling to industrialize in the first place raised another set of issues. Whether major war could be avoided, with its different implications for the future, was another ominous imponderable.

The West's future, toward the end of the twentieth century, was indeed murky—as futures always are. Evolution of specific issues such as the economic problems of the West from the later 1970s onward, or more grandiose scenarios about dramatic transformations, could not easily be read into the decades still to come. Nevertheless, valid possibilities could be usefully debated. It was possible that the West, or western Europe more specifically, had enjoyed a misleading "Indian summer" during the 1950s and 1960s, based on a transient new leadership group, but that its economic and political prospects were glum—that the problems of the 1970s and 1980s, with economic stagnation bumping against fierce popular expectations about consumer and welfare gains, were more indicative of what was to come. It was possible that the Western outlook and personality were in the early stages of some fundamental reshaping, and certainly possible that new technologies and occupational changes portended a dramatic new society in the future—but the extent and precise direction of any transformation remained a matter of guesswork, not fact.

A history of the modern West cannot be ended with a neat blueprint of what is to come, just as it cannot be ended with a dramatic set of events or trends. Western society is still in motion in the late twentieth century, and like any society in motion it sends off diverse signals about strengths and weaknesses, continuities and changes.

A Balance Sheet: The Dynamics of Modern Western History

We cannot pretend to make a conclusive statement about how the contemporary West fits or will fit into the perspective of its modern past. But it is possible to sketch a tentative balance sheet based on some of the underlying factors that have shaped the West since at least the sixteenth century. Several developments, themselves changing in different periods, have been fundamental to the character of Western society in the modern era. The current status of each of these can contribute to a final assessment that cannot predict the future but may help us locate present and possible futures in the context of the past.

Factor one: the West's international standing. From the sixteenth century onward, the West enjoyed clear technological superiority over the rest of the world, starting with its lead in naval gunnery, extending soon to manufacturing and then to land-based (and later air-based) weaponry. From this foundation the West developed a leadership monopoly in the increasingly extensive world economy, enjoying relatively cheap raw materials and selling more expensive processed products, to the steady benefit of its own total wealth.

This favorable world position has at least been seriously modified, and may be in process of substantial transformation, in the later twentieth century, in the new, competitive economic and military climate. The West retains a vital position in world power and wealth, and the results of change may be gradual. But this aspect of the West's modern context seems to be rather fluid, as a result of the West's own internal battles in the twentieth century and the probably inevitable resurgence of a number of other societies in the world. Major changes have taken place in this category.

Factor two: the nation-state. The rise of the nation-state was a staple of modern Western history. This rise was initially visible through reduction of internal rivals to the state's control and the development of improved military and political organization, and it was ultimately expressed also through a growing list of functions, plus new popular loyalties and political focus.

In some respects the nation-state has continued to "rise" in the later twentieth century, even as it becomes a more common political form worldwide. Western nations have extended their educational role and their contacts with individual citizens, through welfare and economic planning activities. The theme of specialized, relatively disciplined bureaucracies continues as well. No obvious internal rivals to the hold of the nation-state have emerged. Changes in groups such as the peasantry may have heightened national consciousness as recently as the 1960s. Yet the twentieth century has produced some new questions about the nation-state form in the West. Particularly in western Europe, the nation-state has proved too small a unit to encompass modern economic activities. Even in the giant United States, multinational corporations split the seams of nation-state control. The nation-state's propensity for devastating war has brought some effort to limit prerogatives, through institutions such as the Common Market; and the intensity of nationalism and possibly national politics more generally may have diminished. There is substantial continuity in this category but also some interesting recent twists and prospects.

Factor three: the capitalist impulse to the economy and social structure, with resultant proletarianization. Capitalism has been much modified in the twentieth-century West, with the rise of corporate forms on the one hand, the development of a more mixed economy with substantial state involvement on the other. Yet the Western economy remains committed to growth and profit-seeking. The nature of proletarianization has changed several times. Initially a gradual process, proletarianization then speeded with population growth, industrialization, and urbanization. The twentieth century has seen substantial adjustments to proletarian status, eased by affluence and mass consumerism. It has also seen proletarianization reshaped by the complexities of white-collar status and the role of knowledge and decision-making control, and not property ownership alone, in defining social position. By the late twentieth century proletarian status reflected not only lack of producing property, but also relatively modest educational levels and relatively low position in the hierarchies of decision-making. Even in its new guise, however, proletarian status still involved considerable powerlessness. Here too, as with capitalism more generally, something of the earlier modern momentum remains. No clearly novel economic and social framework has arisen to replace that which began to take shape four centuries ago. Evolution and change have occurred in this category, but probably not revolution; basic continuity prevails.

Factor four: technology. Technological change, which some have argued described an unusual dynamic in Western history even before the modern centuries, has certainly been a staple of modern Western development. The West has been unusually productive of new technologies and unusually open to their results. By the later twentieth century the West became somewhat less unique in this regard, among world societies, than it had been before. However, the factor continues to describe Western history and prospects in a number of key respects. Western businesses and governments organize to enhance technological change. Public opinion expects such change and either desires it or finds it inescapable.

Yet this is a category in which two quite different sets of questions have arisen in recent decades. First, there is some question as to whether the West is really maintaining its dynamic technological stance, rhetoric to the contrary. Claims that inventiveness and implementation have declined are not conclusive, but they do raise important issues. From another side comes the postindustrial argument that finds the West so open to new technology that a new wave of change is about to transform society, economy, and politics. In this scenario, receptiveness to new technology would form a continuity between modern and postmodern Western history, but the nature of technology would be so radically altered that a new period must be defined. Definite continuity is evident in this category but there are still complex and diverse questions that may suggest radical change is in the offing.

Factor five: a new mentality. As early as the sixteenth century there were signs that ordinary Westerners, as well as formal intellectuals, were beginning to think in new ways. The evolution of modern Western intellectual and popular-cultural life has been complex, but some persistent or recurrent themes have emerged. These include a tendency toward secularization, a heavy reliance on science and presumably rational definitions of the environment, substantial belief in individualism and personal self-control, and a high valuation of the family.

Much of the modern Western mentality continued into the later twentieth century and even underwent some new elaborations. Reliance on science and medicine became if anything more extensive. The scientific battle against death, increasingly focused on hospitals and other medical institutions, moved toward further rationalization and demystification after World War II—to an extent found dangerous by some observers. Definitions of individualism changed; perhaps less stress was placed on competitive achievement and more on expressive leisure and sexuality. But the idea of the individual as a unit and the related emphasis on self-control remain vigorous. Corporate and bureaucratic requirements indeed enhanced efforts to control emotions such as anger in the later twentieth century. The rise of self-improvement books suggested an ongoing belief that the individual should be developed and each person should contribute to his or her own development process.

Efforts to define a modern Western mentality are still bedeviled by diversities and countercurrents. Although the decline of religion is an ongoing theme, it varies with region. Divisions in the formal intellectual sphere, between rationalism and emotionally charged art, set up continuing tensions. Similar tensions emerge in popular mentality—for example, between seeing the family as an intense, emotional unit and vaunting rational self-control in other areas. Some of these complexities, however, maintain tensions that were noted earlier in the development of a modern Western outlook. They warn against oversimplification, but they do not suggest fundamental change of direction.

Yet there may be new and more radical changes to come in this category as well. Throughout most of modern Western history, trends in mentalities, and to some extent in social structure, have been partially divided by gender. Women as well as men were affected by proletarianization and the commercialization of the economy. But whereas male proletarians maintained a central work role, productive, wage-earning labor became ancillary for most working-class women (indeed, for most women of all classes). Relatedly, women were less fully drawn into commercial relationships than men were, although from the nineteenth century onward their activities as consumers involved them in this crucial commercial front. In terms of conventional beliefs, men were expected to express a sense of self, to wield reason and self-control. The rise of science meant, in fact, the devaluing of many traditionally female activities as healers. The divisions in gender values were keenly expressed in the idea of the family as an emotional unit somewhat separate from the public world of work and politics. Women, confined to family but disproportionately responsible for its special qualities, gained new roles and new prestige through this redefinition, but they long failed to gain some of the new rights men gained—as in politics—and by 1800 they actually lost their ability regularly to join in social protest alongside men.

Educational and work gains among women, increasing as the twentieth century progressed and joined by a new and more sweeping feminism, have challenged gender divisions characteristic of earlier modern centuries in the West. These gains apply to women some of the same standards developed previously in men's mentalities, such as rationality and a fuller expression of the self. To this extent they expand on key modern trends. The shift from earlier gender spheres is no small matter, however, either in theory or in potential practical consequences. Thus new patterns of women's work may reduce the intensity of women's commitment to family and the socialization of children. This may in turn challenge many of the ceremonial functions Western families began to display from the sixteenth century onward. Indeed, the rise of the Western family as a center for conversational dining and a key location for emotional bonding, which began in the Reformation era, may have started a historic decline by about 1960, when fast foods and convenience outlets, plus soaring divorce rates, signaled a basic change in direction first in the United States and then in western Europe. More fundamentally still, mother-intensive child-rearing, which according to some historians helped produce the self-conscious, controlled, but intense personalities idealized in the eighteenth and nineteenth centuries among some women as well as some men, may now have to yield to other patterns, perhaps no less valid but different, as children are socialized by a wider variety of agencies including media and peers. Here too, changes in modern gender trends, although building on other modern values, may involve wider shifts in direction.

Relating contemporary Western mentality to previous modern trends is further complicated by widespread belief that a new Western personality is taking shape (in part perhaps because of changing family patterns)—a personality neither traditionalist nor modern. This belief emphasizes a decline of characteristic definitions of individualism and a reduction of certain kinds of self-control, in favor of greater sexual and other indulgence. On yet another front, the rise of new media, particularly television, and perhaps the computer, may ultimately create a post-literate approach to thought and perception, as people depend less on reading, more on other sources of information—with fundamental distinctions in methods of thought resulting between readers and nonreaders. In contrast to traditional oral transmission, reading creates not only access to more information, but also different ways of thinking about information; the spread of reading was an important facet of the development of the modern mentality into our own century. If the late twentieth century sees the beginnings of yet another basic mode of learning, producing still larger amounts of information but also new ways of thinking, the idea of a second, doubtless gradual, revolution in the Western mentality may take on real substance.

Not surprisingly, the verdict on this last fundamental feature of modern Western history—the shaping of beliefs—duplicates the "scores" in most of the other categories. When viewed in the perspective of modern history, the West retains substantial continuity with basic earlier trends: Western society changes, but often within an established framework. Yet there are some new themes, particularly in international context but also in technology or women's roles, that raise questions about continuity, and make it possible not to predict basic change, but certainly to wonder about the durability of the West's modern dynamic.

The twentieth century has introduced more than the usual number of new ingredients into the modern Western brew. Some ingredients hamper the West's ability to retain its modern position as one of the world's most vigorous societies. Others suggest that the West, though possibly still dynamic, may be altering some of its own basic definitions. Yet, even as it faces new uncertainties and prospects, the West continues to be shaped by many of the underlying trends that created its modern characteristics in the first place. A number of its blind spots, as well as its strengths, result from the ongoing impact of factors that seventeenth-century proletarians, or eighteenth-century merchants, or nineteenth-century housewives helped set in motion. Just as reports of the West's collapse have so far proved exaggerated, so the attempts to write off the West's painfully won modern framework in favor of a brave or bleak new world may be premature.

A Balance Sheet: The Dynamics of Modern Western History

SUGGESTIONS FOR FURTHER READING

THE TITLES SUGGESTED IN THIS SECTION are designed to give students a means of following up on the topics covered in this book. The listing is, obviously, far from exhaustive. Leading works are suggested, and also works that will provide access to further bibliographies on subordinate topics (such as individual nations in key periods, or biographies, or case studies). Original sources are not generally listed, but an important way of pursuing additional study in modern European history is to consult works by major intellectual figures or statesmen, and also the increasingly available editions of diaries and autobiographies by more common folk. Books available in paperback are noted with an asterisk.

In addition to following up on special topics through listed books, students can readily advance their knowledge of recent work on leading issues in Western history by consulting several key journals. A standard source on European history is the *Journal of Modern History*. For the newer kinds of social history, see also the *Journal of Social History, Past and Present,* and the *Journal of Interdisciplinary History.*

The Early Modern Centuries, 1500–1800 (Chapters 1–4)

The Renaissance constitutes one of the most intensively studied periods in European history. For good and relatively recent treatments, see *J. R. Hale, *Renaissance Europe: The Individual and Society, 1480–1530* (1978); *J. H. Plumb, *The Italian Renaissance* (1986); and F. H. New, *The Renaissance and Reformation: A Short History* (1977). An older study but valuable in its comprehensive coverage is Myron Gilmore, *The World of Humanism,*

1453–1517 (1962); and for a summary of interpretations, see *K. H. Dannenfeldt, ed., *The Renaissance: Medieval or Modern* (1959). On northern Europe, see also *Johann Huizinga, *The Waning of the Middle Ages: A Study of the Forms of Life, Thought and Art in France and the Netherlands in the Dawn of the Renaissance* (1954). For a recent attempt to show relationships between the Renaissance (in Italy) and ordinary people, see Guido Ruggiero, *The Boundaries of Eros: Sex, Crime, and Sexuality in Renaissance Venice* (1985). On a key nation around 1500, see *J. H. Elliott, *Imperial Spain 1469–1716* (1977). On Renaissance art, consult A. Martindale, *The Rise of the Artist in the Middle Ages and Early Renaissance* (1972) and *M. Meiss, *The Painter's Choice: Problems in the Interpretation of Renaissance Art* (1976). On Renaissance economic life, see *I. Origo, *The Merchant of Prato* (1986).

For an understanding of the social history of Europe around 1500, and aspects of the life of ordinary people, the following studies are particularly useful: Fernand Braudel, *The Mediterranean and the Mediterranean World in the Age of Philip Second* (1976); *Carlo Ginzburg, *The Cheese and the Worms* (1980), a study of peasant mentalities in Italy; and Renate Bridenthal and Claudia Koonz, *Becoming Visible: Women in European History* (1977; rev. ed. 1986) (this book offers essays on women's history in all major periods in European history); *Jack Goody, Joan Thirsk, and E. P. Thompson, eds., *Family and Inheritance: Rural Society in Western Europe 1200–1800* (1978). On recurrent plagues and their impact, see Paul Slack, *The Impact of the Plague in Tudor and Stuart England* (1985), a minor classic.

General coverage of the Reformation can be found in *O. Chadwick, *The Reformation* (1976) and E. H. Harbison, *The Age of Reformation* (1963). For Reformation ideas and their popularization, see Stephen Ozment, *The Age of Reform, 1250–1550: An Intellectual and Religious History of Late Medieval and Reformation Europe* (1980) and *The Reformation in the Cities: The Appeal of Protestantism in Sixteenth-Century Germany and Switzerland* (1975). A vital individual study, using a psychological interpretation, is *Erik Erikson, *Young Man Luther* (1962). On the spread of the Reformation, see *Gerald Strauss, *Luther's House of Learning: The Indoctrination of the Young in the German Reformation* (1978); E. William Monter, *Calvin's Geneva* (1967); *A. G. Dickens, *The English Reformation* (1968). On the Catholic response, see *A. G. Dickens, *The Counter Reformation* (1979) and Hubert Jedin and John Dolan, eds., *Reformation and Counter Reformation* (1980).

On technological change in the 16th century, see William McNeill, *The Pursuit of Power: Technology, Armed Force, and Society since 1000 A.D.* (1982); David Landes, *Revolution in Time: Clocks and the Making of the Modern World* (1985); *Carlo Cipolla, *Guns, Sails and Empires: Technological Innovation and the Early Phases of European Expansion, 1400–1700* (1965). Europe's early expansion is covered in *J. H. Parry, *The Age of Reconnaissance* (1982). The central development of a new world economy, with western Europe at its center, is brilliantly, if controversially, treated in *Immanuel Wallerstein, *The Modern World System: Capitalist Agriculture and the Origins of the European World Economy in the Sixteenth Century* (1974) and *The Modern World System: Mercantilism and the Consolidation of the European World Economy, 1600–1750* (1980). See also *Wallerstein's *The Politics of the World Economy: The States, the Movements and the Civilizations* (1984).

For a basic effort to characterize 16th–17th century change in the wider sweep of European history, see Charles Tilly, *Big Structures, Large Processes, Huge Comparisons* (1985). For developments among the common people in this and later periods, *Peter N. Stearns, ed., *The Other Side of Western Civilization: Readings in Everyday Life, II* (3rd ed., 1984). A sensitive survey of the Reformation period with particular emphasis on social change is *Sheldon Watts, *A Social History of Western Europe, 1450–1720* (1984).

The literature on changes in popular mentalities under the impact of new currents in religion, the economy and medicine is increasingly rich. Key works on the 16th–17th centuries include *Keith Thomas, *Religion and the Decline of Magic* (1975); A. N. Galpern, *The Religions of the People in Sixteenth-Century Champagne* (1976); William Christian, Jr., *Local Religion in Sixteenth Century Spain* (1981); Paul Seaver, *Wallington's World: A Puritan Artisan in Seventeenth Century London* (1985); *Michael MacDonald, *Mystical Bedlam: Madness, Anxiety, and Healing in Seventeenth Century England* (1983); Robert Muchembled, *Popular Culture and Elite Culture in France, 1400–1700* (1985); *Natalie Davis, *Society and Culture in Early Modern France* (1975); *Peter Burke, *Popular Culture in Early Modern Europe* (1978); and David Sabean, *Power in the Blood: Popular Culture and Village Discourse in Early Modern Germany* (1985). Witchcraft has been widely studied. For a fine introduction, see *E. William Monter, *European Witchcraft* (1969).

Changes in family life and outlook form another richly-studied aspect of popular life from the 16th to the 18th centuries. See *Edward Shorter, *The Making of the Modern Family* (1977); *Lawrence Stone, *The Family, Sex and Marriage in England 1500–1800* (1977); *Jean Louis Flandrin, *Families in Former Times—Kinship, Household and Sexuality in Early Modern France* (1977). On changes and continuity in the treatment of children, *Philippe Ariès, *Centuries of Childhood: A Social History of Family Life* (1962); David Hunt, *Parents and Children in History: The Psychology of Family Life in Early Modern France* (1970); and *Linda Pollock, *Forgotten Children: Parent-Child Relations from 1500 to 1900* (1984). Other key family topics are covered in *Michael Mitterauer and Reinhard Sieder, *European Family: Patriarchy to Partnership, from the Middle Ages to the Present* (1984); Peter N. Stearns, ed., *Old Age in Preindustrial Society* (1985); and John Gillis, *For Better, For Worse: British Marriage 1600 to the Present* (1985).

*On demography, E. A. Wrigley and Roger Schofield, *The Population History of England, 1541–1871: A Reconstruction* (1981) and *E. A. Wrigley, *Population and History* (1969). On class structure, Keith Wrightson and David Levine, *Poverty and Piety in an English Village* (1979).

On the religious wars and related political-diplomatic developments into the 17th century, K. H. D. Kaley, *The Dutch in the Seventeenth Century* (1972); *G. Mattingly, *The Armada* (1959); J. H. M. Salmon, *Society in Crisis: France in the Sixteenth Century* (1975); *Wallace MacCaffrey, *Queen Elizabeth and the Making of Policy, 1572–1588* (1981); C. V. Wedgwood, *The Thirty Years' War* (1961); *Keith Wrightson, *English Society 1580–1680* (1982); C. R. Boxer, *The Dutch Seaborne Empire* (1980). A more general account is *Geoffrey Parker, *Europe in Crisis, 1598–1618*.

Popular protest is covered in H. A. F. Kamen, *The Iron Century: Social Change in Europe, 1550–1660* (1971) and Charles Tilly, *The Contentious French*

(1986) (the Tilly book should also be consulted for the structure of popular protest in more recent centuries). For a more nostalgic view of early modern society, *Peter Laslett, *The World We Have Lost: England Before the Industrial Age* (1984).

On the general phenomenon of the new nation-state, see Charles Tilly, ed., *The Formation of National States in Western Europe* (1975). See also Eli Hecksher, *Mercantilism* (1983).

The rise of absolutism can be followed in M. Beloff, *The Age of Absolutism* (1967); J. Wolf, *Louis XIV* (1968); *R. Hatton, *Europe in the Age of Louis XIV* (1979); and for the social as well as political side, *Pierre Goubert, *Louis XIV and 20 Million Frenchmen* (1972). On patterns in central and eastern Europe: H. Rosenberg, *Bureaucracy, Aristocracy and Autocracy: The Prussian Experience, 1660–1815* (1966); *Gordon Craig, *The Politics of the Prussian Army, 1640–1945* (1964); *R. J. Evans, *The Making of the Habsburg Monarchy 1550–1770* (1979); *R. A. Kann, *A History of the Habsburg Empire, 1526–1918* (1974); *Nicholas V. Liasanovsky, *A History of Russia* (1984). On Russia see also Jerome Blum, *Lord and Peasant in Russia from the Ninth to the Nineteenth Century* (1961); and *R. Massie, *Peter the Great* (1981).

Several studies provide excellent introductions to the scientific revolution: *Herbert Butterfield, *Origins of Modern Science* (1965); *A. R. Hall, *From Galileo to Newton, 1630–1720* (1982); R. K. Merton, *Science, Technology and Society in Seventeenth Century England* (1970); *T. S. Kuhn, *The Structure of Scientific Revolutions* (1970). On the wider intellectual implications of the scientific revolution, *Paul Hazard, *The European Mind 1680–1715* (1963), which tries to pinpoint the beginning of a "modern" intellectual outlook.

On the Enlightenment, Peter Gay, *The Enlightenment* (1965); Paul Hazard, *European Thought in the Eighteenth Century* (1954); H. Payne, *The Philosophes and the People* (1976); I. Wade, *The Structure and Form of the French Enlightenment* (1977). An important special study in K. Rogers, *Feminism in Eighteenth-Century England* (1982).

On wider cultural developments in the 17th–18th centuries, Carolyn Lougee, *Le Paradis des Femmes: Women, Salons and Social Stratification in Seventeenth Century France* (1976); Keith Thomas, *Man and the Natural World: A History of Modern Sensibility* (1983)—a fascinating study of changing attitudes to animals and the natural environment; *Norbert Elias, *The History of Manners: The Civilizing Process* (1982)—a classic study of changes in basic self-discipline; *Philip J. Greven, Jr., *The Protestant Temperament* (1981) (on personality styles and childrearing in North America); and *C. Rosen, *The Classical Style: Haydn, Mozart, Beethoven* (1972), on music and society.

Rural society, over a considerable span of time but with focus on 17th–18th century developments, has been studied both through surveys and through regional case studies. See B. H. Slicher van Bath, *The Agrarian History of Western Europe* (1963); *Jerome Blum, *The End of the Old Order in Rural Europe* (1978); *E. Leroy Ladurie, *The Peasants of Languedoc* (1976); Patrice Higonnet, *Pont-de-Montvert, Social Structure and Politics in a French Village, 1700–1914* (1971).

Changes in various aspects of popular life in the 18th century are examined in: Robert W. Malcolmson, *Popular Recreations in English Society:*

1700–1850 (1980); Randolph Trumbach, *The Rise of the Egalitarian Family* (1978); *Paul Mantoux, *The Industrial Revolution in the Eighteenth Century* (1981); R. Wheaton and T. Hareven, eds., *Family and Sexuality in French History* (1980); *Michael Foucault, *Madness and Civilization* (tr. Richard Howard) (1973); Pieter Spierenburg, *Development of the Modern Prison* (1986)—historians have focused on changes in the definition and treatment of "deviants" such as the insane and criminals, and these books can launch further inquiry.

Political revolution at the end of the 18th century has drawn massive attention. Good basic accounts include *R. R. Palmer, *The Age of Democratic Revolution* (1964); *E. J. Hobsbawm, *The Age of Revolution, 1789–1848* (1962); George Rude, *The Crowd in the French Revolution* (1959); *Georges Lefebvre, *The Coming of the French Revolution* (1947). On the dissemination of revolution, *Crane Brinton, *A Decade of Revolution, 1789–1799* (rev. ed., 1971) and O. Connelly, *French Revolution—Napoleonic Era* (1979). More specialized studies on social aspects of the revolution include Lynn Hunt, *Politics, Culture and Class in the French Revolution* (1984); *William Sewell, Jr., *Work and Revolution in France: The Language of Labor from the Old Regime to 1848* (1980); and R. Phillips, *Family Breakdown in Late Eighteenth-Century France: Divorces in Rouen, 1792–1803* (1980).

The Industrial Revolution and the Nineteenth Century (Chapters 5–6)

For the industrial revolution and its basic technological and economic forms, see *Phyllis Dean, *The First Industrial Revolution* (1980) and *David Landes, *The Unbound Prometheus: Technological Change and Industrial Development in Western Europe from 1700 to the Present* (1969). A study of general social development under the impact of industrialization is *Peter N. Stearns, *European Society in Upheaval: A Social History since 1750* (1975). See also *Sidney Pollard, *Peaceful Conquest: The Industrialization of Europe* (1981).

Population upheaval is covered in Carlo Cipolla, *Economic History of World Population* (1962); Michael Drake, ed., *Population in Industrialization* (1969); Thomas McKeown, *The Modern Rise of Population* (1977).

Industrialization's impact on gender and class can be followed up in Louise Tilly and Joan Scott, *Women, Work and Family* (1978); *E. P. Thompson, *Making of the English Working Class* (1966); *John Merriman, ed., *Consciousness and Class Experience in Nineteenth Century Europe* (1979). On the middle classes, C. Morazé, *The Triumph of the Middle Classes* (1968); Patricia Branca, *Silent Sisterhood* (1975)—on the English middle class; *Carl Degler, *At Odds: Women and Family in America, from the Revolution to the Present* (1980).

Cultural developments in the 19th century are covered in George Mosse, *The Culture of Western Europe: The Nineteenth and Twentieth Centuries* (1961); R. Stromberg, *Intellectual History of Modern Europe* (1966); *O. Chadwick, *The Secularization of the European Mind in the Nineteenth Century* (1976); George Lichtheim, *Short History of Socialism* (1970); *Robert Heilbroner, *The Worldly Philosophers* (1967), a somewhat popularized account of the development of economic theory. On Romanticism, *Jacques Barzun, *Classic, Romantic and Modern* (1975); see also F. D. Klingender, *Art and the Industrial Revolution* (1972).

For trends in science and social science an older survey is still very useful: *J. H. Randall, *The Making of the Modern Mind* (5th ed., 1976); see also *M. Ruse, *The Darwinian Revolution* (1979); Martin J. S. Rudwick, *The Great Devonian Controversy: The Shaping of Scientific Knowledge Among Gentlemanly Specialists* (1985)—a fascinating glimpse into how scientific debate operated in the 19th century.

Political trends in the 19th century are easily captured in a number of good national histories. *See Gorden Wright, *France in Modern Times* (3rd ed., 1981); Gordon Craig, *Germany 1866–1945* (1978); Asa Briggs, *The Making of Modern England, 1784–1867* (1967); Louis Snyder, *Roots of German Nationalism* (1978); Theodore Zeldin, *France, 1848–1945* (2v., 1973, 1977); F. D. Scott, *Sweden, the Nation's History* (1977).

Another approach involves focus on political upheaval: *George Rudé, *The Crowd in History: Popular Disturbances in France and England* (rev. ed., 1981); *Peter N. Stearns, *1848: The Revolutionary Tide in Europe* (1974); I. Deak, *The Lawful Revolution: Louis Kossuth and the Hungarians, 1848–49* (1979).

On developments in the family and related matters, see *Jacques Donzelot, *The Policing of Families* (1980), a "social control" interpretation stressing the loss of lower-class autonomy; *John Gillis, *Youth and History* (1981); Angus McLaren, *Sexuality and Social Order: Birth Control in Nineteenth-Century France* (1982); Paul Robinson, *The Modernization of Sex* (1975); Peter Gay, *The Education of the Senses* (1984); Peter N. Stearns, *Old Age in European Society: The Case of France* (1977).

Special studies of women include *M. Vicinus, ed., *Suffer and Be Still* (1972) and *A Widening Sphere* (1981); *R. Evans, *The Feminists: Women's Emancipation in Europe, America and Australia* (1979); *Nancy Cott, *The Bonds of Womanhood: "Woman's Sphere" in New England 1780–1850* (1978); *Bonnie Smith, *Ladies of the Leisure Class: The Bourgeoises of Northern France in the Nineteenth Century* (1981).

Various kinds of changes in popular culture can be traced through: *Stewart Ewen, *Captains of Consciousness: Advertising and the Social Roots of the Consumer Culture* (1976); M. Miller, *The Bon Marché: Bourgeois Culture and the Department Store* (1981); Peter Gay, *Education of the Senses*; Carol Z. Stearns and Peter N. Stearns, *Anger: The Struggle for Emotional Control in America's History* (1986); *Eugen Weber, *Peasants into Frenchmen: The Modernization of Rural France, 1870–1914* (1976); Hugh Cunningham, *Leisure in the Industrial Revolution* (1980) (with a rich bibliography); James Walvin, *Leisure and Society, 1830–1950* (1978); Richard Holt, *Sport and Society in Modern France* (1981); *Harvey Graff, ed., *Literacy and Social Development in the West* (1982); R. D. Altrick, *The English Common Reader: A Social History of the Mass Reading Public* (1957); Fritz Ringer, *Education and Society in Modern Europe* (1979).

Political and diplomatic developments in the later 19th century can be followed in Denis Mack Smith, *Italy, a Modern History* (1969); Robert Kann, *The Multinational Empire* (2v., 1950–64), on Austria-Hungary; *O. Pflanze, *Bismarck and the Development of Germany* (1963); L. Stavrianos, *The Balkans, 1815–1914* (1963).

On imperialism, R. Betts, *Europe Overseas* (1968); *T. Smith, *The Patterns of Imperialism* (1981); and *William Woodruff, *The Impact of Western Man* (1967), this last with an extensive bibliography. See also D. K. Fieldhouse, *Economics and Empire, 1830–1914* (1970) and *Colonialism, 1870–1943* (1981), plus *W. Baumgart, *Imperialism: The Idea and Reality of British and French Colonial Expansion* (1982).

On cultural developments in Russia, Cyril Black, ed., *The Transformation of Russian Society* (1960); R. Zelnik, *Labor and Society in Tsarist Russia, 1855–1870* (1971); T. Emmons, *The Russian Landed Gentry and the Peasant Emancipation of 1861* (1968); *W. Blackwell, *The Industrialization of Russia* (1982).

Late 19th-century social protest can be followed in Edward Shorter and Charles Tilly, *Strikes in France, 1830–1968* (1974); *G. Dangerfield, *The Strange Death of Liberal England* (1961); *Michael Hanagan, *The Logic of Solidarity* (1981); Vernon Lidtke, *The Alternative Culture: Socialist Labor in Imperial Germany* (1985); *Carl Schorske, *German Social Democracy, 1905–1917* (1983); *Albert Lindemann, *History of European Socialism* (1983).

Recent accounts of the alliance system and origins of World War I include *J. Remak, *The Origins of World War I* (1967) and *Lawrence Lafore, *The Long Fuse* (1971). See also A. J. P. Taylor, *The Struggle for Mastery in Europe, 1848–1919* (1954). Arno Mayer, *Persistence of the Old Regime: Europe to the Great War* (1981), interprets 19th-century society and its tensions in terms of the continued strength of the old aristocracy. *Barbara Tuchman, *The Proud Tower* (1972) is a best-seller that captures the moods of the West on the eve of the War. The role of Germany in launching the war has informed much historical debate: for a listing and interpretation of recent work, see David E. Kaiser, "Germany and the Origins of the First World War," *Journal of Modern History* 33 (1983): 442–74. See also *James Joll, *The Origins of the First World War* (1984).

The Twentieth Century (Chapters 7–10)

An excellent general survey of 20th-century history, with ample bibliography, is Robert Paxton, *Europe in the 20th Century* (2nd ed., 1985). On the United States, see *Morris Janowitz, *The Last Half Century: Social Change and Politics in America* (1978); also useful (for earlier periods as well) is one of the better textbooks, such as *Gary Nash, Julie Jeffrey, and others, *The American People* (1986), again with further reading suggestions. An important interpretation of the 20th century, focusing particularly on changes in the West–world relationship, is *Geoffrey Barraclough, *Introduction to Contemporary History* (1964). For a good factual compendium, *Tony Howarth, *Twentieth-Century History: The World Since 1900* (1979).

Another interpretive approach, looking toward the future but with an anchor in 20th-century trends, is *Daniel Bell, *Coming of Post-Industrial Society: A Venture in Social Forecasting* (1976).

National histories form an important guide to 20th-century history as well. In addition to earlier references that cover the 20th century in part, see *Ralf Dahrendorf, *Society and Democracy in Germany* (1979), an important interpretation; A. F. Havighurst, *Twentieth-Century Britain* (1962); John Ardagh, *The New French Revolution: A Social and Economic Survey of France*

1945–1967 (1968) and **France in the 1980s* (1982); Trevor Lloyd, *Empire to Welfare State, English History 1906–1976* (1979); *W. R. Berghahn, *Modern Germany, Society, Economy and Politics in the 20th Century* (1983); *Raymond Carr, *Modern Spain, 1873–1980* (1981); *Donald Treadgold, *Twentieth Century Russia* (5th ed., 1981).

For basic treatments of social and demographic structure, *T. B. Bottomore, *Classes in Modern Society* (1965) and Ralf Dahrendorf, *Class and Class Conflict in Industrial Society* (1959); Michael Young, *The Rise of the Meritocracy* (1958) (a satire); D. V. Glass and Roger Revelle, eds., *Population and Social Change* (1972); T. H. Hollingsworth, *Historical Demography* (1969).

On World War I, *Bernadotte Schmitt and H. C. Bedeler, *The World in the Crucible, 1914–1918* (1984); B. H. Lindell-Hart, *History of the First World War* (repr. 1970). On the war experience, *Paul Fussell, *The Great War and Modern Memory* (1975). For a more interpretive assessment of the nature of modern war, Raymond Aron, *Century of Total War* (1954). On war economics, *Gerd Hardach, *The First World War, 1914–1918* (1977).

On revolutionary Russia, *Sheila Fitzpatrick, *The Russian Revolution, 1917–1932* (1982), is a recent overview with a rich bibliography; see also *Robert Tucker, *Stalin as Revolutionary* (1972); *Alexander Rabinowitch, *The Bolsheviks Come to Power* (1976); and Edmund Wilson, *To the Finland Station*. For developments elsewhere in eastern and central Europe, Arthur G. May, *The Passing of the Habsburg Monarchy 1914–1918* (1966) and Charles Bertrand, ed., *Revolutionary Situations in Europe 1917–1922* (1977). On the Versailles settlement, a good account in Howard Elcock, *Portrait of a Decision: The Council of Four and the Treaty of Versailles* (1972) and Harold Nicolson, *Peacemaking, 1919* (rev. ed., 1945).

On fascism and Nazism, among a host of excellent studies, *Francis Carsten, *The Rise of Fascism* (1980); *Hans Rogger and Eugen Weber, eds., *The European Right* (1965); *Alan Bullock, *Hitler, A Study in Tyranny* (1962); Dennis Mack Smith, *Mussolini* (1982); *Stanley Payne, *Fascism: Comparison and Definition* (1984); *Ernst Nolte, *Three Faces of Fascism* (1969); *W. S. Allen, *The Nazi Seizure of Power: The Experience of a Single German Town* (1984), is an important case study; see also *Richard Hamilton, *Who Voted for Hitler* (1982); and *Karl Bracher, *The German Dictatorship* (1970). *David Schoenbaum, *Hitler's Social Revolution* (1980), provides a nuanced interpretation of the Nazi rise and impact.

For two interpretations of the Holocaust, *Lucy Dawidowicz, *The War Against the Jews* (1976) and Karl Schleunes, *The Twisted Road to Auschwitz* (1970). See also *Rand Hillberg, *The Destruction of European Jews* (1973) and Gerald Fleming, *Hitler and the Final Solution* (1984).

On more general political trends in western Europe, an important comparative interpretation is Charles S. Maier, *Recasting Bourgeois Europe: Stabilization in France, Germany and Italy in the Decades after World War I* (1975); *Raymond Sontag, *A Broken World: 1919–1939* (1971). For the Depression, *Charles Kindleberger, *The World in Depression, 1929–1939* (1973) and, on the American side, John K. Galbraith, *The Great Crash, 1929* (1961). Political results in key states, apart from fascism, can be traced in Nathaniel Greene, *Crisis and Decline: The French Socialist Party in the Popular Front*

Era (1969) and the brilliant book by Annie Kriegel, *The French Communists: Profile of a People* (1972). On an early welfare state, Marquis Childs, *Sweden, The Middle Way* (1936). Goronwy Rees, *The Great Slump, Capitalism in Crisis* (1977), a popularized account on Britain.

The origins of World War II include accounts of the Spanish Civil War: see an indispensable social analysis, Gerald Brenan, *The Spanish Labyrinth* (1960) and Hugh Thomas, *The Spanish Civil War* (1977). Some debate about the direct causes of the war was stirred by *A. J. P. Taylor's clever *Origins of the Second World War* (2nd ed., 1966), which argued that Hitler was in the mainstream of European diplomatic history. Recent syntheses, with more conventional assessments, are *Anthony Adamthwaite, *The Making of the Second World War* (1977) and *Christopher Thorne, *The Approach of War, 1938–39* (1969). On the war itself, *Gordon Wright, *The Ordeal of Total War, 1939–45* (1968); *Alan S. Milward, *War Economy and Society: 1939–45* (1977); Alexander Dallin, *German Rule in Russia, 1941–45* (1981); *Robert Paxton, *Vichy, France: Old Guard and New Order, 1940–44* (1972); Stephen Hawes and Ralph White, eds., *Resistance in Europe, 1939–45* (1975).

On intellectual developments, *H. Stuart Hughes, *Consciousness and Society* (1976), and *The Obstructed Path: French Social Thought in the Years of Desperation, 1930–1960* (1968), on social thought; Theda Shapiro, *Painters and Politics: The European Avantgarde and Society, 1900–1925* (1977); Arnold Hauser, *The Social History of Art* (1951): vol. 4: *Naturalism, Impressionism and the Film Age*; H. R. Hithcock, *Architecture: Nineteenth and Twentieth Centuries* (1977): *Peter Gay, *Weimar Culture: The Outsider as Insider* (1981); *Ronald Clark, *Einstein, The Life and Times* (1971); *Abraham Pais, *Subtle is the Lord: The Science and Life of Albert Einstein* (1982); *Henri Ellenberger, *The Discovery of the Unconscious* (1970), on Freudianism. On religion, *Alec Vidler, *The Church in an Age of Revolution* (1962).

A host of studies convey important themes in popular mentalities, though there is no decisive overall treatment. Raymond Williams, *The Country and the City* (1973), *Communications* (1966) and *The Long Revolution* (1961) traces cultural changes produced by new media and schooling in Britain. Richard Hoggart, *The Uses of Literacy* (1957) blasts mass taste. *Martin Wiener, *English Culture and the Decline of the Industrial Spirit, 1850–1980* (1981) and Andrew Lees, *Cities Perceived: Urban Society in European and American Thought 1820–1940* (1985) deal with important reactions to modern trends. *Roland Marchand, *Advertising the American Dream: Making Way for Modernity, 1920–1940* (1985), treats a major theme. A readable account of British popular culture between the wars is Robert Graves and Alan Hodge, *The Long Weekend* (1940). On leisure, Michael Marrus, ed., *The Emergence of Leisure* (1974) and Benjamin Rader, *History of American Sports* (1985). Two other vital areas of change in mentalities are covered in *René Dubos, *The Mirage of Health* (1955) and Philippe Ariès, *The Hour of Our Death* (1981).

A number of excellent studies treat changes in the rural world in the 20th century: *Lawrence Wylie, *Village in the Vaucluse* (3rd ed., 1974); Julian Pitt-Rivers, *People of the Sierra* (1971); Henri Mendras, *The Vanishing Peasant* (1970); Gordon Wright, *Rural Revolution in France* (1964).

On workers and embourgeoisement, Ferdynand Zweig, _The Worker in
an Affluent Society_ (1962) and J. H. Goldthorpe and others, _The Affluent
Worker in the Class Structure_ (1969), the latter arguing for the continuity of
the working class. See also Richard Hamilton, _Affluence and the French Worker
in the Fourth Republic_ (1967). On working-class protest, an excellent summary with bibliography is Dick Geary, _European Labor Protest 1848–1939_
(1981); see also *D. L. M. Blackmer and Sidney Tarrow, _Communism in
Italy and France_ (1975); James Cronin, _Labor and Society in Britain 1918–1979_
(1984); and, on Eurocommunism, *Howard Machin, ed., _National Communism in Western Europe: A Third Way for Socialism_ (1983).

On economic and social developments since World War II. Thomas
Stark, _The Distribution of Personal Income in the United Kingdom, 1949–1963_ (1972);
A. H. Halsey, ed., _Trends in British Society Since 1900_ (1972); G. Frumkin,
Population Changes in Europe since 1939 (1951); Vernon Bogdanor and
R. Skidelsky, eds., _The Age of Affluence_ (1970); *Anthony Sampson, _New
Anatomy of Britain_ (1971); John Ardagh, _A Tale of Five Cities: Life in Europe
Today_ (1979); *Anthony Giddens, _The Class Structure of Advanced Societies_
(1975); M. W. Kirby, _The Decline of British Economic Power since 1870_ (1981);
Charles Kindleberger, _Europe's Postwar Growth_ (1967).

Studies of women and the family include Jane Lewis, _Women in England
1870–1950: Secular Divisions and Social Change_ (1984); *Eli Zaretsky, _Capi-
talism, the Family and Personal Life_ (1976); Peter Willmott and Michael Young,
The Symmetrical Family (1973); *Christopher Lasch, _Haven in a Heartless World:
The Family Beseiged_ (1975); *Alice Rossi, Jerome Kagan, and T. Hareven,
eds., _The Family_ (1978); *William Chafe, _Women and Equality_ (1977); Hi-
lary Land, "The Changing Place of Women in Europe," _Daedalus_ 108 (1979):
72–92; Patricia Branca, _Women in Europe Since 1750_ (1978); R. Patai, ed.,
Women in the Modern World (1971); S. B. Kamerar and A. J. Kahn, eds.,
Family Policy: Government and Families in Fourteen Countries (1978).

On postwar diplomacy *Charles S. Maier, ed., _The Origins of the Cold
War and Contemporary Europe_ (1975) and *Daniel Yergin, _Shattered Peace: The
Origins of the Cold War and the National Security State_ (1977); *Martin Sherman,
A World Destroyed: The Atomic Bomb and the Grand Alliance (1975); *Walter
Laqueur, _Europe Since Hitler_ (1982); *Alfred Grosser, _The Western Alliance_
(1980) (on NATO); *Robin Remington, _The Warsaw Pact_ (1971); John
Paxton, _The Developing Common Market_ (3rd ed., 1976), a good introduction
with bibliography; Helen Wallace and others, _Policy-Making in the Euro-
pean Community_ (2nd ed., 1983); *Anton W. De Porte, _Europe Between the
Superpowers_ (1979); *Rudolf von Albertini, _Decolonization_ (1982); Prosser
Gifford and William Louis, eds., _The Transfer of Power in Africa_ (1982);
H. M. Sachar, _Europe Leaves the Middle East_ (1972). On a more theoretical
level, *Ernest Haas, _Beyond the Nation State_ (1964).

For postwar political developments, including the welfare state, Ken-
neth Morgan, _Labour in Power 1945–51_ (1984); *Stephen Cohen, _Modern
Capitalist Planning: The French Model_ (1977); Gordon Wright, _The Reshaping
of French Democracy_ (1970); S. J. Woolf, ed., _The Rebirth of Italy_ (1972);
Gordon Craig, _The Germans_ (1983); Philip G. Cerny, _The Politics of Gran-
deur_ (1980), on De Gaulle; *Raymond Carr and J. P. Fusi-Azpurua, _Spain:
Dictatorship to Democracy_ (1981); Lawrence Graham and Douglas L. Wheeler,

eds., *In Search of Modern Portugal* (1983); *E. S. Einhorn and John Logue, *Welfare States in Hard Times* (1982), on Scandinavia.

On eastern Europe: *Richard Barnet, *The Giants: Russia and America* (1977); *Alvin Rubinstein, *Soviet Foreign Policy Since World War II* (1981); Alec Nove, *The Soviet Economic System* (1980); *Seweryn Bialer, *Stalin's Successors* (1980); *Stephen Cohen and others, eds., *The Soviet Union Since Stalin* (1981). The most comprehensive treatment of the smaller East European countries is François Fejtö, *A History of the People's Democracies: Eastern Europe Since Stalin* (1971); see also Jürgen Tampke, *The People's Republics of Eastern Europe* (1983); Timothy Ash, *The Polish Revolution: Solidarity* (1984); *Richard Staar, *Communist Regimes in Eastern Europe* (4th ed., 1982); and *Bennett Kovrig, *Communism in Hungary from Kun to Kadar* (1979).

Accounts of 1968 uprisings include: *Alaine Touraine, *The May Movement, Revolt and Reform* (1971); Raymond Aron, *The Elusive Revolution* (1969); *H. Gordon Skilling, *Czechoslovakia: Interrupted Revolution* (1976).

An interesting set of overviews on Europe comes through Stephen Graubard, ed., *A New Europe?* (1963), written in a spirit of optimism about the postwar renaissance, compared to the more pessimistic appraisals in two issues of *Daedalus*, also edited by Graubard: *Looking for Europe* (Winter 1979) and *The European Predicament* (Spring 1979). See also Ralf Dahrendorf, ed., *Europe's Economy in Crisis* (1982).

PICTURE CREDITS

INDEX